Daniele Manin and the Venetian Revolution of 1848-49

Daniele Manin
and the
Venetian Revolution of
1848-49

PAUL GINSBORG

CAMBRIDGE UNIVERSITY PRESS

CAMBRIDGE

LONDON · NEW YORK · MELBOURNE

Published by the Syndics of the Cambridge University Press
The Pitt Building, Trumpington Street, Cambridge CB2 1RP
Bentley House, 200 Euston Road, London NW1 2DB
32 East 57th Street, New York, NY 10022, USA
296 Beaconsfield Parade, Middle Park, Melbourne 3206, Australia

First published 1979

Printed in Great Britain by
Western Printing Services Ltd, Bristol

Library of Congress Cataloguing in Publication Data
Ginsborg, Paul.
Daniele Manin and the Venetian Revolution of 1848-49.
Bibliography: p.
Includes index.
1. Manin, Daniele, 1804–1857. 2. Venice –
History – 1848–1849. I. Title.
DG678.55.G56   945'.31   78-56180
ISBN 0 521 22077 7

For my parents

Contents

Preface		ix
Abbreviations		xiii
Maps:	*I Italy, spring 1848*	xv
	II The Veneto, 1848	xvi
	III Venice, 1848	xvii
1	Venetian society in the first half of the nineteenth century, 1814–48	1
2	Towards the revolution	47
3	The March days, 1848	84
4	The failure of the Italian republicans, March and April 1848	126
5	The undoing of the Venetian republic, April and May 1848	162
6	Fusion, June to July 1848	210
7	The Mazzinians and the French, July to October 1848	252
8	The winter of the revolution, October 1848 to April 1849	295
9	The last months, April to August 1849	333
10	Conclusion	364
	Bibliography	380
	Note on documents and newspapers	393
	Index	399

Preface

It is now nearly thirty years since Antonio Gramsci's notes on the Risorgimento were first published. In that time they have proved a fundamental source of inspiration and debate for Marxists and non-Marxists alike. Writing first in prison and then in hospital, with very limited access to historical material, Gramsci tried to trace the reasons for the weakness of Italian bourgeois democracy and to uncover the foundations upon which the fascist state had been built. Such an undertaking of necessity involved him in an examination of the Risorgimento, and there are three dominant themes in his analysis of it: the concept of the Risorgimento as a 'passive' revolution, in the sense that the Italian bourgeoisie came to terms with the traditional forces in the peninsula instead of waging a frontal assault on them, an assault which would have involved the active co-operation and material compensation of the lower classes; the importance of the leadership struggle, which saw the liberal monarchists triumph over their opponents, the republicans and democrats; and the great division between town and countryside, a problem deeply rooted in Italian history, and one with which the republicans never came to terms. While admitting the positive nature of the unification of the peninsula, Gramsci reached the inescapable conclusion of the relative failure of the Italian bourgeois revolution, especially when compared with its English and French predecessors:

They [the leaders of the Risorgimento] said that they were aiming at the creation of a modern State in Italy, and they in fact produced a bastard. They aimed at stimulating the formation of an extensive and energetic ruling class, and they did not succeed; at integrating the people into the framework of the new State, and they did not succeed. The paltry political life from 1870 to 1900, the fundamental and endemic rebelliousness of the Italian popular classes, the narrow and stunted existence of a sceptical and cowardly ruling stratum, these are all the consequences of that failure.[1]

[1] Q. Hoare and G. Nowell Smith (eds.), *Selections from the Prison Notebooks of Antonio Gramsci*, p. 90.

Gramsci tried to illustrate the major themes in his analysis with reference primarily to the south and to the critical years of 1859–60. Discussion of his work, such as the renowned Romeo–Gerschenkron debate, has also tended to concentrate on this area, or on the later effects of the events of those years. But it is possible to argue that such an emphasis ignores an equally critical turning point in the Risorgimento – not 1859–60 in the south, but 1848 in the north. In the spring of 1848, with the legendary insurrections of Milan and Venice, and in an international situation of great fluidity, the Italian republicans and democrats perhaps had their best chance of winning the leadership of the Risorgimento and steering it onto another course. I have tried, in what follows, to study this proposition in some detail and to examine the reasons for the republicans' failure, with special reference to Manin and Venice. And, lest I be accused of subscribing to the creation of, in Francis Haskell's words, 'the latest Italian saint', let me immediately say that Gramsci has little to offer on 1848. There is a section in his notes entitled 'Il nodo storico 1848–9', but he takes few steps to unravel this particular 'historical knot'. Indeed, with the exception of one or two important articles, there has been little substantial reinterpretation of any of the Italian revolutions of 1848–9. Gramsci himself talked in the *Prison Notebooks* of the necessity of detailed monographs which would cover the lacunae in his own work, and test the validity of its major themes. That is the purpose of this book.

No overall account of the Venetian revolution of 1848–9 has been written since Vincenzo Marchesi's *Storia documentata della rivoluzione e della difesa di Venezia negli anni 1848–49*, published in 1916, and G. M. Trevelyan's *Manin and the Venetian Revolution of 1848*, published in 1923. Marchesi's is a mammoth work, containing a wealth of detail. But he is not free from the hagiography that so beset Italian history in the decades after unification, and how far his own viewpoint is from mine is best illustrated in his later assessment of one of the principal figures of the Venetian revolution, G. B. Cavedalis: 'He had many of the qualities which today we justly admire in the fascist Duce, the Man who knew how to suppress troublemakers with an iron fist, and how to restore the order and discipline which have sadly been violated for some time in our country.'[2] Marchesi's work is also marred by many incorrect references in the footnotes and by his failure to use the mass of documents in the Venetian state archive. Trevelyan's book is a superb narrative, but is largely a panegyric of Manin and is based for the most part on printed sources and secondary works. I have tried to go further than either of them in my use of primary material from a large number of archives.

[2] G. B. Cavedalis, *I commentari*, vol. 1, introduction, p. xliii.

But I am aware that this does not necessarily imply any greater objectivity of worth, and that I am as much a child of my age as Marchesi and Trevelyan were of theirs. I would also like to say that my own study would have been impossible without the work of the many historians who have preceded me in writing on the revolution and publishing its documents; I would like to pay particular homage to Gambarin and Cessi, and, more recently, Ventura and Bernardello.

Finally, I make no claim to have written a 'definitive' history of the revolution. I could well spend the rest of my life studying it and still not have read all the documentation available. There is at least one area which I have had consciously to neglect for much of the book, and which awaits its historian – that of Austrian policy and rule in the period 1814–66. I have concentrated instead on the Italians themselves, their aspirations, achievements, divisions and failures.

I owe three outstanding debts of gratitude. The first and greatest is to Adolfo Bernardello, communist, schoolteacher and historian. I very much doubt whether this book would ever have been completed without his inspiration and guidance, and whatever merit it may have is in no small part due to him. He has been totally unselfish in sharing his great knowledge of nineteenth-century Venice, and has taught me most of what I now know about the city. As a foreign scholar, I never hoped to find such a friend and collaborator. The second debt is to Brian Pullan, who first suggested to me this subject of research and then as my Ph.D. supervisor guided my subsequent activity with considerable wisdom and tolerance. He was also most patient and helpful at a time when I did not really know what I was doing and, worse, why I was doing it. I could have asked for no more conscientious or friendly supervisor. The final debt is to Norman Hampson, who has kindly read the typescript of this book and saved me (hopefully) from the worst of my mistakes. The errors that remain are not his responsibility.

I would also like to thank the following for their considerable aid and encouragement at one time or another over the last ten years: John Barber, Lucia Bellodi Casanova, Piero Brunello, Mirella Calzavarini, Gaetano Cozzi, Andrew Gamble, Marcello and Stefania Flores, Reinhy and Laura Mueller, Gwyn Williams, Bill Wurthmann; last, and most, Mary Beckinsale, whose humour, fantasy and love have illuminated many an Italian expedition.

Milan, January 1978   Paul Ginsborg

Abbreviations

b.	*busta*
ACPo	Archivio comunale, Pordenone
ACV	Archivio comunale, Venezia
Municip., Atti di Uff.	Municipio, Atti di Ufficio
ASRF	Archivio storico del Risorgimento, Firenze
AST	Archivio di stato, Torino
ASU	Archivio di stato, Udine
ASV	Archivio di stato, Venezia
CC	Camera di commercio, Venezia
CI	Imperiale-Regia commissione governativa di commercio, agricoltura e industria
Pres. Gov.	Presidio di Governo (1814–48)
Gov.	Governo, 1814–48
Gov. Prov. 1848–9	Governo provvisorio, 1848–9
CD	Comitato di difesa
Comm. Milit.	Commissione militare di guerra e marina a pieni poteri
Consulta	Consulta delle provincie venete unite
CPD	Comitato provvisorio dipartimentale, provincie venete
DG	Dipartimento di guerra
MG	Ministero di guerra
MU	Ministeri uniti
OPss	Prefettura centrale ordine pubblico – sorvegliati e sospetti
Pres. Luog.	Presidenza della Luogotenenza veneta, 1849–66
ASVr	Archivio di stato, Verona
DP	Delegazione provinciale
BAM	Biblioteca Ambrosiana, Milano
BBV	Biblioteca civica Bertoliana, Vicenza
BCU	Biblioteca comunale, Udine
BL	British Library
BNF	Biblioteca nazionale, Firenze
FQSV	Fondazione Querini Stampalia, Venezia
HHSAV	Haus-, Hauf- und Staatsarchiv, Vienna
MCV	Museo Correr, Venezia
CPA	Carte della polizia austriaca
Doc. Manin	Documenti Manin
Agg. Manin	Aggiunte Manin
Doc. Pell.	Documenti Pellegrini

MRM   Museo del Risorgimento, Milano
MRR   Museo del Risorgimento, Roma
MS Olivi   Unpublished memoirs of Giuseppe Olivi (see Note on
                             documents and newspapers)
Racc. Andreola   *Raccolta per ordine cronologico di tutti gli atti, decreti,
                             nomine ecc. del governo provvisorio di Venezia, nonchè
                             scritti, avvisi, desideri ecc. di cittadini*, 8 vols., Andreola,
                             Venezia 1848-9

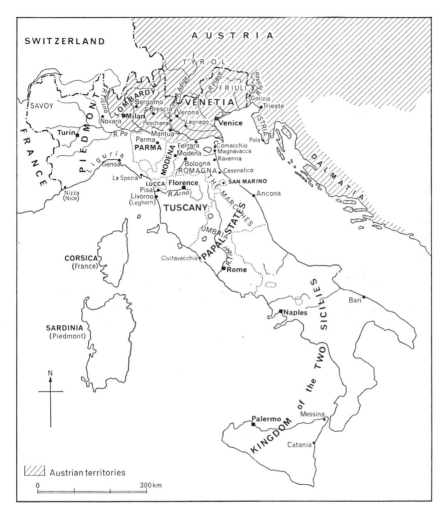

Map I   Italy, spring 1848

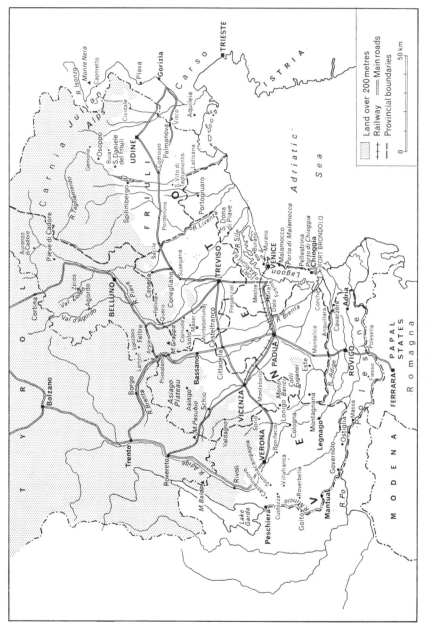

Map II The Veneto, 1848

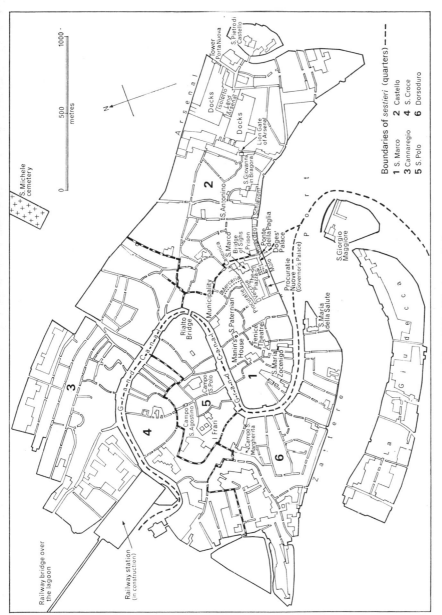

Map III Venice, 1848

S. Michele
cemetery

Railway bridge over
the lagoon

Railway station
(in construction)

Tower
Porta Nuova

S. Pietro di
Castello

Arsenal

Docks

Isolotto
(old Arsenal)

Docks

Lion Gate
of Arsenal

2

S. Antonino

S. Giovanni
in Bragora

P o r t

Bridge
of Sighs

S. Marco

Prison

Ponte
della Paglia

Doges'
Palace

Procuratie Nuove
(Governor's Palace)

S. Giorgio
Maggiore

Veronica

Mercerie

S. Paternian

Municipality

Piazza

Procuratie Vecchie

Molo

Rialto
Bridge

G r a n d
C a n a l

G r a n d
C a n a l

3

Campo
S. Polo

Campo
S. Agostino

I Frari

4

5

Campo
S. Margherita

6

S. Maria
della Salute

Z a t t e r e

Fenice
Theatre

Manin's
House

P. S. Maria
Zocenigo

1

L a   G i u d e c c a

Boundaries of sestieri (quarters) — — —

1 S. Marco   2 Castello
3 Cannaregio   4 S. Croce
5 S. Polo   6 Dorsoduro

1000

500

metres

0

N

I

Venetian society in the first half of the nineteenth century, 1814-48

In June 1814 Lombardy and Venetia, the central and eastern parts of northern Italy, were annexed to the Austrian empire. The crumbling edifice of Napoleonic Italy had provided no great resistance to the invading Austrian armies. The deprivations of the last years of the kingdom of Italy meant that the mass of the population felt little inclined to defend their French masters. Increased levels of taxation and conscription as well as the high mortality rate of the Italian army during the Russian campaign had combined with the bad harvest of 1813 and the ensuing bitter winter to bring destitution and misery to Venice and the Veneto.[1] When Venice fell after a protracted siege, the inhabitants of the city welcomed the Austrians, if only because they recognised in Austrian rule the peace and stability which had been denied them for much of the Napoleonic era.[2] The continuous series of campaigns which had been waged on Venetian soil at last drew to a close. Beauharnais, Napoleon's faithful viceroy, made his peace and retired to the Bavarian countryside. In June 1817 Prince Clemence Metternich came to stay in Venice on his way to Leghorn. He wrote to his wife: 'Yesterday I walked through Venice and it was like being in a city from *The Thousand and One Nights*.'[3] Venetia was to remain in Austrian hands until the outbreak of revolution in March 1848.

---

[1] 27,000 soldiers from the kingdom of Italy went to Russia, of whom only about 1,000 returned. See G. Candeloro, *Storia dell'Italia moderna*, vol. 1, p. 363. For the appalling conditions in the Veneto at this time, see R. J. Rath, 'The Habsburgs and the great depression in Lombardy-Venetia, 1814–18', *Journal of Modern History*, 13 (1941), p. 310.

[2] R. J. Rath, *The Provisional Austrian Regime in Lombardy-Venetia, 1814–15*, p. 356. For a good account of the siege of Venice, during which the canals froze and water ran out, see A. Pilot, 'Venezia nel blocco del 1813–14. Da noterelle inedite del Cicogna', *Archivio Veneto*, 27 (1914), pp. 191–227.

[3] *Mémoires, documents et écrits divers laissés par le prince de Metternich*, vol. 3 (1881), p. 23.

Austrian rule

Austrian government in Lombardy-Venetia has often been presented by Italian scholars, particularly those of the last century, in the most lurid of lights. Intent on denigrating their country's traditional enemy, Italian historians successfully created what Berengo has aptly called 'the black legend of Risorgimento historiography'.[4] While not wishing to subscribe to this legend, it seems impossible to escape the conclusion that the principles and requirements of the Austrians were in contradiction to the needs and aspirations of nearly every section of Venetian society. For many years recuperation from the devastations of war and the slow revival in prosperity masked this contradiction. But as time passed the fundamental conflict of interests between Austrian ruler and Venetian subject became increasingly evident.

No systematic study of Austrian economic and political policy in northern Italy has ever been written, and the period 1815–48 is particularly uncharted territory. But it is clear that Lombardy-Venetia was the most lucrative part of the empire. Wessenberg baldly declared, as early as 1814, that the administration was 'to exploit the Italian provinces to the best advantage of the monarch'.[5] In the average year the Austrians drew between a quarter and a third of the total income of the empire from northern Italy. Gross revenue per head of population was far greater in Lombardy and Venetia than anywhere else in the empire except lower Austria.[6] This was not true for the terrible years of 1814–18, when the crops failed continuously and peasants in the mountain villages of the Veneto starved to death. Then the Austrians remitted taxation and spent considerable sums on distribution of poor relief and an extensive public works programme.[7] But as the crisis passed the imperial government, in

[4] M. Berengo, 'Le origini del Lombardo-Veneto', *Rivista Storica Italiana*, 83 (1971), p. 544.

[5] Wessenberg to Metternich, 13 Aug. 1814. Quoted in A. Sandonà, *Il regno Lombardo-Veneto, 1814–59. La costituzione e l'amministrazione*, p. 74. Since Sandonà's fundamental work and that of J. A. Helfert, *Zur Geschichte des Lombardo-Venezianischen Königsreich*, little has been added to our knowledge. For a relatively recent summary, though not based on fresh archival work, see H. Benedikt, *Kaiseradler über dem Apennin. Die Österreicher in Italien*, especially pp. 111–39.

[6] See the comparative table in M. L. de Tegoborski, *Des finances et du crédit public de l'Autriche*, vol. 1, p. 116. De Tegoborski calculated that in 1837 revenue per head in lower Austria was 14.40 florins, in Lombardy 7.44, in Venetia 7.15, in Bohemia 4.00, in the Tyrol 3.58 and in Galicia 2.49 (one florin = approximately three Austrian lire). The high figure for lower Austria is to be explained by the presence of Vienna.

[7] Rath, 'The Habsburgs and the great depression', pp. 316–20.

spite of considerable outlays on roads and schools, drew an ever-increasing surplus from Italy. By 1845 income from Venetia exceeded expenditure there by over 45 million Austrian lire.[8]

The surplus from northern Italy was vital to the Austrian economy, because the *Hofkammer* (finance ministry) never avoided an annual deficit of considerable proportions. The smallest deficit ever achieved was by Kolowrat in 1830, and he only managed this by introducing the highly unpopular consumption tax, the *octroi*, levied principally on meat, wine and beer. The state debt became an increasingly onerous burden as the years passed,[9] and income from the fertile provinces of Lombardy and Venetia was a vital means of allaying the perennial shortages in the Viennese coffers. Austrian need for the surplus from Italy entailed a whole series of fiscal measures – ranging from the personal tax levied on the peasantry to the export duty on raw silk[10] – which created the unfavourable but well-founded impression that the Italian provinces were the 'milch cow' of the empire.

It is also clear that, within their overall plans for making the empire a self-sufficient economic unit, the Viennese economists ascribed to Venetia the subordinate role of a supplier of raw materials. Other parts of the empire – Bohemia and lower Austria with their cotton industry, the silk workshops of Vienna, and the woollen-processing industry of Moravia – had been singled out as the manufacturing centres. Goods from these areas were therefore introduced into the Veneto with no import duty and easily undercut local products. At the same time prohibitive duties were imposed on the importation of most raw materials into the Veneto. This meant that Venetian industry stood little or no chance of flourishing under Austrian rule.

In political matters, Austria did nothing to mask the basic economic exploitation and quasi-colonial status of the Veneto. Their system of

[8] Sandonà, *Il regno Lombardo-Veneto*, p. 349. In 1825 income from taxation in the Veneto already totalled over 41.5 million Au. lire, while expenditure in the same year was only 16.7 million Au. lire (*ibid.*, p. 339). Austrian road-building, at first to get grain to starving areas and later to facilitate troop movements, was considerable. The backbone of their road system was the 'mistress of Italy', the main road that ran westwards from Mestre to Milan.

[9] C. A. Macartney, *The Habsburg Empire, 1790–1918*, p. 206. De Tegoborski was intent on proving that Austrian finances were not as rickety as everybody made out. He showed that Austrian spending on the administration and the army was less, per head of population, than in either Prussia or France, and that Austria's public debt was not much more than half France's (*Des finances*, vol. 1, pp. 67–8, vol. 2, p. 358). But the major problem, as even de Tegoborski was forced to admit (vol. 1, p. 69), was that Austrian revenue was grossly insufficient to meet her expenditure, however reasonable the latter might have been in comparative terms.

[10] See below, pp. 20–1.

government had two dominant themes – centralisation and control. The Austrian emperor Francis I insisted that all matters of importance (and many of no importance at all) were to be referred to the aulic departments in Vienna and ultimately to the emperor himself. The Lombardo-Venetian kingdom, as the Italian provinces of the Austrian empire were called, existed as a separate entity only in name. The twin governments set up in Milan and Venice had no real powers to take independent decisions. Nor did the viceroy of the kingdom, the mediocre Archduke Ranier, who served as a sort of glorified imperial reporter from his palace at Monza, outside Milan.[11] Requests for orders from Vienna flowed upwards, in Metternich's words, 'like an ascending fountain, a material and moral absurdity, which finishes by drowning the head of state in a flood of minutiae and deprives the state itself of *any means of movement*'.[12]

Centralisation did not necessarily involve such immobility, but the peculiar nature of the Austrian central government and the character of the emperor himself led to the creation of a grotesque bureaucracy and innumerable delays. The relations between the three major Viennese governmental institutions, the *Hofstellen* (aulic departments), the *Staatsraat* (council of state) and the *Kabinett* (cabinet), were never clearly defined. Metternich abhorred this lack of distinction between legislative and executive power. In the absence of a clear hierarchy of command, different parts of the administration became private enclaves of power, vying for the emperor's favour. Kübeck, one of the most perceptive of Austrian statesmen, complained bitterly of the nobility who occupied the chief offices of the state and thwarted any measure that might threaten their feudal privileges.[13] Most Austrian politicians recognised these deficiencies but none seemed capable of carrying through reform.

The principal obstacle lay with the emperor himself. Fearful of delegating any authority, addicted to written reports on the most trivial of subjects, Francis amassed mountains of official papers for his personal attention, and worked through them like a snail. Even the devoted Metternich was forced to admit that his emperor lacked a certain 'speed of execution'.[14] Radvany has commented more bluntly: ' "One has to

---

[11] R. J. Rath, 'L'amministrazione austriaca nel Lombardo-Veneto, 1814–21', *Archivio Economico dell'Unificazione Italiana*, 9 (1959), p. 18.

[12] Letter to Ficquelmont, 8 Jan. 1848, in Metternich, *Mémoires*, vol. 7 (1883), p. 575.

[13] For a lucid account of the Viennese administrative organs, see E. Radvany, *Metternich's Projects for Reform in Austria*, pp. 1–8. *Ibid.*, p. 5 for Kübeck's comments, and pp. 50–1 for Metternich's.

[14] 17 Aug. 1837; Metternich, *Mémoires*, vol. 6 (1883), p. 223.

sleep on this" was his [Francis's] favourite saying; and sometimes he slept for years.'[15]

The emperor's insistence on absolute power for himself also meant the absence of any representative institutions for the Italian provinces. For Francis the unfortunate example of the over-powerful Hungarian Diet, able to negotiate taxation terms with Vienna, was not one to be repeated elsewhere in the empire. He consented only to the establishment of consultative 'congregations' in northern Italy, with very high property qualifications and little power or responsibility. The members of the congregations, drawn exclusively from the nobility and the upper middle class and selected by the emperor himself, were supposed to represent to Vienna the desires and needs of the inhabitants of the kingdom. The congregations soon came to be regarded as worthless for this purpose, though they were lucrative enough for those who sat on them.[16]

The influx of foreign officials was another aspect of the denial of any autonomy for Lombardy-Venetia. While it is dangerous to exaggerate the degree to which Italians were excluded from administrative posts,[17] a large number of those with political or military records as Francophiles lost their jobs after 1815. Former officers of the army of Italy were particularly viewed with suspicion. Indeed one high-ranking Austrian official in Venice, Count Thurn, was convinced that little could be done for the Veneto until that whole generation which had 'fought and thieved its way across Europe' was dead and buried.[18]

Lombards and Venetians, whatever their political past, rarely occupied

---

[15] Radvany, *Metternich's Projects*, p. 13.

[16] There were two central congregations, one at Milan and one at Venice. Each consisted of one noble and one non-noble deputy from every province of Lombardy and Venetia and one deputy from each royal city, of which there were thirteen in Lombardy and nine in the Veneto. The composition of the provincial congregations was less rigid and depended on the extent and importance of the particular province. A minimum annual income of 4,000 *scudi* was required for the central congregations and 2,000 for the provincial (one *scudo* = six Au. lire). Of the inhabitants of Venice in 1846, only 80 had an income in excess of 2,000 scudi, 32 in excess of 4,000 and 44 in excess of 6,000; G. Correr (ed.), *Venezia e le sue lagune*, vol. 2, pt. 1, p. 387. The deputies of the central congregations received 2,000 florins a year for their services (c. 6,000 Au. lire). No systematic study of the role of the congregations in Austrian government has ever been attempted.

[17] The majority of those who had served the French bureaucracy continued to pursue successful careers in the Austrian administration. By 1848 the magistrates in Venice, to take the example of one sensitive area later subject to much unfounded propaganda, were almost exclusively Italians; *Guida commerciale di Venezia*, pp. 168–9. It is impossible to tell merely from the names how many of the Italians were Venetians, but the majority were likely to be. See also Berengo, 'Le origini', pp. 530–4.

[18] ASV, Gov., 1840–4, L 1/1, report of 23 Feb. 1840.

the *highest* posts in the kingdom. Metternich seems to have had an almost racist attitude towards the Italians. He wrote to Apponyi in January 1833: 'They need titles, ribbons and silent senators. They would only have to be allowed to open their mouths for the machine to stop working instantly.'[19] The civil and military governors of Venice, Palffy and Zichy, were both Hungarians, the president of the court of appeal was called Schrott, and Count Thurn was the imperial delegate at Venice, later to be succeeded by Count Marzani, a Tyrolese nobleman.[20]

Few allowances were made for the different traditions and practices of the Italian-speaking provinces. Count Lazansky, who headed the commission of 1814–17 to decide the future administration of Lombardy-Venetia, summarised in five words Austrian thinking in these years: 'Il faut germaniser l'Italie'.[21] The wholesale application of the Austrian legal code aroused great indignation, particularly from the lawyers, for under Austrian law a defendant had no right to employ counsel. Hundreds of non-Italians found employment in the law courts, the most disliked of them being the Tyroleans.[22] In 1821, Count Strassoldo, governor of Lombardy, pleaded that the policy of Germanisation was misconceived and that the Italian administration had to be run by Italians. Little notice appears to have been taken of this sound advice.[23]

---

[19] G. Bertier de Sauvigny, *Metternich and His Times*, p. 190.

[20] Of the twenty-nine top men in the Venetian chancellery and government, eleven were non-Italians and seven were Venetian noblemen; *Guida commerciale*, pp. 94–8. See also the complaints of Giuseppe Olivi about Treviso: 'For many years we had a Grasser as bishop, a Groller as delegate, a Hendel as president of the tribunal . . .' (MS Olivi, pp. 44–5).

[21] Quoted in A. Mariutti, *Organismo ed azione delle società segrete del Veneto durante la seconda dominazione austriaca, 1814–47*, p. 13.

[22] Rath, 'L'amministrazione austriaca', pp. 21–6.

[23] See the letter from Strassoldo to Metternich, 11 Sept. 1821, in Sandonà, *Il regno Lombardo-Veneto*, p. 379. Only in the minutiae of local government did the Venetians have some measure of independence. In the smaller communes, of less than 300 members, all the male landowners met twice a year to approve the actions of their elected deputies. One of these deputies, who had to be amongst the three richest men of the village, would also perform the duties of imperial commissioner if none had been appointed. The influence of the wealthy landowners predominated throughout the local government system. In the larger communes the male landowners elected a council of thirty, of whom at least twenty had to be from among the richest proprietors. In the cities the mayors were appointed by the emperor, and there were high property qualifications for the forty members (sixty in Milan and Venice) of the municipal councils. Austrian officials supervised the functioning of all these organs of local government, but the system was recognised as an improvement on the French one and the most efficient in Italy. See *Venezia e le sue lagune*, vol. 2, pt. 1, p. 377, and Rath, 'L'amministrazione austriaca', p. 21.

One of the principal instruments enabling the Austrians to maintain a close control over their Venetian subjects was the church. After an early clash with the papacy over the selection of the patriarch of Venice, Pope and emperor soon came to close agreement over aims and methods. Francis I clearly established his right to appoint the bishops and archbishops of Lombardy-Venetia and took a personal interest in improving the training, though not the income, of the Venetian clergy.[24] The local priests, particularly in the countryside, were of crucial importance in instilling the correct reverence for Austrian rule into their congregations. In the hill and mountain villages of the Veneto, the sermons of the parish priest often provided the only contact with a wider world. Don Pinzani, parish priest of the hill village of San Daniele del Friuli, had this to say to his flock in 1846:

Render unto Caesar that which is Caesar's and unto God that which is God's. Fear the Lord, honour your priests and respect the king. The will of God is that by his grace you are subject to every human creature appointed by him to govern you. Woe unto him who takes it upon himself to go against any legitimate authority. That would be to reject the authority of God himself, and must lead to damnation.[25]

The influence of the clergy extended beyond the church and into the schools. The Austrians spent considerable sums in establishing a system of state education which was far in advance of any other in Italy at that time. The benefits, particularly in combating illiteracy, were considerable, but the motives for such attention were, in the emperor's immortal words, to ensure that every Venetian was securely 'a patriot for me'. The parish clergy were the principal teachers in the new schools, and in the 1840s the Jesuits, championed at the Viennese court by the pious party of Metternich and Sophie, gained access to the Veneto and took over a number of schools. All students in state schools were obliged by law to confess twice a month, and were given printed certificates in blank,

[24] See the letter of Francis I to Count Lazansky, 20 Jan. 1817, quoted in Sandonà, *Il regno Lombardo-Veneto*, p. 137 n. 1: 'According to the descriptions given me of the Venetian clergy, they lack instruction and education. The clergy there is composed of a mass of ignorant persons of the lowest class, enjoying no public respect, and in no way fit to explain and preach Christian doctrine.' Although the parish priests of the ancient churches of Venice lived quite comfortably, with an income of 700 Au. lire a year, their helpers often lived off charity and the rural clergy were considerably poorer than their urban counterparts. See P. Brunello, 'Rivoluzione e clero nel 1848 a Venezia', fos. 163–4.

[25] *Giornale dei parrochi*, 1 (1846), no. 22, pp. 169–70. Quoted in P. Brunello, 'Mediazione culturale e orientamenti politici nel clero veneto intorno al 1848; il "Giornale dei parrochi ed altri sacerdoti"', *Archivio Veneto*, 104 (1975), p. 150.

which the confessor filled up and stamped with the seal of the church.[26]
In the universities the emperor took great care over the appointment of
staff, and personally selected all professors, librarians and vice-librarians.[27]

The educated Venetian found his world dominated by the police and
the censorship. Kübeck reported delightedly in 1828 that 'the services of
the police are more resplendent than ever',[28] and much of their time was
spent in preventing the proliferation of 'subversive' literature. Among
the books prohibited for university students in 1847 were those of
Lucretius, Dante, Boccaccio, Alfieri, Hugo and Goethe. The list revealed
not only the government's terror of political subversion, but also the
church's fear of those authors who were morally decadent. Often indeed
the upper echelons of the church hierarchy proved more politically reactionary than the Austrian officials. In 1846 Tommaso Locatelli, editor
of the only Venetian newspaper, the *Gazzetta Privilegiata di Venezia*,
announced that he would publish in instalments a history of Napoleon. In
spite of governmental approval, the patriarch Monico fiercely attacked the
idea for fear that 'dangerous books would become too widely diffused'.[29]
Nor was censorship limited to the printed word. Rossini's *William Tell*
was sung at the Fenice, the Venetian opera house, in 1833, with the tyrant
Gessler's title changed from 'governor' to 'administrator'. In 1836 the
whole opera was prohibited because in it 'the story of Swiss independence
appears as an act of rebellion against the house of Habsburg'.[30]

[26] W. D. Howells, *Venetian Life*, vol. 2, p. 211.

[27] For Austrian educational policy, see N. Mangini, 'La politica scolastica dell'-
Austria nel Veneto dal 1814 al 1848', *Rassegna Storica del Risorgimento*, 46
(1957), pp. 769–83. In Venetia by 1845, 85,234 out of a total population of
138,341 boys between the ages of six and twelve were going to school. 14,039
out of 134,318 girls of the same age were also receiving schooling. These figures
compare unfavourably with the Lombard ones and the low number of girls
being educated is particularly striking. See *Annali Universali di Statistica, Economia Pubblica, ecc.*, 87 (1846), p. 192, for a breakdown by provinces for 1844,
and vol. 92 (1847), p. 77 for 1845. For the timetable of a Venetian elementary
school in the 1840s see ASV, Gov. Prov. 1848–9, MU, b. 5, no. 2458, details
from the Scuola elementare maggiore normale di Venezia. Private education, of
which there was a long tradition in Venice, was made subject to the 'Regulations
for private studies' of 1819. These required the submission of regular reports by
independent schools and tutors to government authorities.

[28] MCV, provenienze diverse, 716/c. 11, Kübeck to Lancetti, Dec. 1828.

[29] MCV, Cicogna diary, 1853, p. 6109, looking back to 1846. Published works were
graded in three ways: *admittitur*; *erga schedam*, which allowed distribution to
single individuals with special permission; and *damnatur*.

[30] F. Bertoliatti, 'La censura nel Lombardo-Veneto, 1814–48', *Archivio Storico
della Svizzera italiana*, 15 (1940), p. 63. On the censorship see also the ample
work of V. Malamani, 'La censura austriaca delle stampe nelle provincie venete',
Rivista Storica del Risorgimento Italiano, 1 (1896), pp. 489–521; 2 (1897), pp.
692–726; and *Il Risorgimento Italiano*, 2 (1909), pp. 491–541.

However, the major preoccupation of the Austrian police was with the possible existence of conspiracies against the state. Metternich and the emperor became obsessed with the dangers from this quarter, seeing everywhere a secret society or a lodge of the *carbonari*, the conspiratorial sect that sought to overthrow the governments of Restoration Italy. At first there was some justification for their fears. In late 1818 and early 1819 the police discovered a number of *carbonaro* lodges in the province of Rovigo, at the extreme south of the Veneto. A show trial of thirty-four conspirators followed in Venice in 1821, and some of the convicted received heavy prison sentences. After this the police made fervid attempts to discover other lodges which did not in fact exist. A further spell of intense vigilance followed during the central Italian revolutions of 1831–2, again with very little result.[31] The constant presence of police spies in the Venetian cafés, the habitual opening of correspondence, the impression of permanent surveillance, all contributed to alienate many Venetians who did not dream of revolt. Count Hübner later explained how Austrian policy had backfired in this respect:

He [Francis I] perhaps attached too great an importance to the secret societies which were undermining Italy and . . . he thought that the remedy for this evil lay in keeping a close watch on the so-called intelligent classes of society. This task was carried out by the police, who thereby became one of the chief instruments of his government . . . The effect was to produce in the educated classes a feeling of tacit annoyance with the government and a vague desire for political reform.[32]

If all else failed, the Austrians could always fall back on their final weapon of control, the army. Throughout the Restoration, Metternich maintained that the best safeguard against nationalism and revolution in Italy was a 'forest of bayonets'. Conscription, in spite of the promises made to abolish it after Napoleon had escaped from Elba, was maintained throughout the empire. At the age of twenty each Venetian, unless his

---

[31] Mariutti's work, *Organismo ed azione*, testifies to the small amount of activity of the secret societies in the Veneto after 1821. For Austrian preoccupations about the Veneto in 1831 see Spaur to Metternich, 9 Feb. 1831, HHSAV, Staatskanzlei Provinzen Lombardo-Venezien, fasz. 15, 4, no. 174. Venetian conspiracy in reality was very limited in this period. Virginio Brocchi, a young nobleman from Bassano, organised a revolutionary sect which spread to Padua, Verona and Vicenza, but without tangible results; see F. Della Peruta, *Mazzini e i rivoluzionari italiani: Il 'partito d'azione', 1830–45*, pp. 54–5, and p. 233 n. 58 for Mazzini's complaint of 1834 that Young Italy was virtually unheard of in the Veneto. For the early part of the period see also D. E. Emerson, *Metternich and the Political Police: Security and Subversion in the Hapsburg Monarchy, 1815–30*, chapter 3, 'On guard over Italy', pp. 57–99.

[32] Count J. A. von Hübner, *Une année de ma vie, 1848–9*, p. 19.

family was rich enough to present a substitute, became liable for selection for a period of eight years' military service. Lots were drawn to select the names, and in the average year Venetia sent about 3,000 men to join the army. Much of their time was spent in other parts of the empire because it was Austrian policy to try and avoid concentrating troops in their home countries.[33] The army stationed in Italy, under the able and paternalistic Radetzky, was renowned for being the best in the empire. Metternich and Clam stubbornly tried to resist any attempt to reduce its numbers, though this was sheer folly given the state of Austrian finances. It was also unsound policy for northern Italy. A large standing army meant unceasingly heavy taxation which in times of economic crisis could provoke the very uprising which Metternich was trying to avoid.

In its entirety, Austrian rule in northern Italy from 1815 to 1848 presented a conscious rejection of the semi-autonomy which Maria-Teresa had granted to Lombardy in the mid eighteenth century. Francis I, preferring to follow the example of his uncle Joseph, kept all power in his own hands, allowed very little independence of action to any section of Venetian society, and closely supervised the public and often private lives of his Italian subjects.[34] His system was not infamous in its cruelty nor without its alleviating features. For most of the period the Italian provinces, with few signs to the contrary, welcomed the peace and stability which Austrian rule brought. The public works which the Austrians undertook – poor relief in the great depression of 1814–18, road building and the founding of state schools – aided the revival of prosperity and did a little to combat the backwardness of Venetia. There is no evidence to show that their administration, on a local level at least, was corrupt or dishonest.

On the other hand, the vast financial tribute which the Austrians took from Lombardy-Venetia involved fiscal measures which were deeply resented and which did little to stimulate the economy of the two provinces in these years. The Austrian bureaucracy was renowned for its complex procedures and the exasperating slowness of its workings. The stifling presence of the police and the censorship re-emphasised the Italians' lack of self-government and their subjection to Vienna. In the Piazza San

[33] In 1838 for example the total for Venetia was 3,045 and for Lombardy 3,606; *Collezione delle leggi, istruzioni e disposizioni di massima, pubblicate o diramate nelle provincie venete*, vol. 29 (1838), pt. 1, p. 90. Until 1845, when conscription was standardised throughout the empire, the Italians escaped the lightest. In the Tyrol service was for fourteen years, with another six in the reserve. For some comparisons, see G. E. Rothenberg, 'The Austrian army in the age of Metternich', *Journal of Modern History*, 40 (1968), p. 160.
[34] By an order of Nov. 1829 government employees were forbidden to appear on stage or even to play a musical instrument in public; Sandonà, *Il regno Lombardo-Veneto*, p. 97 n. 1.

Marco an Austrian military band played marching songs while rich Venetians in the Café Metternich discussed every subject but politics.[35] But it was not possible to put the clock back to the age of enlightened absolutism. The revolutionary and Napoleonic period, for all its failings and devastations, had left too strong a legacy. Not only had many of its administrative practices and personnel survived, but also too many new ideas and experiences had become part of northern Italian history. The death of the whole Napoleonic generation was not, as Count Thurn hoped, to see an end to all subversion.

The Venetian countryside

The Veneto is divided into three very different regions. In the far north lie the beautiful valleys at the feet of the Dolomites and the mountains of Carnia. Today the villages of these valleys have become prosperous resorts for winter sports and the *villeggiatura* of bourgeois families during the summer months. But in the first half of the nineteenth century they were still poor hamlets populated by peasants and shepherds, gaining a precarious existence from the products of the rocky and infertile soil.

The hills below these valleys stretch in a long line from above Verona in the west to the furthest confines of Friuli, on the border with present-day Yugoslavia. The Venetian hills were fertile and prosperous, their slopes covered with vines and mulberry trees, their summits often crowned by enchanting small towns like Asolo, Conegliano or San Daniele del Friuli.

Finally, at the foot of these hills the plain stretched outwards as far as the eye could see, until the river Po marked the southern extremity of Venetian territory, and separated the Polesine from the Papal States. In the seventeenth and eighteenth centuries the Venetian nobility had made this flat and fertile land their own, establishing their great estates and building their villas on the banks of the river Brenta and elsewhere. The Po, the Adige, the Brenta, the Piave and the Tagliamento provided the natural irrigation for the area, which became known as the granary of Venice. Today the great fields of maize and wheat are still the most distinctive feature of this part of the Venetian countryside.

[35] Silvio Pellico, the Lombard patriot who was sentenced to many years in the Spielberg for his part in the Milanese conspiracy of 1821, was appalled by the attitudes of the Venetians when he visited the city in September 1820. He described them as nothing but 'chatterboxes' (Mariutti, *Organismo ed azione*, p. 47 n. 3). The Austrian police confirmed that this chatter was not about politics; see, for example, the letter from Lancetti to the governor of Venice, 4 April 1827, quoted in C. Tivaroni, *L'Italia durante il dominio austriaco*, vol. 1, pp. 503–4.

Landowners

During the first two decades of the nineteenth century dramatic changes took place in the ownership of the land. With the fall of the Venetian Republic in 1797 the Venetian nobility were broken forever as a ruling caste. The Napoleonic era was a dismal one for them, as the bulk of taxation and forced loans fell on their heads, and their lands were devastated by the frequent passage of opposing armies. Many began to sell off parts of their estates. In addition, the abolition by the French of the monasteries and nunneries of Lombardy-Venetia – some eight hundred in all – and the freeing of mortmain land by the decree of 1806 placed huge quantities of land on the market.[36] All those who benefited from French rule – members of the French administration, the officer corps of the army of Italy, the suppliers of the French army, and many others – hastened to buy up the acres that were coming onto the market. The Jews were particularly avid buyers. Freed by the French from the traditional restraints on their economic activity, the 5,000 Jews of the Veneto, this 'small but extremely active nucleus of the bourgeoisie',[37] by 1839 owned just over three per cent of the land.

Berengo, comparing the figures of the land surveys of 1740 and 1839, has shown that the Venetian nobility in this period lost nearly half of all the land that they had owned. By 1839 the majority of the hill regions of the Veneto were in the hands of non-noble owners, and the size of the plots, usually between five and one hundred hectares (one hectare = 2.471 acres) testified to the prosperity of the new proprietors. It is impossible to tell exactly who the new landowners were, for though the Austrian land survey lists their names, to try and trace them all would resemble the labours of Sisyphus. Clearly, their occupations varied considerably – some, as already mentioned, had got rich during the French domination, others were *fittavoli* who had begun by renting the land from the nobility and had finished by buying it outright. Others still were wealthy banking or commercial families from Venice, or else those who had made good from the flourishing tourist trade of the city.[38]

[36] M. Berengo, *L'agricoltura veneta dalla caduta della Repubblica all'Unità*, p. 139. Of the 144 noble families known to have existed in 1797, only 94 still had representatives alive in 1846; *Venezia e le sue lagune*, vol. 1, app. III, pp. 37–45.

[37] Berengo, *L'agricoltura veneta*, p. 84; see also pp. 153, 158 and 167. By 1834 church lands totalled no more than four per cent of all land in the Veneto, and much of this was of poor quality.

[38] *Ibid.*, pp. 171–3. A typical example was the wealthy grain merchant Giuseppe Comello, who owned land all over the Veneto by the time of the Austrian land survey. See also the significant work of G. Zalin, *L'economia veronese in età napoleonica*, pp. 219–74. Mirella Calzavarini is at present engaged in writing a full-scale study of this problem, covering the whole of the Veneto.

These changes of land ownership did not result in an agricultural revolution in the Venetian countryside. The first steps in the long process of the transformation of the agrarian economy into a capitalist one had been taken with the freeing of the land from feudal restraints and its acquisition by new sectors of Venetian society. But radical transformations in the means and relations of production, and indeed in what was produced, did not occur until much later in the nineteenth century. Agrarian capitalism did not find the secure foothold in the Venetian plains that it acquired in Lombardy in this period. The majority of Venetian landowners, both old and new, were content with the traditional products of wheat, maize and wine and the traditional means of producing them.

Venetian wheat was of two types. Most of it (*nostrana*) was for the making of bread, but in the more humid areas like the Polesine a variety called *grossa* or *dura* was used for pasta. In spite of the low agricultural prices of most of the period, the landowners' staple income came from these two sorts of grain. Wine was of low quality, and only Bardolino from the shores of Lake Garda, and Valpolicella and Soave from the Veronese, were exported. The Venetian market was thus vulnerable to imported wines, and every chamber of commerce in the Veneto expressed its satisfaction when Metternich doubled the duty on Piedmontese wines in April 1846. As for maize, the majority of it was used for *polenta*, a yellowish cooked flour which formed the staple diet of the peasantry.[39]

The pattern of Venetian agriculture was therefore highly traditional, but a small group of landowners refused to accept this time-honoured immobility. From the early 1830s onwards there is increasing evidence of a current of opinion intent on transforming Venetian agriculture to bring it into line with the great advances occurring elsewhere in Europe. Men like Count Gherardo Freschi of San Vito di Tagliamento devoted themselves to stimulating change on their estates – introducing modern methods, irrigating the fields, reclaiming marsh lands, practising intensive cultivation, founding agricultural associations, publishing journals and paying close attention to the education of their peasantry.[40] The lists of

[39] For the different types of agriculture in the Veneto see G. Scarpa, *L'agricoltura del Veneto nella prima metà del XIX secolo. L'utilizzazione del suolo*, pp. 15–55. See also Berengo, *L'agricoltura veneta*, pp. 243–64 (grain), and pp. 291–304 (wine, and p. 301 for the Venetian reaction of 1846).

[40] Count Gherardo Freschi (1804–93) was one of the founders of the Agrarian Society of Friuli and was its president for many years. He also founded and was editor of the agrarian journal *L'amico del contadino*. Before 1848 he published a number of works on agriculture, including a guide to the breeding of silkworms (San Vito, 1839). For his intense activities as an agronomist and publisher see M. Lucchetta, *Arte tipografica e movimenti politico-letterari a San Vito di Taglia-*

prizes distributed by the local chambers of commerce of the Veneto give a
very good indication of what the most dynamic proprietors were undertaking, and some, like Giuseppe Reali, transferred the practice of prize-
giving to their own estates, rewarding the most industrious and enterprising
of their labourers.[41]

Men like Reali and Freschi represented the continuity of the bourgeois
revolution in the countryside, the link between the freeing of the land
from feudal restrictions and the agrarian capitalism of many decades later.
By no means all the innovating landowners came from the bourgeoisie.
In 1846 Pelizzo made a list of the most enterprising proprietors of Friuli.
Apart from the outstanding example of Freschi, he also included a number
of other noblemen, among whom were Girolamo Venerio and Count
Nicolò di Valvason.[42] Such men were clearly continuing the policies of
high investment and high returns on their estates which had characterised
the economic activity of some of the great eighteenth-century Venetian
noblemen like Andrea Tron.[43] The real distinction therefore was not

mento. I have been informed by the Freschi family that sadly all Gherardo
Freschi's papers were destroyed in the first World War.

[41] See the *Gazzetta di Venezia*, no. 224, 23 Aug. 1869, obituary of Giuseppí Reali.
Reali (1801–69) was well known as one of the richest men in Venice. Before the
revolution he applied for but did not obtain Austrian noble status. He was
president of the Milan–Venice railway company and vice-president of the Venetian
chamber of commerce. For a short biography see P. Rigobon, *Gli eletti alle
assemblee veneziane del 1848–9*, pp. 188–9. Reali's papers appear to have been
dispersed or lost, another sad loss for historians of nineteenth-century Venetia.

The prizes handed out in 1846 by the Venetian Institute of Science, Letters and
Arts give a few examples amongst many of the activities of Venetian entrepreneurs. A gold medal was awarded to Girolamo Lattis for his work of land
reclamation at Caorle (on the coast near San Donà di Piave). He had employed
400 men to reclaim the 3,000 *campi* that he had purchased at Cà Corniani. In
1838 and 1844 he had won medals for similar work undertaken at Altino. The
Paduan Cesare Levi also won a gold medal. In 1843 he had bought a poorly
cultivated *latifondo* of about a thousand *campi* near the mouth of the Po. He
spent 124,000 Au. lire on improving the land and building a new village, and
by 1845 was already getting a return of 14,000 lire a year from the rice that was
being produced there. See *Atti della distribuzione dei premi d'industria fatta
nella pubblica solenne adunanza dell'I.-R. Istituto di scienze, lettere ed arti, 30
maggio 1846*, Venezia 1846. For detailed descriptions of similar land improve-
ments and intensive farming, see the pamphlets of Domenico Rizzi: *Lettera a co.
Gherardo Freschi sui lavori di agricoltura e le industrie campestri*, and *Sui
miglioramenti agrari delle due tenute di Sabbion e Desmontà nel distretto di
Cologna del nob. co. Giov. Papadopoli.*

[42] BCU, F. Pelizzo, *Notizie statistiche della provincia di Friuli* (3 vols., dated 1846,
but never published), vol. 1, pp. 205–11.

[43] For the illuminating example of Andrea Tron's estate at Anguillara in the
province of Padua, see J. Georgelin, 'Une grande propriété en Vénétie au xviiie
siècle: Anguillara', in *Annales, Economies, Sociétés, Civilisations*, 23 (1968), pp.

between noble and bourgeois landowners. It was between those who were trying to introduce more efficient and often clearly capitalist methods into agriculture and those who were not.[44]

Nowhere did the more enterprising of landed proprietors find a better outlet for their energies nor a greater chance of involving their more conservative brethren in the one sector of the Venetian economy in dynamic expansion – silk. The first half of the nineteenth century witnessed striking advances in the production of raw and spun silk in Lombardy-Venetia. High returns were to be had from the planting of mulberry trees, and the great markets and workshops of Europe – in Lyons, London and Vienna in particular – easily absorbed the produce of northern Italy. In this period Italian silk constituted the principal export of the Austrian empire, with de Tegoborski calculating in 1843 that as much as ten-elevenths of Austrian revenue from exports came from silk.[45] Production and profits rose steadily until 1846, but after that the economic crisis of 1846–7, the blights of the 1850s and above all the undercutting of Lombardo-Venetian silk by that coming from India contrived to destroy the great silk boom.

Lombard landowners led the way in sericulture, always produced and manufactured more than the Venetians, and established the principal export market at Milan. But the Veneto also produced vast quantities of raw silk and the figures for the province of Verona bear comparison with any of those in Lombardy.[46] Widespread planting of mulberries had

483–519. However, the nascent agrarian capitalism of Anguillara appears to have remained the exception rather than the rule in the Veneto of the first half of the nineteenth century.

[44] For a stimulating discussion of this question, see S. Soldani, 'Contadini, operai e "popolo" nella rivoluzione del 1848–9 in Italia', *Studi Storici*, 14 (1973), p. 574.

[45] De Tegoborski, *Des finances*, vol. 2, p. 257.

[46] A comprehensive history of the growing and spinning of silk in nineteenth-century Venetia has yet to be written. Details of silk production in the province of Verona for the years 1837–47 are to be found in G. Zalin, *Aspetti e problemi della economia veneta dalla caduta della Repubblica all'annessione*, table 26, p. 150; and for Friuli in the same period, *ibid.*, p. 149 n. 37. See also Berengo, *L'agricoltura veneta*, pp. 305–18, and C. Vanzetti, *Due secoli di storia dell' agricoltura veronese*, pp. 64–5, and p. 71 for a table of the prices of raw silk and cocoons, 1814–48. By 1847 the province of Verona was producing more than four million kilogrammes of silk per year. For a good summary of Italian silk produce and its primacy on the world market at this time, see Sir John Bowring, 'Report on the statistics of Tuscany, Lucca, the Pontifical and the Lombardo-Venetian states, with a special reference to their commercial relations', *Parliamentary Papers*, vol. 16 (1839), pp. 104–9. Bowring wrote (p. 104): 'From the Var to the Isonzo, vast plantations exist of white mulberry, sometimes trained as tall as stately trees, at others pruned down almost to square bushes, but everywhere giving a peculiar and attractive character to the agricultural scenery.'

already begun in the eighteenth century, but was resumed with increased vigour in 1818. The practice of planting them as supports to the vines, as hedges and along the edges of the fields and roads became extremely popular. The Scarpa brothers of Adria, one of the principal establishments for selling mulberry trees in the Veneto, sold nearly one million in the decade 1829–38, and in the light of later political events the list of their customers makes interesting reading.[47]

Giuseppe Olivi, a provincial lawyer in Treviso who was to become the president of the Trevisan revolutionary committee in March 1848, has left a fascinating account of his mounting obsession with the production of silk. In April 1825 he visited Milan and was much impressed by the riches to be gained from silk. He returned to Treviso and in spite of the scepticism of his friends, who called him a 'mulberry maniac', he persevered until in the fifth year of production he obtained 1,600 *libbre* of silk cocoons; 'curiosity had got the better of all the proprietors of the province; when the time came for the silkworms to hatch they could not resist coming to have a look at my silkworm nursery'.[48]

By the 1840s the hills and plains of the Veneto were thickly covered with mulberries and side by side with the production of silk cocoons there developed a silk-spinning industry of considerable proportions. Many landowners built spinning-mills on their estates and employed peasant women for the arduous and delicate task of converting the cocoons into spools of spun silk. Giuseppe Olivi built a 'grandiose spinning-mill' in 1840, equipped with 24 *fornelli*, with the machinery powered by steam and a dormitory on the top floor where the women could sleep. The mill began production in 1844 but with the worsening of economic conditions Olivi could not recoup the sums he had spent and the venture ended in disaster. However, other landowners had considerable success and by 1847 40,000 kilogrammes of spun silk were being produced in the province of Verona alone, of which 15,000 kilogrammes went to other parts of the empire and 25,000 outside it.[49]

These successes could not mask the partial nature of the Venetian silk industry and its failure to graduate to the higher levels of manufacturing.

[47] D. Rizzi, *Adria e lo stabilimento agrario dei fratelli Scarpa*, table at end. Among the purchasers the following were to figure prominently in the revolution of 1848–9: G. B. Benvenuti, who bought 2,550 mulberry trees; Valentino Comello, 1,300; Count Giovanni Correr, 502; Angelo Mengaldo, 6,040; the brothers Treves di Bonfili, 5,854.

[48] MS Olivi, p. 67.

[49] G. Zalin, *Aspetti e problemi*, table 26, p. 150. For Olivi's unhappy experiences, MS Olivi, pp. 77–91. Details of the production of spun silk in Friuli from 1837–52 are to be found in A. Errera, *Storia e statistica delle industrie venete e accenni al loro avvenire*, pp. 249–56.

The Veronese proprietors boasted of the quick returns to be had by selling the spun silk at Milan and thus avoiding all the problems of storage, travel and the fluctuations of the London market. But these quick returns were no substitute for the development of a manufacturing industry, and in the European silk industry of the nineteenth century the Veneto remained in a strictly secondary position as one supplier amongst many.

The same backwardness is to be found in nearly all the manufacturing industries of the Veneto. In 1819 the first Italian steamship, the *Eridano*, had arrived at Genoa from the workshops of Watt. Quite a few steam engines were in use in the spinning-mills of Lombardy and Venetia by the 1840s. But the industrial revolution had not begun to make an impression on the predominantly agricultural nature of Italy in general and the Veneto in particular. Thousands of peasant looms were at work in the Venetian countryside; the loom was often considered an essential part of a peasant girl's dowry. But the handicraft, localised nature of manufacturing was rarely superseded in these years.

Once again, though, the exceptions to this rule are of considerable interest and importance. Among the northernmost hills of the provinces of Treviso and Vicenza, in villages like Valdagno, Schio and Follina, a small woollen-cloth industry was taking the first steps towards transcending the hand-loom weaving of the region. Today this area is the home of Italian textiles and some of the entrepreneurs of the 1820s and 1830s, like Rossi and Marzotto, have given their names to very large-scale concerns. The terrain was exceptionally favourable because of the abundance of flowing water from the mountain streams. At Schio Francesco Rossi and Eleonoro Pasini founded the first factory in 1818 and by 1845 there were four factories employing 540 workers, with modern machinery imported from abroad. At Follina by 1840 there were two large firms, Colles and Andretta, employing 350 operatives each, with smaller firms giving work to another hundred. The Follina cloth was not of the highest quality, being 'suitable for the middle classes', but there was a special *tricot* for trousers which would have done credit to 'any dandy of the jokei-club [*sic*]'.[50]

50 F. Sanseverino, 'Delle fabbriche di pannilana in Follina nella provincia di Treviso, 1840', *Annali Universali di Statistica, Economia Pubblica, ecc.*, 67 (1841), p. 228 (whole article pp. 222–9). For Francesco Rossi's factory at Schio, see *Atti della distribuzione dei premi d'industria … 1846*, pp. 35–6. Again, no history of the early years of the Venetian textile industry has ever been written. Of Venetian industries, only the modest production and marketing of paper has yet received detailed and comprehensive treatment; see A. Fedrigoni, *L'industria e il commercio della carta nel Veneto durante la seconda dominazione austriaca*. For the more developed Lombard industry of the period see the classic work of K. R. Greenfield, *Economics and Liberalism in the Risorgimento. A study of Nationalism in Lombardy, 1815-1848*, pp. 81–127.

The little Venetian industry that existed was frequently to be found in rural settings. The largest mill in the Veneto was the one that spun and dyed cotton at Torre, in the countryside near Pordenone. Here 450 operatives found work and the machinery was powered by a Fourneyron turbine of 100 horsepower.[51] Industrial entrepreneur and innovating landowner often tended to be one and the same person. Giuseppe Reali, who became vice-president of the Venetian chamber of commerce in 1847, owned a wax workshop, a sugar refinery and two brick-factories, as well as a large spinning-mill on his estates in the Veneto.

Thus if the mass of Venetian landowners were cautious and hidebound there was a significant minority who were prepared to experiment. Silk offered them the greatest outlet and return for their talents, but some did not hesitate to invest in manufacturing as well. They did not always succeed, but they represented the forward-looking element in the Venetian countryside, impatient to jolt it from its backwardness. In 1844, on the occasion of the annual distribution of prizes for agriculture and commerce for the province of Friuli, Giovanni Domenico Ciconi exhorted his fellow Friulani to greater efforts in the following terms:

We are on the right road, we are making progress, we are in step with the advances of this century. But we are not employing that energy and urgency which our soil, our ability, the number of our labourers, our geographical position demands of us. Much indeed remains to be done to gain the profits from that capital with which providence has endowed us.[52]

Austrian rule proved a mixed blessing to the Venetian landowners. In political terms the nobility gained some compensation for their increasing impoverishment. The Venetian aristocracy, unlike their Lombard counterparts, had always been Austrophile and Francophobe. In the early years of

---

[51] *Atti della distribuzione dei premi d'industria . . . 1846*, pp. 27–8. By the middle of the century Pordenone had acquired a modest reputation as a manufacturing centre. Pacifico Valussi regretted that no instruction in the techniques of the chemical industry was available, for it would have been of great benefit both to the dyeing section of the cotton factory and the numerous small dyeing workshops scattered through Friuli; P. Valussi, *Rapporto della camera di commercio e d'industria della provincia del Friuli, all'ecc. I.-R. ministero del commercio, ecc . . . 1851–2*, p. 101. For statistics of industry in Friuli in the early 1840s see BCU, Pelizzo, *Notizie statistiche*, vol. 1, pp. 78–81. The most surprising information Pelizzo affords is the existence of 600 weavers of hemp, flax and cotton in Cividale del Friuli, producing goods worth one million Au. lire a year. As there is no evidence of large factories, Cividale must have been an extraordinarily active artisan centre.

[52] G. D. Ciconi, 'Discorso sull'agricoltura friulana', in *Atti della distribuzione dei premi d'industria, 1844, fatta dalla congregazione municipale e dalla camera provinciale di commercio in Udine*, p. 4.

the Restoration the Austrians rewarded them by giving them the most important posts in the administration that were open to Italians, and Francis did not hesitate to offer them all the title of Count.[53] Even so, it was soon clear that they enjoyed only a shadow of the power that they had wielded under the old Republic, and the central congregations which they dominated proved a cruel delusion. For the non-noble landowners Austrian rule had even less to offer politically. Unless they were very rich, bourgeois proprietors were unlikely to find a place on the provincial congregation and had to be content with what limited power they could exercise at village level.

Lack of political influence, though, never aroused the Venetian landowners as much as Austrian economic policy. In 1817 the Austrians decided that a new land survey (the *catasto*) was needed to eliminate evasions and omissions in the direct tax on land. A Giunta was set up in Milan to carry out this survey, and from the very beginning encountered the outright hostility of the Venetian nobility. Under the old Venetian Republic the tax estimate had been drawn up by local government officials, who were often themselves the principal landowners of the neighbourhood. Now, for the first time, the great proprietors had to stand by while their lands were measured and estimated in value. They tried every delaying tactic they knew, and the combination of their obstructionism and the slowness of the Austrian bureaucracy meant that the new tax system began to operate only in 1847, and then just for the provinces of Venice, Padua and Rovigo.[54]

In many ways the land survey represented one of the most positive aspects of Austrian rule. The meticulous enquiry ensured a fairer distribution of the land tax, and the extent and nature of all landed property was noted systematically for the first time. But these advantages were outweighed in the eyes of the Venetians by at least two negative factors. First, the Giunta set up by the Austrians was dominated by the Milanese and the Venetians complained bitterly that they were being discriminated against. Secondly, the tax estimates applied to what was produced on the land as well as the land itself. When the Austrians decided – not unnaturally, in view of the state of their finances – to impose a high tax on the growing of mulberry trees, the Venetian landowners, and the Lombards for that matter, exploded in anger. In vain they protested that the

[53] See the list in Tivaroni, *L'Italia*, vol. 1, p. 506, of important jobs held by Venetian noblemen. The title of 'Count' was widely despised for, as the Italian proverb runs, 'Il conte che non conta, non conta niente' – 'the count who can't count his money counts for nothing'; quoted by Howells, *Venetian Life*, vol. 2, p. 222.

[54] Berengo, *L'agricoltura veneta*, pp. 49–62; also *Venezia e le sue lagune*, vol. 2, pt. 1, p. 368.

government should aid this thriving sector of the agricultural economy, not cripple it at source.[55]

These arguments found further support in the *Hofkammer*'s insistence on maintaining a high export duty for raw and spun silk. This was largely for fiscal reasons – the Austrians had no intention of signing away the estimated two million Au. lire that the duty brought in every year – but it was also to protect the price of raw silk for the flourishing industries of Lombardy and Vienna.[56] The Venetians, though disunited because the Veronese merchants seemed happy to limit their trade to Lombardy, waged an unsuccessful battle to get the duty reduced. The *Hofkammer* did agree to a reduction by a third in 1824, but after that refused to budge. In 1841 Spiridione Papadopoli[57] and Giuseppe Reali, two of the most interesting and significant figures in Venetian society of these years, wrote a long and forceful memorandum demanding that the duty be reduced sixfold.[58] They argued that the amount of oriental silk on the London market had doubled between 1825 and 1835 and was now seriously threatening to undercut the silk from Lombardy-Venetia. This was principally because the high export duty imposed by the Austrians was making Italian silk uncompetitive. Only by denying themselves a reasonable profit were the Lombardo-Venetian growers and merchants staying in the market. They had tried to find other outlets for their silk, and one million of the annual production of four and a half million kilogrammes was being sold in Switzerland, Germany and Prussia. But this

[55] In July 1828 the central congregation of Venice, awakened from its habitual lethargy, demanded no less than a committee of Venetian landowners to sit in judgement on the Giunta's actions. The result was a sharp reprimand from the viceroy, Ranier: 'although it is permitted to the central congregation humbly to represent to His Majesty the needs, desires and prayers of the subjects of this kingdom, it must not be inferred from this that the central congregation of Venice can arrogate to itself the right to query the works of the Giunta' (ASV, Pres. Gov. 1825–9, b. VI, 1/2; quoted in Berengo, *L'agricoltura veneta*, p. 48).

[56] I. A. Glazier, 'Il commercio estero del regno lombardo-veneto dal 1815 al 1865', *Archivo Economico dell'Unificazione Italiana*, 15 (1966), p. 25; also Berengo, *L'agricoltura veneta*, p. 318. In 1847 Viennese manufacturers requested a reduction in the entry duty on oriental silks, thus threatening what was probably the last safe market for Venetian silk; ASV, CI, b. 5, fasc. 11/44, no. 538. In 1838 Vienna had been taking 302,000 *libbre* of Venetian silk; Greenfield, *Economics and Liberalism*, p. 60 n. 35.

[57] Spiridione Papadopoli (1799–1859) belonged to a family of shipowners from Corfu, who had been admitted to the Venetian nobility in the eighteenth century. He was one of the richest and most powerful merchants in Venice, as well as one of the most enterprising. For a short biography see A. Bernardello, 'Burocrazia, borghesia e contadini nel Veneto austriaco', *Studi Storici*, 17 (1976), p. 131 n. 6.

[58] ASV, CI, b. 5, fasc. 11/44, no. 347, 15 March 1841.

was no permanent solution because before long 'those able merchants, the English' would move into these markets as well. Reali and Papadopoli finished by hitting the Austrians in what they knew to be their most sensitive spot. If the *Hofkammer* reduced the duty, the increased export trade would in the long run benefit the finances of the empire by eliminating all the smuggling of silk through Switzerland and Piedmont which was depriving the imperial treasury of considerable sums. But nothing came of this memorandum nor of the many pleas, petitions and reports which followed it on the long road to and around the Viennese aulic departments.[59]

In February 1848, on the very eve of the outbreak of the revolution, Gherardo Freschi, the epitome of the reforming Venetian landowner, summarised in uncompromising terms the Austrians' failings with regard to Venetian agriculture.[60] The backwardness of the Veneto, remarked Freschi, was not to be attributed primarily to 'the ignorance of the proprietors or the failure to apply sound agricultural methods'. The reasons were rather to be found in 'the civil, fiscal, political and penal laws and the procedures related to them, which with regard to agriculture are defective, troublesome and inapplicable'. In elaborating on this statement, Freschi listed the three main problems: excessive taxation of the products of the soil, uncertainties over the rights of land ownership leading to interminable lawsuits, and the remnants of feudal dues and practices which the Austrians had not abolished.[61] Freschi ended by asking for the creation of a special code for agriculture and a special magistracy to enforce it. For once he did not have to wait for a reply; events supplied it for him.

Peasantry

By 1847 the Veneto had over two and a quarter million inhabitants and of these the great majority were peasants and rural artisans. The population rose slowly for most of the period from the Restoration to the middle of the century, but the decade 1837–46 saw a striking increase of 183,082.[62] The plains of Polesine and the province of Padua were the

[59] In its annual report for 1847 the Venetian chamber of commerce asked once again: 'Such a request, it is true, is not new ... but since so many pressing remonstrances of the past have still achieved no effect, we must insist ...'; ASV, CC, b. 184, VI, 26.

[60] G. Freschi, 'Intorno i mezzi di cui abbisogna l'agricoltura per conseguire da vero i progressi che lo stato attuale della scienza le ha preparato', *Atti dell'I.-R. Istituto Veneto di Scienze, Lettere ed Arti*, 7 (1847-8), pp. 77–9.

[61] Freschi mentioned in particular the *pensionatico*, the ancient right of winter pasture in the plains for the sheep of the mountains, as well as the clerical tithe and other feudal servitudes like that controlling the use of water.

[62] The population of the Veneto increased during these years as follows: 1815,

most densely populated areas of the Veneto, having over 400 inhabitants to the square mile.[63]

In general, the Venetian peasantry lived in great deprivation throughout the whole of the period 1815–48. During the first years of the Restoration, from 1814 to 1818, a continuous series of failed harvests plunged many of them below the minimum subsistence level. In the mountain villages of Friuli some peasants were reduced to eating hay, manure and wild berries, others to making bread from the leaves of bean plants. Conditions were not as bad as in some other parts of the empire, where in 'fat Hungary itself' tens of thousands of people died of starvation in 1816–17.[64] But deaths from starvation were reported from Friuli, and bread riots and assaults on tax collectors spread through the Venetian countryside.

Conditions improved quite rapidly after 1818 though the cholera epidemic of 1835–6 took its toll in the Veneto as elsewhere. But many peasants escaped starvation or cholera only to meet an equally dismal fate. Pellagra was rife throughout the Veneto; in February 1817 there were 95,000 reported cases, and the disease continued to plague the Venetian peasants in the following years. The illness was caused by vitamin deficiency, and medical opinion of the time ascribed it to the overeating of polenta and grass. In its final stages, pellagra led to mental derangement; the *pellagrosi* felt themselves to be burning inside, and tried to throw themselves into water.[65]

The incidence of infant mortality among the peasants was very high, their penury and lack of good health remarked upon by all who visited the region. Berengo has summarised the essential features of their lives: 'Food that was devoid of any nutritional value; houses that were cramped, flimsy

1,945,619 inhabitants; 1827, 2,002,204 (+56,585); 1837, 2,074,118 (+71,914); 1846, 2,257,200 (+183,082); Zalin, *Aspetti e problemi*, p. 44. Lombardy's population in 1847 was 2,734,244.

[63] A. Quadri, *Prospetto statistico delle provincie venete*, Venezia 1826, p. 16. No statistics exist to enable us to estimate the number of peasants in this period; see Berengo, *L'agricoltura veneta*, pp. 85–6.

[64] Macartney, *The Habsburg Empire*, p. 200. The best account of conditions in the Veneto in 1816–17 is by G. Monteleone, 'La carestia del 1816–17 nelle provincie venete', *Archivio Veneto*, 86–7 (1969), pp. 23–86.

[65] Terminal male cases from the area around Venice were dispatched to the madhouse on the island of S. Servolo, while the women were accommodated in the civic hospital founded by the Austrians in the Scuola San Marco in 1815; *Venezia e le sue lagune*, vol. 2, pt. 1, pp. 289 and 299–300. See also the discourse by G. L. Gianelli (the medical counsellor of the government at Milan), 'Dei miglioramenti sociali efficaci e possibili a vantaggio degli agricoltori e degli operai', in *Giornale dell'I.-R. Istituto Lombardo di Scienze, Lettere ed Arti e Biblioteca Italiana*, 1 (1847), p. 200.

and unhealthy; pellagra in nearly every family; debts with the landowner, uncertainty in finding work, absolute dependence on the harvest.'[66]

Any detailed description of the peasantry must distinguish between the three areas of the Veneto – the plains, hills and mountains – because conditions, landholding, produce and contracts varied considerably from region to region.

On the plains, where the great estates predominated, the peasantry owned very little land indeed, and then usually in tiny pockets on the fringes of the landowner's vast domains.[67] Some peasant families, who rented the smaller farms (*masserie*, up to thirty hectares) lived quite well, though the contracts which the proprietor might impose differed widely from farm to farm and area to area. On the great estates themselves, often rented out by the landowner or run by a steward in his absence, the ploughman (*boaro* or *bifolco*) came top of the peasant social scale. He and his family would live in the *boaría*, the large brick building with a tiled roof which formed the focal point for each fifty *campi* (19 to 26 hectares), of the great estate. The ploughman usually lived rent free and had the use of a kitchen garden and three-quarters of a hectare in which to grow maize; a third of this he could keep for himself. He also had the right to hire two or three peasant families as helpers and these would live in the *boaría* as well.

Below them came the bulk of the workforce, the *braccianti*, rural labourers. On 11 November of each year, the festival of San Martino, some *braccianti* (*fissi* or *obbligati*) received as a retainer a small amount of maize, which bound them to a particular estate until the harvest had been gathered. Others (*avventizi* or *liberi*) would seek employment in the summer months where they could find it, and for the rest of the year either emigrated to the towns, or else did any sort of odd job on the *masserie* or on large estates, in return for sufficient polenta to keep them alive. The labourers usually lived in the squalid thatched huts which surrounded the main *boaría*; sometimes they were lucky enough to get the use of a small plot of land on which to grow maize. Conditions varied so greatly in the different parts of the plain that it is impossible to come to any accurate conclusions about wages, or even to distinguish clearly

---

[66] Berengo, *L'agricoltura veneta*, p. 223.

[67] Berengo took six sample areas in the various regions of the Veneto (excluding the mountains and Friuli) and found the following amount of smallholding (up to 5 hectares as a percentage of total cultivated land): upper part of the province of Padua, 9.74 per cent; lower part of the province of Padua, 5.36 per cent; Polesine, 7.25 per cent; Trevisan hills, 14.80 per cent; Veronese hills, 28.54 per cent; Veronese plains, 5.51 per cent (*L'agricoltura veneta*, pp. 153–6).

between fixed and day labourers. In general, the *braccianti* would probably receive food, money and other forms of payment to the value of 100–150 Austrian lire each year; the *boari* got 200–240 lire.[68]

In January 1839 Count Pillersdorff, convinced that many peasants in Lombardy-Venetia were living in 'the worst of conditions', ordered an enquiry into Lombardo-Venetian agriculture.[69] The enquiry revealed that in the plains the new landowners were often exacting harsher terms from their peasantry than had the old nobility. This was the considered opinion of Count Thurn and there is evidence of it from a number of areas. At San Donà di Piave, for instance, the authorities lamented the passing of the great ecclesiastical estates of that area into the hands of 'voracious speculators' who 'so as not to lose a penny, torture their peasantry into desperation or immorality'. All the accounts confirm that the landless labourers of the southern Veneto lived appallingly harsh lives.

In the hill regions peasant property was much more widespread, particularly in the province of Verona. Here the great estates gave way to much smaller properties, and the habitual contract between landowner and peasant was that of sharecropping – the *lavorenza* of Verona, the *mezzadria* or *metadia* of the other Venetian hills. Again the specific nature of the contracts differed widely, but in general the peasant received a cottage, a vegetable garden and the use of the landowner's agricultural tools and farm animals. In return, he had to tend the land and deliver 50 per cent or more of its produce to the proprietor. If the labour of his own family was not sufficient, the sharecropper would often employ the sons of the local peasant smallholders on a casual basis.[70]

Peasant conditions in the hill regions were undoubtedly better than in the plains. The peasant had much more of a stake in the land, whether he was smallholder or sharecropper, and this spared him the desperate search for work, the lack of fixed abode and the periods of semi-starvation which were the lot of many labourers on the plains. But the hill peasant's life was far from a mild one. The rapid spread of the mulberry tree in these regions transformed his life and that of his family. The tiresome and exhausting job of looking after the silkworms while they produced the silk cocoons fell exclusively on the peasant families. They had to make room in their cottages for the leaves on which the grubs grew, to ensure an even

---

[68] *Ibid.*, pp. 205–23. The figures for earnings are extremely approximate, taking into account Berengo's comments on the over-optimistic estimates made by Vanzetti for the period 1819–24. Vanzetti relied on the *bracciante* working 250 days of every year (Berengo, *L'agricoltura veneta*, p. 219, n. 4).

[69] ASV, Gov., 1840–4, L1/1. For a recent commentary on the documents of the enquiry, see Bernardello, 'Burocrazia, borghesia e contadini', *passim*.

[70] Berengo, *L'agricoltura veneta*, pp. 202–3.

temperature to prevent the grubs from dying, and to feed them constantly. This usually meant sitting up all night. At the end of this cocoon-spinning period the peasant would most often receive half the cocoons, which he then either sold back to the landlord or to the many Lombard and Austrian merchants who toured the Venetian countryside for this purpose in the spring of each year.[71] S. Laing, a traveller whose account was published in 1842, remarked on the contrast between the fineness of the product and the destitution of those who produced it: 'The people are in poverty in the countryside, notwithstanding the fertility of the soil. It is impressive to see those who raise silk – the most costly material of human clothing – going about their work barefoot and in rags.'[72]

The peasant women and children also found employment in the great spinning-mills that were erected in this period. The small amounts of money they received helped to lessen what was often a chronic indebtedness of sharecropper to landowner. But the work was exhausting and the hours extremely long. Just how long they were can be gauged from the viceroy's decree of 1842 on child employment in mills and factories. Children aged less than twelve were not to work for more than ten hours a day; those between twelve and fourteen not more than twelve hours a day.[73] Silk production undoubtedly brought a little ready cash into the peasant households, but it was sweated labour that had earned it.

In the mountain valleys peasant smallholding predominated, with the *livello*, the long-term lease, as the usual contractual arrangement. Often the plots of land were minute, but even a few acres of fields laboriously created from the rocky terrain were highly prized. Landholding conferred

---

[71] *Ibid.*, pp. 312–13. At Latisana (p. 310) the system of *venti soldi* prevailed by which the peasant would receive one Au. lire (later one and a half) for every *libbra* of cocoons he produced.

[72] S. Laing, *Notes of a Traveller on the Social and Political State of France, Prussia, Switzerland, Italy, etc.*, p. 473. In a later book, *Observations on the Social and Political State of the European People in 1848 and 1849*, Laing went on to ask his readers (p. 391): 'Does it belong to the ridiculous or the sublime, to the meanness or the greatness of human destiny, that a large proportion of our race are occupied all their lives in breeding, feeding, and tending a very ugly disagreeable worm, and spinning and weaving its excrement into ornamental clothing?'

[73] Gianelli, 'Dei miglioramenti', p. 212 n. 37. For evidence of the abuse of this legislation in the spinning and paper mills of Ceneda, in the province of Treviso, see ASV, Gov., 1845–9, dipartimento commercio e navigazione, fasc. XIX, 1/2. Conditions in the woollen-cloth industry were much better. At Follina the operatives worked eleven hours a day in the summer and nine in the winter; Sanseverino, 'Delle fabbriche di pannilana', p. 229. At Schio the Rossi family from the very start used the paternalistic methods for which they were to become famous throughout Italy.

the right to take part in the village assemblies and to enjoy their communal privileges. From their fields the mountain peasantry drew a subsistence crop consisting of cereals, potatoes, chestnuts, vegetables and some wine. In spite of the poverty of their land, the *alpini* were renowned throughout the Veneto for their rude good health, vitality and stamina.[74]

The principal problem in the mountain valleys was that the soil could only feed an estimated three-quarters of the population. Many of the peasantry supplemented the produce of their smallholdings by working the land of the local nobility, wood merchants, or wealthy owners of cattle and sheep. In the district of Agordo, in the province of Belluno, one thousand men found work in the mine producing yellow copper.[75] But for the majority of alpine families the only solution was for their menfolk to emigrate for many months of every year. Twelve thousand men from the province of Belluno habitually came down to the plains, to look for work as labourers on the roads or on the railway being built from Milan to Venice, or else to find any sort of job in Venice itself. In late autumn over seventeen thousand men would leave the mountain villages of upper Friuli, to return to their families only in the summer of the following year. Some of these went to Trieste or Venice, to be porters or waiters. But many also emigrated northwards; the chestnut sellers in the streets of Vienna came from the village of Montanars; the bricklayers and carpenters of Tricesimo and Gemona made their way through Carinthia and Styria looking for work; young peasants from upper Friuli were to be found as far afield as Hungary, helping to make cheeses and sausages and then selling them on their way homewards. Often the women emigrated as well, to work for a few months in the spinning-mills of the hills. With the increase of population after 1837, the flood of emigrants became greater each year.[76]

For the Venetian peasant the period of Austrian rule was certainly preferable to the war-torn years of the Napoleonic era. In the crisis of 1814–18, Austrian aid to the peasantry did not go unnoticed and after 1818 the roving peasant bands and *jacqueries* which had been a significant feature of Napoleonic Venetia seem to have disappeared. None the less, the peasantry found certain features of Austrian rule particularly odious. Conscription to

[74] Berengo, *L'agricoltura veneta*, p. 203; ASV, Gov., 1840–4, L 1/1, letter from the imperial delegate at Udine, 24 July 1839; BCU, Pelizzo, *Notizie statistiche*, vol. 1, p. 160. Ciconi claimed ('Discorso sull'agricoltura friulana), p. 5) that nearly half the male inhabitants of Friuli were landowners, but this is difficult to believe.

[75] ASV, Gov. Prov. 1848–9, CPD, b. 822/Agordo, fasc. 1, letter of 26 March 1848.

[76] Ciconi, 'Discorso sull'agricoltura friulana', p. 26 and n. 58; BCU, Pelizzo, *Notizie statistiche*, vol. 1, pp. 93, 157–8 and 163 (the author comments on the great artisan skills of the people of upper Friuli); Berengo, *L'agricoltura veneta*. pp. 87–8.

the Austrian army, although lighter than in Napoleonic times, was seen as an unmitigated disaster for those peasant families whose sons were unfortunate enough to be selected. For eight years these families had to do without the labour of their younger sons; some of the peasant songs of the time bear ample witness to the sadness and rancour with which the villages bade farewell to the conscripts as they left to serve in some far-flung part of the empire.[77]

The ever-increasing financial difficulty of the Austrian empire also meant a large number of fiscal measures which weighed heavily on the rural poor. In April 1839 the Austrians decided to place on the open market the uncultivated communal lands of the mountain villages. In spite of the protests of the villagers, wood merchants quickly bought up many of the extensive forests of the north, and the peasantry were denied their traditional access for wood and forage. Even before the revolution of 1848 some peasants were driven to violence by these deprivations. In January 1846, sixty villagers from Lamon, in the district of Fonzaso west of Feltre, invaded the woods and about thirty of them fought off the local police. A commission of enquiry found that six thousand peasants in the district had no wood at all, 'either for heating or to build and support their houses. Without this wood the majority of these houses are in such a state of decay that some of them have already collapsed.'[78]

As for taxation, the rural population, with its greater degree of self-sufficiency, suffered far less than the urban poor from indirect taxation on primary products. But two indirect taxes proved a constant source of complaint in the countryside. One was that on *carta bollata*, stamped paper, which was used for every sort of official business and had to be purchased by the peasant himself. In 1840 the Austrians increased the

---

[77] A. Berti, *Canti popolari scritti sui temi di musica popolare raccolta da Teodoro Zecco*, pp. 122ff ('Il disertore'); A. Cornoldi, 'Canti politici e patriottici del Polesine (1848–66)', *Lares*, 13 (1965), p. 130.

[78] ASV, Pres. Gov., 1845–8, fasc. 1, 13/8, no. 446. See also the letter of 8 Sept. 1850 from Baldassare Buja to Jacopo Bernardi arguing that the woods of the districts of Serravalle and Valdobbiadene should be returned to the villagers. Bernardi commented on the letter: 'what have the forestry inspectors done since they came into being so many years ago? Nothing ... at present the price of wood is twice what it was twenty years ago ... it must be said that they let everything go from bad to worse, and it seems as if they had studied how best to destroy the mountain woods' (MCV, archivio Bernardi, b. 36, no number). This problem, of course, was not limited to the Veneto; for the situation in northern Lombardy, see F. Della Peruta, 'Le condizioni dei contadini lombardi nel Risorgimento', *Società*, 8 (1951), pp. 251–2. For a similar erosion of the feudal privileges of the mountain peasantry, see the comments of A. Soboul on conditions in the Pyrenees in his 'Les troubles agraires de 1848', in *Paysans, sans-culottes et jacobins*, pp. 322–3.

severity of this tax with regard to simple dealings which affected the mass of the population. The other tax was that on salt. Salt was a state monopoly, in constant demand in the countryside, and its high price was bitterly resented.[79]

Of direct taxes, that on land ownership caused considerable hardship to the smallholders of the hill and mountain regions. The new taxes deriving from the land survey were in no way progressive, for small and large landowners had their land estimated in identical fashion. The alpine peasantry were also badly hit by the taxes on the transfer, handing down and division of property, transactions that were all too frequent in the mountain valleys as the population increased and peasant land became more fragmented.

Some remnants of the feudal era, particularly the *decime* or clerical tithe, further accentuated the peasants' poverty. But the greatest fiscal burden of all on the rural poor was undoubtedly the personal or poll tax. This tax, which amounted to 5.80 Austrian lire a year, was levied in the Veneto on all men over the age of fourteen and under sixty who lived outside the major cities. The viceroy Ranier, from his palace at Monza, assured Vienna in 1831 that the tax was not exorbitant, as it corresponded to only 'three days' work in a year'.[80] The Mazzinian newspaper, *La Voce del popolo*, gave a more accurate description, soon after the outbreak of the 1848 revolution, of what the tax actually involved:

What the peasant suffers the lack of most is ready money. By continual drudgery the poor man manages to collect together a few lire. From these meagre earnings, for which the peasant has sweated, the tax collector takes the greatest part, and sometimes leaves none at all. You ask a villager what his greatest burden is. He'll reply – the Filippo. The Filippo, or personal tax, is for him a misfortune, a calamity.[81]

In spite of these specific Austrian impositions, there is little evidence of peasant unrest after 1817, and the principal reason for their quiescence

---

[79] Certificates on stamped paper for birth, baptism and marriage cost 75 centesimi per sheet, and a certificate showing the fulfilment of conscription requirements cost 1½ Au. lire; *Guida commerciale*, pp. 74–85. For open criticism of the salt tax and for the multiple uses of salt in the countryside, see Freschi's journal, *L'amico del contadino*, vol. 5, no. 43 (23 Jan. 1847), p. 337.

[80] ASV, Pres. Gov., 1830–4, fasc. IV, 2/4; quoted in Berengo, *L'agricoltura veneta*, p. 73.

[81] *La Voce del popolo*, 31 March 1848, quoted in F. Della Peruta, 'I contadini nella rivoluzione lombarda del 1848', in his *Democrazia e socialismo nel Risorgimento*, p. 95 n. 6. The peasant proprietors were hit harder than some of the landless labourers by the personal tax because the landowners would often pay the tax of those *braccianti* who were bound to their estates; Berengo, *L'agricoltura veneta*, p. 220.

would seem to lie in the series of satisfactory harvests from 1818 to 1844.[82] The prices of grain and maize were often very low in this period, a fact which was of little consolation to the owners of the great estates, but which ensured the peasantry sufficient bread and polenta to stay alive. The rural poor had much to complain of – their lack of land, the severity of the landlords' contracts, the incidence of disease and malnutrition, Austrian conscription and taxation. The number of rural thefts, endemic throughout the period, was but one pointer among many to the deep-rooted discontent of the peasantry.[83] But the Venetian peasantry was not noted for its militancy. The fertility of the soil and the benign government of the old Republic had contrived to keep the rural poor docile for many a generation. The Napoleonic exactions had disturbed this pattern, but did not lead as in southern Italy to a permanent state of peasant insurrection and militancy. As long as the harvests remained reasonably good the Austrians had little to fear from the Venetian countryside.

The Venetian cities

Venice

When the Austrians finally took Venice after the bitter and damaging siege of the winter of 1813–14, they found a city that was all but dead. Many years later the *Quarterly Review* was accurately to catch the desolation of that moment:

the suburbs were deserted and ruinous, life had gradually ebbed from the extremities, and seemed to flutter but faintly in its last retreat at the heart of the city, the Piazza of St. Mark's. The ports, choked up with sand, were inaccessible to larger vessels ... The stores were mouldering in the magazines; the half-finished vessels were rotting on the stocks.[84]

Prosperity was very slow to return to the city. The root of the trouble lay in the loss of trade to the thriving port of Trieste. This city, which by the late eighteenth century had already drawn the craftsmen away from the Venetian arsenal, profited from preferential Austrian policy to attain the

---

[82] A complete record of the annual average prices, up to 1847, of grain, maize and rice from all the provinces of the Veneto is to be found in ASV, Gov., 1845-9, dipartimento commercio e navigazione, fasc. xix, 1/23.
[83] See, among many examples, Rizzi, *Sui miglioramenti agrari*, p. 7. On the depressing effects of the lack of property on the peasants of lower Friuli, see BCU, Pelizzo, *Notizie statistiche*, vol. 1, p. 314. For a very recent and excellent analysis of rural thefts in the province of Verona in the second half of the nineteenth century, and of their general importance, see F. Bozzini, *Il furto campestre*.
[84] *Quarterly Review*, 86 (Dec. 1849), p. 186.

pre-eminent position in Adriatic commerce. Throughout the 1820s few ships apart from local coastal traders entered Venetian waters.[85] Matters were not helped by Francis's decision that Austria had no need of a large fleet because England would look after the seas in time of war. The major part of the Venetian fleet which Napoleon had tried to build up was therefore sold off to Denmark.[86] Venice stagnated:

> Sun-girt City, thou hast been
> Ocean's child, and then his queen;
> Now is come a darker day,
> And thou soon must be his prey.[87]

In 1824 the Venetian general commission of public charity appealed to the emperor, exposing the 'actual state of the inhabitants of Venice'.[88] The population had shrunk from 137,240 in 1797 to 113,827 in 1824. The number of workers in the once famous arsenal had decreased from 3,302 to 773, and, worst of all, those classified as 'in need of public help' totalled 40,764. Venice was the fourth largest city of the empire, after Vienna, Milan and Budapest,[89] but she seemed little more than a picturesque and poverty-stricken backwater.

This profound economic depression gradually lifted during the later decades of Austrian rule. The Austrians' dedication to an improved road system, and their suppression in 1824–5 of their own absurd customs barriers on the Mincio and the confines of the Tyrol, undoubtedly aided the flow of goods to and from Venice. But the greatest single concession granted by them was that of free port status for Venice in February 1830. Under the regulations of the free port most goods coming into and leaving Venice by sea were exempt from tax of any sort. These exemptions aided Venice's transit trade and enabled its citizens to import duty-free goods for consumption or manufacture. The free port, while far from being a panacea for all Venice's ills, or challenging Trieste's commercial supremacy, did aid Venice's trade and coincided with a slow revival in commerce. By

---

[85] Between 1823 and 1829 between 2,600 and 2,800 ships, mostly of very small tonnage, entered the port annually. See G. Luzzatto, 'Le vicende del porto di Venezia dal primo medioevo allo scoppio della guerra 1914–18', in his *Studi di storia economica veneziana*, pp. 26–7.

[86] Macartney, *The Habsburg Empire*, p. 320 n. 1.

[87] P. B. Shelley, 'Lines written among the Euganean hills' (Oct. 1818), in Shelley, *Poetical works*, ed. T. Hutchinson, p. 555.

[88] FQSV, MSS Class IV, DCXI. Alvise Querini Stampalia was a member of the commission.

[89] By 1843 Vienna had a population of nearly half a million, Milan 150,000, Pest 80,000 (and another 40,000 with Buda across the river), Prague more than 100,000; Macartney, *The Habsburg Empire*, p. 265.

the early 1840s the number and size of the ships using the port had reached respectable proportions.[90]

Venice began to flourish again, in spite of a serious outbreak of cholera in 1835 and the European commercial crisis of 1841–3. The great railway bridge across the lagoon was finally completed in 1846 and bore impressive testimony to a new era (for a full discussion of the Milan–Venice railway, see chapter 2).[91] The population of the city slowly began to rise, reaching 122,496 in 1845. Increased savings deposits in the Cassa di Risparmio testified to a revival in bourgeois fortunes; declining trade for the pawnshops indicated an improvement in the standard of living of the urban poor.[92]

The city itself was given a face-lift as more and more visitors began to flock to it. Gaslights illuminated the narrow alleyways and the municipality made every effort to repair damage and decay. By 1846 there were eleven principal hotels, including the Danieli where Ruskin and his wife Effie were to spend their unfortunate honeymoon in 1849.[93] A bathing establishment was founded in 1833; its site was at the mouth of the Grand Canal, near the Punta della Dogana, and was chosen for 'the depth and flow of the water and the magical views of the nearby Piazza San

[90] Napoleon had been the first to grant a free port, but the regulations of 1806 applied only to the limited anchorage and warehouses of the island of S. Giorgio and had not been effective because of British control of the upper Adriatic. The Austrians' concession of February 1830 had been preceded by intensive Venetian lobbying at Vienna by the patriarch Monico, Pietro Dubois and Pietro Bigaglia, the emissaries of the Venetian chamber of commerce. For the limitations of the Austrians' concession, and in particular its failure to stimulate new manufacturing in Venice, see the interesting article by K. R. Greenfield, 'Commerce and new enterprise at Venice, 1830–48', *Journal of Modern History*, 11 (1939), pp. 321–2. By 1843 the number of ships entering the port of Venice had increased to 6,951; the number of foreign ships also rose from 161 in 1836 to 480 in 1845; see G. Luzzatto, 'Le vicende del porto di Venezia', pp. 27–8. For a summary of the long-term effects of the free port, see Zalin, *Aspetti e problemi*, p. 139.

[91] One contemporary American described the railway bridge across the lagoon as 'an artery by which the living blood of today is being poured into the exhausted frame of Venice' (G. S. Hillard, *Six Months in Italy*, vol. 1, p. 83). For the cholera of 1835 see FQSV, MSS Class IV, DCXXXIX. The epidemic lasted from 9 Oct. to 25 Dec.; there were 661 cases, of which 360 were fatal.

[92] For details of the population of the city in 1845 see the section by Count A. Sagredo in *Venezia e le sue lagune*, vol. 2, pt. 1, pp. 384–6. The figures for the Cassa di Risparmio are: 1841 – 1,945 customers depositing a total of 1,766,739 Au. lire; 1845 – 2,448 customers, 3,332,991 Au. lire in deposits; *Venezia e le sue lagune*, vol. 2, pt. 1, pp. 476–7. For the pawnshops, Greenfield, 'Commerce and new enterprise', p. 325 n. 47. The *Gazzetta di Venezia* stated that from Jan. to Aug. 1842 19,564 fewer objects were pawned than in 1841; in 1843, 25,491 fewer than in 1842.

[93] Effie's letters have been published by M. Lutyens (ed.), *Effie in Venice*.

Marco . . . the service is run with great care and *politesse*, with the women
separated from the men'.[94] Six theatres played every night during the
summer season, and the most famous, the Fenice, was swiftly rebuilt after
the fire of 1834. The legendary sopranos Ponti and Malibran were frequent visitors at the Fenice, and Verdi's *Ernani* had its premiere there in
1844.[95] When the emperor visited Venice more than 30,000 visitors
flocked to the city and spent an estimated four million florins. In 1843, a
reasonably typical year, 112,644 visitors came to Venice.[96] By 1848 the
tourist trade was already beginning to assume the crucial position in the
Venetian economy that it occupies today.

Little or nothing has been written on the social classes of the city in these
years and the present inaccessibility of the necessary documents makes
a social history of the city a nigh-impossible task (see Note on documents,
p. 394). The Venetian nobility, as we have seen, entered a period of
decline after the fall of the Republic, though with the Restoration they
regained a little of their power by dominating municipal government.
Only one mayor of Venice of this period came from a family which did
not have its name inscribed in the ancient Golden Book of the nobility.[97]
Some of the new generation of nobility did show a certain openness to the
ideas of the age. Alvise Mocenigo, for instance, introduced steamboats into
Venetian waters, and was always full of projects for improving Venetian
trade, making the port more accessible, and refounding the ancient fortunes of the city. He also had the good sense to marry the daughter of the
Austrian governor, thus bolstering the ailing family fortunes and acquiring the necessary finances for the more crackpot of his schemes.[98] But in
general no reforming wing emerged among the Venetian nobility. This
was in marked contrast to Milan, where the reforms of Maria-Teresa and

[94] *Venezia e le sue lagune*, vol. 2, pt. 1, p. 309.
[95] *Attila* followed in 1846, and after the revolution both *Rigoletto* (1851) and
La Traviata (1853) received their first performances at La Fenice. For the re-
building of the opera house see F. Mutinelli, *Annali delle provincie venete dal
1801 al. 1840*, p. 477. On the Fenice's orchestra under Alessandro da Ponte,
V. Marchesi, *Settant'anni della storia di Venezia, 1798–1866*, p. 81.
[96] Tivaroni, *L'Italia*, vol. 1, p. 505. The diary of Princess Melanie Metternich is
entertaining on the emperor's visit; Metternich, *Mémoires*, vol. 6, pp. 264–5.
[97] *Venezia e le sue lagune*, vol. 2, pt. 1, p. 345.
[98] The complete papers of Alvise Mocenigo are in the ASV and have hardly ever
been consulted. For one of Mocenigo's schemes see ACV, presidio, 1847, document attached to no. 91, 6 March 1846. The port of Malamocco was very difficult
to enter and in 1844 there had been a number of shipwrecks. Mocenigo suggested
that two steamboats should be built with engines of 60 horsepower each to stand
guard at the port's entrance, ready to help ships in distress. The municipality
requested 40,000 lire from the government for the project.

the experience of being the capital city of the kingdom of Italy had combined to revitalise part of the nobility. In Milan a significant section of the aristocracy acquired a reputation for liberal beliefs and economic dynamism. The different development of the nobility of the two cities was to be of considerable importance at the outbreak of revolution in 1848.

The Venetian bourgeoisie had gradually taken over all the manufacturing, trade, commerce and banking of the city. Venice's modest manufacturing had its focal point in the production of glassware of every sort. Murano glass was renowned throughout Europe and the factories of that island, together with the artisan work associated with them, gave employment to about 3,200 women and men in the 1840s. There were also twelve factories employing 1,000 workers producing woollen headwear of various sorts – caps, berets and birettas. Both shipbuilding and silk manufacturing, traditionally two of the most famous of Venetian industries, were in catastrophic decline. Whereas even as late as 1783 there were over 7,000 silk workers, by 1845 the city could not count more than 639 people employed in spinning, weaving and passementerie. In the quinquennium 1841–5, 414 boats were built in the Venetian estuary, but their total tonnage was only 12,873 and 335 of them were fishing boats. A number of other manufactures are worthy of mention: five workshops, employing 180 women and 60 men, produced woollen blankets; thirteen rope workshops employed 530 workers; two sugar refineries, one of which belonged to Giuseppe Reali; a modern factory for producing felt for clothes and carpets, erected in 1841 and equipped with English machinery driven by a steam engine of eighty horsepower; a state-owned tobacco factory, giving work to about 700 Venetians; and an asphalt factory owned by no less a person than Baron Salomon Rothschild, employing 45 people and using one steam engine of sixteen horsepower.[99]

As for trade and commerce, Venice was no longer the entrepot city which had made Rialto the greatest market in Europe. Of Venetian manufactures only glassware and wax products found reasonably profitable outlets in the Austrian empire and elsewhere.[100] However, Venice

[99] For Salomon Rothschild's cement factory see ASV, CC, b. 176, III, 4, no. 1285, Feb. 1847. For other statistics on Venetian manufacturing, A. Bernardello, 'La paura del comunismo e dei tumulti popolari a Venezia e nelle provincie venete nel 1848-9', *Nuova Rivista Storica*, 54 (1970), p. 52. For the silk industry in 1847, ASV, CC, b. 187, IV, 42; Zalin, *Aspetti e problemi*, p. 141 n. 22, and p. 142 table 25 for shipbuilding; Greenfield, 'Commerce and new enterprise', pp. 319–20.

[100] Statistics for exports from Venice to other parts of the Austrian empire for the years 1831–40 are to be found in ASV, CI, b. 5, fasc. 11/60. In 1845 the exporting of glassware to the Russian empire was seriously threatened by the decision of the port authorities of Odessa to increase nineteenfold the import duty on

remained a considerable market for the raw products of its hinterland – grain above all, but also animal hides, timber from the northern provinces, oil, dried and salted fish, straw goods and some minerals. The one exception was raw silk, which went to Milan or was exported directly from the provincial cities of the Veneto. Venice also imported far more than she exported during the whole of this period, and some of the trade in luxury items of foreign manufacture was very profitable. This was particularly true, ironically, of silk goods from northern Europe, which found a thriving market in the many visitors to the city. In all, Venice by 1838 ranked sixth in tonnage of shipments amongst the fifteen leading ports of the Mediterranean – behind Marseilles, Trieste, Constantinople, Genoa and Leghorn, and just ahead of Sira (in the Greek archipelago) and Naples.

If this overall picture is somewhat dismal, it would be a mistake to think that the Venetian commercial and business bourgeoisie was uniformly poor and without resources. When a three-man deputation from the Venetian chamber of commerce went to Vienna in 1835 to bear the condolences of the city on the death of Francis I and to greet the new emperor Ferdinand, they were invited to dine with the Metternichs; Princess Melanie confided to her diary that the three between them possessed thirty million Austrian lire, 'which is no mean fortune'.[101] The Papadopoli family, Giuseppe Reali, the brothers Pigazzi, Angelo and Valentino Comello, the banker Jacopo Treves, to name only some of the most prominent figures, were all extremely rich. Treves, who was Jewish, owned and lived in the Barozzi palace at San Moise, and collected modern painting and sculpture, including a number of Canova's works.[102]

A significant number of the Jewish community apart from Treves were also wealthy. The gates of the Ghetto had been broken down in 1797 and under Austrian rule the Jews were free to own property, be employed by the state and send their children to state schools. Some restrictions still applied, like that forbidding them to be part of the municipal congregation; laws limiting marriage and immigration remained on the statute book, though they were not enforced. Many of the Jews continued to be poor and to live in the Ghetto. But the lifting of the bans imposed by the old Republic on trading, manufacturing and the owning of land enabled

Venetian glass. See the petition of 21 Sept. 1845 to the Austrian emperor from the Venetian glass manufacturers and merchants Dalmistro, Errera, Cerutti, P. Bigaglia, Fratelli Coen di Benedetto; HHSAV, Staatskanzlei Provinzen Lombardo-Venezien, fasz. 40, no number.
101 Metternich, *Mémoires*, vol. 6, p. 16. The three were Giovanni Papadopoli, Jacopo Treves, and Marc'Antonio Zannona.
102 *Guida commerciale*, p. 344. The private archive of the Treves family has not yet been opened to historians, in spite of numerous requests.

many Jews, like the banker and insurance agent Jacopo Levi, to employ profitably the considerable amounts of capital that their families had accumulated as moneylenders.[103]

There were also a number of non-Venetian merchants in Venice who helped to add vitality and foreign capital to Venetian business. The hospitality accorded to merchants of different racial and national origin had been one of the foundations on which Venetian wealth had been built, and some of this tradition clearly remained in the early nineteenth century. Anton Luigi Ivancich, Federico Bertuch, Federico Oexle, and the Englishmen Thomas Holm and Alexander Malcolm were among the most prominent members of Venetian business circles.[104]

Two institutions served this section of Venetian society. The chamber of commerce, composed of twelve members elected annually by the principal merchants and manufacturers of the city, was the main organ of communication between the business classes and the authorities. In addition, a number of businessmen decided in 1839 to found the Venetian commercial company to act as a sort of ginger group, pushing the government and their fellow *negozianti* to further enterprise to improve their own and Venice's fortunes.[105]

Thus, within the general context of the stagnation of Venetian trade

[103] For a comparison with the position of the Jews in the other states of Italy, and the other parts of the empire, see M. D'Azeglio, *Dell'emancipazione civile degl'Israeliti*, pp. 19-24; see also A. Ottolenghi, *L'azione di Tommaseo a Venezia per la emancipazione degli Israeliti*, p. 3. The firm of Jacopo Levi and sons were the general agents for the Lombardo-Venetian kingdom and the Italian Tyrol of the 'I.-R. Priv. Riunione Adriatica di Sicurtà', founded in 1838 and with its head office at Trieste.

[104] The German merchant Friedrich Bertuch has left an interesting account of the revolution of 1848-9 and the years preceding it: *Contributi alla storia del Risorgimento italiano*. He and a young friend from Frankfurt, Karl Aubin, established the principal company dealing in silk products in Venice. Bertuch settled in Venice after the declaration of the free port in 1830, believing that 'those who hastened to make use of this opening were certainly assured of finding a most profitable field of activity' (p. 24).

[105] The Venetian commercial company was founded on the joint stock principle with a nominal capital of 15 million Au. lire divided into 10,000 shares bearing interest at four per cent. Its first exploits were highly successful: it imported over a thousand bales of cotton from New Orleans, and its stock rose to 108. By 1845 the company had run into difficulties, with the stock falling to 92-3, without takers. But it recovered and survived until the revolution; see Greenfield, 'Commerce and new enterprise', p. 320, and MCV, Doc. Pell., b. 44. For the composition of the Venetian chamber of commerce in 1848 see *Guida commerciale*, pp. 150-1. One other Venetian enterprise worthy of mention was the Società Veneta Montanistica, founded in 1839 for the purpose of locating and mining the Veneto's mineral wealth. It had a capital of 2 million Au. lire and its president was Spiridione Papadopoli.

and industry, there existed a number of men with considerable capital at their disposal who wanted to put an end as soon as possible to Venice's backwardness. Their specific activities, which were vital in the gestation of the revolution of 1848, are better examined in the next chapter. Suffice it to say here that with the revival of trade and commerce in the late 1830s and early 1840s their ambitions for Venice increased at an equal pace with their dissatisfaction with certain aspects of Austrian government. The long delays in the implementation of public works, like the new dike for the harbour entrance at Malamocco, and the endless waiting for administrative decisions, proved constant irritants. During the revolution of 1848, the chamber of commerce referred to the Viennese aulic departments as 'the burial ground for petitions and representations'.[106]

The chamber of commerce felt equal anger over some aspects of the taxation system. In 1836 it declared: 'the port of Venice is free, but the books of the merchants are not exempt from the stamp tax; and the registration tax, which does not exist even in Lombardy, besides the burden it imposes, ill accords with the speed of movement that commercial transactions require'.[107] Trieste, less than half the size of Venice, continued to be exempted from taxes that the Venetian merchants were forced to pay.

In addition, although the concession of the free port had benefited Venetian merchants, other Austrian measures, like their persistent refusal to open a branch of the bank of Vienna at Venice, seemed deliberate snubs to the hopes of the Venetian chamber of commerce.[108] Deprived of adequate credit facilities, forced to see the trade of their city consigned to a secondary role beside that of the upstart Trieste,[109] despondent at the unchanging nature of the Venetian manufacturing depression, Venetian businessmen grew increasingly bitter and resentful as the years passed.

Their fellow bourgeois, the professional classes, the lawyers, doctors, university teachers, clerks and officials, had equal cause for dissatisfaction. Numerically, they were not particularly strong – there were only fifty-nine lawyers in Venice – but the only three mutual aid societies in the city had been organised by this section of the bourgeoisie.[110] The lawyers are a

---

[106] ASV, CC, b. 194, III, 9, meeting of 21 March 1849.

[107] Report of the chamber of commerce for 1838, quoted in Greenfield, 'Commerce and new enterprise', p. 331.

[108] See U. Tucci, 'Le emissioni monetarie del governo provvisorio di Venezia (1848–9)', in *Archivio Economico dell'Unificazione Italiana*, I (1956), p. 4 n. 4.

[109] For comparative statistics of the two ports, Zalin, *Aspetti e problemi*, p. 138, table 34; and ASV, CC, b. 180, V, fasc. 22, no. 3223.

[110] These were 'the pious union of chemists, surgeons and doctors', founded in 1836 and boasting 150 members; 'the pious union of lawyers and notaries', and the 'society of the professors of the orchestra of the Fenice theatre', founded

particularly interesting group in the light of the leading part they were to play in the revolution. Denied by Austrian law the right to represent their clients in court, a great deal of their time seems to have been spent in regulating commercial and landowning disputes. In this way close links were often formed between the wealthy members of the chamber of commerce and the lawyers of the city. When the commercial company was founded in 1839 a young lawyer by the name of Daniele Manin soon became a member.

Lack of political power and the heavy hand of the censorship were the *casus belli* for the professional bourgeoisie. Any thoughts of a political career were precluded by the high property qualifications for the central and provincial congregations. This political closed shop was in marked contrast to the system in Hungary where each deputy to the Diet brought with him as his secretary one or more *jurati*, or recent graduates in law. During the Long Diet of 1832-5 no less than 1,500 of these *jurati* attended the debates, among them many of the future leaders of 1848.[111] The Venetian lawyers had no chance of gaining such valuable political experience.

It was among the educated bourgeoisie that the censorship was most resented. Permission to write to correspondents abroad had been obtained with difficulty only in 1824. The Austrians showed themselves profoundly suspicious of Italian intellectuals[112] and unwilling to allow any political matter of public import to be debated openly. The lack of freedom of the press, the often absurd condemnation of the classics of Italian literature, the constant surveillance in the universities and in literary institutes like the Ateneo Veneto, all combined to produce a profound feeling of irritation and emasculation in educated Venetian circles.

The petty bourgeois class was an extensive one, as befitted a city that had lost most of its manufacturing and gained a tourist trade. The number of shopkeepers was significant – there were over 70 hosiery and glove shops, about 100 shops selling silk goods, 25 antique dealers, over 30 shops selling glass objects.[113] Catering for the tourists as well as the locals

in 1831; *Venezia e le sue lagune*, vol. 2, pt. 1, p. 477. In Venice in 1846 there were 1,957 *impiegati* (clerks and civil servants), 866 *professori e maestri* (teachers of one sort and another), 195 chemists, 163 doctors, 79 surgeons, 59 lawyers, 21 engineers and 15 notaries; *Venezia e le sue lagune*, vol. 2, pt. 1, pp. 384–6.

[111] Macartney, *The Habsburg Empire*, p. 247.

[112] See Berengo's comments in 'Le origini', p. 542.

[113] The *Guida commerciale*, pp. 252–359, gives a complete list of all the traders, suppliers, shopkeepers, etc. of Venice. Unfortunately the *fabbricatori, negozianti, mercanti* and *venditori* of any particular item are often grouped together so that it is impossible to tell precisely how many of each there were. For this reason some of the figures cited are estimates.

meant the existence of 28 hairdressing establishments and 101 cafés. The *Guida commerciale* for 1848 listed 76 silversmiths, goldsmiths and jewellers, 108 carpenters, 61 shops selling iron, brass and copperware, 82 shoemaking concerns and 65 tailors' shops. Although no exact figures exist it is clear that Venice was a thriving centre for the sale of artisan goods of every sort. Today it is still possible to see – even in the most tourist-populated quarter of the city, the *sestiere* San Marco – artisan shops whose interiors and products are very similar to those of the 1840s.

Below these small traders and producers, and often merging with them, came the working class of the city. There was clearly no organised proletariat in Venice in the modern sense, but a few factories like the glassworks at Murano and the tobacco factory at S. Croce did have considerable workforces. A large number of men – carpenters, caulkers and the like – found employment in the old arsenal. Their numbers had diminished appreciably since the days of the republic, but by 1848 there were still 800 *arsenalotti*, with another 400 men condemned to forced labour there.

Apart from these few agglomerations of manpower, the Venetian workforce was very dispersed. An enormous number of men and women found employment in artisan crafts of every type – the women often making hats and gloves, the men as tinkers, brassworkers, shoemakers, coopers, tailors, carpenters and smiths. Not surprisingly, a large number of the populace gained its livelihood from the sea, not so much as fishermen, of whom there were many more in the neighbouring city of Chioggia, but as boatmen of every sort. The *vaporetto* (small steamboat) had not yet replaced the gondola as the principal means of transport. The gondoliers would gather at Fusina, where the main road from Padua stopped, to row their passengers across the lagoon to the city. This traffic diminished after the opening of the railway bridge in 1846, but within the city the *traghetti* (ferries) across the Grand Canal remained in full activity. There were also many boatmen using more practical vessels than the gondola for transporting goods from the docks to the markets or shops. Their boats could vary in size from the tiny and primitive *sandoli* to large barges. The *squeri*, or Venetian boatyards, did an active trade in repairing and maintaining this flotilla of small craft.[114]

[114] In June 1841 the Venetian municipality and chamber of commerce heard rumours that Lloyds of Trieste had decided to ask for the concession of a monopoly on steam transport in the lagoon. The Venetians immediately petitioned the emperor, objecting not only to interference in Venetian matters by the Trieste company, but also that the introduction of steam transport would deprive of their means of existence 'that great number of Venice's inhabitants who use their boats to carry goods and persons from one end of the lagoon to the other'; ACV, Municip., Atti di Uff., 1840–4, II, 6/47. The *squero* at San

Servants were another numerous section of the Venetian poor. Howells, the American consul in the city after the revolution, noted that servants were cheap and numerous.[115] Noble and well-to-do bourgeois families maintained an extensive retinue – from the private gondoliers of the house, to cooks, doormen and serving maids.[116] Nearly every middle-class housewife had at least one servant who would live in.

The tourist trade also provided much employment. Gondoliers would hire out themselves and their gondolas at a weekly rate, thus supplying both guide and transport. The big hotels provided jobs for porters, waiters, cooks and maids. But the tourist trade was strictly seasonal, and many Venetian poor often had to rely on the wages and tips of the summer months to last them through the year. In the winter they faced cut-throat competition for what jobs were going from the *alpini* who had come down to the city. Spring was always the most difficult season.

As in all the large pre-industrial centres of Europe, thousands of the poor had no fixed occupation at all, and would live from day to day, with no certainty of finding enough to eat for themselves or their families. In Venice this section of the populace was not as notorious or as numerous as the Neapolitan *lazzaroni* – Naples, after all, had four times the inhabitants of Venice – but they were a considerable percentage of the population. Sometimes they would find temporary work as street sellers of one variety or another – hawking trinkets or chestnuts, or else aiding the street green-grocers and fish vendors. Usually, they would form the bulk of the labourers in the periodic public works projects that the municipality undertook – the filling in of canals, laying of pavements, and of course the construction of the railway bridge, which gave work to a thousand men a day in the early 1840s.

Much was heard of the 40,000 destitute of Venice of these years, but while not wishing to minimise in any way the deprivations of the urban poor, great care must be taken with these figures. They derived from the estimates issued by the commission of public charity of those 'in need of assistance'. The commission had been founded by the patriarch Milesi in 1817, to help the many starving Venetians of those years and to take the beggars off the streets.[117] The commission, true to the long tradition of

---

Trovaso in the *sestiere* of Dorsoduro is the best surviving example of an old Venetian boatyard.

[115] Howells, *Venetian Life*, vol. 2, p. 194.

[116] Even a widow like the Contessa Loredana Gattersburg Morosini employed at the Palazzo Morosini in 1848 three agents, one cook, two gondoliers, two domestic servants, one doorman and two porters. All but two of these were resident in the palace; MCV, Agg. Manin, ix/26.

[117] For details of the foundation, composition and activity of the commission of public charity, see *Guida commerciale*, pp. 160–2 and *Venezia e le sue lagune*,

charity in Venice, gave many types of assistance, like distributing mattresses and blankets, paying for doctors and medicines and aiding the old. In this way the numbers on their books mounted into tens of thousands, but clearly only a fraction of these were absolutely destitute. In reality, the 40,000 aided by the commission consisted mainly of occasionally employed men and their families who had recourse to various sorts of public charity during the winter and spring months of every year.[118]

Those without any means of subsistence at all often ended up in the hated workhouse, which had been founded in 1812. There the men were put to work making mats and ropes, cleaning the streets of the city and lighting the oil lamps. The women made rope and cloth, and did the washing for the workhouse and for outside commissions. Food consisted of one portion of bread and one of *minestra* per day. Payment was made in relation to the amount of work done; all those who did not earn more than 57 *centesimi* per day were allowed to sleep in the institution.[119]

The attitudes of the authorities to the problem of the poverty of this vast mass of underemployed men and women was one of incomprehension, coupled with the classic thesis of the 'undeserving poor'. In 1841 the nobleman Michiel, on behalf of the municipality, wrote a memorandum in response to a government request to suggest means 'to put an end to the begging, idleness and sloth of the poor people of Venice'.[120] Michiel began by making a rather vague plea that the poor should find employment in Venice's non-existent industries. He then went on to advocate more infant schools, 'to inculcate the right and honest road from the beginning', and fewer hostelries 'from which derive an indescribable number of evils'. Having urged that employers give preference to Venetian labourers over those from Friuli and Carinthia, Michiel finished in a truly memorable fashion:

vol. 2, pt. 1, pp. 478–81. Its budget for the years 1817–25 is to be found in *Annali Universali di Statistica, Economia Pubblica, ecc.*, 13 (1827), pp. 288–91. The archive of the commission is in the *Archivio curia patriarcale* in Venice. For annual figures of the number of poor aided by the commission from 1817–48, ASV, Gov. Prov. 1848–9, MU, b. 95, attached to no. 8075.

[118] These were the conclusions reached by the royal institute at Venice. The institute had offered a prize for the best treatise on why the city had so many poor. Fifteen treatises were presented to the institute in 1847 but none was judged worthy of the prize. See the minutes of the assembly of 25 May 1847 in *Atti dell'I.-R. Istituto Veneto di Scienze, Lettere ed Arti*, 6 (1847), pp. 369–410.

[119] *Venezia e le sue lagune*, vol. 2, pt. 1, pp. 479–80. Statistics are given only for days of presence and not for specific numbers in the workhouse. The 'days of presence' declined from 239,014 in 1830 to 114,677 in 1845. There was a special prison for those who tried to beg, with room for fifty prisoners.

[120] ACV, Municip., Atti di Uff., 1840–4, VI, 2/68, no. 9970, minutes of Michiel's memorandum.

It would be no little contribution to the proposed improvement of the populace if the government took firm steps to prohibit marriages between individuals who know nothing of religion or morality, who have no roofs over their heads or beds to sleep on, and who have no means of earning a living. How can we expect anything but bad fruit from such trees?

It is not easy to find any information on the real conditions of the Venetian poor – prices of primary products, wage rates, hours of work, size of families, living conditions, popular culture, etc. Some of the few indications we have about wages are that male silk workers earned 1.50 Au. lire a day, female silk workers 60 centesimi, and dustmen 75 centesimi.[121] We know that after 1818 the price of bread was fairly constant and there is no evidence of urban riots of any sort during these years. Venice was not a city which had exclusively poor quarters. Poor and rich lived in the same streets, and often in the same buildings, with the *piano nobile* reserved for the well-to-do and the basement and attics for the poor. The highly populated quarters of Castello and Cannaregio and the island of the Giudecca were the areas of the city with the greatest concentration of *popolani*.[122] Their houses were often rudimentary; scrofula and rickets were prevalent among their children.[123] Traditionally, the Venetian poor were divided into two clans, the Nicolotti and Castellani, who were bitter enemies and whose ancient rivalry often found more violent outlets than the rowing races of the annual regatta.[124]

[121] Bernardello, 'La paura del comunismo', p. 52 n. 7, and p. 80 n. 96 (100 centesimi = 1 Au. lire).

[122] The population of the six *sestieri* of Venice in 1847 was as follows: San Marco, 20,560 inhabitants; Castello, 33,308; Cannaregio, 26,836; San Croce, 12,420; San Polo, 10,868; Dorsoduro (including the Giudecca), 23,933; *Venezia e le sue lagune*, map at end of vol. 1. We have no statistics for the age of marriage, size of families, etc. of Venetian workers. One list found (ACV, Municip., Atti di Uff., 1845-9, ix, 12/4, no. 6045 (1849)) would seem to indicate that the Venetian poor married early. Of 49 workers under the age of thirty who were about to be made redundant in July 1849 by the commander of military engineers, only two were unmarried, and 41 had at least one child.

[123] One Venetian doctor commented: 'it is surprising that there are not more cases [of scrofula], if one considers the parents' negligence, especially amongst the very poor, the insanitary nature of their homes, and the pernicious use of opiates, with which they hope to soothe the cries of the children suffering from hunger or malnutrition' (*Venezia e le sue lagune*, vol. 2, pt. 1, p. 271).

[124] 'The Nicolotti represent the aristocratic faction of Heraclea, and style themselves "nobile" to this day. The Castellani descend from the democrats of Jesolo ... The Nicolotti wear a black cap and sash round the waist, the Castellani's colour is red' (Horatio Brown, *Life on the Lagoons*, p. 303). Cicogna, in his diary (MCV, p. 6127, 1853), recalls a street fight of April 1845 in the quarter of Castello between the two clans. Two men were killed, one of whom, nicknamed 'Naso', had rowed in the regatta of that year for the Castellani.

The specific grievances that the urban poor held against the Austrians lay with the high level of indirect taxation which affected them far more than it did the peasantry. The state monopolies of tobacco and salt, and Kolowrat's *octroi*, were the principal instruments for taxation on primary products. The salt tax regularly brought in over six million Au. lire to the Viennese coffers. The writers of *Venezia e le sue lagune*, which is largely a panegyric on Austrian rule, had to admit that the annual consumption of salt per head of population of the city had actually diminished since 1812. The other highly unpopular tax, as in the countryside, was that on *carta bollata*, and the lucrative state lottery can be considered as another, slightly more subtle means of depriving the Venetian poor of the little money they earned.[125]

Venice was thus a city which did not expand in any dramatic way in the first half of the nineteenth century, and which was chiefly characterised by the unchanging nature of its economy, its low level of manufacturing and modest maritime trade. If there were a number of very wealthy Venetians, there were also many thousands of very poor ones who gained a living with extreme difficulty. None the less the city preserved its time-honoured tranquillity, and in the latter half of the period became a favourite visiting place for rich European travellers. The late 1830s and early 1840s saw a distinct revival in the city's fortunes and the emergence of ambitious businessmen eager to restore Venice to its former prosperity and importance. The new railway bridge across the lagoon seemed to them a first, vital step to overcoming Venice's backwardness and isolation, to pressing her forward to join the ranks of the modern cities of Europe.

The provincial cities

No other city in the Veneto was even half the size of Venice; Padua had 54,195 inhabitants in 1846, Verona 52,208, Vicenza 31,178, Chioggia 27,702, Udine 23,763, Treviso 19,484, Belluno 12,850, Bassano 11,857, Adria 11,217 and Rovigo 9,694.[126]

Little is known about these provincial centres. Verona was undoubtedly the most thriving and prosperous of them. The Austrians had constructed new roads in the city, including the one along the Adige, and the municipality had designated part of the Palazzo Bra as a huge grain store,

[125] In 1812 annual consumption per head of salt was 6.155 *libbre*. In 1845 it was 5.666 *libbre*; *Venezia e le sue lagune*, vol. 2, pt. 1, p. 372. In 1834, to take an average year, the state lottery yielded over 5.5 million Au. lire; Berengo, *L'agricoltura veneta*, p. 76. It was estimated in 1847 that the lottery was equivalent to an annual tax of 81 centesimi per head of population in the Veneto; *Venezia e le sue lagune*, vol. 2, pt. 1, p. 372.
[126] Zalin, *Aspetti e problemi*, p. 50 table 9.

in which the landowners could deposit their produce until the right moment came to sell it. This meant that the grain market of Verona rivalled that of Venice, and the bi-annual fairs in the city were the most lively in the Veneto.[127] Under the Republic Verona had been famous for its cloth industry, but this had died out in the face of competition from Bohemia and Moravia. On the other hand the spinning of silk had become a major concern in Verona with two large mills and thirteen smaller ones. A large sugar refinery, workshops curing hides, and two cotton-spinning mills founded in 1847 were the other major industries of the city. One of the cotton-mills, owned by Rederer and Grossmajer and situated at Montorio seven kilometres from Verona, employed 250 workers, for the most part aged between twelve and twenty.[128] Verona was also the major garrison town in the Veneto, forming one point in the famous quadrilateral of fortresses, the others being Peschiera, Mantua and Legnago.

Padua was chiefly renowned for its ancient university, although the period 1815–48 was not one of the most distinguished in its long history, the majority of the professors of the time being notable only for their conservatism.[129] Padua also witnessed what was probably the earliest attempt in the Veneto to form a trade union.[130] In February 1847 the imperial delegate at Padua reported to the government that the police had dissolved the mutual aid society of the Paduan bakers. Eighty-eight baking workers had formed the society in October 1846, paying 30 centesimi a week to build up a fund for sickness, old age and unemployment. The police had then received information that the bakers' hands were planning 'to impose onerous conditions on their employers and cause them trouble by demanding higher wages . . . they were already holding illegal meetings on Sundays and feast days in the inns of Zanin and Mangano'. Industry was non-existent in the city apart from six small silk factories with 622 workers.

Vicenza, Udine and Treviso were all provincial capitals and large market towns. Vicenza was distinguished for its many beautiful buildings designed by Palladio, who was born in the city. It had fifteen workshops employing 650 workers producing straw hats, a modest production of

[127] ASV, CI, b. 5, fasc. ii/1, no. 37015, report on the trade and industry of Verona from the provincial delegate of Verona to the Venetian government, 11 Dec. 1832. For the fairs, *Annali Universali di Statistica, Economia Pubblica, ecc.*, 14 (1827), pp. 305–8.

[128] Zalin, *Aspetti e problemi*, p. 160 n. 55, for the names of the proprietors of flourishing factories in Verona. See also O. Cagnoli, *Cenni statistici di Verona e della sua provincia*, pp. 31–5 and 53–65.

[129] See Berengo, 'Le origini', pp. 543–4.

[130] ASV, Pres. Gov., 1845–8, fasc. i, 2/2, no. 805, letter of 4 Feb. 1847.

silkstuffs and a small soap factory. Udine too preserved many striking buildings and paintings from the time when it had been the capital of Friuli, an area of the Veneto which had always had a distinctive history of its own, and which had enjoyed a great deal of independence under the Venetian Republic.[131] The city had two sugar refineries employing 220 workers, two small factories with 180 employees producing cotton, hemp and linen goods, and two workshops with seventy men curing hides. In keeping with the times the municipality had planted 1,500 mulberry trees along the new road that had been built around the city.[132] Treviso and its province were distinguished for being the centre of the paper industry in the Veneto, with more than 2,000 workers deriving a living from it.[133]

Chioggia was rather distinctive, as it was the only large fishing town on the Venetian littoral. Built on a plan which closely resembled the skeleton of a fish, with one large canal running straight down the middle and smaller ones coming off it at right angles, Chioggia had a flourishing fishing fleet and a lively atmosphere somewhat similar to the poorer quarters of Venice and the island of Burano. Apart from fishing, 200 men were employed making boats, and there were 180 linen, hemp and cotton workers.[134]

Finally, there is little to be said about Belluno and Rovigo, at the extreme north and south of the Veneto. Both were small towns, flattered by the title of provincial capitals. Rovigo, being at the heart of the great cereal-producing area of the Polesine, naturally had an active grain market. But it was not the seat of a rich provincial nobility, because most of the landowners came from the other side of the Po, from the Papal States and duchies of Parma and Modena, and left it to their agents to run the great estates.

Conclusion

Venetian society in this period is chiefly characterised by its static nature. The significant achievements of the Napoleonic era, the freeing of property

---

[131] See L. Pilosio, *Il Friuli durante la Restaurazione, 1813–47*, p. 83.

[132] Ciconi, 'Discorso sull'agricoltura friulana', p. 19. For industry at Udine see BCU, Pelizzo, *Notizie statistiche*, vol. 1, pp. 78–81.

[133] In the period 1843–6 Treviso and its province had 29 paper mills in activity; see Fedrigoni, *L'industria*, p. 47. Glazier, 'Il commercio estero', appendix VII, pp. 89–90, has published a letter of 10 Feb. 1847 from the chamber of commerce of Treviso complaining of the prohibitive costs of raw materials for the printshops of the city.

[134] *Venezia e le sue lagune*, vol. 2, pt. II, p. 516, '*Prospetto delle manifatture di Chioggia*'.

from feudal restrictions of ownership, the ending of the economic privileges of a ruling caste of nobility and the breaking down of local markets into the much larger unit of the kingdom of Italy, were not followed up. Apart from the extensive construction of new roads and a number of public works in Venice itself, it is difficult to see what Venetia gained economically from being part of the Austrian empire. The high level of taxation, Austria's condemnation of the Veneto to being a supplier of raw materials, the subordinate position of Venice to Trieste, the impeding slowness of the Austrian bureaucracy and the refusal of credit facilities to Venetian businessmen, all contributed to the long-drawn-out nature of the transition to capitalism in north-eastern Italy.

This slowness of development was not entirely the Austrians' fault. Lack of demographic increase, apart from the period 1837-46, was a major contributing factor. So too was the conservatism of most Venetian landowners, both old and new, whose lack of innovation compared poorly with the activity of their Lombard neighbours. The absence of coal, at this time still the only important source of industrial power, was something the Austrians could do little about. But at a time when the pattern of industrialisation on the Continent was dominated by state intervention and encouragement, the Austrians' contribution in northern Italy seems a paltry one.[135]

In political terms the bourgeois revolution had hardly begun. Although the closed shop of the Venetian nobility had been destroyed forever in 1797, the transference of political power to the bourgeoisie was thwarted by Napoleonic autocracy and made even less progress under Austria. All political power lay with the central government at Vienna, controlled by the emperor, his advisers and the great feudal magnates of the Austrian homelands. What little power the Venetians enjoyed remained almost exclusively in the hands of the old nobility, who formed the majority of the central and provincial congregations and the municipality of Venice. The absence of a long-established representative institution like the Hungarian Diet deprived the Venetian middle class of any experience in public affairs.

Yet it would be wrong to overstress the backwardness of Venetian society. If the Veneto was still at a primitive level of economic development when compared with the most advanced parts of Europe, within Italy it was probably second only to Lombardy. The region's natural fertility, the development of road and rail transport, the great silk boom and the thriving trade and commerce of Venice and Verona in the 1840s, marked Venetia out as one of the most prosperous areas of the peninsula. In political terms as well, the condition of Venice was not much different

135 See E. J. Hobsbawm, *The Age of Revolution, 1789-1848*, p. 211.

from that of the other states of Italy, where native absolutism under Austrian hegemony replaced direct Austrian rule.

Most important of all, it is possible to discern dynamic elements within Venetian society, both in town and countryside, increasingly dissatisfied with the status quo and anxious to see the speedy material development of their native land. The most striking example is the businessmen, bankers and merchants of the Venetian chamber of commerce, some of them extremely wealthy, whose entrepreneurial spirit conflicted markedly with the economic conditions in which they found their city. Elsewhere in the Veneto as well, there was a significant number of improving landowners, merchants and even a few industrialists, the details of whose achievements have often been faithfully recorded by the local chambers of commerce. With the revival of prosperity after 1830, these men had increasing opportunities to use their talents and their capital, but were more hindered than helped by their Austrian masters. They did not dream of revolt, but their very activity could not help but transform them, when conditions changed, from obedient Austrian subjects into sympathisers for the Italian cause.

2

Towards the revolution

The decline of Austrian government

In 1835 the emperor Francis I died. He was succeeded by his son
Ferdinand, a well-meaning simpleton who suffered from epilepsy. The
old emperor had hardly been able to cope with the position of supreme
functionary. The new one did not even try. On either side of him
Metternich and Kolowrat began their long duel which was to end in
revolution. The two statesmen, according to Bellegarde, were the twin
heads of the imperial eagle: 'one looks to the right, the other to the left'.[1]
A system that was so highly centralised could support only with difficulty
the confusion inherent in such a rivalry. Plans drawn up by one state
department were challenged by another, decisions took even longer than
usual to make. The most frequent result was stalemate. All over the
empire there was a gradual decay in the quality of Austrian administration.

At the same time the empire was moving further and further into debt.
The heart of the problem lay with the failure to increase direct taxation.[2]
Kübeck kept floating new loans, or borrowing directly from the great
bankers of Europe, but the end result was that an increasing proportion of

[1] Quoted in Radvany, *Metternich's Projects*, p. 66. Kolowrat told Kübeck: 'Prince
Metternich and I, we both mean well and I greatly respect his intelligence and
character, but we can never understand each other. The prince always adopts a
lecturing manner with me, he tells me that five and three is only eight, that five
times three is fifteen, that there is a great difference between the words "then"
and "once" which the government must keep in mind, that all events are inter-
connected, hence the opium war between the Chinese and English cannot remain
without consequences for our finances, etc. etc. And he tells me all this when I
asked him if he agreed to grant the Northern Railroad a new line to Pressburg'
(*ibid.*, p. 123).

[2] Kolowrat was of the Bohemian nobility and favoured them in administrative
appointments. As a result, the land survey and new tax estimates were successfully
held up in the Slav provinces; Radvany, *Metternich's Projects*, p. 59. Austria's
inability to enforce the new land taxes in most of the provinces of the empire was
a root cause of her economic plight.

imperial revenue had to be devoted to paying the interest and amortisation on the state debt. By 1847 the sums required for these purposes alone almost equalled the empire's total yield from direct taxation.[3] To many Lombards and Venetians the Viennese treasury came to seem like a bottomless pit, into which the wealth of northern Italy poured unendingly.

The Italian alternative

Unfortunately for the Austrians, propaganda for an ever more attractive economic and political alternative to their system increased in the period after 1830. The economic revival of these years led to a considerable strengthening of the bourgeoisie throughout northern Italy, and to a widening of their horizons. Italian intellectuals began to write with increased fervour of the immense advantages that would accrue to every part of Italy if customs barriers were reduced or abandoned, the system of weights and measures unified, a national market established and communications allowed to extend throughout the peninsula.

The disciples of Romagnosi at Milan were in the forefront of this agitation. The learned journals of their city – the *Annali*, the *Rivista Europea* founded in 1838, and Carlo Cattaneo's *Politecnico*, which began a year later – soon acquired a reputation out of all proportion to their circulation. Barred by the censorship from open criticism of the Austrian state, the Milanese writers instead delved deep into the composition of civil society. The volumes of economic and social statistics they compiled often spoke as forcefully as a frontal attack upon the Austrians, Cesare Correnti has left an eloquent description of his enrolment in this painstaking propaganda war:

I resigned myself, an impatient conscript, to the discussion of averages, tables and numbers, which gave us a chance to talk in jargon and in a cipher, and to withdraw ourselves from the mutilations of the censorship, accustomed as it was to sniff only at phrases and epithets. The thing was done. Numbers spoke their language only to those who knew how to read their code; it was the true language of mutes.[4]

Although appalled by the rapacity of English capitalism and the misery of its industrial workers, the Lombard publicists turned to England and France for their models.[5] There they saw at work the 'spirit of the age' –

[3] Macartney, *The Habsburg Empire*, p. 258.
[4] T. Massarani, *Cesare Correnti nella vita e nelle opere*, pp. 62–3 n. 1.
[5] Greenfield, *Economics and Liberalism*, p. 271. See also an article by a Venetian Jew, M. P. Coen, in Racc. Andreola, vol. 1, pp. 742–4, 28 April 1848: 'England must not forget that while the French revolution was both political and social, the

science, harnessed to the new order through free enterprise and association. An economic revolution was sweeping across Europe, and it was vital that the Italians should rid their peninsula of the anomalies that had accrued through centuries of divided rule. Added urgency was given to this national programme by the prospect of the reopening of the Mediterranean trade route to the Orient. *Il mare nostro* seemed to stand once again at the heart of the world. Italy, in turn, stood the chance of acquiring the lion's share of the carrying trade if she could create a customs union and establish free trade.[6]

The political writing that complemented this economic propaganda, while it had many diverse strands, was for the most part liberal, moderate and Catholic. It had as its basis the idea of a federation of Italian states, presided over by the Pope. It became known as the 'neo-Guelph' movement because its protagonists looked back to a semi-mythical epoch of the middle ages when the Italian communes and the Pope (the Guelphs) had united to drive out the foreign emperor and his supporters (the Ghibellines). With the publication of Gioberti's *Primato* in 1843, the liberal Catholic movement became a vast, uncoordinated body of public opinion, above all in Piedmont and the central Italian states, with clear nationalist and political overtones.

This movement had little contact or sympathy with the other major Italian political tendency of the time – Mazzinianism. From the ashes of the central Italian revolutions of 1830–2, Giuseppe Mazzini constructed a new organisation, Young Italy, and a fresh political programme that were to have a fundamental influence on the course of the Risorgimento. Mazzini believed that all history was marked with the idea of progress, granted by God's will to be realised through the destinies of different nations. The task of young Italians was to fulfil the destiny of their nation, through God and the people, and create an independent and united Italy. This new Italian state was to be a republican one and to have its centre at Rome, which would thus enter its third era of world influence. The methods of struggle that Mazzini proposed were, like his political programme, both a continuation and development of the actions of the revolutionary sects. Through education and guerrilla warfare, Mazzini argued, it would be possible first to prepare the people for the struggle against the foreign oppressor and then lead them in successful revolution. Gifted with tremendous enthusiasm and energy, as well as considerable organisational powers, Mazzini was soon able to make his ideas and organisation the

English revolution was exclusively political. The United Kingdom thus presents the pitiable spectacle of enormous riches accumulated by a few, and of a whole people who groan under the weight of poverty and an enormous public debt.'
[6] Greenfield, *Economics and Liberalism*, pp. 209–11.

dominant ones on the left of the Italian national movement.[7] But the young Mazzinians had little or nothing in common with the liberal moderates, who rejected their ideas of insurrection and self-sacrifice in favour of slow and patient work, through diplomatic and other channels, to bring the princes of Italy closer together.

The Venetian bourgeoisie was not in the forefront of the economic and political propaganda of these years. None the less certain sections of it, particularly the lawyers of Venice itself and the Venetian chamber of commerce, were far from indifferent to the agitation which was to reach its climax in D'Azeglio's 'Programme for an Italian national opinion'. The possibility of Venice again becoming a major centre for the carrying trade with the east struck a particularly resonant note. In June 1847 Giuseppe Reali told the Venetian chamber of commerce of the possible future for the city:

Commerce created this city, and commerce must return it to its former splendour; ... they are about to cut a way through the Isthmus of Suez; as you will hear the studies already made provide hope for the successful execution of the project. Venetian commerce fell into decay because the sea route round the Cape of Good Hope closed the land route to the Indies. This route is about to be reopened: steamships have indeed already opened it; this then is our 'good hope'.[8]

It is against this background that we must chart the course of Venetian bourgeois activity in the last decade prior to the revolution. Their actions had no point of reference either with the *carbonari* lodges of the Polesine of the early 1820s or the few Mazzinians active in Venice and the Veneto during the 1830s and 1840s. When the Mazzinian Bandiera brothers founded a secret society called the 'Esperia' in the Venetian navy, they were unable to find any support within the city itself. It was this which in 1844 prompted them, Domenico Moro and fifteen others to flee via Corfu to Calabria, where they hoped to start an insurrection amongst the local peasantry. A few days after landing they were caught and shot by Neapolitan troops.[9] The professional and commercial bourgeoisie of Venice had no time for such heroic but hopeless conspiracies. Rather, they thought of themselves, along with their counterparts throughout

---

[7] An excellent summary of Mazzini's political beliefs is to be found in G. Candeloro, *Storia dell'Italia moderna*, vol. 2 (1958), pp. 194–222. See also the fundamental work of F. Della Peruta, *Mazzini e i rivoluzionari italiani: Il 'partito d'azione', 1830–1845.*

[8] ASV, CC, b. 184, VI, 26, speech of 22 June 1847.

[9] For an ample bibliography by Della Peruta on the Bandiera brothers, see *Bibliografia dell'età del Risorgimento*, vol. I, pp. 255–6.

Italy, as being 'in conspiracy with the overwhelming tendency of the age'.[10]

Greenfield has claimed that it would be wrong to infer that the agitation of these years reflected a movement of the bourgeoisie to gain control of society, since 'the liberal programme was initiated, expounded and propagated, not by an aspiring and self-conscious bourgeoisie, with strong economic interests to serve, but by landed proprietors and a group of intellectuals many of whose leaders were of the aristocracy'.[11] However, the leaders of a revolutionary movement do not of necessity belong by origin to the class in whose interests the revolution is being made. Nor can or does the whole of that class reach the same level of consciousness and aspiration at the same time. All classes are uneven in composition and ideology, containing both backward and advanced elements. The northern Italian bourgeoisie of the 1830s and 1840s could not compare with the English or French bourgeoisie; it was a class still very much in the process of formation. But within its ranks there existed highly ambitious sections and individuals (and certainly not only intellectuals and capitalist-minded aristocrats) whose intentions were quite clear: to seek support for a movement that amounted essentially to 'an attempt by the bourgeoisie to gain control of society'. The history of Venetia in the 1840s is the history of just such a group, composed primarily of a small number of businessmen and lawyers of the city of Venice. They appealed, with increasing clarity as the decade passed and conditions changed, to the commercial and landed interests in Venetian society, in the name of first economic and then political alternatives to the status quo.

The railway question

These elements in Venetian society had an unrivalled opportunity for action with the protracted and complex disputes in the early 1840s over the Milan–Venice railway.[12] The railways assumed immense importance in the writings of Italian publicists of these years. Many writers insisted that a network of railways was an absolute priority, not only to ensure

[10] The phrase is Greenfield's; *Economics and Liberalism*, p. 260.

[11] *Ibid.*, p. 263.

[12] Adolfo Bernardello is at present engaged in writing a full-scale study of the railway question. Some preliminary observations and conclusions are to be found in his review article, 'Un'impresa ferroviaria nel Lombardo-Veneto: la Società Ferdinandea da Milano a Venezia', *Rivista Storica Italiana*, 85 (1973), pp. 186–99. A useful introduction to the problem of railway construction in Italy in general, and the Milan–Venice route in particular, has been written by A. Wingate, *Railway Building in Italy before Unification* (Centre for the Advanced Study of Italian Society, University of Reading, Occasional Papers no. 3).

that ships coming through Suez would unload their cargoes at Italian ports, but also to break down the barriers dividing the Italian states. A constant flow of people and merchandise from one part of the peninsula to another would, they considered, be a revolutionary weapon in combating the ancient municipal rivalries of Italy. Carlo Petitti di Roreto's famous book, *Delle strade ferrate italiane e del migliore ordinamento di esse*, published in 1845, was only the best known amongst a mass of publications on the question of railway building.

When the idea of constructing a railway from Milan to Venice was first seriously discussed, in the Venetian chamber of commerce in 1836, it was recognised immediately as the most grandiose and ambitious scheme of its type in all Italy. It is highly significant that the first impetus to start a railway company for the construction of the 271 kilometres of track should come from members of the Venetian chamber of commerce. Amongst the founders were Giuseppe Reali, Francesco Zucchelli, Pietro Bigaglia, Jacopo Treves and Spiridione Papadopoli. In the first years of the company's existence, the merchants and bankers of the city of Venice held a very large number of its shares, and Venice, although smaller and less rich than Milan, always contributed more to the undertaking. We have here clear proof, as Bernardello has pointed out, of the existence in Venice of 'productive forces in possession of considerable capital, ready to invest large sums in industrial enterprises of no mean stature, and capable of taking sound initiatives, not on the basis of abstract proposals, but with clear aims of profit and capitalist expansion'.[13]

Austrian attitudes to the railway company were not as negative as traditional accounts would have us believe.[14] There were two separate questions involved – the actual construction of the Milan–Venice railway, and the possibility of linking it with other parts of Italy. No evidence exists to show that the Austrians deliberately obstructed the railway's construction. It did take them nineteen months to approve Milani's plans for the route, but this was due more to habitual caution and bureaucratic delay than any sinister motives.[15] They had much more to gain than lose from the railway. It would clearly increase the prosperity of Lombardy-Venetia and would also provide a major link in the chain of communications that the Austrians hoped to extend from Milan through Venice to Trieste, and finally northwards to Vienna. But the Austrians did show themselves absolutely intransigent on the question of joining the 'Ferdinandea', as the Milan–Venice railway came to be called, with any

---

[13] Bernardello, 'Un'impresa', p. 193.
[14] The standard accounts have all followed the line taken by R. Bonghi, *La vita e i tempi di Valentino Pasini*, pp. 86–130.
[15] Wingate, *Railway Building*, p. 27.

of those planned in the other Italian states. The Viennese authorities had no intention of allowing Milan's 'natural' port Genoa, which was in the kingdom of Piedmont, to handle the lion's share of Milanese trade, to the detriment of Venice and Trieste. In political terms, they had even less desire to see a link-up, and Petitti's book, which outlined the long-term political advantages for Italy of a railway system, confirmed their worst suspicions.

A number of disputes racked the early history of the railway company, and the exact reasons for the various positions adopted have not yet been completely unravelled. The most bitter of all was that over Bergamo. The inhabitants of Bergamo were enraged that the proposed route did not run through their city, which was too far to the north and in hilly terrain. They were able to make common cause with a number of Viennese bankers and speculators, particularly the house of Arnstein and Erskeles, who had vested interests in the railway's running from Milan to Monza and then to Bergamo.[16]

For the historian of 1848–9 the details of the dispute are perhaps of less interest than the fact that during it the principal protagonist of the Venetian revolution of 1848–9 appears for the first time. Daniele Manin was at this time a not particularly successful Venetian lawyer in his late thirties. He was half Jewish by origin, his grandparents on his father's side having been converted to Christianity in April 1759, changing their name from Medina to Manin.[17] Daniele was born in 1804 and soon showed himself to be a highly precocious child. At the age of fourteen he had enrolled at Padua university, and graduated in law in July 1821. By then he had already published, albeit with the help of his father, a legal treatise on wills and a translation from Greek of the book of Enoch. He

[16] Erskeles owned the short railway line from Milan northwards to Monza that was in the process of construction, and was afraid that a direct east–west, Milan–Venice railway would detract from the value of his holdings. He therefore spread the rumour in the years 1838 to 1840 that he had in his pocket a concession for the railway to be built from Monza to Bergamo, then from Bergamo to Brescia, and then on to Venice. Speculators were invited to pay for the privilege of reserving shares, and Erskeles in the meantime applied pressure at Vienna to get his route chosen. But the preliminary decisions went against him and he therefore made common cause with the Bergamasque faction to get the railway company to change the route from Milan to Venice; R. Ciasca, *L'origine del 'programma per l'opinione nazionale italiana' del 1847–8*, pp. 372ff; Wingate, *Railway Building*, pp. 29–30.

[17] It was commonly believed that Manin was descended from the Fonsecca family, but the Rabbi Leone Luzzatto showed this to be incorrect; see A. Ottolenghi, 'Abraham Lattes nei suoi rapporti colla repubblica di Daniele Manin', *Rassegna Mensile di Israel*, 5 (1930) (off-print version, p. 4 n. 2).

was conversant in Latin, French, English, German, Greek and Hebrew.

His father Pietro, who was also a lawyer, was undoubtedly the major influence in Daniele's intellectual formation. Pietro Manin was a convinced republican and democrat, and together with his friend, the Friulian lawyer Francesco Foramiti, must have inspired in the young Daniele much of the sympathy for French republicanism that he was later to show. The Manin household was very well stocked with books, and from the diaries and notebooks that he kept it is clear that Daniele read, in spite of the censorship, all the Italian classics, many works of the Enlightenment, Vieusseux's *Antologia*, Silvio Pellico and much else besides.[18]

Daniele Manin always suffered from ill health and was frequently in pain from a stomach complaint of unspecified nature. This seems to have led to long bouts of melancholy, during which he would scribble self-derogatory notes describing the failings in his character.[19] One of these notes ends with the comment 'small in everything'. Another contains this passage: 'I love to rest; I love sleeping and the comfort of a feather bed; I have spent more than half my life idling away my time in a warm bed; I hope to do the same in the future . . .'

In public he presented quite the opposite image. Short of stature, but with a fine speaking voice, his precision of mind and intense energy at moments of crisis were his greatest assets. He was always highly empirical, an impression confirmed by the valuable comments of an English doctor with whom he talked in 1846:

His philosophical creed is that of *explained facts*; his mind tending somewhat to skepticism with regard to subjects upon which he has not *convincing proofs*! This is one of the reasons why Mr. Manin is not of a religious character. Notwithstanding this general tendency to incredulity Mr. Manin's intellect is of an *inquisitive nature* and gives him what may be termed a *philosophical curiosity*![20]

Manin's personal life was a very stable one. After an early romance with Carolina Fossati, the daughter of a Friulian nobleman,[21] he married

---

[18] See the interesting article by A. Ventura, 'La formazione intellettuale di Daniele Manin', *Il Risorgimento*, 9 (1957), pp. 1–21.

[19] MCV, Doc. Pell., xvii/3, and M. Brunetti *et al.* (eds.), *Daniele Manin intimo*, pp. lxv–lxvi.

[20] MCV, Doc. Pell., xx/2. The doctor's name was Castle and he conducted an '*esame frenologico*'.

[21] Manin wrote to Teresa on 15 April 1824 (*Daniele Manin intimo*, p. 47): 'Tuesday evening, while I was strolling on the Riva under the wan light of a fading moon, lo and behold! my mind began to dwell on melancholy, sentimental thoughts. As you will well understand it was not the melancholic nature of these thoughts that was so extraordinary. Melancholia has been my consistent and fraternal companion for many a year. No, it was the *sentimental* content that so astounded me, because I had for some time past abandoned any such ideas and thought

Teresa Perissinotti in September 1825. They appear to have been happy together. In 1826 they had a daughter, Emilia, who suffered from epilepsy and to whom Manin was deeply devoted, and in 1831 a son called Giorgio. Apart from a period of two years, from September 1831 to August 1833, when Manin was forced through lack of work in Venice to go and practise at Mestre, the Manins lived in a house in the heart of Venice, looking over the square of San Paternian. This house was rented from the banker Jacopo Treves.

Manin was won to the Italian cause while still a young man. Many years after the event, he was to tell the historian La Forge in Paris that he and a group of friends, on hearing of the risings in central Italy of February 1831, tried to start an insurrection in Venice.[22] They wrote a proclamation to the citizens of Venice, ran it off on a secret printing press – Manin scorched his hands in the process – and fly-posted it on the walls of Venice. No rising occurred and the Austrian police never found the authors of the proclamation. Although no copy of the proclamation has remained there seems no reason to doubt Manin's story. He was not the sort of man to boast of things he had not done. Indeed, amongst his papers in the Museo Correr there is a diary he kept of the events of 1831–2, which testifies at the very least to his interest in the revolutions.

It was natural that Manin, given his background and social position, should get involved in the railway question. Despite his bouts of indolence and melancholy, he was clearly an ambitious man dissatisfied with the position that lawyers enjoyed under Austrian rule. He was related by marriage to the wealthy and influential Papadopoli family, had been involved in the legal side of a number of commercial transactions, and was a member of the Venetian commercial company.

Valentino Pasini of Vicenza was Manin's closest companion during the fight over the Bergamo route. He too was a lawyer educated at Padua and his father owned one of the woollen-cloth factories at Schio. These two, together with the engineer Pietro Paleocapa,[23] went to Milan in the

they would never return.' For Manin's earlier love affair, see C. Palumbo-Fossati, 'Un amore giovanile di Daniele Manin per una Fossati di Morcote', *Bollettino Storico della Svizzera Italiana*, 28 (1953). The Fossatis had an interesting French background: one of Carolina's brothers was a Napoleonic officer who had been wounded during the Spanish and Austrian campaigns; her sister married a French army officer and after the Restoration went to live in Paris. The family frowned on Carolina's relationship with Daniele Manin, because of his modest origins, and this was one of the reasons for the affair breaking up. But another of Carolina's brothers, Francesco, remained a close friend of Manin and was to take an active part in the revolution.
22 A de La Forge, *Histoire de la République de Venise sous Manin*, vol. 1, pp. 26–30.
23 Paleocapa (1788–1869) studied law and mathematics at Padua before enrolling

summer of 1840 to discuss tactics with those Milanese who were opposed
to the Bergamo route. A number of historic meetings were held in the
Visconti palace. The Milanese were represented by Borromeo, Casati,
Durini and Cattaneo, the Venetians by Manin, Paleocapa and Pasini.
They failed to stop the Bergamo bandwagon at the second congress of
shareholders at Venice in August 1840, but the matter was not settled
once and for all and a commission of enquiry was set up to decide on the
route.

It has often been inferred that the anti-Bergamo group, from the
language they used and their later activity in 1848–9, constituted an
'Italian party' in the railway dispute. The facts, as Bernardello has shown,
do not bear these assumptions out.[24] The Italians involved, did not, as we
shall see, form a united anti-Austrian front. Much use was made of the
word 'national', but nobody at this stage meant by it 'Italian' as opposed
to 'Austrian'. Manin, who on this issue was probably the most advanced
of those involved, undoubtedly used the word in the sense of serving the
interests of Lombardy and Venetia as opposed to Austria. But others, like
Cattaneo, did not automatically attribute to it an anti-Austrian connota-
tion. For most of the businessmen involved the 'national interest' was
simply the prosperity and advancement of the Italian provinces of the
Austrian empire.

After the 1840 congress of shareholders a violent polemic broke out,
and Manin entered the lists against the Venetian lawyer Jacopo Castelli,
who had been hired to represent the interests of the Bergamo faction.[25]
The commission of enquiry decided in favour of the Bergamo route, but
the opposition managed to delay a new meeting of shareholders. During

in the Napoleonic military academy at Modena. He became an officer in the
engineering corps of the army of Italy and took part in Napoleon's Russian
campaign. During the Restoration he became well known as an engineer and in
1840 was appointed director general of public works at Venice.

[24] Bernardello, 'Un'impresa', p. 195. Bonghi (*Valentino Pasini*, p. 295) was probably the first historian to talk of an 'Italian party', and he was followed by all
the later historians of the revolution; I must plead guilty to taking this line in
my unpublished doctoral thesis, 'The politics of the Venetian revolution,
1848–9', fos 42–6.

[25] Jacopo Castelli was born in 1791, the son of an engineering officer in the army
of the Venetian republic. In the 1840s Castelli was considered the leading lawyer
in Venice. For further biographical details see E. Castelli, *Jacopo Castelli, ovvero
una pagina della storia di Venezia nel 1848*. Manin's contributions to the railway
polemics are reprinted in the documentary section of A. Errera and C. Finzi,
La vita e i tempi di Daniele Manin, 1804–48, pp. 1–26. At one stage in
his article 'Altre verità' (p. 25), Manin reminded Castelli that to acquire
immortal fame it was not sufficient merely to drink poison; one also had to be
Socrates.

this time Manin organised a campaign in Venice and the Venetian provinces to persuade local merchants and landowners to buy shares in the company, in the hope of winning a majority of those in favour of the direct route before the next shareholders' meeting. Thus at Verona the lawyer Bertoncelli began an extensive sales campaign. At Padua Luigi Giustiniani did the same; at Dolo the lawyer Biscaro; at Treviso and Conegliano the former Napoleonic officer Angelo Mengaldo; at Vicenza, Pasini. In September 1841 Manin wrote to his colleague in Vicenza: 'Never tire of defending the national cause for which you have fought with so much energy and ability.'[26] The campaign proved more successful in Venice than in the provinces, but a valuable network of contacts was established.

The third congress of shareholders met in Milan in April 1842. It was soon clear that the activity of Manin and Pasini, and their counterparts in Lombardy (Broglio, Strigelli, etc.) had paid off. The majority of share-holders were now Lombards and Venetians, and favourable to the original direct route. Of equal importance, the Austrian government had also declared for this route, thus demonstrating its independence from the Arnstein/Erskeles lobby, and appearing to put the last nail in Bergamo's coffin. But Vienna also offered, because of the importance of the enter-prise, to take it into state hands, and this provoked a complete split in the ranks of the Italian shareholders. Manin, Pasini, the noble landowners of Lombardy and to a lesser extent Venetia, as well as a few bankers – Treves and Brambilla among them – opposed the Austrian offer. Cattaneo and most of the *negozianti* of Venice and Milan were happy to accept state intervention. Genuine differences over what was best for the future of the railway seem to have been at the heart of the split, but we must await further clarification.[27] In any event, those in favour of the independence of the company won the day, and work on the original route from Milan to Treviglio began immediately. Manin regarded the decision to keep the company independent as a tremendous triumph for the 'national cause'. After a deputation including Pasini had visited Vienna, the Austrian

---

[26] Manin to Pasini, 21 Sept. 1841, published in Errera and Finzi, *Daniele Manin*, p. 28. For the sales campaign in the Venetian provinces, see Ciasca, *L'origine*, p. 374 n. 3. Angelo Mengaldo was to be the first commander of the Venetian civic guard in 1848. Born in 1787, he joined the army of Italy in 1804, fought at Wagram, in the Russian campaign, and was decorated by Napoleon. An Anglo-phile throughout his life, in June 1818 he and Byron held a famous swimming race from the Lido to the Rialto. Byron claimed he won but Mengaldo main-tained that he had been tricked into climbing into a gondola. See N. Meneghetti (ed.), *Il Cavaignac di Venezia. Diario inedito del generale Mengaldo, 1848–49*, p. 22.

[27] Bernardello, 'Un'impresa', pp. 194–5.

government was convinced of the viability of the company, and the imperial Resolution of December 1842 gave considerable concessions to it.[28]

At this stage disaster set in, at least from Manin's point of view. The company was making such good progress that the shares rose considerably in value, and most of the Lombards and Venetians who had bought them could not resist the temptation to sell while the going was good. By 1845 the majority of shares was once again in non-Italian hands, and at the congress of that year the shareholders decided, by 917 votes to 34, to hand the company over to the state. Manin fought almost alone against this move, protesting bitterly against the 'national humiliation' of such a policy.[29]

The railway question thus ended in relative failure, in the sense of the railway company losing its independence. But the gains from it had been enormous. It had led to unprecedented discussion of a matter of public importance, and had enabled the most progressive of the Venetian and Milanese bourgeoisie and nobility to meet and talk for the first time. For a lawyer like Manin, prevented by Austrian rule from leading an active political life, the experience of the railway question, the expeditions to Milan and conversation with men of the stature of Carlo Cattaneo, led to an immense widening of his horizons. The campaign he had organised in the Veneto had also brought him into contact with forward-looking elements in the provincial cities. But perhaps the greatest benefit of all was the railway bridge from Venice to Mestre, which was opened in 1846 amidst great festivities.[30] This magnificent bridge, undoubtedly the greatest achievement of the period of Austrian rule in Venetia, ended a millennium of Venice's isolation from the mainland.

The economic crisis of 1846–7

The men who took an active part in the railway question were a small group, without specific political aims. They lacked lasting support from

[28] For details of the concessions, see Wingate, *Railway Building*, pp. 35–6.
[29] The railway was not finally completed until 1857, and the final route presented a partial victory for Erskeles. The line now ran from Treviglio to Bergamo and then back south again to Coccaglio. Most travellers preferred to get off at Treviglio, take horses for the few miles to Coccaglio, and await the train there; see Ciasca, *L'origine*, p. 376 n. 1. Erskeles became deputy governor of the Austrian national bank. Effie Ruskin described his only daughter, Countess Wimpffen, as an 'immense heiress' who never left her bed unless the sun was shining. In 1849 the countess was living in the Palazzo Fini, which was until recently the Grand Hotel. See M. Lutyens (ed.), *Effie in Venice*, p. 98 n. 2.
[30] In 1848 a journey from Venice to Vicenza cost 8.25 Au. lire first class, 6.50 second, and 3.75 third; *Guida commerciale*, pp. 55–62.

the landowners, merchants and professional men of Venice and the Veneto. They could not, as we have seen, be called an 'Italian party' in any meaningful sense. However, in 1846 two events – the European economic crisis and the election of Pius IX as Pope – shattered once and for all, and with extraordinary rapidity, Austrian policy in northern Italy. From being a small number of isolated progressives, men like Manin suddenly found themselves, by the winter of 1847, at the head of a mass movement. What was more, this movement had a clearly nationalist and anti-Austrian character. Looking back on this period the liberal Paduan nobleman Carlo Leoni wrote in his diary in August 1848:

I shall never forget how about three years ago my illustrious friend Tommaseo and I came to the conclusion, after a long discussion on the moral state of the Italian peoples, that *the only hope lay in a process lasting centuries*, so far was Italy from regeneration. But in these three years the great number of important events that have followed one after another, in Europe and Italy, have combined to produce an improvised but most potent political education.[31]

The European crisis of 1846–7 has been described by Hobsbawm as 'the last, and perhaps worst, economic breakdown of the *ancien régime* in economics'.[32] In 1845 the Venetian harvest was poor, with heavy rain and floods being mainly responsible. A year later only the maize crop was reported as being normal, with wheat scarce and potatoes blighted completely. These setbacks were not as serious as in other parts of the empire, such as Bohemia and Silesia, but the Venetian situation was greatly aggravated by the extensive exporting of cereals, particularly maize. As a result prices rocketed. In 1845 the average wholesale price in Venice for a Venetian bushel of wheat was 16.22 Austrian lire, much the same as it had been ever since 1819. In 1846 this average price rose to 18.56 Au. lire, and in the first months of 1847 it leapt to 31.92 Au. lire. A similar catastrophic rise is to be found for maize. The average price paid in Venice for a Venetian bushel of maize in 1845 had been 10.61 Au. lire. For the period February to April 1847 the average price for the same amount was 24.49 Au. lire. The price indexes for the provincial markets reveal an almost identical pattern. The maize prices for the Polesine show the most drastic increase – almost threefold between 1845 and April 1847. This is probably to be explained by heavy exportation across the Po to the adjoining Papal States, where the situation was worse and prices higher. In the far north, in the province of Belluno, the wheat and maize prices seem to

[31] C. Leoni, 'Cronaca, 1848', in *Epigrafi e prose edite e inedite* (ed. G. Guerzoni), p. 475, 28 Aug. 1848.
[32] Hobsbawm, *The Age of Revolution*, p. 203.

have been no greater than elsewhere in the Veneto, but this was the area which suffered most from the failure of the potato crop.[33]

From all over the Veneto in the early months of 1847 reports flooded in to the central authorities of the peasants' suffering. In a crisis of this sort, the labourers of the great plains suffered acutely from their lack of land or food stores. Equally vulnerable were peasants in exclusively wine- and silk-growing regions, in wooded or river areas, and in the mountains. They were all reliant on the local markets, and foodstuffs in these were usually more costly than in the cities, where the greater activity and influx of goods helped to keep prices down.[34]

In some areas desperation turned to violence. In the village of Polesella, on the banks of the Po, more than a hundred villagers gathered on 13 February 1847 to demand bread, and on the same day the granaries of two merchants in the locality were sacked. A little to the west, at Fiesso, at least one death from starvation was reported. In the province of Treviso, two merchants who were transporting grain were stoned by a crowd near Pieve. The peasants tried to steal a sack of maize and shouted that the poor were being left to starve. On the festival of St George in April 1847 the villagers of Cazzano, near Verona, forced the police to seek refuge for the whole day in the house of a local government official.[35]

---

[33] Piero Brunello has recently completed a very detailed article – shortly to be published – on the crisis of 1846–7 in the Veneto. I am grateful to him for allowing me to consult it, and to correct a few earlier inaccuracies. The prices for Venice itself come from ASV, CC, b. 180, v, 28; all the others are from ASV, Gov., 1845–9, dipartimento commercio e navigazione, fasc. xix, 1/23. The crisis reached its peak in June 1847 and did not ease completely until the copious harvest of maize in the late summer.

[34] See the instructive remarks of R. Cobb, *The Police and the People*, pp. 218–20; also G. Monteleone, 'La carestia del 1816–17', pp. 32–3, who notes how the market at Padua deprived the surrounding areas of grain, thus forcing prices up in the rural markets. In 1847 in the village of Mirano near Venice, a local official wrote of two 'foreigners' (in fact from neighbouring Dolo) who bought up the maize 'at any price' so that none was left for the villagers. There was such an uproar that they were forced to give it all back. See ASV, Pres. Gov., 1845–8, fasc. xiii, 7/22, no. 1470. The most striking example of the difference between urban and rural prices is to be found in the Polesine. At Rovigo itself the average price for a *soma metrica* of maize between 15 Feb. and the end of April 1847 was 20.87 Au. lire. The average price in the whole province for the same period was 28.29 Au. lire; ASV, Gov., 1845–9, dipartimento commercio e navigazione, fasc. xix, 1/23.

[35] A long report from Call, the Austrian chief of police at Venice, deals with the incidents at Polesella and Fiesso, as well as describing conditions throughout the Veneto; ASV, Pres. Gov., 1845–8, fasc. xiii, 7/22, no. 966, 14 Feb. 1847. For Pieve, *ibid.*, no. 1690. For Cazzano, ASV, Pres. Gov., 1845–8, fasc. i, 13/4, no. 2814.

Incidents such as these were not grave in themselves, and appear trifling when compared with the contemporary large-scale peasant revolts in the heartlands of the Austrian empire. Even in Lombardy, Croat soldiers had to quell rioting in a number of areas.[36] But the Venetian peasantry was not noted for its militancy, and widespread disturbances of this sort had not been reported since the famine years of 1816–17. In the countryside round Treviso, Giuseppe Olivi recalled that 'the destitute wandered from villa to villa begging for sustenance . . . they eagerly devoured the ears of corn which were not yet ripe . . . My good father spent 16,000 lire in saving our peasantry from starvation.'[37]

In the cities the situation was equally critical. Crop failures meant the destruction of home demand for manufactured goods, and the general European commercial depression of 1846–7 took its toll in the Venetian cities as elsewhere. In Venice there were a series of failures: Federico Oexle, one of the founding members of the Venetian commercial company, and owner of the only power-driven mill in Venice, was forced to suspend payments. So too was the company controlled by Abramo Levi. The Venetian chamber of commerce complained bitterly of 'the extremely difficult conditions for trade of every sort'.[38]

This commercial crisis meant that the urban poor, already seriously affected by rocketing bread prices, found even fewer possibilities of employment than usual, during what was for them the most difficult part of the year. In 1845, to take just one example, there had been 639 silk operatives in the city; by the end of 1847 their numbers had dwindled to 410.[39] Call, the Venetian chief of police, reported on the deterioration in the climate of public opinion and the increased number of menacing letters that he was receiving. One of them ended, 'hunger leads to violent acts: a r—— could take place, and the example of Venice would be imitated in the whole kingdom'.[40]

The plight of Venice's poor was partially alleviated by a shrewd move on the part of six of the richest *negozianti* in the city. Imitating the example of Baron James Rothschild in Paris, they offered 120,000 bushels of wheat and maize at February's prices to the municipality for the months of March to May 1847. They appear to have been motivated by a mixture of philanthropy, fear of rioting in the city, and straightforward desire for profit.[41] The municipality saw to the baking of the bread, which

[36] F. Della Peruta, 'I contadini', pp. 67–8.   [37] MS Olivi, p. 61.

[38] ASV, CC, b. 177, IV, 6; see A. Bernardello, 'La paura del comunismo', pp. 55–6.

[39] Bernardello, 'La paura del comunismo', p. 52 n. 7.

[40] ASV, Pres. Gov., 1845–8, fasc. XIII, 7/22, no. 966, 14 Feb. 1847.

[41] Brunello, in his forthcoming article, puts the accent very much on the third of these motives. Paris was the first city to distribute coupons to the poor which

went on sale at a fixed price from April 3 onwards. The operation proved successful, for the 'municipal bread' forced down prices in the whole city, in spite of the vehement protests of private bakers.[42]

The provincial cities also suffered severely. The bottom fell out of the silk market and there were numerous reports of the unsuccessful attempts of Venetian growers and merchants to unload large quantities of raw and spun silk.[43] At Verona the police reported that on the festival of *venerdì gnocolaro* [*sic*] (Good Friday) the well-to-do of the city, instead of throwing the usual sugared almonds, had seen fit to distribute bread instead. The numbers in the workhouse had greatly increased, and one anonymous letter of 28 March spoke of 'the horror caused by the disorders arising from the great increase in the price of foodstuffs . . . a revolution against the government seems certain. We pray that there may be some remedy.'[44] At Udine women led a riot in the market place and followed it up with nocturnal attacks on the houses of grain merchants. The municipalities of both Udine and Treviso decided to follow Venice's example and either gave away bread to the poor or sold it at a fixed price. At Chioggia on 12 February 1847 a crowd of men and women assembled outside the home of the mayor, crying 'Abbiamo fame, vogliamo polenta!'[45]

The Austrians' reaction during the first months of 1847 was of crucial

they could exchange for bread at a fixed price. When the coupons system was due to finish on 15 March Baron Rothschild ensured that it continued, and offered five million francs for grain and flour. At one stage the municipal authorities of Prague were distributing 25,000 bowls of soup per day; see *Annali Universali di Statistica, Economia Pubblica, ecc.*, 91 (1847), pp. 301–7 and 326. The six businessmen in Venice were Giuseppe Mondolfo, Giovanni d'Angelo Rosada, Thomas Holm, Giuseppe Reali, Federico Oexle (before he ran into financial difficulty), and Spiridione Papadopoli.

[42] The nobleman Michiel reported to the municipality that the gesture of the six had been coldly received by the other merchants of the city. The baking and marketing of the bread cost the municipality 8,459.57 Au. lire, which they considered to be a worthwhile investment. It is interesting to note that of the 37 men employed to bake the bread only six were Venetians by birth; sixteen of them came from the area round San Donà di Piave. See ASV, Pres. Gov., 1845–8, fasc. XIII, 7/22, documents attached to nos. 2751 and 1654; and ACV, Municip., Atti di Uff., 1845–9, IV, 7/45, no. 13165 and document attached to no. 7508. Similar measures were taken in Milan, where the wives of the liberal nobility organised a collection for the poor of the city; Della Peruta, 'I contadini', p. 73.

[43] See, for example, ASV, CC, b. 176, III, 10, and ASV, Gov. Prov. 1848–9, CPD, b. 832/Rovigo CPD, no. 705, 8 May 1848.

[44] ASV, Pres. Gov., 1845–8, fasc. XIII, 7/22, no. 2050 for the anonymous letter to the Venetian government from Verona; no. 1755 for details of the workhouse; and no. 966 for the distribution of bread.

[45] ASV, Pres. Gov., 1845–8, fasc. XIII, 7/22, no. 966 for Chioggia; *ibid.*, no. 1692 for the rioting at Udine; *ibid.*, no. 3292 and MS Olivi, pp. 96–7, for the municipalities of Udine and Treviso.

importance, for the impression they gave was one of both callousness and incompetence. The extreme indebtedness of the Viennese government made it unwilling to reduce taxation at any level. Indeed income from both direct and indirect taxation in the Veneto was greater in the crisis year of 1847 than it had been in 1845 or 1846. The tax on *arti e commercio*, which most affected the business classes of the cities, realised the same amount as in 1845, and only two thousand florins less than in 1846. Revenue from the personal tax, the peasants' bugbear, only slightly diminished in 1847. A report from the province of Belluno in February 1848 revealed just what this meant for the poorest peasantry of the region: 'the poorer classes lack any means of paying the personal tax . . . in lieu of which the tax collector takes their beds and cooking pots, which are often the only ones they have for preparing their food'.[46]

The Austrians also acted much more slowly than most of the other governments of Italy to impose a ban on the exportation of foodstuffs, and to lift import duties on cereals. English speculators bought up a great deal of maize in the Veneto, and Call reported supply ships leaving for Falmouth, Liverpool and London. This was all the more serious because the Veneto usually imported more maize – as opposed to wheat – than she exported.[47] The ban on exportation, finally imposed on 20 February 1847, was not rigidly enforced. Nor, in spite of repeated demands from every quarter of the Veneto, was permission given when it was most needed for the freezing of prices on primary products. Only in February 1848 did Vienna finally agree to allow the price of bread and flour to be fixed by the city municipalities.[48]

[46] *Carte segrete e atti ufficiali della polizia austriaca in Italia dal 4 giugno 1814 al 22 marzo 1848*, vol. 3 (1852), p. 302, no. 677, 12 Feb. 1848. For Austrian revenue from taxation, A. Uggè, 'Le entrate del regno lombardo-veneto dal 1840 al 1864', *Archivio Economico dell'Unificazione Italiana*, I (1956), p. 12, table II. The figures for the tax on *arti e commercio* were as follows: 1845, 168,000 florins; 1846, 170,000 florins; 1847, 168,000 florins. Those for the personal tax were: 1845, 616,000 florins; 1846, 619,000 florins; 1847, 602,000 florins.

[47] This was the considered opinion of Call in his long report of 14 Feb. 1847 (ASV, Pres. Gov., 1845–8, fasc. XIII, 7/22, no. 966). On the ending of import duties see Call to Palffy, 24 April 1847 (*ibid.*, no. 2623). Apparently the viceroy Ranier had agreed to this measure on 26 Jan., but it had not been put into effect. Call reminded Palffy that all the other states of Europe had already adopted similar measures. On the exportation of foodstuffs to English ports, see *ibid.*, no. 1690, and on English merchants buying up maize in the Veneto, ASV, CC, b. 184, VI, 26. Marzani, the imperial delegate at Venice, wrote to the municipality on 2 Feb. 1847 telling them that the viceroy 'is convinced that the fears manifested in some quarters of a future shortage of foodstuffs are completely exaggerated' (ACV, Municip., Atti di Uff., 1845–9, IV, 7/46, attached to no. 1575).

[48] After the ban on exportation there were numerous complaints of supplies being shipped from the small port of Cervignano, south of Udine, and sent south to

Even the Austrian plan to spend more on public works projects in the Veneto was hampered by bureaucratic indecision. Pietro Paleocapa, the director general of public works, soon to become the minister of public construction in the revolutionary government, reported that nothing had been done for the province of Belluno because no plan had succeeded in obtaining the approval of the imperial chancellery.[49]

The Austrians, therefore, had manifestly failed to meet the needs of the population in a time of crisis. They had not reduced taxation, prevented the export of maize, or supplied sufficient employment. Their actions were in marked contrast to the initiatives they had taken nearly thirty years earlier, during the catastrophic years of 1814–18. The peasantry resented deeply the continuation of the personal tax, which in some areas was emptying their households of the few possessions they had. The urban poor felt equal dissatisfaction at the continuing high level of indirect taxation, and the lack of government measures to supply more jobs. As for the Venetian bourgeoisie, the crisis of 1846–7 hit them at exactly the moment when they were confidently announcing the renaissance of their city. The bankruptcies and closures of 1847 represented a serious setback to their expectations. The government, by its unceasing fiscal demands, its persistent refusal to reduce the duty on silk, and its further restriction of credit facilities,[50] left the Venetian chamber of commerce in a state of exasperation and gloom. In general, the disaffection of the Veneto from Austrian rule dates from these first months of 1847.

The election of Pius IX

Six months before the economic crisis hit the Veneto, an event of the

Ferrara from the Polesine and north to the Tyrol from Verona. In Venice between 7 Jan. and 19 Feb. 1847, 86,598 bushels of maize were exported. In March, *after* the government decree, 78,320½ bushels left the port. Seven members of the chamber of commerce wrote to the government on 7 March 1847 and warned that 'it is impossible to say what disorders could take place if the people realise that the ban on exportation is only an illusion' (ASV, Pres. Gov., 1845–8, fasc. XIII, 7/22, no. 1630). For the pegging of bread and flour prices in Feb. 1848 see the letter from the viceroy to Palffy, *ibid.*, *calmiere*, no. 987 (1848).

[49] For Paleocapa's letter on public works, ASV, Pres. Gov., 1845–8, fasc. XIII, 7/22, no. 1951, 25 March 1847. Between Nov. 1846 and May 1847 the Austrians spent nearly four million Au. lire on public works in the Veneto, a considerable part of it going on the Brenta canal; *Annali Universali de Statistica, Economia Pubblica, ecc.*, 92(1847), p. 211. None the less Della Peruta, 'I contadini', p. 73, confirms the general inadequacy of Austrian relief work in northern Italy at this time.

[50] The sovereign resolution of 29 Sept. 1847 suspended the operations of the 'Cassa Straordinaria di Credito'; see Bernardello, 'La paura del comunismo', p. 60.

greatest significance had taken place at Rome – the election of a liberal Pope. As F. A. Simpson has written:

at a time when every considerable monarchy on the continent was sinking deeper and deeper into the reactionary policy of the age, he [Pius IX] was seen to be offering his subjects a series of concessions and reforms: reforms far from inconsiderable in themselves, and naturally hailed with rapture when coming at such an hour, from such a source. For it was in the wilderness that these waters had broken forth; and men fainting for thirst are poor critics of their drink.[51]

The liberal national movement, already glorified by the Romantics, now appeared to be sanctified by the papacy. It was from Rome, albeit unwittingly, that Italian nationalism gained its decisive impetus.

Pius IX carried through a series of long-overdue reforms in his extensive states in central Italy. Soon after his election he granted a political amnesty, and followed this up with a partial liberalisation of the press, the creation of a civic guard to neutralise the influence of the hated police, and the establishment of a consultative assembly in Rome. He did not mean to appear as an example to the rest of Italy, but the reforms could not help but set off a chain reaction throughout the peninsula. For the neo-Guelphs Pius IX's actions were literally a godsend. Hymns of praise were composed in his honour, handkerchiefs and medallions bearing his portrait were sold in their thousands. The cry of 'Viva Pio Nono!' rent the air of every major Italian city. To this was added, with increasing frequency, the twin cry of 'Viva l'Italia!' Agitation spread first to Tuscany and then to Piedmont. In June 1847, on the first anniversary of Pius's election, there were celebrations all over Italy, and in Parma fights broke out between police and demonstrators.[52]

Venetia was slower than most of northern Italy to react to Pius's reforms. There was no active neo-Guelph group in the city, nor any circle of publicists and activists such as was to be found in Milan. None the less Call reported that Venetian public opinion could not help but feel the effects of Pius's election. Manin, in February 1848, recalled that long before the end of 1847 the walls of all the cities and even the smallest villages had been daubed with the slogan 'Long live Pius IX', and that this was frequently accompanied by 'Death to the Austrians'.[53]

Most significant of all, the liberalism of the Pope found fertile ground

[51] F. A. Simpson, *Louis Napoleon and the Recovery of France*, p. 48.
[52] L. Salvatorelli, *La rivoluzione europea, 1848–1849*, pp. 47–51.
[53] For Call's report, *Carte segrete*, vol. 3, p. 122, no. 566, 2 Aug. 1847. Manin made his remarks during his fifth interrogation by the Austrian police on 19 Feb. 1848. He emphasised that the cry 'Long live Pius IX' was 'a political, not a religious one'; see Errera and Finzi, *Daniele Manin*, p. 190.

among the Venetian clergy. The clergy had their own grievances against the Austrians, mainly stemming from excessive interference by the state. They resented the imperial *placet* on ecclesiastical appointments, the censor's revision of the local priest's letters to his parish, the lack of independence of the seminaries, and the ban on bishops' corresponding with the Holy See.[54] The church hierarchy did its best to prevent liberal or nationalist ideas spreading among the Venetian clergy. The patriarch of Venice, Cardinal Monico, in a circular to all the parish priests of the Veneto, urged them to make sure that 'the people are not seduced by the evil scheming of those who wish to use the venerable name of Pius IX as an aid to subvert all religious and political order'.[55] But the religious authorities could not stem the tide. When events reached their climax it was soon clear that many of the clergy had either adopted the national cause, or were unwilling to speak against it. Given their enormous influence in the countryside and the cities, which the Austrians themselves had helped to foster, in the schools as well as the pulpits, this was amongst the gravest blows to be dealt to Austrian control in northern Italy.

On an individual level, the accession of Pius IX meant the arrival for Nicolò Tommaseo of a long-awaited moment. Tommaseo was a scholar of the first order, a man of enormous erudition and energy. One of the most passionate advocates of liberal Catholicism and Italian regeneration, he had spent many of the years before 1848 in exile in Paris. When he was allowed to return he settled in Venice where he lived the life of an ascetic, surrounded by his books.

In his youth Tommaseo had been a strange combination of mystic and libertine; he had remained unmarried, was bad-tempered and arrogant, and suffered fools unwillingly. There was in his writings an element of Christian socialism, influenced by the teachings of Saint-Simon.[56] He believed firmly that the Italian people had first to attain spiritual and moral maturity before the ideal of an independent Italy could be realised. This maturity could only be achieved through the Catholic religion, and from the teachings of an enlightened Pope. At first unsure about Pius IX, Tommaseo, by 1847, had come to see in him the *Papa redentore* whose

---

[54] See the letter of 3 Oct. 1852 from the patriarch Muti, Monico's successor, to the lieutenant of the Venetian provinces, De Toggenburg; ASV, Pres. Luog., 1852–6, b. 224, v, 10/28. This document was first quoted by B. Bertoli, *Le origini del movimento cattolico a Venezia*, p. 64. See also M. F. de Lamennais, *Des maux de l'Eglise et da la société, et des moyens d'y remédier*, pp. 220–1. Metternich, in a letter of 6 April 1844 to the Emperor Ferdinand, urged that bishops should be allowed to correspond freely with the Pope; *Mémoires*, vol. 7 (1883), p. 35.

[55] *Carte segrete*, vol. 3, pp. 125–7, no. 568, 2 Nov. 1847.

[56] See M. Pitocco, *Utopia e riforma religiosa nel Risorgimento. Il sansimonismo nella cultura toscana*, p. 177.

coming he had prophesied in his book *Dell'Italia*. He went to Rome and on 1 October obtained an audience with the Pope.[57] Pius said to him, 'Write words of moderation, as you have always done.' 'That is my path and my duty', replied Tommaseo.

The years 1846–7 therefore witnessed a startling transformation of economic and ideological conditions in the Veneto. The economic crisis had led to the first rumblings of dissatisfaction for many years, and the Austrians had done more to exacerbate than to calm them. The accession of Pius IX meant an enormous growth in the number of adherents to the Italian cause. As G. M. Trevelyan has written, 'Pio Nono did in the first 22 months of his pontificate what he failed to undo in as many years – he made the national cause popular with great classes of men and women whom no radical or intellectual programme would have reached'.[58] It was not just that those Venetian merchants, lawyers, landowners and businessmen who had sought a more dynamic economic future for their homeland now put their aspirations in a national and political context. It was also that the urban and rural poor, who had had good cause to associate their deprivation with the continued high level of taxation, began to make the link between their religion and opposition to Austrian rule. The preconditions for a mass movement existed for the first time.

Cobden's visit and the scientific congress

From the spring of 1847 onwards, Venice was the scene for increasing activity and propaganda by ever-widening circles of the professional and commercial bourgeoisie. Daniele Manin, by his outspokenness, clarity of thought, and ability to organise, became the recognised leader of the liberal and national faction in the city. By the end of the year political demands were being linked with the earlier economic ones in a gathering storm of opposition.

In March 1847 a petition organised by Manin was sent to Vienna begging the emperor to allow the trade from India to come through Venice, rather than Trieste. It was signed by many prominent members of Venice's bourgeoisie, and suggested plans for a new railway from Verona to Innsbruck.[59] On 10 June Manin lectured the Ateneo Veneto, the leading literary and intellectual institute in Venice, on the need to revive commerce. Amongst other things he proposed the establishment of

---

[57] R. Ciampini, *Vita di Nicolò Tommaseo*, pp. 353 and 357–8.
[58] Trevelyan, *Manin and the Venetian Revolution*, p. 166.
[59] MCV, Doc. Manin, no. 17, 10 March 1847. Amongst the 62 signatories were a few noblemen, mainly from the municipality – Correr, Medin and Michiel.

a Venetian commercial journal to combat the influence of the Austrian Lloyd's, and the institution of a training school for merchant seamen.[60]

A week later Richard Cobden arrived in Venice. He was making a triumphant banqueting tour of Italy, and was being received with honour in every Italian city, both as the leader of a successful struggle for reform (the Anti-Corn-Law League), and as a champion of free trade. Those who welcomed him in Venice interpreted free trade as the abolition of customs barriers throughout Italy, and chose to underplay the possible harmful effects of an end to all protection, such as Piedmontese wines undercutting local ones. The municipality would not risk having anything to do with his visit, but Manin and Pasini organised a banquet for eighty, and the mayor, the noble Giovanni Correr, consented to be present. A garden on the Giudecca was selected as the site for the banquet and bedecked with ears of corn for the occasion.[61] There then followed a moonlit trip by gondola up the Grand Canal which was, confessed Cobden, 'sufficiently romantic to excite poetical emotions even in the mind of a political economist'.[62]

On 13 September 1847 the ninth Italian scientific congress, attended by more than a thousand men of learning from all over Italy, opened at Venice. The congresses had begun in Tuscany in 1839. They served the invaluable purpose of bringing together educated men from every Italian state to discuss the scientific innovations of the age and their practical application in Italy. In the absence of a free press, the congresses became one of the most important means of spreading the national economic programme.

The Austrian authorities had given reluctant permission for the ninth congress, which was the largest ever, and there was trouble even before it began. Three of the representatives from the Papal States – the Prince of Canino, Masi and Costabili – created a commotion on the ferryboat crossing the Po, and on disembarking on Venetian territory, Masi cried, 'This land is ours!' He was with difficulty restrained by Costabili from unfurling a tricolour flag on the spot.[63]

A climate of suppressed, and sometimes unsuppressed, nationalism permeated the whole congress. Many of the educated classes from all parts

[60] Errera and Finzi, *Daniele Manin*, pp. 42–4.
[61] Tommaseo's private description of Cobden was: 'deep down the man is a charlatan, but more subtle than most; in other words he is a British charlatan'. See N. Tommaseo and G. Capponi, *Carteggio inedito dal 1833 al 1874*, vol. 2, p. 667 n. 2.
[62] J. Morley, *The Life of Richard Cobden*, vol. 1, p. 440.
[63] See the copy of the report from Vendramini, chief of police at Rovigo, to Call, 14 Sept. 1847, HHSAV, Informations-Büro, Kart. 24, Korresp. mit Polizei-Hofstelle, 1847, vi–xii.

of the Veneto came to listen to the sessions held in the great council chamber of the Doges' palace. Some of the delegates' outspokenness on supposedly 'scientific' subjects must have amazed them. Cesare Cantù, in the geographical section, first quoted Pius IX amidst loud applause, and then outlined the revolution that the railways would bring not only to commerce and industry, but 'to politics as well'.[64] In the agrarian section, which was chaired by the wealthy and liberal aristocrat, Count Giovanni Cittadella of Padua, great sport was had when discussing '*patate*', which in Italian can mean both 'potato' and 'German'. Frequent references to the disgusting *patate* of that year met with surreptitious approval. Manin himself spoke in this section on the necessity for coordinated action by local agrarian associations.[65]

The congress had a tremendous galvanising effect. On 1 November 1847 Guerrieri wrote to Manin from Milan expressing his delight and surprise at the extent of national feeling in a city from which he had hoped for little.[66] The diary of an anonymous Austrophile landowner reveals that the congress made a distinct impression in the provinces as well:

The scientists left on the 29th, triumphant at having awoken the city and the state. They left behind a considerable number of followers who had been seduced by their words and who were now to seduce others in all the cities of the *terraferma* and even in the villages. They travelled from one place to another spreading lies and libels about the Austrian government . . . This accursed sect, which used all its powers to win over the clergy, had all but succeeded. And once the clergy had succumbed, what could we expect from the people?[67]

The lotta legale

Manin now felt strong enough to add to the economic issues of the previous years the political and structural demands that lay closest to his heart. From Cobden's free trade campaign in England both Cattaneo in Milan and Manin in Venice derived the idea of a 'legal struggle' for political expression.[68] Francis I in 1815, afraid of Napoleon and then Murat, had

[64] *Carte segrete*, vol. 3, p. 360, no. 726, 25 Sept. 1847.
[65] *Diario del nono congresso degli scienziati italiani convocato in Venezia nel settembre 1847*, no. 11, 25 Sept., p. 85. Treves, Papadopoli, Reali, Valentino Pasini and Olivi were also members of the agronomy section of the congress. The complete Acts of the congress were never published.
[66] Errera and Finzi, *Daniele Manin*, p. 41.
[67] A. Serena, *Una cronaca inedita del '48*, p. 10.
[68] See C. Cattaneo, *Dell'insurrezione di Milano nel 1848 e della successiva guerra* (revised Italian edition), in his *Opere scelte* (ed. D. Castelnuovo Frigessi), vol. 3, pp. 37–8.

made three promises to his newly acquired subjects: to respect the sentiment of *patria* in the Italian nation; to allow the central congregations to reflect the needs of all; and to permit any citizen to point out to the government the errors of its ways. These promises had never been revoked; they had merely been forgotten. They were now revived by the activists of Milan and Venice and formed the basis for an extensive campaign, which because of its respectability attracted a wide measure of support.

The legal struggle took place in the context of heightening tension throughout Italy. The rulers of both Piedmont and Tuscany had followed the example of Pius IX and made a number of limited concessions in their states. On 3 November 1847 a declaration of principle in favour of a customs union was signed between Rome, Florence and Turin. At Milan, the appointment of a new archbishop was the pretext for further demonstrations in honour of Pius IX, and led to bloody encounters between police and demonstrators; one person was killed and a number wounded. In the autumn, Austrian troops occupied Ferrara, which was in the Papal States, and at the end of 1847 Vienna concluded a defensive/offensive alliance with the reactionary rulers of Parma and Modena, an alliance which Balbo called 'the great line of separation between Austria and Italy'.[69]

In November, in Venice, Manin wrote to the government asking for precautions to be taken against cholera. The tone of his letter reflects the change in the political climate: 'The Venetian Republic in its wisdom knew how to defend its people from contagious diseases. It defended them from plagues; it would have defended them from cholera, if it had broken out during the Republic's lifetime. Governments who dominate a people have a duty in turn to look after the people whom they are dominating.'[70]

On 9 December the *lotta legale* got firmly under way when a little-known member of the Lombard central congregation, Nazari, presented a petition demanding an immediate commission on the grievances of the kingdom. The petition caused an uproar and as a token of respect Nazari received visiting cards from all the liberal nobility of Milan.[71] Manin decided to follow suit in Venice even though he was not a member of any congregation. On 21 December he sent a petition to the Venetian central

[69] Quoted in Ciasca, *L'origine*, p. 540.
[70] Errera and Finzi, *Daniele Manin*, p. lix n. 1.
[71] *Archivio triennale delle cose d'Italia dall'avvenimento di Pio IX all'abbandono di Venezia*, vol. 1, p. 194. This excellent new edition of the *Archivio triennale*, originally edited by Carlo Cattaneo and published in three volumes (Capolago 1850, 1851, Chieri 1855), has been prepared by Luigi Ambrosoli.

congregation, urging the need for a commission of enquiry and stressing that the country had 'many real needs and just desires'. A week later a second Venetian lawyer, Baron Gian Francesco Avesani,[72] submitted another petition supporting Manin's. The same day Avesani received a letter assuring him of 'the absolutely explicit support of the chamber of commerce'.[73]

The chamber's own demands, submitted in January 1848, were rather restrained.[74] They reflected the continued timidity in political matters of the majority of the city's merchants, when contrasted to the more daring and provocative behaviour of the lawyers Manin and Avesani. None the less the requests are worth spelling out, for they constitute an interesting minimum programme as well as revealing the influence of the legal struggle and the scientific congress. The chamber demanded a number of measures to increase the independence of Venice from Trieste and establish equality of treatment by Vienna of the two cities: the abolition of all port duties; the completion of construction works at the port entrance of Malamocco, funds for which had been deleted from the government's estimates for 1848, an action that 'renders the city aghast and afflicted'; the maintenance of the promise given by Ferdinand in 1838 to promote manufacturing industry in Venice; the founding of a bank at Venice 'similar to those established at Genoa and Leghorn'; the ending of the obligation to apply to Vienna before constituting a joint stock company; and the concession of a railway from Venice to Innsbruck. The chamber of commerce also discussed a number of other matters on 13 January but thought fit not to raise them at that stage with the authorities. Among these were the union of the Lombardo-Venetian kingdom with the Italian customs league, and the independence of the chamber of commerce from government supervision.

Nicolò Tommaseo joined the fray two days before the end of 1847, with a speech at the Ateneo Veneto. He presented a brilliant but restrained attack upon the censorship, reminding the Austrians of the third of their

---

[72] Gian Francesco Avesani (1790–1861) was descended from a Veronese noble family and by 1847 was one of the leading lawyers in Venice. His arrogance and harshness of character led to his being disliked in many quarters. For a full biographical note, see Rigobon, *Gli eletti*, pp. 10–21.

[73] ASV, carte Avesani, b. 1, no number, 28 Dec. 1847. In response to these petitions the Venetian central congregation decided to appoint a commission of five of its members to look into the problems. The five were G. B. Morosini, Alvise Mocenigo, Pietro Zen, Dr Antonio Manetti, Carlo Albrizzi and Leonardo Dolfin. At the meeting of 4 Jan. 1848 Morosini read out both Manin's and Avesani's petitions, as well as an address of his own, reminding the Austrians of their promises of 1815.

[74] ASV, CC, b. 188, IV, fasc. 61, no. 1.

promises of 1815 – to permit any citizen to point out to the government the error of its ways. The petition on the censorship which ensued collected over six hundred signatures, and clearly demonstrated the support of the Venetian intelligentsia for the *Lotta legale*. Only two of the professors at Padua university refused to sign.[75]

Protest was not confined to petitions. As Trevelyan has written, 'the opera house, then the magnet and epitome of Italian social life, was that winter invaded by politics'.[76] Verdi's *Macbeth* was playing at the Fenice, and the chorus in Act Four begins with the words: 'The fatherland has been betrayed and implores our aid; brothers, we must hasten to save it.' The house was in uproar night after night, as the harassed police sought to discover from which boxes red, white and green bouquets had been thrown onto the stage.[77]

In Milan the atmosphere was even more fraught. The Milanese had begun a non-smoking campaign in protest against the Austrian state monopoly on tobacco. *The Times* commented piously: 'a people who are behind none of their neighbours in the use of that weed suddenly sacrificed to patriotism what they refused to cleanliness and good taste'.[78] In the first days of January groups of soldiers strolled through the streets of the city, smoking ostentatiously. A conflict was inevitable. On the 3rd, Austrian troops killed five Milanese and wounded more than sixty. From that moment onwards a state of undeclared war existed in Milan.

In Venice no single act of violence of this sort served to polarise opinions, but Manin, encouraged by the manifest signs of support from all quarters, attempted to spread the 'legal struggle' to the provinces. In early January 1848 he wrote to Count Gherardo Freschi, enlisting his support for Friuli:

From the memorandum sent by me to the central congregation, you will see what my opinions are on the legal condition of the kingdom ... If you will consent to my advice, distribute these papers throughout the province, and by means of the authority of your words and your pen, ensure that these ideas become popular. Then the provincial congregation of Udine and the greatest possible number of communal authorities in Friuli must send petitions, demanding these same reforms, so that the resultant outcry is resonant and unanimous.[79]

[75] Ciampini, *Vita di Niccolò Tommaseo*, p. 374.

[76] Trevelyan, *Manin and the Venetian Revolution*, p. 61.

[77] *Carte segrete*, vol. 3, p. 129, no. 571, 31 Dec. 1847.

[78] *The Times*, first leader, 19 Jan. 1848.

[79] F. Planat de la Faye (ed.), *Documenti e scritti autentici lasciati da Daniele Manin*, vol. 2, pp. 565–6.

Tommaseo did the same, writing to Pacifico Valussi for a list of addresses.[80]

In the first days of January 1848 the Jewish community in Venice sent two representatives to see Manin. They were Cesare della Vida, a wealthy businessman who was to ruin his large shipping company in support of the revolution, and Isacco Pesaro Maurogonato, later to be the financial minister of the provisional government of 1848–9. They asked Manin, as the acknowledged leader of the legal agitation, to incorporate the demand for the complete emancipation of the Jews in his reform programme. In return they promised him the unequivocal support of the Jewish community for what he was trying to do. Manin was only too willing to agree.[81]

On 8 January 1848 Manin wrote to the governor of the city, Palffy, remarking that 'it is not to be wondered at that the country, after having waited quietly and in vain for thirty-three years, should now show itself impatient and dissident'.[82] The chief of police reported on this presumptuous lawyer:

It is indisputable that without the effects produced by the writings of *avvocato* Manin, the example of Lombardy would never have found so prompt and widespread an imitation in these provinces ... Manin is a deeply knowledgeable lawyer and an extremely able orator who knows how to express his ideas with remarkable order and clarity.[83]

On the same day as Manin wrote to the governor of the city he presented his second petition to the central congregation.[84] It was an audacious document and marked the climax of the 'legal struggle' in Venice. Manin demanded that the Lombardo-Venetian kingdom should be 'truly national and Italian', independent of the Viennese state departments, and answerable only to the emperor; that the army and navy should be entirely Italian and remain in Italy; that the kingdom's finances were to be separate and controlled by Italians; that the property qualifications for the congregations should be abolished and their powers extended; that freedom of speech was to be established and the scope of police powers investigated; that the kingdom should belong to the Italian customs league; that all fetters on the free development of agriculture – the tithe, the *pensionatico* (winter grazing rights), etc. – should be abolished; that

---

[80] P. Valussi, *Dalla memoria d'un vecchio giornalista dall'epoca del Risorgimento italiano*, p. 69.

[81] Tommaseo was also at the meeting and agreed to write a tract called 'Diritto degli Israeliti alla civile eguaglianza', which is published in Ottolenghi, *L'azione del Tommaseo*, pp. 6–8.

[82] MCV, Doc. Manin, no. 201.

[83] Errera and Finzi, *Daniele Manin*, p. lxxxv.   [84] *Ibid.*, pp. 93–8.

the Jews should be emancipated, a civic guard set up, and the law re-formed.

Tommaseo also drew up a list of demands, but he did not have time to submit them.[85] On 18 January he was putting the finishing touches to his petition to the higher clergy, whom he accused of having 'rendered more unto Caesar than is Caesar's', when he and Manin were arrested.

The last months

In Venice the imprisonment of Manin and Tommaseo proved the decisive catalyst for the national cause. Up to that moment overt agitation had been confined to members of the educated classes, but after the deaths in Milan and the local arrests the movement spread rapidly to the city's poor. The Austrians' action, far from halting the opposition in its tracks, succeeded only in strengthening its popular base.

Objective conditions continued to favour the nationalists. While maize prices had returned to normal, those for wheat remained well above the average. In January and February 1848 a Venetian bushel of wheat still cost between 19.50 and 21.50 Au. lire. The state of employment remained critical. The chamber of commerce reported on 6 March 1848:

As for manufacturing concerns during February, we can do no more than repeat the totally dismal picture which we have had to paint in the previous months. In the absence of any movement of trade, which is our only hope of revival, life is lacking, and the consequences fall on to the class of workers whose conditions can only continue to deteriorate every day.[86]

[85] Tommaseo's demands were more moderate than Manin's, and more concerned with education. He advocated abolition of the personal tax, and the payment of a fixed annual sum towards the cost of the empire. He also requested that Italian soldiers should be asked to fight only against a foreign enemy, and not against any of the other peoples of the empire; see Ciampini, *Vita di Nicolò Tommaseo*, app., pp. 707–10. Manin and Tommaseo were clearly working together at this time. Valentino Pasini came to Venice on 17 Jan., the day before the arrests, to take out for the day his small son who was at the Liceo S. Caterina. He dropped in to see Manin at his house at San Paternian and found Tommaseo there as well. See the Austrian interrogation of witnesses, 9 Feb. 1848, Errera and Finzi, *Daniele Manin*, p. 263.

[86] ASV, CC, b. 187, IV, 6. Details of the grain prices for January and February are also to be found under this reference. The figures are taken from sheets headed *Portofranco di Venezia, prezzo generale compilato nell'ufficio del sindicato della borsa dietro le deposizioni de' pubblici sensali*. On 6 March the imperial delegate sent the municipality a project for instituting labour exchanges in the city, 'so as to give work to the idle'. This seems a somewhat inadequate response to the serious unemployment problem outlined by the chamber of commerce; ACV, Municip., Atti di Uff., 1845–9, fasc. II, 6/71.

The spirit of nationalism was naturally contagious, and it was not difficult for propagandists working among the people to point out the lines on which the coming battle was to be fought: on one side could be seen the national party, represented by the new Pope, the rich Venetians who had seen to the needs of the poor in the previous spring, and the local patriots now under arrest; on the other were the Austrians, the police and the tax collector. An anonymous contemporary relates of these days: 'the imprisonment of Manin and Tommaseo having aroused a general feeling of indignation in every class of the Venetian population, the zeal of our missionaries [*sic*] increased, and the soil was rendered more fruitful'.[87]

As a result, the two ancient Venetian popular clans, the Nicolotti and Castellani, resolved to end their feuding and unite the populace in opposition to the Austrians. As early as 10 January the police had mentioned that the rivals were fraternising as 'Italians', and that in the event of an uprising the revolutionaries could count on the support of a portion of the lower classes.[88] One February morning the Austrians in the city woke up to find the black and red sashes of the two clans intertwined on the altar steps of the great church of Santa Maria della Salute. The same evening a banquet for four hundred celebrated the event. It was difficult for the police to intervene because the real reason for the rapprochement was not voiced, and the mayor himself, Count Correr, paid the banquet a fleeting visit.[89]

Manifestations of protest and of sympathy for the two arrested men assumed a myriad of ingenious forms. Rich and poor alike, while taking their *passeggiata* along the Riva degli Schiavoni, would doff their hats and bow when passing the prison where Manin and Tommaseo were being held. The annual carnival was abandoned and a collection made instead for the families of those Milanese killed or wounded in the fighting of 3 January. Handkerchiefs, scarves, hats and objects of every variety appeared in Venice, bearing the tricolour colours or the portrait of the

[87] MCV, Doc. Manin, no. 3809.
[88] MCV, CPA, vol. 7, no. 801, 10 Jan. 1848. See also the letter of 13 Jan. from Count Agostino Sagredo to Count Faustino Senseverino in Milan. Sagredo recounted that the populace were now taunting the *brigolotti*, as they called the police, shouting at them, 'Sior guerrier, Se digo viva Pio nono, Me menelo in quartier?' (the Austrians had decreed forcible enrolment in the army for anyone who created a disturbance or even shouted 'Long live Pius IX'); see the police copy of Sagredo's letter, HHSAV, Intercepte 35, alt Fasz. 64, no. 55.
[89] MCV, Doc. Manin, no. 3809; this is an unsigned *memoria* dealing with the two clans and their activities. See also H. Martin, *Daniele Manin and Venice in 1848–9*, vol. 1, pp. 51–2. (Unless otherwise stated the English edition is used throughout.)

Pope. Government proclamations were smeared with excrement, slogans were scrawled on walls all over the city, and a police report of 23 January sadly admitted that the 'general bad humour of the populace increases daily'.[90]

The middle classes, imitating their Milanese counterparts, refrained from smoking in public, paraded in black clothes and black gloves, and met at Florian's, the famous coffee house in St Mark's Square, to discuss the political situation. More seriously, eighty-nine of the city's merchants, lawyers and intelligentsia offered to stand surety for Manin if he was released; even Count Correr signed the petition. Most of his fellow nobility refrained from signing, but the Countess Giustinian was one of the leading collectors in the appeal for the Milanese wounded. The British consul Clinton Dawkins, on his return to Venice from Milan, admitted to being thunderstruck at the sudden change in the political climate.[91]

The same pattern of events is to be found in the provincial cities. At Treviso in November 1847 the performances of Verdi's *I Lombardi* at the Teatro Sociale were interrupted by prolonged applause whenever the chorus sang the phrase 'siamo accorsi all'invito di un pio'. On 10 January 1848, after the news of the Milanese killings became better known, the

[90] MCV, CPA, vol. 7, no. 812, 23 Jan. 1848. For the *passeggiata* along the Riva degli Schiavoni, see V. Marchesi, *Storia documentata della rivoluzione e della difesa di Venezia negli anni 1848–9*, p. 97; for the abandonment of the carnival, Martin, *Manin and Venice*, vol. 1, p. 49; for 'patriotic' objects, *Carte segrete*, vol. 3, p. 182, no. 586, 26 Jan. 1848; for slogans, etc., MCV, CPA, vol. 7, no. 775. The following had been daubed on walls in the *sestiere* San Marco: 'Ferdinando va con Dio, cedi il Regno a Pio.'

[91] Consul General Dawkins to Viscount Palmerston, 18 Jan. 1848, in Planat de la Faye (ed.), *Documenti*, vol. 1, pp. 45–7. (Unless otherwise stated, references are to the Italian edition (Venezia 1877) with the original Italian of the documents, not the earlier French version (Paris 1860).) On the funereal fashions and the discussions at Florian's, see MCV, Doc. Manin, no. 3812. Students from the Academy of Fine Arts were held responsible for introducing the prohibition on smoking, and the wearing of feathers in hats to signify support for Italy (*Carte segrete*, vol. 3, p. 197, no. 598, 5 Feb. 1848). The original of the petition in support of Manin's release, dated 24 Jan., is to be found in MCV, Doc. Pell., b. xxxvi/85. The mayor's son, Pietro Correr, was one of a small number of young noblemen who were to play an active part in the revolution. He was to be head of the civic guard in the *sestiere* San Marco during the March days. The Austrian police reported in January 1848 that he was completely estranged from his father (*Carte segrete*, vol. 3, p. 178, no. 581, 25 Jan. 1848). On Countess Giustinian and the collection for the Milanese, C. Tivaroni, *L'Italia*, vol. 1, p. 519. The Bentivoglio family, again of the ancient Venetian nobility, was also pro-Italian; *Carte segrete*, vol. 3, pp. 172 and 185, nos. 574 and 590, 13 and 29 Jan. 1848. The party of *Austriacanti* (Austrian sympathisers) remained strong throughout these months. On 12 Jan. the Venetian chief of police, Call, was given a standing ovation at the Fenice by 'molti signori della città' (MCV, CPA, vol. 7, no. 797).

Trevisan police reported that 'youths like scarecrows from the scum of the people' had started a fight with the police. There were ten arrests.[92] At Udine the chief of police admitted ruefully that 'the deplorable events in Milan ... have provoked a greater attention to political matters and aroused desires hitherto unheard of in the various classes of the population'.[93] At Verona a local nobleman, Count Emilii, was arrested for being the treasurer of the funds collected by the gentlewomen of the city for the Milanese dead and wounded.[94]

The most serious incident of all occurred at Padua. There the university students devised a continuous series of patriotic demonstrations and provocations against the local garrison. On 8 February the soldiers responded by bursting into the ancient and famous Café Pedrocchi, which was a student meeting place, and clearing it at bayonet-point. They then gave chase to the students through the arcaded streets of the city, killing two of them and wounding others. The following day the Paduans saw that at least one Austrian soldier had refrained from cleaning the blood off his bayonet. The university was closed, a number of professors suspended, and the students sent home. Their dispersal only helped to spread news of the Paduan events and hatred for the Austrians to every corner of the Veneto.[95]

These events found an echo in the Venetian countryside, where some signs of discontent were clearly discernible. For this the clergy were probably responsible. Call reported in January 1848:

It has been brought to our notice that there are among the Venetian clergy those who, particularly in the countryside, are attempting to arouse in the

[92] See A. Lizier, 'Prodromi e primi momenti del '48 a Treviso', *Archivio Veneto*, 42–3 (1948), pp. 168 and 179–80. Olivi, the mayor, tried to calm the youths, offering to pay for their drinks if they would disperse quietly.

[93] *Carte segrete*, vol. 3, p. 293, no. 671. The youth of the garrison town of Palmanova were also reported as shouting insults at the soldiers. Palffy advised Pascotini to enrol forcibly all those involved; ASV, Pres. Gov., 1845–8, fasc. 1, 13/7, province of Udine, no. 303 (16 Jan. 1848).

[94] See the letter describing the situation in Verona from Countess Maria Burri to Countess Lugrezia Porcia de Brugnera at Azzano di Pordenone, 25 Jan. 1848. The letter was intercepted and copied by the police; HHSAV, Intercepte 35, alt Fasz. 64, no. 101. Emilii was later released on the orders of Palffy.

[95] Errera and Finzi, *Daniele Manin*, pp. cxii–cxiv, 315–20; Trevelyan, *Manin and the Venetian Revolution*, pp. 72–4. See also the letter from the Paduan professor V. de Castro to P. Paravia, 2 March 1848 (MCV, archivio Bernardi, b. 22, carteggio di P. A. Paravia, no number); and the copy of the letter from Alfonso Porcia in Conegliano to Contessa Eugenia Bolognini, 11 Feb. 1848, where he states (with pardonable exaggeration), 'there is not a village or a villa that does not have a son that was wounded or menaced' (HHSAV, Intercepte 35, alt Fasz. 64, no. 138).

people aversion towards the government and sympathy for its enemies. Whether these insinuations are spread from the pulpit or are mentioned in conversation, the behaviour of the clergy, granted the great influence they exercise on the populace, must always be of the gravest import.[96]

The evidence we have is small, but significant. In December 1847 the local police reported that the villagers of Cornuda, in the province of Treviso, on coming out of church had cried, 'Viva Pio Nono; morte alle Patate!' The Trevisan chief of police denied that the incident had taken place, but recommended that one of the priests of the near-by village of Maser should be relieved of his duties, because of his anti-Austrian sentiments. On 5 December, in the same province, fires were lit on the hills to the north of the provincial capital, and the district commissioner wrote that they were to commemorate the Genoese insurrection against the Austrians in December 1746. From all over the Veneto police officials reported that although the usual tranquillity reigned in the countryside, the poorest peasantry had 'humbly requested' that the personal tax be abolished or reduced. Most striking of all, the Milanese non-smoking campaign, designed to prevent the Austrians from collecting the tax on tobacco, seems to have permeated some villages in the Veneto. At Cavarzere, near Chioggia, on the banks of the Adige, 'the mania for not smoking cigars' had been adopted not by the richer inhabitants of the village, who lived on the right bank of the river, but by the 'coarse and depraved' peasantry and fishermen of the left bank. At Noventa, near San Donà di Piave, north-east of Venice, the local doctor witnessed a large demonstration by the villagers on 16 February 1848. They paraded through the village singing songs in the Friulian dialect, and shouting 'Abbasso il cigaro'. The police, armed with rifles, dispersed the crowd, and claimed that the peasantry had been incited by the *signori* of the area.[97]

Such demonstrations hardly constituted clear-cut peasant militancy, let alone a concerted rejection of Austrian rule. But certain dangerous elements – deprivation, clerical subversion, high taxation and urban disaffection – had combined to arouse the peasantry in some areas of the

---

[96] Errera and Finzi, *Daniele Manin*, p. cix.

[97] For San Donà di Piave, see MCV, CPA, vol. 7, no. 888, 16 Feb. 1848. There were also reports of other '*signori*' stirring up trouble – the Benvenuti brothers from Venice, Count D'Onigo in the province of Treviso and a certain Signora Moretti from Asolo; see Lizier, 'Prodromi', p. 175, and MCV, CPA, vol. 7, nos. 778 and 891. For the villagers of Cornuda, MCV, CPA, vol. 7, no. 778. The priest in question was the chaplain Don Cesare Marson. On Treviso, Lizier, 'Prodromi', p. 173; on demands for the abolition of the personal tax, MCV, CPA, vol. 7, nos. 847 and 850. Finally, on Cavarzere, see MCV, CPA, vol. 7, attached to no. 891, report of 23 Feb. 1848.

Veneto. In the early months of 1848 the Venetian peasantry were not, to judge from the small amount of evidence available, about to embark upon any sort of *jacquerie*. Yet they could no longer be considered as unquestionably loyal to the Habsburg eagle.

The Austrians vacillated in their reactions to the disturbances in northern Italy. In part their hesitancy derived from what had happened in Galicia in 1846. There the peasants loyal to and probably inspired by their Austrian masters had risen up and slaughtered the Polish nobles who had been plotting revolution. The good name of the empire was blackened throughout Europe, for the Austrians seemed prepared to use the peasants' class hatred to defend their own interests. To add insult to injury, in November 1846 Austrian troops occupied the republic of Cracow, thus openly flouting the treaties of 1815.

These events produced a twofold reaction in Austrian government circles. On the one hand, they became acutely sensitive to European public opinion and were therefore unwilling to use iron-fisted tactics in Lombardy-Venetia. This would account for their permitting the inflammatory speches of the scientific congress to go unpunished, and the laxity of the censorship with regard to seditious journals. It might also explain their reluctance to move against the Milanese liberal nobility and their humane treatment of Manin and Tommaseo once they had been arrested.[98] On the other hand, the peasants' actions in Galicia had filled the Austrians with what proved to be quite unfounded faith in the perennial loyalty of the peasantry of the empire. At the beginning of 1848 Marshal Radetzky, the military governor of Milan, wrote a memorandum on the situation in Lombardy. One of its main points was the plan to found a militia composed exclusively of volunteers from the countryside. Radetzky described the peasantry as 'gentle-natured and reasonable', and placed his trust in them. The cities, argued Radetzky, might well have turned against the Austrians, but the countryside would rally to the authorities and aid them in crushing any revolt.[99]

[98] On Manin and Tommaseo's prison conditions, see Trevelyan, *Manin and the Venetian Revolution*, p. 68, and appendix B, pp. 247–8. Palffy had banned a whole number of newspapers in Nov. 1847 without, it appears, much effect; *Carte segrete*, vol. 3, p. 417, no. 773, 10 Nov. 1847, and p. 273, no. 663, police report from Vicenza for Jan. 1848.

[99] A. Lucchini, 'Memoriale del maresciallo Radetzky sulle condizioni d'Italia al principio del 1848', *Nuova Rivista Storica*, 14 (1930), p. 65. Metternich wrote to Buol in June 1846, commenting with satisfaction that the Polish peasantry 'have been governed paternally for more than sixty years and have no intention of risking their tranquillity for utopias that offer them nothing' (Metternich, *Mémoires*, vol. 7, p. 242).

Metternich himself at first favoured a reform programme for Lombardy-Venetia. In December 1847 he talked of the need for a 'radical cure' for Italy, and as late as 23 January was insisting to Ficquelmont, his envoy in Milan, on two immediate provisions: the granting of real powers to the governments of Milan and Venice and the presence of Italian representatives in the central government organs at Vienna.[100] But as the European situation grew more critical, Austrian policy seems finally to have hardened into intransigence. On 23 February a letter of the emperor informed the viceroy Ranier that any measure that 'lessened the bonds between the Lombardo-Venetian kingdom and My Monarchy' was out of the question.[101] On the 25th martial law was declared in the Italian provinces. On 4 March Metternich coldly told Ponsonby, 'It is certainly not in the midst of the dangers of a situation so greatly aggravated by the recent events in France that we should be willing to change anything.'[102]

He was right in a way, for the Austrians seemed in secure control of the military situation. Both Venetians and Lombards were unarmed and Radetzky, at least, knew exactly where he stood: 'Soldiers . . . Against your fearless courage the jealousies of fanaticism and the insane mania for innovations will be smashed, like fragile surf against hard rock.'[103] Confronted by the might of the Austrian empire, the agitation in the Italian provinces stood no chance of succeeding in isolation. At the beginning of March 1848, Manin and Tommaseo were acquitted by the local courts of the charge of conspiracy to excite disorder, but they remained in prison. It seemed likely that a higher court would overrule this decision and condemn them both to long terms of imprisonment.

However, the Lombard and Venetian movement was far from isolated. The unique wave of revolutionary fervour that swept Europe in the first months of 1848 was the decisive factor in transforming the provincial disturbances of northern Italy into national revolution. Palermo gave the lead in the first days of January. There a small group of revolutionaries

---

[100] *Ibid.*, pp. 442 and 581. By 17 Feb. (p. 585) Metternich seems to have convinced himself that Austria's main error was to 'have bored the people'. What north Italy needed was 'to be governed with a firm hand and to be amùsed'. On 19 February (pp. 567–8) he asked a visiting Venetian in Vienna what possible interest Venice could have in common with Italian ports like Genoa and Ancona, its deadly rivals; he seems to have forgotten about Trieste.

[101] ASV, Pres. Gov., 1845–8, fasc. XII, 7/3, no. 1086.

[102] Quoted in A. J. P. Taylor, *The Italian Problem in European Diplomacy, 1847–9*, p. 78.

[103] Order of the day, 16 Jan. 1848; *Carte segrete*, vol. 3, p. 173, no. 576.

publicly proclaimed that they would begin the revolution on King Ferdinand's birthday, 12 January, which was a public holiday. For most of the day the holiday crowds milled around and nothing happened. It seemed that the day would go down in history only as the date of the latest in a long line of crackpot schemes destined for failure. But towards evening the first barricades went up in the popular quarters and the artisans and unemployed of the city gave their support to the insurrectionaries. In the next few days the people of Palermo, aided by peasants from the surrounding villages, succeeded in overcoming the many thousands of Bourbon troops in the city. Ferdinand of Naples was forced to order a withdrawal and within weeks the whole of Sicily except for the citadel of Messina was free of the Bourbon administration. In Naples the crowds took to the streets, demanding consitutional government. Ferdinand, afraid of losing southern Italy as well as Sicily, announced the granting of a constitution on 29 January.

The events in southern Italy had an electrifying effect on the rest of the peninsula. The news reached Venice on 6 February and that evening many of the opera-goers appeared at the Fenice dressed in various combinations of red, white and green. The ballet began with a tune called 'La Siciliana' and pandemonium broke loose. The theatre was cleared by the police and closed from that moment onwards.[104] Elsewhere, immense pressure mounted for the sovereigns of the other Italian states to follow Ferdinand's example and grant constitutions. One by one the Pope, the grand duke of Tuscany and the king of Piedmont yielded; in Turin Charles Albert reluctantly published the details of his famous *Statuto* on 4 March. The king reserved to himself very wide powers. He was the supreme commander of the armed forces, could appoint and dismiss ministers and nominate the upper of the two houses of parliament (the senate). The lower one was to be elected on the basis of a restricted electorate.

These dramatic political transformations in the rest of Italy undoubtedly alarmed the Austrians, but they did not fundamentally alter the relations of power in Lombardy and Venetia. But the revolution in Paris of 24 February, the fall of the 'citizen king' Louis Philippe, and the proclamation of the second French republic, shattered once and for all the world of Restoration Europe. By 29 February Venice knew of the fall of the July government. 'Le vent qui vient à travers la montagne me rendra

---

[104] See the letter from Palffy to the municipal congregation, defending the actions of the troops; ACV, Municip., Atti di Uff., 1845–9, fasc. III, 12/7, attached to no. 1607 (1848).

fou';[105] the Venetians gathered in cafés to listen to readings of newspapers like *La Presse* and *La Nouvelliste* from Marseilles. A report from the city of 2 March noted that 'the workers and the gondoliers talk of nothing but politics'.[106]

The news from Paris had a profound effect in Vienna. Metternich was incapable of stemming the tide of reform and revolution. On 13 March Viennese students, workers, artisans and unemployed flocked to the Hofburg, where the students presented a petition. As the crowd grew the authorities became alarmed and ordered the area surrounding the palace to be cleared. Fighting broke out and the troops opened fire on the un-armed populace. The crowd fled, leaving behind a number of dead. That evening in the working-class suburbs of Vienna, factories were set alight and shops looted. In the Hofburg the glow of these fires could be seen as discussions took place. The Court was divided. Metternich was for stand-ing firm, but the Archduchess Sophie wanted to be rid of him. The anti-Metternich faction triumphed, and the two concessions of a national guard and Metternich's resignation were announced. On the 15th, in response to mounting pressure, the emperor granted a constitution.

Only the boldest spirits in Venice began to think in terms of revolution, but by mid-March reports were circulating of street demonstrations in the capital of the empire. The Venetians waited with bated breath. If the revolution spread to Vienna, anything was possible. On the night of 16 March, as rumours multiplied, an unusually large number of Venetians gathered in the Piazza San Marco; it was decided to hold a large demon-stration the following day. Early on the 17th, the Lloyd's steamer from Trieste brought definite tidings of the revolution in Vienna, the fall of Metternich, and the promise of a constitution for the whole empire. The news plunged the governor of Venice, the Hungarian Count Palffy, into extreme confusion. A large crowd led by three of Manin's friends – the notary Giuriati and the two lawyers Benvenuti and Varè – quickly gathered outside the governor's palace in the Piazza San Marco. The palace was practically unguarded and within moments the Venetians had stormed the staircase, and, face to face with Palffy and his trembling wife, demanded the release of Manin and Tommaseo. Palffy had no idea whether freeing the prisoners would precipitate or postpone revolution; he had received no instructions from Vienna. He decided fatefully to

---

[105] Victor Hugo, quoted in F. L. Lucas, *The Decline and Fall of the Romantic Ideal*, p. 22.

[106] *Archivio triennale*, vol. 1, p. 475. For the influence of the foreign press, *Carte segrete*, vol. 3, pp. 188 and 430–2.

allow them their freedom, and, in the heat of the moment, signed an order for the release of not *Daniele* but *Lodovico* Manin, who had been the last Doge of the Republic.[107] The revolution had obtained its leaders.

[107] Marchesi, *Storia documentata*, p. 103. Manin refused to leave his prison cell until he had made sure that his release had been legally granted.

3

The March days, 1848

The key to the course of the revolution in Venice lies in the relationship between Daniele Manin and the Venetian populace who liberated him and Nicolò Tommaseo on the morning of 17 March 1848. Manin inspired in Venice a devotion to his person unique among the Italian leaders of 1848, and surpassed only by Kossuth in the rest of Europe. The main reasons for this popularity would seem to lie in Venice's tradition of paternalism, the strong municipal pride of its people, and Manin's own deep understanding of the Venetians. It is worth examining each in turn.

Throughout its long history the old Venetian Republic had very rarely been faced with the prospect of popular insurrection. The prosperity of the city, the shrewdness of its ruling class and its developed system of public and private charity helped to create a highly successful model of paternalistic government. The people came to regard the Doge as a beneficent father who represented their interests as well as those of the class to which he belonged. Such attitudes lingered on long after the fall of the Republic and the disappearance of the conditions which had created them. It was only in the twentieth century, with the industrial growth of Marghera and Mestre, that there developed a class-conscious working class eager to break with the past. In the 1840s, the service industries of the tourist trade, the high number of servants in the city, the mingling of rich and poor in the same quarters, all still tended to enforce rather than diminish the time-honoured political traditions of Venice.

Deep-rooted attachment to the city also transcended class barriers. Venice's millennium of history as an incomparably independent and powerful city state, as well as its natural isolation in the lagoon, had created a very strong sense of identity among its inhabitants. Municipal pride was one of the great motive forces of 1848, and the defence of one's city against a foreign aggressor served to unite employer and employed, master and servant. Nowhere was this more true than in Venice.

Manin, as a local middle-class patriot, reaped the full benefit of these factors. His imprisonment made him appear as a martyr, and on his release he became the Venetians' acknowledged leader. As Mengaldo was to write in his diary, 'the people, who had made of Manin their idol, made him also the arbiter of their destinies'.[1] Once granted this power by the Venetian populace, Manin's great ability to gauge their feelings and needs became apparent. Tommaseo asked him sceptically what he expected from 'this people incapable of self-sacrifice'. Manin's reply is of profound significance: 'Believe me, neither you nor anyone else knows the people of Venice. They have always been misunderstood. My boast is that I know them better. It is my only merit.'[2]

Venice is a densely concentrated city; even from the outlying quarters the inhabitants can reach the Piazza San Marco in less than half an hour. There, again and again throughout the revolution, Manin, supported on the shoulders of his friends, or standing on a table, or else leaning from the balcony of the Procuratie Nuove, would talk to the people. He spoke in dialect, using simple words, asking the crowd in the Piazza questions to which they could shout back the answers:

Ho scoverto che vu altri no me amè (*mille voci sì sì sì*) . . . Vu altri disè de sì cola boca, ma no col cuor . . . (*mille voci sì, sì, sì, col cuor, col cuor, e moltissimi battevansi le mani al petto*) . . . Questa xe la terza volta che ve digo di andar via dalla piazza, e vu altri ghe sè ancora . . . Chi no va via, no xe mio amigo, e xe nemigo dell'Italia . . .[3]

The people were Manin's, and they in turn claimed him as theirs. 'Nostro caro padre Manin' was the way in which Domenico Corrao, the head of the Nicolotti clan, referred to Manin in June 1848.[4]

Manin's politics

When Manin was freed from prison on the morning of 17 March it soon became obvious to those closest to him that he was intent on leading a revolution against the Austrians. In view of Manin's dominant role in the March days, it is of great interest to trace the steps that preceded this decision, and to outline his political thinking at this time.

Before their arrest neither Manin nor Tommaseo had believed that

---

[1] Meneghetti (ed.), *Il Cavaignac di Venezia*, p. 41.

[2] La Forge, *Histoire*, vol. 1 (1852), pp. 257–8.

[3] 'I've discovered that you others don't love me (a thousand voices shout "Yes we do, we do") . . . You say that with your mouths but not with your hearts (a thousand voices shout back "Yes, yes, with our hearts, our hearts", and a great many of them beat their fists against their chests) . . . This is the third time that I've told you to leave the Piazza and yet you're still here . . . He who doesn't go away is no friend of mine, and an enemy of Italy' (MCV, Cicogna diary, speech of 5 March 1849).

[4] MCV, Doc. Manin, no. 667, interrogation by the police of Domenico Corrao, 4 June 1848.

revolution was a possibility. Their *lotta legale* had been exactly what its title implied – the attempt, in Cattaneo's words, to constrain the government within 'the hard and prickly confines of the law'.[5] Once in prison, both the Venetian leaders were at pains to establish their moderation. During his first cross-examination by the police, Manin explained the need 'to improve our conditions without bloodshed, without alerting the political equilibrium of Europe established by the Treaties, without waging war on the government'.[6] On 19 February he went as far as to declare that 'a faithful subject must defend the principle of monarchy against this conspiracy of subjects, who wish to make their will prevail over that of the sovereign'.[7] Tommaseo likewise explained that he had tried 'to clarify public opinion, channel it into legal paths, and render it temperate and respectable'.[8] Naturally, with the shadow of some remote Austrian prison looming before them, both men were attempting not to compromise themselves. Their anti-revolutionary feeling, however, was genuine enough.

Yet while Tommaseo remained hostile to any form of uprising, Manin gradually changed his mind. The random notes he made while still in prison reveal the great impression made upon him by the French revolution of February. He copied down from the newspapers allowed to him Victor Hugo's discourse of 14 January:

ce mot merveilleux, ce mot magique, l'Italie qui a si longtemps exprimé parmi les hommes la gloire des armes, le génie conquérant et civilisateur, la grandeur des lettres, la splendeur des arts, la double domination par la gloire et par l'esprit va reprendre . . . la signification sublime et redevenir, avec l'aide de Dieu et de celui qui n'aura jamais été mieux nommé son vicaire, non seulement le résumé d'une grande histoire morte, mais le symbole d'un grand peuple vivant.[9]

Manin tried to calculate the population of the whole of Italy, and estimated it to be nearly twenty-eight million. He asked his lenient gaolers to supply him with books on Venice, as well as maps of the city. His prison notes contain the terse comment, 'Where there is fear there cannot be virtue.'[10] During his last few days in prison, he resolved that if he was released and conditions were favourable, he would attempt a rebellion. It

---

[5] Cattaneo, *Dell'insurrezione*, vol. 3, p. 30.

[6] Errera and Finzi, *Daniele Manin*, p. 135. Planat de la Faye, in her selections from the interrogations (*Documenti*, vol. 1, pp. 53–63, 77–8), omits all paragraphs which portray Manin in a less than heroic light.

[7] Errera and Finzi, *Daniele Manin*, p. 197. When asked about Tommaseo he replied, 'If I am a *galantuomo*, he is a saint'.

[8] *Ibid.*, p. 228.

[9] MCV, Doc, Manin, nos. 55 and 56.   [10] *Ibid.*

was this that distinguished him from all the other leading Venetians in these vital days of March 1848.

However, it was not sufficient to decide on revolution, and on the ancient battle cry of *Fuori i barbari!*, which now meant freedom from the Austrians. Manin later confided to his wife Teresa that he tried during his imprisonment to choose the sort of regime that should replace the Austrian one.[11]

Manin was no theoretician, and was never to write more than the occasional paragraph on political structures. In general terms Tommaseo was right when he wrote that 'Manin imitated the French Republic'.[12] His republicanism derived, in the first instance, from the desire to see the ideals of liberal, bourgeois democracy introduced into Venice. He wanted manhood suffrage with an elected parliament, equality before the law, freedom of the press and freedom of assembly. He rejected the compromise solution of a constitutional monarchy for Lombardy-Venetia, either with an Austrian viceroy or an Italian prince. A monarchy, according to Manin, not only conflicted with the most cherished traditions of his city, but also failed to safeguard the rights of the people. It would lead inevitably to 'a second revolution, and with it a new Iliad of misfortunes'.[13]

Part of Manin's antipathy towards a monarchy came from his belief in the desirability of French republican intervention in north Italy. While he was in prison he had copied out an article attributed to Lamartine, which appeared in *Le National* of 27 February 1848.[14] The author expressed the hope that in the coming battles against the Austrians the Italians would 'permit their French friends to share their danger, and to repay Italy for what she had done for Europe'. Manin was prepared to accept these expressions of altruism at their face value, for he was sufficiently idealistic to believe that the concept of international republicanism – *le secours d'un frère à un frère* – could become a reality. He found no truth in the historical comparisons made by many of his contemporaries with the invasion of Italy by the French king in 1494, or Napoleon's expedition over three hundred years later. The declaration of the second French republic, argued Manin, was the best safeguard against the danger of French aid becoming French conquest.

However, the limits of this French intervention were very clearly defined in Manin's mind. Under no circumstance did he want class warfare

11 Planat de la Faye (ed.), *Documenti*, vol. 1, pp. 159–60.
12 N. Tommaseo, *Venezia negli anni 1848 e 1849*, vol. 1, p. 119 n. 318. He wrote this remark in his copy of Planat de la Faye (ed.), *Documenti*, vol. 1, p. 146, where she deals with Manin's period in prison.
13 Planat de la Faye (ed.), *Documenti*, vol. 1, p. 159.
14 MCV, Doc. Manin, no. 56.

introduced into the Veneto; in June 1848 he wrote to the Venetian representatives in Paris, 'the principal danger of French intervention will be that the war may become . . . a social conflict, that is a war between the haves and the have-nots'.[15] To Manin liberty meant independence from the Austrians, and freedom of association of every kind; equality signified equality before the law; fraternity the brotherhood of all classes and nations. Manin's republic, like Lamartine's, was not, in Marx's words,

the republic which the Paris proletariat thrust upon the provisional government, not the republic with social institutions, not the vision which hovered before the fighters on the barricades . . . the only legitimate republic [to Lamartine] is a republic which is not a revolutionary weapon against the bourgeois order, but rather its political reconstitution, the political reconsolidation of bourgeois society, in a word, *the bourgeois republic*.[16]

From the first moments of his release to the dying days of the Venetian revolution, Manin saw the spectre of what he termed anarchy hovering over Venice. In the Piazza San Marco on 17 March he cried, 'Do not forget that there can be no true liberty, and that liberty cannot last, where there is not order. You must be jealous guardians of order if you hope to preserve freedom.'[17] When Manin spoke of order he meant the maintenance of the social status quo, and the defence of private property against the maraudings of the propertyless.

In this respect Manin's relationship with the lower classes was an equivocal one. At one moment he was confident that he understood them, and that their devotion and obedience to him was secure; at the next, he seemed afraid of them, although they constituted the source of his power. As the course of events unfolded in Paris, his fear increased.

Ideologically, therefore, Manin favoured a republic on the French model. As a shrewd politician and Venetian patriot he also realised the amount of support he would gain through the establishment of a new version of the Republic of St Mark. As Calucci wrote later, 'The lapse of one generation was not sufficient to make fourteen centuries of history be forgotten; and, if few were still alive who had known the old Republic, all had heard their fathers talk of it with tears in their eyes.'[18] Manin knew that the republic would have a dual appeal; it would both recall the

[15] Manin to the Venetian representatives in Paris, Aleardi and Gar, 16 June 1848: Planat de la Faye (ed.), *Documenti*, vol. 1, p. 309.
[16] K. Marx, 'The class struggles in France, 1848–1850' (first published 1850), in his *Surveys from Exile* (ed. D. Fernbach), p. 57.
[17] Trevelyan, *Manin and the Venetian Revolution*, p. 89.
[18] G. Calucci, 'Documenti inediti', p. 321.

ancient glory of Venice and hold out the promise of greater social and political justice.[19]

In the wider context of Italian unification, the Venetian leader was a republican federalist. It is important to stress at this stage, since many historians have accused Manin of deliberately isolating Venice from the rest of Italy, that before 1848 federation was the most widely supported programme for Italian unity.[20] Only Mazzini postulated a single republic for the entire peninsula. Amongst the other Italian political thinkers, the main area of dispute lay in the exact nature of the Italian federation, whether it was to be monarchical or republican, and what weight if any the king of Piedmont, the Pope and other Italian rulers were to have in it. Manin was convinced that the final form of the federation would be republican, though he never excluded cooperation with the Italian monarchs. He insisted only that Venice should be the capital of a new Venetian republic, and should preserve a measure of economic and political autonomy in the new Italy. In this he mirrored Cattaneo's thinking for Milan.

Yet the idea of a strong and united Italy, which would take its place among the great nation states of the world, attracted Manin far more than it did his Milanese colleague. Whereas Cattaneo saw local government almost as an end in itself, Manin considered an exaggerated municipalism to be the principal danger to the unification of Italy. This emerged very clearly even before the revolution. Guerrieri wrote to him from Milan on 1 November 1847, 'I know that above all else you despise municipalism',[21] and Manin when interrogated by the Austrians in February 1848 explained the sending of money to the Milanese wounded as an attempt 'to fight by proof of affection that ill-fated municipalism which is our greatest misfortune'.[22]

17–21 March 1848

The morning of 17 March witnessed the first of the great Piazza scenes of the revolution. Manin and Tommaseo were carried on the shoulders of the crowd the few hundred yards from the prisons to St Mark's Square. There Manin addressed the Venetians for the first time, while above him

---

[19] Manin believed that 'the republic with its traditions of glory and of greatness, with the hope that this word now holds for the most intelligent, will be understood by all, will find an echo in every heart' (Planat de la Faye (ed.), *Documenti*, vol. 1, p. 160).

[20] For a valid defence of Manin against historians like Imbriani, see A. Levi, *La politica di Daniele Manin*, pp. 22ff.

[21] Letter published in Errera and Finzi, *Daniele Manin*, p. 44.

[22] *Ibid.*, p. 178, fourth interrogation, 17 Feb. 1848.

Palffy listened from the balcony of the governor's palace. Manin began by advising moderation, but ended with these words: 'sometimes there come moments when insurrection ... is not only a right but a duty'.[23] Palffy disappeared in anger from his balcony and Manin returned to his family and his house at San Paternian.

Over the next few days Manin confided to his friends the conclusions that he had reached while in prison. He found that none of them agreed with him. Tommaseo was convinced that talk of revolution was premature, and that the Venetians should continue 'a war of reason and of spirit'.[24] When Manin asked him what form of government he believed best for Venice, he replied, 'My friend, I cannot see my way to making any supposition.'[25] To Tommaseo, as to *The Times*, an immediate revolution would have meant that 'the unique fruit has not been brought to maturity by the gradual influence of the sunshine, but scorched and split by the glare of the furnace'.[26]

Of the men who pledged themselves to support Manin[27] and gathered at his house, none agreed on the establishment of a republic. When Manin announced to his friend Leone Pincherle, who was the Venetian agent for a large insurance company, that 'in a few days we will be shouting for the republic', Pincherle looked confused and bewildered.[28]

This group around Manin formed one centre of activity among the Venetians. The other was the municipal congregation, headed by the mayor, Count Correr.[29] The members of the municipality, all from the nobility or upper bourgeoisie, regarded themselves as the true representatives of the city. They were naturally averse to revolution, and the more liberal among them believed that the promise of a constitution left little to be desired. Accordingly, they were at pains to put a stop to any rioting,

---

[23] MCV, Doc. Manin, no. 3838; account of the events of 17 March, dictated at the time by Manin to his daughter. Three other political prisoners, Meneghini, Stefani and Lanza, were released with Manin and Tommaseo.

[24] Tommaseo, *Venezia*, vol. I, p. 59.

[25] Planat de la Faye (ed.), *Documenti*, vol. I, p. 161.

[26] *The Times*, second leader, 6 April 1849.

[27] During the night of 17–18 March a group of citizens, mainly professional men, decided that they would obey only Manin. Apart from meeting at his house, they met at the tailor Angelo Toffoli's. Among those present were the notary Giuriati and the brothers Benvenuti; see Marchesi, *Storia documentata*, p. 110.

[28] Planat de la Faye (ed.), *Documenti*, vol. I, p. 161. Pincherle (1814–82) was Jewish and a lifelong friend of Manin's. For further information see G. Stefani, *Leone Pincherle e Daniele Manin*, and the same author's biography of Pincherle in *1831–1931. Il centenario delle Assicurazioni Generali*.

[29] On the activity of the municipality, see in particular A. Ventura, 'Daniele Manin e la Municipalità nel marzo '48', *Rassegna Storica del Risorgimento*, 44 (1957), pp. 819–29.

and on 17 March appealed to the Venetians to show 'that dignified moderation which has always been the principal characteristic of the Venetian populace, and which you will certainly not wish to betray, especially at a moment in which the intentions of our Sovereign have been manifested in such a way as to secure for us the most hopeful of futures'.[30] They were afraid that further agitation would only serve to endanger social order in the city, and the patriarch, Cardinal Jacopo Monico, whose partiality to the Austrian regime was undisguised, shared this opinion.

The Venetians were thus divided. Those around Manin agreed on the need for further action, but were undecided upon what form it should take. Manin alone wanted to press forward towards revolution, relying on the working people of the city to support him. The municipality, on the other hand, believed that the revolution in Vienna would lead to considerable concessions and deemed it quite undesirable to continue any form of agitation. Although there is no direct evidence, it seems highly likely that most of the bourgeoisie and upper class of the city, including the merchants and bankers of the chamber of commerce, shared the municipality's opinions.

The Austrians, for their part, could call upon a formidable garrison of 8,370 men. Of these 2,160 belonged to the Kinsky battalions, which were mainly composed of Croat troops, and were quartered on the Zattere. There was also a separate Croat battalion of 1,300 men stationed in the arsenal. Many of the remaining troops were Italian – 1,300 belonging to the Wimpffen regiment, 1,100 to the marine infantry battalion, 560 to the five companies of marine artillery, and 500 sailors.[31] The military governor of the city and commander of these troops was an ageing Hungarian, Lieutenant-Marshal Zichy.

During the afternoon of the 17 March, while Manin stayed at home, resting and talking to his family and friends, a large crowd gathered in the Piazza San Marco. At three o'clock troops were called into the square. The police reported that the populace

did not appear very menacing and amongst the multitude that came and went there were many ladies. Jubilation over the constitution which has supposedly been granted was universal ... Two small flags bearing the Italian colours and one with the French were attached to the flagpoles of the Piazza. When the Italian grenadiers took up their positions in the square they were greeted by the crowd with roars of 'Long live the brave Italians.'[32]

[30] BL, 1852.e.9, *avviso* from the municipality, 17 March 1848.
[31] MCV, Doc. Manin, no. 3801; unsigned estimate headed 'Guarnigione di Venezia, 21–22 marzo 1848'.
[32] *Carte segrete*, vol. 3, nos. 622 and 623, pp. 226–7. One man died of apoplexy in

Later in the afternoon the atmosphere became less friendly, and there were
a few skirmishes between the troops and the Venetians. No one was
killed, but there were a number of wounded; one of the sons of the
Piedmontese consul Faccanoni returned home with a bayonet wound in
the stomach.[33] That night a group of men assembled at the Rialto, shouting 'Long live Italy, liberty and Pius IX!'[34]

On the following morning, which was a Saturday, battle was joined in
earnest. At eleven o'clock all was quiet in the centre of the city, but soon
afterwards groups of working men from the Nicolotti clan and students
from Padua began to assemble in the Piazza San Marco.[35] When troops
were called into the square the Venetians broke up some of the paving
stones of the Piazza and hurled them at the lines of soldiers. The Austrian
officers responded by ordering their men to open fire on the crowd. This
they did and the Venetians rushed for cover to the confines of the square,
carrying their dead and wounded into the Café Florian.

Eight Venetians were killed and nine seriously wounded in the fighting
of the morning of 18 March. Although details of all the casualties do not
seem to have survived, the information we have points strongly to the
working-class composition of the crowd. Of the eight killed, two were
boys – Ferdinando Vianello, aged thirteen, and Andrea Sasso, fifteen.
Vianello was employed as an odd-job boy by the painter Molin, and came
from a very poor family of street sellers in Campo San Bartolomeo. Sasso
had been an apprentice carpenter for three months and was the oldest of
six sons of a fruit seller in Castello. Three of the others killed also came
from the Venetian poor; Ridolfo Torre, aged twenty-one, unmarried,
was a glass worker and the only one of his large family to draw a regular
wage. The family was so poor that it had been unable to pay for two
letters sent post restante to Ridolfo from his elder brother who was doing
military service at Gratz. Another of the dead was Vincenzo Decupil, an
unmarried porter aged thirty-six. The fifth was G. B. Longo, a window-
maker aged forty-two. He too was single and lived with his eighty-four-
year-old mother, who was thus deprived of her only means of subsistence.[36]

the Piazza at 4 p.m. For Palffy's account to the viceroy Ranier, written on
17 March, see G. Stefani, 'Documenti ed appunti sul quarantotto triestino', in
La Venezia Giulia e la Dalmazia nella rivoluzione nazionale del 1848–9, vol. 1,
pp. 71–3.

[33] AST, consolati nazionali, Venezia, no. 283, report written at 10 p.m., 17 March
1848.

[34] MCV, CPA, vol. 7, no. 918, *bollettino giornaliero* of the police.

[35] See the letter describing the scene in Venice from Giovanni Burani to Prospero
Antonini, 19 March 1848, in P. Antonini, *Carteggio*, p. 45.

[36] For Vianello, see ASV, Gov. Prov. 1848–9, MU, b. 3, no. 944; for Torre, *ibid.*,
MU, b. 3, no. 897; for Sasso and Decupil, *ibid.*, MU, b. 4, nos. 2078 and 2090;

After the Piazza had been cleared Palffy summoned Pietro Fabris, one of the Venetian deputies of the central congregation, and asked him for his advice. Fabris replied that he had none, but would ask Manin. At San Paternian Fabris found that Manin had a clear line of action to advocate – the formation of a civic guard.[37]

Manin's motives seem clear; the Venetians stood no chance of taking the city unless they were armed. Should Palffy be persuaded to give his consent, the civic guard could share sentry duty with the regular regiments at strategic points throughout the city. This would give the Venetians a chance to fraternise with the Italians under Austrian arms. The revolution could be made only if the citizenry was armed and the Italian soldiers persuaded to desert.

At the same time Manin feared that the middle-class patriots were in danger of losing control of the situation. The *Gazzetta di Venezia* reported that throughout Saturday 'the workers were rioting or demanding money from passers-by'.[38] The last thing Manin wanted was for the Venetian populace to begin to attack private property and vent their anger on the rich as well as the Austrians. He saw the civic guard as an instrument in the hands of the property-owning classes, to be used to secure the social order of the city.

These two strands of thought – the civic guard as a weapon against the Austrians *and* as a defence against 'anarchy' – formed one thread in Manin's mind. However, it was the second line of argument that proved decisive in attracting support for the idea. On the evening of the 17th Manin's followers had dismissed a civic guard as impracticable, but after the fighting of the following morning it came to seem a necessity.

A deputation therefore set out from Manin's house for the governor's palace. It included the notary Giuriati, the lawyers Mengaldo and Benvenuti, Pietro Fabris and the nobleman Nicolò Morosini. Palffy at first refused the request outright, saying that he had made sufficient provisions to guard public buildings. Morosini replied, 'If the military authorities believe it necessary to defend public funds, does your Excellency not find it reasonable that the citizens should wish to defend and guarantee the security of private fortunes and families?'[39] Palffy still refused, but allowed Fabris and Morosini to leave Venice to find the viceroy,

for Longo, *ibid.*, MU, b. 6, no. 2825. Three unemployed workers who had taken an active part in the fight against the Austrians on the 18th asked for and obtained from Manin employment in the tobacco factory; *ibid.*, MU, b. 2, no. 228.

[37] See the Zanetti chronicle, MCV, Doc. Manin, no. 3836, published in full by Ventura, 'Manin e la Municipalità', pp. 824–7.

[38] Racc. Andreola, vol. 1, p. 22. Most of the important extracts from the *Gazzetta* are reprinted in the Andreola collection.

[39] Zanetti chronicle, Ventura, 'Manin e la Municipalità', p. 824.

Archduke Ranier, and request his permission for the civic guard. The two
Venetians were rushed by gondola to the station, the train to Vicenza
delayed its departure until their arrival, and later, on the evening of the
18th, they reached the viceroy at Verona. The archduke gave his consent
on the morning of the 19th and asked, with tears in his eyes, whether it
would still be possible for him to come to Venice to take the waters in the
summer.[40]

Manin, however, had not waited for the result of this expedition, but
had gone from the governor's palace to the municipality, to demand that
they in turn put pressure on Palffy. The municipal congregation complied,
inspired doubtless by the same apprehensions as Morosini, and the
patriarch added his supplications. Palffy wilted before this onslaught from
the city fathers, and on the afternoon of the 18th granted permission for
two hundred civic guards to be armed.[41] Within a few hours, as Trevelyan
has written, 'some 2,000 citizens had been organised in companies and
armed, some with muskets and pistols, others with halberds, spears and
two-handed swords from half the antiquarian collections in Venice'.[42]
The veteran Napoleonic soldier, Angelo Mengaldo, who had helped
Manin during the railway question, was put in charge of the new guard.[43]
In the *sestiere* of Santa Croce the captain of the guard was the nobleman,
Girolamo Gradenigo; in Cannaregio, Pietro Correr, the son of the mayor.[44]
Late in the afternoon of the 18th the civic guard in their white sashes held
their first parade in the Piazza San Marco; Manin himself was at the head
of one of the companies from the *sestiere* of San Marco.

In strategic terms, Palffy had lost the first round. He had consented to
the formation of armed bands of Venetians over whom he had no control.
Disoriented by the events in Vienna, Palffy vacillated continuously

[40] *Ibid.*, p. 826.
[41] Palffy's letter is to be found in ACV, Municip., Atti di Uff., 1845–9, fasc. III,
12/7, attached to no. 338 (1848). He insisted on the 200 guards being chosen
from among '*the most distinguished and upright*' Venetians. The Venetian
newspaper, *L'Indipendente*, commented on 6 April 1848 (no. 5, p. 19): 'To
prevent bloodshed a national guard was conceded, which calmed the lower
classes who were eager for a vendetta.'
[42] Trevelyan, *Manin and the Venetian Revolution*, p. 93.
[43] According to La Forge, *Histoire*, vol. 1, p. 234, Manin convinced Mengaldo of
the need for the civic guard in the following way: ' "The city is in the hands of
the lower classes," Manin said to him; "who will now prevent disorders? We
need a regular force to obtain a regular defence. This regular force can only be a
civic guard; help me to create it." ' Mengaldo had confided his view of the 'mob'
to his diary in November 1847: 'the people, once their passions are aroused,
always tend to lose control and indulge in violent and savage rioting' (Meneghetti,
Il Cavaignac di Venezia, p. 27).
[44] Racc. Andreola, vol. 1, p. 9.

throughout these March days. His weakness infuriated his inferiors and was one of the principal causes of the success of the revolution. So too was the hesitancy of the military governor Zichy, who, unlike Radetzky in Milan, was not prepared to take all power into his own hands so as to ensure his military control of the city.[45]

However, on the evening of the 18th, at the end of what must have seemed a very long day to both Austrians and Venetians, the situation suddenly changed dramatically. At 9 p.m. a special steamer sent by the inhabitants of Trieste arrived in the Bacino San Marco with the news that constitutional government had definitely been proclaimed for Lombardy and Venetia. The *Osservatore triestino* reported: 'The Triestini reached Venice at the most critical of moments; a moment that cannot be described unless in the words uttered by Count Correr, amidst tears of joy: "They have been sent by God"'.[46] The members of the municipality and the Austrians had good cause for jubilation. It seemed as if any plans for revolution would be swamped by the spontaneous rejoicing which greeted the news of the constitution. Many thought that the objectives of the Italian movement had been achieved; late in the night of the 18th the Cafés Florian and Quadri had their names changed to Manin and Tommaseo.[47] Palffy announced his pleasure at being the first constitutional governor of Venice, the Fenice audience applauded the Austrians as they took their seats in the theatre, and celebrations continued throughout the following day, Sunday, 19 March. The chief of police for the *sestiere* of San Marco reported on Monday morning, 20 March: 'Because of the constitution and the concessions granted, yesterday until early in the morning this quarter of the city was full of people of every class. They paraded through the streets happily and without really causing disturbances, and the quarter echoed with their celebrations and shouts of joy.'[48]

The worst seemed to be over for the Austrians, but the period of reconciliation proved only to be an interval between the two acts of the revolution. Persistent rain prevented any more street demonstrations and everyone returned to work on Monday. The Venetians' anger over the shootings in the Piazza had not really abated, and Manin told Mengaldo on the 20th of the people's fury on seeing armed squads from the Kinsky

---

[45] Marzani, the imperial delegate, wrote to Palffy on 19 March saying that Mestre and Chioggia had followed Venice's example and formed civic guards. Marzani added that although he knew it was outside the scope of his powers, he had been unable to restrain himself from ordering the police to intervene to put an end to 'this true state of anarchy' (ASV, Pres. Gov., 1845-8, fasc. 1, 2/4, no. 1517).

[46] *Supplemento all'Osservatore triestino*, 20 March 1848, reprinted in Racc. Andreola, vol. 1, p. 27.

[47] *Ibid.*, vol. 1, pp. 7-8.

[48] ASV, Gov. Prov. 1848-9, OPss, VII, 2, 79.

regiment patrolling the *sestiere* San Marco.[49] By Tuesday, 21 March, definite news was beginning to arrive of the uprising at Milan.[50] A rumour that the Austrians were about to bombard Venice swept through the city.

Manin had continued to lay his plans for revolution. Ever since the 17th he had been making extensive contacts with the Venetian navy, and particularly with Captain Antonio Paolucci, who had been a member of the Bandieras' secret society, the 'Esperia'. Paolucci told him that many of the Italian sailors and marines would back a plan to take over the arsenal and raise the flag of insurrection there. One of Paolucci's friends, Giuseppe Ponti, exercised great influence over the arsenal workers, and was confident that they too would back an uprising.[51] The arsenal was the key to the city. Should the navy be won over and the stores of arms from the arsenal distributed to the people, there seemed a good chance of the revolution succeeding.

During Tuesday 21 March Manin received a letter from the arsenal, unsigned but probably from Paolucci. It warned him that the Croat garrison there was to be reinforced the following day.[52] This news and the fact that Milan was in arms probably prompted Manin to attempt the capture of the arsenal on 22 March.

The evening before the attempt was to be made, Manin summoned a council of friends to his house. There he announced his plans, which were met with general incredulity.[53] Mengaldo refused the support of the

---

[49] See the note written by Manin and signed by Zanetti as well, ACV, Municip., Atti di Uff., 1845–9, fasc. III, 12/7, attached to no. 3401 (1848).

[50] Trevelyan's app. D (*Manin and the Venetian Revolution*, p. 249, 'Want of connection between Milan and Venice, March 17–23, 1848') is quite wrong. Avesani (ASV, carte Avesani, b. 2) had received a note on the 21st headed 'la Corsa (of the railway) del gno. 21'. This reported that news had just reached Venice from Vicenza of the people of Milan taking the castle and capturing Radetzky. The diary of Alessandro Guiccioli published in *Nuova Antologia*, 363 (1932), p. 377, records rumours of street fighting in Milan reaching Venice as early as the 20th. Finally, the minutes of the extraordinary council of the municipality on the morning of the 22nd (see R. Cessi, 'La capitolazione di Venezia del 22 marzo, 1848', in *Atti dell'Istituto Veneto di Scienze, Lettere ed arti*, 106 (1948), p. 29) record Castelli as stating that the news from Milan was of such importance that it should be passed on to the civil and military governors. There was clearly no concerted action between Milan and Venice, but the persistent rumours from Milan without doubt influenced the climate of opinion in Venice.

[51] C. Radaelli, *Storia dell'assedio di Venezia*, pp. 42–3. See also Ventura, 'Manin e la Municipalità', p. 821.

[52] MCV, Doc. Manin, no. 61; letter dated 21 March 1848.

[53] For this crucial meeting, see F. Degli Antoni's 'Ricordi', published in Planat de la Faye (ed.), *Documenti*, vol. I, pp. 139–43; Teresa Manin's account, *ibid.*, p. 161; and the recollections of Bernardi in Marchesi, *Storia documentata*, p. 114.

civic guard for so foolhardy a venture. Even those who agreed that the arsenal should be taken disagreed on the rallying cry of 'Viva la Repubblica'. Most of those present supported instead the cry of 'Viva Ranieri' (the Austrian viceroy). After prolonged discussion some sort of compromise was reached with the simple 'Viva San Marco', but it was a compromise that Manin did not keep.

The members of the municipal congregation had viewed with increasing trepidation the change of mood that had come across the city since the 19th. Manin himself would have little to do with them, but his friend Pincherle had warned them of the lawyer's intentions and asked them, 'On the day when Austrian authority comes to an end in Venice, will the municipality have the strength and courage to assume power?'[54] Correr and his colleagues could not reply to such a question for, with the probable exception of the liberal lawyer Avesani, they had no desire for Austrian authority to cease.

Nevertheless, the pressure of events forced their hand, and news of Manin's decision reached them via Pincherle on the evening of the 21st. That night, at 1.30 a.m., Pincherle and Avesani visited Manin's house. Pincherle later claimed that Avesani agreed on the cry 'Viva la Repubblica', but this seems unlikely. Very early on the morning of the 22nd the mayor himself, Count Correr, came to see Manin. Manin must have told him of his plans, for Correr, when he arrived at the municipal palace later that morning, appeared 'distraught and frightened'.[55]

22 March 1848

On the day of the revolution Manin was preceded to battle by the workers

[54] From the narrative account written by Pincherle and sent to Manin, 9 Nov. 1849. Published by Ventura, 'Manin e la Municipalità', pp. 828–9.

[55] *Ibid.* After Avesani and Pincherle had departed, Manin posted his friend, Giorgio Casarini, outside the door of his house with instructions that he was not to be disturbed. Sometime before 6 a.m. the Piedmontese consul Faccanoni arrived and left the message that he advised Manin to proclaim the republic. See MCV, Doc. Manin, no. 3810, account of Giorgio Casarini, published by Planat de la Faye (ed.), *Documenti*, vol. i, p. 111. There seems no clear reason for this extraordinary piece of advice from Faccanoni, and his dispatch for 22 March never arrived at Turin. See A. Depoli, *I rapporti tra il regno di Sardegna e Venezia negli anni 1848–9*, vol. i, p. 47. On Depoli's highly misleading volumes, see the excellent review article by A. Ventura in *Archivio Veneto*, 66 (1960), pp. 180–93. Gustavo Modena later ascribed sinister motives to Faccanoni's action, claiming that it was 'secure proof of the plan laid by Piedmont to get hold of Lombardy from Austria by raising the bugbear of the republic'. This seems unlikely in the extreme; see Modena's letter to Francesco Dall'Ongaro, 12 Nov. 1851, in *Epistolario di Gustavo Modena, 1827–61* (ed. T. Grandi), p. 152.

in the Venetian arsenal. Their discontent had steadily increased in the first months of 1848, as prices remained high and their own wages unchanged. They had frequently but unsuccessfully demanded a pay increase from Captain Marinovich, the chief supervisor of the eight hundred or so arsenal workers. Marinovich was a merciless taskmaster, and had demanded an agreement of the caulkers and masters of the *squeri* – Venetian boatyards – by which they were forced not to employ any arsenal workmen.[56] Deprived of alternative employment, the *arsenalotti* had no option but to submit to the harsh conditions imposed by their employers. Count Zichy realised that the situation was potentially explosive, and had recommended a pay rise in February. His advice was ignored.[57]

On the formation of the civic guard on 18 March, no *arsenalotto* had been admitted to its ranks, presumably because in the eyes of many, private property needed protection from, not by, these elements of the lower classes. On the 21st the *arsenalotti* petitioned the commanders of the guard, demanding 'with religious impatience' to be allowed at least to join the night patrols.[58] On the evening of the same day many of the workers, on leaving the arsenal, decided to await the departure of their overseer. Some Venetian naval officers immediately called for the assistance of a detachment of the civic guard, and ensured that Marinovich left unmolested that evening.[59]

The following morning Marinovich was rash enough to return to the arsenal without adequate protection. Many of the *arsenalotti* were no longer able to contain their hatred, anger and frustration. Ignoring the efforts of Paolucci to restrain them, they hounded Marinovich through the arsenal and up a tower which stood at its east end, by the Porta Nuova. There one of the workers mortally wounded Marinovich and dragged him down the steps of the tower. At the bottom he was still alive, and asked for a priest. The arsenal workers gave him the reply which he had used so often on receiving their requests for a pay rise: 'forse la prossima settimana' – 'perhaps next week'.[60]

[56] P. A. Monterossi, *Memorie storico-biografiche di Daniele Manin*, p. 11 n. 1.
[57] Marchesi, *Storia documentata*, p. 115.
[58] Racc. Andreola, vol. 1, pp. 30–1, 21 March 1848.
[59] *Il 22 Marzo. Cenni biografici e sul massacro di Giovanni Marinovich*, p. 17.
[60] On Marinovich's murder, see also Trevelyan, *Manin and the Venetian Revolution*, app. C, pp. 248–9. Italian hagiology on the event is extensive – see 'Cenni autentici sulla morte del colonnello Marinovich', in Racc. Andreola, vol. 1, pp. 419–21, 7 April 1848, where Marinovich is 'visibly punished by the hand of God'. And, more recently, Cessi, 'La capitolazione', p. 14, who writes of 'these unprejudiced workers, who, free of any trace of egoism, so magnificently lived out the supreme hours of a noble idea. They demanded neither remuneration nor compensation, and offered disinterestedly, and through devotion to the common good, all the force at their disposal.'

While this was happening, Paolucci sent a messenger to Manin's house. Manin's immediate response shows how much he felt deliverance from the Austrians and maintenance of social order to be different parts of the same battle: 'Now we will have anarchy and very soon the reaction. Our enemies have been presented with a pretext for vendetta. There is not a moment to lose.'[61] He set out for the arsenal, accompanied only by his sixteen-year-old son Giorgio and a couple of friends. He chose a route to avoid meeting any Austrian patrols, and as he walked through the alleys he called to all the civic guards he met to come and join him. By the time he reached the arsenal he was at the head of a small company.[62]

There he immediately took charge of the situation, and none of the *arsenalotti* seem to have resented his authority. The head of the arsenal, Vice-Admiral Martini, was sitting in his office paralysed by the fear of sharing Marinovich's fate. Manin demanded the right to inspect the arsenal to ensure that no preparations for the bombardment of the city were being made. Martini acquiesced and the civic guards took up positions within the arsenal.

Companies from the Wimpffen regiment and the marines now began to arrive outside the arsenal. The civic guard refused them entrance. The Austrian officers ordered their troops to open fire. This was probably *the* crucial moment of the revolution, for had the Italian troops stayed loyal to Austrian discipline, the civic guard and *arsenalotti* could not have held the arsenal. But the Italian troops, many of whom were Venetian peasants, had been infected by the nationalist rejoicing of these days, by fraternisation with the civic guard, and by promises that they would be able to return to their villages if they came over to the Italian cause.[63] They refused to open fire and overpowered their officers. There then began the full-scale mutiny which by the end of the day had deprived the Austrians of more than half their garrison.[64] More and more Italian

---

[61] Teresa Manin's account, in Planat de la Faye (ed.), *Documenti*, vol. 1, p. 163.

[62] The civic guard of S. Pietro di Castello, on hearing of the death of Marinovich, had stationed themselves outside the arsenal gate, to try and control the arsenal workers as they came out. Their platoon leader wrote on 26 March 1848 that they attempted 'to guarantee order in a moment of extreme agitation (and we could do this more effectively because we knew all the workers involved)' (ASV, Gov. Prov., 1848–9, MG, b. 127, no. 248, report of G. B. Fauché).

[63] For this last point see the article in the Venetian newspaper, *L'Imparziale*, of 29 July 1848 (no. 9, p. 34). The article gives no information on how widespread were these promises to the soldiers.

[64] MCV, Doc. Manin, no. 3801. 4,260 soldiers deserted their regiments. Within the arsenal itself, isolated from any contact with other Austrian troops, there was a strong contingent of Croats who could easily have overcome the civic guards during the first hour after Manin's arrival. Fortunately, one of the captains of the civic guard, Francesco Zerman, spoke fluent Serbo-Croat and was able to

troops and Venetian citizens flocked towards the arsenal as news of the uprising spread. Manin forced Martini to hand over the keys to the armament stores; the *arsenalotti* and the populace were armed, and the arsenal was in the hands of the Venetians. From outside the main gate, Manin raised the cry of 'Viva San Marco' for the first time.[65]

During this same period, from about 11.30 a.m. to 2 p.m., Manin's friends had succeeded in taking over the other military keypoint in the city, the cannons in front of St Mark's Cathedral. These cannons, which Lamennais described as 'symbolising the ties which unite the people to the sovereign granted to them by the Congress of Vienna',[66] were manned by Italian grenadiers. The notary Giuriati and Carlo Radaelli, who like Paolucci had been a member of the 'Esperia' society, led a company of civic guards to the Piazza, and persuaded the grenadiers to train their cannons on the governor's palace. Another group of civic guards then took over the entrance and staircase of the palace itself.[67]

The municipal congregation, which that morning had summoned an extraordinary council, learnt of the course of events with growing alarm. At midday, according to Pincherle,

there burst into the council chamber the *arsenalotto* who had killed Marinovich; beside himself and now completely drunk, he boasted of what he had done and told Correr of the extraordinary affection which all the *arsenalotti* had for the mayor, their father. A deep sense of apprehension took possession of those present . . .[68]

At 3 p.m. Mengaldo and the lawyer Benvenuti arrived at the municipal palace. Benvenuti brought news of the fall of the arsenal, and Mengaldo, who had just seen Palffy and Zichy, reported them as ready to reach some sort of compromise with Correr and his colleagues.[69]

The municipality decided to send a delegation, led by Avesani, to confer with Palffy. They had no wish to see Manin at the head of a democratic republic, and even less did they want widespread street fighting to break out in the city. Once at the governor's palace, Avesani with great

deter the Croats from opening fire. See the account by Giovanni Minotto in Racc. Andreola, vol. 1, pp. 52–4.

[65] Minotto's account, Racc. Andreola, vol. 1, p. 50, differs from all the other authorities at this point, claiming that the marines had already raised the cry of 'Viva la Repubblica, Viva San Marco'.

[66] M. F. de Lamennais, *Affaires de Rome*, p. 117.

[67] MCV, Doc. Manin, no. 3259, pp. 10–11; sixteen-page account by S. Bedolo of the occupation of the Piazza.

[68] Pincherle's account in Ventura, 'Manin e la Municipalità', p. 829.

[69] Letter from B. Benvenuti to F. Degli Antoni, 27 June 1850, published in Errera and Finzi, *Daniele Manin*, pp. 369–70.

determination demanded that Palffy should immediately resign power into the hands of the municipality.

There seems little doubt that the Austrian officials were still in a position to refuse this request. General Culoz, the head of the Kinsky regiment quartered on the Zattere, was urging opposition, and the Croats in the arsenal had not surrendered their arms. Both Palffy and Zichy, however, recoiled from the prospect of reducing Venice to a battleground, and preferred to come to terms.[70]

Palffy at first would not consider total surrender, but Avesani would accept nothing less, and stressed that 'every hour, every moment could be decisive'.[71] His sense of urgency was understandable, for while they were discussing, Manin, having rested for an hour in a tavern near the arsenal, prepared to march to the Piazza. An enormous crowd followed him to the Riva degli Schiavoni, where, holding a huge tricolour flag with a red cap on its staff, he raised the cry of 'Viva la Repubblica!'

The immense crowd moved slowly down the Riva and at about 4.30 p.m. reached the Piazza. The argument between Avesani and Palffy came to an abrupt halt. Manin climbed on to a café table and proclaimed the republic with the following words:

We are free, and we have a double right to boast of it because we have become free without shedding a drop of blood, either our own or our brothers', for I call all men brothers. But it is not enough to have overthrown the old government; we must put another in its place. The right one, I think, is the republic. It will remind us of our past glories improved by modern liberties. We do not thereby mean to separate ourselves from our Italian brothers. Rather we will form one of those centres which must bring about the gradual fusion of Italy into one. *Viva la Repubblica! Viva la libertà! Viva San Marco!*[72]

A tremendous cheer went up. Above the Piazza, from the balcony of the governor's palace, Avesani and the municipal delegation watched in dismay. In this enormously dramatic way, the rival Venetian factions for

[70] Palffy escaped retribution from the Austrians, and merely retired from political service. Zichy, however, was court-martialled in 1849, and sentenced to ten years' imprisonment. The emperor pardoned him after eighteen months. See the note by Prunas in Tommaseo, *Venezia*, vol. 1, p. 90 n. 242. *The Times* (first leader, 19 Jan. 1849) slandered Zichy by suggesting that he had 'sacrificed his military duty to his taste for an Italian mistress'. For the Kinsky regiment, see Culoz's report in the Museo Fantoni, Vicenza, published in Marchesi, *Storia documentata*, app. doc. 11, pp. 504–5.

[71] Avesani's account of the conversation is reproduced in Errera and Finzi, *Daniele Manin*, pp. 352–3.

[72] Planat de la Faye (ed.), *Documenti*, vol. 1, p. 114. The translation is Trevelyan's (*Manin and the Venetian Revolution*, p. 113).

power had staked their claim to take over the city at precisely the same moment and in exactly the same place.

The first victory was the municipality's. Manin had hardly completed his speech before he was carried back, half-fainting from nervous exhaustion, to his home. The crowd, not realising that the delegation in the governor's palace was there to nullify at least in part what had just taken place in the Piazza, marched on to the Rialto and Campo San Polo, where the republic was again proclaimed. Palffy handed over power to Zichy, who finally signed a capitulation at 6.30 p.m. This allowed the Austrian troops to leave the city unharmed and with their arms, but consigned to the Venetians the fleet and the fortresses of the lagoon, together with all the military equipment they contained.

A provisional government was declared, with Avesani at its head. It consisted solely of the municipal congregation and its associates and made no mention of Manin or the republic. The intention was clear: to rely on the civic guard to back the government and maintain order, and to limit the revolution to a transference of power from the Austrians to the restricted circle of the municipality, ignoring the popular and democratic elements which had largely determined the course of events.[73]

It was not to be. During the course of the evening it became increasingly obvious that only one man commanded the allegiance of the Venetians and that was Manin. Popular anger at his exclusion from the government grew in intensity, and late at night he issued the following proclamation: 'Venetians, I know that you love me and in the name of this love I ask of you that in the lawful demonstration of your joy you behave in a manner befitting men who deserve to be free.'[74] The failure of the provisional

[73] Correr wrote to Mengaldo that the 'whole city recognises its saviours in the civic guard'; MCV, Agg. Manin, b. xxx/17, no. 77, 22 March 1848. The original of this document is to be found in the Museo Civico, Torino. One half of the municipality – Donà, Giustinian and Michiel, who was himself a member of the provisional government – congratulated the other half in the following terms: 'The respect, admiration and obedience of the citizens will constantly be of the greatest comfort to the provisional government. The municipality in the name of the whole city bears witness to this' (letter published in Cessi, 'La capitolazione', pp. 39–40). Dataico Medin, one of the municipality, in his later *Schiarimento relativo ad una storia vecchia*, p. 14, claimed that the municipality had tried to consult with Manin over a course of action, but this appears to be an attempt to gloss over the fundamental divisions between the two groups.

[74] Planat de la Faye (ed.), *Documenti*, p. 117. Depoli's interpretation of this proclamation is a typical example of the distortions that pervade his book. He claims that Manin 'did nothing to calm his friends' and that the proclamation only advised the populace to contain 'its joy and not its irritation' (Depoli, *I rapporti*, vol. 1, p. 51 and n. 69). Not only is this a far-fetched reading of the document in itself, but it can also be specifically disproved by the note that Manin sent

government to call itself republican incensed many of those who had been in the Piazza in the afternoon: 'The civic guard fraternised with the soldiers of the Wimpffen regiment ... and went through the town with flaming torches, tricolour banners and cockades, shouting *Viva la Repubblica di San Marco*.'[75]

According to Degli Antoni, a group of influential members of the bourgeoisie met hastily in the Café Florian: 'The lawyer Antonio Bellinato was charged to declare to the governing committee their disapproval of the exclusion of Manin from the government and to enjoin the lawyer Avesani to resign from power.'[76] This he did at 3.30 a.m. on the 23rd, after nine hours in power. He confided the government of the city to Mengaldo, who immediately handed over the task to Manin.[77]

At noon the following day in the Piazza San Marco Mengaldo proclaimed Manin president of the Venetian republic, and the names of those whom Manin had chosen to serve under him were read out amidst general acclamation.[78] The ceremony concluded in St Mark's Cathedral with a *Te Deum* for the new government. The patriarch Monico had made arrangements to give his blessing to Avesani's government, and at first refused to do the same for Manin's. Mengaldo forced his hand by telling him that announcements of the *Te Deum* for the republic had already been posted on the walls of Venice. Monico then reluctantly agreed to bless the tricolour flag and the institution of the provisional government of the republic of Venice.[79]

One irredeemable blunder marred the splendour of this moment. During the night of 22–3 March, just before Avesani's government resigned, Massimiliano Maffei, the captain of a Lloyd's steamboat, was entrusted with dispatches ordering the majority of the fleet stationed at Pola to return to Venice. Pincherle swore that Maffei could be trusted, but the Venetians were foolish enough to put Palffy on board the same ship. Once out at sea, the Austrian passengers forced Maffei to head straight for

Mengaldo that evening. In it Manin wrote, 'tonight it is vital that the worthy civic guard redoubles its zeal and vigilance to prevent disorders of any sort'; ASV, Gov. Prov. 1848–9, b. 454, comando della guardia civica, documenti diversi, no. 2.

[75] Burani to Antonini, 22 March 1848, in Antonini, *Carteggio*, pp. 46–7.

[76] Planat de la Faye (ed.), *Documenti*, vol. 1, p. 156.

[77] MCV, Agg. Manin, b. xxix/2, no. 2, the original minutes of the meeting in which Avesani resigned, 3.30 a.m., 23 March 1848.

[78] Report from the *Gazzetta di Venezia*, 23 March 1848, in Racc. Andreola, vol. 1, pp. 89–90. Avesani later claimed that there were only 200 people in the Piazza, but this seems clearly untrue, as the *Gazzetta* refers to 2,000 civic guards on parade, quite apart from the spectators.

[79] See P. Brunello, 'Rivoluzione e clero', fos. 132–7.

Trieste, which the Austrians still controlled.[80] As a result, the Austrians got to the fleet at Pola before the Venetians could, and the lost chance of enjoying undisputed supremacy in the Adriatic was to have the gravest possible consequences for Venice.

Thus in less than a week, and with remarkably little bloodshed, the revolution had been made in Venice and the republic proclaimed. Till the end of his life Manin congratulated himself on not attempting an uprising on 17 or 18 March, which would have led to protracted street fighting and no certainty of victory. The institution of a civic guard had been a master stroke, for its official status had enabled the Venetians to arm themselves and Manin to pose as representing authority in the vital minutes at the arsenal on the morning of 22 March. In general, Manin's tactics and actions between 17 and 22 March were beyond fault, and can be considered as the greatest achievement of his life. He had gone against his own class and his own friends, and successfully used the militancy of the popular forces in Venice to secure a democratic and republican outcome to the insurrection.

The revolution in the provinces

The events in Venice found a resonant echo in the cities and countryside of the Veneto. The news of the fall of Metternich, the release of Manin and Tommaseo, and the promise of a constitution provoked popular demonstrations in all the provincial cities. The municipal congregations of these cities shared the attitudes of their counterpart in Venice. They were scared of the situation getting out of hand, and quickly complied with the

[80] For the intricate confusion leading up to the departure of Maffei, see R. O. J. Van Nuffel, 'Intorno alla perdita della flotta a Venezia', *Rassegna Storica del Risorgimento*, 44 (1957), pp. 784–91. Although the majority of Trieste's population was Italian, the city remained loyal to the Austrians. The great development of Trieste in the first half of the nineteenth century, and in particular from 1841 to 1847 under the governor Franz Stadion, meant that the commercial bourgeoisie of the city saw their future as indissolubly linked with the Austrian empire. In the difficult period of March 1848 the civil and military governors of the city, Salm and Gyulai, showed great skill in keeping the situation under control, in marked contrast to Palffy and Zichy. At Trieste the Austrian authorities avoided conflicts between soldiers and townspeople, granted a national guard, but made sure that moderate elements had a strong presence in it. Thus nearly all the local civil servants enrolled in the guard, as did the head of the territorial civic militia, which was composed mainly of Slav peasants. Orlandini's attempt to march on the governor's palace on 23 March was easily defeated by a counter-demonstration organised by Salm and Gyulai; see the invaluable article by G. Stefani, 'Documenti ed appunti sul quarantotto triestino', pp. 63–110.

decree issued by Archduke Ranier on 19 March, permitting the formation of civic guards. For the most part the municipalities, composed of the provincial nobility or wealthy non-noblemen who had many years of loyal service to the Austrians behind them, tried to make sure that the guards were limited in number and chosen from the ranks of 'respectable citizens'. Thus in Vicenza there were only eighty guards initially, and at Bassano the civic guard was formed of 'landowners, professional men and merchants of known probity, all of whom can provide their own weapons'.[81]

These attempts to establish the class nature of the civic guard were very much in keeping with the traditional picture of this institution. All over Italy in 1848, and in many parts of Europe, the guards were primarily a middle- and upper-class organisation designed to protect the lives and property of the wealthier members of the community against possible attack from the urban and rural poor.[82]

However, a quite different type of civic guard was formed in the Venetian countryside in these days. Most of the village authorities chose to interpret Ranier's decree as allowing the whole of the adult male population to enrol. Often inspired by anti-Austrian motives and apparently undaunted by the possible social consequences of their actions, the rural clergy and many members of the communal deputations put themselves at the head of the militias, which were frequently called 'national' rather than 'civic'. Their actions gave the rural guards a predominantly popular character, and their formation more closely resembled a *levée en masse* than a defence of the class interests of the landowners.

The mood of these days is well captured by the diary of an Austrophile landowner who lived in the village of Cornuda and was horrified by the turn that events were taking.[83] On 20 March he reported that a carriage had passed with 'madmen on board, shouting "Italy is free" and carrying the order for enrolment from the local committee'. Soon after he wrote that 'women of every age are on the roads, rejoicing and crying "we're all Italians"', and that they'll follow the example of the Greeks, of whom

[81] ASV, Gov. Prov. 1848–9, CPD, b. 847/Vicenza, congregazione municipale, no. 1317, letter from the municipality of Bassano, 19 March 1848. They said that a huge crowd had assembled during the day, many of them from the countryside. For Bassano, see also BBV, Gonz. 22.10.27, 'Cronaca del 1848 riguardante Bassano' (a contemporary diary of events in the city). Udine appears to be the exception among the Venetian cities, for the civic guard was open from 20 March onwards to all men between the ages of eighteen and sixty; ASU, archivio comunale, b. 583, no. 1748, announcement by the mayor of the formation of the civic guard.

[82] In Sicily in 1848, for example, Mack Smith has written, 'the national guard was designed as a class militia; it was unpaid, and manual labourers were specifically excluded' (D. Mack Smith, *Modern Sicily after 1715*, p. 419).

[83] A. Serena, *Una cronaca inedita del '48*, pp. 12–13.

the apostles of Satan have given a glowing and wonderful account'. From all over the Veneto there is evidence of large-scale, spontaneous enrolment in the local guard. At Lonigo, a small town to the south of Vicenza, the authorities asked for volunteers on 20 and 21 March. The lists were open to all able-bodied men between the ages of eighteen and sixty, of whom there were an estimated 819 in Lonigo itself. Five hundred and twenty-nine men volunteered in these first two days, 104 of them stating that they came from the neighbouring villages of Monticello, Almisano, Bagnolo, San Toma and Madonna di Lonigo. Forty-eight of them described themselves as either *villici* or *campagnoli*, simple peasants, but it is impossible to tell how many of the ninety *possidenti* were small peasant proprietors. Forty of the volunteers were carpenters, twenty-one tailors, an equal number masons, ten innkeepers and ten shoemakers, six students, four roadworkers and one a shepherd. Forty-nine of the men were unemployed.[84]

The statistics from Lonigo are unique in revealing the social composition of the guard that formed in these days, but the numbers involved in other parts of the Veneto leave no doubt as to the popular base of the local militias. Although the authorities frequently stated that the guards were being instituted to maintain order and tranquillity, the possibility of enrolment for the whole adult male population transformed the militias into something quite different. At Casale, a village near Treviso, 200 men joined in one day, and let the commander of the civic guard of Treviso know that they were 'ready for the signal from him'. At Massa, on the banks of the Po, the district commissioner wrote on 19 March – three days before the success of the revolution in Venice – that 'the peasants are in revolt, crying "Long live Italy and Pius IX"'. At Valdagno, north-west of Vicenza, where Marzotto had built his woollen-cloth factory, the whole population was in the streets on Sunday 19 March, singing, dancing and shouting slogans for Italy and Pius IX. A plaster bust of Pius IX was carried through the town to the church, and the whole congregation knelt before it. The parish priest was wearing a tricolour cockade.[85]

The enthusiasm of the peasantry and rural artisans derived from their hatred of the Austrian tax collector, the sermons of the rural clergy, who seemed particularly favourable to the nationalist cause, and their hopes that a change of regime would mean a lessening in the harshness of their

[84] ASV, Gov. Prov. 1848–9, CPD, b. 847/Lonigo, no number: 'Elenco degl'individui che volontariamente vengono ad iscriversi per far parte dei Ruoli della Guardia Nazionale Civica da Attivarsi in Lonigo'.
[85] For Valdagno, see BBV, Gonz. 24.7.19, G. Soster, 'Valdagno – atti ufficiali e memorie dal 1848 al 1878; ricordi della rivoluzione'. For Casale, see A. Santalena, *Treviso nella seconda dominazione austriaca*, p. 28. For Massa, ASV, Gov. Prov. 1848–9, CPD, b. 832/Rovigo CPD, no. 58.

lives. The promptness of the rural authorities to allow mass enrolment in the guards is less easily explicable. Most of the noble landowners remained resolutely hostile, but those who had recently acquired land and the rural 'intelligentsia' – priests, doctors, lawyers and merchants – were often the principal organisers of the national guards.[86] These middle sections of rural society seemed, for the most part, to be unafraid of the peasantry and confident of their own control in the villages of the Veneto.

The speed with which the revolution triumphed in Venice meant that the provinces avoided conflict with the Austrians and that the rural militias were not called to aid the citizens of the provincial capitals in insurrection. The revolutionaries invoked the help of the peasantry only at the fortress of Marghera, on the mainland side of the railway bridge across the Venetian lagoon. There the Austrian soldiers at first refused to surrender, and all through the night of 22–3 March the tocsin sounded to call the villagers to Marghera. Nearly five hundred of them had arrived by the morning, from Trivignano and other neighbouring communes, but by that time the inhabitants of Mestre, aided by railway workers and deserting soldiers, had forced the garrison to hand over the fortress.[87]

One by one, and sometimes amidst considerable tension, the Austrian civil and military authorities in the provincial capitals followed the example of Palffy and Zichy in Venice and agreed to come to terms. In many of the cities, the Italians themselves were divided between those who supported the municipalities in avoiding any conflict with the Austrians, and those who wanted to expel the foreigner by force. Middle-class patriots, artisans and the Italian troops of the local garrison invariably composed this second group.

At Udine the news from Venice arrived at 2 p.m. on 23 March and by nightfall the Austrian commander had capitulated and retired eastwards with the non-Italian part of his troops. Messengers were immediately sent to the two great fortresses of Friuli, Palmanova and Osoppo, demanding their surrender. At Palmanova the situation was critical, because the Austrian artillerymen were determined to fight. But the local civic guard had taken over one of the gates, and on the arrival of the emissaries from Udine the Italian troops raised the cry of 'Viva l'Italia!' Again the fact that part of the garrison was composed of local troops proved decisive, and the commander agreed to abandon the fortress. General Zucchi, one

[86] Thus at Cologna Veneta, in the province of Verona, the seventeen village ringleaders singled out by the police included four engineers, one chemist, five landowners, one innkeeper, and four local government officials; ASVr, DP, polizia, b. 455, atti riservati, 1845–8, no. 90, report of 30 June 1848.

[87] G. Renier, *La cronaca di Mestre degli anni 1848 e 1849*, p. 17. Also the detailed report by the head of the Mestre civic guard, 30 March 1848, ASV, Gov. Prov. 1848–9, MG, b. 127, no. 186.

of the heroes of the 1831 revolutions in central Italy, was released from his cell and immediately put in charge of the fortress which had been his prison.[88]

At Treviso the mayor, Giuseppe Olivi, was terrified of the 'deplorable state of anarchy' and appealed to the population to obey the authorities and return to work. On the 22nd the municipality issued a proclamation forbidding any citizen not in the civic guard to carry arms in public. None the less a battalion of Italian troops mutinied and the Austrian commander swiftly came to terms.[89] The same pattern of events occurred at Rovigo, though the city was more divided between those headed by the bishop who were ready to accept the constitution, and those who were intent on driving the Austrians out. On the 23rd four hundred Italian soldiers, led by their sergeants and corporals, linked up with the civic guard, and the Hungarian hussars stationed in the city hastily departed.[90] At Belluno Austrian troops withdrew peacefully as soon as news arrived of Zichy's capitulation.

The situation at Vicenza was more fraught, for the military commander there, Major-General the Prince of Thurn-Taxis, had no intention of surrendering even after he had received the news from Venice. The municipality was frantic to avoid a conflict and on 23 March, *after* hearing of Venice's revolution and that all Lombardy was in ferment, they issued the following proclamation, advising complete passivity:

Our province must remain tranquil, it must not provide the soldiers garrisoned here with any pretext for attack, it must continue to provide for its own security in the ways we have already laid down. Furthermore it is of especial importance that there is no movement, either by civic guards or the people, towards the provincial capital or any other rallying point.[91]

The local patriots in Vicenza had no intention of heeding this advice. Valentino Pasini, Manin's close ally during the railway question, the canon Don Giuseppe Fogazzaro, Sebastiano Tecchio and their associates were set on following Venice's example. On the night of 22–23 March, a group of them went to Venice to demand 1,500 muskets for their city. Manin dispatched the arms by rail on the 24th but the Austrians heard of the

---

[88] Zucchi (1770–1867), born in Reggio Emilia, became a general in the Napoleonic army of Italy. After the failure of the revolution of 1831 he was condemned to death, but his sentence was transmuted into hard labour for life, served first at Munchaz, then at Josephstadt and finally at Palmanova.

[89] A. Santalena, *Treviso nel 1848*, pp. 6–11.

[90] See E. Piva, 'La cacciata degli austriaci da Rovigo nel marzo del 1848 e la costituzione del comitato dipartimentale del Polesine', *Archivio Veneto*, 32 (1916), pp. 481–529.

[91] ASV, Gov. Prov. 1848–9, CPD, b. 846/Bassano, municip., no. 719 *bis*

plans and prepared to confiscate the arms on their arrival at Vicenza. Pasini rushed from the city, stopped the train a few miles short of Vicenza, and unloaded the muskets. He then smuggled them back into the city and distributed them among the civic guard.[92]

Vicenza seemed set to fight, but bloodshed was averted by the arrival on the 25th of Lieutenant-Marshal D'Aspre from Padua. This astute officer had decided that all the troops in the western part of the Veneto should march directly to Verona to link with Radetzky should he be forced to retreat from Milan. D'Aspre gambled on obtaining an easy passage for his troops on their way to Verona, and on the city remaining in Austrian hands until his arrival. He therefore hastily came to terms with the Paduan municipality, marched to Vicenza, and after an unsuccessful attempt to wrest 80,000 florins of municipal funds from the determined Pasini, led his eight thousand men out on the Verona road.[93]

Everything therefore depended on the degree of initiative of the nationalist faction at Verona. The strategic importance of their city could not be underestimated. It was the last refuge of the Austrians in north Italy, the key to the Brenner Pass and the principal city-fortress of the quadrilateral. Feelings against the Austrians ran high on 17 and 18 March. At the Teatro Nuovo the flag of the Papal States and the Italian tricolour were unfurled. Then a long chain was made from the shawls and scarves of the women present, and linked the stalls with the gallery in a symbolic gesture demonstrating the unity of all the social classes in their support of the national cause. On the afternoon of 18 March a large crowd assembled outside the Hotel Due Torri, where Archduke Ranier was staying. When he appeared on the balcony there were cries of 'Death to the Austrians'. The soldiers guarding the hotel were insulted and provoked, but refused to react. Their self-discipline probably saved the day and the city for Austria. After three hours a huge thunderstorm dispersed the crowd.[94]

On the 19th the local nobility and municipality hastily formed a 'civic committee', headed by Count Pietro Emilii, whose principal aim was to keep order in the city. They obtained a number of concessions from the viceroy, including the institution of a civic guard. But the civic committee, closely resembling the Venetian municipality in social composition and political objectives, gave strict instructions to the civic guard to discourage any attempts to oust the Austrians from the city. On the 20th a large number of railway workers marched *en masse* from the village of San Michele, where they were quartered, to the Vescovo gate of the city. They found the gates shut, and started to try and force them open. The civic

92 V. Meneghello, *Il quarantotto a Vicenza*, pp. 26–7.
93 R. Bonghi, *Valentino Pasini*, pp. 212–18.
94 R. Fasanari, *Il Risorgimento a Verona, 1797–1866*, pp. 162ff.

guard rushed to the spot, and explained that the city was already in their hands, and that the presence of the railway workers was unnecessary.[95] The workers then reluctantly returned to San Michele and were in this way prevented from performing the decisive role played by the *arsenalotti* in Venice.

No leader with the determination of Manin or Pasini emerged to challenge the authority of the civic committee, or organise the city for insurrection. The crucial days from 22 March onwards were frittered away in spite of the news of successful revolution in Milan and Venice. On the 26th the guards on the ramparts saw D'Aspre's column of troops approaching the city. Verona had been lost for the Italian cause. D'Aspre hastened to send reinforcements to the other fortresses of the quadrilateral – Mantua, Legnago and Peschiera, all of which had also missed the precious opportunity to get rid of their garrisons. With the quadrilateral secure, the Austrians could still nurture hopes of eventual victory.

While the Austrians thus took the first steps to recover from the shock of the revolution, the civic authorities of the provincial cities restrained the peasantry from harassing the retreating troops. In the mountain areas and in the province of Padua there is evidence that the peasant militias were waiting for the signal from the cities to rise in revolt. None came, and where the peasants did set out, as at Valstagna on the afternoon of 22 March, preceded by the village band, they no sooner reached the main town of the area, Asiago, than they were told to go back.[96]

[95] G. Polver, *Radetzky a Verona nel 1848*, pp. 103ff. On 22 March Ranier was to decree the lowering of the price of salt by a quarter and an extension in the category of exemptions from the personal tax; see ASV, Gov. Prov., 1848–9, MU, b. 2, no. 21. The militancy of the railway workers can be judged by a police report of an incident at Caldiero, east of Verona, that took place at sunset on 29 March. The workers apparently attacked an Austrian patrol, disarmed them, and forced them in the direction of Vicenza; ASVr, DP, polizia, b. 461, atti riservati, 1848, police reports for March.

[96] ASV, Gov. Prov. 1848–9, CPD, b. 844/Asiago, 'Spese per la guardia mobile, ecc.', no number; letter of 22 March 1848. For the Paduan countryside, see the letter from Luigi Zanchi to the Venetian government, 25 March; ASV, Gov. Prov. 1848–9, MU, b. 2, no. 438. A typical example of the mobilisation in the countryside between 21 and 25 March was to be found in the village of Tezze near Bassano. The guard was formed of 24 companies of seven men each – 168 in all. Of these, twenty, all of whom had done military service, declared their willingness to leave Tezze if the need arose. The village authorities hoped to requisition arms for half the civic guard, but they were short of ammunition. All this information was sent by the communal deputation to the municipality of Bassano on 21 March, long before any news of successful revolution could have reached the village; ASV, Gov. Prov. 1848–9, CPD, b. 846/Bassano, no. 743.

Only in certain areas of Friuli were the rural civic guards called out, and then strictly as a defensive precaution as the Croat soldiers made their way eastwards towards Trieste. Domenico Barnaba, a Friulian lawyer, has left a fascinating description of this mobilisation in his home village of Buia, thirty-four kilometres from Codroipo.[97] On Sunday 26 March he received a message telling him to bring the civic guard of Buia as soon as possible to Codroipo, where the Croats were expected. Barnaba hastened to the parish priest, who at the end of the mass told the population to assemble immediately in the main square. Barnaba, speaking from the balcony of the *casa comunale*, ordered every villager who had a musket to return to the square at 1 p.m., ready to march to Codroipo. He was greeted with cries of 'Long live Italy! Long live Pius IX! Death to the Croats!' At 1 p.m. Barnaba weeded out those who were unarmed, and this left 300 men, apparently all with muskets, shotguns or arquebuses of some sort. Twelve of them had done military service, and these Barnaba made his officers. They reached the environs of Codroipo at seven in the evening, only to be told the next day to stay out of the town and allow the Austrian soldiers to pass peacefully. Barnaba records that 'a murmur of disapproval' went up from his men on hearing this news, but he distributed 1.50 lire per head, and the villagers seemed happy enough to return to their homes. A similar show of force took place at Spilimbergo on 27 March, when between three and four thousand men assembled, armed with arquebuses, pitchforks and scythes. Sixty men had come all the way from the mountain village of Campone, and the demonstration was led by the archpriest of Spilimbergo and the town band.[98]

Such demonstrations showed clearly that when the provincial authorities appealed for the support of the peasantry during these March days, the response was overwhelming. The villagers of central Friuli were prepared to take whatever arms they had, leave their homes and families and march under the leadership of the local priest, lawyer, doctor or Napoleonic veteran to confront the Austrians. Such impressive testimonies of peasant support for the revolution would have been more widespread if the provincial capitals had had to do battle with their garrisons, or if the municipalities had not issued strict instructions telling most rural civic guards to stay put in their own villages.

For the further development and activity of the rural civic guards, see below, pp. 162–5.

[97] D. Barnaba, *Dal 17 marzo a 14 ottobre 1848. Ricordi*, pp. 32–6.

[98] See the letter of 27 March to the provisional government at Udine, ASV, Gov. Prov. 1848–9, CPD, b. 835/Spilimbergo, no. 1594. Its author, a certain Beltrame, made a tour of the civic guards of the area on 28 and 29 March, and reported that thirty to forty men from each commune knew how to shoot, and given muskets could form the vanguard of the popular forces.

After the Austrians had left, provisional governments were declared everywhere on the *terraferma*. In the major cities the governments were usually a mixture of members of the municipality, leading clergy and local patriots. The most democratic election took place at Padua, where on 25 March a crowd of students and townspeople insisted that the municipal congregation resign and an election by secret ballot be held. This was organised the same afternoon and over 2,000 men voted.[99] Two of those elected were reluctant to serve for fear of being shot by the Austrians at a later date. Giuseppe Olivi, the mayor of Treviso, later confided that similar thoughts had crossed his mind, and that he would willingly have slipped quietly away to his country villa if he could have done.[100] Sometimes the local authorities thought it wise to include representatives of the people; thus at Udine the tinker Gaetano Fabris and the innkeeper Domenico Pletti joined the government.

Each of these provisional governments swiftly dispatched its emissaries to Venice. They were eager to make contact with the Venetian leaders, to discover their intentions and the nature of Venice's new republic.

The first days of the Venetian republic

Manin's first government was composed as follows: Manin himself was president and minister of foreign affairs; Tommaseo was minister of culture and education; Jacopo Castelli, minister of justice; Francesco Camerata, minister of finance; Francesco Solera, minister of war; Antonio Paolucci, minister for the navy; Pietro Paleocapa, minister of public construction; Carlo Trolli, minister of the interior; Leone Pincherle, minister of commerce; and Angelo Toffoli, minister without portfolio.

Manin thus omitted Avesani and all the members of the municipality from his government. In every other way his ministry was an attempt at compromise, an effort to stress his moderation and unite behind him all those who were not militantly Austrophile. It marked a conscious rejection of those who had helped him make the revolution. Only Paolucci, the former Mazzinian, and Angelo Toffoli had played an active part in the events of the 22nd. The French consul reported Toffoli as being a simple workman, but in fact he was an independent tailor who employed several men.[101] The Venetian cabinet contained no equivalent to Blanc and Albert, the Parisian workers' leaders who had joined Lamartine's pro-

---

[99] C. Leoni, 'Cronaca, 1848', pp. 384–6, and doc. B, pp. 539–40. Leoni, whose diary is one of the most interesting of all those kept at this time, was third of the seven elected at Padua, with 638 votes.

[100] MS Olivi, pp. 109–10.

[101] See A. Ventura, introduction to *Verbali del consiglio dei ministri della Repubblica veneta, 27 marzo – 30 giugno 1848*, p. 39.

visional government in February. Manin, somewhat ambivalently, commented later that he had chosen Toffoli 'for his influence among the lower classes, as a symbol of democracy, and in imitation of the French'.[102]

The most extraordinary choice was that of the nobleman Carlo Trolli as minister of the interior. He had served the Austrians for twenty-five years as a councillor in the court of appeals, and had no reputation as a liberal or patriot. It seems likely that Manin selected him in order to have a nobleman in his ministry, and thus reassure the aristocracy of the intentions of his government. But the appointment under him of Luigi Brasil – former Austrian prefect of police – as the new republican chief of police incensed the Venetians, and both men had to resign on 26 March.[103] The ministry of the interior was then given to Paleocapa.

For the rest, the ministers belonged firmly to the Venetian bourgeoisie – 'businessmen (*uomini d'affari*), already well-known, not unpopular', as Manin wrote later.[104] Tommaseo was by far the most intellectually accomplished, his imprisonment had made him popular with the people, and his relations with Manin at this time were good. He was the obvious choice for the most important cultural post of the new republic.

The lawyer Jacopo Castelli had quarrelled with Manin over the railway question, and on 22 March had sided with the municipality and not with Manin. Nevertheless relations between the two men were cordial – Castelli had sent his eldest son to Manin to serve his apprenticeship as a lawyer, and in 1848 had demanded to share Manin's imprisonment.[105] This friendship, and Manin's respect for his elder colleague (in 1848 Manin was forty-four, Castelli fifty-seven) probably prompted Castelli's appointment, in spite of his natural conservatism. He at first declared himself a republican, but his republicanism was inspired more by municipal pride than democratic conviction. Throughout his months in power, he remained deeply uncertain of the political maturity of the Venetian people.[106]

Francesco Camerata, the new minister of finance, had been an economic councillor in the Austrian administration. At the time of the revolution he was a modest man of sixty, with a high reputation for financial expertise. He was completely taken by surprise by the invitation to be part of the ministry, and politically remained a nonentity in the new government.

102 Brunetti *et al.* (eds.), *Daniele Manin intimo*, p. 219.
103 Trolli, in a letter to Paleocapa of 27 March 1848, claimed that 'the unpopular Brasil was not even proposed by me' (MCV, Doc. Manin, no. 3014). On the outcry against them, see BL, 1852.e.8., for handbills by Sernagiotto of the civic guard and the lawyer Giuseppe Soler.
104 Brunetti *et al.* (eds.), *Daniele Manin intimo*, p. 219.
105 E. Castelli, *Jacopo Castelli, ovvero una pagina della storia di Venezia nel 1848*, p. 18. See also P. Rigobon, *Gli eletti*, pp. 66–7.
106 Ventura (ed.), *Verbali*, p. 38.

Tommaseo liked him more than he did any of his other colleagues and described him accurately as 'a fine civil servant, but no minister'.[107]

Little or nothing is known of Solera, except that he was a Napoleonic veteran and was to resign his ministry in the first week of the revolution. Paolucci then became minister of war as well. Paleocapa, as we have seen, had been active over the railway question, but not in the *lotta legale* or what followed it. Again, Manin seems to have chosen him for his professional reputation rather than his political ideals.

The ministry, then, was a collection of individuals well suited for their jobs, but lacking any political cohesion. Manin and Tommaseo were convinced republicans, but the others seem simply to have acquiesced in the establishment of the republic. In the council meetings of the ministry, Manin, Tommaseo, Castelli and Paleocapa emerge as the strong men of the government; Camerata, Pincherle and surprisingly Paolucci are insignificant. Pincherle and Manin were united by close bonds of friendship, as were Paleocapa and Castelli. They were all, without doubt, dedicated to the ideal of Italian nationalism, but this was not sufficient to hold them together in the political trials that lay ahead.

The new republic had been proclaimed, but not defined. During these first few days of liberty, educated Venetians attempted to explain by means of handbills and by articles in the newspapers how exactly they conceived their revolution. The need to establish clearly the relationship between the different classes in the city was of paramount importance to them.

Most of the middle-class Venetian republicans shared the view of their French counterparts who, in Marx's words, believed that 'the classes had been divided by a mere *misunderstanding*',[108] and that rich and poor should live in concord together. The prevalent attitude of paternalism and condescension towards the lower classes was well summed up by Albano Gatte on 24 March:

The rich and educated citizen must not lower himself to the level of those who are poor and uncultured, but must raise them to his own level...Let us concentrate on education, and open free schools where the worker and the gondolier can go for instruction in the evening, so that they can learn their duties as citizens.[109]

The same points appear again and again. There was to be equality before the law, but no economic equality; education for the poor, but no pander-

[107] Tommaseo, *Venezia*, vol. I, p. 127. He called Camerata 'a true republican', and recounted how he used to sit in the kitchen of his house, smoking his pipe, and talking to the servants. See also Rigobon, *Gli eletti*, p. 60.
[108] Marx, 'The class struggles in France', p. 47.
[109] Racc. Andreola, vol. I, p. 116.

ing to idleness; liberty for all, but not to disturb the social order. Gustavo Modena, the famous actor and patriot, summed up the bourgeois republican programme on 29 March:

No communism – No social subversion – No government in the Piazza – Respect for property – Equality for all in the face of the law – Full liberty of thought and word – Free discussion without tumults – Improvement of the condition of those poor who wish to live from their work.[110]

As for the members of the government, Manin himself was strangely silent at this time, but Tommaseo's pen was rarely still. The decree of 24 March which proclaimed the republic contained this sentence specially inserted by Tommaseo: 'The example that we must give is principally one of social and moral reforms, which count far more than political ones.'[111] However, the limits of the social reforms he envisaged had already been made clear in an article published on the morning of the revolution: 'We wish to demonstrate that the fundamental questions of poverty and of work, of merit and of suffering, solve themselves more swiftly through the better use of the fruits of public and private charity, than through the sharing of goods and property.'[112] Tommaseo viewed the problems of the republic from a profoundly religious standpoint and therefore it was moral reforms that mattered most to him. He attempted in the first days of the government to realise his own moral revolution; the republic was to be the instrument for reforming every aspect of Venetian behaviour:

Anyone who insults either a citizen or a stranger, under the pretext of political or other opinions, will be conducted by the civic guard to the nearest parish priest who, assuming the true functions of a citizen priest, will admonish him for the offence committed against the honour of the communal fatherland. He who sins again in this manner will be punished more severely.[113]

[110] *Ibid.*, vol. I, p. 239. Gustavo Modena, born in Venice in 1803, was the son of an actor who forced him to study law, first at Padua, where he was severely wounded in a student riot, and then at Bologna. But Gustavo too soon became an actor and won fame throughout Italy for the force and originality of his interpretations. He was an ardent follower of Mazzini and took part in the ill-fated invasion of Savoy of 1834. There followed a period of exile in London, where he won a name for himself by reciting Dante. Amnestied in 1839, Modena and his company toured Italy with great success in the 1840s. For a recent and detailed biography, see T. Grandi, *Gustavo Modena, attore patriota, 1803–61*.

[111] Planat de la Faye (ed.), *Documenti*, vol. I, pp. 169–70. For evidence that Tommaseo wrote this sentence see Tommaseo, *Venezia*, app. XXXII, p. 356.

[112] Racc. Andreola, vol. I, p. 66, article entitled 'Desiderio di un giornale'.

[113] *Ibid.*, vol. I, p. 154; proclamation, 26 March 1848. For Tommaseo, as Ciampini has written, 'the reign of the Just was about to be manifested anew upon the earth' (R. Ciampini, *Vita di Nicolò Tommaseo*, p. 359).

In a similar, though less exalted manner, the awareness of the dawn of a new era pervades many of the early writings of the Venetians, and lends them a genuinely utopian quality. The letter which Manin and Tommaseo sent to seventeen countries announcing the establishment of the republic expressed the hope that 'our new constitution will only serve to tighten those bonds which sooner or later must unite all peoples'.[114] No nationalism was ever less expansionist, or more infused with the conviction of the imminent reconciliation of all mankind:

You Germans, return in glory to the great Germanic family; we Italians will form part of our beloved Italian family. No more shall we speak of oppressors and oppressed, no more hatred, no more rancour; we shall all be free; we shall all be brothers and friends.[115]

The first few days of the revolution were marked in Venice by an overwhelming spirit of rejoicing and exaltation.[116] Beneath the surface, however, there were considerable social tensions of exactly the sort the Venetian bourgeoisie hoped to avoid. Bernardello has noted how the cry *Adesso comandemo nualtri* – 'now it is we who give the orders', echoed throughout Venice, and how this had a social as well as a nationalist significance.[117] The government had to cope rapidly with a number of incidents of varying gravity. The workers of the tobacco factory threatened to riot against the administration because they had not received any pay and were not prepared to wait. They were only pacified by the swift action of the nobleman Girolamo Gradenigo, head of the civic guard in the *sestiere* San Croce, who paid their wages out of his own pocket. The commander of the port warned the government on 24 March not to leave idle the 1,500 men employed under his authority at Treporti, Lido, S. Andrea and S. Erasmo, lest they became a danger to public order. Many sections of the Venetian lower classes petitioned the government for an improvement

---

[114] Racc. Andreola, vol. 1, p. 357, 28 March 1848. Of the letters sent, that to the United States is particularly charming, and is obviously the work of Tommaseo: 'The ocean divides us, but mutual sympathy brings us close, and liberty, like the electric telegraph, can cross the seas to bring us your example. We will maintain a community of feeling, which is more precious than a community of interests. We must learn many things from you; and we, the eldest son of civilisation, do not blush to admit it' (*ibid.*, vol. 1, p. 355). Only the United States and Switzerland recognised the new republic.

[115] *Ibid.*, vol. 1, p. 449, article entitled, 'Gl'Italiani della Lombardia e della Venezia ai Tedeschi dell'Austria', 9 April 1848.

[116] A delegate from the town of Conegliano reported on 28 March from Venice: 'Here everybody is smiling...' (ASV, Gov. Prov., 1848–9, CPD, b. 834/Conegliano, letter attached to no. 65).

[117] Bernardello, 'La paura del comunismo', p. 65.

in their wages or work conditions. The fishermen of Burano said simply that it was hard for them to survive the winter, and asked the republic to introduce some commerce or industry on to their island.[118]

Faced with this tide of agitation and expectation, the government was compelled to grant a number of concessions. The *arsenalotti* were rewarded for their part in the revolution, foremen and sub-foremen receiving two *talleri* each (12 Au. lire) and ordinary workers one *tallero*. They were also allowed to form their own arsenal guard. Fishermen benefited by the lifting of all fiscal duties on their activity; dustmen had their miserable wages increased from 0.75 centesimi to one lira a day. On 28 March the price of salt was lowered by a third.[119] Most importantly, in mid-April the government decided to return free of charge to their owners any articles in the Monte di Pietà worth under four lire each. This was in response to a good deal of pressure; one anonymous handbill threatened disturbances because 'the people of Venice have not yet gained any advantage from the revolution that they supported'.[120] There were over 100,000 articles to be returned, striking evidence in itself of the condition of the Venetian poor, and the process of collecting them took over a fortnight.[121]

118 For Burano see ASV, Gov. Prov. 1848-9, MU, b. 5, no. 2136, 8 April 1848: the heads of the civic guard of the two fishing villages S. Pietro in Volta and Portosecco (near Pellestrina) asked the new government to provide immediately part of the provisions needed for the inhabitants; *ibid.*, CD, b. 390, no. 15, 29 March 1848. For Gradenigo and the tobacco workers, see Rigobon, *Gli eletti*, pp. 125ff. For the letter of the commander of the port, see ASV, Gov. Prov. 1848-9, b. 440, no. 150.

119 For salt, Racc. Andreola, vol. 1, p. 212. For the arsenal workers, *ibid.*, p. 125 and pp. 127-8, decrees of 25 March 1848. For the fishermen, *ibid.*, p. 210; and for the dustmen, ASV, Gov. Prov. 1848-9, MU, b. 3, no. 1036, 4 April 1848.

120 ASV, Gov. Prov. 1848-9, MU, b. 4, no. 1701, 6 April 1848. A government official in the *sestiere* of San Polo reported angry gatherings of the poor on 6 April after an initial notice had been posted, which threatened to sell all items in the Monte di Pietà if they had not been bought out of pawn by 10 April. He heard plans being laid for a demonstration and an attack on the officials of the Monte, and people 'exclaiming that this was a betrayal executed by the provisional government at the expense of the poorest class' (*ibid.*, MU, b. 4, no. 1810). Both the Monte and the Cassa di Risparmio had been put in considerable difficulties during the March days by massive withdrawals of funds by an alarmed citizenry. The municipality took over the running of both of them on 1 April 1848 and received a grant of 630,000 lire from the new government to keep the Monte from bankruptcy; see M. Brunetti, 'L'opera del comune di Venezia nel 1848-9', *Archivio Veneto*, 42-3 (1948), pp. 31-6. The initial notice of 6 April must have been the first, ham-fisted attempt by the municipality to reduce the Monte's deficit. By 13 April one civic guard reported that he had heard many say, 'if the actual government was run by the poor it could not behave like this' (ASV, Gov. Prov. 1848-9, MU, b. 6, no. 2699).

121 Racc. Andreola, vol. 1, pp. 558-9, decree of 15 April 1848.

A wave of anti-clericalism also swept Venice in the last days of March 1848. The Jesuits, whose close ties with Austrian authority made them a prime target, had their headquarters sacked by an irate crowd on 22 March. Many priests in the city were insulted, threatened or accused of being Austrian spies. The outcry against one parish priest, Don Antonio Cicconi of SS. Apostoli, was so great that he was forced to leave Venice. Manin and Tommaseo did their best to reassure the clergy, promising them the unconditional support of the government, and removing one of their major grievances, the ban on bishops' corresponding with the Holy See. But many of the clergy, thoroughly alarmed by the hostility shown to them under the new political order, remained lukewarm in their support of the republic. This further incensed the Venetians, who contrasted the lethargy of the city's clergy with the enthusiasm of their rural counterparts.[122]

However, the greatest threat to the stability of the new republic derived neither from anti-clericalism nor the demands of the Venetian poor. The four thousand soldiers who had made the revolution possible by refusing to obey their officers on 22 March insisted on being allowed to disband and return to their homes. Freed from Austrian discipline, the soldiers abandoned their barracks and wandered through the streets of Venice. Many of them were drunk; some, having received only fifty centesimi pay in four days, went to the Piazza San Marco and ostentatiously ripped off their tricolour cockades. Others decided to pillage their barracks at San Salvador and had to be restrained by the civic guards.[123]

There is no doubt that the government faced a very difficult situation, but their handling of it left much to be desired. They made no provisions for the soldiers to be properly paid and fed, and at Santa Croce it was

[122] One Venetian handbill complained: 'They neither speak, nor write nor do anything in favour of our most holy of causes' (Racc. Andreola, vol. 1, p. 337). For the Jesuits, see B. Bertoli, *Le origini del movimento cattolico*, p. 18. They also had a substantial amount of property near Mirano, which was promptly confiscated. The Paduan departmental committee thought this a dangerous precedent, but Manin confirmed the decision; see Brunello, 'Rivoluzione e clero', fos. 139–40. For the wave of anti-clericalism see the letter of complaint signed by a large number of Venetian priests, 29 March 1848, ASV, Gov. Prov. 1848–9, MU, b. 3, no. 811; also Brunello, 'Rivoluzione e clero', fos. 141–2.

[123] For the barracks at San Salvador, see the letter of the head of the barracks to the ministry of the interior, ASV, Gov. Prov. 1848–9, MG, b. 127, no. 170, 27 March 1848. The soldiers at first made off with bundles of sheets, blankets, ammunition, and everything else they could lay their hands on. Toffoli twice came to the barracks, and the looting temporarily stopped. It then started again, and the civic guard finally intervened, with the effect of 'putting an end to the thieving and recovering a great part of the goods'. Similar incidents took place two days later at the barracks of S. Cosmo on the Giudecca; *ibid.*, MG, b. 127, no. 64, letter from G. B. Salvi. For other details, including the scene in the Piazza San Marco, *ibid.*, MG, b. 127, nos. 242, 247 and 261, 24–7 March 1848.

again Gradenigo who paid the troops of the Wimpffen regiment out of his own pocket. The war minister Solera added fuel to the flames by threatening to have the soldiers flogged if they did not return immediately to their barracks – an act hardly calculated to endear the new republic to them. Toffoli and Manin went to the barracks and had some success in restraining the soldiers, but never totally calmed them. When a deputation from Udine arrived, requesting that the grenadiers from Friuli be sent home immediately to defend their own province, Manin agreed to let all the troops leave Venice, and for them to take their arms and baggage with them.[124] It was one of his gravest errors, for Venice was deprived in this way of the essential nucleus of regular soldiers around which to form a popular army.[125]

Many of the Venetian bourgeoisie who had supported Manin and the *lotta legale* must have been considerably alarmed at the course of events in the March days. While there had been widespread support for Manin's programme of reforms, the overthrowing of Austrian rule by revolutionary means was quite another matter. As Edward Thompson has sarcastically remarked,[126] 'mill-owners, accountants, company-promoters, provincial bankers, are not historically notorious for their desperate propensity to rush, bandoliers on their shoulders, to the barricades'. It seems highly unlikely that the men of the Venetian chamber of commerce backed Manin rather than the municipality between 17 and 22 March. Austrian concessions went a considerable way to meet the demands of the moderate programme, and Manin's decision to use popular force to establish a republic must have appalled the property-conscious Venetian merchants and businessmen. Nor can the disturbances of the first week of the republic have done much to reassure them of the city's social stability under the new regime. On 24 March Spiridione Papadopoli sent a note to Mengaldo asking for civic guards to protect his house and that of his uncle.[127]

However, Manin acted swiftly to reconcile the commercial classes of the city. His choice of ministers revealed a strong sense of moderation, and the first decrees of the republic emphasised its essentially bourgeois nature. Freedom of the press was established on 28 March, equality before the law for citizens of all religions on the 29th. A series of legal reforms was announced, of which the establishment of the independence of the

---

124 For the deputation from Udine see Ventura, *Verbali*, pp. 84–5; for Solera's threat, *L'Imparziale*, 5 Aug. 1848 (no. 11, p. 41), article signed by 'F. and V.'. The editor of the newspaper denied that the threat had been made; for Gradenigo, ASV, Gov. Prov., 1848–9, MG, b. 127, no. 275, 25 March 1848.
125 See below, pp. 166 ff.
126 E. P. Thompson, 'The peculiarities of the English', *Socialist Register*, p. 325.
127 MCV, Agg. Manin, b. xxx/17, no. 36.

judiciary was the most important. At the same time the government made clear the class nature of the civic guard. On 27 March Mengaldo decreed, in strangely antiquarian tones, that all those 'practising a sordid or abject trade' should be excluded from the guard; all servants and labourers were only allowed to form part of the reserve. The following day the government announced the formation of a new police force to 'maintain the internal order of the republic'.[128]

A number of measures specifically concerning trade and industry stressed the continuity between the new order and the economic agitation of the pre-revolutionary years. The presidents of all the chambers of commerce of the Veneto were no longer to be government officials, but were to be elected by the chambers themselves, so that they could act with 'speed and independence'. Customs duties on cotton and all cotton goods were abolished on 3 April, and this was seen as the first step in the gradual liberalisation of commercial relations. The government also helped smaller merchants whom the revolution had temporarily deprived of funds by repeatedly postponing the date on which bills of exchange had to be paid.[129]

By the end of the first week of the revolution the links between Manin and the bourgeoisie, perhaps endangered by his radical action on the 22nd, were firmly re-established. On 27 March Giovanni and Spiridione Papadopoli offered 3,500 and 1,750 lire respectively for the maintenance of the civic guard in Castello, Jacopo and Isacco Treves gave 5,250 lire, and some days later Angelo Comello also gave a large sum. The chief Rabbi, Abramo Lattes, was so delighted at the ending of all discrimination against the Jewish community that he informed his fellow Jews that military service on the Sabbath was henceforth permitted. As early as 24 March the mutual aid association of doctors, surgeons and chemists had decided to give all their funds to the new government.[130]

---

[128] Bernardello, 'La paura del comunismo', p. 64. For the restriction of the civic guard, Racc. Andreola, vol. 1, pp. 180–1. Other decrees of these first few days included one promising complete security to foreigners of every nation, whatever their previous politics, and the abolition of caning and flogging in the armed forces. This latter decree appears to have come too late (28 March) to influence the wave of feeling among the soldiers in favour of going home. It was also decided to give a state pension to the mother of Domenico Moro.

[129] For the chambers of commerce, ASV, Gov. Prov. 1848–9, MU, b. 3, no. 1524; for cotton, Racc. Andreola, vol. 1, p. 320. The high import tax on Piedmontese wine, instituted in 1846, was also abolished; *ibid.*, vol. 1, p. 347.

[130] The doctors, surgeons and chemists accompanied their gift to the government with a series of demands which went beyond their own professions, and reveal how much the professional bourgeoisie shared a common programme in Venice. They asked for the abolition of the lottery, the simplification of the monetary system and that of weights and measures, the abolition of the tax on stamped paper, the lowering of taxes, the institution of associations for artisans, the

Even the nobility were partially won over. A governmental announcement that was diplomatic if somewhat absurd informed the upper class that the republican epithet 'citizen' would not replace all other titles, but merely precede them. On 24 March nineteen members of the central congregation declared that they accepted Manin's government, and by 2 May one of Manin's correspondents could assure him that 'the nobility, although averse to the republic, support the actual ministry'.[131] Those members of the old nobility who could not abide the new order seem not to have organised a party of opposition, but rather to have retired to their villas in the Veneto, there to await the passing of the storm.

The provinces join the republic

The initial attitude of the provincial provisional governments to the new Venetian republic was one of great suspicion. They had little idea of the nature of Manin's government, and were instinctively afraid of the effect the declaration of the republic might have on the artisans and peasantry of the Veneto. Many also feared the reassertion of Venice's traditional domination of the *terraferma*, as well as its isolation from the rest of Italy, and from Lombardy in particular. In Padua above all there was no great nostalgia for the old Republic. Right up until 1797 the Venetian nobility had been a ruling caste who had allowed the provincial nobility no say in the government. The head of the Paduan government, Meneghini, wrote to Manin: 'The way you have named your republic Venetian, and the crest of St Mark which you have adopted, arouse fears of a too restricted brotherhood, of the revival of ancient and unworkable institutions, of relations of subjection between the capital and the departments.'[132] A handbill from the same city, dated 28 March, stressed 'it is not we who have cried "Viva San Marco"; that cry awakens in us only the memory of misery and fear'.[133]

providing of work, the improvement of the system of charity, the expulsion of *Austriacanti* (Austrophiles) from the administration, and the freedom of trade; see A. Pino-Branca, 'La finanza di guerra del governo provvisorio veneto (1848–9)', in *Studi in onore di Gino Luzzatto*, vol. 3, p. 101. For the proclamation by the chief Rabbi, see Racc. Andreola, vol. 1, pp. 380–1, 5 April 1848. For the donations to the civic guard, Bernardello, 'La paura del comunismo', p. 64.

131 MCV, Doc. Manin, no. 490, unsigned letter to Manin. For the retention of titles, see MCV, Agg. Manin, b. IX/31, where there are the minutes of a letter from Manin to 'Cittadino Principe Andrea Giovanelli'; also *ibid.*, Doc. Manin, no. 574, for the actual decree. For the central congregation, Racc. Andreola, vol. I, pp. 103–4.

132 MCV, Doc. Manin, no. 3543, letter of 27 March 1848. For Meneghini's account of the March days in Padua, MCV, Doc. Pell., b. XXXVI/97.

133 MCV, Doc. Manin, no. 3554. Written by Alessandro de Marchi, head of a

On 24 March Manin formally called upon the provinces to form part of the Venetian republic. The provincial capitals were to acknowledge the authority of Venice, and the smaller towns were in turn to submit to the provincial capitals. At the same time Manin tried to reassure the provincial cities of Venice's intentions:

The provinces ... will form with us a single family without any disparity of rights, since the obligations of all will be equal; and each province should begin by sending a number of deputies, in fair proportion to its size, to decide upon a communal constitution ... the example we must set is of an equality which is not subversive but justly and religiously exercised.[134]

This proclamation was aimed at the provincial ruling class. Manin followed it with two decrees which were designed to win the rural poor to the republic – the abolition of the personal tax and the reduction of the salt tax by a third. The effect in the countryside was enormous. The district committee of Conegliano reported that after the abolition of the personal tax had been announced the whole populace declared itself more determined than ever to defend 'this glorious, reborn regime'. The communal authorities of Montereale wrote that after the news of the decrees reached them the 'enthusiasm of the villagers knew no bounds'; they had 630 men ready to serve the republic. From all over the Veneto there is evidence of the great joy with which the peasantry greeted the government's first actions.[135]

Once the provincial emissaries arrived in Venice they were further reassured about the government's intentions. They discovered that Manin's was not a red republic, that his ministers were moderate men, that they had no wish to hold the provinces in subjection, and that the Venetians opposed any reassertion of their traditional separatism. Dr Francesco Ferro, a member of Treviso's provisional government, wrote from Venice on 23 March:

The republic is proclaimed but it is not the old republic; its constitution will be decided by a constituent assembly, which will be convoked; the new republic is thus in keeping with the times. In conclusion the seat of the government

platoon of the Paduan civic guard, 28 March 1848. For a full discussion of Padua's distrust of Venice, see G. E. Ferrari, 'L'attitudine di Padova verso Venezia nella crisi veneta del quarantotto', in *Miscellanea in onore di Roberto Cessi*, vol. 3, p. 185.

[134] Racc. Andreola, vol. 1, p. 96, 24 March 1848.
[135] For Montereale, ASV, Gov. Prov. 1848–9, MG, b. 127, no. 269, letter of 29 March 1848; for Conegliano, *ibid.*, CPD, b. 834/Treviso, no. 204, 27 March 1848; for the effect in Carnia, see the letter by Angelo Bertuzzi, *ibid.*, CD, b. 390, no. 90, 4 April 1848.

will be in Venice, but all the provinces will have their representatives...
Adhesion is indispensable.[136]

Other envoys recommended the same policy, and one by one, with
numerous provisos, the provincial capitals adhered to the new republic.
Treviso and Padua became part of the new state as early as 24 March,
though the Paduans urged Venice a few days later 'to manifest sentiments
of the widest nationalism'.[137] Belluno and Rovigo adhered without reserve.
Udine agreed on the 28th, while demanding that the republic 'must unite
with us to defend, with all the power at its disposal, this province which is
the key to Italy'.[138] Vicenza finally signed the act of adhesion on 29 March,
but only after a vote had been taken in the main square of the city.
Valentino Pasini harangued the crowd from the loggia of Palladio's
Basilica and then all those in favour of union kept their hats on their
heads, while all those against took them off. In its letter to Venice Vicenza
stressed that it did not want to prejudice by its action 'either the desired
and hoped-for union of Venice with Lombardy, or a special confederation
of these two states, or finally (and most importantly) the general confederation of Italian states'.[139] Provisional departmental committees were
set up in each of the six cities.

The only task that remained was to persuade the lesser towns of the
Veneto to accept the authority of the provincial capitals. Gustavo Modena,
in a letter of 30 March 1848, referred to 'the pandemonium created by
thirty cities all acting independently'.[140] Ancient disputes and desires for
autonomy came very much to the fore. Feltre refused to submit to the
authority of Belluno, Bassano refused to be put under the control of
Vicenza, Chioggia threatened to ally with Trieste if it was denied just
representation, and the Cadore wanted to constitute itself an autonomous
territory.[141] None the less the Venetian government persevered in its
decision to accord only district committees to the lesser cities, and by
the beginning of April, albeit amidst much complaining, all the Veneto
with the exception of Austrian-occupied Verona had adhered to the republic.

[136] Document published in Santalena, *Treviso nel 1848*, pp. 25–6.
[137] MCV, Doc. Manin, no. 3543, 27 March 1848; for Treviso, Santalena, *Treviso nel 1848*, p. 39, doc. v.
[138] MCV, Agg. Manin, b. xiii, fasc. 7, letter from General Prospero Antonini, member of the provisional government of Udine.
[139] ASV, Gov. Prov. 1848–9, MU, b. 3, no. 872, letter signed by Costantini, the president, and the other members of the provisional government.
[140] Letter to C. Cerrini from Treviso, MCV, Doc. Pell., b. xxxvii/26, no. 25.
[141] Ventura (ed.), *Verbali*, pp. 57–8.

Conclusion

The overthrow of Austrian rule in March 1848 and the creation of a new Venetian republic of nearly two million inhabitants was a remarkable achievement. A great share of the credit for the Venetians' extraordinary victory must, as has been said, be attributed to Daniele Manin. At a time when none of his friends shared his analysis of the situation, and all thought revolution an impossibility, Manin persisted in believing that Venice could be freed, and laid systematic plans for putting his beliefs into practice. On the vital day of 22 March he was given invaluable assistance by two elements of the lower classes – the *arsenalotti* and the Italian soldiers in Austrian uniforms. Both these groups espoused the revolution and Italian nationalism for specific reasons: the *arsenalotti* because of their intolerable working conditions, and the soldiers because of the rigours and duration of Austrian military service. With their aid Manin was able to take the arsenal, arm the populace and the civic guard, and declare the republic.

It seems fair to add that without the indecisiveness of the Austrian authorities, Manin would probably never have got so far. Palffy's and Zichy's natural hesitancy was compounded by their confusion at the news from Vienna and their unwillingness to turn Venice into a battleground. It is also clear that Avesani, as well as Manin, realised the Austrians' weakness, and it was he who played the crucial part, once the arsenal was taken, in obtaining a formal capitulation with the minimum of bloodshed.

The swiftness of the Venetian victory deprived the provinces of a major role in the revolution. The municipalities of the major provincial cities showed themselves timid in the extreme, and in the one Venetian city of major strategic importance, Verona, no able and determined Italian faction emerged to combat the restraining influence of the civic committee and to wrest the city from the Austrians. In the countryside the picture was rather different. There the conservatism of the local nobility and large landowners seems to have been submerged in a wave of enthusiasm. The middle sections of rural society – the priests, doctors, lawyers and small landowners – channelled peasant support into the civic and national guards, at the head of which there often emerged Napoleonic veterans, eager after more than thirty years to reassert their military prowess and anti-Austrian sentiments.[142]

The birth of the new republic included many elements familiar to the Venice of previous centuries; the cries of 'Fuori i barbari!' and 'Viva San

---

[142] See, for example, the fifty-five-year-old gilder Marco Natale Pittoni, from Prata near Pordenone, who had fought with Napoleon and Murat; 'Prospetto della guardia mobile di Prata', 11 April 1848 (ACPo, carte della guardia nazionale, 1848).

Marco!', the role of the arsenal workers, the exclusion of the urban poor from bearing arms, the hostility of the *terraferma*, all these were direct links with the city's past. But the power of the old aristocracy had been destroyed for ever, and their place had been taken by the Venetian middle classes. The ideological content of Manin's republic and the social basis upon which it rested distinguished it clearly from its more famous predecessor.

Two grave military errors marred the first week of the republic. The inadequate measures taken to reach the fleet at Pola and persuade it to return to Venice could easily have been avoided. The dispersal of the Italian soldiers garrisoned in Venice was more difficult, if not impossible, to prevent, though in this case Manin does not seem to have acted with the vigour and shrewdness he showed on 22 March. The Venetian ministers could console themselves in part for these losses with the evident enthusiasm of both rural and urban poor for the new republic. The series of concessions granted by the government in its first week of power augmented popular backing for the revolution, a backing which had its foundation in religious fervour and the economic deprivations of 1847–8. Yet were the Austrians to try and return, it was clearly going to be an extremely difficult task to transform this popular enthusiasm into a valid weapon of defence. In such a situation the loss of the fleet and of the nucleus of regular troops were likely to weigh heavily against the survival of the republic.

Such gloomy thoughts were far from the minds of the Venetian republicans at the end of March 1848. Their revolution had not taken place in isolation. The Austrian empire seemed to be disintegrating, to be suffering from 'an incurable stomach cancer, acquired in Hungary, in Bohemia, in Galicia, and in particular in its dearest kingdom of Lombardy-Venetia'.[143] The whole of Italy was in ferment, and the Venetians hastened to make contact with the other Italian powers. In so doing, Manin made plain his commitment to a republican Venice and a federal Italy. It was his own government that was provisional, not the republic. The significance of the new Venetian flag – the Italian tricolour with the lion of St Mark in one corner, was explained as follows: 'With the three colours common to all present-day Italian flags we are professing our allegiance to the Italian commune. The lion of St Mark is the special symbol of one of the Italian family.'[144] But this family was a divided one, and the reactions of its other members to the 'spring-time of the peoples' were to be far from uniform.

[143] Racc. Andreola, vol. 1, p. 536, 'The last will and testament of the Austrian eagle', originally published in Vienna on 24 March 1848.
[144] Ventura (ed.), *Verbali*, p. 80.

4

The failure of the Italian republicans, March and April 1848

The fundamental political division in the Italian national movement of 1848, that between republicans and monarchists, had not come to the fore during the Venetian revolution of 17–22 March 1848. Venice's strong tradition of republicanism, Manin's refusal to compromise, the lack of contact with Piedmont, and the municipality's weakness meant that the republic had been proclaimed and accepted. At Milan, however, the balance of forces was very different and, concurrent with the street fighting against the Austrians, the political battle between monarchists and republicans was waged with great fury.

At stake was nothing less than the future course of the Risorgimento. After over thirty years of what Antonio Gramsci aptly called a 'war of position', the patient and difficult gaining of ground in Italian civil society within the conservative national and international context of the power settlement of 1815, the Italian national movement had at last been able to break into the open. In the situation of great fluidity of March 1848, the 'war of position' had given way to a 'war of manoeuvre'. As the old order reeled under the frontal attack launched in most of the major cities of the Continent, the precise content of the flourishing bourgeois nationalist revolutions became the burning question of the day. In retrospect it is possible to see that the answers given to this question in Italy in March and April 1848, when the room for manoeuvre and for decisive political and military action was at its greatest, exercised a determining influence on the development of the new nation state. The opportunities created by the exceptional wave of insurrections throughout Europe did not recur.

In the struggle for political power created by this exceptional situation, the monarchists' class base in northern Italy lay amongst the liberal nobility and upper bourgeoisie of Piedmont and Lombardy. Their aim was to make Charles Albert of Piedmont the constitutional monarch of a new kingdom of upper Italy, embracing Lombardy-Venetia, Piedmont and the Duchies. This kingdom could then serve as the pivot around which plans for the eventual unity of Italy would revolve. The liberal monarchists aimed to leave the monarch with wide powers, establish a narrow suffrage, aid economic development while safeguarding the social status quo, and limit the power of the common people. To them, as to the young Cavour, the idea of a republic appeared as 'a mortal menace',[1] both because of its implied threat to the whole social order, and because they saw the logic of republican government leading inevitably to the revival of the Jacobin tradition and the resurgence of the Terror.

The republicans and democrats, if not numerically weaker than the monarchists, were far less powerful in socio-economic terms. They were mainly professional men, intellectuals and artisans, active in the great cities but weak in the countryside. Many of them were strongly influenced by Mazzini's ideas, and nearly all greeted with approval the establishment of the French republic of February 1848. They, like Lamartine, wished to establish full-blown bourgeois democracy with adult male suffrage and the liberties of assembly and the press, while at the same time maintaining a harmony between the social classes. For the radicals the Italian national revolution was to rid the country of despotism, whether Italian or Austrian, create its unity and combat its backwardness. Most of them, like Manin, wished to improve the conditions of the lower classes but rejected any socialist ideas. They regarded a constitutional monarchy under Charles Albert as a constraining influence and unnecessary compromise in favour of a king whose patriotism and motives they had good reason to suspect.

The crucial battleground for these different concepts of the Risorgimento was Milan. The Lombard capital was the most prosperous and economically advanced of Italian cities, the centre of nationalist propaganda in the pre-revolutionary years, the scene of the most bitterly fought of all the insurrections of the spring of 1848.[2] What happened at Milan in March was to exercise a decisive influence on the Italian revolution, and to determine in large measure the fate of Manin's republic at Venice. It is therefore necessary to examine in some detail the course of events there.

The cinque giornate *of Milan*

The principal problem to be explained in any political analysis of the five days of insurrection in Milan is the inability of the democratic party in the

---

[1] See R. Romeo, *Cavour e il suo tempo*, vol. 1, pp. 514–17.

[2] For the development of Milan in the first half of the nineteenth century, see M. Romani, 'L'economia milanese nell'età del Risorgimento', in *Storia di Milano*, vol. 14, pp. 675–740. Greenfield has estimated that by 1836 'almost one-half of the population of Lombardy lived in a state of urban or near urban aggregation', and by 1848 Milan and its suburbs had a population of over 180,000; Greenfield, *Economics and Liberalism*, p. 36.

city to establish a republican government. The Milanese uprising was, in the first instance, a spontaneous, popular rebellion; in the five days of fighting which forced Radetzky from the city with the remnants of his Austrian garrison of more than thirteen thousand men, over four hundred Milanese were killed. Of these the majority, as far as we can tell, were either artisans or workmen.[3] The fighting was directed and inspired principally by Carlo Cattaneo and the republicans of the council of war. More than a week after the city had been liberated, the *Times* correspondent remained convinced that only a republic would be acceptable to the people: 'Last night at the Carcano, where the people thronged, "*Viva la Repubblica*" was the prevalent cheer, and even the advocates for Pio Nono were outnumbered.'[4]

The Milanese nobility played the decisive role in preventing the creation of this republic. Unlike the Venetian aristocracy, the nobles of Milan had been traditionally hostile to Austrian rule ever since Joseph II crushed their power in 1786.[5] In 1821 the plot to free Lombardy with the aid of Charles Albert of Piedmont had been led by the high-ranking Milanese nobleman Count Federico Confalonieri, and had the support of a number of the Milanese and Brescian aristocracy. In spite of the failure of the conspiracy, Charles Albert's desertion of the cause, and the consequent imprisonment of Confalonieri in the Spielberg, liberal nationalism and the Piedmontese connection continued to flourish in Milanese noble circles. While paying lip-service to Austrian rule, and occupying important posts in the Austrian administration, many of the nobility looked to Charles Albert for the liberation of Lombardy and its eventual integration into a Piedmontese kingdom of northern Italy. Count Gabrio Casati, the mayor of Milan in 1848, typified this attitude. As Cattaneo wickedly remarked, Casati, 'unable to split himself in two, split his family instead, enrolling

---

[3] *Archivio triennale*, pp. 1157–66, lists 409 persons killed during the fighting (there were many more who were not accounted for). From these 409 I have calculated the social composition as follows: 107 artisans, 41 workmen, 35 shopkeepers, clerks, etc., 12 peasants, 26 servants, 4 students, 3 apprentices, 16 bourgeois (merchants, landowners, etc.), 4 children, 9 others (singer, riding master, comic prompter), and 152 either unemployed or with no employment stated (it is impossible to tell the difference between the two, with the exception of one man who was listed as a beggar). Of those killed 39 were women. See also P. Pecchiai, 'Caduti e feriti nelle cinque giornate di Milano: ceti e professioni cui appartennero', *Atti del XXVII congresso dell'Istituto per la storia del Risorgimento italiano*, pp. 533–7. Pecchiai states that over 1,500 men and women were killed and wounded, but his list certainly does not add up to that number, and he makes no mention of the unemployed or those with no employment stated.

[4] *The Times*, report of 31 March, printed in the edition of 8 April 1848.

[5] See J. M. Roberts, 'Lombardy', in A. Goodwin (ed.), *The European Nobility in the Eighteenth Century*, pp. 79–80.

one son in Charles Albert's artillery, and another at the university of Innsbruck'.[6]

Many of the established elite of Milanese society thus lent respectability to the Italian movement, and provided a leadership which the liberal elements of the bourgeoisie and the clergy welcomed. There also developed in Lombardy, through the works of Manzoni and the activity of Rosmini, a liberal Catholicism which greatly stimulated the neo-Guelph movement.[7] The aristocracy came to appear the natural vanguard of the Italian cause – when Manin came to Milan to discuss the railway question in 1840, he was received by Count Vitaliano Borromeo and entertained at the Visconti palace. A section of the nobility, as Greenfield has shown, were amongst the most active of Lombard entrepreneurs, seeking to introduce agrarian capitalism on their estates, and to accelerate the rate of Lombardy's economic development.[8]

By contrast, the group around Cattaneo was weak, and on many occasions was content to acknowledge the leadership of the nobility. Cattaneo himself, a university professor of immense energy and ability, had not evolved a clear republican position before 1848, and sought rather to obtain a programme of economic and political reform for Lombardy within the Austrian empire. Deeply attached to his own city, Cattaneo's ideal was the independent city-state. He saw the mediaeval communes as the Italian development of the Athenian principle of free association. The great tradition of Italian municipalism had to be preserved at all costs; as R. G. Murray has written, 'By a series of ingenious arguments worked out between 1834 and 1848, he [Cattaneo] managed to root this municipalism both as a tradition and a principle so deep in Italian history that for him it had not become an aspect but the essence of that unique entity known as Italian civilisation.'[9] Cattaneo maintained that Italy was destined by nature to adopt a structure of government similar to that of the United States or Switzerland. He had been brought up under a system so highly centralised that it had deprived the individual of his liberty, and his beloved Milan of its autonomy. The Piedmontese plans were anathema to Cattaneo, for he saw one alien, aristocratic and centralising government replacing another. Declaring himself the ideologue of the Lombard middle classes, Cattaneo urged them to worry first about their own liberty, and only secondly about the unity of Italy.

[6] Cattaneo, *Dell'insurrezione* (revised Italian version), vol. 3, p. 39.

[7] Candeloro, *Storia dell'Italia moderna*, vol. 2 (1958), p. 339. See also Cesare Correnti's 'Memorie', prepared for the *Archivio triennale*, but now published in full by L. Ambrosoli (ed.), *La insurrezione milanese del marzo 1848*, p. 7.

[8] Greenfield, *Economics and Liberalism*, *passim*.

[9] R. G. Murray, 'Carlo Cattaneo and his interpretation of the Milanese revolution of 1848', fo. 391. I must thank Dr Murray for permission to quote from his thesis.

When compared to Venice the absence of any tradition of republicanism in Milan was very striking, and Cattaneo did not seek to put himself
consciously at the head of an anti-Piedmontese republican movement. No
one, for obvious reasons, could openly declare republican or democratic
sentiments – that had to wait till the outbreak of the revolution. Cattaneo's
disaffection from the mayor, Casati, dated from 1844, when they quarrelled
over the production of a guide to commemorate the Milanese scientific
congress of that year.[10] Federal republican influence was probably strongest
at the university of Milan, where Cattaneo taught. Mazzinianism, which
had enjoyed significant support both in Milan and Pavia during the 1830s
and early 40s, in 1848 was still an inspiration for young democrats like
Pietro Maestri and Enrico Cernuschi.[11]

By their action during the economic crisis of 1847, the Milanese
nobility further consolidated their claims to leadership. Mindful of the
events in Galicia, the wealthy liberals, as in Venice, took steps to aid the
starving lower classes. The municipality organised bread subsidies, and
certain noblewomen, led by the Countess Maria Borromeo, wife of
Vitaliano, launched a collection for the city's poor. This *colletta delle
signore* was so successful that it was repeated, on a more organised basis,
at the beginning of 1848. In this way 'the rich, the nobles and the mayor
were praised to the skies as wise, compassionate and courageous; and thus
they grew in the estimation and affection of the people'.[12] In the countryside as well rich liberals took care to aid their peasantry so that the
Austrians, and not the landowners, bore the brunt of the blame for the
crisis conditions. Count Luigi Torelli played the principal part in ensuring
the survival of the provincial Casse di Risparmio, where many peasants

[10] G. Salvemini, 'I partiti politici milanesi nel secolo XIX', in his *Scritti sul Risorgimento*, pp. 46–7. Casati and the municipality produced the nondescript *Milano
e il suo territorio*, while Cattaneo published his famous *Notizie naturali e civili
sulla Lombardia*, which Salvemini describes as 'the most brilliant synthesis of
the geography and social history of Lombardy that has ever been produced'.
Manin was willing to cooperate with Correr in a similar venture at Venice in
1846, and produced a treatise on Venetian law for *Venezia e le sue lagune*.

[11] In Pavia many students were Mazzinians until 1844. Mazzini's influence amongst
the Milanese poor had been strongest before the trial of 1833–5 against his secret
society. It emerged from the trial that over 3,000 artisans and members of the
basso popolo had been inscribed in the society. See F. Della Peruta, 'Il pensiero
sociale di Mazzini', *Nuova Rivista Storica*, 48 (1964), p. 58. For the different
political groups in Milan before the revolution see F. Curato, 'L'insurrezione e la
guerra del 1848', *Storia di Milano*, vol. 14, pp. 325–9.

[12] Correnti's 'Memorie' in Ambrosoli, *La insurrezione milanese*, pp. 17–18. For the
nobles' charitable activities in Milan, see F. Della Peruta, 'I contadini nella
rivoluzione lombarda del 1848', in his *Democrazia e socialismo nel Risorgimento*,
pp. 73 and 75–6.

had deposited their small savings.[13] The rural clergy, much under the influence of the liberal nobility, extolled the virtues of Pius IX and the beneficence of the local landowners.

The radicals could not hope to compete with such activity, and indeed did not attempt to. They had little influence in the countryside and their contribution was limited to the coining of medals of Pius IX and the printing and distributing of Correnti's famous popular almanac, *Il Nipote del Vesta-Verde*, that sold thirty thousand copies in Milan and the provinces in early 1848.[14] But the almanac contained no direct criticism of the moderate programme, and in general the radicals had nothing but praise for the liberals' attempts to win over the lower classes. There was as yet no overt clash of interests between the two sections of the national movement, which seemed to be united under the leadership of the moderates and the auspices of Pius IX.

Yet it was the young democrats who made the most contact with the workers and artisans of Milan itself. One of them, Carlo Clerici, recounted how, late in 1847, they began to build up a network of connections: 'operating as a large group with many contacts amongst the people, we frequented the taverns, slums and factories, not sparing any effort in our attempt to arouse the consciousness of the people'.[15]

The events leading up to the revolution in Milan followed a similar, though more violent, course to those in Venice. On 9 December 1847 Nazari presented his petition for reform to the Lombard central congregation. On 3 January 1848, at the height of the Milanese non-smoking campaign, fighting broke out between soldiers of the garrison and the unarmed populace; there were sixty-four civilian casualties, of whom five died.[16] This proved the fatal turning point for the Austrians, just as the arrest of Manin and Tommoseo rebounded against them in Venicce. From this moment onwards, as Correnti wrote, the people of the towns and countryside made up their minds: 'the Germans are turning against the Pope, the priests and the *signori*, they're slaughtering the poor people in the piazza under the eyes of the archbishop, they're throwing the gentlemen in prison, and they're threatening the *signori* who gave us bread this winter and who love the Pope'.[17]

Up till this time the liberal moderate leadership of the Italian party in Milan had never been in doubt. But the news of the French revolution of

[13] Della Peruta, 'I contadini', p. 77.
[14] See Greenfield, *Economics and Liberalism*, p. 230 n. 138–40, and Curato, 'L'insurrezione e la guerra', pp. 256–7.
[15] C. Clerici, 'Memoria', in *Archivio triennale*, vol. 1, p. 564.
[16] See G. F.-H. and J. Berkeley, *Italy in the Making: 1848*, p. 21 n. 14, for the conflicting estimates of the numbers wounded.
[17] C. Correnti, *L'Austria e la Lombardia*, p. 177.

February 1848 and the declaration of the second French republic sub-
stantially altered the situation. The democrats – men like Clerici, Pietro
Maestri and Enrico Cernuschi – took heart, as Manin had done in his
Venetian prison; the tide of events seemed to be flowing in their direction.
They redoubled their activity and found a ready response amongst the
Milanese artisans and students.[18] The tidings from Paris, however, brought
little joy to the wealthy Milanese liberals. Not only was the prospect of a
new expansionist French republic ominous in itself, but it also served to
swing moderate Milanese feeling back to Austria. The British consul,
Dawkins, reported on 6 March 1848 that

the feeling of hostility to the Austrians, though it cannot be said to have sub-
sided, has at least been put in the background, and appears to have merged in
a general feeling of apprehension at the possible consequences of what has
taken place in France. I think I am correct in this view as regards the great
majority of the upper, and the more rational portion of the middle classes.
Indeed ... the Imperial Government might still rally round it a great number
of persons who, not out of love for the Government, but out of regard for
order would give their support to the authorities.[19]

All this made Charles Albert's proclamation of a constitution doubly
welcome for the liberal monarchists. The news of the *Statuto* of 5 March
1848 was received rapturously by many of the Milanese bourgeoisie and
nobility. Ottolini recounts how they took to wearing grey capes similar to
those of the Sardinian army: 'everyone was talking of Piedmont's 100,000
bayonets'.[20] Count Enrico Martini joined Count Carlo D'Adda at Turin
as unofficial representatives of the Milanese nobility at the court of the
Piedmontese king.

When the revolution broke out in Milan on 18 March 1848, the contradictions inherent in the united front against the Austrians, maintained

[18] Pietro Maestri (b. 1811) was a Milanese doctor; Enrico Cernuschi (b. 1821)
studied law at Pavia university and then worked in a sugar refinery. Before
March 1848 he was notable only for his original mode of dressing, which earned
him the nickname of 'the little Robespierre'; see the article by A. Monti in
Dizionario del Risorgimento nazionale, vol. 2 (1933), pp. 657–8.
[19] 'Correspondence respecting the affairs of Italy, 1846–9', in *Accounts and Papers*,
vol. 28, 1849, p. 503. The French consul, F. Denois, came to almost identical
conclusions: 'the Milanese *seigneurs* aspire to becoming Italian again. They want
to govern themselves, or, to put it more clearly, to govern the rest of the population, but they have not the slightest taste for republican notions. The word
"republic" is a bogy for the vast majority of them, and it is this that explains why
we have marked time here since the momentous happenings of last month';
see F. Boyer, *La seconde République, Charles-Albert et l'Italie du nord en 1848*,
p. 29.
[20] V. Ottolini, *La rivoluzione lombarda del 1848 e 1849*, p. 58.

successfully up until that point, immediately became apparent. The municipal council, led by the mayor, Casati, and consisting of 'old men who belonged to that social class which was rich, refined, and well educated'[21] were terrified as street fighting spread through the city. On the evening of the 18th they, like their Venetian counterparts, issued a proclamation begging the citizens to stop fighting so as to prevent an 'inevitable massacre'.[22] The liberal nobility, with one or two notable exceptions, took little part in the battles that were being waged in the streets.

In the Lombard provinces it was the same story. Della Peruta has shown how great numbers of the peasantry, between 20 and 23 March, rose in support of the insurgents at Milan. In many of the provincial cities of upper Lombardy, in Como, Monza, Lecco, Sondrio, and others, armed peasant bands flocked from the surrounding villages to aid the urban populations in forcing the garrisons to retreat or surrender. However, in lower Lombardy, where most of the peasantry were landless labourers, the municipal congregations of the cities appeared more frightened of the peasants than of the Austrians. At Cremona the municipality refused to respond to peasant demands to harass the retreating Austrians. In the area around Mantua many thousands of the rural population, led by priests, mobilised to take the city, but the municipality hesitated to give any lead and the Austrians were able to secure this vital city-fortress.[23]

In the countryside the radicals were few and ineffectual, and were unable to combat the conservative leadership of the great landowners and the clergy who were under their influence. The peasant movement was thus left without direction. But in Milan itself young democrats like Cernuschi and Manara were among the first to man the barricades. It was they and the working people of the city who formed the great majority of the combatants in the most difficult period of the insurrection, its first two days. They were badly armed and without a general plan, but the barricades they built could only be taken with great difficulty, and many pockets of Austrian troops quickly found their supply and communication lines cut. The bells of every church in Milan rang without stop. Radetzky, who had been boasting of his desire to teach the Milanese a lesson, was forced to abandon his home in the centre of the city and retreat to the castle. From there he declared all acts of resistance high treason and threatened to sack and bombard the city. The fighting went on.

---

[21] C. Spellanzon, *Storia del Risorgimento e dell'Unità d'Italia*, vol. 3 (1936), p. 722.
[22] Proclamation published in Salvemini, 'I partiti politici', p. 61. In fact, most of the municipality had been captured in the assault on the Broletto palace on the evening of the 18th. Thus only two of its members were able to sign the proclamation; Curato, 'L'insurrezione e la guerra', p. 341.
[23] Della Peruta, 'I contadini', pp. 82–8 and p. 85 n. 5.

Carlo Cattaneo had at first refused to join the insurgents. He told his young friends that to fight Radetzky they needed thousands of well-armed and well-led men, and that to think otherwise was madness. But by the evening of the second day, the 19th, the revolutionaries, far from being wiped out, had succeeded in spreading the revolt to the whole eastern part of the city. At this stage Cattaneo decided that he could no longer refuse to be involved, and met the leading insurgents at their headquarters in the Casa di Taverna in the Via Bigli.

This meeting was of crucial importance. The nobility having defaulted, Cattaneo and the young radicals found themselves to be more or less the arbiters of the revolution. As so often happens, the uprising had wrought a dramatic political transformation in the space of a few hours. Instead of the democrats being strictly subordinate to the moderate leadership, they were suddenly the commanders of a popular insurrection in which the majority of the upper classes had refused to participate. At the meeting in the Casa di Taverna pressure was put on Cattaneo to declare a republic: 'That evening some of the young men, inflamed by the battle and embittered because, while they lacked arms and munitions, Casati was being polite to the police, . . . demanded new leaders. The angriest of them wanted to declare the republic immediately, and appeal to Switzerland and France for arms and officers.'[24]

Cattaneo dissuaded them, and he more than anyone else must bear the responsibility for the failure of the republicans to seize the initiative. He argued in favour of a council of war rather than a republic, claiming that the nobility would discredit any republican government by exploiting the popularity of the Piedmontese king with the people of Milan. The princes of Italy, he said, would not come to the aid of a republic. As he wrote later, 'we did not yet know that in those same days the name of the republic was being resurrected at Venice'.[25] A four-man council of war – Cattaneo, Giorgio Clerici, Cernuschi and Terzaghi – was therefore set up, and it directed the fierce fighting of the next two days. Twice in this period Radetzky asked for an armistice; on both occasions Casati seemed in favour of granting it and both times the council of war refused to consider it.

[24] Cattaneo, *Dell'insurrezione*, p. 50.

[25] *Ibid.*, p. 51. Early on the 20th another discussion on forms of government took place at the Casa Taverna. This time Casati was present as well as Cattaneo, and no agreement was reached; see C. Casati, *Nuove rivelazioni sui fatti di Milano nel 1847–8*, vol. 2, pp. 131–2. At 1 p.m. on the 20th the group around Casati issued a proclamation saying that the municipality 'in order to maintain public security' in 'these terrible circumstances' assumed full power on a temporary basis. But this clearly was not a declaration of a new government; see Curato, 'L'insurrezione e la guerra', p. 359, for the text of the proclamation.

By 21 March, in Milan as in Venice, an uneasy duality of power existed among the Italians. On the one hand there were Casati and the liberal nobles who were beginning to regain courage as the battle swung in favour of the Milanese; on the other Cattaneo, the council of war and the republicans. At this moment Count Enrico Martini, who had been having a series of urgent talks with King Charles Albert and his advisers in Turin, managed to get back into Milan disguised as a worker helping to bring salt into the city. With his arrival the battle for power in Milan reached its climax.

Enter Charles Albert

The news of the insurrection of Milan had confronted Charles Albert, king of Piedmont, with a complex and intolerable situation. As a young man he had been the great hope of the Piedmontese liberals, an illusion that was soon dispelled in 1821. Fearful of any disturbances to the status quo, in 1833 Charles Albert had savagely suppressed a Mazzinian plot in his kingdom. But in the 1840s, encouraged by a sizeable section of his nobility, he had begun to move hesitantly towards a more Italian and anti-Austrian policy. Introverted and vacillating by nature, Charles Albert harboured great ambitions for the expansion of his kingdom, but was terrified of losing control of the nationalist movement. For Charles Albert, Italian unity, if it meant anything, meant the gradual rapprochement of the Italian monarchs, with an eventual territorial aggrandisement of Piedmont in northern Italy.

With this view of the Risorgimento as being a movement dominated by the Italian monarchs, the last thing Charles Albert wanted was to get involved in a popular uprising against the Austrians. The news from Milan put him in an impossible quandary. He was influenced against declaring war by the lack of preparation of his army, by Anglo-French pressure, by not knowing whether he could count on the collaboration of the other Italian sovereigns, but above all by the fear that he was about to march to the aid of a Lombard republic.[26] A republican victory in Milan

---

[26] The French opposed any Piedmontese aggrandisement, since it threatened their southern borders. In addition, a large section of Parisian public opinion did not wish to see a possible Italian republican movement suffocated. See below, pp. 148 ff. England wanted to avoid an Austro-Italian conflagration in Italy which might have led to French intervention; she also 'did not want her markets disturbed or her customers impoverished by a European war' (Taylor, *The Italian Problem*, p. 5). For Charles Albert's fear of lack of support from the other monarchs of Italy, see Depoli, *I rapporti*, vol. 1, pp. 26–7. For fears of a Milanese republic, see the letter from Castagnetto to Casati, Torino, 26 March 1848, in V. Ferrari (ed.), *Carteggio Casati–Castagnetto*, p. 18.

would have been worse than defeat by the Austrians; for, with the newly established French republic already seeming to menace his Savoyard border, with the Swiss republic to his north, and with the Genoese tradition of republicanism still very much alive, Charles Albert feared that a Lombard republic could mean the end of his dynasty.

On 19 March Counts Martini and D'Adda, representing the interests of the Milanese moderates at Turin, had an audience with Charles Albert and asked for his intervention. The king replied that to enable him to justify his aggression to the Great Powers, the Milanese municipality would first have to send a message to him asking for his help. After the meeting the Piedmontese statesman, Count Castagnetto, advised Martini to return to Milan immediately to obtain the necessary letter from the mayor Casati. At the same time Castagnetto wrote to Casati, urging him to do everything possible to 'save us from the republic'.[27]

Martini departed, and Charles Albert and his ministers began to wait. They could not afford to delay long, because as soon as the details of the Milanese revolution became generally known, the youth of the Piedmontese towns could hardly be restrained from marching to the insurgents' aid. On 19 March Bianca de' Simoni wrote to Lorenzo Pareto, the Piedmontese minister for foreign affairs: 'we will have a revolution at home if you will not allow our bravest young men to go and meet their destinies. Give orders as an Italian and not as Charles Albert's minister.'[28] As the king hesitated further, and only slowly assembled his forces on the eastern frontier, rumours swept through the kingdom that he was deliberately betraying the national cause. By 24 March Prince Eugene reported from Genoa that the monarchists were in danger of their lives: 'to put it succinctly, here it is the people who are in command, not the government; if the troops do not cross the Ticino, there will be a massacre, for already the people say they have been betrayed, and the soldiers will not restrain the populace'.[29]

The events in Milan were therefore of the utmost importance for the future of the Savoy dynasty. They were also critical for the fate of the republican party in northern Italy. Martini went straight to the Casa di Taverna, where the second Austrian proposal for an armistice had just been refused, exhorted Casati to send a letter requesting Piedmontese intervention, and advised him to form a provisional government. The

27 Ferrari (ed.), *Carteggio Casati–Castagnetto*, p. 7, letter of 19 March. For Martini in Turin, see Candeloro, *Storia dell'Italia moderna*, vol. 2, pp. 172–3.

28 A. Codignola, *Rubattino*, p. 39.

29 T. Buttini and M. Avetta (eds.), *I rapporti fra il governo sardo e il governo provvisorio di Lombardia*, pp. 50–1 n. 3. Dispatch undated, but the editors put it at 23 or 24 March 1848.

mayor, as earlier, did not feel he could act without consulting the council
of war. Cattaneo spoke vehemently against trusting Charles Albert, and
against the monarchists' desire to hand Lombardy to him on a plate:

Signori, reigning monarchs are all outsiders and they do not wish to belong to
any nation; they have interests apart and are disposed always to conspire with
foreigners against their own people. I firmly believe that we must call all Italy
to arms and make the war a national one. If then your Charles Albert will be
the only one to come to our aid, he alone will have earned the admiration and
gratitude of our peoples; and no one will be able to prevent the country being
his. In any case it is useless that you should give it to him; for if he wins, it
will remain his; and if he does not win, it will never be his, not even if you
give it to him a hundred times.[30]

None the less Cattaneo and Cernuschi agreed to formulate a compromise
letter which, while appealing for the aid of all the Italian states, made a
point of adding, 'and especially of neighbouring and warlike Piedmont'.[31]

There remained the crucial problem of the formation of a Milanese
government. Casati at first refused to proclaim a provisional government,
probably because he feared the reaction of the council of war and of many
of those on the barricades. Martini therefore decided to try his luck with
Cattaneo and went into the room where the council of war was assembled.
Martini's action seems inexplicable. Curato has suggested that Martini
was ignorant of Cattaneo's political opinions, but this seems very unlikely,
for Martini was no stranger to the Milanese political scene. Cattaneo recounted that Martini tried to bribe him: 'You know that it is not every
day that you could lend services of such importance to a king?'[32] This
also seems unlikely, for Cattaneo was hardly renowned for being easily
corruptible. In any event, the offer was refused.

At this stage on 21 March Cattaneo relates that he seriously considered
forming his own government from among those sympathetic to the
republic. However, the pre-revolutionary hegemony that the nobility had
exercised over the national movement still weighed heavily with him, and
he felt the need to seek the cooperation of moderate men of high social
standing and repute. He asked Pompeo Litta, a Napoleonic veteran,
scholar and nobleman, and the Marquis Cusani. Both declined. Cernuschi
and Terzaghi, Cattaneo's colleagues on the council of war, then urged
him to convert the council itself into a provisional government. Despite

[30] Cattaneo, *Dell'insurrezione*, pp. 71–2. It should be noted that this is Cattaneo's
account of his speech, written initially in Paris in September 1848. No other
eye-witness has explicitly contradicted this part of his account.
[31] *Ibid.*, p. 72.
[32] *Ibid.*, p. 73. See also Curato, 'L'insurrezione e la guerra', p. 388.

their pleading Cattaneo refused, and with his refusal the last possibility of government by the radicals disappeared.[33]

Why did Cattaneo decline to assume power at this vital moment? In the first place he was a reluctant leader of the revolutionary forces – on his own admission he felt that he had strayed too far from his true role as a publicist and academic. By contrast Manin, in these same days, did not hesitate to take absolute control among the Venetian revolutionaries. Cattaneo also placed too little faith in the Milanese lower classes. His limited, essentially middle-class concept of citizenship – before the revolution he had not been an advocate of adult male suffrage – deprived him of the possibility of seeing an alliance of democrats and populace as an alternative to monarchist rule.[34] In this he was fleeing from the logic of the insurrection, for it was just such an alliance that lay at the heart of its success. Cattaneo underestimated the support for a republic among those who were fighting, and, because of the whole history of leadership by the nobility, he did not believe that the Milanese could do without them at this moment. Above all Cattaneo wanted to avoid dissension while the street battle was still to be won – as he admitted himself, the political battle was lost through his furious insistence on concord at any price.

While in Venice Manin was preparing to take the arsenal and declare the republic, Cattaneo in Milan refused the gauntlet thrown down by Martini. Instead, he limited himself to the rallying cry of 'Fuori i barbari' – 'Out with the barbarians', and to planning the climax of the five days' fighting – the struggle for the Porta Tosa.

Seeing that Cattaneo was making no move, Casati, late on the evening of the 21st, decided to risk declaring his own provisional government. He was influenced in this decision by the moderate democrat Cesare Correnti. Correnti, ever since 17 March, had insisted that in the event of success it was better to allow the nobles to form a government, since 'the oven was hot and the first bread to be baked was bound to be burnt'.[35] This point of view was shared by many other democrats; the nobility had first to take power, and once discredited the republicans could take their place. But in retrospect it is possible to see that such arguments took little

[33] Cattaneo, *Dell'insurrezione*, p. 75.
[34] This point is particularly well made by Della Peruta, 'I contadini', p. 81. He also quotes (*ibid.*, p. 81 n. 3) an article entitled 'Miserere' written by Cernuschi in the Milanese newspaper *L'Operaio*, 20 July 1848: 'There were four of us in the council of war, Clerici, Cattaneo, Terzaghi and Cernuschi. Today we are accused of harbouring stupid ambitions, but then we were the very people who refused to take the power that was practically forced upon us from every quarter, because we did not believe that by ourselves we had enough credit and influence to create a strong, respected and lasting central authority.'
[35] *Archivio triennale*, vol. 1, p. 606: from Correnti's 'Memorie'.

account of the dynamics of the situation. The most favourable moment for the republicans was during the insurrection itself, when their actions had earned them the support of the combatants and the nobility had lost control of the movement. Once Charles Albert intervened the monarchists would be strengthened rather than weakened, and Casati's government would then only be likely to fall in the event of military catastrophe, the last thing that Correnti or any of the republicans wanted to see.

At dawn on 22 March Casati declared his provisional government, with himself as president, and a clear monarchist majority amongst its members. Only Correnti, who was appointed secretary, and Anselmo Guerrieri Gonzaga had republican sympathies. Cattaneo had little choice but to accept this *fait accompli*. He limited himself to asking Casati to create a new committee of war, which would group together all the anti-Austrian forces in the city. Casati agreed, Pompeo Litta was made its president, and its members were Cattaneo, Cernuschi, Terzaghi, Clerici, Carnevali, Lissoni, Ceroni and Torelli.[36] The committee then directed the final military victory of the Milanese as Radetzky withdrew with difficulty from the city.

The last important political proclamation of the *cinque giornate* came on the afternoon of the 22nd. The new government announced to the people,

As long as the struggle lasts it is not opportune to discuss the future political destinies of our beloved homeland. We have been summoned to gain our independence; and the courageous citizens of Milan must now concentrate only on fighting. Once the victory has been won, *a causa vinta*, our destinies will be discussed and decided by the nation.[37]

This declaration, which seemed superficially the only sensible policy to adopt, had the most wide-ranging political implications. Correnti has claimed the credit for it, affirming that it was the only way to prevent the other members of the new government from immediately dedicating Milan to Charles Albert.[38] But, given the political mood of the city, so hasty a fusion of Piedmont and Milan must in any event have been an impossibility.

In fact, Correnti had inadvertently strengthened the monarchists' hand,

---

[36] Cattaneo, *Dell'insurrezione*, p. 76. The committee of war thus united the council of war and the committee of defence. This last had been set up by Casati on the 20th to organise the civic guard and help maintain law and order in those parts of the city which were in the hands of the insurgents. The committee of defence could have endangered the unity of the Milanese military forces, but in fact it cooperated to the full with Cattaneo and his colleagues.

[37] Cattaneo, *Dell'insurrezione*, p. 77.

[38] Massarani, *Cesare Correnti*, p. 130.

for Casati and his colleagues had in one breath excluded the leading republicans from the government, and in the next declared all discussion at an end until the war was over. They had taken crucial political action, and had then denied their opponents, who, after all, were playing the leading part in the insurrection, the right of reply. The policy of *a guerra vinta*, although accepted by the republicans, served in objective terms to disarm them both in Milan and also, as we shall see, in Venice. Any attempt to raise the question of the form of government could now be dismissed as a breach of the political truce. Meanwhile Piedmont, presented with a professedly neutral Milan where political decisions were taboo but where the government's monarchist sympathies were thinly disguised, gained the chance of establishing in Lombardy, and ultimately in Venetia, its own political regime.

Cattaneo only realised at a later date the significance of these events. In September 1850 he wrote to Cernuschi:

When the young have the republic in mind, they will make it. Revolution is the execution of an idea. If there is no idea there can be no revolution. Our people had as their only idea *Via gli austriaci* and that which they had in mind was carried out. Then they could not go forward because no one, ourselves included, had given them any other idea to think about. In this we were all at fault. But we must see to it that we don't make the same mistake a second time.[39]

And in the *Archivio triennale* he commented: 'In most revolutions the masses do not support the audacity of their leaders; in this revolution it was the other way round: *the people were a sword of steel with a wooden point.*'[40]

Even at the time, the republicans made great efforts to regain the ground they had lost on the 22nd. On 25 March the committee of war ingeniously announced, 'the war is over; there remains only the chase', with the obvious intention of reopening the political question without appearing to have broken the truce.[41] Cattaneo found to his surprise that support for the republic was much stronger than he had imagined. G. Ponzio Vaglia, a Piedmontese envoy, wrote to Castagnetto on 31 March, 'the republican party is at the moment the dominant one among the Lombard people'.[42]

---

[39] Letter of 26 September 1850, published in F. Della Peruta, *I democratici e la rivoluzione italiana*, p. 426.
[40] *Archivio triennale*, vol. 1, p. 578.
[41] Depoli, *I rapporti*, vol. 1, p. 127 n. 49.
[42] Buttini and Avetta (eds.), *I rapporti fra il governo sardo*, p. 384. Many observers noted that republican feeling actually increased in the days after 22 March, as a consequence of the slowness of Charles Albert's intervention. Lazzaro Rebizzo,

Casati and the monarchists, however, had no intention of relinquishing the power they had so fortunately acquired. Unlike Avesani in Venice, the Milanese mayor decided that the unpopularity of his government would gradually disappear. He also estimated correctly that Cattaneo would do anything to prevent civil war. Slowly but surely the provisional government consolidated its position.[43] On 31 March the committee of war was dissolved, and by 12 April members of the provisional governments of the provincial cities, for the most part from the old municipal committees, had been incorporated into the new Lombard provisional government. Of these additions only Luigi Anelli for Lodi and Crema was a convinced republican.[44]

Enter Mazzini

The final death blow to republican hopes came with the attitude adopted by Giuseppe Mazzini on his arrival in Milan on 7 April 1848. Mazzini's reputation had declined considerably since the tragedy of the Bandieras' expedition, even though he had always denied knowledge of their intentions. None the less his influence in Milan remained extensive and some of the foremost republicans looked to him for a lead.[45]

While still in Paris Mazzini had made it clear that he believed independence and unity to be the primary objectives. In his view Charles Albert and his army had a decisive role to play in the coming struggles. On his

the official Piedmontese envoy to Venice, stopped at Milan on his way and sent this report of political feeling in the city: 'Everyone is talking of *union*, but each in his own way, and when I referred subtly to the best way for Italy, which is our way, they generally looked at me as if I was talking German' (dispatch of 4 April 1848 from Cremona, published in Depoli, *I rapporti*, vol. I, app. p. 263).

[43] Many observers, like Cesare Cantù, thought that a republic was bound to triumph eventually and failed to realise that power had already passed out of republican hands. Cantù wrote to Tommaseo on 27 March 1848, 'if the federal Italian republic is what you want how much I would like to serve under your flag! But here for the moment we must conceal this, because we need Charles Albert's sword and money from the nobles. We are at work, preparing public opinion' (MCV, Doc. Manin, no. 3853).

[44] Candeloro, *Storia dell'Italia moderna*, vol. 3, pp. 191–2. The government attempted to neutralise Cattaneo by offering him various jobs – special emissary to London, editor of the government's newspaper, general secretary to the minister of war. He refused them all, and wrote to a friend on 10 April 1848: 'Better to be a bird in the woods than a bird in a cage. I have plenty of time in which to choose: I don't want to lose the faith of the good and the courageous' (letter to Baron Anatole Brenier in R. Caddeo (ed.), *Epistolario di Carlo Cattaneo*, vol. I (1949), p. 246).

[45] For Mazzini's own account of these events, see his 'Royalty and Republicanism in Italy', in *Life and Writings of Joseph Mazzini*, vol. 5, pp. 41–155.

return to Milan, Mazzini therefore refused to join the other republicans in demanding immediate elections and a new government, but adhered instead to the political truce and the policy of *a guerra finita*. Between 1846 and 1848, as Salvemini has shown, Mazzini had consistently taken the line that an initial anti-Austrian front was essential.[46] In April 1848 he believed it the tactical duty of the republicans to fight alongside the monarchists. If and when independence was secure, then would be the time to resurrect republican propaganda and to wage the final battle against the moderate party and the Italian princes.

On 26 March 1848, the Mazzinian newspaper *La Voce del popolo* announced, 'Men of good faith, we are not going to circulate absolute principles on social and political questions'. As Murray has commented, 'as a man of absolute principles Cattaneo felt that this was not an auspicious contribution to the first day of a free press'.[47] Cattaneo insisted that freedom came before unity and that Lombardy's traditions and freedom could not be guaranteed in a unified, monarchist Italy. The republican party thus became divided, and had seriously declined in influence by the middle of April.

The Milanese democrats lost the battle for political power in their city during the *cinque giornate*. Their defeat meant Charles Albert's victory. The Piedmontese trod gingerly towards Milan, professing principles of the utmost altruism and patriotism, realising how necessary it was to reassure the Milanese of their good intentions. Charles Albert's first actions implied a complete acceptance of the political truce proclaimed by Casati's government. On 23 March the Piedmontese king declared to the peoples of Lombardy and Venetia that he was marching to offer that aid which 'a brother expects from a brother, a friend from a friend'.[48] His minister of foreign affairs, Lorenzo Pareto, wrote that 'His Majesty's Government, by its armed intervention in the Lombard war, has nothing else in mind but the expulsion of the Austrians from Italy, and wishes to avoid becoming involved in questions of internal politics.'[49]

However, at the same time, Charles Albert justified his intervention to Austria and England on the grounds of the need to prevent the Lombard revolution from developing in a republican manner which would endanger the peace of Italy and his own dynasty. Candeloro has commented acutely

[46] G. Salvemini, 'Giuseppe Mazzini dall'aprile 1846 all'aprile 1848', in his *Scritti sul Risorgimento*, pp. 255–82.

[47] Murray, 'Carlo Cattaneo', p. 39.

[48] For the complete text of the proclamation see Candeloro, *Storia dell'Italia moderna*, pp. 180–1.

[49] AST, sez. I, carte politiche diverse, cart. 26, fasc. 153, letter of 31 March 1848.

that the king's battle cry of 'Italia farà da sé' – 'Italy will go it alone' – derived as much from the need to prevent Lombardy and the Veneto from calling in the French as it did from sentiments of Italian national-ism.[50] The assumptions underlying Charles Albert's entering the war are clearly revealed in a letter from Pareto to the king in the first week of the campaign:

Sire, we are awaiting with anxiety for the moment when you will announce the news that the army commanded by your Majesty has at last encountered the enemy and has put them to rout; this result, which I think inevitable if the enemy risks halting its retreat, will be, I dare to hope, the best argument to persuade every dissenter of the desirability of the intimate union of Lombardy and Piedmont, a union which can alone guarantee the future of our beloved Fatherland.[51]

What would have happened if the Milanese council of war had declared a republic? It seems likely that Charles Albert would have been forced into the war in any event, and that, confronted with a republican Lom-bardy as well as a republican Venice, he would have been obliged to limit his programme, at least initially, to one of fraternal aid. On 31 March Pareto wrote to his brother in Milan: 'In the case of the provisional government being deposed and our running the risk of a republic being declared, here it has been decided that we must nevertheless continue with the same measures.'[52] But once Casati and his colleagues had assumed power in Milan and the republicans had consented to their doing so, a policy aimed at the annexation of Lombardy was the natural next step for the Piedmontese.

The effect on Venice

The news from Milan exercised a great influence on Manin's thinking and the development of the Venetian revolution. Instead of the Milanese insurrection ending in the proclamation of a sister republic, Manin found that his own declaration of the republic had been a unilateral action and was viewed with little sympathy by the new Milanese government. Fear-ing lest he might have jeopardised the unity of the Italian anti-Austrian forces, Manin decided to adopt wholeheartedly the Milanese government's policy of *a guerra finita si deciderà*. He remained a republican, but instead of proceeding to tighten the bonds of the new Venetian state which had

[50] Candeloro, *Storia dell'Italia moderna*, vol. 3, p. 181.
[51] AST, sez. I, carte politiche diverse, cart. 26, fasc. 153. Letter undated, but almost certainly of 31 March 1848. Refers to having just received news of the king's arrival in Pavia, which took place on 29 March at 4 p.m.
[52] Buttini and Avetta, *I rapporti fra il governo sardo*, p. 50.

been established by 1 April, he preferred to stop abruptly in his tracks and to suspend all further decisions about Venice's internal form of government until the end of the war. In this way he hoped to soften the impact of the positive republican action he had taken during the days of the revolution, and to demonstrate that Venice, like Milan, had no wish to damage the Italian cause. Politics were not to interfere with the military effort, in which a brotherhood of Italian states would fight side by side.

Given the importance of this decision, it is of some interest to trace its gestation. During the first week of the revolution Manin received a large number of letters, mostly from Milan, and nearly all stressing the need to unite in the face of the enemy and to delay further political decisions until the Austrians had been defeated. The first dispatch to Venice from Casati and his colleagues, dated 25 March, expressed the hope that 'in constituting a new government, you will have thought of Italian unity. "Independence and Unity", these must be the solemn words on our lips.'[53] Two days later the provisional government of Modena wrote to Venice that 'the assembly of Italian states, once the field has been cleared to allow the wishes of the country to be made known, will shortly decide on the form of our government'.[54]

The most important letters were to Manin himself, from two members of the Milanese provisional government, Count Giuseppe Durini and Gaetano Strigelli. Durini, addressing Manin first as *mio caro* and then as *carissimo*, wrote:

You will understand that the recognised necessity of Piedmontese aid to finish the war has determined us to leave untouched the question of the correct form of government. We could not hope for aid from a sovereign in whose face we waved the republican flag. I say 'recognised necessity' because, in spite of all the heroism that the Lombards have shown, and the Milanese in particular ... it is not reasonable to hope that we can resist a regular army ... Does it not seem fair that a constituent assembly should meet to decide the fate of the nation in a definite manner? ... I speak to you like this because I do not want us to repeat our previous history ... We are now waiting for you to act so that the whole nation can be consulted and so that you do not deprive the nation of this right by opting for one system of government rather than another ... the king arrives at Pavia tomorrow and will put himself at the head of military operations; he will not return his sword to its sheath until the Austrians are beyond the Alps. We have established that he is and must

---

[53] Planat de la Faye (ed.), *Documenti*, vol. 1, pp. 175–6.
[54] Racc. Andreola, vol. 1, p. 317. In Parma and Modena, both dukes were forced to leave, Francis V of Modena on 21 March and Charles II of Parma on 13 April. But in both the duchies the liberal monarchists were far stronger than the republicans, and were able to dominate the new provisional governments; see Candeloro, *Storia dell'Italia moderna*, vol. 3, pp. 203–5.

remain a simple ally . . . We have acted as one sovereign state in liaison with another.[55]

Strigelli's letter of the 27th was much shorter and far ruder, a diatribe against municipal *Kleinstaaterei*: 'As for you, what do you mean to do? Do you want to be a Hamburg, a Lübeck, a primeval Venice?'[56] Jacopo Pezzato, a faithful friend of Manin's in Milan, who was later to become his secretary, warned him on 28 March:

Here the proclamation of the republic at Venice has aroused displeasure. Everyone fears that Venice wants to detach itself from the Italian family so as to return to the particularism of the republic of St Mark . . . the republic is desired by everyone . . . but this provisional government could not and must not declare it. The Sardinian troops would not have marched into our territory to throw the common enemy out of Italy if they had been summoned by a republican government. Charles Albert loves his throne too much, and we need the Piedmontese troops . . .[57]

Only one letter appears to have reached Manin in these days which expressed the opposite point of view. It too is quoted at length, for in juxtaposition with the letters above, it seems to summarise the whole political and military debate of these early days. R. Berlinghieri, a Florentine democrat, wrote on 27 March:

If we are not mistaken, Sicily must already have proclaimed a republican government and at Naples there must shortly be a revolution. Genoa will only wait a few days before imitating her sister Venice. We democrats and republicans are laying plans for our own country . . . Above all else do not allow yourselves, in the name of God, to be deceived by Charles Albert and the princes – hold firm and you will triumph. We are all waiting anxiously to see what Milan will decide. God prevent the Milanese . . . from throwing themselves into the arms of those who now wish to profit from the fruit of their heroic sacrifices . . . But whatever happens, if Venice holds firm, Italy will be saved.[58]

[55] MCV, Agg. Manin, xiii/fasc. 3, no. 2, letter of 28 March 1848. A second, shorter letter, of less importance followed on the 29th; *ibid.*, xiii/fasc. 3, no. 1. Durini (b. 1800) was a lawyer educated at Pavia university who became an Austrian civil servant but then resigned because of his aversion to the Austrian government.

[56] *Ibid.*, xiii/fasc. 3, pt. 2.

[57] *Ibid.*, xiii/fasc. 8, no. 1. Pezzato, according to La Forge, had helped Manin in 1831 to produce the subversive leaflet in Venice after the insurrections in the Romagna. They also worked closely together during the railway question.

[58] MCV, Doc. Manin, no. 3864, letter addressed to Giovanni Carrer in Venice, who sent it to Manin. Berlinghieri was born at Siena in 1795, and was one of the most ardent democrats in Tuscany during 1848–9. For some details of his activities, see C. Ronchi, *I democratici fiorentini nella rivoluzione del 1848–9*, p. 167 n. 58, p. 192, p. 213 and n. 75.

Manin did not see the problem in Berlinghieri's terms, and was far more responsive to the appeals of the Milanese provisional government. On 26 March, probably having received news of the government's action in Milan, Manin wrote to them, 'When the sacred earth of our country is no longer overrun by the foreign oppressors, we will act in concord to establish whatever shall be to our communal profit and glory.'[59] On the following day an article appeared in the Venetian government's newspaper, the *Gazzetta di Venezia*, emphasising the need to delay all further political decisions: 'first we must make sure we continue to exist; then we can begin to think of our conditions of existence'.[60]

By 30 March 1848 it had become clear that Manin meant to adopt the policy of *a guerra finita*. The next problem was to get his fellow ministers to agree. Castelli and Paleocapa at this stage wanted to see the links between the provinces and the capital firmly cemented, so as to allay the suspicions of the departmental committees. On 29 March, at the meeting of the Venetian ministers, they urged the immediate convocation of a Venetian constituent assembly. Manin at first agreed, and it was decided that three councillors from each province should meet in Venice on 5 April 1848, to draw up electoral laws by the end of the month.[61]

Two days later, however, Manin declared his unequivocal hostility to the idea, and came out strongly in favour of delay:

The President [Manin] expressed the opinion that the future of Venice must not be determined until after the expulsion of the Austrians. This was also desired in Lombardy where the proclamation of a republic in Venice had not met with approval... He believed it would be better to nominate a council [from the provinces] which would assist the government.[62]

Tommaseo, Castelli and Paleocapa all expressed their opposition, but Manin, because of his quasi-dictatorial status in Venice at this time, was able to make his policy prevail over the wishes of the other ministers.

---

[59] In 1848 it took 36 hours to get from Milan to Venice. We must allow slightly longer at this time, since it was necessary to circumvent the Quadrilateral. On the Milan–Venice diligence, see Greenfield, *Economics and Liberalism*, p. 66. The minutes of Manin's letter of 26 March are to be found in MCV, Doc. Manin no. 1004. The original letter was in the Archivio Casati at Milan, but has now been destroyed. The letter of 26 March was the second communication of the Venetian government to Milan. The first, written a day earlier, stressed how much municipal discord belonged to the past, and asked what intentions 'rich, beautiful and loyal Lombardy' had for its future destiny; see Planat de la Faye (ed.), *Documenti*, vol. 1, p. 176.

[60] Article reprinted in Racc. Andreola, vol. 1, pp. 173–6.

[61] A. Ventura (ed.), *Verbali*, pp. 87–8. Unfortunately, the minutes of the ministerial meetings are much less complete than might have been hoped.

[62] *Ibid.*, p. 90.

Castelli now had to modify the decree which he had already prepared for the political structure of the Venetian state.[63] The calling of the constituent assembly was postponed indefinitely, and a consultative council from the provinces, the *consulta*, was to meet in Venice instead. This *consulta* was to have advisory powers only.

Manin thus compromised with the independent republican action he had taken on 22 March. It was the first of a number of occasions on which he clearly placed united Italian action above his republican principles. He did not fully trust Charles Albert, but he was not prepared to make Venice the centre of republican opposition to the Italian princes. Milan's clearly stated policy of *a guerra finita* seemed to Manin to assure the Italians of the prospect of each state fighting side by side until the Austrians had been defeated. Manin accepted Durini's argument, which was also Mazzini's, that Charles Albert's army was indispensable to secure northern Italy. By postponing all political decisions it seemed possible to gain the aid of this army without compromising the future, without having to abandon the possibility of a Venetian republic within a federal Italy. Unfortunately, as we shall see, the Venetian republic, once declared, had either to be sustained or abandoned; Manin tried to do both, with disastrous results.

Tommaseo, both at the time and in retrospect, realised that Manin's policy was misconceived. His intransigent republicanism made him sceptical of the value of Piedmontese aid. He wrote to Cantù at the end of March 1848:

We have no other princes to rely upon save those of Savoy: and in the long run they will be unable to satisfy not only the Lombards and the Venetians, but also the Genoese and the Sardinians. Thus they would only open the way to new revolutions. The republic seems inevitable to me if we are to avoid succumbing again to absolute monarchy.[64]

---

[63] Castelli had previously written this preface to the decree: 'Considering the urgency of convoking the constituent assembly and thus interrogating the wishes of the [Venetian] nation so that a permanent government can succeed the provisional one...' On 31 March he replaced it with the following: 'Notwithstanding the urgency for the convocation of the constituent assembly... it is nevertheless in keeping with the spirit of Italian nationalism that we have adopted ... and with our debt of love and respect for heroic Lombardy and our other sisters, that we should wait until they can announce their intentions on the political structure to be deemed most convenient, brotherly and permanent for lands that have common sufferings, sentiments and needs.' See *La Repubblica veneta nel 1848–9*, ed. Il comitato regionale veneto per la celebrazione centenaria del 1848–9, vol. i, *Documenti diplomatici*, pp. 585–6.

[64] MCV, Agg. Manin, xlviii, Tommaseo's unpublished work, 'Venezia, l'Italia, e l'Europa', pt. ii, fo. 18. This work, in five parts, contains all the decrees, letters, etc., collected or written by Tommaseo during the course of the revolution.

Even if the Piedmontese were to beat the Austrians it mattered little to Tommaseo, for Charles Albert 'supported liberty as if it were a ball and chain attached to his foot'.[65] However, it would have been impossible for Tommaseo's opinion to prevail in Venice at this time. Manin's supremacy went unquestioned, and the other ministers acquiesced in his leadership.

The consequences

French aid

The events in Milan and their effect on Manin had a number of crucial results. The first of these was the abandonment of the idea of appealing to the French republic to intervene in northern Italy, a policy that had been clearly emphasised in Manin's prison notes, and one which he was never completely to discard. The failure to declare a republic in Milan, Manin's agreement to a united front against the Austrians, and the widespread acceptance of Charles Albert's battle cry of *Italia farà da sé*, meant that any appeal by Venice for French intervention, with its obvious republican inference, was out of the question. Manin confined himself to sending two envoys to Paris, Zanardini and Nani, to buy arms and request a warship. Zanardini, in his first audience with Lamartine on 9 April 1848, warned him that the unanimous cry amongst the Italians was 'Get the foreigners out of Italy' and that 'the appearance of foreigners under whatever banner and with whatever programme could only be fatal for us'.[66] The Milanese took a similar line. On 27 March Luigi Porro was sent to Toulon to purchase arms, and at the same time the Milanese provisional government wrote to Paris requesting 'the government of the bravest and most generous nation in the world to find the means to aid us in these exceptionally difficult circumstances'.[67] These words created some impression both in Paris and in English diplomatic circles, where they were interpreted as a possible appeal for French republican intervention. In fact the letter as a whole does not have this intention, and ends with the words, 'We will not add anything else, as we do not wish to give a political significance to this appeal.'[68]

[65] R. Ciampini, *Vita di Nicolò Tommaseo*, p. 432. Exact reference not quoted by the author.

[66] See the letter of Zanardini to the Venetian government recalling his first conversation with Lamartine, 10 May 1848 (MCV, Doc. Manin, vol. 9, no. 55).

[67] The full text of the letter is to be found in *Archivio triennale*, vol. 2, pp. 1903–4. A few details of Porro's mission are to be found in MRM, atti del gov. prov. del 1848, fasc. 15, nos. 60–3.

[68] For Abercromby's alarm at Turin, see R. Mosca, *Le relazioni del governo provvisorio di Lombardia con i governi d'Italia e di Europa*, p. 146. See also R. Moscati, *La diplomazia europea e il problema italiano nel 1848*, pp. 13–14.

Lamartine, in any case, had little intention of intervening in northern Italy if he could help it. On 28 March 1848 he told Mazzini that if Italian arms alone did not suffice to defend the revolution, France offered 'her sword to preserve Italy from any invasion . . . We desire no conquests except with you and on your behalf . . . We have no ambitions except in the realm of ideas.'[69] But at the same time he instructed Bixio, the French representative at Turin, to give confidence and authority to the constitutional and liberal party in Italy, rather than to the republicans, whose policies he judged ruinous for Italian emancipation.[70] The more Charles Albert came to appear as the dominant force in the Italian war, the more the French government had to come to terms with the prospect of a greatly enlarged dynastic kingdom on their eastern borders. Far from pursuing a policy of republican aid to northern Italy, Lamartine began to lay plans for a rapprochement with Charles Albert, based on compensation for France in the form of Nice and Savoy, in return for French acquiescence in the establishment of a kingdom of upper Italy.[71]

However, had things gone differently in Milan in March, and had the Lombards and Venetians launched a concerted republican appeal for French aid, the French government might have found it difficult to resist pressure to intervene on their behalf. Parisian public opinion in the early

Lodovico Frapolli, an ardent republican, was sent as the Lombard emissary to Paris, but was limited in what he could do by the hostility of the Lombard provisional government to any idea of French armed intervention; see M. Menghini, *Lodovico Frapolli e le sue missioni diplomatiche a Parigi, 1848–9.*

[69] Speech to the Italian national association, reprinted in Racc. Andreola, vol. 1, pp. 413–17.

[70] See Boyer, *La seconde République*, p. 65. Louis Blanc, though far to the left of Lamartine on home affairs, shared his desire not to intervene to aid the republicans in northern Italy. Mazzini, writing to George Sand on 4 Sept. 1850, recalled an illuminating conversation he had had with Blanc in Paris at the end of March 1848: 'I spoke to him of Europe, and he replied by talking about France and the organisation of labour. I said to him that France could only be saved by intervening in Europe, and he told me that he did not want a European war because it would produce another Napoleon. In any case, he maintained, the great contribution that France had to offer Europe was the organisation of labour; as if the organisation of labour could be achieved in one country alone!' (see E. Passerin d'Entrèves, 'Qualche ulteriore riflessione sull'amicizia tra Mazzini e George Sand', in *Mazzini e i repubblicani italiani. Studi in onore di Terenzio Grandi*, p. 235).

[71] For these plans, see the most recent and carefully documented account of French foreign policy at this time: L. C. Jennings, *France and Europe in 1848*, pp. 88ff; see also A. de Lamartine, *Histoire de la révolution de 1848*, vol. 1, pp. 282–3. For the situation in Paris see MCV, Doc. Manin, vol. 9, no. 26, dispatch of Nani and Zanardini, 30 April 1848, warning the Venetians to expect nothing from the French leaders, as they were threatened by the 'communist party' in the city.

months of the revolution was very much in favour of an intervention in northern Italy. The clubs and newspapers of the left spoke out strongly in favour of spreading the revolution abroad, and aiding both Poland and Italy.[72] On 7 April the French government fanned the flames of speculation by announcing the formation of the army of the Alps, ready to descend into Italy should the need arise. The moderate republicans like Lamartine did not want to use this army, but their principal means of countering the rising tide of interventionist agitation was to point out the hostility of the Italians themselves, including the Lombardo-Venetians, to the idea of the French marching into Italy.

Events reached a climax in Paris in May 1848. On the 15th a massive but confused popular demonstration marched to the national assembly to hand in a petition in favour of French intervention in Poland. The deputies that day were in the midst of discussing both Italy and Poland. The pro-Italian D'Aragon opened the proceedings by asking Lamartine if he would assure the nation that the executive committee was ready for the day when the Italians finally invoked French aid. Wolowski then spoke in favour of Poland and it was during his speech that the demonstrators invaded the national assembly. Their leaders were deeply divided over the course of action to pursue, but for a few hours a new revolutionary government was set up. This proved to be the supreme challenge to the French moderate republicans, both on an internal and an international level. But the *journée* was ill-conceived and totally disorganised. By the evening the national guard had dispersed the demonstrators and the leaders of the left were arrested.[73]

This failure, though, served as a catalyst for Lamartine. At a secret meeting of the five-man French executive committee on 19 and 20 May, he strongly argued for immediate intervention in northern Italy, as the only means by which the whole French nation could be united behind the government. According to Jennings, this was the closest that the French

---

[72] See Jennings, *France and Europe*, pp. 80–1 for the attitude of the Parisian clubs; also the articles in the Parisian newspapers *Le Vrai Père Duchêne*, nos. 1 and 4, 21 and 28 May 1848; and *Le Tocsin des Travailleurs*, no. 2, June 1848.

[73] P. Amann, 'A Journée in the making: May 15 1848', *Journal of Modern History*, 42 (1970), pp. 42–69; L. A. Garnier Pagès, *Histoire de la Révolution de 1848*, vol. 9, pp. 175–266. See also Zanardini's letter to Manin on 15 May 1848, MCV, Doc. Manin, vol. 9, no. 62. Zanardini was an eye-witness to the events, having been inside the national assembly at the time. He wrote: 'Between 100 and 150,000 workers marched on the Assembly, under the pretext of presenting a petition in favour of Poland ... I cannot describe the hideous spectacle ... After three hours of being nearly suffocated I managed to get out ... This evening there are predictions of burnings, barricades, pillaging and other such niceties – poor, poor France and poor liberty!'

republic of 1848 came to going to war.[74] The main objection of the other members of the commission was that the Piedmontese would regard the French action as an invasion. Direct intervention in Piedmont itself could have been avoided by embarking troops at Marseilles and sailing them round Italy to Venice. This was a project which, as we shall see, the French were to take very seriously later in the year. But even then it had to be conceded that the Lombardo-Venetians were unlikely to give the French any warmer a welcome, for they too were committed to the idea of *Italia farà da sé*. After a prolonged discussion Lamartine withdrew his suggestion, agreeing that the hostility of the northern Italians made intervention an impossibility. On 23 May, in his speech to the assembly on the Italian question, Lamartine read out a letter sent to him by the Lombard representative in Paris, Lodovico Frapolli. Frapolli, writing in the name of both Lombardy *and* Venice, made it explicit that both states were opposed to French intervention, for 'reasons of national sentiment'.[75]

Clearly, many factors prevented the French from intervening at this critical moment – Piedmontese opposition, unwillingness to become involved in a European war, an overriding preoccupation with the situation in Paris. But the lack of a call for aid from the republicans of Lombardy and Venetia should not be underestimated in this context. The absence of any such appeal was an important means by which the moderate French republicans could get off the hook, and an important obstacle on 19 May to Lamartine's plans for intervention. In this way the essentially monarchist solution to the political crisis of the *cinque giornate* of Milan cast its long shadow over the prospect of international republican action.

The Venetian provinces

Another, very different consequence of the decisions taken by Manin in the first fortnight of the revolution was the alienation of the provincial committees of the Veneto. The establishment of the *consulta* instead of a full-scale constituent assembly, stemming as it did from Manin's delaying tactics, meant that the provincial leadership had no effective voice within the Venetian government. Instead of being wooed by every possible means, the provincial committees, already alarmed at the possible social implications of the republic,[76] and mindful of Venice's traditional dominance of the *terraferma*, were now offered the tiny and insufficient political morsel of the advisory council. As Tommaseo wrote later, 'such a council,

---

[74] Jennings, *France and Europe*, p. 106. For the meeting of 19–20 May, see Garnier Pagès, *Histoire de la Révolution*, vol. 10, pp. 6–9. Lamartine's point of view was strengthened by the clear British commitment in the spring of 1848 not to get involved even if France entered the war in northern Italy (*ibid.*, p. 72).

[75] Garnier Pagès, *Histoire de la Révolution*, vol. 10, p. 10.

[76] See below, pp. 191 ff.

particularly emanating from a government that called itself republican, was a sort of bad joke'.[77]

The provinces, particularly Padua and Treviso, responded with controlled anger. Both committees immediately petitioned Venice to be allowed to send one or two representatives to become part of the actual Venetian government. Manin refused. The official reason given was that to incorporate members from the provinces into the Venetian government would have been to give it too permanent an appearance, at a time when Manin was trying to stress its provisional nature and to adhere to the political truce.[78] But Manin's refusal was widely interpreted, both at the time and later, as stemming from a desire to prevent the republican group in the government being swamped by moderate representatives from the provinces.[79] It was pointed out, with some justice, that the Milanese had incorporated the Lombard provinces into their new government without it becoming any the less 'provisional'. Certainly, whatever Manin's motives – and the evidence is not conclusive – his creation of the *consulta* showed great insensitivity towards the provincial ruling classes. On 24 March he had assured them that there would be no 'disparity of rights' in the new republic, but he had gone back on his word within a week.

As it was, only the provincial committee of Belluno reacted to the news of the *consulta* by expressing its continued faith in the republic. The other committees, particularly Padua, Treviso and Vincenza, had stressed from the outset the need not to separate the destinies of the Veneto and the rest of Italy. They began to suspect that Manin was doing exactly this, creating a stronghold of republicanism in Venice, and keeping all power in his own hands. Although they had adhered to the republic, these provincial committees started to look to Lombardy and Piedmont for political opinions more in line with their own. In the first days of April Count Sugana of Treviso arrived at Charles Albert's headquarters to stress unofficially the desire of the Veneto for political union with Lombardy and Piedmont. Count Castagnetto wrote to Casati on 8 April 1848, 'it seems to me that the Veneto desires to put itself completely in agreement with Lombardy'.[80]

The problem of self-defence

Even so, Manin need not have lost the Venetian provinces for the republic had he been able to evolve a coherent military strategy. But in the first

[77] Tommaseo, *Venezia*, vol. 1, p. 154 n. 407.
[78] See Ferrari, 'L'attitudine di Padova', p. 204.
[79] See, for example, Ventura (ed.), *Verbali*, p. 56. However plausible this explanation, it is perhaps worth pointing out that there is no written evidence to support it.
[80] Ferrari (ed.), *Carteggio Casati–Castagnetto*, p. 38. For the mission of Count Sugana, see Depoli, *I rapporti*, vol. 1, p. 99.

month of the revolution the Venetian government did little or nothing to plan a vigorous defence of the new republic. Here too, in this most critical of areas, the destiny of Milan and the entry of Charles Albert into the war weighed heavily on the pattern of events in the Veneto. With the creation of a united front against the Austrians, Manin, far from tackling the organisation of a Venetian army, looked increasingly for salvation to the dynastic armies first of Charles Albert, and then later of Rome and Naples. Tommaseo, towards the end of his life, savagely exposed the contradiction in Manin's policy at this time: 'A few days after having raised the cry of the republic, he [Manin] asked for the help of one king, then another and finally a third.'[81] Unlike the Hungarians later in the year, the Venetians could and did look elsewhere than their own cities and countryside for protection from the counter-revolution. Putting his own republicanism into cold storage, welcoming the aid of dynastic armies in the name of the Italian nation, Manin was never forced to analyse the fundamental problem of self-defence until the Italian monarchies had either retired or been defeated. By then it was too late.

In attempting to explain why Manin adopted this line, which was to prove so disastrous, traditional historiography has tended to concentrate on three major points; the lack of any other alternative, given the impossibility of building a Venetian army in the time available; the ruinous effect of the political divisions and municipalism of the Italians; and the all-pervasive euphoria of the Venetians in March and early April, which prevented them from tackling the military problems until it was too late. It is worth taking these in turn, for though each contains undoubted elements of truth, they have tended to obscure as much as they have revealed.

The classic statement of the first point comes from G. M. Trevelyan: 'it is open to question whether either Chatham or Carnot could have called forth an army in so short a time, among a population eminently civilian in its habits'.[82] The creation of a popular army was, without doubt, fraught with difficulty, and the Venetians had little time to gather their forces before the Austrians counter-attacked. It is also true that there was no obvious candidate of outstanding military ability to whom the Venetians could entrust the task of organising their defence. But it is equally undeniable that Venice had sufficient men and equipment to create a far more formidable military force than she did. Quite apart from the numerous civic guards, five battalions of the Austrian army in the Veneto went over to the republic during the March days. It is difficult to believe that Manin would have let the majority of them return to their homes at the end of March if he had not already heard that Charles Albert had entered

[81] Tommaseo, *Venezia*, vol. 1, p. 53.
[82] Trevelyan, *Manin and the Venetian Revolution*, p. 136.

Lombardy with 60,000 men. These soldiers could have formed the nucleus of a republican army, augmented by those who had already done military service. It was absurd to talk of an 'eminently civilian' population when, by the most conservative of estimates, there were well over 60,000 men in the Veneto who had done eight years' military service in the Austrian army.[83] As Beltrame had reported, thirty to forty men in each commune in central Friuli knew how to shoot, and much the same must have been true of other parts of the Veneto. The peasants hated Austrian conscription, but previous historians have tended to assume from this that they would on no account fight for the republic. The evidence from the provinces in the early days of the revolution suggests the opposite. The peasantry, as has been seen, flocked to join the national guards, and in quite a few areas a mobile guard was spontaneously formed, ready to obey the government's orders. There was a shortage of officers, because so many of the middle class had bought their way out of conscription, but the men were there.

So were the arms. The Austrians had taken their arms with them, but had been forced to leave behind in the Venetian arsenal some 30,000 muskets, as well as a large number of cannon. A large number of the muskets had been distributed at random during the chaotic days of 22 and 23 March, some of them disappearing into the Ghetto where the Jews feared a resurgence of anti-semitism. Yet energetic action by the government could quickly have recovered most of them. Even without them, there were 13,000 muskets and pistols, with plenty of ammunition, left in the arsenal at the end of the first week of the revolution.[84] If the Venetians had been left alone to face the Austrians, it is difficult to accept that they would not have made better use of these resources.

On the second point it has been a commonplace of Risorgimento historiography to declare that the war in northern Italy was lost because of 'an orgy of political planning',[85] and that political disaffection ruined

[83] This figure is based on the assumption that about 3,000 men were called up each year in the years 1820–40. In fact, during crisis years like those of 1830–2, the figure was much higher. Many of those called up after 1840 were serving in other parts of the empire when the revolutions of 1848 broke out.

[84] See MCV, Doc. Manin, no. 3940, 'Prospetto delle quantità e qualità delle armi e munizioni da guerra somministrate alle provincie e comuni dal 18 marzo a tutto 20 giugno 1848'. This estimates arms lost between 22 and 25 March at around 10,000. G. Ulloa, in his *Guerre de l'indépendance italienne, 1848–9*, vol. 1, p. 63, writes that there were originally 36,000 muskets. Manin himself, in the ministerial meeting of 3 April 1848, refers to 'about 20,000 stolen and hidden' (Ventura (ed.), *Verbali*, p. 95). For the muskets going to the Ghetto, see the letter from Mengaldo to the government, 3 April 1848 (ASV, Gov. Prov. 1848–9, MG, b. 127, no. 257).

[85] A. J. Whyte, *The Evolution of Modern Italy*, p. 63.

the military effort against the Austrians. It is conceivable that had all northern Italy dedicated itself without delay to Charles Albert, the Piedmontese would have waged a more decisive campaign against the Austrians. But it is clear that in both Milan and Venice, far from sowing discord, the political opponents of Charles Albert went to great lengths to ensure a unity of military action. In Milan the determination of the council of war not to split the Milanese forces was one of the principal reasons for their political defeat. In Venice, Manin's adoption of the policy of *a guerra vinta* was the clearest proof he could give of not wanting political principles to interfere with the war effort. It is true that initially he was reluctant to ask Piedmont for officers or a general.[86] But within days he had changed his mind, and from then on made every effort to secure the effective intervention of Piedmontese and papal troops in the defence of the Veneto. On this account, it seems possible to reprove Manin for taking too little independent action, not too much.

There is considerable substance to the third point. Euphoria did blind many Venetians to the true gravity of the military situation. Manin stated in the ministerial meeting of 28 March that 'time alone, even without any fighting, will induce the Austrians to leave the ex-kingdom of Lombardy-Venetia'.[87] The news of monarchist aid undoubtedly accentuated the exaggerated, if understandable, optimism of the first month of the revolution. However, from Venice itself and especially from the provinces came frequent warnings, even in these early days, not to neglect the building of an army. The Venetian newspaper *l'Indipendente* demanded in its issue of 1 April that the government call up the last three years of Austrian conscripts. As early as 25 March the Paduan departmental committee urged Venice to give serious consideration to a general arming of the people for the purposes of defence. The Trevisan departmental committee was particularly active and perspicacious on this issue. On 28 March it warned Venice of the build-up of Austrian forces on the eastern frontier, and urged that the maximum number of men be sent to Udine immediately. On 13 April it stressed the great danger of reinforcements reaching Radetzky at Verona by marching through the Veneto, and on 20 April it sent Venice a detailed plan for the formation of an army of fifteen thousand men. Specific proposals came even from the province of Rovigo, where Giovanni Battista Oriani, the captain of the civic guard of Adria, wrote on 26 April 1848:

[86] The minutes of the Venetian ministerial meeting of 28 March 1848 read: 'Manin observed that this was a political question and that the request should not be made officially' (Ventura (ed.), *Verbali*, p. 83).

[87] *Ibid.*, p. 85.

The best course of action is to form an organised national army in the Venetian provinces. We must not be frightened by the lack of time. In 1813, in a matter of days, an army of conscripts was collected and trained, and, fighting to sustain despotism, they were among the soldiers who won the glorious battles of Lutzen and Bautzen. Why should it not be possible to obtain the same results now, when we are fighting to preserve our liberty? ... Order immediately a levy of one soldier per hundred population ... in this way, we could, in a short time, make up for the lack of regular troops, and assemble an army of more than 20,000 men.[88]

Far from being blind to the dangers, many of the provincial leaders seemed acutely aware of them.

The fundamental reason for the Venetians' failure to use the resources at their disposal would seem to lie not with the absolute impossibility of the task, or political factiousness, or even all-pervasive euphoria, but rather with the very nature of their republicanism. The reliance on monarchist aid was only the clearest expression of the deep-rooted moderation of the Venetian republicans, their lack of experience, and their exclusively urban view of the revolution.

None of the Venetian leaders took the Jacobin example for their model. Trotsky, in a telling phrase, described the German Frankfurt assembly of 1848 as 'shabbily wise with the experience of the French bourgeoisie',[89] and this applied to the Venetian government as well. Calucci, the Venetian representative in Milan, spoke for them all when he revealed his fears of what he took to be the events of 1793–4:

I too know that in 1793 a small part of France fought and won against the principal European powers and the rest of France put together; but who amongst us would welcome the bloodthirsty enthusiasm of Paris and the means used to arouse it? Who amongst us would welcome a committee of public safety which was prepared to send thousands of citizens to their deaths if they showed themselves less than willing to take up arms?[90]

The apparent ruthlessness of the Jacobins in organising a popular army appalled the Venetian republicans, and made them favour the more civilised alternative of Charles Albert's aid. This was particularly true of ministers like Castelli and Paleocapa who supported the republic more because it evoked ancient and glorious traditions than because it enshrined popular sovereignty.

[88] MCV, Doc. Pell., b. xxxviii/ii (7). For Padua's advice, ASV, Gov. Prov. 1848–9, MG, b. 127, no. 142. For Treviso's letters of 28 March, 13 and 20 April, see respectively ASV, Gov. 1848–9, MG, b. 127, no. 42; *ibid.*, CPD, b. 823/Belluno, no. 864; and A. Santalena, *Treviso nel 1848*, pp. 89–90.
[89] L. Trotsky, *Results and Prospects*, p. 187.
[90] Calucci to Castelli, 25 June 1848, in *La Repubblica veneta*, vol. 1, p. 665.

At the heart of the problem lay the relationship between the central government and the peasantry. In order to have built a popular army, the Venetian leaders would have had to ensure not only urban support but also, as the Jacobins had done in 1793, active peasant participation. An alliance with the peasantry of this sort would have called into question the social conditions of the peasantry, and what concessions could be made to persuade them to fight for the new republic. But such a policy of necessity raised the spectre of class conflict in the countryside. Many of the men of the Venetian chamber of commerce, with whom Manin had worked in the pre-revolutionary years, and who were now giving active financial backing to the republic, were themselves wealthy landowners. The inaccessibility or dispersal of the papers of men like Treves, Reali and Papadopoli makes it impossible to have concrete proof of what they thought on the question. However, they were hardly likely to favour a military strategy which threatened the social stability of the countryside, or gave rise to demands for land by the *braccianti*.

Such attitudes contrasted with those at a local level, where there is evidence to show that far from being afraid of the peasantry, the middle strata of rural society seemed confident of their control over them. The inter-class nature of the rural civic guards was the first and eloquent testimony to this. Many communal deputations posed the problem not so much in terms of an *alliance* with the peasantry, but how best to *use* them. The representatives of the little village of Susegana made this clear in a letter of 6 April 1848:

The peasant is an agricultural instrument. Well handled, he performs splendidly. Left to himself he does nothing. To request the local authorities to move him with persuasion, with blandishments, or even with force, is to fail to understand the situation. What is needed is an edict from on high; in one word, conscription. This, although hateful, is now the only way to get soldiers and is at present absolutely justified by the gravity of the situation and the holiness of the cause. And although one or two may carp, the majority will accept it in good spirits.[91]

The government did not share this point of view. There is no specific evidence that either the Venetian ministers or the great landowners ever actively opposed arming the peasantry through fear of the possible social consequences. But as long as monarchist aid appeared to offer an easier and more effective alternative the Venetian leaders avoided questioning the nature of their backing in the countryside, and its importance in preserving the revolution. They never grappled with the difficult problem

[91] ASV, Gov. Prov. 1848–9, CPD, b. 834/Treviso, attached to no. 1437. The report was sent first to the district committee of Conegliano and then forwarded to Treviso.

of retaining their own leadership of the revolution while appealing for rural popular support, of striking the necessary balance between their own interests and those of the class forces below them, of creating, in this way, their own hegemony.

The dominance of the urban bourgeoisie in Manin's government contributed greatly to this blindness with regard to the countryside. Men like Castelli, Pincherle or Tommaseo had little idea of rural conditions. Although he had a sister at Treviso, Manin himself was not a landowner and had never toured the Veneto extensively. He left Venice only to go to university at Padua, and to serve his early years as a lawyer at Mestre. While Manin had an instinctive grasp of the needs and feelings of the people of the city of Venice, he had no real understanding either of the provincial ruling classes or of the aspirations of the peasantry. In all his copious correspondence of the period, there is hardly a single detailed reference to the problems of the countryside. Manin, like so many of the other republican leaders of 1848, was therefore unable to conceive of an alliance with the peasantry as intrinsically necessary for the survival of the revolution.[92]

Finally, the immaturity of the bourgeois national movement in Venice and the Veneto before the revolution goes a long way to explain the line of action Manin pursued. Venice had for too long been one of the backwaters of the movement, lacking any traditions of struggle, and playing no part in the revolutions of 1830–2. When the revolution broke out in 1848 the Venetians looked naturally for aid and advice to those areas of Italy which had been in the forefront of the agitation of the years 1846–8. This led them both to exaggerate the amount of help they could expect – the Trevisans were convinced that sixty thousand papal troops were coming to their aid[93] – and to underestimate their own potential. Such attitudes were of paramount importance with regard to Venice's relations with Milan. Once the Milanese republicans had failed to give the Venetians that 'sound direction'[94] which they needed, it was difficult, if not impossible, for Manin to avoid following the essentially monarchist strategy of the Milanese provisional government.

Manin's own inexperience of military affairs contributed greatly to this strikingly passive policy. He had not done military service, and his ignorance led him to place an excessive trust in regular troops and dynastic

[92] See Della Peruta, 'I contadini', p. 106, for the way in which neither Mazzini, Cattaneo, Cernuschi nor even Ferrari explicitly posed the problem of an alliance with the peasantry in Lombardy.

[93] A. Santalena, *Treviso nel 1848*, p. 46.

[94] The phrase is Carlo Pisacane's; see his *Guerra combattuta in Italia negli anni 1848–9*, p. 343: 'if the Lombardo-Venetian movement had had a sound direction, and if the people had been less ready to believe in promises ...'

armies, and to belittle the possible efficacy of popular forces. There could be no denying the very real need of regular troops in open battle, but neither Manin nor any of the other Venetian leaders seemed able to envisage, in the decisive first weeks of the revolution, a strategy that systematically utilised popular enthusiasm for the revolution, and combined regular and volunteer forces. This lack of knowledge and experience also led the Venetian republicans to place their faith in ageing commanders who were often convinced of nothing but the hopelessness of forming a Venetian army and the need to appeal to Charles Albert.[95] The Venetians would probably have needed a man of Garibaldi's talents to lead a Venetian army to victory over the Austrians. But the main point is not that the Venetian government failed; it is rather that they hardly tried.

Thus the aid of the Italian monarchs, even though it was never spoken of in Venetian ruling circles as an alternative to self-defence, came in reality to acquire this identity during the first month of the revolution. With the intervention of Piedmont and the likelihood of aid from Rome and Naples, the speed and efficiency with which the Venetians organised their own forces assumed less significance. The Venetian committee of defence, appointed on 1 April as the supreme military body for the republic, decided at its first meeting that in the absence of any army or navy it would confine its attention 'only to the arming and defence of Venice and its estuary'.[96] It was 20 April before Manin asked the committee for details of the forces in the Veneto and their distribution. The committee replied that the possibility of forming a Venetian army did not exist, and that the Venetians should implore Charles Albert to come to their help.[97]

The prospect of monarchist aid appealed to the Venetian ministers on a large number of grounds. It meant that national unity in the struggle, an ideal close to Manin's heart, could be maintained in spite of Venice proclaiming the republic; this was in accord with Milanese insistence on unity at any price, on the need to trust Charles Albert and to delay political decisions till the end of the war. It offered the moderate republicans of Venice and their wealthy supporters an alternative to what they took to be the savage, 'Jacobin' methods that the formation of a popular army entailed. It seemed also to relieve them of the possibility of having to improve conditions on their estates so as to secure continued peasant support. It obviated the necessity for Manin to make his government and his policies less city-based. Above all, it seemed to offer the promise of highly-prized regular troops in the war against Austria, thus sparing the Venetians the

95 See below, pp. 182, 197–8, 217.
96 ASV, Gov. Prov. 1848–9, CD, b. 390, no. 1.
97 ASV, Gov. Prov. 1848–9, CD, b. 390, no. 419 for Manin's letter of 20 April and no. 432 for the committee's reply of 21 April 1848.

arduous task of converting the peasant militias and deserting regiments into a reliable army of their own.

Conclusion

The first war of Italian independence, which opened with the revolutions of Milan and Venice, could initially have gone in one of two political directions. Because the monarchists triumphed, it is difficult to conceive of any other solution, and easy to deny that there could have been a republican alternative. Candeloro, a historian of outstandingly sound judgement, has rightly said that any appeal for French aid by the Lombards 'would have led to an extremely serious break with Piedmont and would thus have had incalculable consequences for the future of the Italian national movement'.[98] Yet it is perhaps worth remembering that before 1848 French intervention, albeit a mixed blessing at the best of times, had contributed far more to the Italian national movement than the house of Savoy. Similarly, republicanism was far from extraneous to the movement, and the Cisalpine, Cispadan and Parthenopean republics of the late 1790s had left strong memories and traditions. It is also worth repeating that federalism, not unification under a single monarch, had been the solution most favoured for Italian unity prior to 1848. Finally, when the anti-Austrian revolutions broke out, it was the republicans, not the monarchists, who put themselves at their head. Without wishing to indulge in idle speculation, or to fall into the dangerous trap of seeing a 'lost revolution' where none existed, it seems possible to insist that in the national and international context of March 1848 a republican strategy for the Italian bourgeois national revolution existed as a viable alternative to subjection to Charles Albert.

That the republicans failed must be attributed primarily to the weakness of the democratic movement in Lombardy before the revolution, and to the hesitancy of its leadership in Milan during it. In the most economically advanced and politically active province of Italy, the progressive wing of the national movement at no stage escaped subordination to the more moderate liberal nobility. During the *cinque giornate* the placing of unity amongst the Italians not only *above* but *to the exclusion of* every other objective robbed the democrats of the commanding position they had assumed.

Once Milan had acquired Casati's provisional government, with Correnti's attempted mediation as secretary only aiding the monarchists in the long run, Venice's republicanism immediately appeared as an isolated act of disunity. Mindful, as were nearly all the republicans of 1848, not to

[98] Candeloro, *Storia dell'Italia moderna*, vol. 3, p. 197.

repeat the 'terrible' lessons of the Jacobins, the Venetians quickly fell in line with what had happened at Milan. They did not abandon all hopes of preserving their republic, but were willing not to re-emphasise its existence while the war was waged. Anxious to preserve Italian unity, desirous of Charles Albert's aid, unwilling and unable to conceive of a forceful policy of self-defence, Manin substantially withdrew from the political position he had adopted on 22 March.

5

The undoing of the Venetian republic, April and May 1848

In Venice and the Veneto the declaration of the republic unleashed, as was only to be expected, a great wave of hopes and illusions. The national cause was embraced by all social classes except the nobility, each hoping to find in it the fulfilment of long-nurtured desires and demands. The spring of 1848 was the time of feverish initiatives, of celebrations, of firm beliefs in the foundation of a new era. It was the time when trees of liberty were again planted in the village squares of the Veneto, when in Venice dozens of newly founded patriotic newspapers celebrated the freedom of the press, when the elite of the city's merchants and bankers met under the elaborate Murano chandeliers of the great rooms of their palaces to plan the new economic ordering of their society. But behind all these manifestations of joy and plans for the future loomed the menace of an undefeated Austria. As the weeks passed, this menace grew ever more apparent, as did the failure of the Venetian government to evolve a political and military strategy which could effectively unite city and countryside, bourgeoisie and lower classes in a concentrated effort to defend the new republic.

Venetian policy and the rural civic guards

During the first fortnight of the revolution, the numbers and organisation of the civic guards grew rapidly in every part of the Venetian countryside. Given the different conditions of the peasantry in the various regions of the Veneto, it would have been natural to expect a high degree of unevenness in their response to the revolution. Certainly the mountain peasantry, with their closely knit communities, their particular grievances over the communal forests, and their traditions of militancy dating from the Napoleonic period, showed themselves the most enthusiastic supporters of the new republic. By 7 April the Sette Comuni, the group of villages on the *altopiano* around Asiago, had offered the Venetian government the services of seven thousand men. High up in the Dolomites and the Carnian

Alps villages like Agordo and Cencenighe formed mobile as well as civic guards, ready to move to wherever the Austrians threatened.[1]

However, mobilisation in both the hills and plains was surprisingly extensive. The reports sent to the provincial capitals or Venice itself stressed the high level of voluntary participation in the guards, though specific details on peasant reactions and expectations are few and far between. Along the whole belt of Venetian hills the guards had reached impressive proportions by the beginning of April. In Bassano and the area round it, about 2,100 guards had enrolled by 7 April, of whom only 500 came from the city itself.[2] The guard at Maser, north-west of Treviso, numbered 500 by 2 April, and of these twenty had gone of their own accord to Castelfranco to join up with other volunteers 'for the defence of our Italy'. Maser had forty firearms and asked for more.[3] At Godego, further to the east, the head of the civic guard, Dr Colledani, wrote that they had 490 men, and the local archpriest, Parolari, added a note to his 'old friend' Manin asking for 150 muskets.[4] In all the hill areas of Friuli, as we have seen,[5] there was great enthusiasm and movement in the last days of March.

The landless labourers of the plains also seemed willing to enrol. As early as 28 March over 3,000 men had joined from the villages round Padua, and at San Donà, in the province of Venice, the civic guard had reached 280 men, 'ready to move at any order of the government'.[6] At Mira, in the same province, the commander of the civic guard, Alessandro Petrillo, reported that the guard could be supplemented by another 2,400 men working on the construction of the Brenta canal.[7] At Pordenone and the villages around it, the guard numbered 5,497, of whom 360 had

[1] For Cencenighe, where there were 36 mobile guards, 200 in reserve and 44 firearms, see ASV, Gov. Prov. 1848–9, CPD, b. 832/Cencenighe, no number. In Agordo the vast majority of the first forty volunteers were peasants, village artisans, or mineworkers; ASV, Gov. Prov. 1848–9, CPD, b. 822/Agordo, municipio centrale, ruoli di volontari. For the Sette Comuni see the minutes of the ministerial meeting of 7 April in Ventura (ed.), *Verbali*, p. 108.

[2] ASV, Gov. Prov. 1848–9, CPD, b. 846/Bassano, nos. 729, 731, 737, 743, 750, 768, 803, 838, 894, 985, 988, 997 and 1,105.

[3] ASV, Gov. Prov. 1848–9, CD, b. 390, no. 76.

[4] ASV, Gov. Prov. 1848–9, MG, b. 127, no. 434, letter of 2 April 1848. Colledani added that the buying of a drum had helped to whip up enthusiasm, but that the peasants were 'always ready to profit from anything'.

[5] See above, p. 111.

[6] ASV, Gov. Prov. 1848–9, MU, b. 2, no. 259. For Padua, see the report of the commander of the civic guard of Padua, *ibid.*, CPD, b. 825/Padova CPD, no. 191. He wrote that 'influential persons are in command of the guard in each commune'. See also the favourable report from the southern part of the province, 12 April 1848; *ibid.*, CD, b. 391, no. 240.

[7] ASV, Gov. Prov. 1848–9, MG, b. 127, no. 18, 26 March 1848.

done military service, and 780 had firearms. There were also another 230 men available from neighbouring Torre, the site of the large cotton factory.[8]

Only on the great estates of the province of Rovigo was the peasant response lukewarm. This is partially explained by the absence in the Polesine of that flourishing middle stratum of rural society that elsewhere was playing so conspicuous a role in the organisation of the civic guard. But the provincial committee of Rovigo was chiefly responsible because they refused to pay the peasants or artisans for serving in the guard. The committee, in the face of protests from various villages, pompously maintained that service in the guard was to be considered 'as the most precious right of nationhood, and as nothing but an honour'.[9] Such an attitude contrasted with other parts of the Veneto, where the guard was paid regularly. In the province of Vicenza, for instance, the commander of the civic guard of Lonigo, Major Trevisan, demanded as much as two lire a day for every artisan and peasant in his guard.[10] He wrote: 'The peasants and artisans have nothing to lose but their lives . . . ; for this reason, if these men are obliged to defend the honour of the country and the lives and property of the rich, they at least have the right to be paid.' His request was immediately granted. In the Polesine the rural poor, deprived of a certain section of the day or night through service in the guard, were

[8] ACPo, carte della guardia nazionale, no number. For the details from Torre, see the letter from G. B. Scotti dated 1 April 1848. Scotti warned that while the men from Torre would come to the aid of Pordenone, there were no volunteers for fighting further afield. As for the province of Vicenza, to take just two examples, the villages of Noventa Vicentina and Pojana, both near Lonigo, had civic guards of 231 and 89 men respectively; ASV, Gov. Prov. 1848–9, CPD, b. 847/Lonigo gov. prov., nos. 37–8, reports of 31 March 1848. A large number of these men had firearms.

[9] ASV, Gov. Prov. 1848–9, CPD, b. 832/Rovigo, no. 29. A similar situation arose in the village of Villafora near Badia, where the peasants refused to do night service in the guard since they were not being paid. They said that they were tired and did not want to leave their families. The commander of the civic guard, who was unusually hostile to them, wrote that the peasants seemed to have enough money to spend in the inns every night and that 'when they go away to work on the railways they abandon their wives, homes and children not just for three hours but sometimes for as much as four months' (*ibid.*, letter of 15 April attached to no. 29). It was also impossible to get any volunteers from three villages near Adria on 9–10 April 1848. In one, Bottrighe, the authorities replied that 'our peasants cannot move because they are bound to landlords who do not live in the commune' (*ibid.*, no. 156 and attached documents (see no. 79 for further examples of three villages near Rovigo)). The only exception in the Polesine appears to be Adria and its district, from which fifty-two men volunteered on 11 April 1848; *ibid.*, no. 317.

[10] ASV, Gov. Prov. 1848–9, CPD, b. 847/Lonigo, gov. prov., no. 38 and attached document.

only demanding a modest fifty centesimi. On being refused it, they withdrew their support.

All over the Veneto, the clergy played a vital role in fostering peasant enthusiasm. Brunello has shown how it was the extra-parochial clergy, particularly the Capuchins, and the lower clerical orders, such as the chaplains, sacristans and seminary teachers, who were the warmest supporters of the revolution. The rural parish priests were better paid and tended to be more socially conservative, but very few of them refused to bless the tricolour flags of the civic guards, and some of them were to be found leading the peasant militias.[11] Most of the bishops of the provinces unequivocally gave their backing to the revolution. Farini, the bishop of Padua, in a circular to his parish clergy of 9 April, spoke of the need in town and country 'to teach the people their duty to defend by force of arms, in the best way possible, the independence we have obtained'. Bellati, the bishop of Ceneda, wrote on 29 March of 'the ever-increasing joy in our countryside', and the bishop of Adria expressed similar sentiments on the 31st.[12]

The belief in a Holy War against the Austrians spread through the rural areas. The commander of the civic guard of Spilimbergo proclaimed on 9 April, 'the Austrians are having to collect criminals and bandits, since no Christian will fight against the vessel of the Redemption, blessed and guided by the immortal Pius IX'.[13] At the small mining town of Agordo, north of Belluno, the municipality, announcing that the kingdom of God on earth was close at hand, planted a tree of liberty 'in the name of the Italian Republic and of all the Republics of sister countries', and so as 'to preserve a popular memorial of this happy and saintly dawn which casts the light of liberty and fraternity on all Italy and on the peoples of the Globe'.[14]

The enthusiasm and vitality of the rural civic guards received a severe

[11] P. Brunello, 'Rivoluzione e clero', fos. 80–95. See also, for Austrian reports on the activities of various priests during the revolution, ASV, Pres. Luog., 1849–66, b. 72, x, 7/1, 1849, no. 428; 1850, nos. 1087, 1555, 2869; *ibid.*, b. 224, v, 10, nos. 12 and 16.

[12] Farini's circular of 9 April is cited in A. Gloria, *Il comitato provvisorio dipartimentale di Padova dal 25 marzo al 13 giugno 1848*, Padova 1927, p. 47 n. 54. A week earlier he had reported to the Venetian government that the peasantry of his province were busy collecting arms; ASV, Gov. Prov. 1848–9, MU, b. 3, no. 1231, 2 April 1848. For the bishop of Ceneda's letter, see MCV, archivio Bernardi, b. 31, no number, letter to Jacopo Bernardi. The bishop of Adria's circular is in Racc. Andreola, vol. 1, pp. 492–3. The bishop of Chioggia, Jacopo Foretti, was less enthusiastic, and on 29 March spoke of his 'state of uncertainty, anguish and trepidation'; see Brunello, 'Rivoluzione e clero', fo. 66.

[13] ASV, Gov. Prov. 1848–9, CPD, b. 835/Spilimbergo, no number.

[14] ASV, Gov. Prov. 1848–9, CPD, b. 822/Agordo, no. 203.

dampener when the Italian troops who had been allowed to leave Venice began to return to their homes. Many of them sold their arms and equipment on the way, and the provincial committee of Treviso complained bitterly to the Venetian government in the following terms:

Soldiers of various regiments, furnished with leave passes and some with arms, are arriving continuously in this city. These individuals are spreading discouragement and ill humour amongst the troops and the citizens, in such a way that the contagion of their cowardice and indifference is becoming dangerous at a moment when it is more necessary than ever to maintain the enthusiasm and patriotism which inspire all our citizens. This committee shares the surprise and deep shock which is universal that the government, instead of helping its brothers by keeping assembled the regiments which were at its disposition, and sending them to aid the *terraferma*, has rather been the instigator of their dissolution.[15]

The Venetian lawyer, Bartolomeo Benvenuti, was at Padua railway station on 30 March to see 'the dismal impression made by the horde of soldiers from the Wimpffen regiment getting out of their carriages to return, still armed, to their homes'.[16]

On 6 April 1848, the village authorities of Susegana gave a very clear picture of the surprise and discouragement that ensued in many communes of the Veneto:

The communal deputation of Susegana has not only invited, but exhorted and begged incessantly both the conscripts of previous years and the soldiers who have returned on leave these past few days, to come to the village hall and enrol again for the military service which is so indispensable in these days. But we must sadly admit that it has been to no avail. Those who have just come home get out of it by saying: 'When our companions present themselves, we'll come along too.' Those who have done their military service, rightly shocked by the incomprehensible dismissal of those who were in Venice, not unjustly reply, 'Why are you asking us? We've done our eight years. They're openly dismissing those who have not yet finished their military service. What's more they're giving them their arms and equipment.'[17]

The example given by the Venetian troops also affected many of the Italian soldiers of the provincial garrisons who had stayed behind after the Austrians had left. Pieri has estimated that in all six thousand regular troops were allowed to disperse in this period.[18]

---

[15] MCV, Doc. Manin, no. 3517, letter of 30 March 1848.
[16] MCV, Doc. Manin, no. 2658, letter of 30 March 1848.
[17] ASV, Gov. Prov. 1848–9, CPD, b. 834/Treviso, attached to no. 1437.
[18] P. Pieri, *Storia militare del Risorgimento*, pp. 369–70. His figures are as follows: 3,000 from Venice, 1,000 from Treviso, 1,000 from Udine, 500 from Rovigo, and 500 customs guards and gendarmes. For the troops from Rovigo, see ASV, Gov. Prov. 1848–9, MG, b. 127, no. 49, letter of 28 March from the mayor of

The grave shock of the return of the regular troops was not mitigated by any coherent Venetian plan to involve the rural civic guards in the war effort. Quite clearly, it would have been impossible to arm all those who had enrolled in the countryside, or to persuade the majority of them to leave their villages. *Campanilismo* was naturally very strong, and it would have needed determined leadership to break, even on a temporary basis, the bond between the peasant, his family and his village. Yet the general enthusiasm of the peasantry, the spontaneous formation of mobile guards in many villages, the example of the mass mobilisation of central Friuli at the end of March, and the power of a sympathetic clergy were not facts which a government more intent on evolving an immediate strategy for the defence of the Veneto would have ignored. Had the Venetian government acted decisively at the beginning of April, it could almost certainly have collected from the provinces many thousands of men who had done military service, and found the firearms with which to arm them.

Instead Manin's government seems to have taken practically no account of what was happening in the rural areas. On 27 March the formation of a mobile civic guard of 6,000 men from the city of Venice was announced, but enrolment in it was voluntary and by 15 April only 3,600 men had come forward. The government then suspended further enrolment until the existing force had been properly equipped. It seemed extremely reluctant to admit the 'mobile' nature of the guard, and indeed only two companies (200 men) crossed to the mainland during the first two months of the revolution.[19] Paolucci, the minister of war, stressed on 4 April that the majority of defensive forces were to be concentrated in Venice. Such an attitude had some merit to it, in so far as Venice, by virtue of its position in the middle of the lagoon, was the most easily defendable city of the Veneto. But any decision to concentrate on Venice was in grave contradiction with the responsibility that the Venetian government had assumed when it persuaded the *terraferma* to become part of the republic. The

Rovigo to the Venetian government, and *ibid.*, CPD, b. 825/Padova CPD, no. 174, letter of provincial committee of Padova of the same date saying that of the 400 soldiers from Rovigo only 198 had arrived in Padua. Treviso alone managed to keep 800 of the regulars together, forming them into the Galateo legion. The provincial committee there built a bridge of boats over the river Sile so that the soldiers returning from Venice would not pass through Treviso and so spread the news of their disbandment; see S. Sardagna, 'I primi errori militari dei Veneti nel 1848, 22 marzo – 8 aprile 1848' (off-print version, pp. 14–15).

[19] For further details, see E. Jäger, *Storia documentata dei corpi militari veneti ed i loro alleati, 1848–9*, pp. 142ff. There were to be ten battalions of 600 men each, and anyone between the ages of twenty and forty could enrol. Pay was one Italian lira a day while in Venice and 1.50 lira outside it. It is interesting to note that every company was to elect its own officers up to the rank of captain; Racc. Andreola, vol. 1, p. 177.

inability of the Venetian committee of defence to include the Veneto in any systematic military plan reveals only too clearly the exclusively urban nature of Manin's government, and a classic split between the needs of town and country.[20]

As a result, the rural civic guards were left in isolation and without any knowledge of what the central government intended or how best they could contribute to the war effort. The Venetian committee of defence supported the idea, not of a central army, but of the formation of *corpi franchi*, volunteer bands from each province. *The corpi franchi* or *crociati* (crusaders) as they were often called, were formed in the most haphazard manner, relying almost exclusively on local initiatives.[21] The volunteers were often a strange mixture of the flower of the patriotic youth and the criminal elements of the cities. Sometimes they aroused more fear than support in the countryside. According to one eye-witness, the motley band of 'crusaders' who set out from Rovigo left a worse impression on the near-by villages than had the brigands of 1809.[22]

[20] The Venetian committee of defence, formed on 30 March 1848, was composed as follows: Giorgio Bua, Galeazzo Fontana, Pietro Stecchini, Lodovico Boniotti, Ermolao Federigo. The choice of Bua to head the committee was Manin's doing; see Ventura (ed.), *Verbali*, p. 83, and Racc. Andreola, vol. 1, p. 249. For Paolucci's comment of 4 April, see Ventura (ed.), *Verbali*, p. 97. He was afraid that the Austrians would try and land troops on the beaches of the Po estuary, and that the Venetians would be powerless to prevent them.

[21] The only instruction about the *corpi franchi* in the papers of the Venetian committee of defence is a circular to the villages in the province of Venice urging them to gather volunteers; ASV, Gov. Prov. 1848–9, CD, b. 390, no. 88, without date but probably of 5 April 1848. What this meant in practice was revealed in the chronicle of the admittedly reactionary archpriest of Mestre, G. Renier: 'A few days after this disgraceful disbanding of men and materials [reference to the regular soldiers leaving Venice] we witnessed the arrival from this same city of recruiting sergeants after new soldiers. They paraded through the little towns and villages with a drum beating and a flag held high by a friar, and managed to scrape together small squads of idle youths and men' (Renier, *La cronaca di Mestre*, p. 32). Clearly, not all the contingents from the countryside were composed of 'idle youths and men'. For one example among many of villagers volunteering at an early date, see the letter of 30 March of the provincial committee of Padua to the *municipio* of Conselve, announcing the arrival in Padua of the forty-eight volunteers from Conselve, Bagnoli and Tribano and saying that they would form part of the Paduan *corpo franco*; ASV, Gov. Prov. 1848–9, b. 825/Padova, CPD, no. 348.

[22] E. Piva, 'Prime armi 1848 (dalle memorie del generale Domenico Piva)', in *1848–1948, Celebrazioni polesane del centenario*, p. 12 and n. 4. In June 1848 the commissioner for public order in the *sestiere* San Marco in Venice was asked to report on how many dangerous individuals there were in his quarter. He replied, rather disconcertingly, that 'many of the violent and suspect persons who were to be found in the squares as vagabonds and beggars have gone to form

Above all, the village guards felt betrayed by the failure of the central government to provide them with arms. The papers of the committee of defence are for the most part nothing but a sad catalogue of demands for muskets from practically every village and town in the Veneto. Because Austrian forces appeared to threaten the Veneto from nearly every angle – Radetzky from Verona, Nugent from Gorizia, the Tyrolese from the north – villages in every province except Rovigo felt the danger of imminent invasion. The Venetian government could not hope to provide for the needs of all the guards, and it would have been folly to disperse firearms in such an aimless manner. But the village authorities were not reassured by any proclamations from the government, or by the announcement of any assembly points to which they could send their best trained men. At Venice Avesani and his group, which included at this time Gherardo Freschi and Isacco Pesaro Maurogonato, realised the failings of the government. As early as 29 March they wrote:

The letters of the provinces are full of complaints that we have abandoned them. Why is this? Because of lack of publicity, lack of reassurance, lack of verbal encouragement. The government claims to have given these to the provincial deputations, but without any proclamations the people of the provinces don't believe it. Give them some publicity, make them understand our good intentions, incite them to fight, at least with words, even if you cannot with men and arms.[23]

Manin's government did not heed such advice. On the vital question of arms, Manin seemed content to take only the mildest measures to recover the muskets lost in Venice between 22 and 23 March. On 3 April he offered rewards to those citizens who saw fit to hand the muskets back, and as late as 9 May Venetian shops were still selling firearms quite openly.[24] The Venetian committee of defence, replying on 2 April to a letter of the provincial committee of Bassano, urged it not to worry, because the Austrians 'when they had 120,000 well-ordered and well-armed men did not know how to resist our insurrection',[25] and that in any

part of the "crusaders" or of the mobile guard, so that it could almost be said that they do not exist in this quarter any more' (ASV, Gov. Prov., 1848–9, OPss, no. 4536, letter of 13 June 1848).

[23] ASV, carte Avesani, b. 2, no number, memorandum to the government. Further memoranda followed on 30, 31 March, 2 and 8 April.

[24] For the rewards offered at the beginning of April see Racc. Andreola, vol. 1, p. 321. The government promised ten Italian lire for every musket and bayonet. For the Venetian shops in May, see the letter of the *consulta* to the government, MCV, Doc. Manin, no. 3231. Only on 2 May 1848 did the government issue a decree exempting all firearms and ammunition from customs duty on entry into Venice; ASV, CC, b. 187, IV, 37.

[25] ASV, Gov. Prov. 1848–9, CD, b. 390, no. 5. Bassano was one of the most active

case papal troops would soon arrive in the Veneto. The arms and cannon that were distributed from Venice went for the most part to the provincial cities.[26] The national guards in the countryside, left without instructions or any sort of arms except pitchforks and shotguns, slowly became disillusioned.

The battle of Montebello and Sorio

The first encounter between Venetian and Austrian troops was to take place west of Vicenza on 8 April 1848. The task of uniting the various volunteer bands and 'crusaders' was given to Marcantonio Sanfermo, a Napoleonic veteran of sixty-five who had been a colonel on the general staff of the army of Italy. The Venetian committee of defence was of the opinion that Sanfermo should take the volunteers eastwards towards the front at Friuli, but Sanfermo was convinced that an invasion from that direction was impossible.[27] He therefore headed westwards towards Verona, gathering recruits as he went.

From the outset it was unclear what function Sanfermo's troop was supposed to serve, whether it was to be a simple observation corps or was to take the offensive against the Austrians. Sanfermo himself seemed undecided on his role, but his men were eager to fight, and he was unable or unwilling to restrain them. The Venetians had little idea of the numbers or morale of the Austrian troops at Verona, and many were confident of an easy victory. Sanfermo was less sure, but at the beginning of April he

of the provincial cities, organising its own 'crusaders' and a company of former Austrian soldiers as a 'mobile column'; ASV, Gov. Prov. 1848–9, CPD, b. 846/ Bassano CPD, no. 1107, and *ibid.*, MG, b. 127, no. 406.

[26] MCV, Doc. Manin, no. 3940, 'Prospetto delle quantità e qualità delle armi e munizioni da guerra somministrate alle provincie e comuni dal 18 marzo a tutto 20 giugno 1848'. In this period 12,207 muskets with bayonets were distributed from the arsenal. Treviso received 800 on 25 March, Vicenza 1,000 on 27 March and Padua 400 on the same day; some of the smaller towns in the Veneto did receive arms – Castelfranco 100, Adria 100, Conegliano 70, etc. There were some very strange decisions taken – the island of Burano, for instance, received 300 muskets. Francesco Restelli, the Lombard representative at Venice, confirmed the Venetians' lack of planning in his dispatch of 6 April 1848: 'Here the war ministry is completely disorganised. Disorganised as far as the techniques of war go, disorganised as well in matters of finance and provisioning. It could not be otherwise. Nobody is directing from the centre the moves of the *corpi franchi* and "crusaders"' (letter published in A. Monti, *Un italiano: Francesco Restelli, 1814–90*, p. 256).

[27] See Sardagna, 'I primi errori', p. 44, and ASV, Gov. Prov. 1848–9, CD, b. 390, no. 64. Before the revolution Sanfermo lived at Padua and had been principally interested in land reclamation and irrigation; see *Dizionario del Risorgimento nazionale*, vol. 4 (1937), p. 195.

was persuaded to lead about two thousand men out of Vicenza towards Verona.

It was highly irresponsible of Sanfermo even to contemplate action against the Austrians in the open field, for his troop lacked both the men and the arms needed for such an action. The confusion over Sanfermo's role and his men's impatience meant that he behaved as if he had an army, when in fact no steps had been taken to create one. Little systematic effort had been made to assemble all the volunteers of the western Veneto before giving battle. The men of Valdagno and Recoaro, for instance, 200 in all, only received instructions from Vicenza to join Sanfermo on 8 April, the day of the battle. The Sette Comuni were not called upon to help at all, although ten days after the battle they were reported as having an organised force of 1,666 men.[28] At Montebello Sanfermo had the Paduan legion, including a company of university students, legions from Vicenza and Treviso, and the *corpo franco* of Schio – about 2,200 men, and probably only a fraction of the number available in these early days of peasant enthusiasm.[29]

Worse still, only five or six hundred of Sanfermo's men had firearms. Sanfermo wrote continually to Venice demanding muskets, and warning that he could not count on the sympathy of the local populations as long as they were deprived of arms. The committee of defence replied that they could not send him any more muskets until those ordered in France and Switzerland arrived.[30] Quite clearly, the committee of defence had decided to keep in Venice the majority of the firearms from the arsenal, and did not rate the supplying of Sanfermo's force as a priority. Under these circumstances it was madness to take on the Austrians. The Venetians at Montebello had four old naval cannon from Venice, mounted on carts pulled by cattle, and the majority of those who were armed had old muskets. Only the 200 former Austrian soldiers from Treviso had more modern muskets.[31]

Against them were at least 3,000 Austrian troops, with two squadrons of cavalry and six cannon, sent out from Verona by Radetzky to make a reconnaissance and collect provisions. The two forces skirmished on the evening of 7 April, and battle was joined the next day at 7 a.m. The

---

[28] ASV, Gov. Prov. 1848–9, CD, b. 391, no. 410, letter from Bellotto in the Sette Comuni, 18 April 1848. For Valdagno and Recoaro see BBV, Gonz. 24.7.19, G. Soster, 'Valdagno – atti ufficiali e memorie dal 1848 al 1878', entry for 8 April 1848.

[29] For the numbers at Montebello, see Trevelyan, *Manin and the Venetian Revolution*, app. F. 'Combat at Montebello', p. 250.

[30] Sardagna, 'I primi errori', pp. 57–8, and ASV, Gov. Prov. 1848–9, CD, b. 390, no. 89, 4 April 1848.

[31] P. Meneghini, *Bozzetti di un crociato*, pp. 8–9.

Venetians at first resisted well, but the Austrians called up reinforcements, and in the afternoon Sanfermo's right flank was turned in the hills near Sorio. The Venetians panicked and Sanfermo, giving the order 'sauve qui peut', drove off in his carriage to Vicenza – he was too old and ill to ride a horse. Many of the Venetians fled, twenty-seven were killed and twenty-nine captured, but the Paduan university students and the men from Schio retreated in good order to Montebello. The Austrians did not follow up their victory, and returned as instructed to Verona.[32]

Although the combat of Montebello and Sorio was little more than a skirmish, and the numbers of dead and wounded were negligible, the psychological effect was considerable. It was the first check to the tide of Venetian success, and showed that the war was not going to be easy to win. The lesson for the Venetians lay in the immediate need to collect together all their forces, ensure they were as well armed as circumstances permitted, and turn those who had served under Austria into the nucleus of their army. It was necessary, as Pieri has pointed out,[33] not to leave the volunteers alone in the open field, but to establish that mixture of trained and volunteer troops essential to any popular army. At the end of May the extraordinary fight put up by Neapolitan and Tuscan regulars *and* volunteers against the whole might of Radetzky's army at Curtatone and Montanara showed what might have been achieved in the Veneto. But the Venetian committee of defence, on hearing of the defeat at Montebello, failed to undertake any serious analysis of it, and decided only to seek fresh generals.[34]

[32] The best account of the battle is undoubtedly Sardagna, 'I primi errori', pp. 67–87. Of the twenty-nine men captured at Montebello, nearly all were young peasants or village artisans from the area around Treviso; MCV, Doc. Manin, no. 3478, report from Vicenza, 12 April 1848. In spite of the sounding of the tocsin, the peasant guards from the nearby villages did not come to the aid of Sanfermo's men, probably because they had no firearms. They were also angered by Sanfermo's decision to destroy three bridges over the river Fratta; see MCV, Doc. Manin, no. 3521, letter from provincial committee of Treviso, 9 April 1848, and ASV, Gov. Prov. 1848-9, CPD, b. 847/Lonigo gov. prov., nos. 48 and 52. F. Molon, in his *Un ricordo del 1848*, p. 49, makes the important point that of the two sides the Austrians were always infinitely better informed of their opponents' movements and numerical strength.
[33] Pieri, *Storia militare*, pp. 371–2.
[34] See Restelli's interesting account of the meeting of 8 April of the Venetian committee of defence; Monti, *Francesco Restelli*, p. 264. The committee decided to ask General Ferrari and Colonel Amigo, who had fought in Algeria and Spain respectively, to come to Venice. Trevelyan (*Manin and the Venetian Revolution*, p. 149) took the battle of Montebello as proof that 'the volunteers were very little use in the open field'.

Peasant agitations and demands

During the same period that saw the build-up and defeat of Sanfermo's forces, a wave of class action by the peasantry swept the Venetian countryside. For the peasantry the declaration of the republic was a unique opportunity to air long-standing grievances and to attempt to improve their social conditions. Their agitations were not particularly widespread or violent, and cannot compare with the contemporary land occupations in southern Italy or the anti-feudal struggles elsewhere in the Austrian empire.[35] They had little effect on the defence of the Veneto in these early weeks, in as much as the peasants' support for the revolution was undiminished, and the rural ruling classes generally kept control of the situation. Although often alarmed by the peasants' action, the local or provincial authorities were never so terrified of the peasantry as to refuse to arm them or attempt to exclude them from the civic guards. But the wave of peasant protests, their half-formed demands and spontaneous, local demonstrations were an important, if fleeting, glimpse of the underlying class tensions in the countryside. The Venetian government's decision to abolish the personal tax and reduce the duty on salt had been greeted with joy by the peasantry. Yet it was clear that their needs went far beyond these two concessions, and that if the government was to keep the rural poor on its side it would have to come to terms with their aspirations and the complexities and contradictions of a highly stratified rural society.

In the mountain areas the actions of the peasantry centred on the restitution of the communal rights and lands of which they had been deprived by the Austrian law of 1839. A petition of 7 April 1848 from the villagers of Maniago in northern Friuli explained how after 1839 the communal lands and forests had been bought up by a few rich 'companies', and how the six thousand poor of the commune had been denied access for cutting wood or grazing their animals on what had been village land for time immemorial. In the villages bordering the woods of Montello, in northern Treviso, the villagers refused any longer to pay the tax imposed on them for collecting mushrooms in the local forest; the tax

---

[35] The most violent incidents that occurred in Friuli were in the extreme east, behind the Austrians' lines. There feudalism still predominated, and the villagers of San Daniele del Carso and Rifembergo burnt all the manorial rolls and other documents. On 26 March 1848 several hundred of them stormed the two castles of Count Lanthier at Rifembergo. The count's gamekeeper and other guards opened fire on the peasants, killing one of them and wounding three. See R. M. Cossar, 'Riflessi goriziani della rivoluzione del 1848', in *La Venezia Giulia e la Dalmazia nella rivoluzione nazionale del 1848–9*, vol. 2, p. 294. On the feudal conditions in eastern Friuli, see P. Antonini, *Il Friuli orientale*, p. 513 n. 1.

collector fled and the peasants entered the forest freely.[36] The most striking incident of all occurred at Auronzo, in the Cadore, soon to be at the heart of peasant resistance to the Austrians. There the villagers invaded the woods *en masse*, and demanded that the former communal forests should be divided up between the families of the village. The provincial committee of Belluno, alarmed at the scant respect of the peasants for private property, demanded that the Venetian government should send 'a force of at least 500 armed men, or failing that a decree declaring the forest to be inviolate'.[37] Manin refused to send any soldiers, but at first drafted a decree instructing the peasants to respect the existing laws. He then appears to have changed his mind, and on 16 April published a more conciliatory decree, inviting the communes of the Cadore to propose new laws which would reconcile both public and private needs. At least some of the peasants interpreted this decree as giving them a free hand, for on 30 April the villagers of Villagrande di Auronzo decided to cut down two thousand trees immediately. The provincial committee of Belluno commented that 'these are the lamentable effects of republican ideas being misunderstood by the inhabitants of that village'.[38]

There is less evidence of peasant protests in the hill areas, but this is not to say that they lacked grievances. The impossibility of exporting raw silk to the Austrian empire deprived many peasant households of what had been their only steady source of cash. In April and May there were widespread fears of a repetition of the grain shortages of the previous years, and in the area round Bassano the villagers tried to prevent grain from being shipped down the river Brenta.[39]

[36] For Montello, see ASV, Gov. Prov. 1848–9, CD, b. 390, no. 90, report of 4 April 1848. For Maniago, *ibid.*, MU, b. 4, no. 2036, 7 April 1848. For the law of 1839 see above, p. 27.

[37] MCV, Doc. Manin, no. 3619, letter of 10 April 1848.

[38] MCV, Doc. Manin, no. 3627, letter of 30 April 1848, which also tells of the actions of the peasants of Villagrande. For Manin's two proclamations to the Cadore, see *ibid.*, nos. 3617 (11 April) and 3625 (16 April). Similar incidents took place at Gemona in Friuli where the peasants stopped the local landlord, Count Groppler, from leaving for Udine, and made him take down the inscription in his house which commemorated that Francis I had slept there. They demanded the freeing of the forests and the communal lands, and the terrified count agreed immediately; ASV, Gov. Prov. 1848–9, CPD, b. 835/Gemona, no. 642, report of 7 April 1848.

[39] See ASV, Gov. Prov. 1848–9, CPD, b. 846/Bassano CPD, no. 1489, report of 1 May from Besica; and the remarks made by Caffo in the provincial consultative committee, 21, 22 and 29 April 1848, in *Le assemblee del Risorgimento*, vol. 2 (Venezia), p. 19 and p. 24. Unfortunately, these minutes of the consultative committee are extremely summary. The peasants in the Bassano area also requested permission to plant tobacco in order to supplement their incomes. Because of the strict state control of the growing and manufacturing of tobacco, the Austrians

However, it was the great plains that saw the most widespread disorders. Because the documents recording these events nearly always use the generic terms *contadino* or *villico* (peasant, villager), it is not possible for the historian to state categorically that it was landless labourers that were involved. But the main areas of protest, the province of Padua, Polesine and the plains east of Venice, were renowned for their great estates and landless peasantry. Although no systematic pattern of demands emerges, in quite a few areas it is clear that the peasants used the revolution to try and take over the government of the villages and to settle long-standing scores with particular landowners. In early April at Concordia in the district of Portogruaro, half way between Venice and Udine, about five hundred peasants invaded the estates of one of the local government officials, and compelled him to sell at half price all his stocks of wine and grain. They then broke into a recently built house and installed a peasant family there. This they did 'in the name of the sovereign people, who now own the house'.[40] At neighbouring San Michele, the villagers invaded the estates of the Venetian nobleman, Alvise Mocenigo. The climax came in mid-April, when a hostile crowd forced the municipal authorities of Portogruaro to resign and elected their own representatives instead. The event had repercussions in Venice, where Avesani and his group complained of the inactivity of the government and its tendency to let such situations drift into anarchy.[41]

On a number of occasions in April 1848 villagers in all parts of the southern Veneto decided to elect their own representatives as the communal deputation, and thus to try and break the stranglehold the landowners exercised over the village communities. In Cartura in the province of Padua *carruolanti* and *villici* were led by the son of an innkeeper, and the provincial committee of Padua wrote to Venice of the contrasts existing 'between the class of landowners and that of villagers'.[42] Similar incidents were reported at S. Pietro in Viminario and Vanzo (province of Padua), at Sorio (Vicenza), at Fiesso (Polesine), Mestre, Cavarzere and Gambarare (Venice). Often the local priests took the side of the villagers. At Gam-

had always prohibited any unauthorised tobacco plantations; see Ventura (ed.), *Verbali*, p. 156, ministerial meeting of 30 April 1848.

[40] See the petition from Avesani's group to the government, 13 April 1848, MCV, Doc. Manin, no. 3192. The petition was signed by Girolamo Lattis, who had been an eye-witness to the events.

[41] *Ibid.* For the occupation of Mocenigo's land, ASV, Gov. Prov. 1848–9, MU, b. 3, no. 1111, 3 April 1848. See also Bernardello, 'La paura del comunismo', pp. 69–70 and n. 56.

[42] ASV, Gov. Prov. 1848–9, CPD, b. 826/Padova, no. 2113, 26–7 April 1848. For some interesting remarks on the composition of the communal deputations in Italy in 1848–9 see Soldani, 'Contadini, operai e "popolo"', p. 599 n. 60.

barare Don Eugenio Bortoloni led four hundred armed villagers to Taglio Mira, forced the communal business to be done in the market square and took the local district commissioner hostage when he tried to quell the protest.[43]

Peasant action against individual landowners was not as common, but there were a few striking incidents involving non-Venetian proprietors. At Legnaro, a village south-east of Padua, the peasants hounded out a landowner of German origin, Emmanuel Edeles. He had doubled the obligations of his peasantry in 1847, and was hated for it. A huge crowd threatened to sack his house on 14 April, the Sunday on which the flag of the local national guard was to be blessed. In their report the communal authorities asked pardon for the disturbances, but added, 'how could this have been prevented at Legnaro, against so great a mass of demonstrators, who included all the members of the civic guard itself?'[44]

Lack of work for village artisans, the price of grain and fear of another disastrous spring also led to peasant protests in a number of areas. At San Donà di Piave, for instance, a crowd armed with shotguns and sticks laid siege to the office of the communal deputation while other villagers guarded the river to make sure that no grain left the village. Four representatives of the villagers demanded that work should be given to the artisans, that the price of grain should be fixed, and that the '*siori*' should not attempt to leave the village. The communal deputation tried to calm the situation by distributing one hundred bushels of maize to the poorest families, but the day after, 26 April, the crowds came back to burn the rolls of the civic guard, fearing that if the Austrians returned the rolls would be used for repressive purposes. At the end of April a *corpo franco* under Giuriati was sent to re-establish order.[45]

The Venetian government's reactions to these peasant protests appears to have been minimal. Occasionally, as at San Donà, they sent troops to help the local authorities, but they never seem to have discussed the causes of the protests, the peasants' conditions and needs. Had Manin tried to

---

[43] ASV, Pres. Luog., 1852–6, v/1, attached to no. 6291 (1853), report of 18 Oct. 1853. For a similar incident at Cavarzere on the Adige, where the villagers had joined in the anti-smoking campaign against the Austrians before the revolution, see Bernardello, 'La paura del comunismo', p. 70 and n. 59. The Venetian government was forced to send 20 gendarmes to re-establish order.

[44] ASV, Gov. Prov. 1848–9, CPD, b. 826/Padova, no. 2079. At Trecenta (Polesine) some villagers threatened to take over the vast estates of Count Spalletti of Bologna; Bernardello, 'La paura del comunismo', p. 69 and n. 51.

[45] Bernardello, 'La paura del comunismo', p. 69 and nn. 52–4. See also reports to the *consulta* on 25 May 1848 (*Le assemblee*, vol. 2, p. 44) on the civic guard of Dolo in the province of Venezia, who were refusing to let grain leave their village.

tackle these problems, he might well have encountered the hostility of many of the wealthy Venetian landowners and merchants on whose financial support he was to rely. But having abolished the personal tax and diminished the salt tax, Manin probably had to go further in order to secure the long-term support of the peasantry. He needed to examine in detail, as the Austrians had begun to do in 1830, ways of improving the contracts and conditions of work of the peasantry, particularly those of the southern Veneto. He could also have taken immediate steps to ensure the peasantry a greater say in the local government of their villages. Clearly, these were measures which would not have resolved in any fundamental way the underlying class antagonisms of the countryside, but they would have been accepted by the peasantry as further proof of the government's good intentions.

To take such initiatives would have been treading on very delicate ground, but there is some evidence that the more liberal proprietors of the Veneto might have welcomed them. The enlightened landowner Gherardo Freschi, the editor of *L'Amico del contadino*, raised the problem of peasant support during the first meetings of the provincial consultative committee at Venice in mid-April. While condemning the invasion of private property at Portogruaro and elsewhere, and ascribing these actions in part to Austrian *agents provocateurs*, Freschi warned of the urgent need to provide moral leadership and material aid for the countryside. At the same time as advocating conscription and a general organisation of all the national guards of the Veneto, Freschi urged the government to regulate the price of bread by government decree.[46] Fortunato Sceriman, district commissioner at Ceneda for many years, was later to advise the setting up of agrarian schools and the reform of the contract system in the Veneto by extending *enfiteusi*, long-term leases of land.[47] But these were lone voices in Venice amidst almost total indifference to the peasant problem, and the Venetian peasantry waited in vain for any further concessions or attention from the republican government.

The defence of Friuli

The Austrian troops which had surrendered at Venice and Udine no sooner reached Trieste than they were reorganised ready to return from whence they had come. General Nugent, the man entrusted with the vital task of reconquering the Veneto, was an Irish career officer who had seen

[46] *Le assemblee*, vol. 2, pp. 13, 16 and 20.
[47] See the interesting article on Sceriman by G. E. Ferrari, 'Spunti di riforma economico-sociale negli scritti d'un funzionario veneto ai margini della rivoluzione', *Rassegna Storica del Risorgimento*, 44 (1957), pp. 350–70. For his argument on *enfiteusi*, pp. 361–2.

fifty-three years of service in the Austrian army. He had the great advantage of familiarity with the terrain on which he had to fight, for thirty-five years earlier he had been quarter-master general of the invading Austrian armies. Nugent hastily ordered a conscription levy of four men in every hundred in the area round Trieste, and in this way he collected and armed some 6,000 troops. Together with the regular battalions and the influx of volunteers from Vienna, many of them students, Nugent by mid-April had a force of some 11,000–12,000 men ready to march through the Veneto and reach the besieged Radetzky at Verona.[48]

The strategic importance of Nugent's mission must not be underestimated. His success or failure would mark a turning point, both for the Italian cause and for the whole European revolutionary movement. Radetzky, without Nugent's relief army, was too weak to risk battle with the Piedmontese forces which were threatening him from the west. In the first fortnight after the revolution the situation not only in northern Italy but in other parts of the empire seemed so desperate for the Austrians that many of them thought there was little to be done but abandon the Italian provinces. The Piedmontese envoy at Vienna, Marquis Alberto de' Ricci, reported on 29 March that a number of 'influential persons' thought that Lombardy-Venetia should have its independence in return for assuming a part of the public debt. On 1 April the minister of the interior Pillersdorff received a deputation of the leading Viennese bankers, merchants and industrialists warning him that a full-scale war in Italy would be economic suicide.[49] For a number of months the Austrian ministers seriously contemplated abandoning Lombardy in order to try and preserve Venetia and the rest of their empire.[50] Radetzky's forces at first represented one of the few remnants of the armies of the old order, and politicians like Pillersdorff were loath to see him compelled to surrender. Radetzky himself always favoured adamant resistance, but if the Venetians had stopped Nugent, there seems little doubt that the Austrians would have tried to make peace with or without Radetzky's consent.

[48] On Nugent see the Earl of Ellesmere (trans.), *Military Events in Italy, 1848–9*, p. 92 (the anonymous author of this work was apparently a Swiss officer in the Austrian army who was in constant contact with the Austrian commanders). The Austrians had already begun to build up their forces on the eastern frontier at the beginning of 1848, and intensified this process after the French revolution of February. This helps to account, at least in part, for the swiftness with which Nugent was able to move onto the offensive, a celerity that no one expected; see A. Venezia, 'Il '48 nel Friuli orientale', in *La Venezia Giulia e la Dalmazia*, vol. 2, pp. 220–1.
[49] See the dispatches of the Marquis Alberto de' Ricci, published in C. Spellanzon, *Il vero segreto di Re Carlo Alberto*, pp. 165 and 167.
[50] Taylor, *The Italian Problem*, pp. 97–8.

What happened in the Veneto was thus of great significance and it would be wrong to assume that Nugent's army was so overwhelmingly strong that the result was a foregone conclusion. Just before invading the Veneto Nugent wrote to Radetzky and, while declining the offer of a detachment of troops from Verona, he stressed that it could take him a considerable time to reach Verona, and that all depended on the opposition he encountered.[51] Time was the essence of it, for the longer it took Nugent, the greater the risk to Radetzky of a decisive action with the numerically superior forces of Charles Albert.

Manin's government made little contribution to the vital defence of the eastern frontier of the Veneto. Of the two companies of grenadiers sent home from Venice to defend Udine, only twenty actually arrived. The provincial committee of Udine complained bitterly that even these had no arms, and were furnished with leave passes by the Venetian government.[52] In the month that elapsed between the triumph of the revolution and Nugent's counter-attack, Venice managed to send only a few hundred volunteers to the front.[53] Brunello has made the important point that many of the Venetian parish priests, following the lead of the conservative patriarch Monico, refrained from advising their parishioners to enrol in the *crociati* against the Austrians.[54] This undoubtedly affected the number of volunteers, but it is impossible to believe that vigorous action by the government would not have produced more positive results.

Most importantly, the Venetians refused to send sufficient arms to Udine, in spite of repeated requests from the provincial committee. On 3 April thirty-five citizens petitioned the minister of war, urging that all the Venetian civic guards who did not know how to use their muskets should give them up for the defence of Friuli. But it was only on 19 April, after the Friulian committee of war had exposed Venice for sending only two hundred muskets and two hundred sabres, that arms were taken from the Venetian civic guard and given to the emissaries from Friuli. By then the decisive battles were being fought and lost outside Palmanova.

[51] R. Cessi, 'La difesa delle provincie venete nel 1848', in *Bollettino del Museo Civico di Padova*, 30–43 (1942–54), p. 217 n. 19.

[52] ASV, Gov. Prov. 1848–9, MG, b. 127, no. 333, letter of 2 April 1848.

[53] The first Venetian 'crusaders', 257 in all, were commanded by Ernesto Grondoni. Grondoni, like Manin, was a lawyer, and was among the forty proscribed by the Austrians at the end of the revolution. In 1859 he entered the Piedmontese army and rose to the rank of colonel. Among the volunteers were the actor Gustavo Modena and his wife as well as the painter Ippolito Caffi. Another 500 'crusaders' left Venice on 8 April, but went westwards to Vicenza; Jäger, *Storia dei corpi militari*, pp. 88ff and 94ff.

[54] Brunello, 'Rivoluzione e clero', fos. 158–61. Grondoni was so furious with the patriarch Monico that he threatened him with the 'anathema of a whole people' if he refused to preach a crusade against the Austrians.

The consignment of arms from Venice never reached Udine before it fell, and was to be used at Treviso instead.[55]

Local action proved far more vigorous. The provincial committee of Udine lowered the salt tax by a half, the greatest reduction of this tax made in all the provinces of the Veneto. It also used both the carrot and the stick on the recalcitrant grenadiers, ordering them to rejoin the ranks immediately on pain of court martial, but offering them double pay and announcing the abolition of corporal punishment in the army. It appealed to all those who normally emigrated for many months of each year to find work, to stay instead and defend Friuli, and offered 1.50 lire a day to the workmen of Udine to help build barricades.[56]

The committee also decided to try and form an army of 10,000 men from all the local militias of the surrounding countryside. The response to this bold initiative was generally enthusiastic. Most of the clergy urged the civic guards to send detachments to the assembly points of Gonars and Trevignano, and some, such as the archpriests of Motta and Spilimbergo, led the militias of their villages. By the middle of April nearly 6,000 men had assembled, striking testimony to the willingness of the Friulian peasantry to fight for the revolution in its first month. The numbers would have been higher had the committee been able to arm more of the men and had the peasants from the mountain villages of Carnia not been forced to remain at home to guard against imminent invasion from the extreme north.[57]

[55] ASV, Gov. Prov. 1848–9, CD, b. 391, nos. 396–7, 541. The muskets were given to Francesco Dall'Ongaro. For the petition to the government of 3 April, *ibid.*, MG, b. 127, no. 274. For the complaints of the Friulian committee of war, which consisted of L. Duodo, G. B. Cavedalis and A. Conti, see their report of 16 April 1848, MCV, Doc. Manin, no. 3604. As soon as Treviso heard of the first Austrian victories Giuseppe Olivi went to see Manin in Venice to implore him to take drastic measures to save Friuli. Unfortunately, we have no details of their conversation; see ASU, archivio comunale, b. 580, R, no. 538, letter of the provincial committee of Treviso to Udine, 19 April 1848.

[56] See the proclamation by the municipality of Udine, ASU, archivio comunale, b. 583, without number or date. For the circular appealing to the Friulani not to emigrate, ASV, Gov. Prov. 1848–9, CPD, b. 835/Latisana, no. 222, 1 April 1848. For the salt tax and the grenadiers, ASU, archivio comunale, b. 583, nos. 12 and 237, 24 March and 2 April 1848.

[57] E. D'Agostini, in his *Ricordi militari del Friuli*, vol. 2, estimates on p. 40 that the total number of volunteers were 5,687 and on p. 45 n. 1, that they were 5,742. It is difficult to understand why G. B. Cavedalis, in his *I commentari*, omits all reference to these volunteers and goes as far as to accuse the peasantry of not defending the cause and of aiding the return of the Austrians (vol. 1, p. 107). On the priests, see ASV, Pres. Luog., 1852–6, b. 224, v, 10/17, for an Austrian report of 11 March 1856 on the activities during the revolution of Don Agostino Casati, archpriest of Spilimbergo; *ibid.*, 1852–6, b. 224, v, 10/7, for a similar

Other parts of the Veneto also sent detachments: Treviso sent as many as 900, with Count D'Onigo, the commander of their civic guard, being particularly active in the organisation of the volunteers. Smaller detachments came from Bassano and Belluno. Many of these men, such as those from Valle near Agordo, were from very distant villages, and travelled for many miles, first in boats down the Piave and then on foot from Treviso, in order to reach the front.[58]

Not surprisingly, the collecting together of these popular forces presented serious problems of discipline, arms and provisioning which were never really overcome. The men lacked experienced officers, many of the peasants had arrived with no proper footwear, payment and food materialised only occasionally, and, of course, most of the companies had no firearms. By 12 April, 130 men from Mortegliano and Codroipo had deserted and many others had begun to complain.[59] This force could only have been effective if it had been well armed, well paid and well led. As Pieri has pointed out, the presence of a few hundred regular troops from the Piedmontese army would probably have worked wonders for the morale of the volunteers and their ability to resist the first Austrian attacks.[60] But

report of 21 May 1854 on Don Gianpiero de Domini, archpriest of Motta. Ellesmere, *Military Events*, p. 96, makes the point that anti-Austrian feeling was particularly strong in the border province of Udine, where 'the vicinity of the German frontier and the influx of German travellers had filled the inns with German landlords and waiters, and had also introduced many Germans into various other employments'. On 7 April the municipality of Latisana begged the rich citizens of the town to contribute for the uniforms of the poorer so that their civic guard would not cut a 'brutta figura' alongside the other companies of the area; ASV, Gov. Prov. 1848–9, CPD. b. 835/Latisana, no. 116.

[58] See ASV, Gov. Prov., 1848–9, CPD, b. 823/Belluno, no. 817 and attached documents for the province of Belluno; *ibid.*, CPD, b. 846/Bassano, nos. 872, 874, 879 and 898, for Bassano and its neighbourhood (the Bassano committee offered 60 lire to every volunteer, to be paid at the end of the war); A. Santalena, *Treviso nel 1848*, p. 71, doc. XVII, for a letter of D'Onigo's of 31 March 1848; finally ASU, archivio comunale, b. 580, R, no. 473, letter from Treviso of 8 April 1848, giving details including the payment of 1.50 Au. lire per day for each soldier.

[59] ASU, archivio comunale, b. 580, R, no. 478, letter from the commander of one of the volunteer battalions, Rosmini, to the committee of war in Udine. The provincial committee of Belluno wrote to their volunteers asking for the return of a certain Captain Badini to Belluno, as his artillery experience was sorely needed. Captain Palatini replied that the men from Belluno had already asked for leave to return home and that only Badini had been able to persuade them to stay. The Belluno committee accepted that Badini would remain, and sent letters, parcels and pipe tobacco to their volunteers on the front; ASV, Gov. Prov. 1848–9, CPD, b. 823/Belluno, no. 817 and documents attached to it.

[60] Pieri, *Storia militare*, p. 370. He estimates that if all the volunteers had been collected together, and a full complement of *guardia mobile* from Venice had

in the absence of any significant help from either Piedmont or Venice, the formation of a popular army on the eastern frontier was an impossible task.

Matters were not helped by the behaviour of General Zucchi, the commanding officer. Zucchi refused to recognise the republic or to go to Venice to confer with Manin, and at first did not believe in the possibility of an Austrian invasion of Friuli.[61] He was convinced that the volunteers were useless, and said that those armed only with pikes should be sent home immediately. He quarrelled seriously with Colonel Conti, a former Austrian soldier who was in charge of the volunteer forces, and resolved to confine himself with what regular troops there were to the fortress of Palmanova. As a result, half-starved, unarmed peasants were left to defend the advanced posts of the Venetian republic.[62]

On 15 April Zucchi ordered about 1,000 of the volunteers to occupy the village of Visco. This they did successfully, and held it on the 17th against about 1,500 Austrian troops.[63] The following day Nugent moved up another two battalions. Conti appealed for regular troops and two cannon to come to his aid, but Zucchi refused the request and the volunteers were forced to retreat. Nugent burnt two villages to the ground as he advanced, and the remainder of the volunteers, terrified by this act and by the Austrian cannon, fled on 19 April. Zucchi wrote a sarcastic letter to Conti the same day, blaming 'your national guards, on whom you put so much store and I none at all'.[64]

been united to the regulars from the Austrian regiments, the Venetians could easily have had an army of 16,000–17,000 men in the first month of the revolution.

[61] Manin wrote to Zucchi on 29 March 1848 asking him to come to Venice to work out 'a plan for a general strategy'; ASV, Gov. Prov. 1848–9, MU, b. 2, no. 425. For Zucchi's views on the slim chances of an Austrian attack and on the Venetian republic, see respectively MCV, Doc. Manin, no. 2662, report of Tommasoni; and Ventura (ed.), *Verbali*, p. 121, ministerial meeting of 14 April 1848. Zucchi's own defence of his actions was that to hold Palmanova was the first priority, while awaiting adequate reinforcements. Radetzky, after all, had adopted the same tactics at Verona; see N. Bianchi (ed.), *Memorie del Generale Carlo Zucchi*, pp. 124–9.

[62] Conti's memoirs are to be found in BCU, fondo Corrente, no. 3851. Conti had seen twenty-four years' military service before 1848 and had been a captain in the Austrian army. He describes Zucchi as 'a frail, nervous little man, rather worn out by age and infirmity, but with eyes that were still bright and which betrayed his southern origin' (Conti, MS, p. 26). For Zucchi's opinion of Conti and the volunteer forces, see ASU, archivio comunale, b. 580, R, nos. 477 and 510. Grondoni wrote to the Venetian committee of defence on 17 April 1848 warning that the peasants guarding vital villages on the front could not be counted on to resist for long; ASV, Gov. Prov. 1848–9, CD, b. 391, no. 402.

[63] Pieri, *Storia militare*, p. 372.

[64] ASU, archivio comunale, b. 580, R, no. 510. The Austrian troops had advanced

The road to Udine was now open. On 21 April Nugent sent an emissary, but he was not even received by the provincial committee. That evening the Austrians began a bombardment of the city that lasted for two hours. Within Udine there were many elements of the population and the soldiers who wanted to resist to the last. But the city was not easily defendable, and after the rout of 19 April the inhabitants could expect no help from the surrounding countryside. Fearful lest the city be razed to the ground, the archbishop, Bricito, agreed to try and obtain favourable terms from the Austrians. His carriage left the city accompanied by a fierce hailstorm and the insults of the populace. By the afternoon of 22 April it was all over. Although at least two members of the provincial committee refused to sign the capitulation, claiming that it was a betrayal of the Italian cause, Udine surrendered and opened its gates to Nugent.[65]

The Austrians were careful to treat the citizens well, and did not attempt to take reprisals. Their policy at this time was to try and reconcile the Italians to Austrian rule by promising them greater independence and liberty. On 19 April Count Hartig, who had been specifically sent from Vienna for this purpose, published a proclamation guaranteeing the Lombardo-Venetians extensive freedoms, and the lessening of taxes on the poor. One of the Austrians' first acts on taking Udine was to grant greater power to the municipalities and communal deputations of Friuli, as well as to absolve local vestryboards from having to send reports to the civil authorities.[66] There is no evidence to show whether these measures had any effect in pacifying the population, but by 27 April the whole of Friuli east of the river Tagliamento, except for the two forts of Palmanova and Osoppo, was in the hands of the Austrians. Nugent encountered further

shouting 'Viva l'Italia', so that at first the volunteers had thought they were reinforcements sent by Zucchi; ASV, Gov. Prov. 1848–9, CD, b. 391, no. 434, letter from the Venetian emissary Domenico Ortis to the committee of defence, 19 April. A day earlier he had reported that the volunteers would have held their positions if they had been helped by Zucchi; *ibid.*, no. 379. The painter Ippolito Caffi had been taken prisoner by the Austrians on 17 April. He and another twenty-two prisoners were taken to Gorizia; Caffi describes how they were spat on and insulted by the local population. But Hartig spared all the prisoners, commissioned a painting from Caffi and freed him and the others after the capitulation of Udine; see Caffi's romantic account in Racc. Andreola, vol. 2, pp. 340–6.

65 For a defence of the archbishop Zaccaria Bricito, see T. Tessitori, 'Zaccaria Bricito (celebrazione del centenario del 1848)', in *Atti e Memorie dell'Accademia di Udine*, 10 (1945–8), especially p. 61.

66 See the 'Istruzioni per la semplificazione degli affari amministrativi nelle provincie italiane' of 24 April 1848, in ASV, Pres. Luog., 1849–66, b. 586, atti del governo militare 1848, no. 30. For Hartig's proclamation of 19 April, *ibid.*, attached to no. 18.

resistance only at Pontebba, north of Udine, where three hundred civic guards from this mountainous district put up a heroic fight for a number of days to prevent the Austrians from reopening communications with Carinthia. The forts of Palmanova and Osoppo, well equipped and valiantly defended, were to stand firm for many months, but the Italian soldiers in them were powerless to halt the Austrians' advance to the river Tagliamento.

Piedmont and Venice

April was a month of cruel disillusion for Daniele Manin. At the same time as the Austrians returned to the offensive in Friuli with a speed and decisiveness that no one had anticipated, it became clear that Manin's political line adopted at the end of March fulfilled neither of its proposed functions – it failed to ensure the delaying of all political decisions until the end of the war, nor did it secure the aid of Piedmont against the invading Austrians.

The first hint that Manin had of Piedmont's intention not to abide by the political truce proclaimed by Milan came with the arrival in Venice of Francesco Restelli, the Milanese representative. At his first meeting with the Venetian ministers, on 5 April, Restelli read out a letter from Count Martini, in which he announced that Piedmont had called for immediate elections in Lombardy, Venetia, Piacenza and Reggio.[67] As the Venetians had decided, only six days earlier, against having any elections because of the political truce, they naturally reacted angrily to the Piedmontese suggestion. Restelli reported that the Venetian ministers did not hide 'their jealousy of and diffidence towards the king of Piedmont, whom under no circumstances do they wish to be king of these provinces'.[68] He went on to

[67] See Restelli's dispatch of 6 April in Monti, *Francesco Restelli*, p. 255. Both Charles Albert and Casati backed elections at this date because of the favourable impression they thought the presence of the Piedmontese army had created; see A. Depoli, *I rapporti*, vol. 1, pp. 128–36. Pareto in Turin quashed the idea because he believed it 'absolutely inopportune' (L. Pareto to G. Pareto, 6 April 1848, in T. Buttini and M. Avetta (ed.), *I rapporti fra il governo sardo*, p. 52). The Piedmontese ministers, convinced that republican feeling was still far too strong, could not understand why Casati agreed to the proposal when the Milanese government had just successfully avoided the elections proposed by the republicans. All of this of course was not known to the Venetians, who were presented only with Martini's letter.

[68] Monti, *Francesco Restelli*, p. 255. Restelli, though sent by the pro-Albertist Milanese government, was a republican. He seems to have favoured an immediate united election as being the only way to establish a Lombardo-Venetian republic, a republic which Charles Albert would then have been forced to recognise; see his letter of 12 April to Francesco Dall'Ongaro in F. Dall'Ongaro, *Epistolario* (ed. A. De Gubernatis), pp. 268–9.

say that 'the Venetian government wishes to postpone the convocation of an assembly until the whole land is free of both Austrian and Piedmontese troops'. At the ministerial meeting of 7 April Manin commented astutely on the marked difference between the Milanese and Venetian governments.[69] Whereas Charles Albert, said Manin, would willingly accept a Milanese envoy to his camp, because the Milanese had 'not closed the way to his ambitions', a Venetian representative would be less welcome since he 'would represent a hostile principle'.

A few days later Lazzaro Rebizzo, the Piedmontese emissary, arrived in Venice and provided some temporary reassurance for the Venetian republicans. He was a friend of Manin's, and brought with him a dispatch of 31 March from the Piedmontese foreign minister, Lorenzo Pareto, which recognised 'the provisional government of Venice'.[70] The Turin government proffered 'those relations of good friendship and that material aid necessary for total independence, which, in the sublime words of Charles Albert, "*a brother must give to a brother, a friend to a friend*"'.[71]

The realities of Piedmontese policy were far removed from such professions of fraternal aid. Charles Albert wrote to Pius IX on 18 April 1848: 'our greatest enemies are not the imperial soldiers but the anti-religious republican party which is operating at this moment with great energy and using the most perverse means to achieve its ends'.[72] The Piedmontese had a mortal and, in the end, exaggerated fear of the republicans gaining total control in northern Italy, which would ruin their plans for uniting Lombardy to Piedmont and threaten the house of Savoy itself. Their political aims were clear: to secure the annexation of Lombardy, isolate the Venetian republicans and then, if the circumstances proved favourable, consume Venice and the Veneto as 'another leaf of the Italian artichoke'.[73] At the end of March the Marquis Ponzio Vaglia was dis-

---

[69] Ventura (ed.), *Verbali*, p. 106.

[70] Depoli (*I rapporti*, vol. 1, pp. 67–8) is intent on proving that this is a unique example in 'the history of diplomatic relations of a monarchist government recognising a republic which has not even sent an official communication'. In fact, the dispatch of the 31st recognised only 'the provisional government of Venice' and made no mention of the republic.

[71] Planat de la Faye (ed.), *Documenti*, vol. 1, p. 199. The italics are in the original text.

[72] P. Pirri, 'La missione di mons. Corboli-Bussi in Lombardia nel 1848', in *Rivista di Storia della Chiesa in Italia*, 1 (1947), p. 74.

[73] The idea of the Piedmontese eating the leaves of the Italian artichoke, one by one, is probably the most famous literary image of the Risorgimento. The Piedmontese statesman, Count Castagnetto, was dubious whether the great powers would let Piedmont have Venice, and was himself content to see Lombardy alone unite with Piedmont; see his letter to Casati of 22 April 1848 in Ferrari (ed.), *Carteggio Casati–Castagnetto*, p. 68.

patched from Turin on an unofficial mission to arouse sympathy for Charles Albert in Venetia. On 31 March he wrote from Milan of his first discussions of the possibility of a Lombardo-Venetian kingdom under the duke of Genoa.[74] This, he concluded, would be 'the first step on the road to the fusion of Lombardy-Venetia with Piedmont'.

In military terms, the Piedmontese had little intention of coming to the aid of the Veneto. The paradox of the first war of Italian independence, as Piero Pieri has pointed out, was 'of a revolutionary war led by a man who feared both revolution and revolutionaries'.[75] In April 1848 the regulars of the Piedmontese army needed to be the fulcrum for the volunteer forces of the entire nation. A Piedmontese brigade was sorely needed in the Veneto to provide the core of the resistance to Nugent. Another should have been sent into the Trentino to cut Radetzky's links to the north and close the circle round the quadrilateral.[76] But the indecision, the timidity and the military unpreparedness of the Piedmontese general staff, when combined with their disdain and fear of the popular forces, meant that during the vital weeks when the Italians held the initiative, the Piedmontese army made little headway. Charles Albert first lost the chance at the end of March of a swift and crushing victory over Radetzky's depleted

[74] AST, carte politiche diverse, 1848, fasc. 132. It is very striking that Ponzio Vaglia had spent the majority of a long letter of 28 March from Milan describing the economic advantages of linking up the railways of northern Italy and driving one through Switzerland to connect with northern Europe. Lorenzo Pareto wrote to his brother on 6 April 1848 (Buttini and Avetta, *I rapporti fra il governo sardo*, p. 62): 'It is no bad thing that Ponzio is going to Venice; he could be very useful as he is very skilful; and besides, not having any official mission, he will be able to discover things that Rebizzo, with his contacts limited to the authorities, will not.' Bianca de' Simoni, Rebizzo's wife, had written to Teresa Manin on the same day: 'I do not like Charles Albert, and I do not like the power of a king, but if the nation gives the law to the king, and the king helps the nation to unite in one aim, with one will, then I accept the king and I even demand him... Make use of this army which now defends you' (MCV, Doc. Pell., b. 10, miscellanea, no number.

[75] Pieri, *Storia militare*, p. 368. Charles Albert actually took steps to discourage and disband many of the volunteer detachments that had formed in the first weeks of the revolution; see E. Rota, 'Del contributo dei lombardi alla guerra del 1848; il problema del volontarismo', *Nuova Rivista Storica*, 12 (1928), pp. 18–25.

[76] Pieri, *Storia militare*, p. 799. There was no doubting the fighting spirit of the Piedmontese army in the first months of the war; M. B. Hanau, the *Times* correspondent, wrote to Robert Campbell from Vallegio on 3 May 1848: 'they are in the highest condition, men and horses, and the soldiers have so much confidence from this continued success that they take themselves to be far superior to the enemy and they demand at every moment to be led against him... *The Times* was right to send me down here' (MRM, archivio Cattaneo, cart. 10, plico xv).

forces, and then remained locked in a war of position on the Mincio throughout April.

On 9 April 1848 the Venetian government decided to send Count Cittadella of Padua and the Venetian lawyer Bartolomeo Benvenuti to Charles Albert's headquarters.[77] There they learned unequivocally that the Piedmontese had decided to put a political price on their military intervention in the Veneto. Cittadella wrote back to Venice on 14 April 1848:

The minister of war [Franzini] has praised the generous sentiments of the king and his sons, but has made us note clearly that Piedmont cannot be inspired by a purely chivalrous spirit and awaits some recompense for its great sacrifices. He did not make it clear of what this recompense should consist, but many of those close to the king have said openly that Piedmont and the Lombardo-Venetian kingdom should form a constitutional kingdom with its seat at Milan ... the fact is that the word 'republic' displeases him and his ministers, and also his troops, who are realists in the most narrow sense ... From this you will see, citizen ministers, that our presence at the camp of the king is superfluous until Venice takes some definite resolution upon its political system and upon its union with, or independence from Lombardy. This resolution should be taken with all possible haste because, in our opinion, until the king knows our intentions and those of the Lombards, the military effort will not proceed with that speed which you and all Italy require.[78]

The Venetian ministers met on 18 April to consider Cittadella's shattering report.[79] Naturally, they did not know that the Piedmontese army was extremely unlikely to intervene in the Veneto whatever political decisions the Venetians took. With their confidence badly shaken after Montebello, and with the news of the massing of Nugent's armies, the Venetian ministers failed to agree on what to do next. Pincherle, overawed by Cittadella's report, asked, 'If we made it understood that the republic is

[77] They were dispatched so as to allay some ministers' fears that if the war was to end swiftly, Venice would not be represented at the 'conventions' that might follow. See *La Repubblica veneta nel 1848-9*, vol. 1, *Documenti diplomatici*, pp. 21-2. Cittadella and Benevenuti were not, as has commonly been assumed, the first emissaries from the Venetian government to Charles Albert. A certain Francesco Maiset had left Venice on 31 March, reached Turin on 4 April and had an audience with the king on 8 April. Charles Albert told him that Lombardy-Venetia had to decide on a form of government, whatever it might be. See his itinerary and report in MCV, Doc. Manin, no. 3688, and ASV, Gov. Prov. 1848-9, MU, b. 5, no. 2613, where he claims his expenses.

[78] *La Repubblica veneta*, vol. 1, pp. 27-8. Benvenuti wrote to Manin (*ibid.*, pp. 24-6, 14 April), saying that he and his colleague were not getting on because Benvenuti was decidedly more republican; he asked to be recalled as he was dying of boredom.

[79] Ventura (ed.), *Verbali*, p. 138.

only provisional, would that be sufficient to content him [Charles Albert]?' Manin refused to consider this compromise. He was determined to salvage Venetian independence, at least until the end of the war, and insisted that the agreed policy of *a guerra finita* be maintained while repeated appeals for aid were made to the Piedmontese king.[80] He also thought that Charles Albert would be forced to intervene in the Veneto in any case, in order to prevent Nugent's troops from reaching Radetzky.

Tommaseo disagreed with this line of action, though he submitted to it. He thought that the council of ministers had no right to continue in the sort of political limbo imposed by Manin's policy: 'Charles Albert has laid down ignoble conditions as the price of his aid, which we cannot by ourselves either accept or reject . . . either we must ask the people what they want or else resign.'[81] Tommaseo favoured the immediate calling of a Venetian assembly to decide on the matter. However, Castelli, Paleocapa and Camerata saw no other solution than fusion with Piedmont. They therefore favoured the calling of a united Lombardo-Venetian assembly, which was what the Lombards wanted, because this would almost certainly have produced a majority in favour of the Piedmontese king.[82] In mid-April Manin was still able to assure the acceptance of his delaying tactic, but as time passed Paolucci and Pincherle gave reluctant support to the fusionist camp. Tommaseo, always sceptical of Charles Albert's military prowess, then sided with Manin, and the split between the two ministerial factions was soon reflected throughout the city.

The first steps in the fusionist campaign were made on 22 April 1848. As soon as the news of Nugent's recapture of Udine reached Venice, Paleocapa was dispatched to Charles Albert's headquarters. Manin gave him strict instructions to solicit aid without making any political promises.[83] Paleocapa ignored these orders and let Castagnetto understand

---

[80] On 16 April Admiral Bua had read out a letter to Charles Albert at the Venetian council of ministers, asking the king to aid Friuli by sending the papal army into the Veneto; Ventura (ed.), *Verbali*, pp. 129–30.

[81] Tommaseo's note read to the council of ministers, 19 April 1848, in Tommaseo and Capponi, *Carteggio inedito*, vol. 2, p. 648 n. 1.

[82] The complicated question of whether to have one or two assemblies to decide on the eventual fate of Lombardy-Venetia dominated the political discussions of these weeks. Behind all the Venetian objections to one assembly lay the fear that the republicanism of Venice would be swamped by the votes of Lombardy and the Venetian provinces. For the different positions, see Restelli's letter to the Venetian government, 11 April 1848, in Monti, *Francesco Restelli*, pp. 271–2, and Calucci's letter to the same government of 19 April from Milan, MCV, Doc. Manin, no. 2050.

[83] For Paleocapa's instructions, see *La Repubblica veneta*, vol. 1, p. 31. Manin continued to implore Charles Albert's aid, and on 28 April (MCV, Doc. Manin, no. 857) added as an inducement, as a result of pressure from Castelli: 'We wish

that Venice was ready for fusion. From this time onwards, the Piedmontese intensified their campaign for the establishment of a kingdom of
northern Italy, and the Lombards for a united Lombardo-Venetian
assembly to decide their political fate.

The alienation of the Venetian provinces

The attempts of the northern Italian monarchists to draw Venice into
fusion with Piedmont and Lombardy were greatly helped by the attitude
of the Venetian provincial committees. For a number of reasons –
principally lack of representation in the Venetian central government, the
prospect of being left defenceless against the Austrians, and fear of the
social disturbances caused by the proclamation of the republic – the provincial ruling classes looked increasingly to Charles Albert for salvation.

The provincial consultative committee, the *consulta*, met in Venice for
the first time on 10 April 1848. There was an immediate fracas. One
of the representatives from Treviso, Dr Giuseppe Bianchetti, declared that
the *consulta* was both premature and illegal: premature because it was out
of order to discuss forms of government and administration while the
military threat was so grave; illegal because the Trevisans had no intention of becoming subject citizens, but wished to participate in the government on an equal footing. Manin, furious, threatened to have Bianchetti
thrown out by the guards. At this the delegates from Treviso walked out.[84]

to repeat that the form of government adopted on 22 March can be changed in
the interests of the communal Italian cause, once the assembly of the nation
meets.'

[84] See Santalena, *Treviso nel 1848*, pp. 56–8. The original delegates to the *consulta*
were: for the province of Venice, Leopardo Martinengo, Giuseppe Reali, Nicola
Chiereghin; for the province of Padua, Giacomo Brusoni, Benedetto Dalvecchio,
Girolamo Faccioli; for the province of Friuli, Luigi Gaspare Gaspari, Gherardo
Freschi, Giandomenico Ciconi; for the province of Vicenza, Gaetano Sbardelà,
Valentino Pasini, Luigi Caffo; for the province of Polesine (Rovigo), Lorenzo
Gobbetti, Dr Vincenzo Tedeschi, Dr Giambattista Lubati; for the province of
Belluno, Giuseppe Palatini, Sante Vanni, Alessandro Miari. The presence of
important figures like Freschi, Reali and Pasini must have made the discussions
of the *consulta* of particular interest, and it is sad that the minutes of the meetings
have come down to us in such abbreviated form. See Racc. Andreola, vol. 1,
pp. 608–9, for complaints against the methods of appointing the representatives;
also the letters from the Cadore, MCV, Doc. Pell., b. xxxvii/26 (12), ad ASV,
Gov. Prov. 1848–9, CPD, b. 823/Belluno, no. 818; and from Lendinara near
Rovigo, MCV, Doc. Pell., b. xxxviii/11 (56). Many felt that there should have
been elections. The Venetian government had also decided to appoint representatives from Verona, to make it quite clear to the Piedmontese that the city
was part of the Veneto, but Aleardo Aleardi and G. B. Malenza refused to come;
Racc. Andreola, vol. 1, pp. 657–8, letter of 21 April 1848.

On 12 April one of them, the monarchist Count Guglielmo D'Onigo, who was also the commander of the civic guard of Treviso, wrote from Venice to Giuseppe Olivi:

the glorious achievement of Manin and Tommaseo, denied by no one, is confined to having established all the elements of an ancient despotism, the despotism of the lion of St Mark ... since they show themselves ungrateful to the Italian constitutional monarchs, they could well come to an agreement with the foreigner, so as to save themselves from a menacing peril, and their states from anarchy; mediaeval history must be our guide at this solemn moment.[85]

The Paduans were equally angry, but decided not to embitter relations further by leaving. On 15 April Castelli wrote to Tommaseo, urging that the Venetians should follow the example of Lombardy, and incorporate the provincial representatives into the government. But Manin remained adamant that until a constitutional assembly was elected, the provinces were only to have consultative status.[86] The Trevisans finally agreed to send three more delegates, and through the skilful work of Valentino Pasini of Vicenza, who remained loyal to Manin, the *consulta* was slowly won round to official policy.[87]

But nothing could mask the increasing gravity of the military situation, and the failure of the Venetian government to take decisive measures to meet the danger. In mid-April Radetzky ordered two battalions to sweep out the Lombard volunteers who were encamped at the village of Castelnuovo, west of Verona. It was an action that had many similarities with that at Montebello, except that Radetzky went one further and ordered the whole village to be burnt down and its inhabitants to be massacred. One hundred and thirteen men, women and children perished.[88] The

---

[85] ASV, Gov. Prov. 1848–9, CPD, b. 834/Treviso, no. 1549.

[86] For Castelli's letter, see Tommaseo, *Venezia*, vol. 1, p. 187 n. 482. Tommaseo wrote to Manin saying that the *consulta* had to act as intermediary between the government and the provinces, and that there should be more exchange of opinions; see MCV, Doc. Manin, no. 4005, without date, but almost certainly of April 1848. On the Paduans, see Ferrari, 'L'attitudine di Padova', pp. 205–6. Manin does not appear to have tried to justify his intransigence in any letter, speech or proclamation of this period.

[87] Pasini's support of a single assembly earned him the distrust of the Vicenza provincial committee, and led to his resignation from the *consulta* on 24 April 1848. Pasini was not in favour of the republic, but believed that the correct legal method for the unification of Lombardy and Venetia was through separate assemblies. See his long letter of 1 May to Durini, in Bonghi, *Valentino Pasini*, pp. 224–9. Durini continued to harbour illusions about Charles Albert: on 24 April he wrote to Pasini saying that in the event of fusion there would be 'a republican monarchy' in northern Italy; *ibid.*, p. 236.

[88] Pieri, *Storia militare*, p. 319, and MCV, Doc. Manin, nos. 3722 and 3725,

Austrian action at Castelnuovo naturally terrified the local authorities of the Veneto. They began to fear that a similar fate awaited them, either from Nugent's troops in the east or Radetzky's in the west.[89] In the absence of any attempts to organise a Venetian army, it looked as if only the Piedmontese army would be able to save the Veneto. The provincial committees reasoned that in the circumstances the political price of fusion with Piedmont was a small one to pay.

Indeed in many quarters the prospect of rejecting the republic and becoming part of a monarchist state was greeted with enthusiasm. Many of the wealthiest provincial landowners and aristocrats had remained indifferent to the national cause and actively hostile to the new republican order. On 11 April 1848 Francesco Comin wrote from Bassano to Manin complaining that 'the upper classes, either from the desire not to endanger themselves or through lack of patriotism, or else from avarice, have done little or nothing for the public good'.[90] At the end of the month the Bassano provincial committee appealed to the rich of the city to aid the unemployed artisans even if they were unwilling to do anything else.[91] Whole sections of the landowning class abhorred the revolution and thought that the Piedmontese monarchy offered much better prospects of social stability.

Such attitudes were reinforced and found a wider social base as a wave of artisan and popular agitations spread through the provincial cities. The artisans were demonstrating against being deprived of their trades by increasing mechanisation. In the Veneto the classic example of this type of protest, which was so strong a motivating force in the German revolutions of 1848, was the action by the coachmen of Mestre in April. They had been rapidly losing work ever since an omnibus company had started a regular service from Treviso and other neighbouring towns to the new railway station at Mestre. The protests of the coachmen reached such

reports of 14 April 1848. One of these described how the Italians of the Haugwitz regiment had threatened to open fire on their fellow soldiers if the killing did not stop.

[89] See, for example, the small town of Asolo in the province of Treviso. There, on 18 April 1848, the leading citizens met to decide the best means of defence. One of them warned that the Austrians, if they met any resistance, would perhaps 'burn down the place as had happened recently at Castelnuovo near Peschiera'. At this meeting it was put to the vote whether the town should erect barricades or not, bearing in mind that it had only 100 civic guards and 52 firearms. Thirty-nine voted against the barricades, ten in favour; ASV, Gov. Prov. 1848–9, CPD, b. 834/Asolo, no. 67.

[90] MCV, Doc. Pell., b. xxxviii/11 (60).

[91] ASV, Gov. Prov. 1848–9, CPD b. 846/Bassano CPD, no. 1405, 28 April 1848. See also the letter from Matteo Petronio to Manin, 20 April 1848, MCV, Doc. Pell., b. xxxix/1 (22).

proportions that Manin had to send Giuriati and a detachment of civic guards to restore order. The coachmen told him that they were starving and could find no work, and that under the republic they had hoped for better things.[92]

In Padua particularly the populace was so active that the ruling class seems to have despaired of there being law and order under a republican government. The coachmen, following Mestre's example, rioted against the Zerman omnibus company, the tailors protested against 'ready-made suits', the hatters against manufactured velvet hats.[93] Giovanni Zoia, a thirty-year-old miller who had been imprisoned by the Austrians after the student riot of 8 February, became the *capo popolo* of Padua. He instituted his own thirty-strong night guard and generally controlled the city. A petition from some of the inhabitants of Padua to Manin complained that 'Zoia and others like him are the despots of liberty and of the lives of the citizens'.[94] The final straw for the Paduan bourgeoisie was a prison riot, with the prisoners demanding to be enrolled in the armed forces. A pitched battle took place for three hours before civic guards and troops managed to quell the disturbance.[95]

Other provincial centres were less turbulent, though at the small town of Este the authorities discovered a plot by sixty 'of the most abject class' to sack the houses of the richest citizens, and at Rovigo there were demonstrations against the Jews, who were believed to be hoarding large sums of money.[96] When combined with the peasant agitations, these popular protests in the provincial cities served to convince even many of those who were loyal to the national cause that the republic was against their class

[92] ASV, Gov. Prov. 1848–9, MU, b. 16, no. 6393, 20 April 1848, report of General Giuriati. Also, Bernardello, 'La paura del comunismo', p. 67 and n. 43.

[93] Bernardello, 'La paura del comunismo', p. 76, and Gloria, *Il comitato provvisorio*, pp. 96ff and p. 104.

[94] MCV, Doc. Pell., b. xxxviii, 11 (59), petition without date from 'gl'abitanti di Padova compromessi'. On Zoia, see also Ferrari, 'L'attitudine di Padova', p. 203 n. 56. After Padua had fallen in June, Zoia made his way to Venice. He was thrown out of the city, but on 20 Aug. 1848 was seen in the Frezzaria, arrested and sentenced to three months in the Casa di Correzione; see ASV, Gov. Prov. 1848–9, OPss, vii, 2, no. 9256. On 5 Nov. he was taken from the Casa di Correzione and put in prison 'at the disposition of the committee of public vigilance'.

[95] Bernardello, 'La paura del comunismo', p. 76.

[96] For Rovigo, see N. Biscaccia, *Cronache di Rovigo dal 1844 a tutto il 1864*, p. 115. In the first three months of the revolution seven rich individuals offered nearly 40,000 lire to the local Monte di Pietà so that the poor could redeem, free of charge, objects pawned for less than 2 lire. The wealthy had done this, said Biscaccia, not out of enthusiasm for the change of government, but from fear of it (*ibid.*, p. 113). For Este, see ASV, Gov. Prov. 1848–9, CPD, b. 826/Padova, no. 2071, report of 12 April 1848.

interests and that they would be better served by the house of Savoy.

Yet if Manin had adopted a more positive policy towards the provinces, it seems obvious that the Albertists would never have triumphed as easily as they did. In Treviso, for example, the republicans were still stronger than the monarchists in mid-April. A letter to Manin from one of the provincial committee, Dr Luigi Malutta, reveals clearly what could have been done:

I have long since decided to give my life for the most holy cause of the democratic republic, and now for the union of all the former provinces, which must have Venice for their centre. There is a party here which is in favour of Charles Albert, and it is headed by Guglielmo Onigo. He has brought with him from Tuscany two Piedmontese, one of whom in particular, by the name of Vitali, spends every day in the cafés and squares, trying to convince the people how damaging republican government is for us, and how much more use a constitutional government under Charles Albert would be. Vitali has been giving away money and on 14 April organised a demonstration by many people outside the office of the departmental committee. They cried 'down with Malutta, Carrobbio and Marzolo', because we are republicans . . . they tried to get the committee to send immediately to Charles Albert for aid, and also for us to submit to his rule . . . I therefore beg you and your colleagues to send republican propagandists to Treviso to arouse in the people sentiments which are in accord with our principles . . . and to keep an eye on the intrigues of the other party, which is much less strong than ours, but which could grow rapidly if we leave it liberty of action . . . my companions and I will do what we can but we have need of your help to sustain us.[97]

Manin appears to have sent G. B. Nicolini in response to Malutta's pleading, but he arrived in Treviso on the same day as the news of the capitulation of Udine: 'You can well understand how here it appears as the end of so many fine promises, and already the news is making its effect felt. For the love of the Fatherland, do not stick to half measures any longer. Only audacity can possibly save us now.'[98] From Vicenza Luigi Masi wrote a similar letter to Manin on 5 May 1848.[99] But the die had already been cast. The provincial republicans were left in isolation by Venice, and a pro-Piedmontese majority quickly formed in each of the provincial committees. At Padua and Vicenza Albertist clubs were founded; that at Vicenza was mainly composed of lawyers, clerics and counts.[100] On

[97] MCV, Doc. Pell., b. xxv/357. Malutta was one of the two members of the committee of Treviso elected by popular acclamation.

[98] MCV, Doc. Pell., b. xxvi/449. G. B. Nicolini was an ardent republican from Ancona who had taken part in the 1831 revolution. In 1849 he was to become secretary to the triumvirs of the Roman republic.

[99] MCV, Doc. Manin, no. 4106.

[100] See A. M. Dalla Pozza, *Nostro Risorgimento. Lettere dal carteggio dei Marchesi*

26 April representatives from the remaining unconquered provinces – Vicenza, Padua, Polesine, Belluno, and Treviso – met at Vicenza. From there they issued a proclamation declaring their disagreement with the republican government of Venice, and insisting that the Lombards and Venetians should unite in a single assembly.[101] The implications, in the light of the Lombard government's drift towards fusion with Piedmont,[102] were all too obvious.

The war in the Veneto and the battle of Cornuda

While these political dissensions undermined the basis of the Venetian state, the Austrians continued their invasion. The disaster on the eastern frontier had stirred the Venetian committee of defence, at least temporarily, into some sort of action. On 16 April, nearly a month after the beginning of the revolution, the committee decided that the Veneto needed 35,000 men and 5,000 cavalry to defend it. This was the first time that they had talked in terms of forming an army. As news of the disasters outside Udine began to filter through to Venice, some attempts seem to have been made to initiate a *levée en masse* in the countryside. Gherardo Freschi wrote to Orlandini urging him to collect 'crusaders' adding that nothing would frighten the enemy more than the sounding of the tocsin and a mass uprising. On 23 April G. B. Nicolini, with the title of Commissar of the provisional government, was sent into the Trevisan countryside and western Friuli 'to encourage the population to rise en masse'. No details exist of his mission, but it was clearly more a frenzied reaction to the Austrian invasion than part of a coherent plan.[103]

At the end of April and the beginning of May, persistent demands came from both Venice and the provinces for the government to introduce conscription. Both Freschi and Valentino Pasini were in favour of conscription, and the *consulta* drew up plans for its enforcement. In Venice a petition was presented to the government demanding a call-up limited

Gonzati su Vicenza nel '48, pp. xli–xlii. At Valdagno on 27–8 April one of the members of the local committee collected signatures for a protest against the republic of Venice and in favour of fusion with Piedmont; see BBV, Gonz. 24.7.19, G. Soster, 'Valdagno – atti ufficiali e memorie dal 1848 al 1878'.

[101] Racc. Andreola, vol. 2, pp. 90–3. For an account of the meeting at Padua see the letter of the representative from Belluno, Canon. Alessandro Schiavo, 26 April, in ASV, Gov. Prov. 1848–9, CPD, b. 823/Belluno, attached to no. 1280.

[102] See below, pp. 204 ff.

[103] See ASV, Gov. Prov. 1848–9, CD, b. 391, no. 432. For Freschi's letter of 20 April, see G. Stefani, 'Giuliani e Dalmati nella guerra d'indipendenza', in *La Venezia Giulia e la Dalmazia*, vol. 3, p. 43. For the committee of defence's plan, see the minutes in ASV, Gov. Prov. 1848–9, CD, b. 391, no. 312.

to those aged between twenty and twenty-five. Conscription was first discussed by the Venetian ministers on 27 April, when they dismissed the idea with the strange comment that 'it would ruin the civic guards'.[104] Castelli raised the question again on 1 May, but Manin procrastinated, saying that provisional measures would have to suffice. This was also the opinion of the new committee of war, set up on 2 May after the committee of defence had been dismissed because of 'its many disorders', a suitable enough epitaph. In spite of the Lombard government urging Venice to adopt its conscription law, the problem was put to one side and on 7 June received the coup de grace when the government passed the matter back to the *consulta*.[105]

It is open to doubt whether, after the 'many disorders' of the first month of the revolution, the population of the unconquered provinces would still have responded to a government decree on conscription. On 22 April 1848 representatives of the little village of Cava Zuccherina, near the estuary of the Piave, wrote to the committee of defence saying that eighty of the villagers would be prepared to go wherever necessary to defend the republic, 'but the lack of arms has sapped the enthusiasm of even the most willing'.[106] On the same day the municipal authorities of Montebelluna reported to Treviso that they had offered pay of six lire a week for each man who enlisted, but with very little success.[107] They said that in the first days many had volunteered willingly, but now nobody could be persuaded; this was because 'of the bad feeling that has arisen, particularly as the result of the total absence of any firearms. There are not more than 200 small shotguns in the whole area, and these are owned by people who under no circumstances will part with them.' The failure of the Venetian government to provide the rural civic guards with any information on the number of arms available, or to incorporate them in

[104] Ventura (ed.), *Verbali*, p. 148. For the petition of 27 April, see MCV, Doc. Manin, no. 3205. For Pasini's view on conscription, see his letter of 16 May to Durini, quoted in Bonghi, *Valentino Pasini*, pp. 232–3.

[105] Ventura (ed.), *Verbali*, p. 196. For the dissolving of the committee of defence, *ibid.*, p. 158. The new committee of war was composed as follows: president, General Pietro Armandi; members, Milani, Cavedalis, Federigo, Fontana. Armandi was Manin's choice, and he described him as 'new and not well known, of extremely moderate opinions' (*ibid.*, p. 160). In the Manin papers (MCV, Doc. Manin, no. 3823) there is an anonymous commentary written after 1849 which maintains that it was impossible to introduce conscription because the peasantry would not have obeyed. Both Trevelyan (*Manin and the Venetian Revolution*, app. E, p. 250), and V. Marchesi (*Storia documentata*, p. 201) attribute this document to Manin, but without providing any proof. The document is certainly not in his hand.

[106] ASV, Gov. Prov. 1848–9, CD, b. 392, no. 612.

[107] ASV, Gov. Prov. 1848–9, CPD, b. 834/Treviso, no. 2267.

any organic plan of defence was clearly having its effect, as was the news that the Austrians had taken to burning any villages which offered resistance.

Yet the general level of peasant enthusiasm remained surprisingly high for a considerable time. Reports from Venetian emissaries indicated strong support in the Paduan and Trevisan countryside in April and early May, and the hill and mountain areas continued to be particularly well disposed. In many villages the civic guard, such as the one 430 strong at Castell'Arzignano in the province of Vicenza, remained in perfect order until the beginning of June. Even in the province of Verona, nominally under Austrian control, there were clear indications of the pro-Italian sentiments of the inhabitants. At Cologna, a large village on the plains south-east of Verona, the local priests were still wearing tricolour cockades at the end of May, and the civic guard had made pikes which they hid when Austrian troops were in the vicinity. Forty 'crusaders' had left the village to help defend Vicenza. The district commissioner lamented that the civic guard which, according to him, had at first served a useful purpose, had since 'established contact with the rebels, taken over the powers of the police . . . and failed to prevent popular excesses'.[108]

Spontaneous and isolated attempts, both comic and tragic, were made to organise peasant resistance against the Austrians. At Canizzano in the province of Treviso twenty peasants, armed with lances and mounted on old farm horses, formed a famous cavalry troop; their commander was an ex-actor by the name of Lanzetti, dressed up as Frederick II. There is no evidence to show what part, if any, they played in the war. But further to the west, in the hills above Schio, the poet Arnaldo Fusinato led the local *corpo franco* and the civic guard of Recoaro in a desperate attempt to defend the pass of Pian delle Fugazze. On 25 April, in bitter weather conditions, the Austrians tried to clear the pass of opposition so as to provide an alternative line of retreat from Verona. They were at first beaten

---

[108] Report of 16 June 1848 to the provincial delegate at Verona; ASVr, I.-R. DP Verona, polizia, b. 455, atti riservati 1845–8, no. 305. See also the report of the inspector of the 'guardia civile di sicurezza' of 30 May, which singled out Dr Antonio Gaspari and the landowner Falghera as the ringleaders; *ibid.*, b. 455, no. 292. For Castell'Arzignano, ASV, Gov. Prov. 1848–9, CPD, b. 844/ Arzignano, comitato distrettuale, no. 973. For Giuriati's reports from the Trevisan countryside, see MCV, Doc. Manin, nos. 2725 and 2743, 1 and 6 May 1848. For the organisation of local resistance in the hills above Bassano, see the letter of 24 April of the Bassano committee to that of Treviso in AST, sezioni riunite, ministero della guerra, corrispondenza per l'armata in Lombardia 1848, mazzo 21, fasc. 52, no. 563. Also the account written in Turin in 1853 by one of the local leaders, Luigi De Stefani, and published by his sons at a later date: *La campagna dei Sette Comuni nel 1848, passim.*

off, having killed two of the Italians and left a number wounded. But many of Fusinato's civic guards, lacking ammunition, had fled, and when the Austrians moved up reinforcements, Fusinato retreated. He wrote to the Venetian committee of defence that it was impossible to hold the pass without the aid of two or three hundred regular troops.[109]

The committee had tried to provide for such needs by setting up a guerrilla force under Papa and De Madice to harass the Austrians from the Veronese and Vicentine hills, and to disrupt their lines of communications. But the idea came to nothing by mid-May. The guerrilla commanders had collected 400 men in a few days, but as the committee never sent them more than 100 *stutzen*, the force soon dispersed.[110]

The Venetian government continued to look to outside aid as the principal means of defence. In mid-April, in response to a Venetian request, the Piedmontese general Alberto La Marmora arrived at Vicenza to take charge of the defence of the Veneto. La Marmora, like Zucchi, was hardly the ideal choice to organise the popular forces of the Venetian republic. He immediately dismissed the possibility of building a Venetian army. On 17 April he wrote to the committee of defence: 'I beg you, gentlemen, not to entertain the thought of a Venetian army, since it does not exist and cannot exist with the forces at our disposal.'[111] As for the peasantry, 'they may get excited for a few moments, but then they relapse into apathy faster than the population of the cities'. La Marmora kept moving around, first from Vicenza to Treviso, then from the Tagliamento back to the Piave, and it proved impossible to get him to stay in one place to train and organise the 'crusaders', militia bands and other volunteers. By early May the Venetians had got no closer to organising an army, and had lost all faith in La Marmora. Manin told Gonzales, the Lombard military attaché, that 'La Marmora had ill corresponded to the faith shown in him by the government when they gave him command of the

---

[109] ASV, Gov. Prov. 1848–9, CD, b. 392, no. 671; see also V. Meneghello, *Il quarantotto a Vicenza*, p. 49, and MCV, Doc. Manin, no. 3492, letter of district committee of Valdagno to Vicenza, 2 May 1848. For the Canizzano cavalry troop, A. Santalena, *Memorie del quarantotto*, pp. 29–30.

[110] ASV, Gov. Prov. 1848–9, CD, b. 391, nos. 349 and 417; b. 392, nos. 637 and 734; and *ibid.*, CPD, b. 844/Arzignano, deputazione comunale, no. 772 and letter attached to no. 685; all of 17–30 April 1848.

[111] ASV, Gov. Prov. 1848–9, MU, b. 7, no. 3176, letter of 17 April 1848. For his comment on the peasants, ASV, Gov. Prov. 1848–9, CD, b. 392, no. 572, letter of 25 April 1848. La Marmora (1789–1863) had first fought with the French and then passed to the Piedmontese army. He enjoyed a reputation as a liberal and had spent many years in Sardinia, where his scientific studies and prowess as an ornithologist had earned him fame. In 1840 he was appointed general in command of the Piedmontese naval school at Genoa.

volunteers, and had never stopped spreading discouragement and diffidence amongst the troops and the people'.[112]

However, more substantial help was close at hand. Convinced of the
strategic need to halt Nugent's advance, and in response to the persistent
pleading of the Venetians and of Massimo D'Azeglio,[113] on 24 April
Charles Albert decided to direct the papal army into the Veneto. This was
not the same thing as sending a Piedmontese brigade, for the papal troops
under Durando acted independently of the Piedmontese army and coordination between the two forces, as we shall see, was non-existent. But
the papal army was certainly better than nothing. Ever since Pius IX's
election in 1846, a profound process of radicalisation had been taking
place in the Papal States. By the time of the outbreak of the 1848 revolutions, the youth of Rome, Bologna and other papal cities was amongst
the most politicised in Italy, and the most ready to take part in a national
war against the Austrians. Strenuous efforts had also been made to put on
a war footing the small regular army, which had been destined only for
internal use for more than three centuries. As a result, in April 1848 the
papal forces numbered some 17,000 troops with 900 cavalry and 22
cannon. Of these 10,000, including 3,500 Swiss troops and another
3,000 regulars, were under the command of General Giovanni Durando,
an ex-officer in the Piedmontese army and an exile since 1831. The
remaining 7,000, all volunteers, were under Colonel Andrea Ferrari
from Naples. Durando was a monarchist, Ferrari a republican.[114]

---

[112] MRM, archivio Bertani, cart. 2, plico 1, no. 11, letter of Gonzales of 4 May
1848. When Ponzio Vaglia reached La Marmora on 26 April he found him
'almost delirious, and as a precaution his pistols had been taken out of his room
an hour earlier'. Ponzio Vaglia told him of the imminent arrival of Durando,
but La Marmora merely replied, 'it is too late; here everything is lost' (AST,
carte politiche diverse, 1848, cart. 24, no. 132, letter of 27 April 1848 from
Venice). However, Lazzaro Rebizzo defended La Marmora in a letter to Franzini
of 19 May 1848: 'He has behaved consistently like a man who is both fearless
and prudent. He could not command the Venetian army because there was no
such thing' (AST, sezioni riunite, ministero della guerra, corrispondenza per
l'armata in Lombardia 1848, mazzo 20, fasc. 36, no. 524). For La Marmora's
own account of his actions, see his *Alcuni episodi della guerra nel Veneto* (ed.
M. Degli Alberti), pp. 1–66.

[113] See MCV, Doc. Manin, no. 2696, where Durando pays tribute to Charles
Albert's generosity in allowing the papal army into the Veneto; letter of 27 April
1848. For D'Azeglio's activities (he was one of Durando's aides-de-camp), see
Massimo D'Azeglio alla guerra d'indipendenza nel '48. Documenti inediti,
pp. 13–24.

[114] For details of the papal army, see Pieri, *Storia militare*, p. 375. Antonio Bonelli,
one of the young Roman volunteers, kept a delightful illustrated diary of the
campaign, which is to be found in MRR, volumi manoscritti, no. 249. His legion
was transported in boats towards Padua, and Bonelli writes of 'the bridges

By themselves these troops stood a reasonable chance of stopping Nugent; if the Venetians had managed to collect and arm 10,000 men to fight by their side, their chances of throwing the Austrians out of the Veneto must have been strong. Nugent, after all, as Pieri has pointed out,[115] was fighting over a terrain rich with natural obstacles, and was facing an openly hostile population, animated by a patriotic clergy. But the Venetian forces by the beginning of May did not number more than 2,000, and their contribution to the crucial campaign on the Piave was minimal.

The situation was made more difficult for the Italians by the fact that Nugent was in constant receipt of reinforcements. By the time that his troops encountered the papal forces, his army numbered 16,200 men, and a second army corps of some 8,000 under Welden had entered the Veneto and was laying siege to the fortresses of Osoppo and Palmanova, as well as garrisoning Friuli. Another 2,000 men had also been sent to Dobbiaco to subdue the Cadore and open the important road that leads from there into the Veneto.[116] Nugent himself reached the river Tagliamento on 25 April to find that La Marmora had ordered the bridge across it to be destroyed. By using the scaffolding from a local church that was about to be

packed with peasants and their women, who rushed in crowds towards the river, shouting at us, "slaughter them, massacre those Croat dogs" '. Bonelli fell in the water, and was only just saved from drowning (pp. 99–100). The advanced guard of the papal volunteers, the *Cacciatori dell'alto Reno*, commanded by Livio Zambeccari, had crossed the Po as early as 3 April. One of them, Luigi Corsini, wrote home on 5 April from the village of Trecenta. His letter is an interesting testimony to the enthusiasm of priests and peasants even in the province of Rovigo where support for the national cause was, as we have seen, less strong than elsewhere: 'For us it has been nothing but a triumphal march through all the little villages hereabouts. They are all up in arms, the women encouraging their husbands and sons to join up to drive out the hated foreigners. I cannot begin to describe the conduct of the priests: they have come to meet us holding huge crucifixes, and the archpriest or curate of each parish gives a small portrait of Christ to every volunteer. We arrived at 11 a.m. in this little town. Three hundred villagers came to meet us, armed with shotguns or forks, with the parish priest at their head, holding a large portrait of Christ. Once in the piazza, they formed a circle, and a monsignor began to speak in a loud voice...' (letter published in G. Natali, 'Corpi franchi del quarantotto', in *Rassegna Storica del Risorgimento*, 13 (1935), vol. 1, p. 195). Felice Orsini, who was later to try and assassinate Napoleon III, was a member of the Zambeccari legion. Gustavo Modena wrote to Manin on 28 April saying that there were many republicans, all friends of his, on Durando's staff, and that the general himself was well disposed towards the republic; MCV, Doc. Manin, no. 2709. This is not an impression confirmed by other contemporaries or by the comments of Prunas in Tommaseo, *Venezia*, p. 284 n. 661.

[115] Pieri, *Storia militare*, pp. 375–6.
[116] See below, pp. 210 ff.

restored,[117] Nugent got across the Tagliamento in three days. La Marmora meanwhile had decided that with the forces at his disposal resistance was useless, and he retreated to behind the Piave. The whole of western Friuli, scene of the extensive peasant mobilisation at the end of March, fell into Austrian hands without a fight. Nugent soon reached the Piave, but he found the bridges burnt and the papal army waiting for him on the other side.

The Austrians responded with a masterly flanking movement to the north. Nugent marched swiftly towards Belluno, encountering little opposition on the way. The main bridge over the Piave at Capo di Ponte, north of Belluno, had been burnt by the local volunteers, but the stone one of the city itself was intact. The provincial committee of Belluno decided that all resistance was useless and the Austrian vanguard crossed the Piave and entered the city on 5 May. Feltre too surrendered without a fight,[118] and by 7 May Nugent had three options open to him: either he could take the most northern road through Borgo and Trent and reach Radetzky that way; or he could drop down into the Venetian plain by way of Bassano; or he could follow the road down the western banks of the Piave by way of Quero and Cornuda, and attempt to capture Treviso before moving on towards Vicenza and Verona. The third route offered the greatest possibilities of reconquering the Veneto before reaching Radetzky, an ambition that lay very close to Nugent's heart.

Durando was not to know this. He had been outmanoeuvred by Nugent and now faced the difficult choice of where to concentrate his forces. The decision was complicated by Venetian insistence that he defend Treviso at all costs. He was slow to realise that Nugent had moved northwards, but he finally decided to concentrate his troops at Primolano, guarding both the Bassano and the Trento roads. But he left Ferrari much further to the south, above Treviso, to guard against the Austrians taking the third alternative. It was probably unwise to split his forces under any circumstances, but it was folly to leave the volunteers without any regular troops to sustain them. Durando let Ferrari have only a hundred dragoons and five cannon.[119]

Nugent in fact chose the southernmost road, and on the evening of

---

[117] See A. Filipuzzi, 'Luoghi comuni nella storia del Risorgimento italiano', in *Memorie Storiche Forogiuliesi*, 56 (1971), p. 47.

[118] At Belluno the provincial committee had 600 armed volunteers against, initially, 1,300 Austrians. The committee decided that it was useless to sacrifice the volunteers, and that they would do better to join the bulk of Durando's army. Nevertheless, as at Udine, the surrender of both Belluno and Feltre provoked serious polemics in the Italian ranks.

[119] The decision was even stranger in view of Durando's and D'Azeglio's frequently expressed contempt for volunteer forces and civic guards.

8 May his vanguard ran up against the first of Ferrari's volunteers. Ferrari immediately sent news of this to Durando. At 7 a.m. on the following morning, 9 May, the battle of Cornuda began. It was to decide the fate of the campaign in the Veneto. All through the morning Ferrari's volunteers resisted bravely as the Austrians gradually piled more and more men into the battle. Ferrari sent urgent messages to Durando imploring his help. Durando replied with a note that reached Cornuda at 12.30 p.m.: 'Vengo correndo' – 'I am coming at the double'. Durando had in fact set out for the battlefield, and had he reached it his regular troops would almost certainly have decided the day in favour of the Italian cause. But Durando had always had a lurking doubt that the Austrian attack at Cornuda was just a diversion, and that the main body of Nugent's troops would break through on the Bassano road. Five miles from the battlefield he was over-taken by a messenger from Primolano: an Austrian column several thousand strong had been sighted advancing towards the Italian positions. Durando had left only a thousand men under Colonel Casanova and no cannon to guard Primolano. Durando decided fatefully to turn back, only to discover that the Austrian column had returned to Feltre without attacking. It was the northern action that was a diversion and the battle at Cornuda the real attack! It was too late. Ferrari's troops resisted throughout the afternoon, spurred on by the knowledge that Durando was coming to their aid. But as no help arrived, and Ferrari was slow to bring up his own reserves, the volunteers grew dispirited. By the late after-noon, after his troops had been fighting for close on twelve hours, Ferrari gave the order to retreat. His right had been turned, and he risked being cut off altogether. The retreat was effected in order as far as Montebelluna, and the Austrians did not follow up their victory, but many of the volun-teers were convinced that they had been betrayed by the monarchist Durando. As Trevelyan has written, 'It was a sorry stream of disgruntled humanity that in the early hours of the morning poured in through the old Venetian gateway at Treviso.'[120]

The casualties at Cornuda had been light – about a hundred in dead and wounded – but the psychological effect was very great. The demoral-isation and indiscipline of Ferrari's volunteers reached such a pitch that the Venetian government felt impelled to call Durando to the defence of Treviso. This meant that Durando was forced to abandon the position he

[120] Trevelyan, *Manin and the Venetian Revolution*, p. 175. For further details of the battle, see Pieri, *Storia militare*, pp. 379–80, and Trevelyan, *Manin and the Venetian Revolution*, pp. 172–4. Also Santalena, *Memorie del quarantotto*, pp. 62–8, including the report of the Austrian commander, Culoz. For the different estimates of Italian losses at Cornuda, see G. F.-H. and J. Berkeley, *Italy in the Making*, p. 261 n. 45.

had taken up further to the west, at Piazzola, blocking the Austrians' route to Vicenza and Verona. Durando's troops repaired to Treviso, and the way to Verona was of necessity left open.[121]

The battle of Cornuda was thus decisive in allowing the Austrian relief force to link with Radetzky. Although Durando was principally to blame for the defeat, and Ferrari cannot escape criticism because of the misuse of the troops at his disposal, the lack of any significant Venetian force by their side in mid-May was also of vital importance. Carlo Gonzales, a Lombard military attaché with General Ferrari's troops, commented acutely some days before Cornuda on the Venetians' failure:

Everywhere in the Veneto precious and irretrievable time has been and is being lost in hoping for help from other parts of Italy. It is almost as if the Venetians were not sons of the same benign and pious Italian mother, and do not feel the same obligation to fight for the holy cause and independence. General Ferrari has justly noted that the absence of Venetian regiments in the crusading army to which all the other peoples of Italy have contributed, apart from indelibly blotting the honour of the Venetians, has deprived the Roman legions of the great advantages accruing from knowledge of local conditions.[122]

At the crucial moment in the campaign in the Veneto the brunt of the fighting had been borne, not by Venetian troops, but by papal volunteers.

The papal allocution, 29 April 1848

While the papal troops were failing to halt Nugent's advance in the Veneto, an event equally damaging to the Italian cause took place in the city from which many of them had come. Pius IX had been extremely hesitant about consenting to the departure of the papal army and the volunteers, and had much preferred his approval of the Italian cause to be expressed in the less dangerous project of a league of Italian states. Castellani, the strongly pro-republican Venetian representative at Rome, reported enthusiastically on the project of each state immediately sending

---

[121] On the condition of Ferrari's troops, see his letters to the Venetian government, MCV, Doc. Manin, nos. 2787–9, 13–14 May 1848. The villagers of Pederobba, north of Cornuda, had resisted with shotguns and stones on 8 May, as the Austrians advanced on the eve of the battle. The land in these parts belonged to Guglielmo D'Onigo, who had been very active in forming the local civic guard. Two of the peasants were caught and shot. In Cornuda on 10 May a sixteen-year-old peasant was shot for wearing a medallion of Pius IX and having a tricolour cockade; Santalena, *Memorie del quarantotto*, p. 73 n. 1, and app. II, pp. 129–31.

[122] MRM, archivio Bertani, cart. 2, plico 1, no. 8, letter to the Lombard government, 3 May 1848.

representatives to Rome for a congress under the presidency of the Pope. He hoped that Venice too would be granted representation at the congress. This news received a warm welcome in the Venetian council of ministers, where Manin declared that support of the congress would enable 'any accusation of municipalism on our part to be rebutted. A declaration of solidarity with the Italian federation would conserve our political personality.'[123] But Piedmont remained adamantly against the plan. The Piedmontese government had no wish for the military aid of the other Italian monarchs to be diluted into a talking-shop at Rome, let alone that Lombardy and Venetia should be independently represented. The congress foundered on this hostility, and Pius IX could no longer hope to use it as an alternative to direct military intervention in the war against Austria.

On 5 April at Bologna Durando issued an order of the day to his troops. It had been written for him by Massimo D'Azeglio and gave the impression that the Pope approved of the war as being one of civilisation against barbarism, and thus not only national, but also profoundly Christian. Pius was reluctantly prepared to let Durando's troops cross the Po, but only so long as they did not act in his name. D'Azeglio's proclamation profoundly upset him, and he hastened to issue a strong disclaimer. Meanwhile reports began to reach Rome of the growing anger in Austria and the Catholic regions of Germany against the Pope. There was even talk of an imminent schism. Deeply concerned that he might destroy the unity of his spiritual kingdom by continuing to support the Italian cause, however circumspectly, Pius IX, in his allocution of 29 April, declared that the papacy could not support either side in a feud between Christians. At one stroke he deprived the Italians of their spiritual leader and shattered their illusions of a national religious war. The neo-Guelphs were destroyed overnight as a leading force in the Risorgimento. The ministry in Rome, which was composed of a majority of lay members, immediately resigned, thus initiating that chain of events which was to culminate in the flight of the Pope from Rome and the declaration of the Roman republic of 1849.

Although Pius's allocution had an immediate and profound effect in Rome, its full consequences were not widely understood in the Veneto, and made no appreciable difference to the war effort. Those in Venice who did understand the allocution's significance managed to conceal it for a considerable length of time. There are numerous examples of the reverence with which the Venetians continued to treat Pius's name throughout the summer of 1848. As late as 2 July the Venetian newspaper

---

[123] Ventura (ed.), *Verbali*, p. 163. Castellani had an audience with the Pope on 7 May. Pius told him that the declaration of the republic had not pleased him, but he understood that 'Venice could not have done otherwise' (MCV, Doc. Manin, no. 1543, Castellani's dispatch to the Venetian government).

Fatti e parole began an article: 'Evviva Pio Nono . . . Pius IX is our hope,
our pledge of future victories, of future unity.'[124] But the gravity of Pius's
action could not be masked forever.

The triumph of the monarchists in Lombardy and the Veneto

After the fall of Belluno and Feltre, and the defeat at Cornuda, tension
reached breaking point in the Venetian council of ministers. Castelli,
Paleocapa, Camerata and Pincherle demanded the acceptance of the
principle of a united Lombardo-Venetian assembly; at this stage this was
little more than a euphemism for the eventual fusion of Lombardy and
the Veneto with Piedmont. Tommaseo insisted that only the Venetians
had the right to decide whether the republic should cease to exist. Manin
still stuck firmly to not making any further political decisions: 'to go back
on these [the government's principles] in the hope of obtaining more help
would be to make it understood that the government was ready to cede
ground in the event of danger and thus perhaps be disposed to capitulate
in an extreme situation'.[125] The question was put to the vote, the republicans were outnumbered. The following day, 12 May, a decree proclaimed
the Venetians' agreement to a united Lombardo-Venetian assembly.
Manin felt obliged to sign it, even though he came close to resigning on
the issue.[126] Tommaseo refused.

In the event, the Venetian decree was irrelevant, for on the same day,
12 May, the Lombard government decided openly to break the political
truce which the Milanese had brought into being. They announced an
immediate plebiscite which was to ask the Lombard people to choose
between having Charles Albert as their king, or the continuation of the
policy of *a guerra finita*.

Throughout April the Milanese republicans had been steadily losing
ground. At the beginning of the month fusion with Piedmont had seemed
a very remote possibility, but by 25 April Calucci, the Venetian emissary
to Milan, wrote to Manin that the Albertists were fast becoming the
strongest party and enjoyed the backing of the whole of the nobility.

[124] *Fatti e parole*, no. 19, p. 73, 2 July 1848. See also, for further evidence on the
same point, Brunello, 'Rivoluzione e clero', fos. 173–4. Pius did try temporarily
to calm the storm at Rome. In early May he protested that he did not wish to
condemn the Italian cause, consented to the Roman troops remaining in northern
Italy under Charles Albert's command, and sent a letter to the Austrian emperor
begging him to desist from the war; Marchesi, *Storia documentata*, p. 246.
[125] Ventura (ed.), *Verbali*, pp. 169–71.
[126] See Manin's conversation with Restelli, reported in Restelli's dispatch of 12 May
in Monti, *Francesco Restelli*, p. 326. Restelli told Manin that it would be a
crime against the fatherland if he resigned, and that he was absolutely necessary
to Venice.

Albertist clubs were being founded and petitions were circulating.[127]

When the military peril became clearly apparent early in May, the fusionists intensified their activities. They were able to point to Charles Albert as the only salvation for Lombardy, because the Lombard government had done little more than Venice to form its own army. It did decide on a policy of conscription, but never accompanied it with those elementary concessions necessary to ensure peasant backing. The personal tax, for instance, was not abolished until 25 June, and the weight of governmental fiscal policy fell on the urban and rural poor. The great landed proprietors formed the social base of Casati's government, and this meant that even fewer overtures were made to the peasantry in Lombardy than in the Veneto. None the less the first call to arms of the 1826 and 1827 classes, on 19 April 1848, met with little resistance from the peasants, who still believed that they stood to gain something from the revolution. But as the summer wore on, with the low prices of agricultural products, the impossibility of exporting raw silk to the Austrian empire, the forced loans and increased requisitioning by the Piedmontese, the Lombard peasantry turned against the *signori* whose government had given them so little. Lombardy managed to gather twelve thousand men by mid-June, but it was in the face of increasing opposition on the part of the rural population. By July the first cries of 'Viva Radetzky' were to be heard in the Lombard countryside.[128]

Faced with a situation that was clearly going against them, Cattaneo and Ferrari resolved in desperation to overthrow the provisional govern-

---

[127] MCV, Doc. Manin, no. 2056. On 18 April Alessandro Porro, a member of the Lombard provisional government, had written to Count Petitti di Roreto, Piedmontese councillor of state, that 'an immense majority which has not yet shown itself... is in favour of the most complete fusion possible' (letter published in A. Corbelli, 'I partiti politici in Lombardia nel '48', *Rassegna Storica del Risorgimento*, 12 (1935), p. 827).

[128] F. Della Peruta, 'I contadini', pp. 97–9. For Lombard recruitment, see Rota, 'Del contributo', pp. 26–7. The Lombards were worse off for arms than the Venetians, for there was no arms deposit in Milan comparable with the arsenal at Venice. Gaetano Strambio reported from Milan to Venice between 16 and 21 April on the Lombard government's failure to organise militarily or to appeal to the peasantry: 'The weakness of the Lombard military provisions is fatally acting to snuff out that zealous enthusiasm which the barricades had aroused amongst our people... the government will soon call upon the enormous numbers of our peasants to exercise the two most solemn acts in the political life of a nation: *the defence of the country and the right to vote*. This peasant class, so important and so neglected by the immorality and indifference of the Austrian regime, cannot enter into the spirit of the new political order if there are not *tangible* measures taken to satisfy their interests, and to persuade them that in this new order of things lies their best guarantee for the improvement of their lives' (ASV, Gov. Prov. 1848–9, DG, b. 372, diversi, lettere private, no number).

ment, set up a republican one, call a Lombard assembly and demand the intervention of France. On 30 April Cattaneo, Ferrari and Cernuschi went to Mazzini to plead for his support of their plan of action. Mazzini refused outright, and in the face of his intractability, any chance of decisive action by the republicans disappeared.[129]

In the first days of May the pressure on the provisional government to break the political truce became overwhelming. The provincial committees of Bergamo, Brescia and Cremona declared openly in favour of union with Piedmont. Turin sent propagandists; Gioberti, having only returned to Turin on 29 April, was in Milan ten days later. The provisional government was in any case strongly inclined to Piedmont, and were not unhappy to yield to the pressure being put on them. On 12 May, after a large demonstration in Milan in favour of fusion, the Lombard government, reassured from Turin of the liberal intentions of the king – Charles Albert had not been the least autocratic or the most consistent of monarchs – proclaimed the plebiscite. In vain the remnants of the republican party protested at the undemocratic nature of the referendum; in vain Mazzini, furious at having taken at their word Casati and his colleagues, accused them of betraying their own policy of a *guerra finita*. Even an attempted uprising on 29 May in Milan, led by Fortunato Urbino, did not delay the plebiscite, for the crowds refused to follow Urbino's suggestion that Casati be deposed, and the demonstration fizzled out.[130]

Francesco Dall'Ongaro was in Lombardy on voting day, and wrote this report of it for the Venetian paper *Fatti e parole*:

The question to be decided under all these words like union, fusion, dedication, constitution, was always the same: do you want a king or not? . . . Those who favoured the king went among the peasants, the tradesmen and all the simple people, announcing the choice to be between Charles Albert and the Austrians; either to give themselves to Piedmont immediately, or to return to Austrian rule. I heard them with my own ears. Naturally the simple people, faced with such an alternative, put their names or crosses where the government and the provincial committees wanted.[131]

Della Peruta has also found evidence that many peasants voted for the king hoping that he would protect their interests better than the *signori* had done.[132] The Lombard results, made known on 8 June 1848, showed

[129] A. Monti, *Un dramma fra gli esuli*, pp. 3–22.
[130] G. Candeloro, *Storia dell'Italia moderna*, vol. 3, p. 199. For the protest of the Milanese republicans, see MCV, Doc. Manin, no. 517, handbill of 29 May 1848. Mazzini's declaration of 12 May is published in Racc. Andreola, vol. 2, pp. 83–4.
[131] *Fatti e parole*, nod. 14, pp. 53–4, 27 June 1848.
[132] Della Peruta, 'I contadini', p. 100, quoting from the anonymous article, 'Sulla sorte dei contadini in Lombardia', in *Italia del popolo*, vol. 2, p. 542.

that of 661,626 adult males having the right to vote, 561,000 voted for fusion and only 681 for a delay.

As soon as they heard the news of the Lombard plebiscite, the Venetian provincial committees decided to follow suit. On 16 May Vicenza explained the plebiscite in the following terms: the policy of *a guerra finita* was a noble idea, but it had been taken in vain. There had been too much discussion, too many petitions concerning the political destinies of northern Italy. The political truce no longer had any meaning. It was time to make a decision.[133]

Manin sent Dall'Ongaro to Treviso to speak against the plebiscite. The republican Malutta reported: 'Our Dall'Ongaro spoke frankly and well, but it is all in vain, the proclamation [for the plebiscite] is already published, and many emissaries are collecting signatures: the outcome is certain – surrender to Charles Albert.'[134] Republicans also went into the villages around Padua, but the provincial committee ordered their arrest.[135]

Nevertheless many districts in the provinces refused to hold the plebiscite, at least not until the central government had given them permission. From the Cadore Giovanni Coletta wrote to Venice affirming the continued faith of the *alpini* in the republic. Massa, Occhiobello and Adria in the province of Rovigo, and Bovolenta near Padua refused to open the registers until they had heard from Venice. Asiago in the province of Vicenza, despite the threats of the provincial committee, would have nothing to do with the plebiscite, saying that it smacked of 'thanklessness and ingratitude towards the government which has always beneficently replied to every request'.[133] But the vast majority in the provinces were in favour of fusion with Piedmont, hoping vainly that Charles Albert could or would defend them against reconquest. In the province of Padua 62,259

---

[133] MCV, Doc. Manin, no. 3506, proclamation from the committee of Vicenza. The Venetian satirical newspaper, *Sior Antonio Rioba*, poked fun at the whole idea of *a guerra finita* on 19 July 1848 (no. 5, p. 20): 'They tell us that at Brescia Tuscans, Piedmontese, Neapolitans, etc., have been so well received by the Brescian families, and have got on such intimate terms with the daughters of these families, that there are now many, many marriages planned there. But when the soldiers left for the front again, serious disagreements took place. The soldiers wanted to put off all plans till the end of the war – *a guerra finita si deciderà* – while the girls refused to wait so long and wanted to get married immediately.'

[134] MCV, Doc. Manin, no. 2418; letter to Manin without date, but obviously of May 1848.

[135] Ferrari, 'L'attitudine di Padova', pp. 215–16.

[136] MCV, Doc. Manin, nos. 3505 and 3513, 2 and 3 June 1848. For the Cadore, see P. Rigobon, *Gli eletti*, p. xvii. For the province of Rovigo, see Marchesi, *Storia documentata*, p. 193. For Bovolenta, MCV, Doc. Manin, nos. 3594–5.

voted for the Piedmontese king, 1,002 for *a causa vinta*; in the province of Vicenza, 56,328 for, 520 against; in the province of Rovigo 23,605 for, 1,276 against. Whole districts or villages tended to vote one way – Pettorazza Grimani (in Rovigo) had 333 votes for *a guerra vinta* and none for Charles Albert.[137] But the overall result was not in doubt; by 5 June the Piedmontese and the Austrians had between them reduced the Venetian republic to the city itself and the lagoon surrounding it.

Conclusion

The leaders of revolutions are sometimes allowed by circumstance a breathing space in which to establish themselves in power and to reflect with care upon their policies. The Venetian republicans had no such luck. The Austrians were on them within a month, forcing them into decisions, into improvising, into seeking immediate remedies for a difficult military situation. And while the Austrian relief army continued its relentless advance from the east, from the west Piedmontese political pressure for the dismemberment of the republic became ever more insistent.

The only way that these twin dangers could have been combated was by a vigorous republican strategy of self-defence. Had Manin been able to harness popular enthusiasm for the revolution into an effective fighting force, he might have halted Nugent's invasion and resisted Piedmontese pressure. But neither he nor his ministers were ever equal to this task. Manin had been a superb and incisive leader during the March days, but he was at a loss to know how to react to the very different conditions of April and May. He had accepted the Milanese demand for postponing all political decisions, trusting that this would ensure him the military aid of Piedmont and the inviolability of the republic. In fact the opposite happened – no Piedmontese brigade moved into the Veneto, and the political truce was broken by the very men who had proclaimed it. Monarchist aid acquired a political price.

While this realisation dawned upon the Venetian republicans, they provided in only the most confused and slapdash way for their own defence. This was partly because of the difficulties of the situation, but largely because of their own incompetence and the belief in imminent salvation at the hands of the Piedmontese or papal armies. Manin's inexperience of military matters, when combined with his unfortunate choice of advisers, made for a whole series of disasters. Brave local

---

[137] MCV, Agg. Manin, ix/13 for the results from Rovigo, 1 June 1848; *ibid.*, ix/17, for the province of Padua; and Dalla Pozza, *Nostro Risorgimento*, pp. li–lvi, for the province of Vicenza. The results from Treviso were not made public because of the change in the political climate of the city. See below, pp. 213–18.

initiatives and the ardour of the first mobile civic guards were suffocated through the lack of any general plan of defence. The six thousand peasant militias outside Udine and the two thousand volunteers with Sanfermo at Montebello were proof enough that large numbers of men were willing to fight. But the enthusiasm at a local level must be contrasted with the total lack of clarity at the centre, with the war ministry distributing arms aimlessly throughout the Veneto, forming a Venetian mobile guard that never moved from Venice, and never talking seriously about the possibilities of conscription.

Behind the problems of self-defence lurked the social problems that the new republic encountered. The Venetian republicans were moderates, and most of the provincial leaders were not republicans at all. The invasions of estates and forests, and the artisan demonstrations in the provincial cities, gave added weight to the political arguments in favour of Piedmont and against the formation of a popular army. But while these elements of class tension cannot be ignored, the general control of the middle strata of rural society over the peasant civic guards was never in doubt, and nor was that of the bourgeoisie over the artisans in the cities (with the possible exception of Padua). Many of the provincial committees and local communal deputations were not slow to suggest to the government ways of forming an army, or of ensuring continued popular participation, but this advice tended to fall upon deaf ears.

The gravest indictment of the central government came with the battle of Cornuda. The presence of Durando's army was Charles Albert's answer to the persistent requests for help from the Venetians, and critics like Massimo D'Azeglio then pointed out with some justice that it was high time for the Venetians to contribute to stopping Nugent. Had Manin been able to field an army of even ten thousand men to supplement the papal regulars and volunteers, Nugent's difficulties would have been seriously increased. As it was, the Venetian contribution at this most crucial of moments was minimal, and it is hardly surprising that the unconquered provinces then turned en masse to Charles Albert for salvation. Isolated from Lombardy and discredited in the eyes of the provincial committees, Manin's republican government had conspicuously failed to meet the considerable demands made upon it.

6

Fusion, June to July 1848

With the defection of the unconquered Venetian provinces to Piedmont, it was assumed that the city of Venice would be dragged, an unwilling dog on a Lombard lead, into a new kingdom of upper Italy. As the summer of 1848 reached its height, the Venetian republicans struggled for survival, but in increasingly difficult circumstances. The forces working against them were to triumph in three different spheres of action: in the general military and political situation of northern Italy; within the city of Venice itself, amongst the different classes of its population; and on an international scale, with Austria's renewed self-confidence, the refusal of the other Italian governments to consider French aid, and the cataclysm of the June days in Paris.

The resistance in the Cadore

Although for the Venetians the military situation continued to deteriorate throughout early May and June 1848, a number of events combined to prevent the total rout that seemed likely after Cornuda. One of these was the protracted fighting in the mountain valleys of the Cadore. The resistance there was one of the most dramatic and significant incidents in the defence of the Veneto. The population of the Cadore had a long tradition of loyalty to the Venetian Republic, dating from the beginning of the sixteenth century, when they had defended the Veneto from Emperor Maximilien's troops and received a gift of salt from a grateful republican government. Under the old Republic the Cadore had enjoyed a large measure of independence which disappeared under Austrian rule. The Austrian law of 1839 decreeing the sale of communal lands and forests further alienated the mountain peasantry, and after the deprivations of 1847 and the Austrians' harsh insistence on collecting the personal tax, the valleys of the Cadore were ripe for revolt.

At first it seemed that the area would suffer the same fate as the rest of the Veneto; at the end of March a number of Cadorini warned the provincial committee of Belluno that their villages were 'quite well disposed, but lack any organisation or means of defence'.[1] The Austrians were already preparing to attack from the north, through the Tyrol by way of Dobbiaco, so as to open up another valuable line of communication. But for once the Venetian government was sensitive both to peasant demands and military necessity. Manin issued his decree placating the peasantry who had invaded the woods of Auronzo, and promised new policies for the former communal lands and forests;[2] he also dispatched an outstanding young officer, Pier Fortunato Calvi, to organise resistance. Calvi, aged thirty at the outbreak of the revolution, had been trained as a military engineer in Vienna. He was an able and inspiring leader who soon won the confidence of the local authorities and the peasants. On 25 April he wrote to the Venetian committee of defence saying that he could count on 6,000 men eager for battle, but that they had only 199 *carrabine de cacciatori*, 20 percussion rifles, 1,000 shotguns in bad condition, and five cannon (which he had brought from Venice).[3] The Venetian government responded by sending 400 *stutzen* and 1,650 pounds of powder. Calvi formed six companies of *corpi franchi*, about 400 well-armed men, and organised another 4,000 local civic guards, equipping them with shotguns, lances, pitchforks, etc. He also ordered large stores of boulders to be collected ready to roll down on the Austrians as they advanced through the narrow gorges that led to the main town of the area, Pieve di Cadore.

The first alarm came at the end of April, when 2,000 troops under Major Hablitschek moved into the Cadore from the north. On 29 April the Cadorini rose *en masse*, with the bells of the churches sounding the tocsin and priests at the head of each company. Battle was joined at Chiapuzza on 2 May. Calvi, with a copy of the capitulation of Udine on the point of his drawn sword, led his *corpi franchi* with such courage and clear-sightedness that Hablitschek's troops were soon forced to retreat. A week later Culoz sent six companies to attack from the south, along the road that follows the valley of the Piave. Calvi had prepared a formidable ambush, the effect of which was ruined by the undisciplined enthusiasm of some of the civic guards, who opened fire and launched their boulders before Calvi gave the signal. Their precipitate action cost the Cadorini a number of casualties and the loss of a cannon. But Calvi reorganised the ambush for the following day, 8 May, and the Austrian column was

---

[1] ASV, Gov. Prov. 1848–9, CPD, b. 823/Belluno, no. 262, no date but received in Belluno on 1 April 1848. See also the appeal of the Cadore to the Venetian government for 1,000 muskets, 28 March 1848, *ibid*., MG, b. 127, no. 268.

[2] See above, p. 174.

[3] ASV, Gov. Prov. 1848–9, CD, b. 392, no. 615.

caught fair and square by an avalanche of boulders. In some confusion they retreated back towards Belluno.[4]

In the fortnight that followed, two further attacks were launched against the Cadore. Hablitschek's forces were again repulsed, this time at the pass at Venas, and a column coming westwards from Tolmezzo ran into another ambush at the Passo della Morte. Throughout May Calvi received invaluable help from the Cadore's committee of defence, which had been elected at Pieve on 25 April. But the Austrians were determined to stamp out the resistance, and Nugent entrusted the task to the second relief army under Marshal Welden. Welden moved eight thousand troops to the confines of the Cadore, and prepared a simultaneous attack on three different fronts, from the north, the south and the east.

The first battle of this fresh attack took place on 27 May, when Austrian columns tried to move through the valley of Zoldo so as to attack the flank of the defenders of Venas. The civic guards from Zoldo and the neighbouring villages put up such a fight that the Austrians completely failed in their objective. Then, on 28 May, came the full might of the three-pronged attack. The earlier battles had helped to discipline Calvi's men, and with great determination and ingenuity they succeeded in repulsing all three Austrian columns. The Cadorini, with only four hundred muskets and their ambushes of boulders, had resisted the determined attack of eight thousand Austrian troops.[5]

This extraordinarily tenacious defence could not last. By the end of May Calvi was running short of ammunition and food supplies. All the grain in the area was forcibly requisitioned, but without help and reinforcements from the central government the Cadore could not survive for long. The Austrians were also beginning to learn the arts of mountain warfare, and to take to the mountain paths instead of following the roads that ran along the bottom of the gorges. On 4 June at the Mauria Pass Calvi had to give way in the face of overwhelming numbers. The Austrians then overran the whole of the Cadore, with the last flames of resistance dying at Agordo and Zoldo. Calvi, with a price of ten thousand florins on his head, managed to escape and eventually reached Venice. There he

[4] See G. Moreno, *Calvi e la difesa del Cadore*, pp. 31ff. Also MCV, Doc. Manin, no. 3759, letter from Dr Gabriele Gregori in Pieve, 30 April 1848, describing the *levée en masse*. On the Austrians' first defeat see the letter from the canon Antonio Schiavo to Manin, 3 May 1848, published by R. Barbiera in 'L'insurrezione del Cadore nel 1848' *Rassegna Storica del Risorgimento*, 9 (1922), pp. 144–7.

[5] Moreno, *Calvi*, pp. 54ff. In a letter of 25 May to Zoldo Calvi, Palatini and Coletti wrote that 'whatever happens we will fight like the Spanish' (ASV, Gov. Prov. 1848–9, CPD, b. 823/Pieve di Cadore, no. 415). The civic guard were paid 1.50 lire a day at Zoldo and 2.12 lire per day at Lorenzago; see MRM, archivio generale, Cadore, reg. no. 36976, nos. 1 and 5.

became head of the legion of the *Cacciatori delle Alpi*, and played a significant part in the defence of the city in 1849.[6]

The exceptionally favourable terrain had undoubtedly aided the peasantry of the Cadore, and made theirs something of a special case. But to explain the protracted resistance of the Cadore only in terms of terrain is to miss other vital elements. Even though the Venetian government eventually abandoned the Cadore to its fate, it had initially shown some sensitivity to the needs of the area. Manin's attempt to meet peasant demands over the communal forests and the sending of Calvi with a sizeable number of muskets were initiatives which greatly contributed both to reviving the Cadore's traditional loyalty to Venice and to supplying it with the means to resist. Had such sensitivity and foresight been applied at all consistently elsewhere, the history of the defence of the Veneto might have been a very different one.

Treviso and the military council

When Ferrari's troops fled in confusion to Treviso after the battle of Cornuda, it seemed likely that the city would soon follow the examples of Udine and Belluno, and capitulate without resisting. The indiscipline and demoralisation of the papal volunteers went a long way to confirm this impression. On 10 May, with the air thick with rumours of betrayal, some of the papal volunteers seized three Italians who had the misfortune to be in the city at the time – Scapinelli, the ex-governor of Reggio, Desperati, the former chief of police of Modena, and Puato, a merchant from Este. Denouncing them as spies, the volunteers and some Trevisans flung them into a cart, which they towed round the city. At the end of this macabre procession, the three men were beaten to death.[7] This was one of the very few excesses committed by the Italian revolutionaries in 1848–9. Ferrari immediately responded by leading his men out northwards, hoping to restore their morale by means of a successful skirmish. But they had only

---

[6] When Venice fell in August 1849 Calvi went to Piedmont, but he always felt the need to return to the Cadore. Eventually he tried to do so, only to be caught by the Austrians at Cogolo, and executed at Mantua in 1855. The best short account of the defence of the Cadore in 1848 is by Pieri, *Storia militare*, pp. 390–7. On food requisitioning at the end of May see MRM, archivio generale, Cadore, reg. no. 36976, nos. 45 and 46. For details of the final Austrian victory in the Cadore, C. Fabris, *Gli avvenimenti militari del 1848 e 1849*, vol. 2 (1898), pp. 148–52.

[7] The best account of the murders is in Santalena, *Memorie del quarantotto*, pp. 85–9, based on Cicogna's description. Cicogna was secretary of the tribunal which heard the case against a number of Trevisans in 1850–1. Sentences were passed of 8, 10, 16 and 18 years of forced labour. The papal volunteers appear to have escaped the Austrians' wrath.

gone a few kilometres along the main road before the Austrian artillery caught them full square. The road was lined with broad and deep ditches on either side, which made it impossible to escape from the Austrians' deadly fire. Panic ensued. The whole of Ferrari's column turned around and fled back to Treviso.

Ferrari then decided that many of his troops were probably more of a menace than an aid to the city, and departed with them to Venice, where some were discharged and the rest were kept to man the lagoon forts. He left behind in Treviso two battalions of grenadiers and four battalions of Roman and Venetian volunteers with seven cannon; in all about 3,600 men under the command of the Napoleonic veteran, General Guidotti. Appalled by recent events and deciding that a heroic gesture was needed to stiffen resistance in Treviso, Guidotti led out forty volunteers, among whom was the renowned Barnabite friar Ugo Bassi. They charged the Austrian lines until Guidotti fell dead and Bassi was seriously wounded. Guidotti's death did mark a turning point, and spirits revived in the city.[8] Nugent was slow to launch any attack and then decided, after persistent orders from Radetzky, to leave Treviso unconquered and head towards Verona.

In the second half of May Treviso witnessed the founding of the military council for all volunteer corps. This was undoubtedly the most serious and interesting attempt to form an army of the volunteer forces existing in the Veneto. The council contained some of the finest radicals in Italy. Its military commander, Colonel Antonio Morandi, had considerable experience of revolutionary war; born in 1801, he had taken part in the insurrections at Modena in 1821–2, fought in the Greek war of independence, and participated in the central Italian revolution of 1831. He was captured after the battle of Novi, tried and imprisoned in Venice, but staged a spectacular escape and returned to Greece until 1848.[9] The president of the council was the young Giuseppe La Masa, one of the outstanding leaders of the Palermo revolution of January 1848, who had brought about a hundred Sicilian volunteers across Italy to the Veneto. Its secretary was Antonio Mordini, who later played an important part in the Tuscan events of 1849. Other prominent members included Gustavo Modena, Francesco Dall'Ongaro, Luigi Fabrizi and the Englishman Hugh Forbes. These men, mostly ardent republicans, saw the necessity of gathering all the volunteers in the Veneto under one command, and of harnessing popular enthusiasm in some coherent military fashion. They shared the faults which Gramsci later ascribed to the *Garibaldini* – a lack of awareness of the real needs of the peasantry, and an excessive belief in the

[8] Marchesi, *Storia documentata*, p. 165.
[9] *Dizionario del Risorgimento nazionale*, vol. 3 (1933), p. 638.

efficacy of an elite volunteer corps. But they did have the fierce enthusiasm and courage which found their highest expression in Garibaldi's Sicilian expedition of 1860, on which many of them were to go.

On 22 May La Masa wrote to Manin, asking him for his full support:

It is useless to tell you that if you continue to put your trust in Durando and in help from the Italian kings our cause is lost ... All that remains for Italy is the force which has raised the people in insurrection and has compelled the princes to give their reluctant support; I am talking of the educated classes [*la forza intelligente*] who have enrolled *en masse* in the volunteer corps and who, angry at being betrayed, will now fight with new vigour and in increasing numbers. Venice must rely on this force alone – Venice which is the citadel of liberty and Italian independence ... Have faith in those of us who are young and who have been hardened by the political struggle; old generals have led too many Italian revolutions to a bad end.[10]

Modena followed up La Masa's tirade to Manin with a similar one to Tommaseo:

All you members of the Venetian government still put great faith in the help of the praetorian guards of the two monarchs who are in fact bound by the diplomacy which has already organised the counter-revolution in Italy and Germany. Such help is worse than foreign aid ... You have agreed to our project to unite all the volunteer corps into a truly Italian army to be put at the service of Venice for the time being ... How should we achieve this end? By sending Morandi all the volunteers in your pay and all those who will come from every part of Italy. But what is the Venetian minister of war doing instead? He is keeping all the volunteers dispersed in small groups at Vicenza, Padova, Venice, Mestre. What can they do if they are scattered about like this? What can they hope to achieve? Nothing, except to demoralise each other ... Should Manin read these lines he must not take offence at the sharpness of my tone.[11]

Despite this last appeal, it was clear that there was a deep division of opinion between the council and the men whom Manin had entrusted with the war effort. On 2 June Morandi attended the Venetian council of ministers to report on the situation at Treviso. The Trevisan national guard had been mobilised, and the council had about eight hundred men

[10] MCV, Doc. Manin, no. 2839. On the Sicilians in the Veneto see G. La Masa, *Documenti della rivoluzione siciliana del 1847–9*, vol. 1 (1850), pp. 266–70. La Masa wrote that his volunteers had marched from Sicily to Ferrara in ten days. Many of them were officers who served as simple soldiers, and many were veterans of the January revolution in Palermo.

[11] T. Grandi (ed.), *Epistolario di Gustavo Modena, 1827–61*, pp. 85–6. The date of the letter is uncertain, but is probably of 27 May. See also his letters to Tommaseo of 21 May (MCV, Doc. Manin, no. 4227), 31 May and 2 June (Grandi, *Epistolario di Gustavo Modena*, pp. 86–7).

under its command.[12] Morandi said that his troops would only serve under the republican flag, and that at Treviso the petitions for union with Piedmont had only obtained five hundred signatures, after which they had been suppressed. The council had in fact been at work politically as well as militarily, and had made use of noted orators like Nicolini and Gavazzi to persuade the Trevisans against fusion.[13] As a result, the plebiscite in the province of Treviso never took place. All this pleased Manin greatly at a time when he felt he had been duped politically by Piedmont and Lombardy, and deserted by the other Venetian provinces. Morandi returned to Treviso and the following day led his troops in a brilliant minor action on the banks of the Sile, where 250 Austrian troops were put to flight at Porte Grandi, and over eight hundred cattle were taken back to the city.[14]

However, this action marked the height of the council's success. Armandi and Paolucci, respectively the president of the Venetian committee of war and Venice's war minister, feared the council's policies. The council represented a possible threat to their own authority, its politics were too radical, and if allowed to develop it was bound to alienate Charles Albert. Manin, although initially favouring the council, in the end allowed

[12] For the meeting of the Venetian ministers, see Ventura (ed.), *Verbali*, p. 189. The mobilised Trevisan national guard numbered 240 men and there were another 200 Trevisan *crociati*. The estimate of 800 is based on the letter that Mordini sent to the Venetian committee of war on 26 May; ASV, Gov. Prov. 1848–9, MG, b. 382, presidenza del ministero e del comitato della guerra, riservati (carteggio non protocollato), no number. Mordini claimed that the council had control of 3,310 troops, but his list included a large number of men at Vicenza, Venezia and Padua who were not in fact answerable to the council. The letter also asked that Hugh Forbes be made chief of Morandi's staff.

[13] Antonio Bonelli heard both Gavazzi and Nicolini, and disliked their anti-Piedmont sentiments; see his diary in MRR, volumi manoscritti, no. 249, pp. 213–15. On 25 May the council had published an appeal to the Trevisans, urging them not to vote in the plebiscite: 'the people by their revolutions have created the provisional governments; only the people, legally represented in parliament, can decide the fate of any part of Italy' (Racc. Andreola, vol. 2, pp. 161–2). Olivi, the mayor of Treviso, gave his consent to the Trevisan national guard coming under the orders of Morandi (ASV, Gov. Prov. 1848–9, MG, b. 382, riservati, no. 174), but in his later memoirs confided that he was terrified of the council because of its tendency to 'communist doctrines and sanguinary measures'. He wrote that 'it was the great misfortune of the city to become the centre of the most fanatical republicans who, with the consent of Manin, set up a committee of war'. Olivi attempted to counter the council's influence by founding a committee of public security and securing the support of the more moderate papal officers; MS Olivi, pp. 112–13.

[14] See the account from the commune of San Michele del Quarto to the municipality of Mestre, 4 June 1848, in ASV, Gov. Prov. 1848–9, MG, b. 382, riservati, attached to no. 145. See also Morandi's description, written at a much later date; A. Morandi, *Il mio giornale*, pp. 99–105.

himself to be overruled by his military advisers in Venice. His decision was made easier by the council's attempt to enrol papal troops in its ranks, an action which provoked a furious letter of protest from the papal commissioner Aglebert, and which deprived the council of some of the sympathy it had acquired during its brief existence.[15] Manin then acquiesced in Armandi's decision not to send the council any arms or to recognise its authority. La Masa came to Venice to plead the council's case. At this time the Cadore was still in arms and La Masa urged that four thousand men should be sent to aid Calvi. It was to no avail. Manin preferred the advice of Armandi, and without the Venetian government's support the council could not develop.[16]

It is probable that, even had Manin backed the council to the full, its formation came too late to change fundamentally the course of the war in the Veneto. The peasant enthusiasm and mass mobilisation of the March days were no longer present at the end of May. Twelve years later in Sicily, the men who had formed the military council at Treviso were to find a much less formidable enemy army, and social conditions that were more favourable to their cause. But it seems difficult to deny that the council, had it been properly supported by Manin, would have used to the full the limited room open for manoeuvre in the Veneto at the beginning of June. At the very least the plan to send help to the Cadore would have

[15] ASV, Gov. Prov. 1848–9, MG, b. 382 riservati, no. 171, for Aglebert's letter to Armandi of 8 June 1848. Ninety of the papal troops under Lieutenant Landriani had decided to join the council, and Morandi had apparently accepted them. Tommaseo had initially been favourable to the council, as can be seen from his letter to Dall'Ongaro of 28 May 1848, MCV, Agg. Manin, XLVIII, Tommaseo's unpublished work 'Venezia, l'Italia e l'Europa', pt. II, p. 241. But in his much later work, *Venezia negli anni 1848–9*, vol. 2, p. 29, he dismissed the council as being of little use.

[16] See La Masa, *Documenti*, vol. 1, pp. 269–70 for his attempt to persuade Manin about the Cadore expedition. On 6 June Armandi wrote to the council saying that he could not find any evidence in Venice to show that the council had government approval, and that unless the council could produce some he would have no alternative but to refrain from any further correspondence; ASV, Gov. Prov. 1848–9, MG, b. 382, riservati, no. 151. Pietro Armandi (1778–1855) had a distinguished Napoleonic career, reaching the rank of colonel. He took an active part in the revolution of 1831 in the Papal States and was elected minister of war and the navy in March of that year. But he proved a failure because although an able military instructor, he was quite incapable of organising a revolutionary war. Exiled to Paris, in 1843 he published a military history of elephants (*Storia militare degli elefanti*). His services had been refused by Rome in 1848 before being accepted by Manin. Later in the Venetian revolution he was emarginated from the highest echelons of the Venetian military command, and in June 1849 was demoted from the rank of general for his criticisms of the evacuation of Fort Marghera; see the note by G. Di Peio in *Dizionario biografico degli italiani*, vol. 4 (1962), pp. 219–21.

prolonged the war in the northern mountains and kept Welden's army tied down for many more weeks. At the most Morandi might have formed a small but effective fighting force to serve as a constant thorn in Radetzky's eastern flank. But Manin's refusal to abandon the cramped conservatism of his military advisers, and their inability to conceive of a vigorous plan of self-defence, meant that the plans of the council were never put to the test.

Vicenza

After the battle of Cornuda, Durando still hoped to stop the Austrians from reaching Verona, and took up positions to the west of the river Brenta, at Piazzola. His intention was to abandon Treviso, and he ordered Ferrari to join him as soon as possible. But both Ferrari and the Venetian government were adamant that Treviso was not to be left to its own devices, and Durando, who relied on the Venetians for payment and supplies, had no option but to leave his position at Piazzola and march towards Treviso. He reached the southern environs of the city on 18 May, at which the Austrians promptly broke camp and marched swiftly towards Vicenza and Verona, along the main road that had now been left open for them. Nugent had had to abandon the command because of the recurrence of an old head wound, and General Thurn took over the Austrian troops.[17]

Thurn reached Vicenza on 20 May 1848 and hoped that the city would succumb, as Udine had done, at the first signs of a serious attack. But Vicenza had much better natural defences, the spirit of resistance was strong among its citizens, and various volunteer corps from the Papal States had arrived to aid the local civic guard which was under the command of the tough old soldier Domenico Belluzzi.[18] The Schwarzenberg

---

[17] On 19 May the municipal authorities of Castelfranco wrote to the provincial committee of Treviso, recounting how the town had been suddenly occupied that day by 15,240 Austrian troops. The Austrians were intent only on reaching Verona, the municipality had supplied all their needs, instructed the population not to resist, and everything had gone off peacefully. The authorities of Castelfranco were amazed at the amount of detailed and accurate information the Austrians possessed on everything to do with the town – the size of the civic guard, the number of cannons, guns, etc.; ASV, Gov. Prov. 1848–9, CPD, b. 834/Treviso no. 4571.

[18] Belluzzi was born in Bologna in 1783 and died at Turin in 1853. In 1802 he enrolled in the Napoleonic army, and reached the rank of captain. In 1831 he took part in the revolutions in the Papal States and in 1848 at the age of sixty-five was made a colonel. After the fall of Vicenza he went to Bologna, and then in September 1848 returned to Venice where he was made a general.

brigade, aided by cannon and rockets, attacked the Porta Santa Lucia, but were vigorously beaten off by the battalion of the Alto Reno under Zambeccari and a battalion of the papal mobile guard. The Austrians lost about one hundred men and the Italians nearly the same number. Once again the volunteer forces had shown that they were far from useless.

During that night Thurn made a complicated detour round the north of the city and on 21 May found himself at Olmo, on the main road to Verona. Meanwhile Durando had arrived post haste at Vicenza with the mass of his army, and from Venice, by train, came a most unexpected contingent – Manin and Tommaseo, at the head of a thousand troops, among whom were Antonini's legion of Italian volunteers from Paris.[19] It is not clear what prompted Manin into this action, for he has not left any explanations of his conduct. Possibly the news from the Piedmontese camp, where Martinengo had written on 16 May that 'any help from the Piedmontese for the moment seems to me to be out of the question',[20] made Manin realise that aid for Vicenza from Venice was essential. It seems likely that he wanted to counteract all the accusations circulating in the provinces at this time about Venice's municipalism. He must certainly have felt powerless, sitting in Venice while the Veneto was reconquered, and the expedition to Vicenza served to overcome this frustration. Be that as it may, the presence of Manin in Vicenza, and the fact that he had brought his sixteen-year-old son with him, had a profound effect on the people of the city. It was to be the only time that Manin left Venice during the eighteen months of revolution.[21]

A council of war was hastily assembled. Manin demanded that the Italian forces immediately attack Thurn's rearguard. Antonini agreed, but Durando, almost certainly correctly, pointed out that it would serve little purpose. None the less the Venetians and volunteers sallied forth from the city, backed up by a few companies of Swiss troops. Some hard fighting ensued, during which Antonini lost his right arm and Manin and Tommaseo showed themselves to be fearless under fire. But the

---

[19] Giacomo Antonini (1792–1854) had been to Moscow with Napoleon, fought in Poland in 1830 and with Mazzini's expedition in Savoy, and in 1844 had been arrested as an accomplice of the Bandiera brothers. He was exiled to Paris where in 1848 he formed the Italian Legion. For details of this legion and its arrival in Italy, see A. Arzano, 'L'arrivo della legione Antonini in Italia nel 1848', in *Memorie Storiche Militari*, 6 (1912), fasc. 3, pp. 505–49.

[20] *La Repubblica veneta*, vol. 1, *Documenti diplomatici*, p. 38.

[21] A hundred of Vicenza's leading citizens signed a letter to Manin thanking him for making the expedition; see Trevelyan, *Manin and the Venetian Revolution*, p. 180. On the other hand, 93 Venetians, many of them from the civic guard, signed a petition of 22 May urging Manin never to leave Venice again; MCV, Doc. Manin, no. 500.

Austrians gave as good as they got and in the evening marched on towards Verona.[22]

At this stage Radetzky, who had so eagerly been awaiting the relief army, gave Thurn orders not to enter Verona but to go back to Vicenza and compel the city to surrender. Until Durando and the volunteers were tamed, Radetzky feared for his freedom of action in the campaign against Charles Albert. He also wanted a larger area of supplies for his army and an extra link with Austria by means of the road running north-west from Vicenza. Thurn returned to Vicenza on the night of 23–24 May, with nearly 18,000 men and 42 cannon. The city's defenders, who now numbered 11,000 in spite of the return to Venice of Antonini's legion and the Venetians, had not been inactive. The dykes of the river Redone had been cut, with the result that the land to the south-west of the city had been flooded. This made Thurn's task doubly difficult, for he had to reach and take the Berici hills, which lay to the south of the city and were the key to Vicenza. The Austrians made only slow progress in the night, but finally managed to instal their cannon at 5 a.m. and begin the bombardment of the city Many hundreds of cannon balls fell within the walls, but did little harm either to the buildings or the spirits of the inhabitants. From the Berici hills, which the Austrians did not succeed in taking, the Swiss artillery of the papal army peppered the Austrian positions below, and succeeded in silencing some of their cannon. The gate of Santa Croce was attacked three times, but was defended gallantly. Before 9 a.m. Italian regulars and volunteers counter-attacked, and put the Austrians to flight at bayonet-point. Thurn ordered a general retreat, and this time Radetzky allowed him to enter Verona.[23]

Vicenza had thus been successfully defended on two separate occasions, and this gave new heart to all the Italian forces fighting in the Veneto. None the less Nugent and Thurn had achieved their main task. In little more than five weeks they had brought 18,000 men to join Radetzky and in so doing had vitally changed the balance of forces in the north Italian war.

The Neapolitans

One force was conspicuous by its absence in this early and most decisive

22 For the council of war, see the account of L. G. Sanzin, 'F. e L. Seismit-Doda nelle vicende del 1848–9', in *La Venezia Giulia*, vol. 3, pp. 507–8. His report is based on a letter of Federico Seismit-Doda. Antonini's dictated account of the fighting is to be found in MCV, Doc. Manin, no. 3773.
23 For the second battle of Vicenza, see Trevelyan, *Manin and the Venetian Revolution*, pp. 180–1, and Pieri, *Storia militare*, pp. 384–5.

phase of the first war of Italian independence – the army of King
Ferdinand II of the Two Sicilies. Before the revolution Ferdinand's army,
which numbered 60,000 in peace time, and could be increased to 80,000
in time of war, was considered by many observers to be superior to that of
Piedmont.[24] Ferdinand and the Neapolitan aristocracy did all they could
to avoid sending the army northwards, but liberal pressure was too strong,
and they were forced to allow 10,000 men to leave. The commander of
this force was the sixty-five-year-old Guglielmo Pepe, lifetime *carbonaro*
and patriot, and hero of the Neapolitan revolution of 1820–1. Pepe had
fought under Napoleon and Murat, and had narrowly escaped death
while still only a boy defending the Parthenopean republic of 1799 against
the sanfedist reaction. He had considerable experience of revolutionary
war, and was author of a number of military tracts which stressed the
need to combine regular and popular forces, and to use to the full the
natural advantages which the Italian terrain offered insurrectionary forces.
He was loved and respected by the few officers in the Neapolitan army
who were liberals and nationalists, but had little sway over the majority of
his army, who remained strictly royalist and resentful of the ageing general
whom Ferdinand had been forced to welcome back from exile and appoint
as their commander.[25]

Pepe's march towards the Po was hindered by the king and court, who
tried desperately to play for time. Pepe was told categorically that he was
not to cross into Lombardy-Venetia until he received specific orders from
the king. Precious weeks were lost, in spite of Pepe's efforts; by the time
of the battle of Cornuda the Neapolitans were still strung out between
Bologna and Ferrara. Charles Albert had agreed to their going into the
Veneto, and had they crossed the Po in the first half of May their presence
could well have been the determining factor in the Venetian campaign.
But while the Austrians moved with extreme speed and decisiveness, the
Italians were painfully slow to marshal their forces.

In the event, it was the Neapolitan fleet, not the army, that arrived in
Venice first. On 16 May hundreds of small craft raced out to welcome
the Neapolitans as they sailed into Venetian waters. A banquet for over
100 persons celebrated the event. Restelli reported that in his opinion
Manin proposed two toasts which were less than tactful: one to the
Sicilians 'who were heroically fighting for their independence'; and the

---

[24] Pieri, *Storia militare*, pp. 173–5.
[25] For further details on Pepe, see Trevelyan's splendid description, *Manin and the
Venetian Revolution*, pp. 183–4: 'His whitening hair was crowned by a cocked
hat with an enormous white feather, and he still dragged clanking at his heels a
sabre of the size that had been fashionable when the world was young in the days
of Joachim Murat, *fils d'aubergiste* and King of Naples.'

other to 'those who were still fighting for the cause of independence, and not for dynastic gain or self-interest'.[26] This last was all too transparent a reference to Piedmont. But at the very moment when Manin's resentment against Charles Albert was at its height, the Piedmontese fleet too arrived at Venice. This meant that the combined Italian fleet was far superior to the Austrian one, even though the Venetians, having lost the fleet at Pola in the first days of the revolution,[27] could only contribute two brigs and two corvettes. The overall commander, the Piedmontese admiral Albini, was unable to make much of this opportunity. The Austrian fleet escaped hurriedly to the harbour of Trieste, where it was protected by three large shore batteries. Albini and the Neapolitan admiral, Cosa, decided not to attack, but began a type of blockade. This succeeded only in arousing the anger of the British and of the German confederation, who made dire threats of reprisals in the event of damage to their commerce or to any of their merchant fleet.[28]

The blockade of Trieste had hardly begun when news reached the north of the triumph of the counter-revolution at Naples. On 13 May the deputies of the lower house of parliament, elected on a restricted suffrage throughout the southern mainland, met for the first time in Naples. An immediate squabble broke out between deputies and king over the exact powers of the parliament. Many of the deputies from Cilento and Calabria had been accompanied to the capital by local squads, and these soon spread the rumour that the king was preparing a coup d'état. Crowds gathered in the main streets, and the king ordered his Swiss regiments to occupy key positions in the city. The deputies tried to calm the crowds and reach a reconciliation with the king, but to no avail. On 14 May the first barricades were erected and on the 15th battle was joined. The insurgents were not more than a thousand strong, of whom only three hundred were Neapolitans – radical bourgeois, artisans, and a section of the national guard. The rest were from the Cilento, from Calabria and from Sicily. The royal troops were supported by the *lazzaroni*, ever faithful to the Bourbon crown; various houses and palaces adjacent to the barricades were looted and their occupants massacred. The resistance on the barricades, although tenacious, could not survive the overwhelming assault by the troops, and by the end of the day Ferdinand II had become the first

---

[26] Monti, *Francesco Restelli*, p. 339, dispatch of 18 May. Alessandro Poerio, the Neapolitan poet, gives the best description of the arrival of the Neapolitan fleet, in a letter to his mother of 18 May 1848; see V. Imbriani, *Alessandro Poerio a Venezia*, pp. 41–3.

[27] See above, pp. 103–4.

[28] The best description of the naval manoeuvres of these weeks has been written by G. Stefani, 'La flotta sardo-veneta nell'Adriatico e il blocco di Trieste', in *La Venezia Giulia*, vol. 2, pp. 1–103.

monarch in Europe to turn the tide of revolution. He did not yet feel strong enough to return to absolute monarchy, but the attempted rising provided him with the pretext for the immediate recall of his troops and fleet from the north so as to ensure the internal order of his kingdom. By a quirk of fate 15 May was also the day which saw the failure in Paris of the popular demonstration in favour of Poland. The events in both Naples and Paris were to weigh heavily against the survival of the revolution in northern Italy.

Ferdinand's orders reached Pepe at the moment when he had decided to wait no longer to cross the Po, and to go forward with or without royal approval. He tried in vain to get the bulk of the Neapolitan force to follow him. The officers were fearful of having their possessions confiscated and their families disgraced, the men of losing the only employment they had ever known. Pepe managed to cross the Po with only two battalions of volunteers and one of regulars, along with a number of outstanding officers from the artillery and the engineers. He received a great welcome in Venice, where he was quickly appointed commander-in-chief of the Venetian forces.[29] But though Pepe and his men were to be invaluable to Venice, they were only a fraction of the monarchist forces on which the Venetians had placed their hopes. The Neapolitan fleet followed the example of the army, and left Trieste to sail back to southern waters.

Manin, Mazzini and Venetian politics

While the military situation worsened, the Venetian government came under unceasing pressure to abandon the republic. On 31 May the unconquered provinces published an *indirizzo intimidatorio*, threatening to break off all relations with Venice within three days. They urged Venice to change its form of government since it was repugnant to the Italian princes, and particularly Charles Albert, who in their opinion was the primary source of aid.[30] Feelings in the provincial cities and towns ran very high against *la città dominante*, because it was generally believed that only Venetian political intransigence was preventing Charles Albert from sending troops into the Veneto. The walls of the city of Padua were daubed with anti-Venetian slogans.[31] In Rovigo Giovanni Maria del Pedro, the commissioner for war, reported that the provincial committee

---

[29] For Pepe's first review of his troops in the Piazza San Marco, see the description by the Neapolitan colonel F. Matarazzo in his manuscript, 'Memorie storico-politico-militari sulla campagna del Veneto e sulla difesa di Venezia nel 1848–9' (MRM, archivio generale, reg. no. 34386, p. 68).

[30] Supplement of the *Gazzetta di Venezia*, no. 133, 2 June 1848.

[31] A. Gloria, *Il comitato provvisorio*, p. 107.

would send no money from taxes to Venice, since the latter 'was in the process of isolating itself from the rest of Italy'.[32]

This was also the period when Venice's unpopularity in the rest of Italy was at its height. Most Italian observers could not understand why Venice had both failed to defend the *terraferma* and insisted on maintaining its republicanism. It seemed a dual recipe for disaster. Quite apart from the onslaughts in the Piedmontese and Lombard press, the influential Florentine journal, *La Patria*, lamented on 2 May that 'the Venetians, after alienating the provinces through their improvident action, and leaving them without defence, are now starting to repeat the historical testimony of their ancient government'.[33] Carlo Poerio wrote from Naples to his brother Alessandro that the Venetian republic had 'retarded and compromised the Risorgimento'.[34] The moderate Milanese republican, Cesare Correnti, commented, 'even what is being said in all Italy about the incapacity and weakness of Venice is not strong enough'.[35] Only F. D. Guerrazzi, in the *Corriere Livornese*, chose to ignore Venice's military failure in favour of emphasising the lack of municipalism in Manin's policy, and its fidelity to the Milanese programme of 22 March.[36]

Faced with this climate of marked hostility, Manin remained obdurate for a number of days. He felt increasingly mistrustful of Charles Albert, a king who, in Manin's opinion, had clearly violated the terms on which he had crossed the Lombard border. The Venetian leader was afraid that the Piedmontese were preparing a worse betrayal, a re-enactment of Campoformio, by which Venice would be sold to Austria as the price of

[32] MCV, Doc. Manin, no. 2719, date unclear, 8? June 1848.
[33] MCV, Doc. Manin, no. 1533, *La Patria*, no. 238, included in a dispatch from Castellani. For the Lombard press, see MCV, Doc. Manin, nos. 3241-4, copies of the Milanese newspaper *Pio IX*, 23–5 May 1848, particularly the article of P. A. Paravia published on 24 May. The newspaper compared Genoa's sacrifice with Venice's selfishness, and stressed the necessity of a constitutional monarchy, 'on the one hand to save us from communism, on the other to reinforce the struggle against the oppressor'. Also BL, 1852.e.8, for a letter from the Circolo Nazionale of Genoa to their Venetian brothers, urging union (29 April 1848); MCV, Doc. Manin, no. 532, Milanese handbill (no date), asking if Venice wanted to become like San Marino; *ibid.*, no. 535, an unpublished article by Manin reproving Gioberti for calling the Venetian government a 'mediaeval oligarchy' (20 June 1848). Finally, MCV, Doc. Manin, no. 2071, dispatch from Calucci in Milan, 17 May 1848: 'the sympathies of Europe are aroused by one principle – that of nationalism. If we Italians split up, and debase that principle by arguing over forms of government, we will lose all impetus'.
[34] Imbriani, p. 136.
[35] Correnti from Ferrara to the Lombard provisional government, 18 June 1848, MRM, archivio Bertani, cart. 4, plico xxi, no. 24.
[36] *Corriere Livornese*, 6 June 1848. Reprinted in Racc. Andreola, vol. 2, pp. 304–5.

Piedmont's annexation of Lombardy. Venice, according to Manin, had to be kept in Venetian hands, for once the city belonged to the Piedmontese they could dispose of it as they wished.[37]

In an attempt to find a political and military alternative to fusion with Piedmont, Manin therefore thought seriously of inviting Mazzini to Venice. The end of May 1848 found Manin in his most radical mood since the March days. He felt very strongly that the Piedmontese had distorted the nature of the war for their own ends, that the future of north Italy would be a bleak one under the suspect Charles Albert: 'the present war is not a war of the princes, but of the people; not a dynastic or municipal war, but a national one; not a war of conquest, but of liberation'.[38]

These feelings corresponded very closely to those of Mazzini, who had denounced both Lombardy and Piedmont for the abandonment of the policy of *a guerra finita*. On 20 May 1848, the first number of Mazzini's *L'Italia del popolo* proclaimed: 'we reject the formation of a kingdom of upper Italy'.[39] Manin wrote to Mazzini on 28 May, asking him to 'defend us, not because I seek the approval of others, but because in defending us you defend the cause of Italian liberty, which until now has had no other refuge outside the Venetian lagoons'.[40] Mazzini wrote back, offering Venice the aid of a number of volunteer legions, including the Poles and a Franco-Italian force four thousand strong. Manin politely refused these, and in the end he decided not to invite Mazzini to Venice. He was dissuaded by Tommaseo, who thought the two men were incompatible, and perhaps by the realisation that Mazzini would push Venice into an open split with Piedmont. This Manin wanted to avoid at all costs, for, in the last analysis, he trusted more in the efficacy of Charles Albert's army than in Mazzini's various offers of volunteer troops. Manin could write that the war should have been a war of the people, but in practice he was prepared only to put his trust in a dynastic army.

At the end of May 1848, Manin still hoped that this dynastic army would march into the Veneto and towards victory without Venice's giving itself to Charles Albert. However, by this time he stood not only in

[37] As early as 23 April the Venetian government, in the minutes of a letter to Calucci, had shown itself suspicious of a possible treaty between Charles Albert and the Austrians (MCV, Doc. Manin, no. 2054). For Manin's fears at this time, see his unpublished notes (MCV, Agg. Manin, xiii/i, no. i), undated, but obviously of the period 12 May – 3 June 1848.

[38] MCV, Agg. Manin, xiii/i, no. i.

[39] Quoted in Candeloro, *Storia dell'Italia moderna*, vol. 3, p. 198.

[40] Letter of 28 May 1848, published in the interesting article by G. Gambarin, 'Il Mazzini, il Tommaseo, il Manin e la difesa di Venezia', *Archivio Veneto*, 5 (1929), p. 322.

opposition to his envoys in Milan and at Charles Albert's headquarters,[41] but also alone in the Venetian council of ministers. He tried to argue that any fusion with Piedmont would create civil war in Venice, but the rest of the government was solidly against him. Camerata, the minister of finance, warned that Venice could not survive financially in isolation. Tommaseo, up to that point Manin's most loyal ally, wanted an assembly because he was convinced it would confirm Venice's republicanism. The threat from the provinces to set up a rival government on the *terraferma* also weighed heavily in favour of an immediate popular vote. Manin was forced to give in. A decree of 3 June fixed the convocation of a Venetian assembly for the 18th of the same month. Venice and its province were to elect, by adult male suffrage, two hundred representatives to decide whether or not to continue the policy of *a guerra finita*. No mention was made of the kingdom of northern Italy, but it was clear that if the assembly voted against *a guerra finita*, fusion with Piedmont and Lombardy would not be long in following.[42]

Outvoted by his own ministers, Manin saw the ideal of a federation of Italian states, of which a Venetian republic would be one, fading in the face of Piedmontese determination to unite northern Italy under Charles Albert. On 7 June Manin wrote to a French friend of the dangers of fusion:

It is vital that the Italian states, in their composition and extension, should be based upon historical tradition. Peoples who have different origins and customs should not be forced together, because otherwise civil war will follow the war of independence. Finally, no state should be refused the republican form of government if it feels better suited to it than to the transitional stage of a constitutional monarchy.[43]

Yet fusion seemed the only way to secure Charles Albert's aid, and most Venetians, including Manin, still thought the king could intervene in the Veneto if he chose to. On what proved to be spurious grounds of military necessity, the Venetians prepared for their election.

Venice and the elections

In the eleven weeks of the revolution the city of Venice had not altered fundamentally. Its most striking feature was the enthusiasm of the poor

[41] See the letters from Calucci of 24 May 1848 (MCV, Doc. Manin, no. 2077) and Martinengo of 21 May (*La Repubblica veneta*, vol. 1, p. 45).

[42] Racc. Andreola, vol. 2, p. 230.

[43] Letter to M. de Cormenin, written in French, in Planat de la Faye (ed.), *Documents et pièces authentiques laissés par Daniel Manin*, Paris 1860, vol. 1, pp. 264–5.

for the new republic. This was all the more remarkable in view of the difficult economic conditions in which the city found itself. The suspension of trade with Austria and the absence of tourists had a grave effect on the sale of artisan goods and the seasonal employment upon which so many Venetians were reliant. The handbills of the time are full of references to the precarious conditions of many sections of the Venetian poor.[44]

None the less, popular enthusiasm for the revolution was undisputed, and in trying to explain this most historians have emphasised the nationalism of the Venetians and their adulation for Manin. G. M. Trevelyan, for instance, has written: 'The enthusiasm of the working-class, which gave to the President's position its real strength, was personal and patriotic, an offering to Manin, to Venice and to Italy'.[45] Undoubtedly, Manin's own magnetism helped greatly to popularise the new political order. So too did municipal pride and the idea that the city was once again an independent republic. But it is important to note that a number of shrewd economic measures served to cement the alliance which Manin formed with the Venetian lower classes. Without these measures it is dubious whether popular support for the republic would have survived as long as it did.

In the first place, the government was willing to guarantee employment in a number of state or municipal concerns. At the tobacco factory of Santa Croce the 700 workers, both men and women, showed an independence and militancy which seem quite modern. Early in April they declared that they wanted to elect their own foremen. It had to be explained to them 'one by one' that 'they were acting on a mistaken belief, since the existence of the republic did not mean that employees could nominate their immediate superiors'.[46] In May they petitioned for economic parity with their colleagues at Milan. But it soon became clear that lack of primary materials and opportunities for exporting the finished products would mean a cut in the numbers employed. The manager of the factory warned that rioting would greet any sackings, and the government decided instead to pay a daily subsidy to the 300 women workers who were in danger of losing their jobs. This subsidy continued till the fall of the provisional government.

Similarly, as we have seen,[47] the government made sure that the 1,500 workers at Treporti, Lido and S. Erasmo who were under the orders of

---

[44] See for instance Racc. Andreola, vol. 1, pp. 581–2, handbill of 16 April 1848 from 'a mother'. Also *ibid.*, vol. 1, pp. 623–4, handbill of 18 April from Antonio Bernardini, complaining that conditions were worse than during the blockade of 1813–14.
[45] Trevelyan, *Manin and the Venetian Revolution*, p. 138.
[46] See Bernardello, 'La paura del comunismo', p. 78.
[47] See above, p. 116.

the commander of the port had sufficient work.[48] At the arsenal the need to construct a fleet meant that by October 1848 the number of workers employed there had risen to 2,172.[49] If work in the artisan shops and tourist trade had slackened considerably, the government seemed to be providing some sort of substitute.

Manin's ministry also responded to the constant popular pressure to raise wages. Although adamantly in favour of not interfering in relations between employer and employed, the government's example in raising the wages of those workers under their or the municipality's control was one that was widely imitated. In this way dustmen, arsenal workers, lamp-lighters, bakers' hands, tailors, shoemakers and smiths all received wage rises in the first months of the revolution.[50] Government action on taxation was also enlightened. The reduction of the salt tax and the abolition of all duties on fishing were well received, as was the decision to do away with the tax that gondoliers paid for each passage they made within the city.[51]

Perhaps most crucial of all, as soon as grain prices showed signs of rising, the republican government decided to peg the price of bread. On 23 May 1848 the new provisions came into force. The price of white bread was fixed at 24 centesimi per *libbra*, and brown bread (*pane semolei*) at 20 centesimi per *libbra*. In the face of widespread protests from the bakers, the price of white bread was allowed to rise to 26 centesimi, but that of the cheaper bread remained the same. The government's price fixing was a considerable success, for by the end of August 1848 the cost of the two types of bread had only risen by a couple of centesimi.[52]

[48] The workers on the Lido fortress complained bitterly to the government against the harshness of the engineer in charge of the works, and of his foreman: 'The barbarous and unjust way in which these two men, who can hardly be called human, tyrannise over the workmen needs to be exposed. They are reducing our so-called wages to almost nothing, an act which is certainly not compatible with the policy of this new government which, so we understood, seeks to reward every worker in proportion to his labour. The actions of these two men are in direct contradiction to the professed aim of lessening the sufferings of citizens who have languished under Austrian repression for so many years' (MCV, Doc. Manin, no. 3923, a complaint signed by 42 workers at the Lido. No date, but obviously of this period).

[49] MCV, Doc. Manin, no. 2244, 5 Oct. 1848.

[50] Bernardello, 'La paura del comunismo', pp. 80–1. In April the bakers' hands marched down the Mercerie demanding a wage increase. Their leaders were arrested, but the police were forced to release them when a menacing crowd gathered outside the Questura.

[51] *Ibid.*, p. 80 n. 97. For the measures on salt and fishing, see above, pp. 117 and 122.

[52] The measures of 23 May immediately followed a series of riots directed against bakers' shops. For details of the price fixing, see ACV, Municip., Atti di Uff., 1845–9, IV, 7/49, no. 4946 (1848). Mengaldo, the head of the civic guard, wanted

All these measures, when combined with the handing back of the smaller items pawned at the Monte di Pietà, served the government in good stead in its relations with the Venetian lower classes. But there was another side to Manin's policy, and this consisted in elaborate security measures to restrict social unrest. Bernardello has documented the widespread fear of 'communism' amongst the Venetian bourgeoisie at this time,[53] and various incidents and demonstrations served to increase their apprehension. Some of the Venetian artisans whose livelihood was threatened by new machinery saw the revolution as an opportunity to assert their rights. An 'illegal association' of felt-hat makers began a campaign of sacking all those shops which were stocking up with cheaper cardboard hats. Various print-workers threatened to smash the new machine of the government's printer, Andreola, which was 'the reason why many of us are deprived of the income by which we maintain ourselves and our families'.[54] In addition, on 30 April a group of sixty *popolani*, forty of whom were armed with large sticks, tried to stage a demonstration in the Piazza San Marco. The reasons for their action are not clear. The gendarmes forced them to disperse, but they split up into small groups and wandered through the city till late at night.[55]

In response, on 7 May 1848 Manin set up a committee of public vigilance. It asked for a fort on the Lido to be put at its disposal, and on 13 June drew up a list of those likely to disturb the public order. These suspects were for the most part from the Venetian poor, and were porters, boatmen and street sellers.[56] The committee also advised Manin to discontinue the sermons which three radical preachers – Fathers Gavazzi, Bassi and Tornielli – were giving daily in the Piazza San Marco.[57] The committee reported that Bassi and Tornielli had said things 'which alarm us greatly and which are likely to arouse among the poor hatred for the rich and noble classes'.

the price of rice, beans and pasta to be controlled as well, because the decree of the 23rd had not sufficed to 'calm the restlessness of the people'; see his letter of 24 May to the municipality (*ibid.*, no. 5084). But the municipality did not comply.
[53] Bernardello, 'La paura del comunismo', *passim*.
[54] See the petition of June 1848 to the government, MCV, Doc. Pell., b. xxxviii/11 (11). On the hatters, ASV, Gov. Prov. 1848–9, OPss, vii, 2, no. 3271.
[55] See the gendarmes' report of 1 May 1848 in ASV, Gov. Prov. 1848–9, b. 649, corpo di gendarmeria, no number.
[56] ASV, Gov. Prov. 1848–9, OPss, vii, 2, nos. 3250 and 4466.
[57] MCV, Doc. Manin, no. 3035, report of the committee of public vigilance, 9 May 1848. Following the sermons in the Piazza a mass of *Crociati* had threatened to sack some houses in Cannaregio on the pretext of searching for arms. The committee said that the preachers were attracting so much attention that the poor refused to go to work.

In his attitude to the Venetian lower classes, Manin thus combined shrewd economic interventions with constant surveillance. His approach to the bourgeoisie was, hardly surprisingly, much less double-edged. In spite of the difficulties of the economic situation, the government made very clear its good intentions in the limited time available to it. The export tax on silk was more than halved, and to encourage the silk industry in the Veneto raw silk was freed of any import charge. On 27 April the import duties on cotton, iron, dyestuffs, granulated sugar and coffee were reduced by 20 per cent. The government's aim was clearly to move away from Austrian restrictionism towards a free trade economy. Such a policy would have stimulated many parts of the Venetian economy, though some manufacturers were quick to point out the perils for certain sections, for example for Murano glass when faced with Bohemian competition.[58]

The government also approved plans for an Italian Lloyd's company, though circumstances prevented their realisation. The company was to rival the Austrian one of the same name, and was to acquire or build steamships which would transport goods and passengers between Venice and the various Italian ports. The first patrons of the new company were to be Giuseppe Reali, Antonio Luigi Ivancich, Jacopo Treves, Andrea Giovanelli and Spiridione Papadopoli.[59]

On 5 June 1848 the Venetian chamber of commerce presented a number of requests which would probably have formed the basis of the government's economic policy had the revolution survived. They asked that products manufactured in Venice should receive tax concessions when sold on the *terraferma*; that fiscal burdens on merchant shipping be removed; that a national bank be set up, as at Genoa and Leghorn; and that the monetary systems of Lombardy-Venetia, Piedmont and the Papal States be standardised. They also requested a number of other measures which they agreed to delay because of the difficult military, financial and political situation. These included a completely new commercial code, the use of the Milan–Venice railway for transporting goods, and the further

---

[58] ASV, Gov. Prov. 1848–9, MU, b. 2, no. 283, letter of 28 March 1848 from four makers of blown glass from Murano – Bonifacio Santi, Bernardo Andreotta, Francesco Zanetti, Francesco Suardi. They complained that the trade in Murano glass had been declining for some time, but did not give details. Also the letter of 16 April from Francesco Braida of Udine and Giuseppe Vittorelli of Treviso, owners of two of the biggest sugar refineries in the Veneto, warning that any reduction in the import duty on sugar cane could only harm them, for their warehouses were full of unsold sugar; *ibid.*, MU, b. 7, no. 3072.

[59] See the minutes headed 'first ideas', written on government paper, but without date; MCV, Doc. Manin, no. 3191. It was also part of the plan to have one English and one French sponsor.

reduction of the export duty on raw silk, to be viewed in the general context of pan-Italian agreement on duties and taxation. The chamber concluded by stating that 'it shares with the class it represents that faith and hope that derive from the constant proof the government has given of being persistently vigilant and active in securing the interests of this city'.[60]

It was not only the merchants and businessmen amongst the Venetian bourgeoisie who supported the new political order. Far from dismantling the Austrian administration, the new government guaranteed, with very few exceptions, the jobs and salaries of those who had been employed by Austria. This was a constant source of complaint from many patriots, for while the petty officials and clerks lived modestly enough, the medium- and high-ranking administrators enjoyed considerable incomes. Thus in the superintendence of finance the chief official drew 6,000 lire annually under the republic, while the average salary was around 1,500 lire.[61] By maintaining these salary levels, the government avoided a disgruntled officer class and gained continuity and efficiency in the administration. But with workers' wages around 300–450 lire a year, the contrast between rich and poor in the new republic remained very marked.

In general, the members of the educated classes felt that the new republic represented their interests. They particularly welcomed the new freedom of association and of the press, and the market for five-centesimi newspapers was soon completely saturated. These measures, when combined with the greater freedom in the universities and schools and the abolition of the censorship, meant that an exuberant climate of intellectual freedom permeated Venice.[62]

[60] ASV, CC, b. 194, III, fasc. 9, no. 43. There were seventeen demands in all. See also the notes of 18 April of the finance minister explaining that fundamental reforms of customs duties and tariffs should await the deliberation of the whole nation; ASV, Gov. Prov. 1848–9, b. 434, consulta, fasc. 14, no. 23.

[61] See ASV, Gov. Prov. 1848–9, b. 462, comitato di pubblica sorveglianza, 7 May – 17 July 1848, for a list of all *impiegati* and their salaries. Of the 121 employees in the finance offices, four joined the *Crociati* and one became a lieutenant in the mobile civic guard. See also MCV, Doc. Pell., b XXXVIII 11 (101) for a list of those given employment directly by the new government. For example, Manin's two principal secretaries, Pezzato and Zanetti, were paid 375 and 300 lire per month.

[62] Over 100 newspapers appeared during the revolution. They were nearly all about five or six pages long, and very frequently repeated each other. With a few exceptions, they are less useful to the historian than might be supposed. On 8 April 1848 *Il Libero Italiano* published a scathing attack on Charles Albert. Numerous copies of the newspaper were burnt in protest in the Piazza San Marco. There was a strong movement to have the newspaper suppressed, but Manin refused; see MCV, Doc. Manin, nos. 848, 3062, 3203, 3593; Racc. Andreola, vol. 1, pp. 463–7, 497–9, 521; *L'Indipendente*, no. 9, p. 35, 11 April

Among the clergy and the nobility, the twin pillars of the old establishment, enthusiasm for the new order was naturally rather mixed. The upper echelons of the church hierarchy, and the patriarch Monico in particular, remained aloof from the national cause. Some of the parish priests followed the patriarch's lead, but the lesser and extra-parochial clergy were as patriotic as on the mainland.[63] As for the nobility, most of them would have nothing to do with the new government. A few, like Marco Grimani, gave donations to the civic guard or allowed the courtyards of their palaces to be used for drilling new recruits. The Bevilacqua were one of the few nationalist aristocratic families (the Giovanelli were another), and gave the republic their castle near Legnago to be used for military purposes. It was briefly defended by Zambeccari and the legion of the Alto Reno, but was then burnt to the ground by the Austrians. Five members of the old aristocracy were actually elected in June 1848 to the Venetian assembly. But most of the nobility retired discreetly to their villas, or, like Alvise Mocenigo and his Austrian wife, left the Veneto altogether and sought refuge in cities like Florence that were as yet relatively undisturbed by revolutionary fervour.[64]

One of the most pressing problems that the Venetian government had to

1848. On education see the decree in Racc. Andreola, vol. 1, p. 176, announcing a commission to advise the government on scholastic reform. See also N. Tommaseo, *Venezia*, vol. 1, p. 143 n. 381, for details of Tommaseo's writings, decrees, etc. while in office. One of Tommaseo's first acts was to throw open the archives for use by the general public. The only evidence I have so far found of new schools being opened in this period is a 'Hymn for the opening of schools in the arsenal', MCV, Doc. Manin, no. 3261. The provincial consultative committee wrote to Tommaseo on 12 May 1848 stressing the need for the political education of the masses. They suggested special courses in Italian history so as to convince people of the justice of the national cause. They commented that 'the people are paying us for our apathy by riots, excesses and corruption of every sort'. Tommaseo replied agreeing with them, but saying that the first task was to make the priests and teachers aware of their duties. To meet this need, he had commissioned a number of educational tracts from young authors, with titles ranging from 'Liberty and Equality' to 'What is Fidelity?'; ASV, Gov. Prov. 1848–9, b. 434, consulta, fasc. 33, no. 140.

[63] See Tommaseo, *Venezia*, vol. 2, p. 84. Even some of the patriarch's entourage were favourably disposed; one of them, Ignazio Zorzetto, always wore a tricolour cockade during 1849, and after April 1849 sported a red sash as well; B. Bertoli, *Le origini del movimento cattolico*, pp. 15–16.

[64] For Mocenigo's letters of the period, ASV, fondo Mocenigo, b. 150. For Guglielmo and Girolamo Bevilacqua, MCV, Doc. Manin, no. 1671, letter of early April 1848. For Marco Grimani, MCV, Agg. Manin, xxx/17, nos. 26–7, letters of early April 1848 from Grimani to Mengaldo. See also the letters of Giovanni Querini Stampalia, in FQSV, MSS Class ix, 17, 7.

confront was that of finance. When the Austrians capitulated, they left behind considerable amounts of money with which the republicans met the first needs of the revolution. It also emerged that the Venice–Milan railway company, which was state-owned by 1848, had over five million lire in its Venice offices. The new government decided to assume control of the company, and on 13 April arranged for three million lire of the railway's funds to be loaned to the republic.[65] But these early windfalls were soon eaten into by the very heavy expenditure of the first months of the revolution. Manin had agreed that Venice should pay and provision the papal troops, an outlay which in September 1848 the papal government refused to repay.[66] In addition, the Venetian provinces provided very little income for the central government before they were reconquered. Padua did pay 692,507 lire in taxes, but the only other contributions in taxation were 72,174 lire from Belluno and 600 lire from Treviso.[67]

By May 1848 the situation was becoming critical, and the government decided to launch a loan of ten million lire. The details were published in a decree of 14 May. The loan, which offered interest of 5 per cent, was guaranteed by the nearly 30,000 shares in the railway company, which had become state property. It was to be repaid over six years, from 1849 to 1854. The loan was called a voluntary one by the government, and has been so described by most historians, but it was nothing of the sort. The expected contributions from individuals were fixed by a government commission and the provincial committees. Venice was to provide 4½ million lire, Padua 2½ million, Vicenza 1,400,000, Rovigo 1 million and Treviso 600,000.[68]

The list of individuals in Venice and the amount each had to pay make extremely interesting reading, for they give the historian some indication of the relative wealth of the best-known figures in the city.[69] Of course the

---

[65] ASV, Gov. Prov., 1848–9, MU, b. 5, no. 2391.

[66] Dispatches of Castellani to Manin, 2 and 4 Sept. 1848, in *La Repubblica veneta*, vol. 2, *Documenti diplomatici, carteggio di G. B. Castellani*, pp. 269–70, 276–7.

[67] See MCV, Doc. Manin, no. 3149, a summary of Venice's finances up to the end of 1848.

[68] ACV, Municip., Atti di Uff., 1845–9, 1, 5/10, copy of the decree attached to no. 4878 (1848). Each contributor had to pay in three equal rates in May, June and July. The German merchant Bertuch refers in his memoirs to 'the so-called voluntary contributions which were sollicited and which it was impossible to refuse' (F. Bertuch, *Contributi*, p. 812. Bertuch was assessed at 5,000 lire in this first loan.

[69] ASV, Gov. Prov. 1848–9, reg. 1224: 'Elenco delle somme individualmente attribuite alle Ditte domiciliate od aventi entità tassabili nella suddetta Provincia per la formazione del prestito dei 10,000,000 di lire correnti'. In all there were 682 names. For an introduction to the financial policy of the government, which however gives no details of individual contributions, see A. Pino-Branca, 'La

figures must be treated with some care. For instance, Giuseppe Reali, the
president of the Venetian chamber of commerce, was only called upon for
28,000 lire, which was reduced on appeal to 20,000. He was later to lend
the government much greater sums, and his low rating in this first loan
must be ascribed to a temporary shortage of liquid capital. But the same
names and relatively similar amounts appear with great regularity in all
the loans that the government was to undertake, and these first figures are
therefore a fairly sound guide. The list contains 682 names and its most
striking feature is the very substantial wealth of a number of merchants
and businessmen, most of whom had long been active in the Venetian
chamber of commerce. Jacopo and Isacco Treves, the bankers, were
required to lend no less than 225,000 lire, as was the company of Angelo
Papadopoli. The brothers Pigazzi were called upon for 100,000 lire,
G. B. Sceriman 70,000, Angelo and Valentino Comello 50,000 each,
Spiridione Papadopoli 50,000, Antonio Ivancich 40,000, Jacopo Levi and
sons 30,000, Angelo Maria Rosada 20,000. As for the old nobility, we
clearly cannot be absolutely certain that the sums asked for corresponded
to their actual wealth. Much of their resources was tied up in land, and
the government may have treated them with care for fear of their outright
hostility. None the less there is evidence of noblemen who had little to do
with the revolution being asked for and paying very large sums, while
the few nobles in favour of the revolution were often able to pay relatively
modest amounts. In general, and allowing for all possible qualifications, it
seems difficult to avoid the conclusion of a marked decline in noble
wealth. One or two families still paid huge amounts: Pietro and Andrea
Giovanelli 275,000 lire, Vettore Pisani 210,000, Loredana Gattersburg
Morosini 80,000, Pietro Zen 32,000, Leopardo Martinengo 24,000. But
many noblemen, even those playing a leading part in the fate of the city,
seemed able to pay comparatively little: Giovanni Correr 4,000 lire, Luigi
Michiel 2,000 lire, Luigi Donà 3,000, Giovanni Gritti 6,000.[70]

finanza di guerra del governo provvisorio veneto (1848–9)', in *Studi in onore di
Gino Luzzatto*, vol. 3, pp. 95–125.

[70] Of all the old nobility, the Giovanelli family were assessed for the greatest
amount by the revolutionary government. The Giovanelli entered the Golden
Book at the time of the war of Candia, and made their fortune through banking
and the silk trade. On the death of his father Andrea in 1860, Giuseppe Giovanelli
decided to discontinue the practice of weekly distributions of alms outside the
gates of the family palace in the parish of Santa Fosca. He did this 'to avoid
gatherings of persons who were not always respectful and obedient', and instead
gave the city's charity commission 1,800 lire annually. Giuseppe became a
senator in 1866 and when he died in 1886 left an inheritance of at least fifty
million lire, an enormous sum for those times; see T. Sarti, *Il parlamento subalpino e nazionale. Profili e cenni biografici di tutti i deputati e senatori creati dal
1840 al 1890*, pp. 522–3. Alvise Mocenigo wrote to his agent Pasqualini on

Both Padua and Rovigo immediately complained about the quotas attributed to them. Venice refused to allow any reductions, but did consent to the minimum individual loan being lowered to 500 lire in these provinces. The authorities in the Polesine found themselves in particular difficulty because of the large number of absentee landowners.[71] But with the reconquest of the provinces, the Venetian government was forced to raise Venice's quota to six million lire, appealing this time to the less wealthy in the city, with a minimum contribution of 200 lire. Of this six million, 5,141,354 lire was successfully collected,[72] but practically nothing came from the provinces. By mid-June the financial situation was still grave, and this lent added force to those who argued that there was no salvation for Venice outside a kingdom of northern Italy.

As the campaign for fusion warmed up, and the future of the republic was seen to be in danger, Venice became increasingly divided. This division was largely along class lines. The lower classes regarded the republic as their republic, and Manin as their leader. The gondoliers started singing a song which began, 'Fusion is really confusion', and ended, 'but as for us, it's fine by us, as long as Manin stays'.[73] The letters that Manin received in these days show that many of the Venetians regarded him with absolute adulation – 'Manin, padre della patria e padre mio'.[74]

When the decree announcing the elections for the assembly was made public, there were immediate demonstrations of protest. Zennari, the government secretary, wrote to Calucci at midnight of 3 June 1848 saying that the streets had been filled since five in the afternoon with people crying 'Long live the republic, we want Manin'. On the fourth, a Sunday, a number of fishermen armed with spiked sticks invaded the Piazza. Their leader, Domenico Corrao, who was also head of the Nicolotti clan, was arrested. When interrogated he replied that he had gone to the Piazza

---

17 May 1848: 'Here the loan is already under way. I do not know what amount they have decided to tax me; knowing my financial state, I hope it is only for a little' (ASV, fondo Mocenigo, b. 150, no number). Mocenigo was in fact asked for only 5,000 lire.

[71] ASV, Gov. Prov. 1848–9, b. 525, fasc. 1, nos. 6235 and 7497 for letters of 17 and 31 May from the provincial committee of Rovigo; *ibid.*, no. 6148 for the Paduan complaint of 20 May.

[72] Brunetti, 'L'opera del comune di Venezia', app. 3, pp. 124–5.

[73] Marchesi, *Storia documentata*, p. 243, no. 110.

[74] MCV, Doc. Manin, no. 481, anonymous, April 1848. Also in the same letter: 'He who dies protected by God dies blessed – he who lives protected by Manin cannot suffer.' Other examples of the same sort of letter are *ibid.*, nos. 511, 512, 526, 527, 534.

to 'make known the plight of us fishermen at this time, and to acclaim our Manin, crying for that reason "Evviva la repubblica" '.[75]

The republic also received the support of two middle-class groups. The 'Republican Club', which held meetings throughout April and May 1848, consisted mainly of local professional people who for ideological reasons were averse to a kingdom of upper Italy. They included the notary G. D. Giuriati, Carlo Radaelli, who had been a former member of the Bandieras' secret society, the Benvenuti brothers, the priest G. B. Tornielli, the lawyers Antonio Bellinato and G. D. Manetti, and the wealthy merchant Angelo Comello. Their profession of faith, drawn up on 20 April, began:

LIBERTY, EQUALITY, FRATERNITY!

We have come together to proclaim, sustain and defend the principle of democratic republicanism. This principle best expresses the moral dignity of Mankind, and best develops the power and courage of our peoples in their struggle for the independence, unity and liberty of Italy.[76]

The club decided in April that it should urge the government to form a national army as soon as possible, by calling up all those between twenty and twenty-five years of age. It also agreed on the necessity of a programme of popular education. But it never numbered more than twenty-five to thirty people, and in spite of the intention of most of its founders to acquire a mass following, the club never had more than a very limited weight in Venetian politics.[77]

The second group was probably more powerful, though it was not organised in any systematic way. A number of influential merchants and businessmen were, for economic reasons, averse to fusion. They feared that with Milan the capital and Genoa the principal port of the new

---

[75] MCV, Doc. Manin, no. 667, police interview with Domenico Corrao, 'aged 54, married with five children, no criminal record, Catholic and illiterate', 4 June 1848. For Zennari's letter see G. Calucci, 'Documenti inediti', p. 93. For the pre-occupations of a conservative member of the municipality, see the letter of Luigi Michiel to Martinengo, 27 May 1848: 'the arrogance of the people grows greater every day, and we of the municipality are under surveillance by various popular leaders (*capi del popolo*)'; *La Repubblica veneta*, vol. 1, p. 54. There was another, very similar demonstration, on 17 June, this time by about 60 fishermen; see Marchesi, *Storia documentata*, p. 232.

[76] MCV, Agg. Manin, xxx/9, no. 1, 20 April 1848. On 26 April (*ibid.*, no. 4), on the proposal of Bartolomeo Benvenuti they changed the word 'unity' to 'union'.

[77] *Ibid.*, nos. 6–11. The discussion of the national army took place on 27 April, and for the resulting petition, see above, pp. 194–5. Tornielli pointed out the many difficulties that could arise in the provinces if the government tried to enforce a call-up of those aged between 20 and 25. Radaelli said he had already petitioned the government once, but the excuse then had been the shortage of arms.

kingdom, Venice would be reduced 'to less than Chioggia'.[78] It is not possible to tell how many of the members of the chamber of commerce felt like this, for the matter was never put on the agenda and the chamber did not take up an official position for or against fusion. But there exists a revealing letter of 24 June 1848 from the Jewish banker Angelo Adolfo Levi to Manin.[79] Levi insisted that, in the event of fusion, Venice should retain its free port; that half the ships of the new kingdom should be made and repaired in the Venetian arsenal; that Venetian steamships should reopen communications with the Levant, and not allow Lloyd's of Trieste to pre-empt them; and that a special Venetian consulate should be established in Alexandria, to ensure that the trade from the projected Suez canal should come through Venice.

These two groups apart, the mass of the bourgeoisie and upper classes were in favour of Charles Albert. Many supported the king believing him to be their military saviour; many others saw him as a saviour of a different sort – as the lawyer Baron Gian Francesco Avesani wrote in a speech prepared for the assembly: 'Revolution under a monarchy is an exception; revolution under a republic is a rule. Let us place ourselves as soon as possible under the protection of a monarch, which is protection both from the war with the Austrians and from civil war.'[80] Monarchist clubs were formed and met in cafés all over the city. They were sponsored, according to one account, 'by the nobility, who do not want to lose their coats of arms; ... the frightened who see anarchy and disorder coming from democracy; and the rich who fear communism'.[81]

When it was announced that elections were to take place, many Venetians urged that it was dangerous to put so much power in the hands of the people. They favoured instead a two-tier system of election. The mass

[78] G. Berti to Martinengo, 2 June 1848, in *La Repubblica veneta*, vol. 1, p. 86. Valentino Pasini wrote to Visentini in May 1848: 'The city of Venice contains among its inhabitants many who believe that their material interests would be compromised if Venice was not to remain a capital city, if it lost its free port and the industries that have developed there, and if it was forced to compete on equal terms with Genoa for the trade of the whole of northern Italy. It is wanton self-deception not to realise that the republic is also the political formula which corresponds to many material interests, some clearly understood, others less so' (letter published in Bonghi, *Valentino Pasini*, p. 231).

[79] MCV, Doc. Pell., b. xxv/349, letter of 24 June 1848. Bertuch recounts (*Contributi*, pp. 25–6) that whenever the English merchant Malcolm was asked if he was for Austria or Italy, the Republic or the Monarchy, he replied invariably and imperturbably, 'I am for commerce.'

[80] Avesani's speech is published by A. Ventura in his article, 'L'Avesani, il Castellani e il problema della fusione', *Archivio Veneto*, 45 (1955), pp. 128–39.

[81] Racc. Andreola, vol. 2, pp. 17–18; article by the lawyer Giacomo Mattei, entitled 'The clubs of Venice', 2 May 1848.

of the population would vote only in the preliminary round, and those elected by them would then choose the actual deputies to the assembly. Manin refused to contemplate such a system and thereby clearly differentiated himself not only from the more conservative elements in his own city, but also from the Piedmontese. The Venetian democrats saw the enfranchisement of the adult male as a permanent feature of their political system; in contrast, the Piedmontese monarchists, while using plebiscites to justify their fusionist policies, were in future years quick to revert to the practice of a restricted electorate once the annexations were complete.[82]

Pre-election propaganda in Venice was not particularly virulent. Many of the people were guided by what the parish priests had to say, and they in turn followed the lead of the patriarch and urged their flocks to choose wise and responsible men. Quite a few of the parish clergy felt that they best fitted this description; eight priests from the city and three from Murano and Burano were elected. Avesani attempted to get as many monarchists into the assembly as he could. Cesare Levi, editor of the pro-republican newspaper *Il Libero Italiano*, published lists of recommended candidates, but Varè of *L'Indipendente* simply advised the people to 'choose the men most likely to bring the greatest happiness to the greatest number'.[83]

When it came to voting on 9 and 10 June 1848 the population as a whole remained apathetic, either through incomprehension or awareness that the assembly threatened the republic. Zennari, the secretary to the government, estimated that two-thirds of the electorate had not voted.[84] The city and neighbouring towns and villages voted by parishes, and each parish, according to its size, elected a certain number of representatives. Anyone could stand in any parish; there was no residential qualification and no apparent limit to the number of parishes a candidate could contest. The turn-out in some areas was very low: in the parish of S. Pietro di

---

[82] Manin's friend, Valentino Pasini, made this point very clearly in a letter to Lorenzo Pareto of 22 May 1848 (Bonghi, *Valentino Pasini*, p. 245): 'These direct votes without an assembly and by means of signatures [the methods used by the Piedmontese] have always been adopted when liberty was on the decline, never when it was on the ascendant. They are good for giving a decorative tinsel of legality to a constitution born of a *coup d'état*.' On the Venetian objections to direct adult male suffrage, see Rigobon, *Gli eletti*, p. xvi.

[83] *L'Indipendente*, editorial, 7 June 1848. For Cesare Levi, *Il Libero Italiano*, 5–7 June 1848. For Avesani, ASV, carte Avesani, b. 2, for his papers throughout June 1848. On the Venetian clergy and the election, see Rigobon, *Gli eletti*, p. xxxix, and P. Brunello, 'Rivoluzione e clero', fos. 185–96. The parish priest of SS. Ermagora e Fortunato announced a meeting in his church at 8 a.m. so that he could explain the government's decree. The bells of the church were to be rung from 7 a.m. onwards (MCV, Doc. Manin, no. 3437, handbill of 5 June 1848).

[84] Zennari to Martinengo, 11 June 1848, *La Repubblica veneta*, vol. 1, p. 118.

Castello with a population of 10,000, the three representatives together polled only 538 votes. In S. Francesco della Vigna – having a population of 4,000 – only 155 voted. At Cavanella d'Adige, in the commune of Chioggia, Domenico Penso won the election with four votes. The numbers of those voting was average in the towns of Chioggia and Dolo, and high on the islands of Burano and Murano.

Of the leaders of the revolution, Tommaseo surprisingly did best, being elected in eight different parishes. It remains a mystery whether or not Manin let it be known that he did not wish to be elected in more than one parish. The figures merely show that he was elected in four. The Jews were well represented in spite of the parish system. In all 193 deputies were elected, and they tended for the most part to be respected members of the bourgeoisie, regardless of whether they were monarchist or republican. Lawyers, doctors, parish priests and merchants made up the great majority of the assembly.[85]

The end of the resistance in the Veneto

While Venice went to the polls to elect the first constituent assembly of its history, the final disasters overtook the defenders of the Veneto. Once Thurn's forces had reached Verona, Radetzky decided that he was strong enough to take the offensive against Charles Albert. He and his brilliant chief of staff Hess conceived an audacious plan to march to Mantua and attack the Italian forces from the south, before Charles Albert had time to re-deploy his army. On the evening of 27 May the Austrian army left Verona and reached Mantua extremely swiftly. But on the 29th they were held up by the heroic and tenacious defence of the Tuscans and Neapolitans at Curtatone and Montanara.[86] Their unexpected resistance gave time for the Piedmontese to gather their forces at Goito, and seems to have thrown Radetzky into some confusion. After the battle the Austrians did not move fast enough, and at Goito found the Piedmontese ready to fight with considerable vigour. Radetzky had to order a withdrawal, and his elaborate manoeuvre to catch the Piedmontese unawares had ended in total failure.

However, while Charles Albert did nothing in the next ten extremely precious days, except to celebrate the battle of Goito and the fall of the Austrian fortress of Peschiera, Radetzky and Hess turned defeat into

[85] For a breakdown of the composition of the assembly, see Rigobon, *Gli eletti*, pp. xli–xliv. For the detailed election results see the printed sheets to be found in BL, S.H. 632/2 (formerly 1852.e.7), and also in MCV, Doc. Manin, nos. 3430 and 3431. These results were not published until 28 June 1848. As for the Jews, Isacco Pesaro Maurogonato polled 155 votes in S. Geremia, Jacopo Treves 34 in S. Maria del Giglio, Samuele Olper 32 in S. Marziale.   [86] See above, p. 172.

victory. Deciding that Charles Albert's by now notorious immobility
meant that Verona could be left with only a small garrison, Radetzky
marched with the bulk of his army, 30,000 men and 124 cannon, to
subdue the defiant city of Vicenza. He knew he had little time to lose, for
news had just reached him of the second revolution in Vienna, which
promised unforeseeable consequences for the Austrian army in northern
Italy.[87] At dawn on 10 June, destined to be a boiling hot summer's day,
the Austrians launched their attack on Vicenza.

In Vicenza Durando had 11,000 men and 36 cannon. The crucial
defensive positions were on the Berici hills – the wooden fort of the Bella
Vista, the Villa Guiccioli and its grounds, the sanctuary of the Madonna
del Monte. A little lower down, the famous Palladian Villa Rotonda was
another vital strong point. The Austrians under Culoz at first made little
impression on the determined defence of the narrow spur of the Berici
hills, but the defenders of the Villa Rotonda – the Roman university
students, *i bersaglieri del Po*, and volunteers from Schio and Faenza –
were soon in trouble. The position had no cannon and was under constant
fire from the howitzers of the Clam brigade. The Italian volunteers
resisted well for some time, but at the critical stage Durando, who had
kept back 1,000 of the Swiss, sent up no reinforcements to the Rotonda.
Eventually its defenders were forced to retreat to the Villa Valmarana and
then, after another prolonged holding operation, to the city itself.

On the Berici hills Culoz had taken the Bella Vista but his progress was
slow. Fierce fighting raged all morning in the wooded grounds of the
Villa Guiccioli. At two in the afternoon some of the Swiss, led by Enrico
Cialdini, tried to counter-attack but were beaten back with heavy losses.
Cialdini himself was seriously wounded. Slowly but surely the Austrians
gained ground. In the last desperate defence of the Villa Guiccioli Massimo
D'Azeglio, who together with Cialdini had been in charge of the Italian
troops on the Berici hills, was also gravely wounded. Durando, with his
remaining reserves, came up to the Madonna del Monte to organise the
final resistance. The battle raged furiously in and around the great church
of the hill sanctuary, but the Austrians were not now to be stopped.
Durando and the remnants of the defenders of the hills retreated back
down the porticoed road which leads from the sanctuary into the city.

The defence of Vicenza itself was now hopeless, for the Austrians
commanded the Berici heights and could bomb the city at will. Durando
ordered the white flag to be hauled up on the tower of the Piazza dei
Signori. But the civic guard and population of Vicenza would not hear of

[87] The party which favoured making peace in Lombardy, and calling Radetzky
home to subdue the insurrection in Prague, was growing stronger as the weeks
passed. See below, p. 245.

surrender. They too had taken an active part in the fighting, particularly at the gate of Santa Lucia, where the Austrians had been repulsed and their general, Prince Wilhelm Thurn-Taxis, mortally wounded. Shots were fired at the white flag and it was soon replaced with a red one. The Austrians reacted by continuing the bombardment through the night until 1 a.m., and by then even the Vicentini realised there was nothing left but to treat with the enemy. This Durando did, and secured terms by which the papal army was to march out of the city with the full honours of war, but was to promise not to take up arms against the Austrians for three months. On the morning of the 11th Durando's army filed out by the Porta Monte. The resistance offered by all the combatants, regulars and volunteers, Italians and Swiss, in the face of far superior numbers, had been heroic. The price in dead and wounded on the Italian side was never exactly established, but was around two thousand. The official Austrian losses were 141 dead, 451 wounded and 140 dispersed.[88]

The terms given to Durando may appear generous, but Radetzky was in a hurry to get back to Verona lest Charles Albert had belied his reputation and tried to take the city. But the Piedmontese king did not begin operations against Verona till the morning of 13 June. By then Culoz's brigade and the whole of the first army corps were safely back in the city. Charles Albert had missed his chance yet again, in what Pieri has aptly called 'the war of lost opportunities'.[89]

The immediate consequence of the fall of Vicenza was the capitulation of both Padua and Treviso. The Venetian government decided that it was useless to try and defend Padua and that rather than risk losing the 5,000 troops likely to be involved, among them Pepe's Neapolitans, it was better to concentrate all defence in Venice. Needless to say, the Venetian decision was hardly popular in Padua, and crowned what can at best be called the uneasy relations between the two cities during the revolutionary period.[90]

[88] The best description of the third battle of Vicenza is by Trevelyan, *Manin and the Venetian Revolution*, pp. 189–95; see also Pieri, *Storia militare*, pp. 386–90. Belluzzi's criticism of Durando after the battle is published by R. Cessi, 'La difesa', app. doc. no. 12, p. 266. The day after the battle some Croat soldiers, enraged because the Servite fathers of the sanctuary of the Madonna del Monte had taken part in the fighting, cut into 32 pieces the famous picture of the banquet of San Giorgio by Paolo Veronese, which was in their refectory. The emperor Franz Joseph later ordered the painting to be restored.

[89] P. Pieri, 'La guerra regia nella pianura padana', in *Il 1848 nella storia italiana ed europea* (ed. E. Rota), p. 169.

[90] The mayor of Padua, Meneghini, wrote to Venice denouncing the incapacity of the provisional government; published in Cessi, 'La difesa', app. doc. no. 15, pp. 270–3. At the same time as Pepe was telling the Paduan garrison to retire to Venice, Armandi was ordering them to stay put; A. Noaro, *Dei volontari in Lombardia e nel Tirolo e della difesa di Venezia nel 1848–9*, p. 74.

At Treviso a council of war had been formed and the volunteers were eager to fight. But when Welden began to bombard the city the leading officers changed their minds and voted 18 to 4 in favour of coming to terms. La Masa and many of the younger officers were all for fighting their way to Venice, but Zambeccari reached agreement with the Austrians before they had a chance. Welden conceded the same terms as had been given to Vicenza, and another 4,000 troops were thus excluded from the war for three months. As with all the cities of the *terraferma*, Treviso's capitulation immediately led to furious polemics as to what could and should have been done.[91]

As the cities of the Veneto fell one by one, the peasantry too withdrew from what had always been for them an unequal and unrewarding fight. The Venetian government had made no further attempts to rally them and had granted no concessions since the initial ones of the abolition of the personal tax and the reduction in the price of salt. With the coming of the wheat harvest, the mass of the peasantry in the unconquered areas abandoned the civic guards in order to attend to the fields. None the less isolated pockets of resistance remained, the most notable being in the villages on the Brenta above Bassano, and at near-by Énego, one of the Sette Comuni. On the evening of 6 June the citizens of Bassano could see the glow of fires in the northern mountains that loom above their city, sure sign that all the villages in those parts were up in arms. It took the Austrian columns a good week to overcome a resistance that relied exclusively on shotguns and boulders.[92]

The Austrians did their best to make their peace with the peasantry. On 14 May Count Hartig, the official Austrian 'pacifier' in northern Italy, published an interesting appeal 'to the good peasantry'.[93] In it he claimed that the Austrian army was coming 'to liberate you from the despotism of the agitators who constrain you to exchange the plough for the sword and involve you, your families and your belongings in slaughter and destruction, so that famine will follow war'. These agitators, continued Hartig, were from a social class which should have known better. But, clearly afraid of inciting the peasantry to another Galician-style massacre, Hartig urged them to forgive their social superiors and 'to respect their rights, their possessions, their persons. In this way you will be known as true Christians, as good subjects, as reasonable men, qualities

---

[91] See the account by La Masa, *Documenti*, vol. 1, pp. 271–3. See also the part of the Olivi manuscript published in A. Santalena, *Treviso nel 1848*, doc. LXII, pp. 231–2.

[92] BBV, Gonz. 22.10.17, 'Cronaca del 1848 riguardante Bassano', entries for 5–11 June 1848. See also Pieri, *Storia militare*, p. 397.

[93] ASVr, I.-R. DP, b. 461, atti riservati 1848, no. 252.

of which your respected class has always been able to boast.' On 31 May Marshal Welden followed up this proclamation by abolishing the personal tax in all the reconquered regions. He also took care to distribute the very heavy requisitioning load as evenly as he could.[94] For the peasantry there was now very little to choose between the two sides, except that the Austrians were obviously winning.

By mid-June 1848 the only two isolated pockets of Italian resistance in the Veneto were the Friulian fortresses of Palmanova and Osoppo. At Palmanova Zucchi and the garrison of former Austrian troops, aided by one hundred Piedmontese artillerymen, had been subjected to continuous bombardment. After the fall of Vicenza the Austrian fire intensified and Zucchi was prepared to yield. But the fortress was extremely strong, all the soldiers and population wanted to continue the fight (Palmanova housed a small town within its walls), and Zucchi was forced to continue the battle for another few days. He then surrendered on favourable terms on 24 June, to the fury of nearly all the defenders. There was no doubt that the fortress could have held out much longer, but Zucchi, with little prospect of Venice coming to his aid, could see no point in going on.[95] At Osoppo the commanders, the Bolognese Licurgo Zannini and the Friulian Leonardo Andervolti, were far more determined, especially the latter, who in 1860 was to go with Garibaldi to Sicily. The village below the fortress kept the garrison supplied for a long time until the Austrians sacked and burnt it on 9 October. In the fort, Andervolti quelled a riot against Zannini and generally kept spirits up. On 15 August the birthday of Napoleon was solemnly celebrated by the garrison, with the singing of the 'Marseillaise' and Italian patriotic songs. The fort eventually sur-

---

[94] For the personal tax, see M. Berengo, *L'agricoltura veneta*, p. 74 n. 2. For the plight of the peasantry in some areas of the Veneto as a result of Austrian requisitioning, see the letters of the municipality of Conegliano to Call and Hartig (ASV, Pres. Luog. 1849–66, atti del governo militare 1848, documents attached to nos. 1 and 106, 23 and 27 May 1848). The Austrians had taken all the cattle the peasantry possessed, leaving them no farm animals with which to plough. The authorities pointed out that in the absence of any of the usual commerce and industry (silk, etc.), and the resulting shortage of cash, the peasantry had nothing left but the land. Welden replied on 12 June (*ibid.*, attached to no. 157) by rotating the provisioning burden between Pordenone, Sacile and Conegliano.

[95] Pieri, *Storia militare*, pp. 398–9. Cessi, 'La difesa', app. doc. no. 116, pp. 273–7, publishes the critical report on Zucchi's conduct made by Count G. Volpe. On 19 June 1848 Mengaldo proposed to the Venetian government that a relief expedition of four infantry battalions, 200 cavalry and six cannon be sent to Zucchi, but the idea was not adopted; see MCV, archivio Bernardi, b. 112, copy of the letter at the front of Mengaldo's diary.

rendered on 13 October 1848, and the survivors were allowed to go to Venice, where they helped to form a Friulian legion.[96]

Venice and Europe

With the fall of Padua and Treviso, Manin decided to delay the convocation of the Venetian assembly, originally planned for 18 June. He justified this decision primarily on the grounds of the need to defend the city,[97] but he was also inspired by a sudden hope that fusion with Piedmont could yet be avoided, for on 13 June a petition signed by over a thousand Venetians called upon their government to appeal for French aid immediately.[98]

This petition was the pretext for Manin to reopen the question of outside intervention in the Italian war. The Veneto had given itself to Charles Albert, but apart from the hundred artillerymen sent to Palmanova at the end of March and the dubious donation of General La Marmora, the king had not sent a single one of his own soldiers to prevent the Veneto's reconquest. By mid-June it could seriously be questioned if the fusion of Venice with Piedmont would serve any military purpose at all. Many Venetians had come to share the opinions expressed by Gherardo Freschi in the *consulta* on 24 May,[99] when he stated that recent events had convinced him that 'the Italian war is no longer purely a war of independence, fought by the people in alliance with their princes, but is the war of absolutism against the liberty of the Nations'. Manin, however, had no wish to cast himself in the role of a latter-day Lodovico Sforza. In spite of what he called Piedmont's 'political usury', Manin was not prepared to make a unilateral Venetian appeal to the French. His fidelity to the national as well as the Venetian cause made it imperative for him to ask the opinion of the other Italian states before taking any action.[100] Accordingly, messengers were dispatched on 14 June to Milan, Florence, Rome, Palermo and Charles Albert's headquarters.

[96] Pieri, *Storia militare*, p. 399. For details of the siege see also A. Faleschini, 'Corrispondenze di Licurgo Zannini e Leonardo Andervolti dopo l'assedio di Osoppo del 1848', in *Atti dell'Accademia di Scienze, Lettere e Arti di Udine*, 10 (1945–8), pp. 147–68; and his 'L'assedio di Osoppo nelle memorie di Leonardo Andervolti', in *ibid.*, pp. 169–96 (p. 189 for the commemoration of Napoleon's birthday).

[97] After the fall of Padua and Treviso, Austrian troops moved up to Mestre, on the edge of the Venetian lagoon.

[98] The text of the petition was displayed at eight cafés throughout the city; see Racc. Andreola, vol. 2, p. 318.

[99] *Le assemblee del Risorgimento*, vol. 2, p. 41.

[100] Tommaseo appears to have played an important part in ensuring that the other Italian states were consulted. See his letter to Manin, MCV, Doc. Manin, no. 657, 13 June 1848.

The response was unanimously hostile. Charles Albert, hardly surprisingly, would not discuss the matter further, and 'declared that he would do what he could for the defence of the Veneto'.[101] Corsini from Florence, Marchetti from Rome, Ruggero Settimo from Sicily deplored any idea of French intervention. Only the Milanese were mildly sympathetic, but noted that they were now Piedmontese subjects and that in any case they preferred to invoke French aid only in dire extremity.[102] Faced with such a barrage, the Venetians were forced to drop the idea.

In any case, by the beginning of June the French politicians were thinking along very different lines. After the failure of the demonstration of 15 May and the subsequent decision of the French executive committee not to intervene militarily in northern Italy,[103] plans went apace for a compromise solution to the Italian war. Bastide and Lamartine seem to have approved a deal by which Lombardy would secure its independence from Austria, Venice would get a liberal constitution under Austrian rule, and, hopefully, France would get Savoy. On 10 June 1848 the French ambassador at Innsbruck, Delacour, proposed this line of action to Wessenberg, and met with a favourable response.[104]

Apart from the successful march of Nugent's relief army to Verona, things had been going from bad to worse for the Austrian empire. The demonstrations in Vienna on 15 May had successfully forced the emperor to agree to abandon all property qualifications for the primary vote in the Austrian elections. On the 17th Ferdinand decided to flee to Innsbruck. The Bohemians were in open revolt, and after the Piedmontese success at Goito, the emperor's advisers thought seriously of coming to terms in Italy, if only to be able to send Radetzky against Prague. The financiers

---

[101] *La Repubblica veneta*, vol. 1, p. 139.

[102] See Calucci's report from Milan, 16 June 1848, MCV, Doc. Manin, no. 2095. In May the Lombard provisional government had been terrified of 'the French hordes'; see their letter to Restelli published in *La Repubblica veneta*, vol. 1, pp. 636–7. However, by the beginning of July, the French consul at Milan could report that 'all classes and nearly all the parties' wanted French intervention. This was almost certainly as a result of a growing lack of faith in Charles Albert's ability to win the war, and the triumph of Cavaignac in the June days in Paris; see F. Boyer, *La seconde République*, p. 175. For the replies from Florence, Rome and Sicily, see respectively MCV, Doc. Manin, nos. 1092 (19 June 1848), 1073 (21 June 1848), and 1121 (29 June 1848).

[103] See above, pp. 150–1.

[104] Taylor, *The Italian Problem*, pp. 122–3. Denois, the French consul in Milan, had made a similar proposition to Casati in the middle of May, but had met with a clear refusal. On 11 June Delacour, encouraged by Austrian willingness to compromise on the previous day, proposed that they give up Venice as well. Wessenberg would not hear of this, and the French did not raise the problem of Venice again. See Boyer, *La seconde République*, pp. 148–50. The Venetian

to whom Austria owed much of her national debt were at pains to point out that the empire could not afford to continue the Italian war, and Viennese business interests were all for a quick settlement.[105] As early as 20 April 1848 Pillersdorff had suggested to a ministerial council that Austria should recognise the independence of Lombardy, and by early June this seemed the best way for them to avoid disaster. Wessenberg therefore wrote to Casati on 13 June, offering him the independence of Lombardy, and at the same time asked England to put pressure on the Italians to accept this proposal.[106]

In London, Palmerston had been meeting regularly with Hummelauer, the Austrian special emissary to the British government. The British had favoured Charles Albert from the outset, since his success would have meant the end of republicanism in northern Italy, and thus have lessened the likelihood of French intervention and a probable European war. The establishment of a kingdom of upper Italy therefore met with British approval; but whereas Palmerston told Hummelauer that it would suffice for Austria to abandon Lombardy, Lord Minto and Russell insisted that Venice too should be granted her independence. Palmerston was overruled by this strong pro-Italian lobby in the Cabinet, and instructed Ponsonby at Innsbruck to declare that Britain could not mediate on the basis of Lombard independence alone.[107]

This was a blow to the Franco-Austrian proposal, but there remained the hope that the Italians would accept without English prompting. Charles Albert was certainly beginning to favour a compromise solution of this sort, even though fusionist propaganda had reached its height in Venice at this time. The Piedmontese king, disillusioned by the lack of military aid he had received from his fellow Italian sovereigns, and doubting every day the ability of his troops to withstand another Austrian attack, was to write to Franzini from Roverbella on 7 June 1848: 'If we can obtain, with

representatives in Paris had great faith in Bastide, the French minister of foreign affairs appointed on 12 May 1848. Bastide did give orders for the arms requested by Venice to be dispatched, but at the same time he was telling the Austrian ambassador that France 'would prefer Austria's keeping the greater part of her Italian possessions to Sardinia's aggrandisement'; see R. Moscati, *La diplomazia*, p. 49.

[105] Macartney, *The Habsburg Empire*, p. 344.

[106] For further details of feeling among the Austrian ministers at this time, see H. M. Smyth, 'Austria at the crossroads: the Italian crisis of June, 1848', in *Essays in the History of Modern Europe* (ed. D. C. McKay), pp. 63–78.

[107] Taylor, *The Italian Problem*, pp. 108–9. Palmerston was first overruled on 24 May 1848. On 3 June 1848, in a note to Hummelauer, he repeated that England did not consider Lombard independence sufficient. See N. Bianchi, *Storia documentata della diplomazia europea in Italia, 1814–61*, vol. 5 (1869), p. 268.

English mediation, Lombardy and the Duchies, we will have concluded a fortunate war; a little state like ours, defying the colossal Austrian empire, will have made superb acquisitions without historical parallel . . . To desire more would be rash.'[108]

The Lombard government, however, rejected all ideas of deserting Venice. Restelli wrote to Manin saying that the Milanese would never tolerate another Campoformio, and the French and Austrians had to abandon their proposal.[109] Then, on 23 June, the Parisian working class rose in insurrection, and all thoughts of French intervention in northern Italy, whether diplomatic or military, had to be abandoned. While all Europe waited anxiously for news from the city that was the nerve-centre of revolution, Cavaignac succeeded in crushing the revolt at the cost of thousands of lives. As for the Austrians, they took heart from the fact that Italian victories seemed to have come to an end, and decided to trust in the force of arms and give Radetzky a free hand.[110] They were not to be disappointed.

The Venetian assembly

Venice remained ignorant of many of these transactions and attitudes, and only knew that Lombardy had refused an Austrian offer of independence. But, in any case, the news of the June days in Paris destroyed any illusions Manin may have harboured about French aid as an alternative to fusion. Venice's financial state was growing more critical every day. The money raised from the forced loan and the 600,000 lire offered spontaneously by Venetian citizens was calculated to last only until the first weeks of July, for Venice was now spending at the rate of three million a month.[111] The

---

[108] N. Bianchi (ed.), *Scritti e lettere di Carlo Alberto*, p. 62.

[109] Restelli to Manin, MCV, Doc. Manin, no. 1046, no date. Antonio Beretta was sent to Charles Albert to inform him of the Lombard decision. The king remarked only that 'the reply of the government is worthy of the city of the Five Days', but invited Beretta to pass into an adjoining room where his staff and generals were conversing. They reacted quite differently, upbraiding the Lombard government for not accepting, and complaining that it had no understanding of the situation; see G. Visconti Venosta, *Memoirs of Youth, 1847–60*, pp. 96–7.

[110] The decisive meeting took place on 23 June 1848; Smyth, 'Austria at the cross-roads', pp. 75–6. Wessenberg had previously sent Radetzky an order to seek an armistice with Charles Albert as soon as possible. Radetzky refused and sent Prince Felix Schwarzenberg to Innsbruck to argue his case.

[111] See the letter from Manin to Pareto, 21 June 1848, published in *La Repubblica veneta*, vol. 1, pp. 150–2. Cesare Correnti was in Venice at this time and did his best to get finance for Venice from Lombardy; see his letter to the Venetian government of 19 June announcing that 50,000 lire would be arriving in three

military situation was also far from reassuring. Although Venice was garrisoned by more than 13,000 men – Venetians, Ferrari's papal troops, Pepe's Neapolitans, Antonini's volunteers from Paris, a Lombard legion, etc. – many of the men were undisciplined and their material conditions were very poor. The commanders of the papal and Venetian troops at Fort Marghera reported on 25 June on the terrible state of the fortress. There were no latrines, the whole place stank, it was infested by insects and mosquitoes, wine and food sellers came and went as they chose, and the wine was being diluted with lagoon water.[112] There had already been one revolt by a whole battalion. With similar reports coming in from the Lido, where many men were sleeping on the beaches, the government had every reason to fear an Austrian attempt to take the city by a *coup de main*.[113]

It was on these grave financial and military worries that Count Enrico Martini, the Piedmontese special envoy, played with great effect on his arrival in Venice on 17 June.[114] Martini, it may be remembered, was the emissary that Charles Albert had sent to Milan during the March days, when he had made every effort to avoid the declaration of the republic and to secure the immediate dedication of the city to Piedmont. Martini, a shrewd if unscrupulous operator, knew that he held the trump cards. He made it clear to Manin that in return for an immediate summoning of the assembly and a vote in favour of fusion, the Piedmontese would send 2,000 regular troops to the city and arrange substantial financial aid. The deal was one which Manin could not afford to refuse. On 21 June the Venetian council of ministers decided to convoke the assembly for 3 July 1848.[115]

days' time from the Lombard provisional government; MCV, Doc. Manin, no. 1042.

[112] See the *promemoria* from Augusto Aglebert, Pietro Correr and Luciano Beretta, ASV, Gov. Prov. 1848–9, DG, b. 372, documenti non protocollati, Marghera, no. 650.

[113] See the letter from Amigo to Armandi, ASV, Gov. Prov. 1848–9, b. 382, MG, riservati, no. 110. Matters were not helped by a dispute between Armandi and Antonini about who had overall command; see their exchange of letters, 14 June 1848, *ibid.*, no. 198.

[114] On Martini's mission, see G. Quazza, 'La missione Martini a Venezia e il problema della fusione', in *Il Risorgimento*, 3 (1951), pp. 121–35; R. Cessi, 'La missione Martini a Venezia nel giugno 1848', *Archivio Veneto*, 50–1 (1952), pp. 139–54; and the strongly pro-Albertist Depoli, *I rapporti*, vol. 2, pp. 369–405.

[115] The date of 3 July was fixed so as to allow further news from Rome to reach Venice. Castellani and others had been making strenuous efforts to assemble a national Diet there, which Manin could have put forward as a political alternative to fusion. However, Castellani's plans never came to fruition; see his

During the ten days that preceded the first session of the assembly, it became obvious that if the republicans were to stand their ground when the assembly met, there was a serious risk of civil war breaking out in the city. The committee of public vigilance informed Manin on 1 July that the lower classes alone were still strongly in favour of the republic, and that alarming reports of their intentions had been reaching the committee. A shoemaker at S. Francesco della Vigna had declared that on 3 July the city would be sacked and he personally intended to break into the house of a local dignitary, the *cavaliere* Paravia. A boatman at S. Benedetto had been heard to remark that it would be better to become French subjects than to put the city in the hands of a king; one of his friends stressed the need to arm on 3 July to counter demonstrations in favour of Charles Albert. Padre Tornielli told the banker M. P. Coen that if the outcome of the assembly was an '*Albertinata*' (a vote for Charles Albert), he did not dare to continue collecting money for the national cause in Cannaregio, since he would risk getting himself killed.[116]

On the other side, the civic guard, drawn up in the Piazza by Mengaldo, held a massive demonstration in favour of fusion on 29 June. Manin was furious and officially reproved the leaders: 'While the lowest classes of the people have restrained themselves and calmly await the imminent vote of the assembly, the noble corps of the civic guard have set a terrible example by trying illegally to influence the vote, thus endangering the very public order that they are supposed to be preserving.'[117]

In this atmosphere of acrimony and tension, and with the news of the civil war in Paris fresh in the deputies' minds, the assembly met in the Doges' palace on 3 July 1848. Those who attended were forbidden to bring sticks, umbrellas or arms of any sort into the council chamber. The first day passed quietly enough, with Manin, Castelli and Paolucci reading

letters to the government, 12–14 June 1848, in *La Repubblica veneta*, vol. 2, pp. 115ff.

[116] MCV, Doc. Manin, no. 4166, undated letter from Coen to Manin. For the incidents at S. Benedetto and S. Francesco, see respectively ASV, Gov. Prov. 1848–9, OPss, vii, 2, no. 5625, 1 July 1848, and *ibid.*, no. 5218, 24 June 1848. For the report of the committee, see Marchesi, *Storia documentata*, app. doc. xv, p. 516.

[117] MCV, Doc. Manin, no. 666. The navy also presented a petition in favour of fusion on 23 June 1848 (*ibid.*, no. 662). There is strong evidence, from Mengaldo's letters, of Castelli's and Paleocapa's aid in organising the civic guard demonstration (see MCV, Agg. Manin, xxx/17, nos. 7–9, 17, 18). Castelli suppressed the republican newspaper *La Staffetta del Popolo* on 29 June 1848 on the grounds that it was endangering the public peace. Tommaseo wrote to Manin urging him to act so that 'we do not repudiate the principles for which we have suffered and are still suffering' (MCV, Agg. Manin, xlviii, 'Venezia, L'Italia, e l'Europa', pt. ii, fo. 462).

accounts of the diplomatic, financial and military activity of the republic. Manin justified the policy of *a guerra finita* by reiterating that it 'had been proclaimed and repeated by the Lombard government from the very beginning'. There were a few jeers from the fusionists.[118]

The following day, the 4th, was the decisive one. It began with Tommaseo declaring prophetically that if Charles Albert could have helped Venice he would already have done so, and that there was therefore no point in fusion. His discourse was greeted with silence and disapproval. Paleocapa then spoke at length, amidst much applause, in favour of immediate fusion, and Avesani cried that Venice had simply to follow Pareto's advice: *Fate la fusione.*[119] Manin then spoke. He intended to avoid civil war, and knew that only if he accepted fusion would the lower classes do likewise. He also realised that the majority of the deputies were against the continuation of the republic. Manin therefore urged those who still supported him to sacrifice their principles and vote for fusion, while reserving the right to fight again another day:

The enemy is at our gates, counting on our divisions. Let us give him the lie. Let us forget all parties today. Let us show that today we are neither royalists nor republicans but that we are all citizens. To the republicans I say – the future is for us. All that has been done or is being done is provisional. The decision belongs to the Diet at Rome.[120]

To the cheers of the whole assembly Castelli rushed across to Manin and cried 'he has saved Venice'. By 127 votes to 6, Venice became part of the kingdom of upper Italy.

Conclusion

The vote of 4 July marked the end of the first and most decisive phase of the Venetian revolution. The republic proclaimed by Manin in the Piazza some three months earlier had been unable to survive either politically or militarily. Once Lombardy had decided, first in March and then in May, against the republic and in favour of Charles Albert, the Venetian republicans were left in isolation in a predominantly monarchist Italy. They could probably have maintained their independence had they been able to forge a substantial military force to fight alongside the papal army in the

[118] Racc. Andreola, vol. 2, p. 448. For the regulations governing attendance see BL, S.H. 632/2 (formerly 1852.e.7), Paleocapa's instructions of 1 July 1848.

[119] Racc. Andreola, vol. 2, pp. 472–7. For Tommaseo's two discourses planned for the assembly, and his preface to them, *ibid.*, vol. 2, pp. 462–7. The speech that Tommaseo gave in the assembly was a shortened version of his first discourse; he never had an opportunity to deliver his second discourse because of Manin's intervention.

[120] Trevelyan's translation, *Manin and the Venetian Revolution*, p. 203.

campaign against Nugent. But in spite of significant incidents of fierce resistance, particularly in the Cadore and at Vicenza, no unified Venetian army emerged to take its place with Durando's regulars and Ferrari's volunteers in the fight to stop the Austrian relief army from reaching Verona. The incapacity and conservatism of Manin's military advisers, and Manin's lack of clarity on this most vital of issues, prevented any systematic attempt to utilise the pro-revolutionary popular forces of both town and countryside. In an admittedly difficult situation, the generals and ministers of the Venetian republic responded with a fatal mixture of caution and chaos, resulting in a narrow policy of waiting upon monarchist aid. Such a policy was never seriously challenged. The council for all volunteer corps at Treviso represented a fleeting possibility of an alternative, but it was deprived of governmental support before it had time to flourish. In the period of the revolution which gave them most space for manoeuvre and the distinct possibility of final victory, when the Austrians were far from invincible and the European situation was favourable to the revolutionary cause, the Venetian republicans were unable to capitalise on their brilliant victory of 22 March.

Within Venice itself, Manin was far more successful. His astute provisions for the well-being of the Venetian lower classes and his great capacity as a popular leader ensured him mass support even in time of economic crisis. Manin also made it clear to the bourgeoisie of the city that he embodied their interests and would not tolerate social unrest. In political terms his insistence on adult male suffrage for the Venetian assembly and his unwillingness to curb basic freedoms such as that of the press were in strident contrast to the attitudes of the liberal monarchists of Piedmont and elsewhere. All these attributes mark Manin out as a bourgeois republican leader in the classic mould. Although defeated in the assembly, Manin's reputation as the founder of the revolution and his ability to rule the city went undisputed. Both were to be put to the supreme test in the dark months of resistance that lay ahead.

7

The Mazzinians and the French,
July to October 1848

Custozza

The incorporation of the city of Venice into the kingdom of upper Italy
proved to be the peak of Charles Albert's success. While the odds against
his army's beating the Austrians grew longer every day, the Piedmontese
king had managed none the less to make maximum political capital from
the mere presence and position of his troops, upstage on the Italian theatre
of war. As long as these troops remained undefeated, Charles Albert
appeared to most Venetians and Lombards as the only person who could
prevent complete Austrian victory. No political sacrifice was therefore too
great to be certain of his aid.

Yet the uneasy Piedmontese combination of political victory and
military stalemate could not be prolonged for ever. On 23 July 1848 the
storm broke. Radetzky, who had received further reinforcements after the
battle of Vicenza, mounted a fierce and concentrated attack on the Piedmontese positions around Custozza. The Piedmontese army, spread along
a far too extensive front, and deprived by the confusion in its high command of any clear directives, was soon forced to retreat. Radetzky gave
the Piedmontese little chance to recoup, and in the next week pursued
them vigorously across the length of Lombardy. Demoralised, exhausted,
and half-starving, Charles Albert's troops fell back towards Milan.

The Piedmontese generals were all for abandoning Milan to its fate,
but the king, fearful that the Milanese would immediately declare a
republic and call the French to their aid, ordered the army to prepare to
defend the city.[1] The Milanese formed a committee of defence, consisting
of Maestri, Restelli and Fanti, and steeled themselves for a new encounter
with Radetzky. Soon after 8 a.m. on 4 August Radetzky launched his

---

[1] The debate as to whether Charles Albert deliberately intended to betray Milan to
the Austrians has been long and polemical. The most fervent denunciation of
Charles Albert has come from Cesare Spellanzon in his *Il vero segreto*. But see
also the balanced and magisterial account of Candeloro, *Storia dell'Italia moderna*,
vol. 3 (1960), pp. 270–4.

attack on Charles Albert's troops, who had taken up defensive positions outside the walls of the city. By mid-afternoon he had succeeded in driving them back into the city itself. In spite of this defeat, and all that had preceded it, the Piedmontese army was still substantially intact. The Milanese were determined to resist to the last, and Radetzky was in fact extremely preoccupied about his position.[2] He had advanced so far and so fast that he now found himself in the midst of enemy territory with only 37,000 men, in front of a city that he knew was going to fight and with the serious risk of a general insurrection in northern Lombardy. On 1 August the Milanese committee of defence had appealed for a *levée en masse* in the countryside. Notwithstanding the many delusions of the spring and summer, many thousands of the hill and mountain peasantry answered this call and began to stream towards Milan.[3] To add to Radetzky's worries, the Milanese had sent Giuseppe Garibaldi, recently returned from South America, to try and organise the peasant bands of the north. At the very least he hoped to harass the Austrians and cut their lines of communication.

The situation, then, while obviously grave for the Italians, was not without hope. But Charles Albert had had enough. On the evening of 4 August he sent emissaries to Radetzky's camp, and by the following morning had agreed to give up the struggle. The Salasco armistice, signed by Charles Albert on 7 August, stipulated that the Piedmontese were to abandon Lombardy and Venetia, Milan and Venice to the Austrians. In return, Radetzky agreed not to cross the Ticino into Piedmontese territory. When rumours of the capitulation began to circulate in Milan on the morning of 5 August, an angry crowd for a time besieged Charles Albert in the Palazzo Greppi. The committee of defence, after a heated discussion with the Piedmontese generals Bava, Olivieri and Salasco, asked Zucchi, who had come to Milan after the fall of Palmanova, to lead the Milanese in a fight to the end. But they had asked the wrong man, for Zucchi, as we have seen, had little faith in popular forces, and little appetite for such a battle. After Zucchi's refusal the committee of defence, hopelessly disillusioned, abandoned what was by now an impossible

[2] Pieri, *Storia militare*, p. 336, and also his 'Carlo Cattaneo storico militare della prima guerra d'indipendenza', in *Studi sul Risorgimento in Lombardia*, vol. 1, p. 42.

[3] Della Peruta, 'I contadini', pp. 102–5. Even in some parts of the Lombard plains the earlier enthusiasm for the national cause had not died away. The newspaper *L'Eco del Po* reported on 20 July 1848 that in the village of Commessaggio, south-west of Mantua, the peasants still wholeheartedly supported the national guard and 'abandoned the urgent work of the field to take up their guard posts and join the patrols' (quoted by R. Giusti, 'L'agricoltura e i contadini nel Mantovano (1848–66)', *Movimento Operaio*, 7 (1955), p. 378 n. 55).

struggle. A third of the population of Milan chose to go into exile rather than receive Radetzky back into their city.

Charles Albert, by first appearing to want to defend Milan and then totally abandoning it, had destroyed all possibility of popular resistance. Milan, the city which in the five days of March had achieved one of the greatest of all urban insurrections, and which was widely regarded as the very heart of anti-Austrian resistance, was forced to accept back Radetzky's troops without a single shot being fired. Whatever Charles Albert's intentions may have been, the Italian republicans and democrats can hardly be blamed for accusing him of open betrayal in respect of his conduct between 1 and 5 August 1848.

In the immediate aftermath of this disaster, it came to appear that there were only two possible ways by which the Italian war of independence could be salvaged. The first, based on Mazzini's rallying cry of 'The war of the king is over, the war of the people begins', sought to demonstrate that guerrilla warfare waged by the whole Italian people could still bring victory. The second, dependent upon the European balance of power, urged French intervention in the north Italian war. It is the purpose of this chapter to examine the development of both these lines of action, the one Italian and populist, the other European and diplomatic, in relation to Venice's continued resistance against the Austrians.

The July government

After the vote for fusion had been taken in the Venetian assembly on 4 July 1848, a caretaker government was elected the following morning to control the city until power could be handed over to the Piedmontese. Manin received the largest number of votes for a place in this 'July government', as it came to be known, but he refused to become a part of it: 'I am and I will remain a republican. In a monarchist state I can be nothing . . . Also I am tired and worn out by the strains of these three months; physically I can do no more, believe me.'[4] Castelli therefore became president, as well as minister of justice, culture and public order. His fusionist colleagues in the former ministry, Paleocapa, Camerata and Paolucci, became respectively ministers for public works and education, finance and the navy. Giuseppe Reali, the president of the chamber of commerce, and Leopardo Martinengo, the republican nobleman who had been Manin's emissary to Charles Albert's headquarters, were the only new members of the government. Both were extremely reluctant to accept

---

[4] Planat de la Faye (ed.), *Documenti*, vol. 1, p. 353.

office, but were persuaded by the government's need for men of renown and prestige.[5]

Castelli and his colleagues were fortunate enough not to be faced by an immediate military crisis. By July Marshal Welden had only been able to assemble some nine thousand troops for the siege of Venice, and had no real idea of how he was going to penetrate the city's superb natural defences. His men were spread out in a long line on the edge of the lagoon and many of them had fallen sick with malaria. On the Venetian side, Pepe overestimated the force he was facing and organised no sorties worthy of note.[6] But many of his men were laid low with malaria and he had his hands full trying to transform the many thousands of volunteers in Venice into a cohesive fighting force.

However, if the July government had little to fear from the Austrians for the time being, within the city it was faced with the grave problem of the Venetian people's overt hostility to the new order of things. The decision for fusion had not been greeted with any enthusiasm, and, as in Milan, there was a noticeable reaction in favour of the republic. When the two thousand Piedmontese soldiers promised by Martini arrived in Venice, the *basso popolo* were much angered by the fact that instead of being sent to the forts of the lagoon, the troops were detailed to maintain public order in the city itself. The Piedmontese, who showed great patience and tolerance, were treated as foreigners by the Venetians, who found their dialect practically incomprehensible. Dall'Ongaro relates that 'the good women of Castello and S. Marta' remained in complete ignorance as to the identity of 'this *sior Carlo Alberto*'.[7] Dionisio Zannini, a Roman lawyer who had recently become Castelli's secretary, and who had acquired a high reputation for street oratory, tried to explain without much success that Charles Albert was 'a republican king, a real Enrico Dandolo'. The reaction was invariably the same: 'Nu no volemo che el nostro Manin e el nostro Tommaseo.'[8] On 30 July Manin, in a typical gesture, appeared as a simple civic guard on sentry duty in the Piazzetta. The republican Paduan Carlo Leoni, whose diary is amongst the most informative sources for this period, recounted that two to three hundred people stopped to

[5] A. Ventura, *Lineamenti costituzionali del governo provvisorio di Venezia nel 1848–9*, pp. 69–70.
[6] Pieri, *Storia militare*, p. 401. See also Marchesi, *Storia documentata*, p. 262.
[7] F. Dall'Ongaro, *Venezia l'undici agosto 1848*, pp. 12–13.
[8] *Ibid.* Enrico Dandolo was the blind Doge who led the Venetian expedition to capture Constantinople in 1204. See also Castelli's letter to the municipality of 26 July 1848, complaining that the Venetian boatmen were swindling and insulting foreign soldiers; ACV, Municip., Atti di Uff., 1845–9, 7/46, attached to no. 7027 (1848). For the Piedmontese troops, A. Della Marmora, *Alcuni episodi della guerra nel Veneto* (ed. M. Degli Alberti), pp. 90–102.

admire Manin's conduct and to applaud him: 'This man', wrote Leoni, 'is destined for great things and it is true to say that he is adored by the Venetians.'[9]

The Venetian middle-class republicans, taking their cue not from Manin's conciliatory speech in the assembly, but from his refusal to become part of the ministry, were also not slow to express their disapproval of the new order. Castelli, alarmed at the possible subversive influence of the republican newspapers, banned for a second time *La Staffetta del Popolo*, imprisoned its editor, and temporarily prohibited publication of *Fatti e parole* and *Sior Antonio Rioba*. The content of these papers, although critical of Charles Albert and his myrmidons, was far from inflammatory.[10]

Castelli's high-handedness was taken as sure proof that the democratic liberties established under the republic were to be abolished. On 8 July Dall'Ongaro, Vollo and Valussi, the editors of *Fatti e parole*, appealed to Manin for help. He refused to get involved, but Tommaseo wrote a furious letter to Castelli: '. . . repair this scandalous injustice! In a country that declares itself free, to imprison the author of a newspaper article, as well as the owner and editor of the newspaper, without trial or examination – Austria could not have done worse. I am ashamed for the ministry.'[11]

The July government's only reply was to set up a new council of vigilance to report on the growing discontent.[12] Yet what really frightened them was not so much native Venetian hostility, although this could not be underestimated, as the attitude of the large numbers of refugees and troops who had been flowing into Venice ever since the middle of June. Martini dismissed them as '12,000 blackguards from every corner of

[9] C. Leoni, 'Cronaca, 1848', p. 450. V. Rovani, *Daniele Manin*, pp. 73–7, is rather silly, pontificating against the insincerity of Manin's gesture.

[10] The following anecdote, taken from *Sior Antonio Rioba* of 19 July (no. 5, p. 20), is typical of its mild humour: 'A Venetian gentleman, accustomed to being rowed by two boatmen, but now reduced to employing only one, remarked to his gondolier the other evening: "Nane, why aren't you as happy as you were in the first days of the revolution? Perhaps you're not pleased with what we've done?" Nane, with the wit for which Venetian gondoliers are renowned, replied: "It's true, *lustrissimo*, I was very happy as long as I believed that the revolution would make me become like you; but now that I see instead that you're becoming like me, all my hopes have gone for nothing." '

[11] Marchesi, *Storia documentata*, app. doc. xvi, 517. For the appeal to Manin from Dall'Ongaro, Vollo and Valussi, see MCV, Doc. Manin, no. 673. On the same day all the leading journalists of the city handed a protest to the government; Racc. Andreola, vol. 3, pp. 12–13.

[12] Racc. Andreola, vol. 3, pp. 57–8. There were seven members of the council, supposedly 'belonging to different classes'. However, two were magistrates, two were merchants, one a lawyer, one a professor of law, and the last a landowner.

Italy'.[13] There were Ferrari's papal troops, Zanellato's volunteers from Vicenza, Antonini's legion from Paris, the Lombard legion, Calvi's *Cacciatori delle Alpi*, Pepe's Neapolitans and a host of smaller groups from the Veneto. Often they had no uniforms, and many of them were sleeping out on the Lido beaches.

The government coped as best it could with this massive influx of volunteers into the city. It sent many of them to man the island forts around the city, and thus eased the serious problems of accommodation, provisioning and sanitation. But even with many of what Paleocapa called 'the *canaille*'[14] confined to the middle of the lagoon, it was obvious that the whole balance of power in Venice had changed. For by the beginning of August the loyalties of many of the leading personalities amongst the newly arrived volunteers lay not to Manin (whom Castelli hoped to rely upon to control the Venetian *popolani*), nor to Charles Albert, but rather to the political and military programme of Giuseppe Mazzini.

The war of the people

Mazzini, as we have seen, had given his support to Charles Albert at the beginning of the war, believing that the political battles against the monarchy could be waged *after* military victory had been secured. The Piedmontese army had seemed indispensable, and the Milanese declaration for *a guerra finita si deciderà* appeared to set a limit upon possible monarchist territorial gains. At the start Mazzini was confident both of Charles Albert's ability to defeat the Austrians, and of the republicans' own ultimate victory once the war had come to an end.

Instead the opposite happened: the Piedmontese made great political but very little military progress. Disillusioned by the Lombard provisional government's decision to break the political truce, Mazzini wrote to Manin on 18 May from Milan: 'I am sickened by what they are doing here to secure Charles Albert's triumph; sickened by the provisional government;

---

[13] Letter from Martini to Pareto, 17 June 1848, in G. Quazza, 'La missione Martini', p. 125. On 16 June 1848, in view of 'the extraordinary number of people arriving from the *terraferma* and in particular volunteers from Padua', the committee of public vigilance ordered an inspection of the papers of all those in lodging houses or rented rooms; ASV, Gov. Prov. 1848–9, OPss, VII, 2, no. 4731.

[14] Ventura, *Lineamenti costituzionali*, p. 71. The ministers' attitude must be contrasted to that of some of the refugees, like Cesare Correnti, who wrote to Achille Mauri (T. Massarani, *Cesare Correnti*, p. 155): 'Come and suffer with us here; if the Italian cause must die, Venice is a magnificent, immortal cemetery. Here we must protest, fight and die ...'

sickened by nearly everything.'[15] Through June and July Mazzini's newspaper *L'Italia del popolo* ceaselessly criticised the conduct of the Piedmontese in establishing a kingdom of upper Italy before they had beaten
the Austrians. At the same time Mazzini grew increasingly aware that he
had seen the military problem in the wrong terms. As the Piedmontese
made less and less progress, it became clear to him that Cattaneo had been
right and that he had been wrong; Charles Albert's army would never
secure Italian independence by itself. To Mazzini the defeat at Custozza
came as no surprise. In many ways it was a relief. At last, he argued, the
war could become a people's war. From Como and with the help of
Cattaneo and Restelli, Mazzini transformed the Milanese committee of
defence into the 'Italian national committee for insurrection'. Forced into
exile, the committee quickly settled for Lugano as its headquarters.[16]

The 'war of the people' was to be a guerrilla war, waged at every level
by the population of Lombardy-Venetia, in the towns and the countryside,
against the Austrian occupying forces. Mazzini exhorted the people to

divide the enemy so as to destroy him more easily. Prevent the concentration
of Austrian troops in one place. Wherever a single, detached Austrian regiment is quartered, attack it in the streets, in the squares, from behind barricades, inside houses, from the rooftops, with every sort of weapon, from
muskets to knives, from stones to boiling water. Aim to kill their officers. In
the countryside destroy bridges and roads, cut down trees, cut the enemy's line
of retreat. Wherever an Austrian shows himself, knife him. Every hedge should
seem to hold an ambush for him, every lodging certain death . . . Every man
fit to fight should be a soldier of the insurrection, every woman a sister of
charity for the insurrection, every old man, every priest an apostle for the
insurrection.[17]

This clarion call to arms is open to criticism on two levels. In the first
place, the moment had long since passed when a massive response could
have been expected from the people of Lombardy and Venetia. In March
and April 1848 the enthusiasm of the peasantry, the preaching of the
clergy, the formation of the civic and national guards, and the initial concessions made by the new governments in both town and countryside, all
meant that a real possibility existed of mass participation in the war of
independence. But in August and September, with the whole of the Veneto

[15] Mazzini's letter is published in G. Gambarin, 'Il Mazzini, il Tommaseo, il
Manin', pp. 319–20.

[16] *Ibid.*, pp. 345ff. Also G. Mazzini, *Scritti editi ed inediti*, vol. 35 (1922), pp. 342–4,
for a description of the famous soprano Giuditta Pasta, a staunch republican,
giving a recital for the exiles in Lugano. She was fifty in 1848 (letter to Emilie
Hawkes, 21 Sept. 1848).

[17] From the proclamation for the planned uprising in the Val D'Intelvi, 29 October
1848, Mazzini, *Scritti*, vol. 38 (1922), pp. 253–6.

reoccupied, with the disillusionment of many of the Lombard peasants, the capitulation of Milan and the total absence of any regular troops, the task facing the revolutionaries was many times more formidable. At the time when the greatest possibilities had existed for a successful 'war of the people', Mazzini had backed the wrong horse.

Secondly, the generic nature of Mazzini's propaganda lessened the likelihood of a positive response. As Della Peruta has written, Mazzini had 'no deep awareness of the stratified world of rural Italy, of the peasants without land, the tenants and sharecroppers suffocating under the burden of exorbitant and semi-feudal contracts, the day labourers reduced to absolute misery'.[18] The lack of any specific social content in Mazzini's political thinking, his inability to tackle the fundamental questions of agrarian reform, meant that although the Lombardo-Venetian peasantry might have understood the kind of war he wanted them to wage, they simply had no good reason to wage it. In the towns, where newspaper propaganda was far more extensive, where municipal pride transcended class barriers, nationalism was not the exclusive preserve of the middle classes. But in the countryside, with so large a degree of isolation, illiteracy and suspicion, Mazzini's vague imprecations to revolt 'in the name of God and the people' fell upon deaf ears.

However, it would be quite wrong to dismiss out of hand the new Mazzinianism of the autumn of 1848. Its real value lay not in any successful exhortation to mass action, but in the inspiration it afforded the flower of the middle-class Italian republicans. In its own terms Mazzini's programme was a complete failure. The people as a whole did not rise up to hound out the oppressor. Yet the *ideal* of the people's war, of fighting *per Dio e Popolo* to establish a republic and the unity of Italy, inspired the radicals to unequalled heights. It enabled them, whenever they were in power, to make maximum use of the limited resources available to them. The dedication, courage and determination of the members of the Action Party, as it came to be called, led them to attempt the impossible, and, after more than a decade of failure, finally to achieve it in Sicily in 1860.

In 1848 the first to try and translate Mazzini's thinking into action was no less a person than Giuseppe Garibaldi. Undaunted by the news from Milan, he seized two paddle-steamers on Lake Maggiore, disembarked at Luino accompanied by about a thousand men, and then routed an Austrian force some five hundred strong. Before the battle he had made a fiery proclamation to the Italians, believed to have been written for him by Mazzini:

---

[18] Della Peruto, 'Il pensiero sociale di Mazzini', p. 56.

In the name of God and the People I have been elected by the citizens of Milan and their representatives to be a leader, a *Duce*. Our aim is to make Italy independent. I therefore cannot accept the humiliating armistice made by the king of Piedmont with the hated foreign power which dominates our country. The king does not scruple to preserve his crown at the price of cowardice and defeat.[19]

But if Garibaldi refused to be discouraged, his followers and the local peasantry were, and he soon found his numbers dwindling rapidly. After skilfully evading the Austrians for some time, and beating them off at Morazzone, Garibaldi had no option but to seek refuge in Switzerland. In the late evening of 27 August, Garibaldi, disguised as a peasant and accompanied by no more than thirty followers, finally managed to cross the Swiss border. [20]

The foundation of the Italian Club

Mazzini's ideas very quickly spread to Venice, carried by the refugees and volunteers who had arrived from the *terraferma*. Among them were several members of the council for all volunteer corps, including its secretary Antonio Mordini, and two of Garibaldi's most famous lieutenants in 1860, Nino Bixio and Giuseppe Sirtori. Bixio soon departed for Paris, where his brother Alessandro had been seriously wounded during the June days.[21] Sirtori stayed and became second in importance only to Manin during the last months of the Venetian revolution.

Giuseppe Sirtori was thirty-five in 1848. Born in Lombardy and a very close friend of Cesare Correnti, he had at first entered a seminary and become a priest. However, in 1844 he renounced his vocation and with it the contemplative life. In February 1848 he fought on the barricades in Paris, and was one of those responsible for forcing Lamartine to declare the republic at the Hôtel de Ville. Returning to Milan after the *cinque giornate*, Sirtori formed a republican club opposed to the kingdom of upper Italy, and thus came into contact with Mazzini. Once the Lombards had decided for fusion he left Milan on 28 May, having been elected as a junior officer in the volunteer battalion of Agostino Noaro. The battalion went first to Pavia, was then transported down the Po to Rovigo, and reached Venice in mid-June.[22]

19 D. Mack Smith (ed.), *Garibaldi*, p. 17.

20 Pieri, *Storia militare*, pp. 337–43.

21 C. Lazzarini, *N. Bixio*, p. 33. A letter from Mordini's father to him, urging him not to interest himself in politics or support the republic, has found its way into the Manin letters; MCV, Doc. Manin, no. 3096, letter of 13 June 1848.

22 The Venetian newspaper *L'Operaio* gave a good biography of Sirtori on 25 June 1849 (no. 66, pp. 261–4). See also N. Tommaseo, *Venezia*, vol. 1, p. 273. There

Sirtori was tall and bearded, with a deep and powerful voice. He said little, but was always concise and logical. He was impassive, distant and universally respected. Ulloa commented that he was made more to command than to obey, and his absolute fearlessness under fire soon won him renown as well as promotion. Politically, this 'soldier priest from the Middle Ages', as Tivaroni called him,[23] was at this time very close to Mazzini. The battle for a democratic Christian republic had to be fought, according to Sirtori, with absolute fanaticism; there could be no half measures.

In the last days of July regular gatherings of the leading Venetian and non-Venetian republicans were held in Giuseppe Giuriati's house in Venice. On 20 July *Fatti e parole* defended the citizens' right of association,[24] and at the beginning of August, as rumours of Charles Albert's headlong retreat reached the city, it was decided to hold a large public meeting in the Casino dei Cento in Campo Santa Margherita. On 2 August 350 people crammed into the small hall to discuss the military situation. In view of the dilatory performance of the Venetian committee of war, it was decided that a delegation from the meeting should request the government to form a new committee of defence. The delegates appointed were Sirtori, representing Lombardy, Mordini for Tuscany, Virgili for Naples, Giannini for Rome, Solerni for Sicily, and Albrizzi, Rossetti, Gregoretti and Talamini for the Veneto.[25]

Castelli naturally refused the meeting's request, and on 3 August another large gathering was held at the Casino dei Cento. On this occasion the *Circolo italiano*, the Italian Club, was founded. Its professed purpose was to meet daily to discuss all matters of importance, and to make recommendations to the government, but from the outset it was clear that

are two biographies of Sirtori which are both inadequate for the Venetian period of his life: G. De Castro, *Giuseppe Sirtori*, and C. Agrati, *Giuseppe Sirtori*, '*Il primo dei mille*'. For an extraordinary letter on religious matters sent by the young Sirtori to Cesare Correnti, see Massarani, *Cesare Correnti*, pp. 493–5.

[23] Tivaroni, *L'Italia*, vol. i, p. 579.

[24] *Fatti e parole*, no. 37, pp. 141–2, 20 July 1848. For the meetings at Giuriati's house, see A. Abruzzese, 'Il Circolo italiano a Venezia negli anni 1848–9', *Rassegna Nazionale*, 58 (1927), p. 13. This is the only work to have been published on the club. It has no footnotes, and is in many places inaccurate.

[25] Article from *L'Indipendente* of 2 Aug. 1848, reprinted in Racc. Andreola, vol. 3, pp. 191–2. The sentiments expressed by the Neapolitan Girolamo Ulloa in a letter to Nicola Fabrizi of 31 July 1848 must have been common to many of the volunteers in Venice at this time: 'So now we need the French. Poor Italy! That's the work of Pius IX and Ferdinand II . . . I believe that there's nothing else for it but to get the liberals to rise *en masse*, destroy the retrograde party, and put ourselves on a popular footing. Blood and energy are going to be needed to liberate Italy' (MRR, b. 517, no. 51 (1)).

the club was a centre for the republicans and all those sharing Mazzini's ideas.

While the club was discussing its constitution on the 3rd, a crowd of about five hundred Venetian workmen arrived in Campo Santo Margherita. Some were drunk, many were carrying sticks, and they began to shout abuse at those inside the Casino dei Cento. Quite how they had been assembled and what they thought was happening was not clear, but two separate republican sources claim that Castelli's secretary Zannini had spread the word that *Austriacanti* were meeting in the Campo.[26] It looked as if a fight would break out, but Samuele Olper, a Venetian republican, went up to one of the workmen whom he knew, embraced him, and the moment of tension passed. The crowd dispersed, some went in to listen to the discussion, and according to Olper, 'in the end a few of the workmen decided to become members of the club'.

The incident was illuminating in a number of ways. Because the government, for fear of further accusations of tyranny, did not dare to ban the club, Zannini appears to have employed the classic right-wing tactic of exploiting the ignorance of the *popolani* to persuade them to break up a meeting of radicals. His attempt cruelly exposed the lack of contact between the Mazzinians and the 'people' whose war they were about to launch. The Venetians who went along to the club were predominantly middle-class; many of them had been members of the republican club which had flourished in May and June. Most were professional people – doctors, lawyers, notaries and academics – or else shopkeepers and merchants. Amongst the non-Venetian members the class base was wider, but this merely reflected the very mixed composition of the volunteer corps themselves. The club was to make almost no attempt to work amongst the Venetian poor, or to interest them in its ideas.

None the less, in the explosive situation created by the rumours of Charles Albert's defeat, the club was an obvious threat to the Albertist government. On 3 August Tommaseo published a leading article in *Fatti e parole* which demonstrated the influence that Mazzini had already gained among the Venetian republicans:

Venice has promised to share the destinies of Lombardy under any circumstances. Well, a new situation, both urgent and honourable, has arisen. Threatened again by the common enemy, Lombardy has now realised that the

26 Dall'Ongaro, *L'undici agosto 1848*, pp. 74–6, and Olper's account of the incident written to Manin in 1851 (MCV, Doc. Manin, no. 3817). In its meeting of 3 August the club passed a special vote of thanks to Sirtori who was the spokesman for the delegation demanding a new committee of defence. The president said that Sirtori should be offered Venetian citizenship; *Fatti e parole*, supplement to the edition of 2 Aug. 1848.

war has to be fought in a new way so as to make it, as it was originally, national and popular. The Lombards have created a committee of defence which, having complete power, will wage the war decisively. It will gather together our forces, brush away any obstacles, dismay the kings, and inspire the brave to battle. Venice for its salvation and its honour must do the same.[27]

What this meant in practical terms was outlined in the same newspaper two days later:

Garibaldi in Milan has already proclaimed a war of insurrection; he has raised a great flag around which all the youth of Italy has gathered. We have heard that General Pepe too is now prepared to wage guerrilla warfare in the Veneto ... We can only fight Austrian enthusiasm with Italian enthusiasm ... each family to be a platoon, each wall to be a fortress.[28]

On 7 August 1848 the Piedmontese commissioners, Colli and Cibrario, arrived to take over the reins of government. News of Custozza, though not of the complete defeat of the Piedmontese, had reached Venice, and by all accounts the solemn ceremony of fusion resembled a funeral procession.[29] The Piedmontese persuaded Castelli to share power with them, and the rest of the July ministry, as well as the defunct provincial consultative committee, were to assist the three commissioners.

These constitutional arrangements provided the republicans with a good issue on which to fight. Paleocapa had left Venice to become a member of the new government in Turin, and this meant that the Venetian assembly should have met to elect both his and Castelli's successors. The commissioners, however, were afraid to summon the assembly, which enjoyed far more popularity than they did. Instead, on 9 August, as the first disquieting reports of the fall of Milan spread through the city, Colli, Cibrario and Castelli wrote to Albini, the admiral of the Piedmontese fleet at that time in Venetian waters, asking him to send a warship to anchor in the Bacino San Marco.[30]

---

[27] *Fatti e parole*, no. 51, p. 197. From 28 Aug. until 6 Oct. 1848 the newspaper assumed the subtitle of 'Giornale del Circolo italiano'.

[28] *Ibid.*, no. 53, pp. 205f. Pepe had written a book called *L'Italia militare e la guerra di sollevazione*, which was first published in Paris in 1836, and reprinted in Venice in 1849. The July government attempted unsuccessfully to combat the gathering crescendo of republican activity by issuing two proclamations on 2 Aug., one reminding the people not to confuse the right of association with illegal reunion, and the other obliging those non-Venetians who could not justify their residence in the city to leave it within 24 hours; Racc. Andreola, vol. 3, pp. 188–90.

[29] See, for example, A. De Giorgi, 'Venezia nel 1848 e 1849', *Archivio Veneto*, 11 (1876), p. 22.

[30] The minutes of this letter are in MCV, Agg. Manin, xiii/fasc. 9, no. 4.

The republicans reacted strongly. On 10 August a meeting of republican deputies was held in Santello's house on the Salizzada San Canzian. Among the twenty-eight who attended were Manin, Tommaseo, Olper, Varè, the editor of the influential *L'Indipendente*, and Ferrari-Bravo, one of the most prominent Venetian members of the Italian Club. A protest in favour of the assembly was prepared. Manin, who had taken no part in the Italian Club and who had refused to criticise the July government, argued against publishing the protest on the grounds that it could only 'lessen the faith of the people in the government at this crucial time'. Tommaseo, however, said that it should be published immediately and that 'they must do something more', though he did not specify what. The protest, signed by thirty-four deputies including Manin, was presented to the government later on the same day.[31]

Fatti e parole also launched into the attack on 10 August with a leader which began, 'A government which has no confidence in the people does not merit the people's confidence'.[32] Tommaseo further fanned the flames by publishing in *L'Indipendente* a scathing attack on the government's use of Austrian laws to repress its critics. It was clear that events were building up to a climax, though no one foresaw how dramatic that climax was to be.

11 August 1848

Early on the morning of 11 August Marshal Welden announced to the Venetians the definite conclusion of the Salasco armistice. Welden made special reference to its fourth article: 'The Sardinian land and sea forces should leave the city, the forts and the port of Venice, and return to Piedmont.'[33] The news, although disbelieved by some because it came from an Austrian source, spread swiftly, and many Venetians took it to mean that Charles Albert was surrendering Venice to the Austrians. A wave of disquiet swept through the city.

That afternoon the commissioners, Colli, Cibrario and Castelli, held a meeting with the members of the provincial *consulta*. Castelli said that as soon as Turin confirmed the armistice, Venice should once again become independent. The two Piedmontese, who to their credit had no intention of surrendering Venice to the Austrians, agreed to resign from power as

---

31 MCV, Doc. Manin, no. 717 for an account of the meeting, 10 Aug. 1848; and no. 719, for a copy of the petition. Manin had seen the commissioners briefly on 9 Aug.; see Cibrario's account, published by Planat de la Faye (ed.), *Documenti*, vol. 1, pp. 573–9.

32 *Fatti e parole*, no. 58, p. 225.

33 Marchesi, *Storia documentata*, p. 271.

soon as official news arrived, and to create a committee of defence whose members were to be chosen from the assembly. They also agreed that the assembly should meet as soon as possible, and fixed its reunion for 10 a.m. on 13 August.[34]

They were prevented from realising this plan by a huge crowd which gathered in the Piazza San Marco on the evening of the same day. Hungry for definite news, fearing the imminent capitulation of the city, and angry that Piedmontese aid had proved to be such an illusion, the crowd, which consisted mainly of Venetians, raised cries of 'Death to the commissioners!' Whether this demonstration of hostility to the Piedmontese had been planned or not remains uncertain.[35] It was by now an established pattern in the Venetian revolution that, at every crisis, the people would assemble in the Piazza underneath the Procuratie Nuove, from which the government, whether it was Austrian, Piedmontese or Venetian, could give a direct account of its actions.

Colli and Cibrario were unable to control the situation. They had no definite news of the armistice, and were determined not to resign until an official dispatch arrived. They appeared on the balcony of the Procuratie Nuove and tried to gain time by reading an account of the fall of Milan from the *Pensiero italiano*. This, they said, was the only certain news they had. Their inability, however, to say anything about the armistice only further incensed the crowd. At this point, according to Montanelli, Giuseppe Sirtori leapt onto a table in the Piazza and swore on his own blood that the Milanese could never have surrendered, and that if the city was in Austrian hands it could only have been betrayed. There were cries from those around him of 'Viva Milano! Viva il capitano lombardo!' Sirtori, Cattabeni, Mordini and a few others then forced their way up the staircase of the ex-governor's palace and broke into the room where Colli, Cibrario and Castelli were gathered.[36] They tried to persuade the commissioners to resign immediately, but Colli and Cibrario steadfastly refused to do anything until official news of the armistice reached them. It can only be surmised what Sirtori and Mordini intended to do next. It

---

[34] See the handbill published by the government on 11 Aug., MCV, Doc. Manin, no. 3446; also Ventura, *Lineamenti costituzionali*, p. 88.

[35] My account of the events of the evening of the 11th is based on Marchesi, *Storia documentata*, pp. 272–3, who correlates Cibrario's report, Dall'Ongaro's book and Manin's account to the assembly on the 13th. See also G. Montanelli, *Memorie sull'Italia*, pp. 541–3.

[36] Sirtori was able to do so because the cries from the crowd in the Piazza drowned Mengaldo's attempt to sound the alert for the civic guard; see Meneghetti (ed.), *Il Cavaignac di Venezia*, p. 46. The commissioners obviously wished to avoid using Piedmontese troops to restore order, in case they were forced to fire on the Venetians, which would have had catastrophic consequences.

seems likely that they would have tried to form a committee of defence to
organise resistance in the city and to work closely with Mazzini's national
committee of insurrection. But their attempts to cajole the two Piedmontese into resigning were interrupted by the arrival of Daniele Manin.

That afternoon Castelli had asked Manin to come and confer at 8.30
p.m. with the commissioners at the Procuratie Nuove. While the crowd
was gathering in the Piazza earlier in the evening, Manin had been
browsing in a bookshop in the Mercerie. He was found there by a friend,
Giorgio Casarini, and together they hurried to the ex-governor's palace.[37]

As soon as Manin had taken stock of the situation, he assured the commissioners that he would restore peace in fifteen minutes and told Sirtori
that he intended and was prepared to prevent anarchy. Colli and Cibrario,
although they repeated that they could not resign, agreed to desist from
further acts of government. Manin then came out on to the balcony over-
looking the Piazza. His sudden and unexpected appearance on the balcony
from which he had often addressed the people in the previous months
had a striking effect on the crowd below. Total silence fell in the Piazza.
Manin, in a strong and clear voice, told the crowd of the commissioners'
decision, and then added: 'The day after tomorrow the assembly will
elect a new government. For these forty-eight hours I shall govern.' At
the words *governo io*, the whole Piazza exploded with enthusiasm. Manin
urged the Venetians and Italian volunteers to take up arms and make
sure that the Austrians knew immediately that there was no possibility of
the city surrendering. In a climate of overwhelming enthusiasm, equal to
that of 22 March, the crowd dispersed, and the civic guard and soldiers
returned to man the forts defending Venice. Neither Sirtori nor Mordini
had contradicted what Manin said, but what was in effect an attempt by
the leading Mazzinians to overthrow the July government had been fore-
stalled by Manin's hold over his own people.

Manin and the creation of the triumvirate

At the time the events of 11 August were not interpreted in this light. In
early August Manin's attitude towards the Mazzinians was an ambivalent
one, and many of them must have held strong hopes of winning him over.
Although he had not taken part in the meetings of the Italian Club, Olper
and Varè, two of his friends, were enthusiastic members.[38] There was no

[37] See the account by G. Casarini in MCV, Doc. Manin, no. 3816. According to
Casarini the crowd kept shouting, 'Why should we go on serving the servants of
a king who has betrayed us?'
[38] Olper was completely under Manin's sway. See his letter of 17 Oct. 1848 (MCV,
Doc. Manin, no. 4109): '...well or ill, you will always be Papà Manin'.

question on the evening of 11 August of the club opposing Manin's
decision to rule the city for two days. On the contrary, *Fatti e parole*
welcomed what he had done,[39] and the obvious faith of the Venetian
Mazzinians in Manin made it all the more easy for him to dominate the
situation. Sirtori and Mordini may not have been happy about being so
brusquely eclipsed by Manin, but they probably expected him as a republican to favour their way of thinking.

In fact, Manin had moved decisively to the right during the period that
he had been out of power. The side of his character which placed order
above all else had been considerably strengthened by the reports that had
reached Venice of the June days in Paris.[40] The workers' struggle there
appeared to him as a new form of barbarism, and as something that could
happen in every major European city unless the leaders of the revolution
placed internal order foremost on their list of priorities. On the evening
of 11 August, Manin, in conversation with Cibrario, had referred
scathingly and apprehensively to the '*popolaccio*'[41] in the Piazza below,
forgetting that it was exactly this *popolaccio* who had brought him to
power on 22 March. In 1849 Cicogna commented astutely: 'Manin,
although he holds the whip hand over the Venetian rich and poor alike, is
never the less afraid whenever the people gather together.'[42]

This meant that for Manin the new Mazzinianism appeared more
dangerous than attractive. From August until Venice surrendered the one
recurrent theme, amounting almost to an obsession in all Manin's pronouncements, was the need to maintain strict internal order and to prevent
the people from discussing political questions. On 20 August, in an
account of the events of the 11th sent to the Piedmontese minister of
foreign affairs, Manin wrote that 'the city would have fallen into anarchy'
if he had not intervened.[43] In November, when he heard that Garibaldi,
who would have made a superb commander of the Venetian fleet, wanted

Tommaseo estimated that Varè was Manin's front man in the republican opposition, a role which he apparently played 'with courtesy and dignity' (Tommaseo,
Venezia, vol. 2, p. 53).

[39] *Fatti e parole*, no. 61, p. 237, 13 Aug. 1848.
[40] *L'Imparziale*, no. 2, 5 July 1848: 'After four days of indescribable horror, the
terrible drama which has been playing in Paris has finally come to an end –
Anarchy has lost.' See also the dispatch from the Venetian representatives in
Paris, Aleardi and Gar, 26 June 1848: 'We are awaiting the announcement at
any time of the total repression of the insurrectionaries. For the great part led
astray by unknown agitators, they have shown a heroism in battle worthy of a
better cause' (G. Biadego, *Aleardo Aleardi nel biennio 1848–9. Carteggio inedito*,
p. 60).
[41] Cibrario's report, quoted by Ventura, *Lineamenti costituzionali*, p. 53.
[42] MCV, Cicogna diary, 5 March 1849.
[43] MCV, Doc. Manin, no. 868, rough draft of the letter of 20 Aug. 1848.

to come to Venice, Manin wrote to Tommaseo: 'He [Garibaldi] is not suited to defending these forts ... indeed if he came, we would fear for the city's tranquillity, the conservation of which is not the least of our worries.'[44]

Manin's accentuated social conservatism led him to assess the war effort in rigidly conventional terms at a time when most republicans were adopting Mazzini's heterodox opinions. An acute observer, Federico Seismit-Doda, commented in 1849 that while Manin was 'courageous, honest and devoted to his own city', he was also 'slow to venture, slower still to act, ready to come to terms with the strongest but distrustful of the most daring'.[45] Salvation, according to Manin, could only come from the large, trained armies of either Piedmont or France. The Piedmontese troops had impressed him, as had Colli and Cibrario. Manin was probably alone amongst Venetian republicans in refusing to condemn Charles Albert after Custozza or dismiss the possibility of a fresh Piedmontese intervention. He hoped that his more flexible attitude towards political questions would earn Venice Piedmontese aid, and in this he was not to be totally disappointed. As for French intervention, Manin had always been in favour of the idea, and its appeal was reinforced by the fact that General Cavaignac, now at the head of the republic, had given ample proof while suppressing the June 'anarchy' of his being a republican of the right sort.

In keeping with these views the first thing that Manin did during the night of 11–12 August was to send an emissary to Paris to invoke French aid. The choice of the emissary caused some difficulty. At first Manin appears to have selected Sirtori, perhaps bearing in mind the latter's experience in Paris in February, perhaps because he wanted him out of Venice.[46] But then he changed his mind and summoned Tommaseo instead. Tommaseo, who had become increasingly critical and jealous of Manin, came reluctantly, muttering that he had no intention of making himself 'the footstool for anyone's ambition'.[47] He had spent many years in exile in Paris and spoke French fluently, but his temperament was hardly suited to diplomacy; again Manin's motives may have been mixed. In view of Tommaseo's high prestige, his temporary support for Mazzinian ideas and his swingeing attacks on all those who limited the freedom

---

[44] *La Repubblica veneta*, vol. 1, p. 474, letter of 17 Nov. 1848.

[45] L. G. Sanzin, 'F. e L. Seismit-Doda', in *La Venezia Giulia*, vol. 3, p. 549.

[46] MCV, Agg. Manin, xxx/5, no. 6 is a pass, dated 11 Aug. and signed by Manin, for Sirtori to travel to Paris 'by land and sea, accompanied by his secretary'. This may of course have been written after Tommaseo's departure, but it seems unlikely.

[47] MCV, Doc. Manin, no. 3816, Casarini's narrative.

of political criticism, it may well have seemed a relief to have him out of the city. Tommaseo at first refused the mission, but then consented and left Venice the same night.[48]

The Venetian assembly reconvened on 13 August 1848.[49] The nobleman Carlo Trolli, who had been Manin's first choice for the ministry of the interior in March, and who was strongly Albertist, declared that the Piedmontese commissioners should resume power. He was howled down and the assembly, in recognition of what Manin had done on 11 August, and in view of the gravity of the military situation, offered to create him dictator. Manin declined on the grounds of military incompetence, and chose instead to share power in a triumvirate, with Colonel Giovanni Battista Cavedalis and Admiral Leone Graziani.

Cavedalis, fifty-four years old in 1848, was a Friulian nobleman who had received his education at the Napoleonic military academy at Modena. He qualified as an engineer and fought under Beauharnais in the last campaigns in northern Italy. In 1815 he was allowed into the Austrian army as a lieutenant, but retired to private life in 1828. He became well known as a hydraulics expert and on the outbreak of the revolution became captain of the civic guard of his home town of Spilimbergo. He was called to become a member of the committee of defence of Udine, and after the fall of the city came to Venice. A severe and conservative man, Cavedalis was on the right of the Italian political spectrum, being far closer to the liberal monarchists than the republicans. He was thus naturally averse to any attempt to coordinate a general insurrection with Mazzini's committee at Lugano. Graziani was a likeable, easy-going senior naval officer, whose daughter was the widow of Attilio Bandiera. He tried to refuse the post of triumvir as being too important for him, and this was probably a just estimate of his own talents. Graziani lacked dynamism

---

48 For Tommaseo's own description, see *Venezia*, vol. 2, pp. 118–22. Gambarin (*La Repubblica veneta*, vol. 1, p. 246) is convinced that Manin sent Tommaseo because he thought him the best man for the job. For Tommaseo in Paris, see below, pp. 284ff.

49 One of Manin's first acts during the night of 11–12 Aug. was to order the arrests of the Albertists Zannini, Soler and Prati. He justified this action on the grounds of saving them from the people's anger. This was all the more necessary, he said, because Zannini had been found 'exhorting his supporters in Cannaregio to a violent counter-demonstration'; see Manin's letter to the prefect of public order, MCV, Doc. Manin, no. 3065, 13 Aug. 1848. Castelli was shattered by what had happened and wrote a sad letter to Manin on 12 Aug., asking him to clear his name of any imputations of treason (MCV, Doc. Manin no. 4019). Manin did this in the assembly on the 13th. Castelli then left Venice for Florence, to try and sustain his failing health. From there he was called to Turin by Paleocapa, was made a councillor of state by Charles Albert, but died on 18 March 1849.

and while he was in charge little progress was made in the vital task of building up the navy.[50]

Once the assembly had approved Manin's choice of fellow triumvirs, Manin announced his intention not to re-declare the republic. In view of the need to put the fight against Austria before all else, explained Manin, Venice had had to have 'a government that is provisional in every meaning of the term . . . its members must belong to no political party: the only party is that which will defeat the Austrians'.[51] Manin's insistence in not reaffirming the principles of 22 March dismayed most of the republicans in the city, and some of his closest supporters.[52] It was a very grave blow to Mazzinian hopes of republican unity.

The final demonstration of Manin's lack of sympathy for the Mazzinian programme came over the question of the proposed committee of defence. The Italian Club petitioned Manin stressing the need to give a new committee the most wide-ranging powers. On 15 August Manin did appoint a new council of war, but its powers were limited and its relationship with Cavedalis and with Pepe, the commander-in-chief, was never clearly defined. Four out of five of its members – Milani, Ulloa, Mezzacapo and Mainardi – were fine and dedicated soldiers. Milani had played an active part in trying to organise the volunteer corps in the Veneto, Ulloa was an intrepid Neapolitan and a member of Pepe's staff, Mezzacapo built up a first-rate artillery brigade, the *Bandiera e Moro*, during the winter of 1848–9, and Mainardi was a Mazzinian lieutenant in the navy. But at the head of the new council was Admiral Bua, who in March and April had also headed the first, incompetent committee of defence. Bua and Cavedalis together meant that the 'war of the people' was never considered, and that the spirit and inspiration of the finest radicals never permeated, until far too late in the revolution, the highest echelons of the Venetian military establishment.

[50] For further biographical details on Cavedalis and Graziani, see P. Rigobon, *Gli eletti*, pp. 68–9 and 127–8. On Cavedalis see also the introduction by V. Marchesi to Cavedalis's *I commentari*.

[51] For the proceedings of the assembly, see Racc. Andreola, vol. 3, pp. 310–15 and 324–33.

[52] Castellani from Rome had exhorted both Manin and Castelli to proclaim the republic without delay; see, for example, *La Repubblica veneta nel 1848–9*, vol. 2, Documenti diplomatici, carteggio di G. B. Castellani, p. 194, letter of 7 Aug. 1848. For the memorandum from the Italian Club on the new committee of defence, see MCV, Agg. Manin, ix/44, no. 1. The memorandum is one of four from the Italian Club to the government, all undated, but which must belong, because of their content, to the period 11–13 Aug. 1848. The others are of no particular importance.

The Mazzinian challenge

The Italian Club in Venice did not allow itself to be deterred by Manin's hostility to its ideas. During August and September 1848 the club gradually built up its numbers and the strength of its arguments. At first it was careful not to offend Manin or to question the triumvirs' authority. On 18 August the secretary, Ponzoni, noted that 'the club has already decided to aid a government that has need of rapid results and to transmit to it realistic ideas and measures, as Manin himself desires'.[53] *Fatti e parole* went so far as to approve Manin's decision not to re-establish the republic.[54]

Much of the discussion in the club during the evenings in August, and even later, was devoted to mundane matters concerning the city's welfare. A finance committee was set up, and Cenedese read a report on the state of Venice's provisioning. On 24 August there was an endless debate on the wells of Castello, and on 23 September most of the meeting was taken up with complaints about the wine tax.[55] The club also made a number of proposals relating to the military effort.[56] Varè strongly criticised the system by which officers in the civic guard had to buy their own uniforms. This, he argued, meant that only the rich could afford to become officers, and led to a military elite of wealth and not of talent. A memorandum was sent to the government requesting reforms in this field, and also requesting that the civic guard should be allowed to elect all its officers up to the rank of commander-in-chief.

Other *circoli* in Italian cities sent messages of sympathy and encouragement to the Venetians, and these were read out during the meetings of the Italian Club. Siena, Leghorn and Genoa all urged the Venetians not to capitulate, as their city constituted the last bulwark of Italian independence and liberty. The Italian Club replied on 20 August by organising a proclamation, signed by over 21,000 Venetians, which stated that, despite all the errors committed since 22 March, 'a nation of 24 million cannot perish, as long as it desires to fight'.[57]

---

[53] ASV, Gov. Prov. 1848–9, b. 821 contains the minutes of the meetings of the Italian Club from 18 Aug. to 23 Sept. 1848. Ponzoni's remark is to be found on p. 10 of the minutes of an undated meeting, but almost certainly of 19 Aug. 1848.

[54] *Fatti e parole*, no. 90, p. 359, 12 Sept. 1848. The article continued: 'the right to establish our own form of government, to make the great decision for monarchy or republic, is for all Italy to decide, once it is free from foreign armies, and once its deputies have assembled in the future Italian Diet'.

[55] ASV, Gov. Prov. 1848–9, b. 821, respectively the meetings of 27 and 24 Aug. (minutes of the meeting, pp. 5–9), and 23 Sept. (pp. 2–4).

[56] *Ibid.*, 19 Aug. (p. 6).

[57] Racc. Andreola, vol. 3, pp. 408–9. For the messages of sympathy see ASV, Gov.

By the end of August Dall'Ongaro could report that the club had 150 regular members. On 8 September the general commanding the civic guard, Marsich, and Colonel Bragadin both became members. On the 11th the club moved to the larger Sala Comploy at San Luca. A special platform was erected in it so that women could listen, even though they were forbidden to take part.[58]

The move to San Luca opened a new phase in the club's life. From Lugano Mazzini conceived the idea of turning Venice into a centre of radical action. He planned to establish a pan-Italian government there, which could coordinate the Lombardo-Venetian insurrection with events in other parts of Italy. Unaware of the way Manin was thinking, Mazzini sent Maestri to Venice to persuade him, as a first step, to declare a republic for Lombardy and Venetia. Pietro Maestri had played one of the most prominent parts in instigating the Milanese insurrection in March, and was widely respected for his honesty, courage and firmness of principle. On 5 September 1848 Mazzini wrote to Mordini, 'I consider my friend Maestri's mission as of vital importance for the Italian people, and I hope that once you are convinced by what he has to say, you will use all your influence and energy to support him'.[59]

On his arrival in Venice Maestri appears to have made little headway with Manin, but the Italian Club was quick to approve Mazzini's new strategy, and did not abandon hope of persuading Manin to accept Maestri into his government.[60] From this point on, the club gradually shook off the caution of August. On 19 September a grand reunion of exiles from the Venetian provinces took place, and a day later Sirtori presided over a

---

Prov. 1848–9, b. 821, meeting of 22 Aug. (p. 1) for Leghorn, 23 Aug. for Genoa and Siena.

[58] *Fatti e parole*, no. 89, p. 353, 11 Sept. 1848. For Dall'Ongaro's report, ASV, Gov. Prov. 1848–9, b. 821, 26 Aug. (p. 6). For Marsich and Bragadin, *Fatti e parole*, no. 86, p. 341, 8 Sept. 1848. Manin had replaced Mengaldo by Marsich as head of the civic guard, principally because Mengaldo was in Paris, but also because Manin had not forgotten Mengaldo's organisation of the civic guard demonstration at the time of the fusion crisis. When Mengaldo returned from Paris, he was only given a minor command in Chioggia.

[59] Mazzini, *Scritti*, vol. 35, p. 311. See also his letter of 7 Sept. to Lamberti in Florence (*ibid.*, p. 313): 'We are trying to persuade Venice to proclaim a republic, first for Lombardy-Venetia, then for Italy.' Also his letters to Ruffoni, Cattaneo and Frapolli in Paris (*ibid.*, 8 and 12 Sept., pp. 317 and 325–6). On 19 Sept. Mazzini launched an appeal for Venice, calling it 'the heart of Italy' (*Scritti*, vol. 38, pp. 231–2).

[60] See the letter from Dall'Ongaro to Tommaseo, 21 Sept., in R. Ciampini, *Vita di Nicolò Tommaseo*, p. 502. Dall'Ongaro added: 'I cannot say whether we will succeed or not, because Manin will be afraid to let the Lombards take him in hand, for he admits their superiority to him.'

similar gathering for all the Lombards in the city. It was decided to set up a joint assembly which would represent to the government the needs of all the non-Venetians. *Fatti e parole* pointed out on 21 September how easy it would be to establish a Lombardo-Venetian government in Venice. Two new *circoli*, both affiliated to the Italian Club, were founded. One was for military personnel and the other, 'the Club of the Veneto', boasted over four hundred members shortly after its establishment.[61]

Mazzini redoubled his efforts to radicalise the Venetian government. On 22 September he wrote a long letter to Manin, appealing to him to transform Venice into a strong, aggressive, republican state.[62] Five days later *L'Indipendente* announced the receipt from Lugano of a proclamation denouncing Gioberti's attempt to found a National Association in Turin, 'that city which was formerly the Garden of Eden of the Jesuits, and which is now the Mecca of the liberal monarchists'.[63] Mazzini's proclamation ended with this advice:

Let us destroy the monarchs who up to now have been the vermin which have sapped our strength. Venice is republican; let the other Italian cities take their destinies in their own hands and make Venice their capital; it is to Venice that we should send representatives, arms and assistance. This is the true path to UNION . . . only the REPUBLIC will save Italy.

Fatti e parole followed this lead by suggesting that the Italians should imitate the Germans and set up a Frankfurt parliament in Venice. On 28 September the newspaper made its first indirect attack upon Manin: 'a leader of the people can rely on no other support except the faith which he inspires, and his people's love. If, because of his own mistakes or the mistakes of others, this love, this faith begins to fail, he is done for and must fall from power'.[64] Large numbers of non-Venetian troops were

[61] ASV, Gov. Prov. 1848–9, b. 821, 22 Sept. 1848, and Marchesi, *Storia documentata*, p. 300. See also *Fatti e parole* no. 93, p. 369, 15 Sept. 1848; no. 97, pp. 385–6, 19 Sept.; and no. 99, p. 394, 21 Sept. For the Lombards, Racc. Andreola, vol. 4, pp. 144 and 167ff. On 13 September the club appointed Tommaseo in his absence as their first president and Dall'Ongaro announced that in the past week the number of members had increased considerably, and that more and more well-known Venetians were attending the meetings.

[62] Gambarin, 'Il Mazzini, il Tommaseo, il Manin', pp. 356–7. Pincherle, Manin's former minister of commerce, was at Lugano from August to October, 1848, and wrote a number of letters to Manin, outlining and supporting Mazzini's plans (e.g. MCV, Doc. Manin, no. 2009, 31 Aug., and no. 2017, 5 Oct.).

[63] Reprinted in Racc. Andreola, vol. 4, pp. 199–204. *Fatti e parole* began a campaign at this time against Paleocapa and Castelli. Thus 29 Sept., p. 426: 'the viceroy of Egypt has offered Castelli a lucrative stipend for ten years, as he is going to give them a new code of laws. We await news of a fusion of Egypt with the kingdom of Cyprus and Jerusalem [over which Charles Albert claimed suzerainty]'.

[64] *Fatti e parole*, no. 106, p. 424.

now flocking to the clubs. The Italian Club approved Benvenuti's suggestion to increase efficiency by dividing the club into three sections concentrating on military affairs, politics and the economy, with each section
reporting back to the general assembly. The club had become in effect a
council outside the government. At the end of September, in anticipation
of the arrival of delegates from the Genoese Italian Club, a new executive
was appointed. Alessandri and Dall'Ongaro were elected from the Veneto,
Sirtori and Revere from Lombardy, Mordini from Tuscany, Fabrizi from
Modena, Masi from Rome, and Carrano from Naples.[65]

The October crisis

1 October 1848 was the day of reckoning for the Mazzinians in Venice.
In the morning an article by Dall'Ongaro appeared in *Fatti e parole*
reproving Captain Mazzuchelli for failing to capture an Austrian ship that
had run aground. Dall'Ongaro made no attempt to hide the contempt in
which he held Venice's military leaders:

Generals, admirals, ministers of war past and present; in five months of
calculating and prudence you have squandered the fruits of a victory won with
superlative courage in five days. The People have gone forward without you
and in spite of you. You have always retarded them or made them turn back.
Is this the sum total of your achievements? Beware, because everyone *thinks*
so, and many are already *saying* so. Perhaps the day will not be far off when
the People, undisciplined, imprudent and fearless, will attempt another coup.[66]

The same evening Giuseppe Revere and Mordini both delivered speeches
at the Italian Club. Revere, who was a well-known poet and dramatist as
well as a regular contributor to Mazzini's *L'Italia del popolo*, had
accompanied Maestri to Venice. His speech was a moderate one, demanding only that 'all the democratic forces of the nation should meet at
Venice', and that the Lombard and Venetian exiles had a right to some

[65] *Ibid.*, no. 108, p. 430, and no. 109, p. 433. Dall'Ongaro was unsure whether the
  club should press for the clear declaration of a republic: 'Would the provisional
  government of the United States of Italy not suffice?' (letter to Tommaseo, without date, but of late Sept., quoted in Ciampini, *Vita di Nicolò Tommaseo*, pp.
  502–3). See also the letter from Venice written by the Bolognese patriot Francesco
  Pigozzi to Carlo Fenzi, 28 Sept.: 'Here the Italian Club is still keeping all the
  population in high spirits, and they remain well disposed ... Many believe that
  Venice, the only free and popular government in Italy, should, in our present
  plight, call a national congress to meet here. I believe that all those who are with
  us must support this idea, and send to Venice deputies from the various provinces.
  The Lombards and the Venetian provinces have already chosen theirs' (ASRF,
  archivio Fenzi, filza 67, 7, no. 201).
[66] *Fatti e parole*, no. 109, p. 434.

sort of representation. Mordini used far stronger language. He began by accusing the government of being surrounded by a *camera nera*, and continued:

No account has been taken of the courageous youth which has gathered here to fight the war of insurrection; corruption has penetrated every level of the administration; no tribunal of war has been instituted. The government, to remedy these evils, should call a new assembly for which the Lombard and Venetian exiles will be eligible, since it was for Venice that Milan sacrificed her liberty . . . ; this way the Italian cause will be saved.[67]

Manin had been watching the growth of the club and the development of its strategy with great attention. A letter he wrote to Castellani in Rome on 20 September shows that, albeit cautiously, he seemed to be moving towards the Mazzinian position:

I believe that it would be a good idea to set up this Italian parliament in Venice . . . The best brains of Italy, gathered here, could form the nucleus. If you believe it is a good idea, cooperate, but be extremely careful, because the government must not take the initiative. From this you will see that we agree upon ends, though we differ somewhat over means and timing. I write in private as a friend to a friend, and not as anything else.[68]

But as the Italian Club became more brazen in its criticism, Manin made up his mind to crush it. The threat that the club presented was obvious: more and more non-Venetian soldiers, who had no special loyalty to Manin, were coming to support Mazzini's ideas. The commander of the Venetian civic guard had become a member of the Italian Club; Tommaseo, though in Paris, had become its first president. A whole rival power centre seemed to be forming, ready to question Manin's authority if he continued to reject Mazzini's plans for Venice. If it came to a battle, Manin knew he could rely on the support of most Venetians, but the prospect of civil strife was hardly one he welcomed.

Manin was also under pressure from the right wing in the city to do something about the club. The nobleman Girolamo Dolfin Boldù wrote to Manin on 1 October 1848, expressing his fears for the fate of Venice:

You must not delude yourself: republicanism amongst the Venetian people has not the same meaning as elsewhere. You yourself when you declared the

---

[67] *Ibid.*, no. 111, pp. 444f, 3 Oct. 1848, for both Revere and Mordini. During this crisis Varè's *L'Indipendente* gave much fuller coverage and from 6 Oct. assumed the task of reporting on the club's activities. On Revere, see C. De Franceschi, 'G. Revere e il Circolo italiano di Venezia', in *La Venezia Giulia*, vol. 3, pp. 281–96.

[68] *La Repubblica veneta*, vol. 2, p. 318.

Republic on 22 March were certainly not thinking of Mazzini! . . . The news-papers *Fatti e parole* and *Sior Antonio Rioba* are trying to introduce new ideas amongst the people, especially the uneducated, ideas which are worse than those of the red republicans.[69]

Giuseppe Reali, president of the chamber of commerce, and one of the principal financial backers of the government, was equally concerned. In one of his few surviving letters, he wrote to Jacopo Castelli that Dall'Ongaro was set to introduce the Terror into Venice, that the patriarch was to be deposed and that four guillotines were to be erected in prominent positions in the city.[70]

Manin had a less sensational view of Mazzinian aims, but did not underestimate their potential danger. Fortunately for him, General Pepe was on his side, and Manin could therefore be quite sure of his orders being obeyed. On 2 October Mordini, Formani and Revere were arrested. When the civic guards went to Mordini's lodgings, he tried to get them to wait outside. They grew impatient, broke in, and found Mordini, half-dressed, burning some of his papers. Formani was later released, but both Mordini and Revere were expelled from Venice. A few days later, a similar fate befell Dall'Ongaro.[71] On 3 October Manin also decided to forbid all soldiers in the city to attend the clubs, unless the government gave them special permission. Deprived of some of its ablest leaders and prevented from building a solid base in the armed forces, the power of the Italian Club had been smashed. Little hope now remained to the Mazzinians of transforming the city's politics.

At the time there was a strong reaction against what Manin had done. One hundred and sixteen officers and N.C.O.s from the Roman and Lombard legions protested at the 'violation of citizens' liberties'. How-ever, the outcry was not as great as it might have been, since Manin astutely conciliated while he suppressed. On the same day that he banned all soldiers from the clubs, he announced that the assembly would meet

[69] MCV, Doc. Manin, no. 4091.

[70] Marchesi, *Storia documentata*, app. doc. XXIV, p. 522.

[71] For the arrests, see MCV, Doc. Manin, nos. 3086–90. No. 3090 is the report written by one of the guards sent by the committee of public vigilance to arrest Mordini and Revere. Dall'Ongaro, in a vigorous letter of self-defence written to Tommaseo on 27 Oct. 1848, maintained that the club had taken no steps to proclaim the republic, but had 'many times suppressed or adjourned Falconi's motions which tended in that direction . . . On seeing Manin becoming ever more narrow and in fact municipal in his ideas, we wanted to adopt in the face of all Italy a more Italian strategy . . . they accused the club's committee of desiring power and I in particular wanted to be *minister of culture*! We would be able to laugh at that if circumstances were different' (Tommaseo, *Venezia*, vol. 2, app. IX, pp. 397–403).

on 11 October to draw up new electoral laws.[72] This seemed to hold out the promise of immediate representation for the dissident non-Venetian elements in the city. The moderate wing of the Italian Club, who had disapproved of Mordini's speech and had grown alarmed at the club's new-found aggression, welcomed Manin's declaration as proof that he intended to move slowly towards a Lombardo-Venetian government. Varè persuaded the club's executive committee, who had resigned in protest, to resume their duties and await the result of the assembly.[73]

They were to be bitterly disappointed. In the assembly Manin, secure of his position, reaffirmed his policy of political non-commitment, and the new electoral laws were not completed till December 1848. The moderates were delighted. Reali wrote to Castelli, 'Manin has moved with energy and arrested many of the most fanatical . . . ; he is no longer the man of 22 March'.[74] The assembly passed a vote of confidence in the triumvirate by 105 votes to 13. After it, Manin emphasised once again the need to avoid giving way to impatience, and the necessity of not abandoning the policy of expectation, 'the only one which at the moment can save Venice, and with Venice, Italy'. The Mazzinian challenge in favour of a more positive republican policy had been repulsed, and its vehicle, the Italian Club, reduced to a shadow of its former self. At the end of October the attempted Mazzinian rising in the mountainous Val d'Intelvi, on the confines of Lombardy and Switzerland, failed ignominiously. The strategy of the 'war of the people' could not have got off to a worse start – rejected in Venice and crushed in the Val d'Intelvi. Mazzini was now forced to abandon the north and transfer his attention to the more fruitful terrain of central Italy.

---

[72] There was great controversy over whether the July assembly had any legal power at all, since it had been convoked to decide only upon the question of fusion. See the pamphlet by the lawyer M. Costi, *Della illegalità della Assemblea convocata in Venezia pel giorno 11 ottobre 1848*, Venezia 1848. For the officers' protests, see Racc. Andreola, vol. 4, pp. 277–8, 3 Oct. 1848.

[73] *Fatti e parole*, pp. 447–8, 3 Oct. 1848. Olper (MCV, Doc. Manin, no. 3817) says that some members of the club greeted Mordini's speech with whistles and jeers.

[74] Marchesi, *Storia documentata*, app. doc. xxiv, p. 522. For Manin's pronouncements in the assembly, see Racc. Andreola, vol. 4, pp. 302 and 309. One of the most reasoned criticisms of Manin's policy of 'prudent expectation' came from Giovanni Ferrari-Bravo, councillor at the criminal court and an active member of the Italian Club. In a letter to 'the electors of the parish of S. Zaccaria in Venice' (*ibid.*, vol. 4, pp. 336–9, 12 Oct. 1848), he wrote that Venice should strive to be the cause of events rather than merely being affected by them: 'If, in our critical condition, we allow our future to be determined by events over which we claim no control, we are no better than the pilot who in a tempest abandons his vessel to the fury of the wind.'

The quest for French intervention

One of the reasons for Manin's adamant refusal to abandon his policy of 'prudent expectation' was his belief that the Venetian government should do nothing to upset the delicate diplomatic negotiations which he hoped would lead to the fulfilment of his cherished dream of French intervention in northern Italy. As long as all Italians had adhered to Charles Albert's *Italia farà da sé*, it had been impossible for the French to join the Italian war. Time and again from March until June 1848, the French representatives at Turin had warned Paris that if the Army of the Alps marched into Italy, its troops would be greeted not as liberators but as conquerors. The Piedmontese monarchists, of course, had more to fear from the French republicans than had the other north Italians, but in the nationalist euphoria of the early months of the war every Italian hoped that French aid would not be necessary.

However, the longer Charles Albert took to win a decisive victory, the more the idea of French aid returned to the fore. In June the Venetians had wanted to appeal to the French, but the opprobrium of the rest of Italy had prevented them from doing so.[75] In August, with Charles Albert in full retreat, there was no stopping them. Even before Manin had reassumed power, Castelli had written in confidence on 4 August to the French foreign minister, Jules Bastide, appealing to France's 'generosity' in the event that Venice might once again be left alone to face the enemy.[76] Manin used much the same language in the letter he sent to Paris with Tommaseo on the night of 11 August: 'The life of a people who have contributed not a little to European civilisation now depends on the immediate assistance of the heroic French nation.'[77] The letter mentioned that the Piedmontese navy and troops would soon have to leave the lagoon, but said nothing about Venice's future political state. However, on 14 August, after the triumvirate had been appointed and a provisional government agreed upon, Manin wrote again to Bastide, making it clear that Venice was no longer under Piedmontese rule and had regained her independence. Angelo Mengaldo was immediately despatched to Paris with this letter.[78]

[75] See above, pp. 244–5.
[76] MCV, Doc. Manin, no. 938, draft of the letter to Bastide. Castelli also wrote on 5 Aug. to Vasseur, the French consul in Venice.
[77] *Ibid.*, no. 941.
[78] *Ibid.*, no. 942. The fact that Venice did not again become a republic appears to have made little difference in Paris. Only on 1 Oct., after all hope of French intervention had disappeared, did Tommaseo write that the new Venetian government 'is not recognised, and no one knows whether we are still Piedmontese or what we are' (*La Repubblica veneta*, vol. 1, p. 371).

As it was, before either Tommaseo or Mengaldo arrived in Paris, the French had already come close to marching into Italy. The standard view taken by Italian historians has been that the French were consistently 'duping' the Italians by promising intervention without ever meaning it. This is not strictly true. Neither Bastide nor Cavaignac wanted war; like Lamartine they would have preferred to have revised the treaties of 1815 and to secure Italian independence by means of a European congress. In the summer of 1848 they had good reasons for non-belligerence: any French intervention was likely to aid Piedmontese aggrandisement and create a strong Italian kingdom on the French republic's south-east borders; the attitude of some German states and sections of Prussian public opinion meant the possibility of German aid to Austria in the event of French hostility; the internal situation of France was utterly unconducive to launching a major war – the economy was in a terrible state and large numbers of regular troops were tied down in Paris and Lyons; finally Cavaignac, as aware as any of his contemporaries of the lessons of the first French revolution, feared that a foreign war would reactivate the revolutionary process he had so savagely tried to halt in June.[79]

Nevertheless there was a distinct possibility that war would be forced upon the French leaders. From March onwards the reiterated policy of the republic had been that, should Radetzky crush the Italians, France would not hesitate to intervene. On 28 July 1848, as news of Charles Albert's rout filtered through to Paris, Bastide told the assembly: 'Italy knows that we desire her independence and that we are ready to help her if, by chance, her successes turn to disasters.'[80] A strong pro-Italian lobby in the French assembly, led by the radical republicans and having the support of Lamoricière, the minister of war, and the assembly's foreign affairs committee, was ready to keep the foreign minister to his oft-repeated promises. As A. J. P. Taylor has written: 'Cavaignac and Bastide were very unwilling to go to war, but they had committed themselves so far – and relied so much on foreign affairs to enhance their prestige – that

---

[79] Karl Marx was not slow to point out the glaring contradiction between the earlier internationalist principles of Cavaignac and Bastide, and their actual practice in 1848: 'this one day of rule destroyed 18 years of opposition for the *National* ... an irony of history made Bastide, the former foreign affairs editor of the *National*, French Minister of Foreign Affairs, so that he could refute his articles one by one, with each of his dispatches' ('The class struggles in France', p. 68). For details of the French position, and the influence of German opinion and internal affairs, see Jennings, *France and Europe*, pp. 147–70. However, the army of the Alps, although depleted, still numbered 45,000 infantry by 11 Aug., with 6,500 cavalry and 72 pieces of artillery; see the letter from Ricci to Pareto, AST, carte politiche diverse, cart. 25, fasc. 141, no number.

[80] Bianchi, *Diplomazia europea in Italia*, vol. 5 (1869), p. 293.

in certain circumstances it would have been very difficult for them to have avoided intervention.'[81]

Such circumstances arose with the headlong Piedmontese retreat towards Milan at the end of July. The French republican government was understandably reluctant to fight on behalf of Charles Albert alone. But, as Cavaignac said to Normanby on 1 August 1848: 'If, in consequence of actual or imminent oppression, there came a popular appeal for assistance from the Italian people ... no government established here would long be able to resist the demand for armed intervention in Italy.'[82] This 'popular appeal' in fact arrived at Paris on the same day that Cavaignac had his audience with Normanby. Its bearer was the Marquis Anselmo Guerrieri Gonzaga, who had been sent by the committee of defence appointed by the Lombard provisional government to defend Milan. Guerrieri requested immediate armed aid in order to prevent the fall of Milan.

For a week France hovered on the brink of war. Count Gustave Reiset, the French envoy in Turin, in his dispatch to Bastide on 30 July stated: 'In spite of all the desire I feel to see the peace and calm of Europe, I believe that we are honour bound to come to the aid of our Lombardo-Venetian brothers, and that consequently our intervention is unfortunate but inevitable.'[83] *The Times*, in an eloquent first leader of 4 August, showed itself extremely apprehensive about French intentions:

Ever since February there has been a floating idea that France was sooner or later to be absorbed in the Italian gangrene ... Sixty thousand Gauls were to purge a classic soil from the barbaric invasion. The knight-errant was to rescue the maiden and return ... [But] there is revolution in every step of that army from its inaugural review in the Champ de Mars, to the 'Te Deum' of victory in the cathedral of the Doges.

In Paris certain Italian envoys made frantic efforts to push the French into Italy. Lodovico Frapolli, Milan's first representative in Paris after the *cinque giornate*, later sent Manin an account of what he and his colleagues had tried to do: 'We emissaries of every sort, past and present, from Lombardy, Venice and Tuscany, exerted all the pressure we could on the

[81] Taylor, *The Italian Problem*, p. 196. For the pro-war pressure on the French leaders, see *The Times*, second leader, 8 Aug. 1848, and Jennings, *France and Europe*, p. 141.
[82] Taylor, *The Italian Problem*, p. 138. Bastide wrote in 1858: 'had we gone to the help of Piedmont we would have given the world the strange spectacle of a democratic government sending its soldiers to their deaths in order to establish a powerful kingdom on our own borders' (J. Bastide, *La République française et l'Italie en 1848*, p. 60).
[83] Published in Spellanzon, *Il vero segreto*, p. 189.

government and the men of influence in France. For fifteen nights and days we had no rest; we worked so hard that the ministry of foreign affairs practically became our permanent residence.'[84]

These interventionists were opposed by a combination of Piedmontese and English diplomacy which skilfully played upon France's unwillingness to get involved. The Piedmontese Alberto Ricci left Turin at the same time as Guerrieri Gonzaga left Milan, and ostensibly with the same purpose – to seek immediate French aid. However, both Ricci and the Marquis Brignole Sale, the Piedmontese ambassador in Paris, were apprehensive about the possible implications for the Savoy dynasty of French republican troops marching through Piedmont. Instead of joining forces with the Lombard and Venetian envoys, Brignole and Ricci disowned them. On the evening of 3 August the two Piedmontese, accompanied by Guerrieri Gonzaga, met Cavaignac and Bastide for over two hours. It was clear from the start that the Italians were split, with only Guerrieri Gonzaga pressing for immediate armed intervention. Cavaignac was able to use the Italians' disagreements to dominate the meeting, which broke up inconclusively.[85]

The Piedmontese line in Paris was a clear one – no French troops in northern Italy but a joint Anglo-French diplomatic mediation instead. Brignole and Ricci thought that if both France and England brought pressure to bear upon the Austrians, Piedmont might still be granted Lombardy in return for her five-month campaign. Such thinking was not exactly in accord with the new government of the kingdom of upper Italy. Count Casati, the former mayor of Milan and head of the Lombard provisional government, had left Milan to preside over the new ministry in Turin. While all his actions since March had shown him to be no friend of republicanism or the French, in the desperate situation after Custozza Casati was prepared to push for French armed intervention to save his native city. But Charles Albert was not. Casati wrote at least twice to the king's headquarters seeking permission to call in the French, but Charles Albert procrastinated for as long as possible. It was only on

[84] The original, dated 10 Oct. 1848, is to be found in MCV, Doc. Pell., b. xxiv/ 281. It was published on 3 Nov. 1848 in Racc. Andreola, vol. 5, pp. 33–8.

[85] See Jennings, *France and Europe*, p. 151. Brignole wrote to Bastide on 7 Aug. reminding him of the voluntary fusion of Lombardy-Venetia into the kingdom of upper Italy, and arguing that as a result Guerrieri and all the other emissaries enjoyed no official status and were to be ignored; see V. Adami, 'Dell'intervento francese in Italia nel 1848', *Nuova Rivista Storica*, 12 (1928), p. 155. Bastide wrote in his book: 'When M. Ricci showed his credentials and proved to us that he alone represented at Paris the government of the king, to whom Lombardy unfortunately had given herself, we were compelled to accept his words' (*La République française*, p. 60).

4 August that the Piedmontese government finally wrote to Paris seeking French 'cooperation'. The dispatch did not arrive until the evening of 6 August, and Brignole and Ricci had thus enjoyed nearly a whole week in which to canvass actively for mediation.[86]

They found willing allies in the English. Palmerston and his representative at Paris, Lord Normanby, were intent on preventing the local war in north Italy from becoming a European conflagration. The English had nothing to gain and their markets to lose in a full-scale European war. Yet they did not hesitate to offer advice on the Italian question and most of it, in spite of Queen Victoria, was pro-Italian. In May 1848 Palmerston had informed a disgruntled Hummelauer in London that the British Cabinet considered Austria would be better off without her Italian possessions. On 22 July Bastide proposed Anglo-French mediation on the basis of Lombardy going to Piedmont and Venetia remaining Austrian, though with a greater degree of autonomy than previously (he was at the same time furiously reassuring the Venetians in Paris of France's intentions to stand by Venice). Palmerston at the time rejected these proposals as being too anti-Italian.[87]

However, after Custozza, Normanby in Paris realised he had to act swiftly to avert the danger of Cavaignac and Bastide being hoisted with a petard not of their own making. On 5 August he had a long and decisive meeting with Cavaignac and Bastide. The danger of war was clear:

Upon every occasion on which I have seen General Cavaignac within the last few days, he has expressed the greatest anxiety for a prompt understanding upon the Italian question. Every day it is evident that he dreads some event which, by exciting the popular feeling here, may overpower his pacific resolves. I am bound to add that I have also received intimations in society and from most of the principal members of the Assembly of all the differing parties

[86] Boyer, *La seconde République*, pp. 195–6, 208–9. In asking for French cooperation the Piedmontese government made it clear that there would be no question of Nice and Savoy going to the French in compensation, and asked that the French troops should make no republican propaganda and should avoid marching through Savoy. Cavaignac's terms for intervention, as Jennings reveals (*France and Europe*, p. 154 n. 25), were naturally somewhat different. Among Cavaignac's personal papers there is an undated and unpublished policy statement which, in the event, was never presented to Charles Albert. The statement made it clear that any Franco-Sardinian military operations were to be under French command, that Lombardy and Venetia were to be allowed to decide at the end of the war whether they wished to 'be re-united with Sardinia', and that Piedmont was in no way to compromise the independence of the other peoples of Italy.

[87] Jennings, *France and Europe*, pp. 145–6. Palmerston wanted the Austrian border to be on the Piave, thus leaving Venice and the majority of the Veneto in Piedmontese hands.

amongst the friends of peace and order, impressing upon me the urgency of the case; the desire they have that the crisis should be averted by an immediate co-operation on our part; and saying that if something was not done within the next few days, a further reverse on the part of the Italians, or any great town taken, with the aggravating circumstances which would probably attend such an event in the present feeling of both parties, would create such an indignation throughout France as would for the time overbear all prudential considerations, and would render it impossible for the Government to resist the demand for armed intervention.[88]

Normanby therefore, acting on his own initiative in this meeting of 5 August, proposed Anglo-French mediation on the following basis: Lombardy was to become part of the kingdom of Piedmont; Venice would be sacrificed. She was to remain under Austrian rule with a separate administration and government; Parma and Modena were to be allowed to decide their own fate. Cavaignac disliked the prospect of Piedmontese aggrandisement. He was also worried lest the mediation terms committed France to aiding Austria in securing Venice's surrender. But, however unsatisfactory the terms, they were infinitely preferable to war, and the French leaders gratefully accepted Normanby's initiative.[89]

There followed another two days of considerable tension, with the French and Normanby awaiting Palmerston's approval from London. On 7 August, after the official Piedmontese request for French cooperation had been presented, Cavaignac again saw Normanby, and warned him that he would very soon be forced into 'at once working the Telegraph to order a prompt compliance with the demand from Turin' unless there was immediate agreement on the joint mediation. Normanby could only blame 'the uncertain weather of the English Channel' for not getting a speedier reply from Palmerston;[90] Bastide asked for a little more time from Ricci, who was only too happy to give it him. Then, on the 8th, to everyone's relief (except that of the Lombard and Venetian envoys), Palmerston's acceptance of Normanby's proposal arrived in Paris. It came at the right moment, for a day later definite news arrived of the fall of Milan. Paris was in uproar, and only the announcement of mediation served to quieten the storm. It had been a close thing. As Normanby wrote later: 'had the news of the capture of Milan preceded the acceptance of mediation, I believe that decisive steps would have been taken which must have rendered an European war inevitable'.[91]

[88] Normanby to Palmerston, 5 Aug. 1848, quoted in Jennings, *France and Europe*, pp. 152–3.
[89] Taylor, *The Italian Problem*, p. 140.
[90] *Ibid.*, p. 142.
[91] Letter to Palmerston of 1 April 1849, quoted in Taylor, *The Italian Problem*, p. 140. Jennings (*France and Europe*, chapter 7) strangely does not allude at all

Paradoxically, it was probably the survival of Milan, and not its capture, that would have been most likely to cause war. Charles Albert made his own armistice with the Austrians on 9 August, on terms that immediately caused Casati's government to resign. But had Milan still been under siege from the Austrians at this stage, France's principal objection to intervening – that of aiding the growth of Piedmont – would no longer have applied. An extended defence of Milan, accompanied by an independent and passionate appeal from the Lombards and Venetians in Paris, would have put Cavaignac and Bastide in a situation where all their unwillingness and Nomanby's skill could not long have withstood the pro-war lobby. In this light, the gravity of Charles Albert's actions between 1 and 5 August, which effectively deprived Milan of any chance of organising her own resistance, cannot be underestimated.[92]

The Venetian expedition

Anglo-French mediation had provided an outlet for the tension in Paris after Custozza, but the Italian question remained very much on the French agenda throughout August 1848. By the end of the month a new crisis had developed, and this time it directly concerned Venice.

Tommaseo, having left Venice on the night of 11–12 August, reached Florence on the 13th, Genoa four days later, and finally arrived in Paris on the 20th. He was shortly joined by Mengaldo, whom he disliked. As Aleardi was still in the French capital, the Venetian government had three Parisian emissaries, all bearing different instructions, all staying at the same hotel (the Bristol in the Place Vendôme), and each living one floor above the other. Tommaseo resented the others' presence, and there was therefore very little coordination between them.[93]

to Taylor's convincing thesis that British action was a crucial factor in preventing France from intervening in the tense days that followed Custozza. Taylor writes (*The Italian Problem*, p. 142): 'The extreme impatience which Cavaignac displayed in the intervening three days [5–8 Aug.] is a clear and decisive indication that France was very nearly involved in war and that war was only averted by the prompt action of Normanby and Palmerston.' There is some confusion as to when the news of the fall of Milan reached Paris. Taylor (*ibid.*) says it was 7 Aug., but Boyer (*La seconde République*, p. 223) claims that information only arrived on the evening of the 9th and that even then it was considered as doubtful.

[92] See Pieri, *Storia militare*, p. 336 for the possibilities of Milanese resistance.

[93] Tommaseo recounts how, in order to save money, he ate only bread and an apple for lunch, and then hid the apple cores from the servants at the opulent Hotel Bristol; Tommaseo, *Venezia*, vol. 1, p. 151 n. 399. Aleardi went back to Italy in September, but Valentino Pasini then arrived to further safeguard Venice's interests in Paris. Pasini wrote to Manin on 2 Oct. 1848: 'I must tell you, my friend, what I could have told you a week after I arrived in Paris. It is

By mid-month the Italian presence at Paris had reached ridiculous proportions. Mazzini decided that the moment had come for an alliance between France, Switzerland and republican Italy, and therefore dispatched Cattaneo and Ruffoni to Paris on 9 August. Their arrival only helped to swell the already crowded expatriate ranks. Cattaneo, writing in English to his English wife, commented accurately on the excessive number of emissaries, and the confusion that reigned amongst them:

Here there are many who give out themselves as charged with powers from Lombardy, such as Lugo, Guerrieri, Bargnani, Frapolli, besides me and my companion. This is not well ... There are also other people who write and speak, but the whole of them very ill-informed and full of prejudices, such as De Filippi, Sega, Ronna. The princess [Cristina di Belgioioso] is to open her saloon next week, she is full of zeal, but, as you see, there is not a trace of the political *man of business* in all this.[94]

None the less, despite the presence of so many envoys and the persistence of personal antagonisms,[95] the Venetian request for aid did put new pressure on the French. The significance of the Venetian appeal, presented on 23 August to Cavaignac by Tommaseo, was twofold. At this time Venice, unlike Milan, was both unconquered by the Austrians and independent from Piedmont. The standing of her emissaries could therefore not be disputed as Brignole and Ricci had disputed the rights of the Lombards in Paris. And, in aiding Venice, the French republicans were

sad that Tommaseo, for all his good qualities, has such an exaggerated sense of *amour propre*, and such a frantic jealousy of any other person ... He is certainly necessary in Paris in order to satisfy the Venetians who believe him more useful here than he could possibly be. Although a man of extraordinary talents he lacks those qualities which appear of secondary importance, but which are essential to a diplomat. He lacks patience, he has little knowledge of the world, he has a limited grasp of facts, he does not have the ability to choose between what should and should not be done, and his judgments are based too much on personal considerations' (MCV, Doc. Manin, no. 2436 (not published in Bonghi, *Valentino Pasini*)).

94 Caddeo (ed.), *Epistolario di Carlo Cattaneo*, vol. 1 (1949), p. 271, letter of 28 Aug. 1848.

95 Frapolli refused to be one of Cattaneo's colleagues, despite Mazzini's instructions. Tommaseo wrote that Cattaneo saw no one and was not representing Italy. He added, with a grain of truth, that for Cattaneo 'Milan is the Jerusalem of the new Israel'; see Ciampini, *Vita di Nicolò Tommaseo*, p. 503. On the other hand the Princess Belgioioso sought to make up for having supported the monarchist position. She wrote to Cattaneo at this time from Grenoble (MRM, archivio Cattaneo, cart. no. 4, plico xiv, no. 38): 'Now that we shall be in the same ranks how I regret and regret and regret having contributed to leading my fellow citizens astray.' For an interesting account of Princess Belgioioso's life and an assessment of her writings on 1848, see the introduction by S. Bertone to C. di Belgioioso, *Il 1848 a Milano e a Venezia*, pp. 5–48.

not furthering the dynastic ambitions of Charles Albert, nor had their conduct to be bound by any provisos from Turin.

Tommaseo made good use of the strength of Venice's position by hastily publishing an *Appel à la France*. This shrewdly appealed to the French sense of honour, which Tommaseo knew to be a strong emotive factor in French politics:

I will not speak of the hopes of material advantage which might encourage France; I would blush to narrow and lower the question in taking from it the grandeur which alone gives it importance in my eyes. It is in one single consideration that I sum it up. France has in this moment the right to aid us by the most effectual means, because she has the duty to do so.[96]

It is unlikely that Cavaignac or Bastide felt deeply moved on reading Tommaseo's appeal. They would undoubtedly have ignored it had they been sure that the mediation was to be accepted by both Austria and Piedmont. But whereas Piedmont was quick to agree, Austria showed every sign of refusing. The French leaders had only been able to temporise in early August by claiming mediation as a viable alternative to war. If Austria now refused mediation, Cavaignac would be forced to choose between armed intervention or a humiliating repudiation of France's oft-stated promises to Italy.

Unfortunately for Cavaignac, by mid-August Austria felt strong enough to resist English and French pressure to join them at the conference table. Wessenberg, the Austrian foreign minister, fortified by Radetzky's victories in northern Italy and by German and Russian backing, held an audience on 22 August with the English and French representatives in Vienna, Ponsonby and Delacour. He diplomatically informed them that while the Austrian cabinet did not decline the Anglo-French offer, it could not see its way to accepting it. What this meant was more clearly spelled out on 24 August, when Wessenberg informed the Austrian ambassadors of the European capitals that since Lombardy had now been reconquered, 'discussion about its future will be to no avail'.[97]

Wessenberg's refusal caused consternation and anger among the French council of ministers. Throughout August Cavaignac and Bastide had been trying to persuade the English that if Austria refused, diplomatic mediation should give way to *armed* mediation by the two countries. Cavaignac had proposed armed mediation as early as 9 August, in response

---

[96] N. Tommaseo, *Appel à la France*, p. 8. Jennings (*France and Europe*, pp. 195ff) has a good analysis of French public opinion at this time and quotes de Tocqueville writing to his friend Beaumont: 'The only wish here is to save the honour of France and, above all, to preserve peace' (p. 195).

[97] Boyer, *La seconde République*, pp. 259–60.

to the Austrian invasion of the Legations.[98] He told Normanby that Austria 'had no more right to Bologna than to Lyons'. In the next two weeks, Gustave de Beaumont, the new French ambassador at London, kept insisting to Palmerston on the necessity for joint armed mediation, though he did not stipulate its precise nature. Palmerston refused to consider Britain getting involved militarily in northern Italy, saying that he had already gone as far as he could to defuse the situation.

However, the Venetian request for help when combined with Austrian intransigence lent new urgency and content to the French idea of armed mediation. The French decided to prepare a military expedition to Venice. In Marseilles more than three thousand troops were put on alert, and at Toulon frigates from the Mediterranean fleet took on board three months' provisions. On 29 August Bastide wrote to Beaumont in London: 'Venice must be occupied without delay ... The republic approaches the decisive moment when it may have to appeal to the force of its ideas.'[99] Bastide further instructed Beaumont to make every effort to gain British cooperation, with the aim of winning for Venice either 'an Anglo-French garrison or a French garrison and an English naval division'.

Clearly, part of the French plan was to threaten the occupation of Venice in order to scare the Austrians into accepting diplomatic mediation. Pressure on the English served to make Palmerston, in his turn, warn

[98] Jennings, *France and Europe*, pp. 175–6.
[99] Taylor, *The Italian Problem*, p. 157 and n. 2. Jennings (*France and Europe*, p. 187 and n. 67) has by far the clearest account of the preparation of the expedition to Venice, based on an examination of two Marseilles newspapers, *Gazette du Midi* and *Le Sémaphore de Marseilles*. That some news filtered through to Venice about the French preparations can be seen from the documents in ACV, Municip., Atti di Uff., 1845–9, viii, 5/32 (1848). These contain details of arrangements made between 20 and 25 Sept. for the lodging of '5,000 French troops who are about to arrive'. The Zichy, Brandolin and Rezzonico palaces were to be put at the disposal of the French. In early September Manin received an extraordinary 'secret letter', dated 26 Aug., and apparently from General Oudinot, commander of the army of the Alps (MCV, Doc. Manin, no. 800). But the letter's contents and its ungrammatical French throw considerable doubt upon its authenticity: 'Voulant profiter du Courrier qui part aujourd'hui pour la Lombardie, je vous adresse mon cher ami Manin, comme sachant que vous êtes le président de la République de Venise et que vous ne cessé de veiller à la défense de cette ville, Recevez en conséquence ce conseil d'amitié; c'est d'écrire au Général Garibaldi, qui se trouve en ce moment en Lombardie, lui dire que lorsque la lutte recommencera avec les barbares autrichiens, de fair sonner le tocsin dans toutes les parroisses de la Lombardie, et que, dans le cas que les médiations de l'Angleterre et de la France seraient sans éffets et qu'après le délai expiré de l'armistice, le soulévement soit général dans toute l'Italie que la réusite sera certaine, en faisant fuir où exterminer l'étranger pour l'indépendance de l'Italie. Je suis avec 80 mille hommes en attendant de vous donner l'accolade fraternelle. Tout à vous, Oudinot.'

Austria of the dire consequences of their continued refusal. But it would be incorrect to maintain that the French were only playing an elaborate diplomatic game, without any serious intention of sending troops to Venice. All the participants in and observers of the situation in Paris were convinced of the strong possibility of French armed intervention. Angelo Mengaldo, the Venetian emissary, had two important audiences with Cavaignac, one on 29 August and the other, to which he was suddenly summoned, on the evening of the 31st.[100] On the first occasion, Cavaignac questioned him 'with great urgency' on the condition of Venice and whether the city could hold out until the arrival of French troops. On the 31st, in the presence of Normanby, Cavaignac 'asked new and more penetrating questions as to the state of Venice and its ability to resist'. Mengaldo thought that this second audience had been decisive in securing intervention. Tommaseo saw Bastide on 30 August, and wrote home full of hope about French intentions.

By 3 September Thom, the Austrian chargé d'affaires in Paris, was writing to Wessenberg: 'The opinion that the French government only wants to intimidate us and that it will not press matters to extremes seems to me very hazardous.'[101] The English were equally alarmed. *The Times* warned its readers: 'There is reason to apprehend that the protracted resistance of the Republican party in Venice and the solicitations of M. Tommaseo, its emissary in Paris, have shaken those resolutions of the French government, which seemed to promise the maintenance of the peace of Europe.'[102] Normanby confided in his diary, 'I fear that the additional difficulty I have lately found in controlling the impatience of General Cavaignac in those questions of foreign policy immediately under discussion, arises from a growing conviction, urged upon him by many, that the best safety for the Republic is to be found in war.'[103] On 31 August Palmerston tried to urge his Cabinet colleagues to agree to joint armed mediation in Venice, as a means of controlling French actions in Italy. He was overruled, but made it clear that he thought the French would go on regardless.[104]

---

[100] For both conversations, see Mengaldo's diary in Meneghetti, *Il Cavaignac de Venezia*, pp. 50–2. On 19 Aug. the French had decided to send two warships into Venetian waters to discourage an Austrian attack on Venice from the sea. Austria persistently refused to include Venice in the armistice, pointing out that under the terms of the Salasco armistice, all Piedmontese troops and ships should have left Venice, which could now only be treated as a rebel city.

[101] Taylor, *The Italian Problem*, p. 159.

[102] *The Times*, first leader, 5 Sept 1848.

[103] The Marquis of Normanby, *A Year of Revolution from a Journal kept in Paris in 1848*, vol. 2, p. 199, entry of 6 Sept.

[104] Taylor, *The Italian Problem*, pp. 154–5. Palmerston wrote to Russell on 30 Aug.:

The crunch came at a secret meeting of the French council of ministers held probably on 3 or 4 September 1848.[105] Bastide, who had always struck Venetian emissaries as being particularly well disposed towards their city, spoke in favour of ordering the expedition to set sail from Toulon immediately. Lamoricière, the minister of war and a consistent proponent of intervention, supported Bastide. They were opposed by Cavaignac. The two sides failed to reach agreement, the matter was put to the vote, and Cavaignac won the day by a majority of one. Orders were then sent to Marseilles cancelling the organisation of the expedition.

Manin's much-cherished dream was thus denied fulfilment by the slenderest of margins. British refusal to cooperate in the venture was probably the crucial reason for Cavaignac's eventual opposition. Normanby had warned him that any action was premature, that the Austrians had not yet definitely rejected the diplomatic mediation, and that any drastic French move could well alienate the British Cabinet. Cavaignac was no Napoleon – the risk of isolation in a European war was one he was not prepared to take. France's lack of preparation for war must also have weighed heavily with him. Mengaldo, in spite of his optimism of 31 August, came to the reluctant conclusion a few days later that the French

'With regard to Venice, it seems to me that we have to choose whether there shall be peace or war between Austria and France, and whether we shall deliberately let France loose to settle the affairs of Italy in her own way or not. If she goes to Venice without our consent and sanction Austria will consider it an act of war, and the next step will be the entrance of France into Lombardy. If we associate ourselves morally and politically with the move, Austria will not venture to treat it as war, but will deal with it as an element of negotiation ... France now says that if the negotiation is declined she must send a garrison to hold Venice, that she will do it without us if we prefer, but that she prefers doing it with our concurrence. Do we believe what she says or not? If we do not, then let us give her a civil answer, and take the chance of our incredulity being well founded. But if we believe she will go on, and that is my belief, we must say something about it' (G. P. Gooch (ed.), *Later Correspondence of Lord John Russell*, vol. 1, pp. 340–1). Russell replied on the same day that if Austria rejected mediation he was not prepared to go any further but would rather maintain a peaceful attitude; see his letter quoted from the Palmerston papers by O. Barié, *L'Inghilterra e il problema italiano nel 1848–9*, p. 174.

105 Jennings again gives the best account (*France and Europe*, p. 192), based on D. Stern, *Histoire de la révolution de 1848*, vol. 2, pp. 522–3. No minutes of the meetings of the council of ministers seem to have survived. F. A. De Luna, *The French Republic under Cavaignac*, pp. 357–8, has nothing to add and makes a number of factual errors, e.g. (p. 358), 'France late in September dispatched an expeditionary force of 3,000 troops from Toulon, but recalled it after a few days.' All the historians who deal with the international situation in these weeks make the mistake of assuming that Venice was once again a republic after 11 Aug. 1848.

ministers were too preoccupied by 'the highly uncertain state of affairs in Paris and the provinces' to intervene in northern Italy.[106]

Fortunately for the French their abandonment of Italy was to be partially masked by a quite independent Austrian decision to accept in principle the Anglo-French mediation. Wessenberg, like Palmerston, became convinced between 29 August and 2 September that the French meant what they said. Delacour had more or less issued him with an ultimatum in Vienna, and Thom had been told by Normanby that if the Austrians persisted in their attitude war was inevitable. In some considerable haste Wessenberg therefore decided to accept the mediation. Even so, he thought that his acceptance had come too late; on 9 September he wrote to the Austrian ambassadors at St Petersburg and Berlin saying that he feared the French expedition had already set sail.[107] If that was the case, he continued, then 'Austria awaits the outcome of the crisis with calm and with the confidence that comes from knowing that she is in the right'.

The French expedition had not sailed. On 7 September Bastide frankly admitted to Thom that 'we find ourselves, or to speak more accurately we have put ourselves, in a very embarrassing position'.[108] The following day Paris knew of the Austrian change of heart. Surprised and grateful, Bastide hurried to communicate the news to the assembly.

In fact, the terms on which Wessenberg had accepted the mediation made nonsense of it. Although he had been greatly alarmed by the apparent intentions of the French, Wessenberg had also been careful not to lose control of the situation. While accepting the mediation in principle, he emphasised that the bases proposed by the French – Austrian abandonment of Lombardy, etc. – were quite unacceptable to Vienna. He suggested that new proposals be put forward, which would correspond more closely to the position after Custozza and the fall of Milan.

This was a clever move. The Austrians had no real intention of coming to any agreement, and were only playing for time. Palmerston realised this and was angry at the French for so eagerly accepting what amounted to a death sentence on the mediation.[109] But Cavaignac and Bastide, in order to save face, to extricate themselves from their 'very embarrassing

---

[106] MCV, Doc. Manin, vol. 9, no. 97, letter to Manin begun on 2 Sept. 1848, finished on the 4th.

[107] Letter published in R. Moscati, *La diplomazia*, app. 1, pp. 86–8. See also Boyer, *La seconde République*, pp. 272–3.

[108] Taylor, *The Italian Problem*, p. 161.

[109] *Ibid.*, pp. 164–5. Carlo Leoni wrote in his diary on 7 Sept. 1848: 'Today the *Gazzetta* says that the government has received notification from Vienna that Austria accepts the Anglo-French mediation. To accept the mediation means little; what matters is that they accept the conditions...' (Leoni, 'Cronaca, 1848', p. 482).

position', were only too prepared to clutch at any straw thrown them.

The second crisis of French aid to Italy in little more than a month thus ended with a vague acceptance of the Anglo-French mediation. The French expedition to Venice, which would have had major implications for the Italian republicans and the wider European revolutionary movement, was replaced by a seemingly endless debate as to where the conference of the Great Powers should take place, who was to be invited and what was to be discussed.

Stalemate

As the last months of 1848 slipped away, the Great Powers pursued the question of mediation with less and less enthusiasm. After the October revolution in Vienna had briefly raised and then dashed Italian hopes, Austrian policy became increasingly intransigent under the hard-headed Prince Felix Schwarzenberg. The new Austrian prime minister aimed to conciliate France while himself making no concessions. This policy was an unqualified success. On 15 September Bastide had renewed his appeal to Britain to aid France in preventing the reconquest of Venice. But Palmerston firmly refused to get involved in any joint armed mediation, and warned Cavaignac that any unilateral French action would be regarded most unfavourably. All French attempts to get Venice included in the armistice proved fruitless, and Bastide had to content himself with an assurance from Wessenberg that Austria would not attempt the recapture of Venice in the immediate future. In any case, as the French presidential elections approached, French interest in northern Italy rapidly declined. Cavaignac switched his attention to Rome, hoping that aid to the Pope would earn him the Catholic vote needed to offset the rise of Louis Napoleon. After Pius IX's flight from Rome in November, Cavaignac, amidst great publicity, offered the Pope sanctuary in France. But his plan backfired, for Pius chose to remain at Gaeta, as the guest of the king of Naples.[110] This last failure proved a fitting end to Cavaignac's and Bastide's vacillating and unprincipled Italian diplomacy.

Tommaseo, Pasini, and other Italian envoys stayed in Paris, kicking their heels and bickering.[111] Pasini in particular made every effort to

---

[110] Jennings, *France and Europe*, pp. 246–50. On Schwarzenberg see Taylor, *The Italian Problem*, pp. 171–80.

[111] See Gambarin, in *La Repubblica veneta*, vol. 1, p. 249; Meneghetti, *Il Cavaignac di Venezia*, p. 57; MCV, Doc. Manin, nos. 2448 and 4139, letters from Pasini and Serena to Manin, 18 Nov. and 11 Dec. 1848. Cattaneo also remained in Paris in September and October, preparing for publication his work on Milan in 1848. Although few authors ever write books as memorable as Cattaneo's, the rest of us can glean some comfort from the fact that he too suffered more than

hasten the conference, and gain Venetian representation at it. But he was fighting a losing battle, since to French indifference and Austrian intransigence was added England's determination that Venice should return to Austria. Palmerston, in a letter of 16 October 1848, bluntly told Manin:

I have to inform you that it forms no part of the proposals made by the British Government to the Government of Austria for the pacification of Italy that Venice should cease to be 'under the Imperial Crown', and that consequently it would be wise for the people of Venice to come to an understanding with the Austrian Government.[112]

Clearly, any earlier British sympathies for Venice had been replaced by preoccupation lest the city remain a potential *casus belli*. Beaumont, France's ambassador in London, observed: 'To Lord Palmerston the success of Venice in defending itself is a great nuisance.'[113]

Eventually, early in February 1849, British, French and Piedmontese representatives did actually arrive in Brussels in anticipation of the opening of a congress there. However, Schwarzenberg continued to procrastinate on the bases for any discussion. On 24 February 1849 Palmerston refused to give Austria a written guarantee that Britain would not demand the ceding of Lombardy to Piedmont, and with this refusal 'the mediation may be said to have virtually come to an end'.[114] The Austrians decided against sending a delegation to Brussels, and the congress never began.

The Venetians, in the end, received only one substantial benefit from the French republicans. On 19 August 1848, as we have seen, the warship *Jupiter* and the frigate *Psyche* were sent by the French government into Venetian waters to ensure that the city did not fall before the French government had made up its mind whether to intervene or not.[115] Then in September, as some compensation for the failure of the Venetian expedition to materialise, Bastide ordered the two ships to remain and two more, the *Asmodée* and *Brazier*, joined them. Ostensibly they were to

---

a little self-doubt during its production. He wrote in English to his wife on 22 Sept.: 'Anna my dear, My poor book is printing. I never was so unfortunate in my life as in this first essay before a foreign public. I felt under the pressure of imbecility. I was in necessity of doing and undoing at least four times. Never in my life I scribbled so much and so uselessly. All this made me unhappy at the utmost. In my present circumstances I have the distaste for life at such a tempting extremity, that if my existence was not a necessity in this moment for (*Epistolario di Carlo Cattaneo* (ed. R. Caddeo), vol. I, p. 290). you, I would have given it away. My dear, I feel as if upon the rakes...'

112 For the original, see MCV, Doc. Manin, no. 965.
113 Quoted in Taylor, *The Italian Problem*, p. 167.
114 *Ibid.*, p. 213.
115 See above, p. 288 n. 100; also Boyer, *La seconde République*, pp. 269–70.

safeguard the interests of French citizens in Venice. In the event, the four French ships, all of which stayed through the winter of 1848–9, served to restrain the Austrians from imposing too vigorous a blockade on the besieged city. Schwarzenberg realised that it was better to allow essential food supplies to go through than to risk rekindling French anger over the fate of Venice.

Conclusion

Venice's fate in the autumn of 1848 was decided, both on a local and international level, within the space of a few weeks. It was in early September that the French council of ministers, having assembled an expedition to sail to Venice, voted by a majority of one not to send it. And it was less than a month later that Manin decided to crush the Mazzinian opposition in Venice, and reject plans for Venice to become a republican centre. Giuseppe Mazzini was convinced that the two areas of activity, the local and the international, were closely linked and that united republican pressure on the French would force them to intervene. Obviously unaware that early September had been the decisive turning point, Mazzini, still full of hope, wrote on 22 September to Manin, outlining his strategy:

We can expect nothing from the Piedmontese as far as the war goes . . . ; from France we can expect little if we leave them to diplomacy . . . We know all the conditions and habits of the French; and in addition I am very well acquainted with the desires and nature of Bastide. We need to create in France a situation from which they cannot escape unless by dishonour or war . . . Proclaim the republican government; call Lombardy and Italy to follow you, make the call in the last resort to the national Italian constituent assembly (not to an Italian Diet). We will follow you immediately. And the Lombardo-Venetian-Ligurian insurrection must bring in France by the very nature of things.[116]

Such thinking reflected the excess of voluntarism which so often characterised Mazzini's proposals. It was extremely doubtful, as the failure in the Val d'Intelvi was to show, that the objective conditions existed for a Lombard insurrection, let alone a Venetian or Ligurian one. Equally, it is unlikely that the re-proclamation of the Venetian republic and united action by the northern Italian republicans would have made much difference at Paris in August and September 1848. Fear of isolation in a European war and the grave internal situation of France decided Cavaignac against the Venetian expedition, not the disunity of the Italian republicans, or their lack of ideological clarity. This is not to say that the actions

[116] Gambarin, 'Il Mazzini, il Tommaseo, il Manin', pp. 356–7.

of the republicans in Lombardy-Venetia had no influence on French policy in 1848. Their decision to make no clear appeal to the French in the early months of the war had been a major reason for French non-intervention. But by late August 1848 they only had limited leverage on republicans of the Cavaignac variety, whatever they did.

However, if Mazzini greatly overestimated the possible effect in Paris of united republican action, he was probably on much sounder ground with regard to Italy and Venice. At a vital moment, when Charles Albert had been discredited and the initiative had clearly swung to them, the Italian republicans remained divided and without a focal point. This was not Mazzini's responsibility, but Manin's. Had Manin chosen to re-declare the republic after 11 August and adopt the programme of the Italian Club, he would have made Venice the heart of anti-Austrian resistance, and attracted to it all those who at a later stage were to flock to Rome, Giuseppe Garibaldi included. Instead he followed a conservative and insular policy. Fearful lest social order be disturbed, unwilling to break with Piedmont, Manin chose to wait upon events, rather than himself try to influence them. If Mazzini was guilty of an excess of voluntarism, Manin after 11 August erred in the opposite direction. Lacking any breadth of concept, or any confidence in the programme of the radical republicans, Manin refused Venice the possibility of becoming the centre of Italian insurrectional activity. As a result, the city waited for a French expedition that never arrived, and as the autumn mists enshrouded the lagoon, Venice's isolation, both physical and military, increased.

8

The winter of the revolution, October 1848 to April 1849

The French decision not to intervene in northern Italy was but one event amongst many which confirmed the turn to the right on a European scale in the autumn and winter months of 1848. After the French expedition to Venice had been voted down, Venetian hopes were once more raised by news that filtered through of the October revolution in Vienna. For a fortnight it seemed possible that events at the heart of the empire would again prove, as they had done in March, the decisive driving force for Italian liberation. But the workers and students of Vienna could not survive Windischgrätz's onslaught unaided. The Viennese revolution had begun when troops destined for use against the Hungarians were forcibly prevented from leaving the capital, and it was only at the hands of the Hungarians that the revolution could be saved. However, the Hungarian generals, having defeated Jelačic and reached the Austrian border, hesitated before taking the last and greatest leap into illegality – the invasion of Austria itself. Kossuth hastened to the border to urge the army across, but precious days had been lost and even then General Moga, the Hungarian commander, acted with little enthusiasm. On 30 October Jelačic halted the Hungarian army at Schwechat, a few kilometres from Vienna. Two days later Vienna's desperate resistance to Windischgrätz finally crumbled. The chance of taking Habsburg forces between two fires had been irretrievably lost. This lack of united action between the Viennese revolutionaries and the Magyar army was probably the most clamorous example of the complete failure of the revolutionary forces to combine on an international scale in 1848. Coming hard on the heels of French non-intervention in northern Italy, it provided clear proof that the struggle against the counter-revolution would be waged only on a national or even municipal basis.

The defeat of the Viennese revolution saw the triumph of the most able and intransigent of the Austrian statesmen of 1848–9 – Prince Felix Schwarzenberg. He became prime minister on 21 November and six days later outlined to the Viennese Diet his project for a constitution which would reconfirm the centralised nature of the empire. He aimed to make as few concessions as possible to the various nationalities of the empire while relying on his army chiefs to overcome all remaining resistance. In the winter of 1848–9 the focal point of resistance in Italy was Venice, and Schwarzenberg did not hide his desire for the immediate subjugation of the city. In February 1849 he wrote to Thom:

As long as the revolutionary government in Venice still stands as a living symbol of the subversive spirit which arouses Italy, as long as the so-called Republic of St Mark offers an asylum to all the entrepreneurs of revolution who have come to no good elsewhere, ideas of order will not be able to triumph in the rest of the peninsula.[1]

The military situation

Schwarzenberg may have wanted to reduce Venice as quickly as possible, but a number of serious obstacles lay in his path. Having accepted the Anglo-French mediation, the Austrians had to be careful what they did. They had always refused to include Venice in the armistice, but Schwarzenberg realised that an all-out attack on Venice might well arouse French public opinion and undo the good work of August and September. It was much better to let the mediation die a slow death than risk provoking France. In any case, the Austrians lacked the necessary forces to start a serious siege of the city. The Hungarians, and not the Italians, were the major Austrian preoccupation in this period, and most of the army of Italy was with Radetzky in Lombardy, guarding against a possible Piedmontese renewal of the war. Marshal Welden had 21,000 men in the Veneto in October 1848, but a third of these were on the sick list. The Austrian troops stationed on the mainland opposite Venice were to suffer severely from malaria throughout the winter.

Facing them was a city determined to resist and endowed with considerable natural defences. Venice was not going to capitulate like Udine, Padua or even Vicenza. The lagoon, with its tides, sandbanks, and intricate system of channels, was a potentially fatal hazard for enemy boats trying to reach the city, as many of Venice's opponents had discovered in the past. The city was also surrounded by a network of island forts, a legacy of both the Republican and Napoleonic eras. Clearly, any siege of Venice was going to be, as it had been in 1813–14, a long and exhausting task.

With the enemy at their watery gates, the Venetians at last set about the task that they had so signally avoided in the early months of the revolution – the formation of an efficient fighting force. For this Pepe and

[1] Dispatch of 6 Feb. published in Moscati, *La diplomazia*, app. i, p. 115.

Cavedalis must take most credit.[2] Although they came from very different backgrounds – Pepe the southerner, *carbonaro* and life-long revolutionary, Cavedalis the cautious former Austrian officer from Friuli – they shared a Napoleonic past and the conviction that Venice would not survive for long unless her troops were properly disciplined and organised. Their efforts were given added impetus by the long-awaited arrival in September 1848 of 6,000 of the promised French rifles. By 8 October the Venetian forces consisted of no less than 19,372 men.[3] The nucleus of this force was the six infantry legions of just under 10,000 men in all. The majority of the soldiers were Venetians but many had also come from the Venetian provinces, either after the surrender of their native cities or else when the Austrians threatened the reconquered areas with a fresh wave of conscription. The sixth legion mixed Venetians and Neapolitan volunteers, and there were many contingents from other parts of Italy – 600 Lombards, 1,200 men from Bologna and 3,700 from the three papal regiments which had been in Venice since early summer. There were also 100 Swiss. The crack artillery company, the *Bandiera e Moro*, included many university students and was to perform prodigious feats in 1849.[4]

At the end of October the army commanders resolved to take some action. They were spurred on by the news from Vienna and had formed a Hungarian legion in the hope that some of the Hungarians stationed on the shores of the lagoon would desert to Venice.[5] Pepe decided to attack Mestre, the small town on the mainland side of the railway bridge. It was defended at this time by 1,500 Austrian troops with six cannon.

[2] For short biographies of Pepe and Cavedalis, see above pp. 221 and 269.

[3] MCV, Doc. Manin, no. 2936, list drawn up by the cavalry and infantry superintendence. When the 6,000 rifles arrived in Turin there appears to have been some doubt as to whether the Piedmontese would send them on to Venice. In Turin Paleocapa, to his credit, wrote an insistent letter to Casati as the then prime minister demanding that the rifles be sent immediately: 'I hope that it will not be possible to say that having abandoned Venice it is now Piedmont's wish to deprive her of the means by which she can defend herself' (AST, carte politiche diverse, cart. 25, fasc. 150, no. 40).

[4] The most complete and painstaking account of the Venetian army is to be found in Jäger, *Storia dei corpi militari*. For the Bandiera and Moro company, see *Memorie istoriche dell'artiglieria Bandiera–Moro, assedio di Marghera e fatti del ponte a Venezia, 1848–9* (Documenti della Guerra Santa d'Italia, vol. 10); also the account by Tomaseo of their role in the defence of Marghera in Racc. Andreola, vol. 7, pp. 333–4. For the Friulani fleeing to Venice, see the letter from Manin to Tommaseo, 17 Nov. 1848, MCV, Doc. Manin, no. 2329. The Swiss role in the defence of Venice has been most interestingly described by J. Debrunner, *Aventures de la compagnie suisse pendant le siège*. A very good breakdown of Venetian forces in early November 1848 is to be found in the list drawn up by the chief of staff, MCV, Doc. Manin, no. 2939, 4 Nov.

[5] Racc. Andreola, vol. 4, p. 402.

On 27 October, advancing under the cover of mist, some 3,000 Venetians took the Austrian garrison by surprise, and after fierce house-to-house fighting put them to flight. The Venetians held Mestre for a few hours but then on Pepe's instructions withdrew to the fort at Marghera, taking with them 500 Austrian prisoners and a few cannon. Pepe's order of the day, written after the battle, made special mention of the Lombards Sirtori Rosaroll and Cattabeni, who, 'courageous to the point of fool-hardiness', had driven out the Austrians at bayonet-point.[6]

The sortie to Mestre was highly successful in its own way, for it served to raise Venetian spirits after the long series of defeats earlier in the revolution, and for the first time it gave them confidence in the value of volunteer troops. But it formed no part of a wider strategy to take advantage of the Austrians' temporary weakness, nor did it form the prelude to guerrilla action in the Veneto. The sortie to Mestre mirrored in military terms Manin's political decision not to make Venice the centre of insurrectional activity for Lombardy and Venetia. There was no liaison between Venice's army commanders and the attempted insurrections in the Val d'Intelvi, the Valtellina and the Bergamasco, which also occurred at the end of October. These flickerings of Lombard revolt, upon which Mazzini placed so much hope, were quickly and savagely extinguished by Marshal Haynau.

Cavedalis was insistent that little could be done until the Venetians were properly trained, and there was much substance to his argument. In addition, many of the Venetian troops were suffering from the cramped, insanitary conditions of the forts and the rigours of winter; in early November over five thousand of them were on the sick list. Manin too was against further military action, hoping that the good offices of Piedmont and France could still get Venice included in the armistice.

But it is also clear that a strong undercurrent of dissatisfaction and subversion continued in the Lombard and Venetian provinces for many months after the Austrians had returned. To take just one example, in February 1849 at the village of Solagna near Bassano, the inhabitants

---

[6] Jäger, *Storia dei corpi militari*, p. 271. The Italian Club had urged the government to take some military action just before the Mestre sortie in fact took place. On 15 Oct. they pointed out that the Austrian army was again without orders from Vienna, and that discord between Hungarians and Croats was growing in its ranks; MCV, Agg. Manin, IX/35. During a skirmish two days before the Mestre sortie, Alessandro Poerio, the Calabrian poet, was hit twice in the right leg. The leg was amputated, but he died of the wound on 3 Nov. 1848. Poerio, although sickly and short-sighted, had enrolled as an ordinary private under Pepe, and came north with the Neapolitans to fight for Italian independence. Other outstanding figures in the Mestre battle were Ugo Bassi and Francesco Baldis-serotto; Marchesi, *Storia documentata*, pp. 318–20.

stoned four soldiers who had shot dead a local youth while he was trying to escape arrest. He and his companions had been caught singing patriotic songs. The village was fined 3,000 Austrian lire and had fifty soldiers garrisoned there.[7] Austrian requisitioning was severe and anyone caught in possession of firearms was immediately shot. There is evidence from various parts of the Veneto of small numbers of peasants and artisans being put to death for this offence.[8] These isolated acts of defiance could not have led to a general uprising in this period. But the Venetians made no further attempts to harry the Austrians, either by sorties or by forming guerrilla bands in the Venetian hills. As the months passed, Cavedalis's purely defensive thinking, at first the only sensible policy, came under increasing criticism.

By the end of February 1849 the number of troops in the Venetian army had dropped to 17,396. The main reason for this drop was that all but one hundred of the Roman soldiers, tired of being cooped up in Venice, had been sent back to the Papal States. Five of their senior officers had complained about living conditions, and Cavedalis had responded by denouncing the licentiousness and ill-discipline of the Roman volunteers.[9] But in spite of this loss, all the defences of the city had been considerably strengthened, and when the Piedmontese general Oliverò came to Venice in February he was greatly impressed both by the state of the fortifications and by the discipline of the army.[10]

No such praise could be applied to the Venetian navy. The Piedmontese

[7] BBV, Gonz. 22.10.27, 'Cronaca del 1848 riguardante Bassano', 11–22 Feb. 1849, no pagination.

[8] See, for instance, A. Benedetti, *Pordenone e i paesi del Friuli occidentale nel Risorgimento*, pp. 131–2 nn. 36–8. Of the seven men shot in or around Pordenone in this period, two were fishermen, one a peasant, one a tenant farmer, one a sailor, one a carpenter and one a bricklayer. On 6 Nov. 1848 Alvise Mocenigo, who was in Florence by this time, wrote that the letters from his agents 'are full of horrendous stories of Austrian violence' (ASV, fondo Mocenigo, b. 150, letters 1848, no number). The wool factory of Alessandro Rossi at Schio was doing a roaring trade because no one would buy Austrian cloth; see the letter from Alessandro's brother Giovanni to Valentino Pasini of 24 Nov. 1848 in G. Rossi, *Lettere dal sacerdote Giovanni Rossi, profugo in Firenze a Valentino Pasini a Parigi, ottobre–novembre 1848*, no pagination.

[9] On 4 November 244 soldiers were under arrest, of whom 92 came from the second papal regiment alone; MCV, Doc. Manin, no. 2939, report from the chief of staff. For the papal complaints see MCV, Agg. Manin, 1/32, letter of 22 Oct. 1848. Cavedalis also had plenty to say about the Lombard legion, some of whom he said were no better than scum, while others he dismissed as 'under the influence of communist propaganda' (Cavedalis, *I Commentari*, vol. 2, p. 35).

[10] G. Pepe, *Histoire des révolutions et des guerres d'Italie*, p. 204. The chief of staff's report on the Venetian army is to be found in MCV, Doc. Manin, no. 2999.

fleet returned to Venetian waters on 27 October, the Turin government having used the Austrian failure to return abandoned siege material from Peschiera as an excuse for breaking the conditions of the Salasco armistice, and sending their ships back to Venice. Together with the four French ships stationed in Venetian waters, the Piedmontese fleet was able to ensure that the Austrians never maintained an effective blockade in these months. The small imperial fleet was in poor condition in any case, and would probably have been unable to prevent supplies from reaching Venice. All this lulled the Venetian leaders into a false sense of security. With the easy-going Graziani in command of the navy, little was done to build up an independent Venetian fleet.

One of the crucial problems that should have been tackled at this time was the acquisition of a steam-powered vessel. Although the Venetians had a number of well-equipped sailing frigates, they had no steamships and could thus be easily outmanoeuvred should the wind fail them. Earlier in 1848 Nani and Zanardini, the first Venetian representatives at Paris, had started to make enquiries about purchasing a steamship. But in early May they had been told to drop the idea by Manin because 'in a few days the Neapolitan fleet will be here with five steamships of the line'.[11] This was yet another striking example of the Venetians relying, with dire consequences, upon the Italian monarchs in the early part of the revolution. In October Manin issued fresh instructions, this time to Serena and Lombardo, to find the right ship, but neither they nor Pasini were able to make a satisfactory purchase In January 1849 Manin seemed convinced that the French government would aid Venice in this matter, but a month later Pasini was forced to admit that he had been obstructed at every turn.[12]

Once again it is possible in retrospect to see that a number of Venetians thought more clearly than Manin or Graziani on this issue. As early as September 1848, Luigi Fincati, one of the ablest of the Venetian naval officers, warned Manin of the possible consequences of neglecting the navy. His initiative was followed by the Italian Club, who in December urged the government to speed up the construction of the frigate *L'Italia* and to make full use of the arsenal. Many other letters were written to the government on the same subject, but little or nothing was done.[13] The Venetians were to pay dearly for leaving to others the task of controlling

[11] MCV, Doc. Manin, vol. 9, no. 31, copy of Manin's letter of 3 May 1848.
[12] The details of Serena and Lombardo's attempts are to be found in MCV, Agg. Manin, XLIX/6 and 9–34. Pasini tried to obtain a steamer of 120 h.p. capable of bearing two cannon; see Bonghi, *Valentino Pasini*, pp. 379, 391, 395, 420–1 (for Manin's instructions of 24 Jan. 1849), and 493.
[13] Fincati's letter is published in Marchesi, *Storia documentata*, app. doc. XXIII. For the Italian Club see MCV, Agg. Manin, IX/47, letter of 5 Dec. 1848. See also MCV, Doc. Manin, no. 806, 8 Nov. 1848, letter of Giovanni Minotto to Manin's

the Adriatic; Tommaseo, as usual, found a pungent way of summing up the government's failure: 'the former queen of the seas ... became a slave-girl, and the winged lion no more than a water rat'.[14]

Finances

Venice was safe from land and sea, but a more insidious threat, that of bankruptcy, threatened her in the autumn of 1848. The loans of May and June had scarcely sufficed until the Piedmontese took over, and after 11 August the economic situation looked grim indeed. The city needed an estimated three and a half million lire a month, of which 2,700,000 were being spent on the war effort. Income from taxation was only in the region of 300,000 lire a month, and the government thus had the unenviable task of trying to find more than three million lire a month in order to survive.[15]

The crisis was immediate, for the provisions that reached Venice by sea had to be paid for in metallic currency, of which there was an acute shortage. On 16 August 1848 the government ordered every citizen to consign to the mint within forty-eight hours all the gold and silver he or she possessed. Cicogna, the ageing secretary to the court of appeal, whose diary is amongst the most informative of the period, tells us of the family who gave only a small amount of silver to the mint and the rest to their gondolier who hid it under his bed. But the ruse was discovered, and Cicogna comments on the need 'never to trust servants'. As Cicogna himself is credited with handing in silver worth a paltry 167 lire, he had obviously found a more secure hiding place for his family valuables. Others were far more generous, Jacopo Treves contributing gold and silver worth over 40,000 lire, Spiridione Papadopoli 18,658 lire and Leopardo Martinengo, the nobleman who had been Manin's emissary to the camp of Charles Albert, 12,895 lire. Manin himself gave valuables worth over 1,000 lire, the principal of which was his own silver cigarette case. In all, well over 1,300,000 lire's worth of gold and silver were collected in this way and melted down for use as coinage. But despite this measure, and many other generous gifts, the Venetian mint could only issue coins to the value of 2,238,082 lire during the seventeen months of the revolution.[16]

secretary, Alessandro Zanetti: 'Speak to Manin about the navy. I fear that those in power know less than their subjects about what is really happening.'

14 Tommaseo, *Venezia*, vol. 1, p. 71.

15 MCV, Doc. Manin, no. 3155, unsigned estimate of Venice's needs in the period March 1848 – April 1849.

16 Tucci, 'Le emissioni monetarie', pp. 2–3. The majority of this money was made up of *talleri levantini*, which were worth six Au. lire each. The full details of

Coins took time to mint, and at the end of August the government could not afford to wait. It wrote to the chamber of commerce on 3 September praising the 'willing patriotism of this valuable class of citizens' and demanding an immediate loan of 175,000 florins (525,000 lire) in hard cash.[17] Giuseppe Reali, as president of the chamber, had the task of collecting the money, and encountered some resistance. One firm of bankers, the Coen brothers, said that they could not pay since all exchange with Milan and Trieste had long ceased. The wood merchant G. B. Cadorin said that he had sacrificed everything in the Cadore and could only pay if the government lifted the ban on the exportation of timber. But Reali would not take no for an answer and all the money was collected. The principal contributor was the firm of Jacopo Levi and sons with 16,000 florins, closely followed by Angelo Papadopoli and Jacopo Treves with 14,000 florins each.

The melting down of precious metals and the aid of the chamber of commerce eased the government's immediate shortage of metallic currency, but they did not solve the long-term problem of financing the revolution. On 31 August Venice appealed to all Italy to come to its aid, and announced details of a new 'Italian' loan for ten million lire. Twenty thousand shares of five hundred lire each were to be issued, interest was 5 per cent, and repayment was promised in five years. The loan was guaranteed by a special mortgage on the Doges' palace and the Procuratie Nuove, the government buildings on St Mark's Square. Gherardo Freschi, the liberal landowner from Friuli who had been so active in promoting economic change before the revolution, was entrusted by Manin with the task of collecting money throughout the peninsula. By mid-November he was in despair. He wrote to Manin: 'I can assure you that travelling through Italy one finds so few who really cherish national independence that one loses all courage, all faith in the future.'[18] By the end of February 1849 only just over half a million lire had been received. In October 1848 the whole peninsula contributed just 26,000 lire, in November only 100,000. At a time when Venice was held in high esteem throughout Italy for her continuing resistance to the Austrians, the lack of material assistance she received was a terrible indictment of the national movement.[19]

who gave how much are to be found in ASV, Gov. Prov. 1848–9, reg. 1250. The July government had asked the patriarch to contribute church plate but Cardinal Monico, following instructions from the Pope, refused; see Bertoli, *Le origini del movimento cattolico*, p. 17 and p. 44 n. 45. Cicogna's entry in his diary (MCV) is of 17 Sept. 1848.

[17] ASV, CC, b. 188, iv/57, no. 4706.

[18] MCV, Doc. Manin, no. 2031, 11 Nov. 1848.

[19] For details of the money contributed, see Pino-Branca, 'La finanza di guerra',

Faced with imminent bankruptcy, the government decided to risk issuing large amounts of Venetian paper money. The main exponent of the idea was Isacco Pesaro Maurogonato, a young Jew who had graduated in law from Padua university and was a friend of Manin's. A bank of Venice had been set up in July with the intention of providing the credit facilities which had for so long been denied Venetian businessmen by the Austrian government. The bank had a capital of four million lire, was supported by most of the wealthiest bankers and merchants in Venice, and was seen as the ideal vehicle for the issue of paper money.[20] On 19 September the triumvirs announced the first issue of *moneta patriottica* to the value of three million lire, in one-, two-, three-, and five-lire notes. The government proudly announced that forty-two of the richest citizens in Venice had voluntarily underwritten the new paper money by a loan of three million lire, but although many contributed of their own free will, the forty-two had no option and were assessed in proportion to their wealth, to the tune of 22,000 lire in every million. Once again, the register for the loan reveals the enormous resources of certain Venetian companies and families: Andrea and Pietro Giovanelli, Jacopo and Isacco Treves and the Papadopoli company all contributed in the region of 350,000 lire, while Vettore Pisani paid 200,000 lire, the Pigazzi brothers 177,000 and Loredana Morosini Gattersburg 160,000. The wealthy glass merchant Antonio Giacomuzzi refused to consign the 85,000 lire for which he had been estimated, and on 16 October the government ordered his factories and shops to be seized.[21]

Other forced loans to underwrite the *moneta patriottica* followed at regular intervals. In October one hundred and fifty of the lesser fortunes

p. 102. See also the appeals from the Venetian government to Tuscany: Manin to Gino Capponi, 2 Sept. 1848 (BNF, G. Capponi, ix/35); the triumvirate to Montanelli (MCV, Doc. Manin, no. 1095, 1 Nov. 1848), and his negative response (*ibid.*, no. 1096, 8 Nov. 1848). The Italian clubs of the various cities of the peninsula gave over 400,000 lire (Pino-Branca, 'La finanza di guerra', p. 124). Tommaseo in Paris meticulously collected and noted all the small sums offered by Parisians for the Venetian cause: 'Marie Dodie, domestique, pour deux mois, deux francs' (Ciampini, *Vita di Nicolò Tommaseo*, pp. 494–7).

20 Tucci, 'Le emissioni monetarie', pp. 4–8, Pino-Branca, 'La finanza di guerra', pp. 105–8. 8,000 shares of 500 lire each were issued. Many were sold immediately, but the municipality also selected from the tax lists those who would be cajoled into buying them. The bank was immediately to lend the government one and a half million lire, at 6 per cent, repayable in six-monthly instalments. By 8 May 1849 only 3,469½ of the bank's shares had been sold. See also Racc. Andreola, vol. 4, p. 135 for a list of the bank's main sponsors, 19 Sept. 1848; and a letter from the municipality to Bortolo Lazzaris, of 19 Aug. 1848, asking him for his support (MRR, b. 917, no. 72/4).

21 ASV, CC, b. 188, iv/57, no. 6. For full details of the forty-two contributors to the loan of three million, see ASV, Gov. Prov. 1848–9, reg. 1258, no. 1.

of the city were estimated for a loan of two million lire, and in November all those who had not yet contributed were required to raise a loan of one million lire. Finally, in April 1849 the government demanded that those who had originally been estimated for more than 24,000 lire should again raise the capital for a loan of three million. It is testimony to the wealth of this group, their patriotism and the government's insistence that all but 18,000 lire of this last loan was successfully collected.[22]

The draconian measure of repeated forced loans brought in many millions of lire, but it was still not enough. Sources of wealth other than the city's richest individuals had to be sought. In October 1848 the idea was floated of making some of Venice's greatest works of arts sureties for an international loan. Tommaseo was instructed to look into the possibility and reported that six and a half million francs could be raised, provided that the pictures were taken to London and held until the loan was repaid. The pictures would be exhibited in London and the public charged admission, two-thirds of which would go to Venice and one-third to those making the loan. Venice had twenty years within which to repay the loan, after which the pictures would be sold. Manin at first agreed and a special commission selected fifty-eight masterpieces, worth an estimated fourteen million lire.[23] But there was strong opposition for fear of losing the pictures forever, and in the end Manin agreed to adopt the plan only in absolute extremity.

In early November the government and its advisers came forward with another proposal. The triumvirs asked the municipality to approve a super-tax on all its goods, which would bring in twelve million lire over the next twenty years.[24] If the municipality gave its consent, the government would then go ahead with further issues of paper money, to be called

[22] Information on this last loan is to be found in ASV, Gov. Prov. 1848–9, b. 607. Once again the major contributors were Jacopo and Isacco Treves (360,000 lire), Pietro and Andrea Giovanelli (360,000 lire), and the Papadopoli company (350,000 lire). Vettore Pisani contributed 200,000 lire, the brothers Pigazzi 177,000, Loredana Morosini Gattersburg 160,000. Giuseppe Reali was able only to loan 27,000 lire by this time, one of the smallest contributions. For the lesser loans of two million and one million lire, of Oct. and Nov. 1848, see ASV, Gov. Prov. 1848–9, reg. 1258, nos. 2 and 3. The government managed to repay many of the loans fairly rapidly, so that large amounts of the *moneta patriottica* were withdrawn from circulation and publicly burnt. This was the main reason for the *moneta patriottica* always being 1½–2½ points higher in real value than the *moneta comunale*.

[23] Marchesi, *Storia documentata*, pp. 295ff; Ciampini, *Vita di Nicolò Tommaseo*, pp. 493–4. All the great Venetian artists were included in the list, with the strange exceptions of Giorgione and Carpaccio.

[24] See in particular the work of Brunetti, 'L'opera del comune di Venezia', pp. 37–67.

moneta comunale. The triumvirs said they wanted to issue communal rather than governmental money because 'speculators might with justice throw doubt upon the stability of the government, while the commune cannot perish'. On 6 November the municipal council met to consider the proposal. There were a number of murmurings against the government's financial policy. One councillor said that since landowners and merchants were being asked to bear the lion's share of the sacrifices, they should be better represented in the government's finance committee. His speech met with considerable approval. But when the vote was taken, an overwhelming majority of the councillors, 43 to 4, agreed to support the plan. The only proviso they made was that the other Italian states should agree to accept Venetian paper money as legal currency. They also agreed to stand additional surety for the loans financing the *moneta patriottica*. In 1849 the municipality supported further issues of paper money and by the end of the revolution over 27 million lire's worth of *moneta comunale* had been printed.[25]

Manin made strenuous efforts to get the governments of Tuscany, the Papal States and Piedmont to recognise the Venetian paper currency, but without success. Only the Piedmontese, while not accepting the communal money as legal tender, took some steps to aid Venice. In January 1849 the house of deputies in Turin voted a subsidy of 600,000 lire a month to Venice. This act, together with the return of the Piedmontese navy to Venetian waters, did much to repair the damage done to Piedmont's reputation by the Salasco armistice and the events of 11 August.[26]

Fortunately, the Venetians themselves quickly adapted to the novelty of a currency that had no intrinsic value. But there was far too much paper money circulating in Venice, and as the months passed it slowly

---

[25] Tucci, 'Le emissioni monetarie', pp. 8–12. The demand for the other Italian states to recognise Venice's paper money was made by the nobleman Nicolò Priuli, during the course of a long speech which was subsequently published: N. Priuli, *Venezia all'Italia. Discorso pronunziato nell'adunanza del consiglio comunale di Venezia, il giorno 6 nov. 1848.* On 28 May 1849 further communal money was issued, guaranteed by the salt and tobacco produce in the hands of the commune, and further issues followed on 28 June and 12 August 1849, guaranteed this time by additional taxes of six million lire each.

[26] MCV, Doc. Manin, no. 910, letter from Sebastiano Tecchio in Turin to Manin saying that the Piedmontese had voted 110 to 7 in favour of the subsidy. For Venetian efforts to gain recognition of the paper money, see Manin's letter to Piedmont, AST, carte politiche diverse, cart. 25, fasc. 150, no. 47, 24 Nov. 1848, and his letter to Mamiani in Rome, MCV, Doc. Manin, no. 1078, 27 Nov. 1848. Also Montanelli's reply to the request (*ibid.*, no. 1082, 6 Dec. 1848), and Manin's discouraged report to the assembly on 22 Feb. 1849 (*ibid.*, no. 1079). For a detailed exposition of Venetian finances at the end of 1848, see the memorandum sent to Pasini in Paris (*ibid.*, no. 2460).

but inexorably lost value. By the beginning of April 1849 it was worth only three-quarters of its face value. The issuing of paper money can nevertheless be judged a considerable success, without which the city would have faced the ignominy of a speedy capitulation for financial reasons alone. Pesaro Maurogonato and the other financial advisers of the government showed themselves to be ingenious as well as practical, though the toll taken on the commercial and banking families of Venice was a very heavy one. Some businesses, like that of the wealthy merchant Cesare della Vida, never really recovered from the strains imposed upon them during the revolutionary years.[27]

Social conditions and government policy

No great social disturbances rocked Venice during the autumn and winter of 1848–9. The predominant thought in everyone's mind was the struggle against the Austrians and the chances of the city's surviving the onslaught that all knew to be imminent. As with any city under siege, the population felt a heightened sense of solidarity in the face of the enemy. In earlier months the Venetians had been roundly criticised by the rest of Italy for their republicanism and supposed insularity. But now their city was the only one in the whole of Lombardy-Venetia that still flew the Italian flag. After 11 August the Venetians discovered a new self-respect, a new seriousness of purpose that found its clearest expression in the creation of the army and the prolonged defiance of their city.

This is not to say that Venice was devoid of social tension or that the fundamental class divisions of its population had disappeared. The Paduan Carlo Leoni, writing his diary in Venice in early September, gave an interesting and acute account of the conditions of the different sections of the population:

Commerce has all but ceased; the *terraferma* is cut off and there is no trade but that in foodstuffs. The boatmen are busy enough, and indeed the lower classes are in fine fettle and better than before. But it is the proprietor and merchant who are really suffering. The proprietor, in whom resides the real wealth of Venice, is as hard hit here as on the mainland. He has had to say goodbye to all his silver and now eats with wooden spoons. He has had to pay for the loan, for shares and other lesser financial tricks. The merchant no longer sells his wares and is weighed down by the same burdens as the proprietor. Thus these citizens are far from content, but the people are gay and cordially curse the Germans. The middle class which made the revolution and carried through the almost unbelievable liberation of Venice, are very much to the forefront and very active in the civic guard ... Manin asks for and obtains

[27] For a biographical note on Della Vida, see Rigobon, *Gli eletti*, pp. 88–9.

perfect tranquillity, sending away troublemakers and imprisoning a few of the populace who were threatening to sack and pillage.[28]

Leoni was right enough that the Venetian working classes were in good spirits in September, content that Manin was back in power and that the fight against the Austrians was on. But he overestimated the material well-being of the Venetian poor, and ignored the significant problems that they faced. The absence of the tourist trade in the summer of '48 deprived many of them of the cash that usually saw them through the winter and spring. The committee of public vigilance reported early in September on the growing bands of ten- to fifteen-year-olds who were begging in St Mark's Square and spending the night on the café chairs or the steps flanking the arcades.[29] Although we lack anything but occasional references to prices during this period, it is clear that tobacco, wine and meat all became dearer.[30] With commerce at a standstill, the artisans of the city faced a very grave crisis. They petitioned the municipality and the government for work, and at the end of December a commission was set up to look into their conditions. It found that there were over two thousand unemployed, five times the September figure.[31]

Certain sections of the Venetian working class moved onto the offensive, repeating and developing the demands that had been made at the outbreak of the revolution. At Murano in January 1849 the glass-blowers and glaziers downed tools, refusing to go back to work until they received a wage increase and a fund had been set up for their fellow workers who were ill, disabled or old. The employers responded with a lock-out, and tension ran very high on the island. At first the authorities thought of using force to destroy what they considered to be an illegal workers' league,

[28] Leoni, 'Cronaca, 1848', p. 480. See also the letter from Venice of the Tuscan doctor Uccelli to Carlo Fenzi, 7 Feb. 1849, saying that Venice was not dominated by 'the guillotine or by torture ... here there is a pure and sincere love of independence, without the disturbing shadow of Robespierre and Marat' (ASRF, archivio Fenzi, filza 67, 8, no. 313).

[29] ASV, Gov. Prov. 1848–9, OPss, no. 10387, 3 Sept. 1848.

[30] The price of tobacco was raised on 23 Aug. 1848; Marchesi, *Storia documentata*, p. 293. As early as the beginning of Oct. 1848 Vasseur, the French consul, was complaining that there was not enough meat even for the rich; Planat de la Faye, *Documenti*, vol. 2, p. 23. An extra tax of 1.80 lire for every quintal was placed on wine so as to bring in extra funds for the commission of public charity; see the copy of the letter from Toggenburg to the minister of finance, 6 April 1851, ASV, Pres. Luog. 1852–6, b. 229, fasc. vi, 5/2, no. 24850.

[31] ACV, Presidio, 1849, no number, draft of the report of the commission, 8 Jan. 1849. The figure quoted was 2,070, but its approximate nature was stressed. For some of the petitions to the municipality, see ACV, Municip., Atti di Uff., 1845–9, ix, 12/4, nos. 8688, 8723, 8851, 10386, 10658, 10660, 10716 (1848), and 3022, 3126 (1849).

but they were dissuaded by the great number of workers involved. After lengthy negotiations a settlement was reached which was a substantial victory for the workers. The employers agreed to pay an obligatory minimum wage and to provide subsidies for the old and disabled.[32] A similar dispute, though on a smaller scale, concerned the bakers' hands in Cannaregio. In April 1848 the baking workers had succeeded in forcing the bakers to pay them by the day and not, as had always happened before, by piece work. Then in February 1849 the workers demanded an increase of the daily rate. This incensed the employers, who appealed to the government. But Manin replied that he did not consider it the government's business to intervene in the economic relations between bakers and their employees.[33]

In general, Manin seems to have continued the twofold policy which characterised his earlier actions in this field, combining a concerted attempt to ensure that working-class conditions were not unbearable, with police vigilance and the rigid maintenance of public order. It was Manin who insistently petitioned the municipality in September and October, demanding that it draw up a proper programme of public works to reduce the growing numbers of unemployed. The municipality responded by employing stonemasons and labourers on the construction of the dike at Alberoni, and employing others in the dredging of canals, the cleaning of streets and the repair of the window and door frames of public buildings. By April 1849 more than seven hundred men were on the municipality's pay-roll.[34] Of course, it was the war effort which absorbed most of the unemployed, either directly into the infantry regiments or in the arsenal or else in repair work on the forts. But the government also kept a careful watch in areas other than unemployment. For instance, the price of bread continued to be controlled and only in April 1849 was allowed to creep up again by two centesimi per *libbra*. And, after repeated reports of shop-keepers abusing government regulations on the price and weight of bread, the central provisioning committee set up permanent local committees to safeguard the conditions under which basic foodstuffs were sold, so as 'to prevent complaints and discontent amongst the poorest part of the population, who are worst hit by abuses'.[35]

[32] See Bernardello, 'La paura del comunismo', p. 100 and n. 143.
[33] ACV, Municip., Atti di Uff., 1845–9, IV, 7/46, attached to no. 1483, 12 Feb. 1849.
[34] ACV, Municip., Atti di Uff., 1845–9, IX, 12/4, no. 2827, 27 April 1849. Manin reported to the assembly on 26 Feb. 1849 that whereas only 800 men had been employed in the arsenal before the revolution, there were now 2,300 at work there; MCV, Doc. Manin, no. 3389. See also Brunetti, 'L'opera del comune di Venezia', pp. 82–3, and Bernardello, 'La paura del comunismo', p. 87.
[35] ACV, Municip. Atti di Uff., 1845–9, IV, 7/59, no. 1167, 6 Feb. 1849. For the

However, it would be incorrect to present Manin as some kind of precursor of social democracy. His policy of non-interference in economic relations between employer and employed, if it benefited the workers in the bakers' dispute, also had its negative side. In a reply of January 1849 to the director general of public works, Manin said it would be dangerous to fix wages, because 'the government might be credited with the unwarranted intention of interfering with contracts between masters and journeymen, and of guaranteeing work and food to all those who have need of it'.[36] The profound social conservatism of a government which thought in terms of charity rather than of social policies appears from an appeal by the committee of public vigilance in August 1848. The appeal, approved by Manin, asked the rich to continue to employ their servants: 'We are asking you to give solemn proof that our feelings are in perfect accord on the need for this provident charity, so that we can remove the danger that may arise from the sufferings of that class which is by fate destined to live on the bread of others.'[37]

Almost no social reform was undertaken during what Tommaseo described as 'the long empty months from August onwards'.[38] In February 1849 Manin did ask for a commission of enquiry into the Venetian workhouse, but the commission took three months to report and then suggested very little. Conditions in the prisons went unaltered and, rather surprisingly, no overhaul of the educational system seems to have taken place.[39] Manin, in his statement to the assembly of 26 February 1849, revealed his

raising of the price of bread in April 1849, see the interesting letter of 19 April from the provisioning committee of the city to the government; ASV, Gov. Prov. 1848–9, MU, b. 117, no. 12611. The committee said that they needed more money urgently to acquire grain, and reiterated that 'the lower classes would be exposed to severe suffering and there would be dangerous riots if price control, after being in operation a year, was to be abandoned'. The government had wanted to tax every *traghetto* (ferry across the Grand Canal by means of gondola), but after an impassioned plea by Father Tornielli on behalf of the boatmen, the idea was abandoned; see P. Brunello, 'Rivoluzione e clero', fo. 181 n. 2.

[36] ASV, Gov. Prov. 1848–9, MU, b. 68, no. 951; quoted by Bernardello, 'La paura del comunismo', p. 88 n. 111.
[37] Racc. Andreola, vol. 3, p. 389, 22 Aug. 1848.
[38] Tommaseo, *Venezia*, vol. 1, p. 142.
[39] On the lack of any change in education, see, amongst others, Vollo's comments in his newspaper *Per tutti* in March 1849; A. Pilot, 'Il *Per tutti* di G. Vollo', *Rassegna storica del Risorgimento*, 14 (1927), pp. 405–14. Also MCV, Doc. Manin, no. 3194, Samuele Olper to Manin, 5 Dec. 1848. Even the physical education which Tommaseo had introduced was allowed to lapse after he went to Paris. On the prisons see Tommaseo, *Venezia*, vol. 1, pp. 140–1. On the workhouse, ACV, Presidio, 1849, no number, report of the commission of 27 April 1849.

fear of the possible effects of social change: 'A popular government must first and foremost look after the needs of the people. It must not, however, arouse in them unfounded or subversive pretensions, or vain hopes which are always followed by disillusionment.'[40] The committee of public vigilance was always extremely fast in clamping down on any individuals whom they thought threatened the public peace, and on at least one occasion had to make a public apology for wrongful arrest.[41] The general picture that emerges in these months is of a government sensitive to working-class needs and enjoying considerable popularity, but unwilling to interfere with the traditional social and economic structures of the city, and wary of the slightest signs of unrest.

Opposition and repression

The principal opposition within the city to Manin's government, the Italian Club, had been crushed at the beginning of October, but this did not see an end to all criticism, or even an end to the clubs. A number of radicals and journalists continued to use the freedom of press and assembly to expound social, political and religious ideas which were anathema to the new Venetian establishment.

The first to fall foul of the authorities was the anti-clerical and satirical paper, *Sior Antonio Rioba*. It spoke scathingly of the Pope and poked merciless fun at the patriarch, rightly casting aspersions on his patriotism. By the beginning of December Cardinal Monico could stand no more, and forbade the faithful to read the newspaper. On 3 December the radical preacher Ugo Bassi, in a sermon in the Piazza San Marco, violently attacked the patriarch and his advisers, whom he accused of being either 'Jesuits or lovers of Austria'. After Bassi had finished speaking a large crowd started to move towards the Palazzo Querini Stampalia, which was the cardinal's residence at this time. Civic guards blocked the way and dispersed the crowd, but the incident provoked a tremendous outcry from the city fathers. The municipality wrote to the government urging it to act against Bassi for creating such a scandalous scene, and some of the leading figures of the city, including Reali, Papadopoli, Martinengo and Bigaglia, published an open letter in support of Monico. But Manin steadfastly refused to take action against either *Sior Antonio Rioba* or Ugo Bassi.[42]

40 MCV, Doc. Manin, no. 3389.

41 Bernardello, 'La paura del comunismo', p. 88 and n. 112. The apology was given to Pietro Bonlini and his friends, after they had been imprisoned, tried and found not guilty of suspected 'communism'.

42 For the whole incident see A Pilot, 'Il patriarca cardinale G. Monico contro *Sior Antonio Rioba*', in *Rassegna Nazionale*, 43 (1923), pp. 136–9.

The case of Marc'Antonio Canini and the 'People's Club' ended some-what differently. Canini was a young Venetian who had begun to study law at Padua, but in 1847 was forced to flee the university for having organised an anti-Austrian student protest. He went to Tuscany but after the revolution soon returned to Venice. Canini, who was then twenty-five, enrolled in the artillery and began to press for the democratic election of officers. But neither Manin nor Cavedalis would countenance such pro-posals, and Canini resigned in protest. In December he and Father Gavazzi, a popular and radical preacher, turned their attention to founding the People's Club in Cannaregio, one of the most working-class areas of the city. The idea of the club was to further the political education of the Venetian poor, but no details have come down to us of what exactly took place. Canini himself was a primitive socialist at this time, believing that the profits from men's labour should be shared equally amongst them.[43]

The club flourished and on 11 January 1849 Canini felt confident enough to publish the first edition of his own newspaper, *Il Tribuno del popolo*. It was not in the least inflammatory, and its front page stressed that the three bulwarks of life were 'Religion, Fatherland and Family'. But the next day both he and Gavazzi were arrested; Canini was thrown in prison, and Gavazzi expelled from the city. On 14 January 1849 Manin wrote to Gavazzi, justifying his actions, and at the same time providing a very clear account of his political attitudes:

I am sorry about what has happened; but you must realise that we have assumed the sacred task of defending Venice at any cost, and that Venice can-not be defended unless it be kept in tranquillity and concord. Both of these might well have been compromised by the People's Club, by the class of people called on to constitute it, by the insolence of some of the persons who intended to lead it, and by the socialist theories that were being preached there. You know that these seductive theories might quickly carry away the excitable and ignorant artisans of this city, and lead them to put such ideas into fearsome practice. This would imperil society, and bring ruin upon those poorer classes whose cause they espoused. France has lately furnished a terrible example of this. Now if these theories have produced such fearful consequences at Paris, which is menaced by no external foe, reflect how much more fatal they would be to Venice, besieged and blockaded and with the enemy at its very gates.[44]

---

[43] On Canini see Bernardello, 'La paura del comunismo', pp. 91ff. Manin inter-vened on the question of democracy in the army on 30 Nov. 1848, observing that 'the excessive love of discussion, the mania for innovation, the converting of an army into a debating assembly, make it difficult for the individual soldier to maintain that discipline without which no militia can be properly ordered'; ASV, Gov. Prov. 1848–9, MU, b. 58, no. 7120, quoted by Bernardello, p. 95.

[44] Planat de la Faye (ed.), *Documenti*, vol. 2, pp. 158–60. The full text of the letter has been published in English in *The Revolutions of 1848. Document Collection*, p. 101.

Canini languished in gaol for six weeks. During that time he wrote to Manin, protesting against his continued imprisonment without trial, and against the misapprehensions under which Manin was labouring.[45] He denied preaching class hatred, but said his intention had been to establish night schools for the people, and to build up support for an Italian constituent assembly. He complained bitterly of the way in which the government had neglected the education of the poor. At the end of February he was finally released, but a week later was rearrested and expelled. He then made his way to Rome via Ravenna, and was shortly to become secretary of the Roman republic's commission for the barricades of the city.[46]

Other critics of the government were less harshly treated, but nearly all were subject to harassment in one form or another. Giuseppe Vollo, another young Venetian, though no friend of Canini's, began to publish his own paper, the *Per tutti*, on 5 March 1849. Its declared aim was to 'arouse anger', and it was deeply critical of the policies – or lack of them – of the government. It survived until 16 April 1849, when an article headed 'Manin at Gaeta', accusing Manin of being a prisoner surrounded by '*austriacanti* and conservative politicians' was too much for the committee of public vigilance. The paper was suspended and Vollo exiled to Ravenna.[47]

Two other radical newspapers, the *San Marco* and *Il Precursore*, were more fortunate. The *San Marco* lasted for over three months, from December 1848 to March 1849, and during that time its young editors, Bernardo Canal and Giovanni Piermartini, did not hesitate to expose the continuing inaction of the triumvirate.[48] Opposed to communism, which they took to mean the abolition of private property, Canal and Piermartini favoured instead a kind of moralising and reforming socialism. They were outspoken in their condemnation of 'a social system which for centuries has meant that . . . there are a few dispensers of wealth oppressing the rest of the population who are forced into lives of drudgery and humiliation'. The *San Marco* also declared itself in favour of the principle of the right to work, 'the inspiration of Raspail, of Ledru Rollin and other Frenchmen who are the only true supporters of the Italian cause amongst

[45] Canini's two letters of 13 and 18 Jan. 1849 are published by Bernardello, 'La paura del comunismo', app. I and II, pp. 111–13.
[46] *Ibid.*, pp. 104–5.
[47] Pilot, 'Il *Per tutti*', pp. 13–14. Vollo had played an active part in the People's Club, but was hostile both to Canini and his ideas, and would not help him when he was in prison. Vollo was allowed back to Venice in the summer.
[48] Canal was born in 1824, Piermartini in 1826. Both had been educated at Padua University. For the history of the newspaper see G. Gambarin, 'Il giornale *San Marco*', *Archivio Veneto*, 75 (1964), pp. 44–67.

that nation'. While profoundly Christian, Canal and Piermartini attacked the conservative Venetian clergy and the continuing obligation of students to confess five times a year: 'reconciliation with God must be commended, not commanded'. They advocated the establishment of night schools for the people, and claimed that the impetus for law reform of the first days of the revolution had not been maintained. The magistracy was reactionary, the delay in hearings enormous, the freedom of the press constantly infringed. As for administration, they castigated a top-heavy bureaucracy in which senior officials were drawing large salaries at a time when the poor were beginning to starve.[49]

Il Precursore, which flourished between November 1848 and February 1849, was conceived as a less popular newspaper than the *San Marco* and more as a review of the social and political ideas of the time. Its editor was another Christian socialist, Pacifico Valussi, who believed that socialism 'was a peaceful means for the reordering of society, a scientific discovery to be applied by means of persuasion'. In February 1849 Valussi founded another club, the San Martino, in the popular quarter of Castello. But he was careful to avoid falling foul of the authorities as Canini had done, and made it clear that the club would concern itself not with socialist ideas, but with the 'civil education of the people'. The club flourished for a number of weeks, but once again we have no details of how many people went to it and what was discussed there.[50]

By the beginning of April 1849 most of the radical newspapers had ceased publication and the clubs had fallen into decay. They are perhaps of more interest to the historian for the advanced ideas they expressed than for the real influence they had on Venetian society at this time. At no stage did the work of these Christian socialists lead to any sort of organised opposition amongst the Venetian poor. Manin and the committee of public vigilance kept a close watch on the radicals' activity, and whenever they felt threatened by them, as with Canini and the People's Club, they moved swiftly to destroy the danger. The support of the Venetian popular classes for Manin was thus never seriously brought into question in these months.

The second election

One fundamental reform remained unaltered during the course of the

[49] Gambarin, 'Il giornale *San Marco*', pp. 51–2. For the editors' opposition to the obligation to confess, see *San Marco*, no. 54, 25 Jan. 1849. For their remarks on the French, *ibid.,* no. 56, 27 Jan. 1849; and on the social system, *ibid.,* no. 13, 13 Dec. 1848.
[50] Bernardello, 'La paura del comunismo', p. 99 and n. 140. On *Il Precursore*, see *ibid.,* pp. 91–2.

revolution – the establishment of universal manhood suffrage. 'We have just passed a great turning point in the story of the world', wrote *The Times* on 1 January 1849; 'the majestic creations of policy or of time have been submitted to the suffrages of the casual populace.' In December 1848 the Venetian triumvirate decided to hold new elections in January of the following year. An electoral commission was set up to devise a more satisfactory way of voting than by parishes. The commission decided to have one representative for every 1,500 voters, and to split the city and the lagoon into fourteen electoral areas. Venice itself was divided into eight, and provided eighty-three representatives. Chioggia formed two electoral areas, the outlying islands and villages of Murano, Burano, Torcello, Pellestrina and S. Pietro in Volta one each. The real innovation was the provision of two constituencies for the army and navy. This meant that non-Venetians had the opportunity to vote, and the measure was seen as a sop to those who in September had pressed for a pan-Italian assembly.[51]

The electoral campaign was far more intense than the previous one in June. Manin's own feelings on it are revealed by some jottings he made prior to the voting: 'There are honest men among the republicans, and there are honest men amongst those who are not republicans – what we must do above all else is to choose honest men, who have the true good of the country at heart, regardless of their political opinions.'[52]

Election lists, recommending certain candidates, were circulated in nearly every constituency. Some were divided between republicans and Albertists; others named suitable lawyers, priests, doctors or noblemen. Many broadsheets advised citizens to consult the parish priest or some *gran galantuomo* if they were not sure for whom to vote. At the end of December Manin wrote to all the parish priests of the city, urging upon them the importance of the coming election:

The vast mass of the people, ill-accustomed because of their long slavery to the exercise of their political rights, may fail to understand the great importance of what they are being asked to do ... It is essential that each one of you, both privately and from the pulpit, makes it understood how the act of voting is the

[51] Rigobon, *Gli eletti*, pp. xxiii–xxv. The commission consisted of Manin, Calucci, L. Pasini, Pesaro Maurogonato and Martelli. See also MCV, Doc. Manin, no. 3374, 24 Dec. 1848, for the electoral laws. As there was no polling station on the Giudecca, Manin ordered the municipality to lay on boats to transport the voters free of charge across the Giudecca canal to Dorsoduro; ACV, Municip., Atti di Uff., 1845–9, III, 12/11, no. 405, 14 Jan. 1849.

[52] MCV, Doc. Manin, no. 3413, no date, four sides of Manin's writing under the heading 'general scope of the meeting'. The document appears to be the notes for a speech made at a meeting prior to the elections. The notes are obviously not of the period preceding the first election, because there are references to the Anglo-French mediation.

expression of national independence and the dignity of a free citizen. Under an absolute government the people are nothing, and can be disposed of secretly, according to personal ambitions. But under a free government the people are everything. If they cannot meet in the piazza to discuss and decide, they must do so by means of representatives, whom they directly and freely mandate.[53]

The Italian Club enjoyed a new lease of life during the campaign, creating committees in every constituency. Through Varè's newspaper, *L'Indipendente*, they recommended a large number of republicans, but were careful not to offend Manin's susceptibilities, and stressed 'probity' and 'patriotism' as the qualities for which the electors should look.[54] The *San Marco*, mindful of Canini's fate, published a leader in favour of Manin on 21 January 1849. But the newspaper was also harshly critical of a list of candidates proposed by the parish priest of San Pantaleone. This criticism enraged a number of parishioners, and resulted in a warning being given to the editors by the prefecture of public order.[55]

One electoral meeting was of special interest – that of the gondoliers on 16 January 1849. More than three hundred of them gathered in a large hostelry called the Malcanton. They had asked the government for three representatives to chair the meeting, and Manin sent the republican nobleman Giovanni Minotto, and two Albertist lawyers, Alvisi and Rensovich. The main speaker was Girolamo Galli, called *il musico*, a gondolier in the service of the banker Coen. Hardly surprisingly, his speech was a model of moderation. Having condemned 'the errors of socialism', Galli went on: 'We wish to have the same rights and duties as other citizens ... but we do not want to appropriate for ourselves what is

[53] MCV, Doc. Manin, no. 3825, letter of 28 Dec. 1848. For examples of electoral propaganda, see Racc. Andreola, vol. 5, pp. 441–2, 475 and 487–9. In the third electoral district, consisting roughly of the *sestiere* San Marco, 200 electors met on 17 Jan. 1849 and selected a list of 'recommended candidates' for the constituency. Another meeting for the same purpose, and in the same constituency, was held the following day (ASV, carte Avesani, b. 2, no number, broadsheet of 19 Jan. 1849).

[54] Rigobon, *Gli eletti*, p. xxx. This was not the opinion of another famous Mazzinian, Gustavo Modena, who had left Venice by this time and felt free to express himself. In a letter of 10 January 1849 to Orazio Cerini in Venice, Modena wrote, 'The assembly will not be made up of those who cried with joy when the republic was proclaimed; it will be composed, as usual, of lawyers, writers, poets ... if Venice gave me an assembly of men from the market, from the streets, from the boats, ready to put an end to soft talk, to all reserve, to cautious lawyers and disguised Jesuits ... I would say to you: I'm coming immediately, and I wouldn't waste a moment before setting out'; see T. Grandi (ed.), *Epistolario di Gustavo Modena*, pp. 98–9.

[55] The editorial in praise of Manin appeared in no. 50, 21 Jan. 1849. For the election list in S. Pantaleone, see Gambarin, 'Il giornale *San Marco*', p. 57 n. 55.

not ours. The rich should remain rich so that they can give us work, and we will always have respect for our masters.'[56]

More than 29,000 electors went to the polls, out of a possible 42,000. When the results were published on 30 January 1849 there were very few surprises. Since anyone could stand for any constituency, the leading figures of the revolution were all elected more than once. Manin was elected for all the constituencies of the city and that of the soldiers, and received over 11,000 votes. Cavedalis was the next most popular, with over 7,500 votes and election to eight constituencies; he was followed by Tommaseo with 5,200 votes and seven constituencies. The Italian Club did well: Sirtori came third in the army list, with 2,660 votes, after General Rizzardi and Cavedalis. His high poll perhaps reflected his bravery during the Mestre sortie as much as it did his politics. Other prominent members of the club who were elected included Ferrari-Bravo, Minotto, Varè, Giuriati and De Camin. Gian Francesco Avesani was the most successful of the Albertists. In class terms, the composition of the assembly differed very little from that of the previous one; professional men dominated, and the only representatives of the poor were two gondoliers.[57]

Gioberti, Montanelli and events in Rome

Before describing the political struggles that developed in the new Venetian assembly, it is worth returning briefly to look at developments in the rest of Italy after the Salasco armistice, and to see Venice's reactions to them. Most of the Italian moderates abandoned ideas of renewing the war of independence, preferring to adopt a policy of waiting upon events not dissimilar to Manin's, and to place their hopes in the Anglo-French mediation. The radicals and democrats, on the other hand, moved onto

[56] Planat de la Faye (ed.), *Documenti*, vol. 2, pp. 160ff. See also F. Federigo, *Del periodo politico e della vita intima di D. Manin*, pp. 114–18.
[57] Rigobon, *Gli eletti*, pp. xxx–xxxi. Anyone who was elected more than once chose the constituency he wanted to represent. By-elections were then held in those constituencies that, because of this procedure, found themselves short of representatives. MCV, Doc. Manin, no. 3291, 9 Feb. 1849, is a large list giving all the results of the election; *ibid.*, no. 3402, the unprinted results of the first voting. Twenty-six inhabitants of the tiny island of Lio Piccolo, five miles from Torcello, wrote to the government complaining that they had been deprived of the vote. They said that on 21 Jan. the parish priest Francesco Pavan had announced through his deputy, Friar Ambrogio, that the 21st was the only day for voting. Because so few people had been at mass, and because of the distance of the island from the nearest polling station at Torcello, the inhabitants of Lio Piccolo had in effect been deprived of the vote (ASV, Gov. Prov. 1848–9, b. 437, 'L'assemblea permanente', fasc. 1, letter of 2 Feb. 1849).

the offensive in the central Italian states and attempted to set up an Italian constituent assembly as the first step in a strategy of united action against the Austrians.

Gioberti

The first concrete proposal for a pan-Italian meeting came not from the Mazzinians, but from Gioberti in Turin. The new Piedmontese government, led by Alfieri and Pinelli, was distinctly moderate. While proclaiming its intention to reorganise the army and attack the Austrians again, the government in reality hoped that the mediation would bring Piedmont some small territorial acquisition, like the duchy of Parma, as a tardy reward for her war efforts. Gioberti, though by no means a democrat, saw that such a policy, narrowly Piedmontese in its outlook, ran the danger of losing Piedmont the initiative in Italy at precisely the moment when she most needed to re-establish her reputation after the great blows of Custozza and the Salasco armistice. He therefore made common cause with the Piedmontese democrats and was soon recognised as leader of the opposition. His first action, in a campaign designed to keep Piedmont as the nucleus for a united Italian offensive against Austria, was the summoning of a federal congress in Turin for 12 October 1848, under the aegis of 'the National Society for the Union and Confederation of Italy'.

One of Gioberti's many problems in launching this congress was to persuade the Venetians to send representatives. Castelli and Paleocapa were already in Turin, but they had no official standing. Gioberti, therefore, first sent Manin a highly flattering letter on 19 September, praising Venice for its resolution and dedication to the national cause. Then, on 25 September, Gherardo Freschi wrote to Manin telling him that Charles Albert was thinking of forming a more radical government, with Brofferio at its head. Manin was to be offered the ministry of foreign affairs. Manin's reply has been lost, but it was definitely a refusal.[58]

Gioberti was not discouraged by this obvious indication of Manin's desire to keep Venice uncommitted. On 9 October 1848, he and eleven other Piedmontese deputies wrote a long letter to the Venetian triumvirate. In it they urged that the old Venetian consultative assembly, consisting of two representatives from Venice and each of the provinces, should reassemble as soon as possible in Turin. In that way, Gioberti argued, the

---

[58] Gioberti's letter of 19 Sept. 1848, MCV, Doc. Manin, no. 870. Freschi's letter, *ibid.*, no. 2014. Castellani, Venice's representative in Rome, attempted to organise a counter-congress in Venice. Manin was cautiously enthusiastic, but Castellani sent out the invitations too late, and by 2 October he had to report that 'everyone is going to Turin' (*La Repubblica veneta*, vol. 2, *Documenti diplomatici, carteggio di G. B. Castellani*, p. 357).

318

Manin and the Venetian revolution

July votes for fusion would be confirmed, and the links binding northern Italy into a single kingdom would be strengthened. The alternative, wrote Gioberti, was for

... the Queen of the Adriatic to reduce herself to the narrow proportions of a Hanseatic city, and to succumb in a short time from misery and deprivation.[59]

Manin's reply of 26 October was brutally frank:

To reopen the political question and thus to introduce an element of discord among the people and the army would be highly imprudent at a time when we are completely surrounded by enemy troops. It would put into the gravest danger this citadel of Italian liberty, which since 11 August has been and will be impregnable. This is because we have restored and maintained internal concord. When, through the work of the Sardinian army or through other events, our military situation improves, we will have greater freedom of action. But today it would be tantamount to betrayal to create a dangerous situation in the city, simply for the vague possibility of military aid. If you cross the Ticino again, we will talk.[60]

Gioberti's congress therefore went ahead without any representatives from Venice. Various individuals, such as Count D'Onigo from Treviso and Professor Negri from Padua were present, and Pincherle, Manin's former minister of commerce, went along as an observer.[61] Paragraph 2 of article 2 of Gioberti's programme insisted on 'the maintenance of the union of Piedmont with the Duchies and with the Lombardo-Venetian provinces, forming a kingdom of upper Italy under the dynasty of Savoy'. This was obviously anathema to the Venetians, and no support at all came from the city for Gioberti's efforts.

In any case, by the end of October, the congress at Turin was being superseded by more realistic plans. On 21 October 1848 Pincherle wrote to Manin from Turin: 'The federal society is losing ground every day. The Tuscan proposal for a constituent assembly has opened most people's eyes. Whereas in Turin there is nothing but gossip and rhetoric, the Tuscan plans are a real and important possibility.'[62]

Montanelli and Tuscany

Tuscany had taken little part in the first months of the revolution. The

59 MCV, Doc. Manin, no. 871*a*. Avesani also received a copy of the letter at a later date. Gioberti commented that the triumvirs, overwhelmed by the cares of office, might have forgotten it; ASV, carte Avesani, b. 1, letter of 17 Oct. 1848.
60 MCV, Doc. Manin, no. 871.
61 For Pincherle's comments on Turin and the congress, see MCV, Doc. Manin, nos. 2017–18, letters of 5 and 11 Oct. 1848.
62 *Ibid.*, no. 2024.

government of Cempini and Ridolfi had avoided any major commitment, and the only Tuscan intervention in the war effort had been the valiant defiance of Radetzky by the small Tuscan force at Curtatone and Montanara.[63] But after the Piedmontese defeat at Custozza, the Tuscan democrats were able to tap growing popular dissatisfaction with the grand duke's meagre contribution to the national cause. Demonstrations in Florence called for the resignation of the ministry and a more active policy. Gino Capponi took over the reins of government, but he too was unable to restrain the growing tide of discontent. The thriving port of Leghorn was the focus for this discontent and the driving force behind the Tuscan revolution. Although the working classes of the city were by no means homogeneous – there were clear distinctions between the artisans on the one hand and the numerous dockers and construction workers on the other – a broad democratic and popular front had been formed in the city under the leadership of Domenico Guerrazzi. Municipal dislike of Florence, poor economic conditions and a genuine devotion to the national cause combined to make Leghorn a city which needed very little to be provoked into insurrection. The spark was supplied by the friar Alessandro Gavazzi, who, as we have seen, was later to be expelled from Venice. The Tuscan authorities refused to let Gavazzi preach, arrested him and escorted him to the frontier. When the popular classes of Leghorn heard of the treatment afforded Gavazzi, they rose in revolt on 25 August, took over the city's fortress and imprisoned the governor. All subsequent attempts by the Tuscan government to suppress the insurrection by force were heavily defeated. By 12 October 1848 Capponi had no option but to resign, and a new ministry was then formed, headed by Guerrazzi and Giuseppe Montanelli.

Montanelli, an author and journalist of considerable reputation, had become a popular hero for the part he had played at Curtatone and Montanara, where he had been seriously wounded. A moderate democrat with many similarities at this time to Manin, he was greeted with great enthusiasm when he visited Leghorn on 8 October. He used the occasion to make a resounding speech on the necessity for an Italian constituent assembly, which would meet at Rome and give Italy the national government she needed to wage successful war against Austria. 'What', asked Montanelli, 'was lacking in all those forces which rose up to fight for our independence? We lacked unity of leadership, we lacked a national government, we fought as Piedmontese, as Tuscans, as Neapolitans, as Romans, and not as Italians. This was the primary reason for our failure.'[64]

[63] See above, pp. 172 and 239.
[64] *Corriere livornese*, 8 Oct. 1848, quoted in Candeloro, *Storia dell'Italia moderna*, vol. 3 (1960), p. 303.

During October Montanelli, as the new head of the Tuscan government, made great efforts to spread the idea of the constituent assembly throughout the rest of Italy. He wrote to Venice and Manin replied in confidence on 30 October. It is an extraordinary letter, worth quoting in full, for in it Manin, encouraged by the triumph of the democrats in Tuscany and the news from Vienna, seems to have moved temporarily to a position much closer to that of the Mazzinians:

In March, when I proclaimed the Venetian republic, I declared that territorial and political questions had to be definitely decided by the whole nation according to the general interests of Italy. In July, when I was forced to give way to the party propagating lamentable fusionist propaganda, I said that everything that was being done was provisional and that the Italian Diet at Rome would make the final decisions. My opinions of March and July have not changed. From this you will see to what extent we are in substantial agreement.

But I cannot agree with you when you say that the recommencement of the war must be deferred till the constituent assembly nominates a central power to direct it. No central power can be elected in a short enough time to meet our war needs. I firmly believe that our cause will be lost if we do not make use of what has happened in Vienna, and if we let popular enthusiasm languish. You must also consider that because of her increasing financial difficulties Venice will not be able to resist for long. We have never had an armistice and in these last few days we have again taken the offensive.

In the absence of a central power which will direct the war with only the national interest in mind, we much have two centres of action in order to avoid the disasters of July and August. Let me explain. I am convinced that England will happily abandon the Veneto to Austria. I also have strong reason to believe that Piedmont will allow this to happen, provided she gets Lombardy. And indeed, if a fresh war is waged only by Piedmont, it is highly probable that she will make a pact with the Adige as the dividing line. So we must leave Piedmont to fight in Lombardy, as her interests so dictate, and let the other Italian forces concentrate in the Veneto. They must aid the army that we have gathered in Venice, and the population of the *terraferma*, who will rise up in arms if they know that help is not far away.

You could well send your Tuscan militias into the Veneto, commanded by the brave General Garibaldi; and you could also encourage the population of the Papal States to cross the Po to aid us, whether their government wants it or not. Our experience of the war of the princes has been all too painful. Now it is time for an awe-inspiring and formidable war of the people.

We must do what we can for each other. Long live Italy.[65]

Manin thus agreed on the need for a constituent assembly, but emphasised that military aid was the essential priority. If the Tuscan democrats

[65] Ciampini, *Vita di Nicolò Tommaseo*, app. p. 713. Ciampini does not tell us in which archive he found this letter.

could seriously help Venice in this way, Manin was prepared to embrace the idea of the war of the people, and even to approve Garibaldi as the head of Tuscan militias operating in the Veneto. This was to be in stark contrast to his position a month later when he rejected the idea of Garibaldi coming to Venice itself, for fear of disturbing the internal tranquillity of the city.[66]

Montanelli, in fact, had little to offer in military terms, because Tuscany had never had a large regular army, and no provisions had been made to meet the new situation. But Manin's reply did not deter him from going ahead with his plans for the Italian assembly. On 7 November 1848 Montanelli circulated his proposals to all the other Italian governments. Briefly, he envisaged a two-stage plan. The first stage was to elect by adult male suffrage an assembly to meet at Rome, which would concentrate exclusively on measures to defeat the Austrians. Once independence had been achieved, the assembly would then move on to decide on a constitution for the new Italy. Montanelli asked all the states which were not under foreign rule, including Venice, to send their representatives as soon as possible to Rome.[67]

Hardly surprisingly, the Piedmontese reply was somewhat evasive. While welcoming any agreement between the Italian governments which would aid the war effort, Perrone did not agree that representatives should necessarily be elected by adult male suffrage. He also made it quite clear that any Piedmontese participation was dependent upon the recognition of the kingdom of upper Italy. As Manin totally rejected this, the prospects for the assembly looked dim indeed. But at this moment yet another twist in the long and complicated saga of the Italian revolutions of 1848 took place, and the focus of interest shifted once again, this time to the upheavals in Rome.

Rome, Venice and Piedmont

During the summer of 1848 Pius IX had moved further and further away from the national cause. He had refused to admit that his army was in fact fighting the Austrians, and had become increasingly estranged from the moderate but distinctly nationalist Roman government, led by Terenzio Mamiani. After three months of continuous conflict Mamiani resigned and on 16 September the Pope replaced him with Pellegrino Rossi. Rossi was a capable and strong-minded man, convinced that the renewal of the war would be useless, and that order and economic stability had to be restored to the Papal States. While wishing to preserve the limited liberal

---

[66] See above, p. 268.
[67] The copy of Montanelli's circular sent to Venice is to be found in MCV, Doc. Manin, no. 3336.

constitution granted by the Pope, Rossi was not prepared to further Montanelli's plans for an Italian assembly, and showed himself highly suspicious of both the aims of the democrats and the aspirations of Piedmont. Such attitudes aroused the immediate hostility of the popular and national clubs at Rome, which exercised considerable influence at this time. On 15 November Rossi, on leaving his carriage to enter the new session of the Roman chamber of deputies, was stabbed to death. Although never clearly proven, it seems almost certain that Rossi's assassin was Luigi Brunetti, the son of the renowned Roman popular leader, Ciceruacchio.

Pius was thus deprived of the one man who he hoped could restore order and stability to his states. Worse was to follow for him. The People's Club met on the evening after Rossi's assassination and drew up a list of demands to be presented to the Pope, including the names of a new ministry and the acceptance of a committed war policy against Austria. In support of these demands, on 16 November a huge crowd besieged the Pope in the Quirinale. The Swiss guards opened fire on them, but this only served to incense the crowd further. More than ten thousand people surrounded the papal palace, a barricade was erected and a cannon trained on the principal entrance of the Quirinale. The Pope hastily summoned the lawyer Galletti to tell him that he agreed to the names of the new ministers, and Galletti then with difficulty persuaded the Romans to disperse. But it was clear to all that a complete break had taken place between the Pope and his Roman subjects. On 24 November Pius, disguised as a simple priest, fled from Rome and sought refuge at the Neapolitan port of Gaeta, where he was received by King Ferdinand II of the Two Sicilies.

From Gaeta Pius IX made it clear that he had renounced liberalism once and for all, and that there was no hope of a reconciliation between himself and his subjects, barring their total submission. His intransigence, which was to continue for the rest of his life, isolated the moderates like Mamiani who remained in Rome, and greatly strengthened the democrats' hand. A large number of radical exiles were also beginning to flock to the capital, including Garibaldi, Cernuschi and Maestri. In a matter of weeks the balance of power in Rome shifted dramatically to the left. The acting government decided to hold elections based on the principle of adult male suffrage, and on 21 January, much the same time as the second Venetian election, 250,000 men went to the polls. The result was a distinct victory for the democrats, and on 9 February 1849 the new Roman assembly, by an overwhelming majority, declared the Roman states a republic.

The startling developments at Rome confronted Manin with a quite new situation. For the first time since the beginning of the revolution, a significant part of Italy other than Venice had declared itself in favour of a republic. The need to react to what had happened in Rome was made all the more urgent by the fact than on 16 January the Romans had made clear their support for the Italian constituent assembly, and declared that the first hundred deputies elected for the Roman parliament would also be the Roman representatives at the national assembly. Manin decided for the first time since resuming power in August to emerge from his diplomatic shell and enter into negotiations. For once he was bolder than Tommaseo, who still nurtured neo-Guelph illusions about Pius, and was incensed at the murder of Rossi.[68]

On 27 January 1849 Manin dispatched a senior civil servant, Francesco Venturi, to Florence, Rome and Turin, so as 'to hear the proposals of the three governments, and to see how they can be put into effect'.[69] He was encouraged to take this initiative by a marked improvement in the internal situation of Piedmont. The Perrone–Pinelli government had fallen on 4 December and had been succeeded by one headed by Gioberti. Determined to push ahead with his ideas of an Italian confederation now that he was in power, Gioberti accepted Montanelli's proposals regarding the first stage for a constituent assembly. He also dissolved the Piedmontese parliament, called new elections and was rewarded with a chamber of deputies which had a democratic majority. In Tuscany as well, the impetus for an Italian constituent assembly was gathering strength, and on 22 January a proposal was made to the Tuscan parliament that thirty-seven deputies should immediately be elected by adult male suffrage to the Italian national assembly.

Manin instructed his emissary with great care. Any reference to the kingdom of upper Italy was to be deleted from the constitution of the assembly, and Venturi was to make sure that each state should send an equal number of representatives to Rome, rather than a number proportionate to its population, as Tuscany and Piedmont were suggesting. At the same time Manin wrote to Gioberti, saying that the new Venetian assembly was about to meet, and that it was 'extremely likely that Venice will declare her desire to adhere to the Italian constituent assembly'.[70]

---

[68] Tommaseo went as far as to invoke French intervention in order to prevent the Pope from falling under Austrian influence. See his two articles in *Ere Nouvelle* of 30 Nov. and 5 Dec. 1848, and the comments of Ciampini, *Vita di Nicolò Tommaseo*, pp. 508–12, and Gambarin in *La Repubblica veneta*, vol. 1, *Documenti diplomatici*, pp. 253–4. The Italian Club wrote to the government on 12 Dec. 1848 asking it to condemn what Tommaseo, in the name of the Venetian people, had said in Paris (MCV, Agg. Manin, ix/48). Manin decided to recall Tommaseo, who left Paris on 11 Jan. 1849.

[69] MCV, Doc. Manin, no. 3346, copy of Venturi's instructions.

[70] *Ibid.*, no. 3344, letter of 27 Jan. 1849.

Venturi's first dispatch from Rome, dated 4 February 1849, was guardedly optimistic.[71] He reported that Gioberti was prepared to compromise on the two major points: each state was to be equally represented at the first stage of the constituent assembly, and 'the indirect recognition of the independence of Venice was to be admitted'. But Venturi also added that he thought that Rome and Florence had gone too far too fast, and had put the participation of Piedmont at risk. Manin welcomed Venturi's dispatch and in his reply of 10 February seemed firmly committed to going ahead.[72] He urged Venturi to obtain 'a formal declaration of welcome from the Roman government for the Venetian deputies to the constituent assembly, as representatives of an independent state', and asked whether the deputies should be sent straight to Rome, or their departure be delayed a few weeks.

However, having got this far, Manin's enthusiasm for the assembly cooled appreciably over the next few weeks. Part of the reason was his fear that Venice, if she associated too closely with the increasingly radical central Italian governments, would be compromised in the eyes of the Great Powers. The grand duke of Tuscany, Leopold II, greatly alarmed at the course of events in his state, decided to follow the example of Pius IX, and by means of the British steamship *Bulldog* reached the haven of Gaeta on 23 February. A few days earlier a huge demonstration had been held by the democrats in Florence. Mazzini was there, and wrote an enthusiastic account in English to his friend Mrs Susan Tancioni:

On Sunday last, we have a great demonstration, and we proclaimed here the republic and unity with Rome; I spoke to the people in the square of the Palace of the Government; was half killed by their embraces; the tree of liberty was planted; but the Government did not yield; only they were obliged to give a proclamation in which they declare themselves favourable to our opinion and wishing to have it shared by all the Tuscan provinces.[73]

The Venetian representative in Florence, Tommaso Gar, was rather less enthusiastic, and the moderate Milanese democrat Cesare Correnti, previously so critical of Venice, wrote to Manin: 'In truth, the more experience I have of the affairs of the other Italian states, the more I learn to admire and love Venice.'[74] Castellani, the Venetian emissary in Rome and himself a convinced republican, warned Manin repeatedly of the revolutionary nature of the new regimes in Tuscany and Rome: 'Before

[71] *Ibid.*, no. 3353.
[72] *Ibid.*, no. 3352.
[73] HHSAV, Informations-Büro, Kart. 25, no. 194, a copy made by the Austrian police of this intercepted letter, 22 Feb. 1849.
[74] MCV, Doc. Manin, no. 761. See also Tommaso Gar's dispatch of 22 Feb., *ibid.*, no. 1253.

Venice sends deputies, it would be better to wait and see how things develop.'[75] Similarly, Pasini wrote from Paris that Lord Normanby thought Rome was in the hands of demagogues: 'Drouyn de Lhuys affirms that neither Florence nor Rome has a regularly constituted government, but both are in the hands of a few subversive individuals . . . the situation in the central states reflects also on us.'[76] This last report was the most damaging of all, because the Great Powers had at last assembled their representatives at Brussels and Manin was still hoping that some positive settlement, like an independent Lombardo-Venetian state, could emerge from the negotiations.[77]

Even so, Manin's attitude might not have changed if either Florence or Rome could have offered substantial financial or military aid. But both their armies were in a pitiful condition, and their finances were precarious. Venice's last hope of getting another Italian state to accept its paper money faded on 8 January 1849, when Muzzarelli reluctantly conveyed to Castellani the Roman government's refusal. In the same month Manin wrote to Vieusseux in Florence asking him if Tuscany would buy twenty million cigars from Venice. The minister of finance wanted to accept, but feared that the consequent slackening of production at the Florentine tobacco factory would provoke 'a revolution among the workers', some seven hundred men who included 'the scum of Florence'.[78] The Tuscan government also upset Venice by its insistence on proportional representation for the assembly. An angry Venturi, in his dispatch to the triumvirs of 20 February, pointed out the consequences of this proposal: 'It would be absurd . . . if Venice, which has an army and navy superior to the combined forces of Tuscany and Rome, had to send to the constituent assembly not more than four or five deputies.'[79]

But by far the most important element in the situation was the attitude of Piedmont. While Gioberti had initially given the impression of being sympathetic to the idea of the constituent assembly, by the latter half of February he was more interested in plans to intervene militarily to restore

[75] Castellani to Manin, 27 Jan. 1849, in *La Repubblica veneta*, vol. 2, p. 560.
[76] Dispatch of 28 Feb. 1849 in Planat de la Faye (ed.), *Documenti*, vol. 2, p. 217. *The Times* called the Romans an 'infatuated and miserable race' and Pasini also reported that the Lombard and Piedmontese emissaries in Paris did not hesitate to denounce the central Italian states.
[77] For the Brussels congress see above, p. 292. For Manin's illusions about a possible favourable outcome see, for example, his instructions to Venturi of 27 Jan. 1849 (MCV, Doc. Manin, no. 3346).
[78] Vieusseux to Manin, ASV, Gov. Prov. 1848–9, MU, b. 72, no. 2211, quoted by Bernardello, 'La paura del comunismo', p. 78 n. 91. For a copy of Muzzarelli's letter to Castellani see MCV, Doc. Manin, no. 1081.
[79] MCV, Doc. Manin, no. 3360.

the grand duke of Tuscany and the Pope to their respective thrones. He had broken with the Piedmontese democrats and as Charles Albert had always detested him, it was not long before he was forced to resign. But with or without Gioberti, it was clear that Piedmont alone could offer Venice the military and financial aid she needed. Between January and March 1849, Sebastiano Tecchio, who had been one of the departmental committee of Treviso, and was now the Piedmontese minister of public works, wrote a series of letters to Manin from Turin.[80] In them he stressed again and again that Piedmont was about to renew the war, that the army would fight only for the king, and that the Italian constituent assembly was aimed at the elimination of the Italian princes. He advised Manin to continue to adopt an attitude of 'prudent reserve', for 'only Piedmont can fight the war, and Piedmont can do so only with Charles Albert'. That Piedmont alone was aiding Venice was self-evident: the subsidy of 600,000 lire a month, the presence of the Piedmontese fleet in Venetian waters and the mission of General Oliverò were all concrete proof of the fact.

Manin therefore let the idea of the constituent assembly drop. On 23 February he wrote to Venturi, 'the constituent assembly is useless without the adhesion of the Sardinian government'.[81] On the 28th Carlo Fenzi, the Tuscan emissary to Venice, reported that Manin had said to him, 'in view of the difficulties in which Venice finds herself, we must avoid anything which may offend Piedmont, whose help we consider essential'.[82] Venturi eventually returned to Venice, and Venetian deputies were never sent to Rome. Manin, whose support for 'the war of the

[80] See, in particular, the letters of 19 and 30 January and 4 March 1849 (MCV, Doc. Manin, nos. 895, 904, 913). See also the extract from a letter of Gherardo Freschi in Turin to Manin, making much the same points as Tecchio; *ibid.*, no. 3351, 7 Feb. 1849. That Manin still harboured much resentment at the behaviour of Piedmont during the period of fusion can be seen from his letter of 3 Feb. 1849 to Rebizzo, the former Piedmontese envoy in Venice. Manin said that he had always wished Rebizzo well, 'even when under the guise of diplomacy you were making fusionist propaganda for Piedmont in my poor Venice, and stirring the unthinking provinces to revolt. When I prophesied the funereal consequences of these machinations, you, even if you did not say it, judged me in your heart to be a fanatic and a madman. But if this madman had been listened to, many calamities and disgraces would have been avoided. And if this madman had not persisted with his fantastic ideas, Venice would now be in the hands of the Austrians, and the honour of Italy irreparably lost' (MRR, b. 80, no. 55).

[81] MCV, Doc. Manin, no. 3358.

[82] Bianchi, *Diplomazia europea in Italia*, vol. 6 (1869), p. 114. Fenzi, the son of the wealthy Florentine banker Emanuele Fenzi, had been sent by the Tuscan government on 11 Feb. 1849. Antonio Mordini, now secretary of state for foreign affairs in Florence, asked Manin to cancel the order banning him from Venice, and wanted to keep the honorary rank of captain in the Venetian army (MCV, Doc. Manin, no. 4105, 10 Feb. 1849).

people' had been so clearly stated in his letter to Montanelli at the end of October, thus reverted by February to the careful cultivation of Piedmont. Manin's empiricism led him to only one conclusion – that Charles Albert and not an Italian constituent assembly was the only possible saviour of his beleaguered city.

The assembly in Venice

The new 'permanent' assembly, as it came to be called, convened in Venice for the first time on 15 February 1849. It did so against the background of the radicalisation of central Italy and the debates over the constituent assembly which have been charted above. Indeed, two days before the assembly met, a crowd gathered in the evening in the Piazza San Marco to demonstrate in favour of the Italian constituent assembly. The demonstration was organised by the Italian and the People's Clubs, and Manin came out to speak to them.[83] After its relative success in the elections, the Italian Club had taken on a new lease of life, and it was clear that Manin could no longer expect to govern without opposition.

In the month that followed the opening of the assembly, a great battle was waged for the control of Venice. Giuseppe Sirtori, at the head of a surprising number of representatives, attempted to push the government towards the left. His aim was not to topple Manin – that would have been impossible – but to force him to share power with the radical members of the assembly, rather than with more conservative figures like Cavedalis and Graziani. He also tried to get Manin to adopt a more positive attitude, both towards the waging of the war and relations with Tuscany and Rome. The political battle was thus very similar to that waged at the end of September, except that this time it was fought out within the confines of the assembly.

The opening shots were fired when Sirtori asked the assembly to insert, as a preamble to each of its decrees, the Mazzinian slogan 'In the name of God and the People'. Tommaseo supported him and the motion was passed. Then, on 27 February, a petition signed jointly by the Italian and People's Clubs was presented to the assembly.[84] The clubs complained of the 'absolute military inactivity' of the past four months, and asked for a new military commission to be set up. Manin tried to dismiss the petition by saying that the clubs were taking popular sovereignty into their own hands; he moved that the assembly pass to the business of the day. Sirtori

[83] Marchesi, *Storia documentata*, p. 373.

[84] ASV, Gov. Prov. 1848–9, b. 437 (L'assemblea permanente), fasc. for the proceedings of 28 Feb. 1849, containing the original petition from the clubs. For the adoption of the slogan 'In the name of God and the people' see Racc. Andreola, vol. 6, p. 308.

opposed him, replying that by submitting a petition the clubs had clearly recognised that 'sovereignty does not lie with them, nor with the government, but with the assembly'. Sirtori's speech was greeted with applause, and the clubs' demands were forwarded to the commission for war. There they were conveniently forgotten, but the significant fact was that a majority of the assembly had been persuaded to vote against Manin, albeit on a minor point.

Fortified by this success, the radical deputies prepared a direct attack on the composition of the government. On 3 March the triumvirate announced that since the constitution of the assembly had been finalised,[85] they would resign from power. Ferrari-Bravo, a Venetian member of the Italian Club, immediately proposed that a ruling commission of nine should replace them. The assembly decided to postpone for two days the vote on whether or not to take Ferrari-Bravo's proposal into consideration.

During the next two days rumours spread through the city that Sirtori was trying to force Manin out of power in order to hand Venice over to the Austrians. Varè, a level-headed deputy who was certainly no enemy of Manin's, later accused the committee of public vigilance of complicity in spreading these rumours.[86] On the morning of 5 March 1849, soon after the deputies had gathered inside the Doge's palace, an enormous crowd collected in the Piazzetta. With shouts of 'Death to Sirtori' the crowd, unopposed by the civic guard, surged into the courtyard of the Doge's palace, clearly intending to invade the assembly. But before they could get any further they were met by Manin, sword in hand, standing at the top of the Giant's Staircase. He told them that if they wanted to interrupt the proceedings of the assembly, they would have to do so over his dead body. The crowd was extremely reluctant to disperse, and Manin had to come out and talk to them three times before the Piazzetta was finally cleared.

[85] MCV, Doc. Manin, no. 3372, a large pamphlet dated 1 March 1849, laying out the rules for the assembly. The presidents and vice-presidents of the assembly were to be elected for a month at a time. The assembly was split into three sections, drawn by lots; each section would discuss the relevant issues amongst themselves, before the final debate and voting in the full assembly. There were four permanent committees of the assembly: for the army and navy; for finance, trade and commerce; for the legal code; and for internal administration. Each committee was composed of eleven representatives and no one could belong to more than two of them. There were new elections for them every two months. Any representative could attend the meetings of the committees, but had no voting rights.

[86] The committee offered their resignation, which Manin refused to accept. Tommaseo, in the assembly of 7 March, said their inaction was not attributable to evil intentions, but rather to somnolence. Stefani, the vice-prefect of public order, was a well-known Albertist; MCV, Doc. Manin, nos. 3118, 3126, 3128, 3450.

De Giorgi has described it as the most serious popular disturbance of the revolution.[87]

After this, the assembly decided by 61 votes to 48 not to take Ferrari-Bravo's proposal into consideration. The pro-Piedmontese Avesani then moved that the triumvirate be given unlimited powers, and should consult the assembly only in the case of a change in the political condition of the city. Avesani's move was obviously an attempt to prevent the radical elements in the assembly from exercising any political power. A committee, headed by Tommaseo, was set up to examine the proposal. It decided by five votes to four against the proposal, and recommended that the previous powers of the triumvirate should be considered as adequate. The assembly adopted the recommendation by 72 votes to 36.[88]

Avesani's attempt to emasculate the assembly thus came to grief, but the triumvirate were confirmed in power, and the radicals' offensive had foundered again on the rock of popular support for Manin. After the incidents of 5 March Sirtori commented to a colleague, 'we are forced to admit that here at Venice there is not a people, but only a man'.[89] On 7 March Olper proposed that Manin be appointed president of a new government, whose members he should select. Sirtori made a number of amendments, all of which were overwhelmingly defeated. Manin became president and reappointed Cavedalis and Graziani for the army and navy, as well as Calucci for justice and internal affairs, Da Camin for education, culture and charity, and Pesaro Maurogonato for finance.

The first act of the new president was to adjourn the assembly for a week. Manin had originally wanted to make the adjournment last a month, for he feared that feelings were still running very high. He was advised against doing so by his friend Malfatti, in a letter of 7 March. Malfatti's letter presents an unrivalled picture of the balance of political forces in Venice at this time:

I must confess that the introduction of foreigners into the Venetian assembly has caused me great anxiety. Already you can see that these men are of the

[87] A. De Giorgi, 'Venezia nel 1848 e 1849', p. 35.

[88] MCV, Doc. Manin, no. 3370, handbill of 5 March 1849, reporting the proceedings of the assembly of that day. Tommaseo, as chairman of the committee, had the casting vote. He firmly supported Sirtori and Ferrari-Bravo, and opposed any increase in Manin's power.

[89] De Giorgi, 'Venezia nel 1848 e 1849', p. 36. Vollo, in *Per Tutti* (no. 5, 9 March) leapt to Sirtori's defence with a leader in Venetian dialect reminding the Venetians of Sirtori's heroic part in the Mestre sortie. Carlo Fenzi, the Tuscan emissary, in a letter of 10 March to his father, wrote that 'Manin has a popularity amongst the common people that surpasses all belief'; see M. Nobili, 'Corrispondenza tra Emanuele e Carlo Fenzi nel 1849', in *Rassegna Storica del Risorgimento*, 26 (1939), p. 286.

extreme Left and are against the government. Cavedalis's discourse,[90] while full of home truths, was imprudent. It has strengthened that confounded left wing, and has made your position more difficult. From my observations, which I think are accurate, there are . . . 36 votes firmly for the government, and 19 firmly for the Left. . . . The 19 of the Left are difficult to win over because they are either foreigners, or else hot-headed patriots of confused ideas who have allowed themselves to be dominated by the foreigners. What we must do is win over all those representatives who can be classified as 'wavering'.[91]

While the assembly was in recess, Venice received new affirmations of friendship from the Roman republic. Mazzini had become one of the triumvirs of the republic and addressed a proclamation to the Venetian people: 'Italy will be made, and no force will be able to unmake her, on the day when the men of Venice walk in the Campidoglio, and share their votes, their hopes, and their thoughts with the men of the Eternal City.'[92] On 5 March Castellani wrote saying that the Roman assembly had matched the Piedmontese by voting Venice a subsidy of 100,000 scudi (600,000 lire). 30,000 of this was to be brought immediately to Venice by Guiccioli. In return the Venetians assigned four cannon for the defence of Ravenna.[93]

This ad hoc mutual aid was much welcomed by both Romans and Venetians, but it was clear that the Roman leaders wanted to go beyond it, and tighten the bonds between Tuscany, Rome and Venice, so as to create a democratic bloc in contrast to monarchist Piedmont. This idea was taken up by the opposition in Venice when the assembly reconvened. On 14 March Sirtori urged the assembly to declare 'its solidarity with Rome and Tuscany'.[94] Manin said that questions of party should not be raised, and attention should be given only to the defence of the city. Sirtori replied that his words had been spoken not out of love of party, but for love of his country. The debate was postponed till the following day, but

---

[90] Malfatti's reference is to Cavedalis's report on the army of 22 Feb. 1849, when he told the assembly that a besieged city could not be turned into a debating society.

[91] MCV, Doc. Manin, no. 4098. The letter is marked *urgentissima*. Bartolomeo Malfatti (1802–65) was chief administrator of the civic hospital in Venice from 1841 onwards. He was elected to both the July and the permanent assemblies.

[92] Marchesi, *Storia documentata*, app. doc. xxvii, p. 524.

[93] The main reason for this Venetian generosity was the fear that Austrian troops would occupy both Ancona and Ravenna, and thus cut off the supply of foodstuffs that came from those ports. See the letter sent by the government to Vasseur, 19 Feb. 1849, MCV, Doc. Manin, no. 2510. For Mazzini's letter of thanks, 4 April 1849, see MCV, Agg. Manin, xvi/4. On the Roman subsidy, see *La Repubblica veneta*, vol. 2, pp. 613ff and 622, Castellani's dispatches of 5 and 8 March 1849.

[94] See Ventura, *Lineamenti costituzionali*, p. 133.

in the meantime dramatic news arrived in Venice – Piedmont had broken its armistice with Austria and once again declared war. On 15 March, amidst mounting excitement, Manin ordered the assembly to go into recess for a fortnight while hostilities were resumed.

Novara, and resistance at all costs

By March of 1849 King Charles Albert of Piedmont felt that he had no option but to go to war again, even if the chances of success were considerably more limited than a year earlier. His personal prestige and that of his dynasty had been badly damaged by the defeat at Custozza, the incidents at Milan and the Salasco armistice. Both his honour and the future of the Savoy dynasty were now at stake, and an honourable defeat was far preferable to a humiliating abandonment of the struggle against Austria. By March also any hope he may have had of territorial recompense through the Anglo-French mediation had faded completely. In addition, the Austrians were heavily involved in the war with Hungary and the longer the Piedmontese delayed the more chance there was of Vienna being able to pick off its enemies one by one. Finally, the finances of the kingdom could not for long support the maintenance of the army on a war footing. Serious efforts had been made to reorganise the army, and a Polish general of some reputation, Chrzanowski, had been invited to take overall command. Most of the Piedmontese generals and officers were pessimistic about the outcome of a new war against Radetzky, and resentful of the appointment of an outsider as commander-in-chief, but few felt that there was really any alternative.

For two weeks Italy was gripped by the war fever that had characterised the early days of the revolution. Mazzini told Castellani in Rome that he would have preferred to have had the war delayed by two months so that central Italy could have led the offensive. If Piedmont lost, said Mazzini, the cause of national independence would be set back by many years; but if Piedmont won, the republican party would be lost forever. Castellani commented curtly to Manin that in his opinion 'the Piedmontese war effort is preferable to the cowardly inertia of Tuscany and of Rome. These two states could at most preserve themselves but never, as things are at the moment, wage war against Austria.'[95] In Venice, maps of Lombardy were laid out on the café tables of the Piazza, and rumours of Austrian defeat proliferated.[96] Amidst wild rejoicings, General Pepe left for Chioggia to lead a sortie into the southern Veneto against the

[95] *La Repubblica veneta*, vol. 2, p. 638, Castellani's dispatch of 17 March 1849.
[96] These details come from a long poem which appeared in *Per tutti*, no. 26, 30 March 1849.

Austrians. His plan was to penetrate deep into the Polesine and, if possible, link first with the Roman troops that were concentrating at Bologna, and then with the Piedmontese. On 17 and 18 March detailed plans were drawn up for the expedition. A first column of 4,610 men was to break through the enemy lines and would then be followed by a second of 1,845 men, including the Alpine legion under the legendary Calvi.[97]

Pepe did not go so far or so fast as he hoped. The Austrian line proved difficult to break and the first few days of hostilities were confined to a series of skirmishes north of Brondolo. But the Venetians had far from despaired when suddenly the most shattering news arrived from Piedmont, and put an end to all hopes of a Venetian offensive. After only a few days of the new campaign, Charles Albert's army had been totally outmanoeuvred and outfought by Radetzky at Novara. The king had abdicated in favour of his son Victor Emmanuel II, and a new armistice had been signed which included the provision that the Piedmontese fleet should again immediately leave Venetian waters. Radetzky was left undisputed master of northern Italy.

On 2 April 1849, the Venetian assembly met behind locked doors, in the great Council Chamber of the Doge's palace. It was a solemn moment. The only Italian force regarded as capable of opposing the Austrians had been totally crushed. Manin asked the assembly if Venice wished to continue to resist. There was a unanimous cry of 'Yes'. 'At any cost?' 'At any cost.' Manin was granted unlimited powers, a huge red flag was hoisted on the central flag pole in St Mark's Square, and many Venetians from then onwards wore a red ribbon in their buttonholes.[98] With great bravery the city prepared to face the full onslaught of the Austrian army.

---

[97] See the order of the day, signed Ulloa, of 17 March 1849 and Cavedalis's *urgentissima* of 18 March 1849, in ASV, Gov. Prov. 1848–9, DG, b. 342, fasc. 2691, nos. 7983 and 8067. Pepe had written to Charles Albert on 15 Feb. 1849, urging him to go to war again, and concluding his letter: 'I, averse by nature to monarchy, will none the less acclaim from the bottom of my heart Charles Albert as king of Italy as soon as he crosses the Isonzo again' (AST, carte politiche diverse, cart. 25, fasc. 150, no. 55).

[98] See R. Fulin, 'Venezia e Daniele Manin', *Archivio Veneto*, 9 (1875), pp. 169ff, and Marchesi, *Storia documentata*, pp. 392–3 n. 67.

9

The last months, April to August 1849

For five months Venice was to withstand every Austrian attempt to force her into subjugation. With no hope remaining, the Venetians rivalled the Romans in the heroism with which they defended their city. G. M. Trevelyan, in describing Garibaldi's defence of Rome, wrote: 'If the Englishman does not know when he is beaten, the Italian sometimes knows it and does not care.'[1] It was like this with the Venetians; as the summer reached its height, and the Austrian guns intoned their incessant message across the lagoon, Venice began to starve. As more rye was mixed with the dwindling supplies of wheat, what bread there was became increasingly unpalatable. A chicken cost a working man his week's wages, there was no wine, and butter could not be bought even by the rich. Then, to these deprivations were added the horrors of bombardment and finally the ravages of cholera. Throughout it all, the Venetian people did not once raise their voice to demand surrender. On 13 August 1849, when Manin spoke to the Venetians for the last time from his balcony on the Piazza San Marco, he was so overcome with emotion as to be unable to finish what he had been trying to say. Stepping back into his study, he murmured to those nearest to him, 'Such a people! To be forced to surrender with such a people!'[2]

Venice and Rome

After the Piedmontese defeat at Novara, only Tuscany and the Papal States remained to fight alongside Venice against the counter-revolutionary forces which were by now dominant in Italy and Europe. The city of Genoa did rise in revolt against the Savoy dynasty, and Mazzini held out great hopes that another corner of the peninsula would be won for the republican cause. But after a few days Genoa capitulated to La Marmora, and the new king, Victor Emmanuel II, was able to hold his kingdom together.

[1] G. M. Trevelyan, *Garibaldi's Defence of the Roman Republic*, p. 209.
[2] H. Martin, *Manin and Venice*, vol. 2, p. 220.

The democrats and republicans fared little better in Tuscany. As the threat of Austrian invasion loomed large, Guerrazzi was given supreme power, but he proved totally unequal to the task. Most of the Tuscan moderates had by this time abandoned the revolution, and the landowners and priests began to use their influence on the peasantry to provoke insurrections against Florence and Leghorn. On 26 April 1849 15,000 Austrian troops under General D'Aspre marched into Tuscany. They met fierce resistance only at Leghorn, where the populace had forced the municipality not to surrender. The city was occupied by the Austrians on 11 May, and the popular leaders, Bartelloni and Ghilardi, were shot. The grand duke returned to his dominions some two months later.

This left only the Roman republic, which was to organise a famous resistance, lasting until 2 July 1849, against the various armies which threatened its borders. By a savage twist of fortune their principal enemy and eventual conqueror was the French army under General Oudinot which had originally been assembled to aid the Italian cause. But Louis Napoleon, the new French president, now sought the support of the traditional and clerical elements in French society by restoring Pius IX to his throne. He and his ministers believed mistakenly that it was possible to restore the Pope without his abandoning all the constitutional achievements of the period preceding the assassination of Rossi. Napoleon justified his intervention in terms of preventing the Austrians or Neapolitans getting to Rome first, and re-establishing absolutist rule in the Papal States. Oudinot therefore landed at Civitavecchia and the soldiers of the French republic moved against the republic of Rome. As they neared the city, they found the trees and walls by the roadside covered with placards bearing the text of article 5 of the French constitution – that the republic would never use force to suppress the liberties of other peoples. Oudinot expected Rome to fall without a fight, so great had been the propaganda all over Europe about the disorder and incompetence of the Roman government. But on 30 April the forces of Garibaldi, Masi and Galletti completely routed the 6,000 French troops, who retreated in some disorder. Garibaldi wanted to follow up this brilliant victory, but was restrained by Mazzini, who still hoped that Napoleon could be persuaded to change his mind. He did not, but the Roman resistance was to continue, against all odds, for another two months.

During this time, when the republicans and democrats of Rome and Venice were fighting for their lives, and in the process creating two of the most glorious episodes of Risorgimento history, it would have been natural to expect the two cities to have been locked in fraternal alliance, aiding each other in any way that circumstances permitted. This was not the case. Manin consistently refused any formal alliance with the Roman republic. In the Venetian assembly of 2 April 1849 one of the members of the Italian Club, Samuele Olper, proposed that commissioners should be dispatched immediately to both Florence and Rome. On the 3rd he wrote to Manin, urging a life or death pact with the central Italian states.[3] Manin did not agree; he argued in the assembly that Venice should not be shown to align herself politically with any other Italian state: 'We are not talking any more of an offensive war . . . we can do nothing but resist.'[4]

Behind this statement there lurked a deep mistrust of and hostility to the Roman republicans, the causes of which are to be found in both the nature of Manin's republicanism and his interpretation of events in Rome. Manin had not wanted either Mazzini or Garibaldi in Venice, and since resuming power on 11 August 1848 had consistently underplayed his own republicanism. He had also, as we have seen, stressed internal order as of the highest priority for Venice. Gustavo Modena, writing from Rome in January 1849, wickedly observed that if the time came for Venice to surrender, 'the assembly will fade away and Manin will shed tears for his country, but will console his conscience by repeating to himself: "everything is lost except for legality, and I now give this back to Heaven in the same immaculate condition as when I received it from Professor Cramer [of Padua university]"'.[5] Mazzini's overt hostility to Piedmont, the power of the clubs at Rome, the popular demonstrations that preceded and followed Pius IX's flight from the city, all these were elements which Manin disliked and which he had sought to combat in Venice. In a letter of 30 April 1849 Manin gave instructions to Castellani, Venice's emissary to Rome, which clearly condemned the Roman republicans.[6] Manin told Castellani 'to obtain for us at least that moral support which could be of use to us', but only on condition that 'things should return to the state that they were in before 16 November'. While Rome was in the hands of the republicans, Manin wanted very little to do with it.

Castellani himself must take a fair share of the responsibility for Manin's attitude. The Venetian emissary at Rome, although a firm republican, was no Mazzinian, and never ceased to paint the Roman republic in the most lurid of lights. He was harshly critical, with some justification, of the incompetence of the republican government at Rome, but did less than justice to the heroism demonstrated by the Roman army and populace from 30 April onwards. Even those who were openly hostile to the republican cause, like the Wurtemberg consul Kolb, paid greater tribute

[3] MCV, Doc. Manin, no. 842.
[4] Fulin, 'Venezia e Daniele Manin', p. 171.
[5] Grandi (ed.), *Epistolario di Gustavo Modena*, p. 99.
[6] *La Repubblica veneta nel 1848–9*, vol. 2, *Documenti diplomatici, carteggio di G. B. Castellani*, p. 709.

to the Roman resistance and republican leaders.[7] When Oudinot finally took the city at the cost of many a republican life, Castellani wrote him a note that can only be judged as cringing and inexcusable: 'My government has never feared French armed intervention in the Italian question. Revolutions come and go, but civilisation remains, and France is its worthy propagator and guardian.'[8]

Part of Castellani's antagonism to the Roman republic stemmed from its failure to keep its promises to aid Venice financially. Of the 100,000 scudi voted by the Roman assembly only 30,000 were actually delivered. In a conversation of 9 April 1849 Mazzini reproached Castellani for the fact that while Rome was proposing 'a strategy of active union', Venice insisted on remaining in 'patient isolation'.[9] With controlled fury Castellani pointed out that Venice had paid for the papal troops in the Veneto the previous year, and had contributed some five million lire and 26 cannon: 'We now need three million lire a month to survive; you and Tuscany should pay two of them between you.'

The Venetians also hoped that by dissociating themselves from Rome, which was so compromised in the eyes of the Great Powers, Venice might yet be treated as a special case and Austria be persuaded to grant her a measure of independence. On 4 April Manin wrote to both England and France, appealing for their intervention on behalf of his city. Palmerston and Drouyn de Lhuys responded by giving the same advice; there was

---

[7] See his dispatch of 4 May 1849 published in R. Moscati, *La diplomazia*, p. 145. Opinion was sharply divided amongst those who left Venice for Rome at this time. Samuele Olper, having been strongly in favour of the Roman republicans while in Venice, changed his mind when he got there. He wrote to Rensovich on 24 April 1849 (MCV, Doc. Manin, no. 4110): 'I think that it needs only the smallest of attacks, either internal or external, to make the city give in; this is the fault of the government, not the people ... I have spoken three times and at length with Mazzini, and I am now convinced that our Manin is worth a hundred Mazzinis.' On the other hand Federico Seismit-Doda wrote to Bianca da Camino on 29 April 1849: 'The assembly here acts with divine grace, as does the Triumvirate. Oh! If you could only read the reports of the assembly's sessions and the decrees approved by these young deputies.' Castellani remained adamant in his condemnation of the republic long after it had fallen. In a long and interesting letter of self-justification, written to Giuseppe Gabussi in November 1851, he admitted that Rome had been defended with glory, but that the city had been governed 'without thought, without courage, without genius, without virtue'; see R. Giusti, 'Le vicende della Repubblica romana del 1849 nel carteggio di Benedetto Musolino, G. Battista Castellani, Filippo de Boni ed altri democratici', *Archivio Veneto*, 66 (1960), p. 72.

[8] *La Repubblica veneta*, vol. 2, p. 749. Enrico Dandolo and Luciano Manara, two of the young leaders of the Milanese *cinque giornate*, were amongst those killed in the defence of Rome.

[9] *Ibid.*, pp. 675–6.

nothing left for Venice, in their opinion, but to make peace with Austria on any terms.[10] Palmerston said that he had not failed to notice 'the good order which has been preserved within the city', but the time had come to surrender. Both these replies had been received by the beginning of May and effectively put an end to any lingering hopes the Venetians may have had of salvation by means of European diplomacy. Even so, Manin continued to refuse open support for Rome, and the Roman republic fell some two months later without ever having been recognised by Venice. This unjustifiable reluctance to grant Rome some sort of recognition in its hour of greatest peril was the *reductio ad absurdum* of Manin's policy of 'prudently waiting upon events'.

The defence of Fort Marghera

While the French moved slowly on Rome, the Austrians prepared to reduce Venice. After Novara their army increased in strength to 30,000 men, under the command of the infamous Lieutenant-Marshal Haynau, who had just earned himself the title of the 'butcher of Brescia' for his barbaric suppression of that city's revolt against the Austrians. Brescia had risen in insurrection after the news of Piedmont's renewal of the war, and under the leadership of the republicans Cassola and Contratti had fought off the Austrian troops for more than a week. Haynau finally put down the revolt amidst atrocities and summary executions. Between 600 and 1,000 Brescians lost their lives.

As Albini and the Piedmontese fleet had had no option but to leave Venetian waters for good, the blockade of Venice began in earnest.[11] There was at first little shortage of food, since the government had built up copious reserves. Bread and vegetables were plentiful, but by the beginning of May firewood was practically unobtainable. Although the city was peaceful and spirits high, an ominous increase in the number of beggars bore witness to the continuing impoverishment of the lower classes.[12]

On 4 May 1849 the Austrian artillery opened fire on Fort Marghera, which lay near the point where the railway left the mainland to bridge the lagoon. Earlier in the revolution Marghera had been strongly fortified

[10] Palmerston's letter was dated 20 April 1849, that of Drouyn de Lhuys, 27 April; MCV, Doc. Manin, nos. 962 and 951.

[11] See the letter from Albini to Manin, 10 April 1849; MCV, Doc. Manin, no. 929. The French ships also left, bearing the foreign residents of the city. The *Pluton* later returned and was to stay until Venice surrendered.

[12] V. Marchesi (ed.), 'Diario di un anonimo (Venezia dal maggio al 16 agosto 1849)', in *Miscellanea veneziana (1848–9)*, entry of 4 May, p. 131.

by the amiable Venetian general Rizzardi,[13] and it was garrisoned by 2,500 Neapolitans and Venetians, among them the *Bandiera e Moro* artillery company. On the first day of the assault seven thousand cannon balls were fired at the fort. Radetzky and other Austrian dignitaries looked on from a tower in nearby Mestre, believing that the Italians would capitulate by the evening. They were quite wrong. Marghera was gallantly defended for three weeks, until hardly a gun in the fort was working, and one man in six had been wounded. On 15 May Sirtori, who played a leading part in the defence of the fort, wrote to Tommaseo of the heroism of the Italian soldiers.[14] One of the Lombard engineers, Valli, had had to have his left foot amputated. When the operation was finished he kissed Sirtori 'with an angelic smile such as I have never seen. Dear Tommaseo, such examples are a sublime school of heroism. Witnessing them increases a hundredfold one's will to resist.'

Long after the Austrian grand dukes had tired of waiting, the inhabitants of Venice continued to stream to the western flanks of the city, or to its highest bell towers, to watch the spectacle and admire the bravery of their troops. Finally, on 27 May, just before the Austrians launched another massive assault, the commander of the fort, the intrepid young Neapolitan Girolamo Ulloa, decided that the resistance could not continue. The fort was abandoned overnight and its garrison was saved from having to surrender. Sirtori and the Neapolitan Enrico Cosenz, another of Garibaldi's bravest lieutenants in Sicily in 1860, were the last to leave. They successfully spiked the remaining guns and Sirtori mined the adjacent fort of S. Giuliano, which blew up when the Austrians occupied it.[15]

The Venetians immediately destroyed five arches of the railway bridge so that it could not provide the Austrians with a gateway to the city. At the far end of the truncated bridge a battery of guns called 'San Antonio' was set up. Against all odds the Italians held this battery, as Trevelyan has written, 'for week after week of that truceless midsummer war above

[13] N. Tommaseo, *Venezia*, vol. 1, pp. 194–5. See also n. 495 where Tommaseo describes Rizzardi as 'a mild man, even when he had been drinking, and he certainly drank'. Rizzardi, like so many of the leading military figures of 1848–9, had been a Napoleonic soldier who emerged from retirement at the time of the revolution.

[14] BNF, fondo Tommaseo, 130/36, no. 4. For the number of wounded, see Trevelyan, *Manin and the Venetian Revolution*, p. 226.

[15] Trevelyan, *Manin and the Venetian Revolution*, p. 227. Tommaseo (*Venezia*, vol. 1, 223), pays tribute to the gondoliers who braved the hail of bullets to carry munitions to Marghera and return with the wounded; Marchesi, in his *Storia documentata*, p. 413, makes the same point with regard to the *arsenalotti*. For the letters of one of Marghera's bravest defenders, see C. Rosaroll, *Assedio di Malghera 1849. Lettere del colonnello barone Cesare Rosaroll-Scorza, comandante la lunetta n. 13*.

the shimmering lagoon'.[16] Two of the position's commanders – the Venetian Coluzzi and the Neapolitan Rosaroll – were killed defending it. The third, Cosenz himself, survived four wounds including a sabre cut across the face, and kept the guns firing till the very last.

The military commission

Within Venice few despaired, but confidence in the military members of the triumvirate, Cavedalis and Graziani, diminished considerably. Dissatisfaction with the lack of coordination between the various authorities in the city – the triumvirate, General Pepe, the municipality, the civic guard and the committee of war – reached its height after the fall of Marghera. Ulloa, for instance, complained angrily to Manin in a letter of 10 June that the railway bridge had been blown up, but his exhausted soldiers had not received the necessary help in the vital task of clearing away the debris.[17] The commanders of the Venetian outposts had been promised several hundred workmen by the municipality; in the event only about sixty turned up to help remove those pieces of the destroyed bridge which might have aided the enemy's advance. Neither Pepe nor Ulloa had any power to order the municipality about, and Ulloa was particularly bitter that his troops, who had been severely tested in the previous weeks, had not received any substantial aid.

It was with Cavedalis in particular that the young and frequently radical officers who had distinguished themselves during the Mestre sortie and the defence of Marghera were growing impatient. Ulloa wrote a scathing letter to Fabrizi on 24 March 1849, recounting how the 'cowardly' Cavedalis had given the order to retire during a sortie near Brondolo because he had mistaken the Lombard legion for an Austrian column.[18] Manin had then approved 'the wise orders' of Cavedalis. 'Is it possible', asked Ulloa, 'to go on any more with this rabble?' Later Fabio Uccelli wrote to Sirtori complaining of the 'provincial nepotism' shown

---

[16] Trevelyan, *Manin and the Venetian Revolution*, p. 228. The Florentine Carlo Fenzi wrote home on 4 July 1849, calling Rosaroll 'the Ajax of our army'. He continued: 'In general, the Neapolitan officers that we have here all show an extraordinary bravery and are of the highest quality; perhaps they are the best the Bourbon king had in his army'; see M. Nobili, 'Corrispondenza', p. 312.

[17] ASV, Gov. Prov. 1848–9, b. 118, presidenza ed esteri, riservati, 1849, letters of Ulloa 9 and 10 June 1849, no number.

[18] MRM, archivio generale, reg. no. 36976 (N. Fabrizi). A month later Ulloa wrote again to Fabrizi (*ibid.*, 24 April 1849), expressing the opinion that 'in these moments Manin is moving closer to the real republicans'; but by June it was clear that Manin, although often seeming to draw near to the radical republicans, was in reality a firm supporter of men like Cavedalis.

by Cavedalis in his appointments.[19] Many officers, especially the non-Venetians, had a very low opinion both of Cavedalis's politics and his military prowess.

On 3 June 1849, at a crowded meeting of the Italian Club, an invitation was issued to all soldiers as well as citizens to come every Sunday to discuss the problem of the coordination of defence. As this was in defiance of the ban imposed on 2 October 1848 on military participation in the club, Manin immediately closed it down. But agitation for a new military commission with wide-ranging powers continued to grow. On 6 June a deputation from the civic guard asked Manin to dismiss the old committee of war, over which the lethargic Admiral Bua still presided. On the 9th Tommaseo, now completely estranged from Manin, wrote to him demanding that the navy take some action, that a committee of the assembly be appointed to inspect any letters that Manin wrote to the Austrians, and that a military commission be established. Then, on the 11th, three of the Italian Club, the engineer Manzini, the abbot Lazzaneo and Michele Caffi, were arrested on the charge of having organised a meeting of officers with the aim of getting rid of the committee of war.[20]

This struggle was taken up in the assembly and resulted in the only major victory of the radicals during the revolution. Sirtori's popularity had rapidly increased as a result of his part in the defence of Marghera. On 31 May, in the assembly's election for a committee to decide whether to treat with the Austrians, he came third with sixty votes. A fortnight later, when another committee was set up to deal with the same problem, Sirtori topped the poll with 105 votes, practically all the assembly voting for him. The committee reported on 16 June; it recommended that resistance should continue, and also that 'a military commission should be appointed with full powers'. It further stipulated that the commission should consist of Ulloa, Sirtori and a young lieutenant in the Venetian navy, Francesco Baldisserotto.[21]

Manin seems to have been resigned to giving way at this stage. He

[19] BAM, carte Sirtori, ii/58, letter of 21 July 1849.
[20] Marchesi, 'Diario di un anonimo', p. 140. See also the interesting little pamphlet by M. Manni, *La commissione militare dittatoriale dal giugno all'agosto del 1849*. The author obviously took part in these events, but his memoirs are written so long afterwards that he has mistaken a number of dates. For Tommaseo's letter, see Ciampini, *Vita di Nicolò Tommaseo*, p. 542. For Manin's closure of the club, see Racc. Andreola, vol. 7, pp. 327–8.
[21] Fulin, 'Venezia e Daniele Manin', pp. 175 and 181. Baldisserotto (1813–91), who came from Vicenza, had been active in the navy during the days leading up to 22 March 1848, and he had distinguished himself in a sortie from the fort at Treporti, as well as at Mestre. It was hoped that his youth and courage would bring new fire to the Venetian navy.

limited himself to saying in the assembly that while under normal circumstances a diarchy in Venice would not be tolerable, he would make every effort to overcome any difficulties that arose. The assembly voted 93 to 18 in favour of the commission. Manin announced the decision to the crowd that had assembled in the Piazzetta, and, in contrast to the events of 5 March, the news was greeted with shouts of joy.[22] Thus, after eleven months, the idea for which the Italian Club had first campaigned was finally realised.

Almost the first act of the commissioners was to order the release of the three members of the Italian Club arrested on the 11th. Manin reluctantly agreed, and it became clear that supreme authority in the city now rested with the commission. The committee of public vigilance promptly resigned, stating that it had lost 'all moral power'; it took Manin a fortnight to persuade Carlo Zambaldi, its president, to withdraw his resignation.[23]

The details of the activities of the military commissioners will never be known in full, for, on leaving Venice at the end of the revolution, they destroyed all but one *busta* of their papers.[24] However, from the papers of Giuseppe Sirtori and other sources, it is possible to reconstruct the broad outline of their policies. They were determined to instil into every part of the Venetian army and navy the same absolute determination to resist that they themselves felt. In order to do this, they tried to remove from positions of responsibility all those officers who had been over-cautious and conservative in the past, and who by June of 1849 had given the battle up for lost. Admiral Bua was dismissed, Armandi was demoted from the rank of general, Mengaldo was sent off to Fort Brondolo, and a host of other senior officers lost their posts to younger men. On 21 July, for example, 26 officers including two colonels and two lieutenant-colonels were put on half pay because they had contributed little or nothing to the resistance. All leave was cancelled and Sirtori wrote to Cavedalis denouncing the excessive bureaucracy that he had built up at the war department.[25]

The military commissioners also made every attempt to recruit fresh

[22] MCV, Doc. Manin, no. 3839, Vasseur's diary. See also Fulin, 'Venezia e Daniele Manin', pp. 182–9. Pepe was so hurt at not being included as one of the commissioners that he threatened to leave Venice. A compromise was hastily arranged, and he became honorary president of the commission.

[23] MCV, Doc. Manin, nos. 3134–7. Zambaldi and Rensovich both insisted on resigning again, and for good, on 24 July 1849. Rensovich wrote, 'the principles now dominant in Venice are absolutely opposed to my own' (*ibid.*, nos. 3143–4).

[24] See ASV, index 177.

[25] BAM, carte Sirtori, III/24, minutes of Sirtori's letter of 13 July 1849. For the measures of 21 July, see ASV, Gov. Prov. 1848–9, b. 413, comm. milit., no number.

soldiers so as to keep every part of the fortifications well defended. A report of 15 June showed that the total number of men in the army had dropped to 14,424, and of these 1,035 were in hospital. Sirtori at first considered conscription and Morandi, the former commander of the council for all volunteer corps at Treviso and by now a general in the Venetian army, suggested a call-up of all those who had done military service in the years 1845–7. His advice does not seem to have been taken, but the commission's constant appeals for new men met with a ready response; by 25 July numbers in the army had risen to 16,574.[26] One section in particular, the Venetian civic guard, was radically transformed. Reports reached Sirtori that the civic guard, which had played so memorable a role at the beginning of the revolution, had fallen into decay. This was because of the widespread exemptions from service granted to civil servants and the middle classes, and only the artisans and working classes of the city were continuing to perform the duties assigned to them. On 7 July the commissioners asked Marsich, the commander of the civic guard since the previous August, to supply them with another 400 men.[27] Marsich replied that he could meet the demand only by mobilising the civic guard's reserve, which constituted 'the most destitute part of the population'. The reserve was mobilised, and the commissioners also put an end to the abuses of the previous months.

In the navy less seems to have been done, perhaps because Baldisserotto was not of the calibre of the other two commissioners. But Admiral Bucchia was appointed the new commander-in-chief, and attempts were made to put an end to the demoralisation that had infected both officers and men after the many months of inactivity under Graziani. At Chioggia, the military commission decided that the local landowners and most of the committee of the city were not to be trusted. For the rest of the revolution, therefore, Chioggia was put under a special military commission of its own to ensure, as Sirtori put it, that the city 'will resist with dignity'.[28]

In all, the tireless and implacable activity of the military commission

[26] ASV, Gov. Prov. 1848–9, MU, b. 111, no. 11289 for details of the army on 25 July 1849; BAM, carte Sirtori, 11/47 for details of 15 June. Earlier in the summer (3 May 1849) Sirtori and Cosenz had made a tour of the Venetian army and reported to General Pepe that the only sections of the army that left something to be desired were the Venetian line regiments which had previously been the Venetian mobile civic guard; BAM, carte Sirtori, 11/35. For Sirtori's considerations on conscription and the general military state of affairs on 29 June 1849, see BAM, carte Sirtori, 11/70; *ibid.*, 111/46, for Morandi's suggestions.
[27] BAM, carte Sirtori, 111/12. For the condition of the civic guard see the reports from the second and third battalions, 5 July 1849, *ibid.*, 111/8, *c* and *d*.
[28] *Ibid.*, 11/70.

contributed greatly to the heroism with which Venice was defended in the summer of 1849. In his history of the revolution Vincenzo Marchesi, no lover of radicals, was forced to admit that 'the defence of Venice in its last two months was better conducted and better organised than at any stage previously'.[29] Sadly for the Venetian cause, the commission had come too late, for in June 1849 there was no room for manoeuvre, and no possible outcome except eventual surrender. But the activities of the commission, like those of the defenders of Rome, gave the emphatic lie to those like Cavedalis who maintained that the radicals were incapable of discipline and that under their command the army would degenerate into a factious hothouse of political discord. Instead the commission succeeded in implanting their own spirit of self-sacrifice and determination, feelings well summarised in the letter that the young Tuscan radical Carlo Fenzi wrote from Venice on 11 May 1849 to his wealthy, anxious and disapproving father:

My conscience impels me to destroy and hunt out the enemy from my country at whatever cost, at the cost of burnt-out cities, ravaged fields, or social disorders. In a word, as I have told you on many an occasion, I would blow up half Italy to get rid of the Austrians. The independence of Italy is for me, and will be till I die, the purpose of my life. And so, once and for all you must accept that I am not under the evil influence of anyone; my actions are spontaneous, the product of my intelligence and my will.[30]

Venice, Hungary and Austria

While the Venetians strove to withstand the Austrian assault, they received encouragement from only one foreign power – Hungary. Indeed, it was only in Hungary that the turn towards counter-revolution had been contained, and that the will to resist had been translated into an effective army. Although Kossuth and Görgey, his greatest general, were increasingly at loggerheads as the revolution went on, they had managed to assemble a most reliable fighting force – 152,000 men with 450 guns. Nearly all the Magyar regiments of the Austrian army had gone over to the insurgents' side, and the recruitment campaign that Kossuth had carried out in the great Hungarian plains in September 1848 yielded thousands of men willing to enlist in the *Honvéd*, the Home Defence regiments. Sporting a tricolour sash and carrying a national flag, Kossuth

---

[29] Marchesi, *Storia documentata*, p. 429.

[30] Nobili, 'Corrispondenza', p. 303. Guglielmo Stefani wrote to Jacopo Serravalle in Trieste on 29 June 1849, telling him of the heroic defence of the city and his part in it. He added, 'Who could have predicted this when we were vegetating together at Padua?' (MCV, archivio Bernardi, b. 35, no number).

had been able to appeal to the peasantry to fight for the national cause, something that no Italian leader had succeeded in doing in 1848. Because the April laws had both ended feudalism for many of the peasantry and promised the landlords state compensation, Kossuth was able to unite landlord and peasantry in a way that was unique in Europe in 1848–9. The conservative nobleman Pázmándy wrote to Csányi on 5 October 1848: 'we have too many men; they have arrived here but without suitable clothes; these peasants are so poor they do not deserve to be armed'.[31] But armed they were, and in spite of many setbacks in the winter of 1848–9, the Hungarian army survived intact and in May and June 1849 won a series of spectacular victories, retaking Budapest and sending the Austrian troops under Welden scurrying back towards Vienna. If Venice was to be saved, the Hungarians alone were her likely saviours.

Tommaseo had originally thought that it would be the Serbo-Croats and not the Hungarians who would fight alongside the Italians against the imperial forces. Throughout the revolution, Tommaseo never tired of writing proclamations to the Serbo-Croatians (he was Dalmatian by birth), appealing to them to unite with their Italian neighbours. As late as April 1849 he addressed an appeal to Jelačic, beginning: 'Up till now, the Croats have gained neither liberty, military glory nor the least shadow of power'.[32] This may well have been true, but Kossuth's strident nationalism made the Serbo-Croats irreconcilable enemies of the Magyar cause, a division which the Austrians exploited with considerable skill. Jelačic rallied his co-nationals to the side of the emperor, and as a result Tommaseo while in Paris found more in common with the Hungarian Count Teleki, who was also seeking French aid. The two struck up a friendship, which Tommaseo would have liked to have seen extended to an alliance between the two powers they represented. But because of Manin's refusal to take any diplomatic initiatives at this time, Tommaseo's project came to nothing.[33]

---

[31] Quoted in G. Ember, 'Louis Kossuth à la tête du Comité de la Défense Nationale', in *Studia Historica Academiae Scientiarum Hungaricae*, 6 (1953), p. 19 n. 9. See also F. Fejtö, 'Hungary, the war of independence', in F. Fejtö (ed.), *The Opening of an Era, 1848*, pp. 313–49.

[32] Ciampini, *Vita di Nicolò Tommaseo*, p. 428. See also Tommaseo, *Venezia*, vol. 1, p. 109 n. 291. From May to July 1849 Tommaseo edited a journal called *Fratellanza dei Popoli*, which advocated in messianic tones the brotherhood of all nations, and the need for Serbo-Croats, Hungarians and Italians to unite; see the article by G. Rutto, 'Tommaseo e la *Fratellanza de' Popoli*', *Rassegna Storica del Risorgimento*, 62 (1975), pp. 3–16.

[33] Tommaseo wrote to Sirtori in August 1849: 'If the agreements reached by me in September had been drawn up into a formal treaty, the war would have taken another direction, both for them and for us' (Ciampini, *Vita di Nicolò Tommaseo*, p. 492).

None the less, contacts continued to take place between Venice and Hungary. In October, as we have seen, a Hungarian legion was formed in Venice under Lajos Winkler, and in December the Hungarian emissary in Italy asked the Venetians to issue a proclamation to the thousands of Italians serving in the war against Hungary, urging them to lay down their arms. Manin's proclamation had little effect, but a legendary Italian legion under Colonel Alessandro Monti was to fight by the side of the Hungarians until the bitter end.[34]

Five months later, in May 1849, when only Hungary, Venice and Rome continued to defy the Austrians, Kossuth sent General Bratich to Manin to conclude a defensive/offensive alliance. Kossuth at this time had great hopes of being able either to conciliate the Serbo-Croats or failing that to send a Hungarian army under Bem through Croatia, Styria and Carinthia to occupy Fiume and Trieste. The Hungarian and Venetian armies could then link up, and the Hungarians in Radetzky's army be persuaded to desert. Bratich outlined these plans to the Venetians, and Manin at last emerged from his diplomatic shell. On 20 May 1849 the alliance between Hungary and Venice was signed at Duino: Hungary promised to provide Venice with a substantial financial subsidy, and Venice agreed to create a strong diversion to the east of the city as soon as news arrived of a Hungarian column reaching Trieste.[35]

All through the summer the Venetians kept hoping that the treaty that had been signed was the prelude to a successful Hungarian expedition to the Adriatic. When the alliance was first announced the Venetian paper money suddenly regained much of its lost value, and rumours about the Hungarians were always rife in Venice – Kossuth had put aside 500,000 lire for Venice in a Parisian bank, an army of fifty thousand was marching on Trieste, the Austrians had been beaten in Transylvania, Haynau was in disgrace.[36] But these were no more than the fantasies of a besieged city.

34 See A. Pierantoni, *Il colonnello Alessandro Monti e la legione Italiana in Ungheria*, and F. Bettoni-Cazzago, *Gli italiani nella guerra d'Ungheria, 1848–9*. For the Hungarian request for a Venetian proclamation, see MCV, Doc. Manin, no. 969, letter from Turin, 2 Dec. 1848.

35 For two letters from Kossuth to Manin, April–May 1849, MCV, Doc. Manin, nos. 971–2. For further details of the alliance, *ibid.*, no. 974. For Kossuth's hopes at this time, see M. Jászay, *L'Italia e la rivoluzione ungherese del 1848–9*, pp. 148–9.

36 See Marchesi, *Storia documentata*, p. 406. Mengaldo wrote in his diary on 16 July 1849: 'It is impossible to see how we can continue to resist if the Hungarians delay their arrival. But everyone securely believes that they will arrive in time' (Meneghetti (ed.), *Il Cavaignac di Venezia*, p. 79). On 26 June 1849 Manin sent Tommaso Gar to Hungary as the Venetian chargé d'affaires; MCV, Doc. Manin, no. 980. A month later (27 July 1849) Manin received a letter from Frederic Szarvady, the secretary of the Hungarian legation in Paris, telling of Russian

In fact, Schwarzenberg had asked for the aid of Czar Nicholas I, and once the Russians intervened the Hungarians were hopelessly outnumbered; they were opposed by 328,000 men armed with 12,000 cannon. Furthermore, in spite of all Hungarian and Italian efforts to reach a reconciliation with the Serbo-Croats, Jelačic and Garašanin stood firm in support of Austria. The Hungarians never began the long march towards Trieste but, divided and demoralised, were forced into total surrender by the beginning of August. On 18 August 1849 Manin ordered the publication of two telegraphic dispatches he had just received; they told of the defeat of Hungary and the surrender of Görgey.[37] It was the reactionary powers who had combined, not the revolutionaries.

While most Venetians continued to trust in Hungary, Manin did not fail to consider a direct approach to Austria, in an attempt to gain favourable terms. On 5 May, after the bombardment of Marghera had just begun, Radetzky invited the Venetians to surrender, promising only a general amnesty and a safe passage out of the city for those too heavily compromised by the revolution. But by the end of May the Austrians, preoccupied by the Hungarians' successes and by their own lack of progress against the Venetians, instructed de Bruck to begin negotiations. The Venetian assembly, meeting in secret session, decided by 98 votes to 4 to meet the Austrian minister and hear what he had to offer. On 3 June 1849 Giuseppe Calucci and Giorgio Foscolo, both of whom knew de Bruck personally, met him at Mestre. De Bruck said that he had been entrusted with the task of drawing up the future constitution of the kingdom of Lombardy-Venetia. While remaining within the Austrian empire, the region would be granted a house of deputies and senate, which would enjoy full legislative powers. If Venice surrendered immediately, she could become part of this kingdom or else an imperial city like Trieste, or alternatively a separate kingdom of Venetia could be formed, with Venice as capital. Calucci and Foscolo said there was no question of surrender, and returned to report to the Venetian government. Manin then asked de Bruck to be more explicit about what rights the Venetians would enjoy under any new constitution. De Bruck replied evasively, saying that he had only been airing certain ideas, that precise terms were to be negotiated, but that in any case Venice would do better not to become an imperial

defeat and the rout of Jelačic (*ibid.*, no. 986). For the temporary rise in the value of the paper money, see Marchesi, 'Diario di un anonimo', p. 138. On 5 June 1849 paper money to the value of 130 lire was worth 100 lire in metallic currency. By the beginning of July, however, the paper money was worth only half its face value.

[37] MCV, Doc. Manin, nos. 3274–5.

city. He also sent the Venetian government a copy of the imperial constitution of 4 March 1849.

These negotiations were inconclusive and de Bruck had been less than clear, but they did leave some hope that Venice might salvage a measure of independence by agreeing to terms. Manin reported to the assembly on 16 June, and the deputies agreed that the talks should go on. Accordingly, Calucci and Lodovico Pasini were sent to Verona to meet de Bruck on 21 June. They found that his position had hardened, and that in reality he had little to offer beyond some form of provincial statute to be appended to the imperial constitution once Venice had surrendered. Their worst suspicions were confirmed by the letter that de Bruck wrote to the Venetian government on 23 June, which, apart from some financial concessions, amounted to an ultimatum to surrender.[38]

In the assembly of 30 June 1849 Manin gave a full account of the negotiations with de Bruck, and Varè then proposed that the assembly should move on to the order of the day, 'and let Europe be the judge between Austria and Venice'. Varè's motion was passed by 105 to 13, but not before Nicolò Priuli and the abbot Pietro Canal, both noblemen, had spoken in favour of accepting de Bruck's terms. That evening some four hundred Venetians demonstrated outside Priuli's palace, and shattered some of its windows. Some of the crowd then went on to the Piazza San Marco where Manin harangued them for their behaviour, telling them that 'they were not the people, but only a fraction of them'. He said that the army was short of sappers, and personally came down into the square to enlist those who had been demonstrating.[39]

The starving city

Conditions in Venice deteriorated quite rapidly in the summer of 1849. With the Austrians tightening the blockade around the city, bread prices, which had been so successfully pegged for much of the revolution, could not be held down any longer. By 20 May 1849 the best white bread cost 32 centesimi per *libbra* while the standard type of bread, *pane semolei o traverso*, cost 26 centesimi per *libbra*. A year earlier the two types had cost 24 and 20 centesimi each. By 16 June the stocks of wheat in the city

---

[38] For further details of these negotiations, see Marchesi, *Storia documentata*, pp. 420–3, who gives the most complete account. See also Planat de la Faye (ed.), *Documenti*, vol. 2, pp. 351, 366–9 and 393.

[39] Marchesi, 'Diario di un anonimo', pp. 146–7. According to this account, only twelve men came forward, and some of the others present, workmen to judge from the way they were dressed, laughed at those who had enrolled for 'having been caught in the trap'. See also the fragmentary diary of L. Carrer, entry of 30 June 1849, MCV, provenienze diverse, 730.c.iv.

were running low, and the government ordered rye to be mixed with it. Bread baked from this mixture went on sale at 26 centesimi per *libbra*, but it was much darker than the normal Venetian loaf and was widely regarded as indigestible and unpleasant to eat.[40]

While bread was getting much dearer and declining in quality, the government did all it could to limit price rises of other foodstuffs. On 29 May price limits were fixed for practically every other article which was regarded as a prime necessity – cheese, ham, oil, beans, rice, peas, *baccalà* (dried salt cod), wood and coal. None the less these articles also gradually became more and more scarce and costly. Wine was beginning to run out by the end of June, and innkeepers were mixing it with water. By the end of July, the government felt forced to control the sale and price of fish, which was still being caught in reasonable quantities in the lagoon. Only the three central markets of Rialto, Burano and Chioggia were allowed to sell fish, under the strict supervision of the inspectors sent out by the provisioning committee.[41]

The resilience and patriotism of the Venetian lower classes in the face of such hardship amazed every observer. The report of those who, after Marghera, made a door-to-door collection for the needs of the troops, reveals extraordinary sacrifices on the part of the poorest inhabitants of the city:

In one house they found a woman who was ill. She apologised for not having any straw mattresses to spare, but then gave one of the mattresses off her own bed . . . One family, whose son had been tragically killed at Marghera a few days earlier, gave a pillow, asking forgiveness for not being able to give more.[42]

In July Tommaseo, accompanied by the parish priest, made a collection in one of the poorest parishes in the city, S. Giovanni in Bragora. He collected more than 700 lire, a remarkable amount in view of the condition of the city and the fact that, as Tommaseo himself wrote, 'everyone knew that the end was not far away'.[43]

But though the Venetian poor were prepared, for the most part, to resist to the last, their class antagonism towards the rich inevitably increased with the dwindling of food supplies in the city. Rumours spread that the

[40] ASV, Gov. Prov. 1848–9, commissione centrale annonaria, b. 509, VIII, 1, nos. 4946 and 5771.
[41] *Ibid.*, commissione centrale annonaria, VIII, 1, no. 7318, 26 July 1849. For the extension of price controls on 29 May, see *ibid.*, MU, b. 117, no. 12611. For wine, see Marchesi, 'Diario di un anonimo', p. 145: 'True wine no longer exists, and he who buys it drinks something that is certainly not what it is called.'
[42] MCV, Doc. Pell., b. xxxvi/87, undated, but obviously of the period immediately after the fall of Marghera.
[43] Ciampini, *Vita di Nicolò Tommaseo*, p. 546.

wealthier members of the community were hoarding food. In the assembly of 5 July Tommaseo proposed a rationing system, the drastic reduction of the number of cakes baked, that white bread should be reserved only for the ill and for children, and that a doctor should supervise the production of the rye bread so that 'our daily bread does not become a daily bomb in the stomachs of the people'.[44] He also insisted that all private stores of foodstuffs should be denounced and confiscated. He was opposed by Manin and other members of the government who maintained that rumours of private food hoards were greatly exaggerated and that to institute a search for them would be to invite civil war in the city.

The situation continued to decline. Bread queues grew longer and the number of destitute on the books of the commission of public charity steadily increased. The committee of public vigilance suggested that soup kitchens be set up throughout the city, and sent the municipality a recipe for bean soup, and a suggested price. But more drastic measures were necessary. On 15 July Oexle's mills ceased to function and the next day there was a terrible shortage of bread. Father Tornielli wrote to the military commission describing the desperation and anger of the people:

For God's sake, there is no bread left! Yesterday it was the people of Castello who were furious; today the fury is everywhere. This morning there was a lamentable scene in Campo SS. Giovanni e Paolo. The women who had gathered to buy bread were swearing and praying, and tearing the earrings from their ears and the wedding rings from their fingers ... We must not wait until the People take matters into their own hands.[45]

After the scenes of the 16th, the provisioning committee decided to introduce rationing immediately. Each head of a family was issued with a card on which were written details of his dependents and the amount of bread and flour that the family needed daily. The parish priest and two citizens were to verify the details. In this way the government managed to secure

[44] *Ibid.*, p. 549.
[45] BAM, Carte Sirtori, III/28, d. *Ibid.*, III/28, f, for news of Oexle's mills ceasing to function. For the suggestion of soup kitchens, see ACV, Municip., Atti di Uff., 1845–9, III, 12/3, attached to no. 4359, 12 June 1849. Bread that was confiscated from bread shops because its price or weight contravened the regulations was distributed to the poor of the various parishes; see the lists in ACV, Municip., Atti di Uff., 1845–9, IV, 7/59, attached to no. 7041 (1848). For the report of the commission of public charity of 5 May 1849, see ASV, Gov. Prov. 1848–9, MU, b. 95, attached to no. 8075. Hand mills for producing flour were put on sale at a low price to try and offset the charges of those who controlled the main mills in the city; ACV, Municip. Atti di Uff., 1845–9, IV, 7/50, attached to no. 4347 (1849), letter from Maurogonato to the municipality, 11 June 1849. Venice did not run out of water, because provision had been made for the sinking of a number of artesian wells, which supplied the city throughout the siege.

a more egalitarian distribution of bread and relative calm outside the bread shops until the very last days of the siege.[46]

Rationing may have quietened the situation, but it did little to ease the minds of many of the upper bourgeoisie and nobility. By now, few of them had any faith left in the revolution, and wanted it to end before further disasters befell them. They had been subjected to unceasing forced loans, and social tension in Venice in the summer of 1849 was increasing daily. As early as June there had been a demonstration by boatmen on seeing 150 of the richer Venetians depart for Trieste. According to Cicogna the boatmen shouted: 'Venetian pigs, you and so many other *signori* are getting out and leaving us to face the dangers ahead.'[47] By July the would-be defectors included one of the most notable supporters of the revolution, Giuseppe Reali, the president of the chamber of commerce. His sugar refinery had been requisitioned by the government and turned over to the production of nitre. Reali complained of the damage done to it, demanded compensation of 1,565 lire and requested to leave the city. Manin ordered the compensation money to be paid but refused Reali his passport.[48] Friedrich Bertuch, the German silk merchant, did not try and leave, but instead built up a large reserve supply of dry bread from the end of June onwards. He was also lucky enough to have a well in the court-yard of his home, from which he and his neighbours drew their water. On 10 August there was only enough water for his own family. His house was then besieged by the local poor, who threatened to set it alight unless he distributed what water he had. A few days later his son was unwise enough to write on a wall poster: 'Venetians, it is time to surrender, your cause is lost.' Bertuch's house was immediately surrounded by 'a few dozen of the saddest and most infamous specimens of humanity', who cursed and swore at 'the evil German'. Fortunately for Bertuch, his

[46] Marchesi, *Storia documentata*, p. 449 n. 50. On 17 July Giustinian and Ferrari-Bravo of the provisioning committee elected by the assembly wrote to the military commission complaining of the soldiers who were jumping the queues outside the breadshops, 'jostling and alarming those poor women who in great numbers and for many hours have been waiting for their much-needed provisions' (BAM, carte Sirtori, III/31,*a*). In some of the outlying districts, bread and drink failed to arrive during this crisis of provisioning which occurred in mid-July 1849; see the letter from Milanopolo on the Lido to Baldisserotto, 17 July 1849, MRM, archivio generale, N. reg. 36976 (N. Fabrizi).

[47] Quoted in Marchesi, *Storia documentata*, p. 432 n. 66.

[48] ASV, Gov. Prov. 1848–9, MU, b. 95, no. 8153, and b. 111, nos. 11247 and 11318. The French brothers Pierre and Henri Dubois de Dunilach were bankers resident in Venice at this time, and sent letters to the various banking houses of Europe, regretting the continued resistance of the city, and the fanaticism of those who held power in it; see the Archivio Dubois de Dunilach, lettere copiate 1849, *passim*.

neighbour was a captain in the civic guard, and he managed to disperse the crowd by distributing money. Bertuch comments in his memoirs that 'especially during the last weeks before the surrender, very few of the rich or the notables were spared several hours of acute anxiety'.[49]

Bombardment and the cholera

The Venetian assembly met on 28 July 1849 to consider the declining situation of the city. Manin by this time seems to have lost faith in the continuation of the revolution. With the radicals in supreme military control and the danger of social warfare in the city growing by the day, the cornerstones of Manin's policy – moderation and social order – had been destroyed. He said in the assembly that the Hungarians had so far managed to keep none of their promises; they had sent no money, no ships and no troops. He asked the deputies if it was feasible for Venice to continue to resist. Maurogonato reinforced what Manin had said by stating that the Venetian coffers would be empty by 20 August. Sirtori and Ulloa, however, insisted that Venice could still survive, and they found an unexpected ally in the conservative lawyer Gian Francesco Avesani, who spoke in favour of resistance to the last. Baldisserotto said that there was still the hope that the navy could break the blockade, and the assembly voted in favour of continuing the struggle.[50]

They had reckoned without the latest plans of their adversaries. During the night of 29–30 July 1849, less than thirty-six hours after the assembly had met, the Austrian artillery began to bombard the city. By raising their guns to maximum elevation, the Austrians managed to reach the western quarters of the city; the lightest cannon balls fell just short of the Piazza San Marco. At first the Venetians were terrified, and there were scenes of panic in the popular quarter of Cannaregio. But they soon realised that the cannon balls were relatively harmless, for, unlike a modern shell, they did not explode on impact, but merely dropped from a great height. None the less, as the night wore on, hundreds of Venetians left their homes in the western quarters of the city and congregated in the Piazza San Marco. Tommaseo, who later presented the assembly with a graphic description of the events of that night, said that the Piazza had 'never been honoured by a more dignified or moving gathering of people'.[51]

In the days and nights that followed, the Austrians bombarded Venice at the rate of a thousand projectiles every twenty-four hours. The most dangerous of these, which exploded like a modern shell, only reached the

[49] F. Bertuch, *Contributi*, p. 90. For the preceding events, see pp. 77–9 and 88–9.
[50] Fulin, 'Venezia e Daniele Manin', pp. 192–205.
[51] Tommaseo's speech of 31 July 1849, in Racc. Andreola, vol. 8, pp. 292–3.

western boundaries of the city. The Austrians tried to render the cannon balls more effective by making them red hot before firing, with the hope of burning down significant sections of Venice. These red hot cannon balls were nicknamed 'Viennese oranges' by the Venetians, because of the way they illuminated the night sky above the city. But the Austrians did not have sufficient furnaces to heat every cannon ball in this way, and the fires they did start were fairly effectively contained by a reinforced Venetian fire brigade. The number of casualties was small, and the Venetians soon came to terms with the bombardment and even profited from it. The military commission offered money for each cannon ball that was recovered and taken to the arsenal, where the iron could be turned into more ammunition for the Venetian troops. The French consul reported with unspoken delight that a cannon ball had dropped into the bed of the British consul, Clinton Dawkins – the two men were at different ends of the political spectrum, and had very divergent views on Venice's continued resistance. Dawkins escaped unharmed. Every commentator has noted that the bombardment, far from cowing the Venetians into surrender, strengthened their resolve to fight on.[52]

The western quarters of Venice were gradually evacuated. The fish market moved from the Rialto to the Riva degli Schiavoni, the fruit and vegetable stalls to Campo San Zaccaria. The fire brigade and the gendarmes kept guard over the deserted quarter of Cannaregio, to prevent looting and damage. A committee of three, including Jacopo Treves, who unlike his associates Reali and Papadopoli stayed faithful to the revolution till the bitter end, was appointed by the assembly to find work and housing for those citizens who had left one part of the city to seek refuge in the other.[53]

After the Venetians had recovered from the initial shock of the bombardment, the radicals of the military commission decided to make a number of desperate sorties to try and aid the provisioning of the city. On 1 August, Sirtori at the head of 1,200 men set out from Fort Brondolo at the southern extremity of the lagoon. His forces took the enemy outposts by surprise and returned triumphantly with 175 cattle, some wine, corn and an Austrian flag – one of the very few captured by the Italians in the wars of 1848–9. That evening, in celebration of the sortie, Rossini's *William Tell* was sung at the Fenice, the opera being punctuated by the

[52] Marchesi, *Storia documentata*, p. 441. For the French and British consuls, see the entry in Vasseur's diary for 19 Aug. 1849, MCV, Doc. Manin, no. 3839. For the 'Viennese oranges', see Bertuch, *Contributi*, p. 67. For Dawkins, see H. Hearder, 'La rivoluzione veneziana del 1848 vista dal console generale inglese', *Rassegna Storica del Risorgimento*, 46 (1957), pp. 734–41.

[53] Racc. Andreola, vol. 8, p. 293. The other two were Priuli and Bigaglia.

noise of falling cannon balls.[54] But the victuals that Sirtori's men had captured sufficed to feed the city for an estimated three hours. When another sortie was made the following day from Treporti, at the other end of the lagoon from Brondolo, the Venetians found that the Austrians had been tipped off and were waiting for them in strength. There was no chance of penetrating the Austrian defences and the sortie had to return empty-handed. The Austrians, in any case, had issued strict instructions to the peasants to remove all their cattle from the area round the lagoon, on pain of being shot.[55]

One group in the city now campaigned in earnest for surrender – the patriarch Monico and a small number of nobility who had remained in the city. On 2 August Girolamo Dandolo drew up a petition urging capitulation, and after it had been signed by a number of other noblemen, he obtained Manin's consent to present it to the assembly for consideration. But the assembly never discussed it because word spread rapidly that the patriarch was advocating surrender. On the morning of 3 August a large crowd of soldiers, civic guards and Venetian poor attacked the Palazzo Querini Stampalia, where the patriarch was living. Books, furniture and paintings were thrown in the canal, and the palace's assailants were only pacified by the arrival of Tommaseo and Jacopo Bernardi. Shouts of 'Andemo al Daniele' and 'Abbasso i signori' went up, for it was well known that a number of nobility had left their palaces once the Austrian bombardment had started, and had sought refuge in the Hotels Daniele and Vapore, on the Riva degli Schiavoni close to the Palazzo Querini Stampalia. But before the crowd moved on, gendarmes arrived in force and blocked their way. After a while they succeeded in dispersing the crowd, and the patriarch immediately fled to the island monastery of San Lazzaro, from which he denounced Manin and the whole revolution.[56]

[54] Martin, *Manin and Venice*, vol. 2, pp. 180–1. For detailed reports on the Brondolo sortie from those officers who took part, see BAM, carte Sirtori, iii/55, *a–u*. See also ASV, Gov. Prov. 1848–9, MU, b. 117, no. 12851, petition from the owners of the animals captured, 19 Aug. 1849.

[55] Five people had in fact been shot at Piove di Sacco on 5 July 1849. For the failure beyond Treporti, see the report of 3 Aug. 1849 to the military commission, BAM, carte Sirtori, iii/60.

[56] San Lazzaro was, and still is, an Armenian monastery. For Monico's letter to Manin of 17 Aug. 1849, see Bertoli, *Le origini del movimento cattolico*, pp. 22–3. For the riot, see Marchesi, *Storia documentata*, pp. 453–4, and Debrunner, *Aventures*, pp. 282–3. Also, for extensive quotes from Cicogna's diary, A. Pilot, 'L'assalto al palazzo del patriarca cardinale Monico a Venezia nel agosto 1849', *Rassegna Storica del Risorgimento*, 11 (1924), pp. 121–7. A letter of 4 Aug. 1849 from the commander of the gendarmes to the committee of public vigilance shows that the local civic guard did not help the gendarmes to quell the riot, but were

Like so many of the popular disturbances of the revolution, the exact origins of the demonstration of 3 August remain unknown. One account tells of the notary Giuriati reading out the names of the signatories of the petition to a crowd outside Florian's. The Austrians later tried to arrest him and Ippolito Caffi as the main instigators of the riot. Tommaseo himself does not escape suspicion, for Cicogna was to write in his diary that Querini Stampalia told him that Tommaseo had been inciting the crowd outside the palace, and not trying to calm them. However, since there were no arrests or interrogations, the problem of whether the demonstration was spontaneous or contrived, and of its exact size and social composition, are likely to remain unanswered.[57] But whatever its origins, the incident at the Querini Stampalia made it clear that any talk of capitulation was premature and would be rudely silenced.

In the aftermath of 3 August rumours swept through Venice that the lower classes were planning to sack the houses of the wealthy on a systematic basis. Throughout the summer the committee of public vigilance had been at work, arresting and imprisoning those whom they thought a danger to public order. For example a twenty-year-old carpenter, Antonio Milani detto Piansi, had been arrested after he had led a group of men to requisition flour and wood. Piansi had distributed the provisions equally amongst the poor of his quarter, keeping none for himself. The committee of public vigilance reported that Piansi had previously been seen in the Piazza with a group of his friends, crying 'Viva la Repubblica'. He was sentenced to a month's imprisonment. In August after the incident at the Querini Stampalia, indiscriminate arrests were made. One hundred and thirty-one boatmen, porters, streetsellers, etc. were detained for fear that they would be the instigators of a general sacking of the city.[58] The last weeks of the revolution saw a clear break in the alliance which Manin had so astutely preserved with the Venetian lower classes. While they wanted to fight to the last, and to share out on an equal basis the remaining resources of the city, Manin thought resistance hopeless and incidents like that of 3 August a prelude to social war. It was no secret that Manin and the committee of public vigilance worked closely together, and the escalation of the committee's repressive policies was bound in the end to reflect upon Manin himself.

favourably disposed to the actions of the crowd; ASV, Gov. Prov. 1848–9, MU, b. 117, no. 12779.

[57] For the large number of papers that the Austrians collected on the riot, see ASV, Pres. Luog., 1849–66, b. 29, fasc. 1/21, Venezia provincia, no. 357. For Cicogna's conversation with Querini Stampalia, MCV, Cicogna diary, 18 April 1860.

[58] See Bernardello, 'La paura del comunismo', p. 108. For Piansi, *ibid.*, p. 107 and n. 159. On 28 July 1849, 161 workers were dismissed by the commander of the

To Austrian bombardment, famine, and the fear of civil war was added perhaps the worst of the scourges which Venice had to bear in the summer of '49 – the cholera. The first cases were reported in early July, and the epidemic had reached frightening proportions by August. Between 11 July and 21 August the minimum number of cases reported per day was 306, and the maximum number of fatalities in one day was 247, on 17 August. By 23 August 2,788 people had died in the epidemic, well over 1.5 per cent of the total population of the cities and forts of the Lagoon at this time. On 6 August the municipal medical officer of health, Giacomo Duodo, wrote an anguished letter to Manin: 'Who can prevent the disproportionate overcrowding of the people in small, damp houses? Who can change their meagre diet of unhealthy foodstuffs?'[59] Nearly every family lost a relative, and the government prohibited the mournful sound of priests ringing their small bells while on the way to administer the last rites. By mid-August the overcrowded quarter of Castello, to which many of the inhabitants of Cannaregio had fled to escape the bombardment, was witnessing the most macabre of scenes. Sufficient provision for burying all the dead had not been made, and the corpses were being left out in the open in the square of S. Pietro di Castello. The sacristan of the church wrote of 'the stink of the decomposing corpses, made all the worse by the summer weather; and the barracks near-by, packed out with soldiers, increases the possibilities of the spread of the contagion'.[60] The soldiery were particularly prone to the cholera, for the unhygienic conditions of the forts, and their situation in the midst of the marshes, lowered the resistance of the men. Carlo Fenzi wrote home lamenting the almost complete absence of ice, and the large number of his companions who were falling sick.[61] To join the militias defending Venice was, for many of the young Italian volunteers, the realisation of a supreme and cherished ideal. The reality, as always in war, was squalid and horrific.

military engineers because of lack of work. There was general panic as to what to do with them, but in the end jobs were found.

[59] MCV, Doc. Manin, no. 783. For the statistics on the cholera, see the small register in the Manin papers (*ibid.*, no. 797). Of the fatalities 1,621 were men and 1,167 were women.

[60] Letter quoted in M. Brunetti, 'L'opera del comune di Venezia', p. 99. For the government prohibition to priests, Marchesi, *Storia documentata*, p. 488 n. 15.

[61] Nobili, 'Corrispondenza', p. 318, letter of 26 July 1849. On the same day the surgeon major of the Lombard battalion wrote to his commanding officer complaining that many of the men being discharged from the military hospitals were in a worse state than when they were admitted; letter quoted in C. Agrati, *Giuseppe Sirtori*, p. 104.

The Venetian assembly

With the prospect of death from either disease or starvation facing all Venetians, the assembly met on 5 August 1849. While it was deliberating the Venetians were voting for the third time in the revolution. The 'permanent' assembly had been elected for six months only, and its mandate was due to expire in August. But although the people went to the polls, few details have survived of the result of this third election, and the new assembly never had a chance to meet before the city fell.[62]

On 5 August, Sirtori, against the wishes of Manin, had forced through another loan of five million lire from the municipality. As a result Maurogonato had resigned, and Manin pleaded with the deputies to discuss the material conditions of Venice which, he said, had 'declined terribly'.[63] The scene was thus set on the 6th for the last great battle between Manin and Sirtori, the two men who had dominated Venetian politics since August 1848.

The assembly opened with the news of the serious spread of the cholera.[64] Avesani claimed that the epidemic was under control, but Manin denied it, and told the assembly that he advised surrender: 'whether from exhaustion or for other reasons, it is my sad duty to say that I have ceased to have any hope'. He said that if the assembly wished to fight on till the last piece of bread and the last grain of powder, it should assign power to Avesani, Sirtori, or Tommaseo, or else to Sirtori alone. Avesani immediately declared that if Manin left the government there would be civil war. Ulloa said that he was now convinced that the city could not be provisioned from the land. Cavalletto speaking for the Alpine legion and Francesconi for the *Cacciatori del Sile* said that they had 1,400 men ready for any expedition, however arduous. Ulloa replied that he had not asked for men, but a concrete plan for supplying the city. Manin then said that he wanted to make it perfectly clear that the military commission had done everything possible to defend the city, and that Sirtori's sortie had

---

[62] Because of the bombardment many parts of the city had no chance of meeting the minimum quotas required to return deputies to the assembly. Sirtori was returned for the army, as was Carlo Mezzacapo, the lieutenant-colonel in command of the *Bandiera e Moro* artillery company; see BAM, carte Sirtori, iii/88, and Rigobon, *Gli eletti*, pp. xlvii–xlviii. See also ACV, Municip., Atti di Uff., 1845–8, iii, 12/11, nos. 5770, 6266, and 6638 (1849) for further minor details.

[63] For Maurogonato's resignation, see his letter to Manin, MCV, Doc. Manin, no. 3158, 30 July 1849. For the proceedings of the assembly of 5 Aug. 1849, see Fulin, 'Venezia e Daniele Manin', pp. 205–12.

[64] For the historic debate of 6 Aug., see Fulin, 'Venezia e Daniele Manin', pp. 212–27, and the account kept by Tommaseo which is published by R. Ciampini, *Studi e ricerche su Nicolò Tommaseo*, pp. 349–56.

been brilliantly executed, so much so that they had captured an Austrian flag, 'something which the Piedmontese never achieved'.

The assembly continued to debate the problems for some time, during which Father Tornielli appealed to Manin to lead out all the citizens and troops of Venice in a desperate sortie against the Austrians. Minotto finally came to the crux of the matter by proposing that Manin be given full power to treat with the enemy as he saw fit. Sirtori immediately leaped to his feet 'to declare frankly that Manin is now not capable of governing the city, because he no longer enjoys the confidence of either the troops or the people'. Manin thanked Sirtori for his frankness and agreed that his own popularity had declined; this was, he said, because he stood for an ideal that in the present circumstances could not be realised. Benvenuti tried to defend him, but Sirtori insisted that 'Manin cannot remain in the government, because his name is associated with capitulation'.

This was too much for Manin. Exhausted though he was, he was not going to be thrown out of government by Sirtori. He demanded absolute power, saying that over the last few months he had been little more than 'a name on a piece of paper'. He asked if he could count on Ulloa and Baldisserotto in the event that the assembly granted him full powers; they replied that he could. Sirtori thus found himself isolated from his colleagues. Father Tornielli suggested a compromise: Manin, Pepe and Sirtori could hold power together. Sirtori rejected this, and Manin then left the assembly while the vote was taken on conferring full powers upon him. The deputies voted 56 to 37 in his favour, instructing him 'to act in the way in which he considers most suitable for the honour and salvation of Venice'. The only proviso was that any decision to surrender had to be ratified by the assembly. Manin returned to the assembly, but declared that the numbers voting against him were too large to inspire confidence. He asked the minority in the assembly to give an undertaking to cooperate with him to the full. According to Tommaseo there was an ominous silence, broken finally by Sirtori, who said that Manin's request was an unnecessary one. Manin replied that Sirtori's reply did him honour, and the protracted meeting ended with all the deputies promising to act for the good and honour of the country.

Manin thus regained the position of supremacy that he had lost in June 1849, but this last bitter discussion in the assembly had largely been an academic one, for Venice was dying on its feet. On 8 August handbills went up all over the city, signed by a certain Tondelli, advocating a mass sortie and urging the people to gather that evening in the Piazza San Marco. Tommaseo was known to be in favour of a *levée en masse*, as were Belluzzi and Morandi, who certainly knew more about such things than Tommaseo. But Pepe and Ulloa dismissed the idea as pure folly. None the less a fair number of Venetians gathered in the Piazza on the evening of the 8th. There Manin told them that a sortie was out of the question, but that he had received news that Giuseppe Garibaldi, fleeing from Rome, would soon reach Venice. One of Garibaldi's followers, who had just arrived in the city, then confirmed the story.[65] The crowd dispersed, hoping that Garibaldi's arrival might ring some miraculous change in the city's fortunes.

In fact, Garibaldi was still some way from Venice, with very little hope of reaching it. Ever since the fall of Rome, he had been with difficulty moving northwards through the Papal States, accompanied by an ever-dwindling band of supporters. At the beginning of August they finally reached the Adriatic at Cesenatico, and set sail for Venice in fishing boats. But at dawn on 3 August the boats were intercepted by the Austrian fleet, and Garibaldi's was run aground on the coast near Comacchio, still many kilometres from Chioggia. With his wife Anita dying in his arms Garibaldi tried to avoid the Austrian patrols and head towards the refuge of the Venetian lagoons.[66]

In Venice Sirtori was doing everything he could to get information about Garibaldi's whereabouts. On 9 August he sent Lieutenant Baruffaldi, who knew the area south of Chioggia extremely well, to try and trace Garibaldi and help him into the city. On the 11th Sirtori received news that Garibaldi had definitely been sighted at Messola, some thirty-six kilometres south of Chioggia. His informant said that Garibaldi had been dressed like a peasant, in a corduroy jacket, and that an expedition could easily reach him, because the Austrian garrisons were very small in that locality. But on 14 August Baruffaldi reported that all traces of Garibaldi had been lost. He had definitely been in Messola, and had been reported near Ariano, but had not been sighted after that. Sirtori decided against an expedition into the area, perhaps fearing that Garibaldi was already dead. In reality Garibaldi had never been at Messola but had been forced southwards into the Comacchio lagoon. On 4 August Anita had died at the Guiccioli dairy farm at Mandriole. A heartbroken Garibaldi then abandoned all attempts to reach Chioggia. Aided by the local patriots and peasantry he escaped out of the area and eventually out of Italy itself.[67]

The navy

In Venice the number of cholera victims increased daily, and the Austrians

[65] MCV, Doc. Manin, no. 3820, chronicle of Zennari, secretary to the government. For the idea of the *levée en masse*, see Marchesi, *Storia documentata*, p. 481.
[66] Trevelyan, *Garibaldi's Defence*, pp. 288ff.
[67] BAM, carte Sirtori, III/75, 80, 85 and 96,*b*.

continued to shell the city. The efforts of the Venetian troops were hampered by the very large number of those sick – nearly three thousand on 18 August[68] – and by the shortage of ammunition. The Venetian powder factory suffered serious explosions twice in July, and there was very little potash left by the middle of August. It was obvious to all that the end was now very near. On 13 August Manin joined one of the street patrols in the area under Austrian bombardment. He helped to put out a fire near the Frari church and in celebration his patrol drank a rare bottle of Valpolicella, and shared five loaves between them, 'two white and three black as the night'.[69] The many non-Venetians who were helping to defend the city began to think of what chances they had of escaping death from starvation or the cholera and returning eventually to their homes. The abbot Jacopo Bernardi, who came from the hill village of Ceneda in the Veneto, toured the lagoon preaching in the small churches of its villages and islands. He wrote to his mother, 'going and coming back I could see from the boat our mountains in the far distance, and my heart and my thoughts went out to you, to the family and to my friends . . .'[70]

One last hope remained – the navy. If the Venetian fleet could be persuaded to put to sea, there was a chance that it might break the Austrian blockade. All through the last months of the revolution dissatisfaction had grown at the continued inactivity of the navy. Baldisserotto and the new commander, Admiral Bucchia, had at first been optimistic, but quickly became disillusioned. The problem was that while the Austrians, under the Danish admiral Dahleroup, were making great efforts to refurbish their fleet, the Venetians under Graziani had done little or nothing. By April 1849 the Austrians could boast a navy of 2,500 men, many of them Italian, and fourteen ships with 110 guns (of which 72 were large-calibre). The Venetians had only 600 sailors and eight ships armed with 100 light cannon. Most important, the Austrians had the use of six steamships from the Lloyd's company of Trieste. The Venetians had only one, the *Pio Nono*, and discipline was so poor aboard it that in June the military commission was forced to court-martial seventy of its crew and sentence three of them to death. All the mistakes that the Venetian leadership had made with regard to the navy – the failure to secure the Pola fleet on 23 March 1848, Manin's decision not to purchase further steamships in May 1848, and the appointment of Graziani in August – had now

[68] See the report to the military commission in BAM, carte Sirtori, III/110. The total number of troops on 18 Aug. was given as 15,323.

[69] MCV, Doc. Manin, no. 3819, account by Giorgio Casarini, who accompanied Manin on the night of 13 August 1849.

[70] J. Bernardi, *Affetti e dolori. Alla memoria di una madre*, pp. 15 and 18.

to be paid for. An ill-equipped and ill-disciplined Venetian fleet, composed almost completely of sailing vessels, confronted a technically superior and better trained Austrian force.[71]

In the assembly of 28 July Baldisserotto stressed how difficult it might be for the Venetian fleet to get back into port once it had set sail. Unless favourable winds coincided with high tides, most of the fleet faced the real danger of being cut off on the high seas. Nevertheless, in the face of criticism from Sirtori, Baldisserotto promised that Bucchia was only waiting for the right moment before making a sortie. But Bucchia, although an honest and much-liked officer, had been unable to animate the crews of the Venetian vessels or to prepare them for the desperate enterprise. Had Garibaldi reached Venice, he might have succeeded where Bucchia failed. But he did not, and Bucchia seemed loath to commit himself to action. Five days passed and still nothing happened. Tommaseo then issued an 'Address to the Venetian Navy' thanking them in advance for the definite promise – which they had never made – to set sail immediately. Bucchia was furious, but since the whole city was hourly expecting the fleet's departure, he had no option but to make a sortie. The Venetian navy duly set out on 8 August, but returned two days later without having encountered the Austrians, and having captured only one ship carrying a cargo of wine.[72]

The failure of this expedition only further demoralised the Venetian crews. On 14 August Bucchia wrote to Manin:

I am not the master of every circumstance, and morale is not only declining, but has reached the lowest depths. The crews are now in such a state that I cannot even answer for them for a minute, let alone for an hour. And even if I can count on the men aboard my own ship where I have won the affection of many, I cannot for the other vessels.[73]

Manin immediately wrote to the military commission suggesting that Lieutenant Paita should replace Bucchia. But Bucchia stayed in command,

---

[71] For the resurgence of the Austrian fleet, see J. Benko von Boinik, *Geschichte der K.-K. Kriegs-Marine während der Jahre 1848 und 1849*. The best account of the Venetian navy in the last months of the siege is undoubtedly pt. 3, ch. 12 of Marchesi's *Storia documentata*, pp. 461–77. Only one of the three sentences of death against the crew members of the *Pio Nono* was in fact carried out; the other two men received ten years' imprisonment instead; Marchesi, 'Diario di un anonimo', p. 145.

[72] Marchesi, *Storia documentata*, p. 470. For Tommaseo's address to the Venetian navy, see Racc. Andreola, vol. 8, pp. 286–8. Marchesi produces some evidence to show that both Manin and the military commission had ordered the fleet not to sail out of sight of the city, lest the populace took their disappearance as a sign of treason (p. 470).

[73] Marchesi, *Storia documentata*, p. 472.

and the fleet was persuaded to put out to sea a second time, on 16 August. For the whole day near S. Pietro in Volta the two fleets watched each other from a distance of about four miles. Then towards evening the Austrian frigate *Bellona* and their steamship *Vulcano* moved towards the Venetian vessels *Lombardia* and *Pillade*. The Austrians fired without effect and the Venetians replied, upon which the Austrians retired immediately. This little encounter did much to encourage the Venetian sailors, and Baruffaldi reported that Bucchia hoped to engage the Austrian fleet on the 17th, provided the winds were favourable.[74] But the Austrians avoided the encounter, and Bucchia returned to port on the 18th. Cholera had begun to spread amongst the crews, and Bucchia said it was inhumane and pointless for the navy to remain at sea any longer. In the days that followed, the fleet did not again leave port, and this abysmal performance was sad testimony to the decline of a great naval tradition.

Surrender

On 13 August the provisioning committee was forced to change the quantities of wheat and rye that were being used to bake Venetian bread. From now on it was to be four-fifths rye, and would be sold for 25 centesimi per *libbra*. Even so, the committee had to inform Manin that the city would run out of bread by 24 August. On the 16th the political committee of the assembly wrote a last letter to Manin:

The cannon balls of the enemy are now reaching Murano, and part of that island's population is flocking into the already overcrowded streets of Venice ... Numerous citizens are ill in damp rooms on the ground floor, without ventilation and without light. Often they are forced to lie in the same bed as dying men or corpses. The dead are not being buried because of the shortage of gravediggers, and those that there are refuse to carry the bodies to places which are under bombardment from the enemy.[75]

74 BAM, carte Sirtori, iii/107, report to the military commission from Lieutenant L. Baruffaldi. There is evidence that the military commission ordered a conscription of sailors at Chioggia, in the hope of replacing some of the recalcitrant crews of the Venetian navy. But the Chioggians were less than willing to be conscripted at this stage of the revolution; see the report of the military command of Chioggia to the military commission, 15 Aug. 1849, BAM, carte Sirtori, iii/102.
75 MCV, Agg. Manin, xxix/4, no. 4. For the declining quality of bread, see ACV, Municip., Atti di Uff., 1845–9, iv, 7/59, no. 6653 (1849). For the provisioning committee's estimate of when the city would begin to starve, MCV, Doc. Manin, no. 788. It was only in the last days of the siege that the people began to eat the pigeons of St Mark's Square, which were widely regarded as sacred birds; Marchesi, *Storia documentata*, p. 458 n. 16.

Two days later there was a serious bread riot on the Giudecca.[76] A crowd of between three and four hundred persons invaded the offices of the president of the local provisioning committee. He distributed all the bread he had, but the crowd then stormed the warehouse where stores of rice for the sick were being held. The commission's president was compelled to distribute a *libbra* of rice per person, but he then recounted that the crowd got out of control completely and carried off all the bread, rice and money that they could find. They threatened to return the following day armed with knives to demand a general distribution of wheaten flour.

Such reports must have greatly alarmed an exhausted Manin, and on the 19th he heard the definite news of the Hungarians' surrender. There was now no hope and Manin decided to treat with the enemy. Ironically, just at the moment when Venice chose to surrender, conditions showed signs of improving. The cholera epidemic abated considerably,[77] and Admiral Dahleroup informed Vienna that if Venice resisted till the end of August the blockade would have to be partially lifted, because of the appalling state of three of the Austrian steamships.[78] Manin was aware of neither of these facts when he decided to surrender. Even so, his was the right decision, for the Venetians could not have relied on the navy to provision the city adequately, and the Austrians had too strong a grip on the Venetian hinterland to hope for help from that direction.

Accordingly, on 19 August Cavedalis, Medin and Priuli set off in two gondolas flying white flags. At first they gained no concessions from the Austrians, but on the 22nd Hess and de Bruck arrived at Mestre, and terms were speedily agreed on. On the whole, the Austrians were lenient to their adversaries. All the officers who were subjects of the emperor and who had fought against him, all the other Italian soldiers, and forty Venetian citizens were to leave Venice. The communal money was to be reduced to half its face value, and then be withdrawn from circulation as soon as possible. The patriotic money was to be withdrawn immediately. Cavedalis was to remain a hostage until the city was reoccupied, but the Austrians gave him a written promise that there would be no reprisals against Venetian citizens.[79]

One last crisis rent the beleaguered city. Manin, on hearing of the

---

[76] ACV, Municip., Atti di Uff., 1845–9, IV, 7/67, attached to no. 6816 (1849), report of Berti, the president of the the provisioning committee of the district.

[77] MCV, Doc. Manin, no. 797. The number of fresh cases on 23 Aug. was 123; up to that date the minimum number of fresh cases for any day had been 306. The number of those who recovered rose from 26 on 17 Aug. to 125 on 23 Aug. Fatalities per day had fallen from 247 on 17 Aug. to 95 on 23 Aug.

[78] See the letter from Dahleroup to Gyulai, the minister of war, published in Marchesi, *Storia documentata*, app. doc. XL, p. 534.

[79] *Ibid.*, pp. 483–6.

Austrian terms, ordered the Venetian soldiery to be given ten days' pay, while the other Italian soldiers were to receive sufficient for three months. Some of the Venetian soldiers, bitter at having to surrender, scared of being forced back into the Austrian ranks, and disillusioned at what they mistakenly took to be Manin's ingratitude, revolted on 23 August. According to a report sent to the military commission, about fifty to sixty artillerymen occupied the 'Rome' battery at the near end of the railway bridge and turned its guns on the city.[80] At the same time the garrison at Murano sacked parts of the island. The soldiers on the 'Rome' battery announced that they would never surrender, and that they wished to continue the struggle on the mainland, under the command of Sirtori or Ulloa.

The municipality was terrified and urged Manin to let the Austrians deal with the rebels. Manin refused and he and Ulloa led a party to the railway bridge to parley with those in possession of the guns. An exchange of shots followed, but on the morning of 24 August the revolt collapsed, and Ulloa, having disarmed the men, let them go unpunished. That afternoon, at 2 p.m., Manin's government officially ceased to function.[81]

On 27 August 1849 Hungarian whitecoats occupied the Piazza San Marco. On the 28th General Gorzkowsky entered the city. At 3 p.m. on the same afternoon, the French ship *Pluton* left Venetian waters, bearing into exile Manin, Sirtori, Tommaseo, Pepe and others of the Venetian leadership.[82] The Venetian revolution was over.

[80] BAM, carte Sirtori, III/119a, report from Major Mathieu, chief of staff of the first military district, 7.30 p.m., 23 Aug. 1849.

[81] ASV, Gov. Prov. 1848–9, MU, b. 117, no. 12742, minutes of the final declaration of the government (not signed by Manin). For Ulloa's five-page account of the events of 23–4 Aug., written in his own hand, see MCV, Doc. Manin, no. 3821.

[82] Dispatch of Vasseur to de Tocqueville, 28 Aug. 1849, in Planat de la Faye (ed.), *Documenti*, vol. 2, p. 529. At the end Manin was generous to his political enemies. He ensured that Sirtori was taken on board the *Pluton*, and that his former critics were granted sums of money as they departed for exile. His friends Giuriati and Zanetti both received 3,000 lire of government funds, but Pacifico Valussi (1,500 lire), Bernardo Canal (900 lire) and Giuseppe Vollo (500 lire) were also well treated; ASV, Gov. Prov. 1848–9, MU, b. 117, no. 12618.

 10

Conclusion

Looking back on the complex and dramatic chain of events in Italy during 1848–9, it is possible to discern two distinct periods. The first, stretching from the insurrection in Palermo in January 1848 to the defeat of Charles Albert at Custozza in July, was characterised by an international situation of great fluidity and expectation. With the revolutions in both Paris and Vienna, and the subsequent nationalist agitations in nearly every part of the Austro-Hungarian empire, the European balance of power established after 1815 was destroyed in a matter of weeks. When Metternich and Guizot, both refugees from their own countries, met on the steps of the British Museum, it was clear to all observers that an era had ended. The spring and early summer of 1848 were to determine the nature of the new phase in European history, and to set the pattern of historical events for a number of decades. In Italy in these critical months everything seemed possible. The bourgeois nationalist movement, after fighting for many years a war of position within Italian society, a war punctuated by the occasional Mazzinian folly, was able at last to emerge into the open, and confront both the Austrians and the reactionary elements within the peninsula. But this war of movement, so rich in content and so full of hope, was of short duration. By July the republicans had lost the political initiative, the Pope had abandoned the cause, Ferdinand II had staged the counter-revolution in Naples, and Charles Albert, having established the kingdom of upper Italy, was crushed by Radetzky's troops outside Verona.

The second period, from the fall of Milan in August 1848 to the surrender of Venice just over a year later, has to be set in an international context no longer favourable to the revolutionary cause. From the June days in Paris onwards, the European counter-revolution had gathered force at considerable speed, as whole sections of the bourgeoisie sought an understanding with the forces of the old order in the face of the peril from below. Furthermore, the revolutionaries failed to combine, while the reactionaries did. Republican France did not intervene in northern Italy or Poland, and in the end Louis Napoleon was to send the former army of the Alps to crush the republic at Rome and restore the Pope. The Hungarians failed to move fast enough to save the second Viennese revolution, and were in their turn overwhelmed by the combination of Austrian and Russian troops. Thus although in this second period the republicans and democrats seized the initiative in Italy, particularly in the central states, they did so at a time when the European tide was running against them, and the prospects of eventual victory had considerably diminished. By the summer of 1849 the Italian revolutionary movement was reduced to the heroic but hopeless defence of two cities – Venice and Rome.

In analysing the contribution of Manin and the Venetians to these events, the decisiveness of the first period, from March to July 1848, becomes very apparent. In the early days, both before and during the March insurrection in Venice, Manin proved a superb leader. In his *lotta legale*, the legal struggle for reforms within the Austrian system, Manin was able to unite the progressive sections of the Venetian commercial and professional bourgeoisie in a carefully orchestrated campaign. The *lotta legale* was led by the radical lawyers and intellectuals of Venice and the provincial towns. Men like Pasini and Tommaseo had fundamental objections to the repressive character of Austrian rule – the activities of the police, the rigours of the censorship, and the injustices of the penal code. They also had no chance of gaining political power, which lay in the hands either of foreigners or the aristocracy. They were backed with increasing vigour by the merchants, businessmen and bankers of the Venetian chamber of commerce. Giuseppe Reali, Jacopo Treves and Spiridione Papadopoli were in no sense revolutionaries – Reali, for instance, had applied for Austrian nobility before the revolution. They would much have preferred accommodation and integration within the imperial system to a policy of open opposition. But their economic interests forced them to line up with Manin and his associates. The extortionate rate of Austrian taxation, the inefficiency of the bureaucracy, and above all the limitations imposed on entrepreneurial activity by the economic system of the empire pushed the most powerful members of the Venetian chamber of commerce into consideration of Italian alternatives to Austrian rule.

However, during the March days themselves, the bourgeois bloc which had been created in the *lotta legale* was broken, and by Manin himself. It was his supreme achievement to realise that the Austrians *could* be thrown out of the city, and to seize the opportunity presented on 22 March. While the city fathers and many of Manin's own friends, including Tommaseo, thought the Austrian concessions a significant victory, Manin pursued an uncompromising policy that was both anti-Austrian *and* republican. In order to carry through his plans, Manin had to rely on the active support of the popular classes of the city. This was no passive revolution. The arsenal workers, stirred by Austrian intransigence over both wages and taxation at a time of economic hardship, and their passions aroused by propaganda in favour of a Holy War, both preceded Manin to battle on the morning of 22 March, and lent him vital support when he arrived, almost unaccompanied, at the arsenal gate. And, much later on the same day, it was the working people of the city and the deserting rank-and-file soldiers who marched through Venice protesting against the exclusion of Manin from Avesani's moderate provisional government. It was their pressure that ensured Avesani's resignation and the establishment of a republic with Manin at its head.

Venice's brilliant victory was soon imitated by the provincial cities of the Veneto. In some of them, like Vicenza, bourgeois leaders with ideas similar to Manin's wrested the initiative from hesitant and fearful municipal councils. In nearly all, the Austrian garrisons, disconcerted by the news from Venice, decided not to fight but to come to terms similar to those agreed by the vacillating Palffy at Venice. But in one city, Verona, the most important of them all, no leader of Manin's kind emerged, nor did the Austrians show any intention of surrendering. The failure to secure Verona was of enormous gravity for the Italian cause, for Radetzky found there the haven he needed after the battering his troops had received at Milan.

None the less, by the beginning of April 1848 the Venetian republic, stretching throughout north-eastern Italy, had come into being. The prospects of its survival, given the general international situation and the trouble faced by the Austrians elsewhere in the empire, seemed reasonably bright.

Yet once made, the revolution did not progress. In seeking to understand why this was so, the parallel events at Milan are of the greatest importance. Lombardy was economically the most advanced region in Italy and Milan its most dynamic city. Before the revolution, the Milanese publicists had been in the forefront of the 'conspiracy in open daylight' against the Austrians, and the city's non-smoking campaign had culminated in the bloody street battle of 3 January 1848. In the nationalist agitations preceding the urban insurrection of March, Venice and Venetia had been very much the junior partners in the Lombardo-Venetian kingdom. It was natural, therefore, for the Venetians to look to Milan for their lead. But though the Milanese rose against the Austrians in the legendary *cinque giornate*, though the insurrectionaries were very largely artisans, urban poor and unemployed, and were led by a group of young radicals and democrats headed by Carlo Cattaneo and the council of war, no sister republic to the Venetian one was proclaimed.

It is in Milan in March 1848 that the leadership struggle in the Italian nationalist bourgeois revolution finds one of its most dramatic battlegrounds. Cattaneo was approached twice by the young radicals and urged to proclaim a republic. Twice he refused for fear of alienating the moderate liberal nobility who had been the leaders of the national movement in the city before the revolution. Anxious to preserve a united front against the Austrians, Cattaneo allowed political power to slip through his hands and Casati to form a provisional government of ill-concealed monarchist sympathies. Thus although the popular insurrection in Milan, as in Venice, was led by the radicals and democrats, the chance was lost of replacing the Lombardo-Venetian kingdom by a united Lombardo-Venetian republic.

It is quite impossible (and also dangerous) to try and assess how successful such a republic would have been. It might well have waged unsuccessful war against Austria, or succumbed swiftly in the face of the monarchist challenge. Its leaders could well have failed to sustain the popular alliances which were at the heart of French republican success in 1793–4 or Kossuth's Hungary in 1848–9. All one can say is that a republic in Milan as well as in Venice would have dramatically altered the political balance of power in northern Italy. It could have served as a counterbalance to Charles Albert's Piedmont and might, had it survived, have acted both as a pole of attraction and an example to the bourgeois democrats in other parts of the peninsula – Genoa, Leghorn, Bologna, and other cities of radical traditions.

It would also have posed the Italian problem in quite different terms on the European stage. In the spring of 1848 Austria was at her weakest. The empire threatened to be torn apart by the nationalist uprisings in Bohemia, Hungary and northern Italy. In Vienna itself the revolutionary ferment amongst the lower classes and the students heightened the confusion and despair in imperial ruling circles. The Austrian ministers were under constant pressure from leading members of the Viennese bourgeoisie to abandon their Italian possessions and not to bankrupt the empire by trying to launch a full-scale war of reconquest. At the same time Palmerston was making it quite clear to Hummelauer in London that the British considered it correct and necessary for Austria to withdraw immediately from Lombardy-Venetia. Palmerston on no account wanted Austrian stubbornness in northern Italy to be responsible for setting the French armies once more on the march. As for the French themselves, the shallowness of Lamartine's promises to Italy was apparent to many observers. But the army of the Alps was no mirage, nor could anyone deny the existence of a large body of public opinion in Paris favourable to the Second Republic's intervention in a war of national liberation, be it in Poland or in Italy.

In such a situation, uniquely favourable to the revolutionary forces in Italy, an unequivocal appeal by the Lombardo-Venetian republicans for French aid might have had the most far-reaching of consequences. It was to the French republic that the young Milanese radicals urged Cattaneo to turn on the evening of 19 March. And it was to France that Manin had always looked with sympathy, from the time of his imprisonment onwards. Had it been clearly established in March and April of 1848 that the Lombardo-Venetians wanted French help, there seems little doubt that in Paris the Italian cause would have far exceeded the Polish in popularity. Had a republican appeal been made at this time, the principal pretext for Lamartine's recalcitrance – the hostility of *all* the northern Italians to French intervention – would have disappeared. The pressure on the French government would then have been very great indeed. And had a French expedition set sail for Venice, Austria's position would have been further weakened and the whole course of the Italian and French revolutions drastically altered.

However, such conjecture is as futile as it is fascinating, because the number of variables involved (not least the attitude of Piedmont) makes it quite impossible to predict what might have happened. In the event Casati, not Cattaneo, emerged victorious in Milan on 22 March. The Milanese provisional government proclaimed a ban on all political discussion till the end of the war, and Venice's declaration of a republic was then widely regarded either as an isolated act of disunity, or else, as Pisacane always maintained,[1] the mere resurgence of an ancient municipal tradition. Charles Albert's battle cry, *l'Italia farà da sé*, became the dominant one in northern Italy, and rendered the concept of international republican aid both inconceivable and unpatriotic. Even Venice at this stage was not prepared to receive French help. Consequently, as Marx noted, 'there were no great foreign implications to kindle energy, to accelerate the revolutionary process, to drive forward or throw overboard the [French] Provisional Government'.[2]

In Italy, the net result of Cattaneo's political decisions between 20 and 22 March, paradoxical though it may appear, was to turn an insurrectionary war into a dynastic one, and a bourgeois revolution based on the active participation of the popular classes into a passive one. The Venetian republic was, *by itself*, too moderate in content and too short-sighted in action to present an alternative to monarchist hegemony in northern Italy. Manin's response to the political outcome of the Milanese *cinque giornate* was not to tighten the bonds of the new Venetian republic, but rather to

[1] See the letter from Pisacane to Cattaneo, 17 April 1851, MRM, archivio Cattaneo, cart. 5, plico xvii, no. 43.
[2] Marx, 'The class struggles in France', p. 48.

accept the ban on all political discussion until the end of the war. Rather than try and form a republican army which utilised popular enthusiasm for the national cause, Manin turned more and more to dynastic armies for salvation from reconquest. But in order to survive politically, the Venetian republic had to show that it was able to defend itself from Nugent's invasion. Once it was clear that the Venetian ministers were relying almost exclusively on Charles Albert and the papal army to do the fighting for them, the days of the Venetian republic were numbered.

This question of self-defence lies at the heart of Manin's failure in the period March–July 1848. Through a mixture of moderation, ignorance and sheer incompetence, Manin never posed in a concrete form the question of the formation of a Venetian army. He was convinced, or allowed himself to be convinced by his dubious military advisers, that any energetic action in this direction was an impossibility, and that there was no option but to rely on Charles Albert.

One of the fundamental reasons for such an attitude was Manin's lack of knowledge of the countryside, and his city-based politics. The revolution in Venice had been accompanied in the villages of the Veneto by the formation of national and civic guards, and the enthusiastic support of many sections of the peasantry for the new republic. The preaching of the rural parish priests in favour of the national cause, the enthusiasm of the middle strata of rural society for the revolution, the new government's abolition of the hated personal tax and its reduction of the salt tax, these were all elements which served to win the peasantry to the republic. But Manin was unwilling and unable to try and transform this rural enthusiasm into an effective fighting force. His ignorance of the countryside meant that he was unable to realise the possibilities inherent in this situation, to appeal to his natural allies in the rural areas – the provincial lawyers, the Napoleonic veterans, the lower clergy – to overcome the more conservative elements in the provinces and help transform the national guards into a republican army. Instead the provinces were left to put up a sporadic and uncoordinated resistance to Nugent. This resistance had moments both of mass participation (the assembly of 6,000 peasants in the area east of Udine) and significant success (Calvi's tenacious defence of the Cadore), but was never able to overcome the lack of coherent planning or direction from Venice. Manin visited the provinces only once during these critical months, when he made a day trip by railway to help defend Vicenza. His attitude is in striking contrast to that of Lajos Kossuth in Hungary, perhaps the only 'Jacobin' of 1848 in Gramsci's sense of the word. While Kossuth spared no effort to tour the villages of the Hungarian plain in September 1848 to persuade the peasantry to enlist in the *Honvéd*, Manin remained tied to Venice itself. He refused to envisage the possibility of a popular army, declaring that he knew nothing of military affairs and that defence was a problem for others than himself. The division between Italian city and countryside was never more apparent.

This is not to suggest that the formation of a popular army was an easy task, nor that victory over Nugent would have been easy to secure. The fate of Sanfermo's ill-led and ill-equipped volunteers at Montebello and Sorio was warning enough of what disasters might have befallen untrained peasant militias. But it is perhaps worth bearing in mind a number of points. The Venetian arsenal possessed enough muskets to arm a sizeable army. At least 60,000 of Venetia's population had served eight years of military service in the Austrian army. There was no obvious candidate to lead a Venetian army, but Morandi, Belluzzi and Calvi all showed signs of real military ability in these first months. At a later stage of the revolution, Venice *did* form an effective fighting force of some 16,000 men. Nugent's army itself was not a highly trained fighting unit, but was composed at least in part of volunteers and hastily conscripted peasants from the area round Trieste. It was probably the weakest link in the Austrian chain. At the decisive battle of Cornuda, Ferrari's papal volunteers managed to resist Nugent's troops for a whole day; had a significant Venetian force been fighting by their side, the Austrians might well have been turned back. This would have been of great significance, for Radetzky made no headway until the relief army from Trieste reached him. Had Venetian and papal troops stopped Nugent, the Viennese politicians might seriously have considered abandoning their Italian possessions, as the British were urging them to do, with or without Radetzky's consent. Even with Radetzky reinforced, Wessenberg was still prepared to offer Lombardy its independence on 13 June.

It is probably incorrect to maintain that any *lasting* alliance between the moderate Venetian republicans and the bulk of the Venetian peasantry could have been made. Such an alliance, if not impossible, would certainly have been unequal. Any major social concessions to the peasantry would greatly have alarmed the rich landowners and merchants on whom Manin relied for financial support and to whom, at the end of the day, he was clearly committed. Sooner or later a strategy which in effect used a peasant army to secure the bourgeois revolution was bound to be broken by the class tensions which divided landless labourers from estate owners, and mountain smallholders from the speculators who bought up their villages' communal forests. In this respect one must be careful to stress the real limitations, in the long term, of the proposed alliance between bourgeois republicans and rural poor which lies at the heart of Gramsci's writings on the Risorgimento.

However, this is not to imply that for the peasantry it made no difference what specific form of government was created during the bourgeois revolution in the Veneto. Manin's republic, had it survived, would almost certainly have allowed the peasantry a freedom of expression and of self-organisation that they had not previously known. Although Manin himself was singularly unaware of peasant needs, the logic of the republic must have in time forced the peasant question onto the centre of the stage. Even in the brief interlude of 1848 it is possible to see the beginning of this process. Significant sections of the peasantry used the declaration of the republic to raise long-harboured social grievances, to stake their claim to lands they considered theirs by right, to demand and even to impose representation at a local level. The fundamental contradictions between peasant and landlord were bound to remain and develop, but the survival of a republic based on adult male suffrage and the basic bourgeois freedoms would have produced a social and political dynamic quite different from that possible under either the Austrians or the Piedmontese.[3]

In the event the republican alternative was crushed before it had time to develop. In the spring of 1848 time was of the essence. Between March and July the game was played and lost. In that time the Venetian republic was overrun by Austrian troops and dismembered by the dynastic ambitions of Piedmont. Manin, till the end of his life, blamed the fusionist politics of Piedmont for the failure of the first war of independence.[4] But

---

[3] Gramsci's writings on this question raise a problem which lies outside the scope of this work, but which it may be worth mentioning briefly. It is a problem that concerns the connection between bourgeois and proletarian revolution. Gramsci's prison notes on the Risorgimento tend to take it for granted that an advanced bourgeois revolution, such as the French or the British, was of much greater advantage not just to the bourgeoisie but also to the working classes. A 'bastard' revolution, such as the Italian one, not only excluded the masses from the life of the state, but also opened the way for the suppression of democratic liberties and the crushing of the workers' movement. All this seems incontestable. But there are two sides to the coin. From a British point of view it must be asked whether an advanced bourgeois revolution does not conceal perils of its own for the working-class movement. The bourgeois revolution was so successful in Britain that the bourgeoisie, by a whole series of ideological mechanisms and material concessions, has been able to a great extent to integrate the British working class into the bourgeois state. In Italy the retarded or uncompleted bourgeois revolution undoubtedly led to the savage repression of the working class and the landless labourers, and was the historical basis from which Fascism developed. But it also, by its very alienation of the lower classes, helped to create an intransigent, antagonistic and at moments revolutionary working-class movement. Gramsci, writing in a prison cell after the terrible defeats of the 1920s, tended to see *only* the disadvantages of the Italian experience, so much so that at times his notes on the Risorgimento read like a manual for the enlightened bourgeoisie. This is a question to which I hope to return in greater depth at a later date.

[4] See his article in *Siècle*, 20 June 1853, quoted in A. Levi, *La politica di Daniele*

there was an element of self-deception in this. Manin failed, at the critical moment in the revolution, to forge a political and military strategy for the survival of the republic. Deprived of an effective lead from Milan, he was unable to conceive of the creation of a republican army based, on however temporary a basis, on the support and active participation of the popular forces in the Veneto.

This was not the failure of Manin alone, but of all the Venetian leaders. Tommaseo was more aware than Manin of how much military aid could be expected from Piedmont, and the political price to be paid for it, but he offered no coherent alternative. Furthermore, it was inconceivable that he could have replaced Manin at the head of the republic. Tommaseo was frequently right, but he was no leader of men, and after the role Manin had played in the March days his position was not one that could easily have been questioned.

Manin's dominance was also based on the fact that he was as successful within Venice itself as he was unsuccessful outside it. From 22 March onwards he created a link between himself and the lower classes of the city that was only broken in the last weeks of the revolution. This link was founded on all the qualities that historians have traditionally ascribed to Manin – his great understanding of the Venetians themselves, the simplicity and power of his oratory, his consummate skill in controlling and dominating difficult situations like 11 August 1848 and 5 March 1849. But Manin combined these qualities with shrewd economic measures designed to hold the allegiance of the popular classes: the restitution of small objects pawned at the Monte di Pietà, the rewards to the *arsenalotti* after 22 March, the wage increases granted to municipal workers, and above all the effective pegging of bread prices for much of the revolution – these were the constituent elements upon which the alliance between Manin and the Venetian poor was based. And when all this was combined with Manin's firm commitment to the right of all adult male Venetians to have the vote, his extraordinary popularity in Venice becomes easier to understand.

At the same time Manin took care to control any claims by the lower classes which he considered to be unjustified. Through the committee of public vigilance he kept a close watch on the internal order of the city, and was swift and often ruthless in suppressing any signs of what he took to be social disorder. He was determined to prevent a situation arising in Venice such as had occurred in Padua, where a *capopopolo* like Zoia had seemed to exercise more power than the provincial committee itself. He

Manin, p. 37: 'I believed and I still believe that the propaganda for the annexation of the Lombardo-Venetian provinces to Piedmont was the principal cause of the failure of the war of independence.'

needed to act in this way to gain the continued backing of the other element in Venice on which he heavily relied – those whose wealth was constantly being taxed through forced loans. The fortunes of men like the Giovanelli, the Papadopoli, Treves, Pisani and Bigaglia were the economic power house on which the revolution rested. To cajole them into further sacrifices, Manin had to appear as the supreme guardian of social order in the city.

As the first period of the revolution drew to a close, Manin temporarily lost his control in Venice. The bourgeoisie of the city became convinced that only Manin's insistent republicanism was preventing Charles Albert from sending troops to their aid. Manin was forced to sacrifice the republic, and Piedmontese commissioners took over the running of the city, which was incorporated into the kingdom of upper Italy. But the monarchist triumph was extremely short-lived, for their military capabilities did not match their political pretensions. By 11 August news had reached Venice of the Salasco armistice. Manin then triumphantly resumed power.

The second period of the revolution, which stretched from August 1848 to August 1849, presented far fewer chances to the Venetians of ultimate success. The Austrians now controlled the whole of Lombardy and the Veneto, and the international situation, with the exception of what was happening in Hungary, was swinging firmly in their direction. But it was to the international situation that Manin turned in the early hours of 12 August, dispatching a grumbling Tommaseo to Paris to seek French intervention in the northern Italian war.

The idea of French aid had never been far from Manin's mind in the early part of 1848. But with Cattaneo's failure in Milan, and the consequent isolation of the Venetian republicans, the possibility of a Venetian appeal to the French in the early part of the revolution had had to be ruled out. Manin limited his emissaries in Paris to asking for arms and recognition. When Lamartine came closest to intervention, in the aftermath of the debacle of 15 May, the undoubted hostility not only of Piedmont but also of Lombardy and Venice was one of the principal reasons that forced him to abandon the project.

It was only after the defeat of Charles Albert that Manin finally felt that he had a free hand. But in August the favourable conditions of the spring no longer existed. Austria had been greatly fortified by Radetzky's victory and the suppression of the Prague insurrection, and Cavaignac and Bastide were extremely reluctant to get involved in a foreign adventure. None the less it was not easy for the French leaders to refuse Venice's appeal because they relied very heavily on foreign policy to maintain their prestige, and Austria seemed intent on humiliating the French by refusing to accept the Anglo-French mediation. At the beginning of September it looked very much as if the French would send a garrison to Venice, an action which would have totally changed the situation in northern Italy. Palmerston and many other observers were convinced that the French were intent on going ahead with the expedition. But at the critical secret meeting of the French ministers, Cavaignac, alarmed by dire English threats of French isolation in an international war, spoke against the Venetian expedition and won the day by the narrowest of margins. The French troops, who had already embarked on frigates ready to sail round Italy to reach Venice, were then ordered to disembark again.

With the French decision against aiding Venice, the city was left to its own devices throughout the winter of 1848–9. Cavedalis and Pepe built up an efficient army to safeguard Venice from any Austrian attack, and Manin continued his successful policy of social alliances within the city. But he had moved substantially to the right since March 1848, and after the June days in Paris was obsessed with the maintenance of order in Venice. He also adopted a highly cautious foreign policy, refusing to re-declare the republic and urging an attitude of 'prudent reserve' upon the Venetians.

These ideas soon came into conflict with those of the radicals and republicans who had gathered to defend Venice as the last bulwark of Italian freedom, a freedom defined as both independence from Austria and liberty from the discredited Italian monarchs. The Mazzinian idea of making Venice a centre for insurrectional activity rapidly gained ground amongst the non-Venetian volunteers. Dall'Ongaro, Mordini, Fabrizi and Sirtori attempted to put pressure on Manin through the Italian Club, and Mazzini sent Maestri to persuade Manin to make Venice the republican heart of all Italy. But Manin remained adamant in his policy of not committing Venice to any particular political line, and crushed the Italian Club when it seemed to threaten his power.

It is doubtful whether the programme of the Italian Club, had it been put into practice, would have substantially altered Venice's eventual fate. Mazzini's conversion to the idea of a people's war had come too late in the revolution to evoke a response from the artisans and peasantry of Lombardy-Venetia. By October, as the abortive rising in the Val d'Intelvi showed, there was little chance of a fresh wave of insurrection breaking out. But Manin's 'prudent reserve' meant that the spirit of self-sacrifice and determination which characterised the Mazzinian radicals never permeated the defence of Venice until resistance was all but hopeless. It was Manin's responsibility that the military commission, which did so much to animate the defenders of Venice in the summer of 1849, was not set up the previous autumn. And it was Manin who refused to let Garibaldi come to Venice, on the grounds that he might disturb the social order of the city. In this way the Venetian fleet was deprived of the one man who stood a chance of inspiring its sailors and breaking the Austrian blockade.

In 1849 Giuseppe Sirtori and a group of radical deputies in the Venetian assembly attempted to force Manin out of his shell and draw Venice closer to the radical regimes of Tuscany and Rome. Sirtori's attempt to oppose Manin's policies foundered on the mass support that Manin continued to enjoy within Venice itself. After the demonstration of 5 March it was clear that any attempt to replace Manin or limit his power would be the occasion for an insurrection by the Venetian populace. While the radicals tried to arouse enthusiasm for a people's war, the Venetian lower classes reserved their loyalty and devotion for Manin and their own city. Sirtori also failed because Rome and Tuscany had nothing to offer Venice in the way of financial or military aid. Manin could point to the Piedmontese fleet in Venetian waters and the monthly subsidy from the Turin parliament as tangible evidence of the rewards which a non-committed policy had brought to Venice. But after Charles Albert's second defeat, at Novara, only Rome and Venice remained to resist the Austrians. Manin still refused to recognise the Roman republic, a refusal that represented the nadir of Venice's relations with the rest of the revolutionary forces in Italy.

In 1849, the Venetian militias and volunteers from all over Italy participated in a heroic and long-sustained defence of the city. On the publication of Planat de la Faye's selection from Manin's papers, G. Visconti Venosta wrote to Senator Fornoni:

The glorious resistance of Venice, narrated in these documents, was for our country one of those events which will remain in the history of our people as a most honourable landmark, as a perennial inspiration.[5]

Manin, for the good order which he maintained in Venice, earned the dubious honour of unceasing accolades from *The Times*:

Whilst the rest of Italy has been disgraced or polluted by recreants and assassins, Venice has still found within her walls men able to govern, and a people not unworthy to be free ... We regard the defence of Venice and the administration of D. Manin with the admiration and sympathy due to a people who are still contending for the restoration of their ancient independence, without having allowed themselves to fall into any of the excesses of modern revolution.[6]

[5] MCV, Agg. Manin, b. xxx/19, no. 22, letter of 27 Feb. 1877.
[6] *The Times*, first leaders, 19 Jan. and 17 Aug. 1849. See also second leader, 2 Sept. 1849.

But for all this praise, Palmerston curtly told Manin that the British government's only advice to the Venetians was to surrender. For all the good order that Manin kept in the city, he was unable to prevent it from reconquest. He had relied for too long on the military advice of those advanced in years and devoid of imagination. By the time Sirtori gained military power in June 1849 it was too late to reform the navy and secure the Adriatic for the Venetians. Above all, Manin's conservatism in the last months of the revolution contrasted poorly with Mazzini's conduct in Rome during the same period. Manin's obsession with public order meant that he lacked the breadth of vision which inspired Mazzini to tell the Roman assembly: 'We must act like men who have the enemy at their gates, and at the same time like men who are working for eternity.'[7]

G. M. Trevelyon wrote at the end of his book on Manin:

It was the masterpiece of Italian good sense that Italians proved capable of taking an impression, of learning the lesson of their failure in 1848 – not like the Germans abandoning their faith in free institutions and dreaming mere blood and iron, but finding a single policy on which to agree, and adhering to it in the face of all Europe till it had become an established fact.[8]

Perhaps the opposite is true. The republicans, with few but notable exceptions, learned the wrong lessons from 1848. They became convinced that the most important feature of the Risorgimento was the struggle for independence and unity, to which the democratic and republican beliefs that they had held in 1848 were to be sacrificed. Dazzled by Cavour's transformation of Piedmont, drawn magnetically towards the revitalised Piedmontese monarchy and army, the republicans abandoned their principles one by one. Few of them heeded the warning that Cattaneo gave in his analysis of the failure of '48:

the courtiers continued the cry amongst us: *out with the barbarians: Italy will make herself*. But the events at Messina, at Genoa and at Rome have shown that a barbarian can be German, or French, or Italian; and that *every nation has its own barbarians*.[9]

The myth was created of the republic having divided the Italians, while the monarchy would unite them. Thus while the liberal monarchists of Piedmont gained in strength, the Action Party was fatally weakened by the defection of so many of those who had been republican leaders in 1848.

[7] Trevelyan, *Garibaldi's Defence*, p. 93.
[8] Trevelyan, *Manin and the Venetian Revolution*, p. 244.
[9] 'Considerazioni sulle cose d'Italia nel 1848', in Cattaneo, *Opere scelte* (ed. D. Castelnuovo Frigessi), vol. 3, pp. 328–9.

Manin, together with Garibaldi, was the foremost amongst them. On leaving Venice, the *Pluton* bore Manin to Marseilles, where his wife, afflicted by cholera, died a few hours after they had docked. Manin never fully recovered from the terrible shock of being forced into exile and losing Teresa in the space of a few days. He settled in Paris, where he lived with his customary modesty and gave Italian lessons to earn his keep. His beloved daughter Emilia died in 1854, and Manin, exhausted by his efforts in the revolutionary years and tired of life, followed her to the grave in 1857. He was fifty-three. But before he died he made it clear that he would sacrifice his republicanism and support Victor Emanuel if the Piedmontese monarch united Italy. In a conversation he had with Nassau Senior on 24 April 1857, a few months before his death, Manin went as far as to say:

I would take Murat, the Pope, Napoleon Bonaparte, the devil himself for king, if I could thereby drive out the foreigners and unite Italy under a single sceptre. Give us unity and we will get all the rest.[10]

Manin was far from being the only leading republican of the Venetian revolution who took this line. Tommaseo, Castellani, even Sirtori,[11] decided over the next decade to abandon their republicanism and support Victor Emanuel II. None of them heeded what Pisacane and Cattaneo, in very different ways, were trying to say: that Victor Emanuel might unite the peninsula, but he would not bring it liberty. None of them analysed the republican failure of 1848–9 in its own terms, and sought to rebuild the republican alternative on the basis of a strategy of popular alliances. Because of these many defections in the years after the revolution, the left wing of the bourgeois nationalist revolution never regained the strength it had enjoyed during 1848–9.

Nor did conditions ever favour them again in quite the same way as they had in the spring of 1848. In post-revolutionary Europe, the schemes of Cavour and the prospect of a monarchist Italy made far more sense than anything else, and this was one of the principal reasons why so many of the republicans went over to the monarchist side. In a Europe that was predominantly anti-republican, and with an imperial France, there seemed little chance of a republican Italy being either permitted or supported. And in Italy itself, many of the factors that had contributed to the startling successes of the spring of 1848 no longer existed. The clergy had gone

[10] Nassau Senior, *Conversations with M. Thiers, M. Guizot, and Other Distinguished Persons During the Second Empire*, vol. 2, p. 127.

[11] For Tommaseo, see Marchesi, *Storia documentata*, p. 500 n. 18. For Castellani, see his letter of 6 Nov. 1851 to Gabussi in Giusti, 'Le vicende della Repubblica romana', p. 69. For Sirtori see Tommaseo, *Venezia*, vol. 1, p. 278 n. 649, and p. 279 n. 650.

over decisively to the side of reaction. Cardinal Monico, the patriarch of Venice, proclaimed in 1850 that 'between Catholicism and liberalism as understood by the modern reformers, there cannot nor will there ever be any agreement',[12] and these words were repeated faithfully by the parish clergy. The belief in a Holy War against Austria had died with the revolution, as had the neo-Guelph party. In Venetia the years after the revolution saw a rapprochement between the Austrians and those wealthy elements of the Venetian bourgeoisie who had supported Manin. The revolutionary period had been an economic disaster for the Venetian bourgeoisie, and they now followed a path, not of direct confrontation, but of gradual merging with the old forces in Venetian society. As for the lower classes, their lot certainly did not improve, as blights on silk and wine devastated the Venetian countryside in the 1850s, and the famine of 1853 brought starvation to both urban and rural poor.[13] Discontent was rife in the Veneto. In 1850 the Austrians set up at Este a military court which acted with great savagery against the peasants and artisans who were the great majority of those brought to trial. In little more than three years the court pronounced many hundreds of death sentences.[14] But with the exiling or flight of so many of the professional and intellectual bourgeoisie, there no longer existed the leadership capable of transforming the deprivations of the lower classes into a systematic attack upon Austrian rule. The extraordinary alliance of class forces that had taken place in early 1848 was not to reoccur.

When Venice and the Veneto finally became part of the kingdom of Italy in 1866, it was not as a result of a popular uprising, but through the good offices of Napoleon III and the might of the Prussian army. A plebiscite gave the customary overwhelming majority in favour of becoming part of Italy, but this was the first and last chance to express their political opinions that most Venetians of that generation were to enjoy. It was not till shortly before the first World War that all adult male Venetians gained the political rights that their fathers and grandfathers had enjoyed in the elections to Manin's assemblies of 1848 and '49. Nor did the new kingdom offer any prospect of improving the conditions of the urban and rural poor. Indeed, in 1868 the Italian parliament decided to introduce the hated *imposta sul macinato*, the tax on flour, into the Veneto. There were

---

[12] Quoted in Bertoli, *Le origini del movimento cattolico*, p. 9.

[13] For the famine of 1853, see ASV, Pres. Luog., 1852–6, b. 229, vi, 1/1; b. 231, vi, 10/2; and buste 244–6, xi, 4/13.

[14] See A. Da Mosto, *L'archivio di stato di Venezia. Indice generale*, vol. 2, pp. 80–1. The papers of the court have just become available for consultation (see Note on documents, p. 394, entry for Archivio di stato, Venezia). Piero Brunello drew my attention to this source and is at present at work on the papers of the court.

violent riots in many areas, accompanied by cries of 'Death to the *signori*, long live Pius IX, long live Religion'.[15] The unification of Italy had come to mean to the Venetian lower classes an increase in their economic obligations, an anti-religious monarchist movement that offered them nothing and refused them political participation. In this way the failure of the revolution of 1848–9 cast its long shadow over the life of the new nation state.

[15] M. Sabbatini, *Profilo politico dei clericali veneti, 1866–1913*, p. 26.

Bibliography

Abruzzese, A., 'Il Circolo italiano a Venezia negli anni 1848-9', *Rassegna Nazionale*, 58 (1927)

Adami, V., 'Dell'intervento francese in Italia nel 1848', *Nuova Rivista Storica*, 12 (1928)

Agrati, C., *Giuseppe Sirtori, 'Il primo dei Mille'*, Bari 1940

Amann, P., 'A Journée in the making: May 15, 1848', *Journal of Modern History*, 42 (1970)

Ambrosoli, L. (ed.), *La insurrezione milanese del marzo 1848*, Milano, Napoli 1969
  Archivio triennale delle cose d'Italia dall'avvenimento di Pio IX all'abbandono di Venezia, 2 vols., Milano 1974; originally edited by Carlo Cattaneo (q.v.)

Antonini, P., *Il Friuli orientale*, Milano 1865
  Carteggio, Udine 1913

Armandi, P., *Storia militare degli elefanti*, Paris 1843

Arzano, A., 'L'arrivo della legione Antonini in Italia nel 1848', *Memorie Storiche Militari*, 6 (1912)

Atti della distribuzione dei premi d'industria fatta nella pubblica solenne adunanza dell'Imperial-Regio Istituto di scienze, lettere ed arti, 30 maggio 1846, Venezia 1846

Baccini, G., 'La stampa periodica in Venezia nel 1848-9', *Rivista delle Biblioteche e degli Archivi*, 27 (1916)

Barbiera, R., 'L'insurrezione del Cadore nel 1848', *Rassegna Storica del Risorgimento*, 9 (1922)

Barié, O., *L'Inghilterra e il problema italiano nel 1848-9*, Milano, 1965

Barnaba, D., *Dal 17 marzo a 14 ottobre 1848. Ricordi*, Udine 1890

Bastide, J., *La République française et l'Italie en 1848*, Bruxelles 1858

Belgioioso, C. di, *Il 1848 a Milano e a Venezia* (ed. S. Bortone), Milano 1977

Benedetti, A., *Pordenone e i paesi del Friuli occidentale nel Risorgimento*, Pordenone 1966

Benedikt, H., *Kaiseradler über dem Apennin. Die Österreicher in Italien*, Wien 1964

Benko von Boinik, J., *Geschichte der K.-K. Kriegs-Marine während der Jahre 1848 und 1849*, Wien 1884

Berengo, M., *L'agricoltura veneta dalla caduta della Repubblica all'Unità*, Milano 1963

'Le origini del Lombardo-Veneto', *Rivista Storica Italiana*, 83 (1971)

Berkeley, G. F.-H. and J., *Italy in the Making: 1848*, Cambridge 1940

Bernardello, A., 'La paura del comunismo e dei tumulti popolari a Venezia e nelle provincie venete nel 1848–49', *Nuova Rivista Storica*, 54 (1970)

'Un'impresa ferroviaria nel Lombardo-Veneto: la Società Ferdinandea da Milano a Venezia', *Rivista Storica Italiana*, 85 (1973)

'Burocrazia, borghesia e contadini nel Veneto austriaco', *Studi Storici*, 17 (1976)

Bernardi, J., *Affetti e dolori. Alla memoria di una madre*, Pinerolo 1860

Berti, A., *Canti popolari scritti sui temi di musica popolare raccolta da Teodoro Zecco*, Padova 1842

Bertier de Sauvigny, G., *Metternich and his Times*, London 1962

Bertoli, B., *Le origini del movimento cattolico a Venezia*, Brescia 1965

Bertoliatti, F., 'La censura nel Lombardo-Veneto, 1814–48', *Archivio Storico della Svizzera Italiana*, 15 (1940)

Bertoni Jovine, D. (ed.), *I periodici popolari del Risorgimento*, vol. 1, Milano 1959

Bertuch, F., *Contributi alla storia del Risorgimento italiano*, Venezia 1911

Bettoni-Cazzago, F., *Gli italiani nella guerra d'Ungheria, 1848–9*, Milano 1888

Biadego, G., *Aleardo Aleardi nel biennio 1848–9. Carteggio inedito*, Verona 1910

Bianchi, N., *Storia documentata della diplomazia europea in Italia, 1814–61*, 8 vols., Torino, Napoli 1865–72

Bianchi, N. (ed.), *Memorie del generale Carlo Zucchi*, Milano, Torino 1861

Scritti e lettere di Carlo Alberto, Roma 1879

Bibliografia dell'età del Risorgimento, 3 vols., Firenze 1971–5

Biscaccia, N., *Cronache di Rovigo dal 1844 a tutto il 1864*, Padova 1865

Bonghi, R., *La vita e i tempi di Valentino Pasini*, Firenze 1867

Bowring, Sir J., 'Report on the statistics of Tuscany, Lucca, the Pontifical and the Lombardo-Venetian states, with a special reference to their commercial relations' (1837), *Accounts and Papers, Reports from Commissioners*, vol. 16 (1839).

Boyer, F., *La seconde République, Charles-Albert et l'Italie du nord en 1848*, Paris 1967

Bozzini, F., *Il furto campestre*, Bari 1977

Brown, H., *Life on the Lagoons*, London 1884

Brunello, P., 'Rivoluzione e clero nel 1848 a Venezia', Tesi di laurea, Università degli studi di Padova, facoltà di lettere e filosofia, 1973

'Mediazione culturale e orientamenti politici nel clero veneto intorno al 1848: il "Giornale dei parocchi ed altri sacerdoti"', *Archivio Veneto*, 104 (1975)

Brunetti, M., 'L'opera del comune di Venezia nel 1848–9', *Archivio Veneto*, 42 (1948)

Brunetti, M. *et al.* (eds.), *Daniele Manin intimo*, Roma 1936

Buttini, T. and Avetta, M. (eds.), *I rapporti fra il governo sardo e il governo provvisorio di Lombardia*, Roma 1938

Caddeo, R. (ed.), *Epistolario di Carlo Cattaneo*, 4 vols., Firenze 1949–56

Cagnoli, O., *Cenni statistici di Verona e della sua provincia*, Verona 1849

Calucci, G., 'Documenti inediti relativi al primo periodo della rivoluzione italiana nel 1848', *Atti del Regio Istituto Veneto di Scienze, Lettere ed Arti*, 6 (1870–1)

Candeloro, G., *Storia dell'Italia moderna*, 7 vols., Milano 1956–74

Carte segrete e atti ufficiali della polizia austriaca in Italia dal 4 giugno 1814 al 22 marzo 1848, 3 vols., Capolago 1851–2

Casati, C., *Nuove rivelazioni sui fatti di Milano nel 1847–8*, 2 vols., Milano 1885

Castelli, E., *Jacopo Castelli, ovvero una pagina della storia di Venezia nel 1848*, Venezia 1890

Cattaneo, C., *Dell'insurrezione di Milano nel 1848 e della successiva guerra* (first version, *L'Insurrection de Milan en 1848*, published in Paris in 1848; revised Italian edition, Lugano 1849), in C. Cattaneo, *Opere scelte* (ed. D. Castelnuovo Frigessi), vol. 3, Torino 1972.

Cattaneo, C. (ed.), *Archivio triennale delle cose d'Italia dall'avvenimento di Pio IX all'abbandono di Venezia*, 3 vols., Capolago 1850, 1851, Chieri 1855; re-edited by L. Ambrosoli (q.v.), 2 vols., Milano 1974

Cavedalis, G. B., *I commentari* (ed. V. Marchesi), 2 vols., Udine 1928–9

Cessi, R., 'La capitolazione di Venezia del 22 marzo 1848', *Atti dell'Istituto Veneto di Scienze, Lettere, ed Arti*, 106 (1948)
'La missione Martini a Venezia nel giugno 1848', *Archivio Veneto*, 50–1 (1952)
'La difesa delle provincie venete nel 1848', *Bollettino del Museo Civico di Padova*, 30–43 (1942–54)

Ciampini, R., *Studi e ricerche su Nicolò Tommaseo*, Roma 1944
Vita di Nicolò Tommaseo, Firenze 1945

Ciasca, R., *L'origine del 'programma per l'opinione nazionale italiana' del 1847–8*, Milano, Roma, Napoli 1916

Ciconi, G. D., 'Discorso sull'agricoltura friulana', in *Atti della distribuzione dei premi d'industria 1844, fatta dalla congregazione municipale e dalla camera provinciale di commercio in Udine*, Udine 1845

Cobb, R., *The Police and the People*, Oxford 1970

Codignola, A., *Rubattino*, Bologna 1938

Collezione delle leggi, istruzioni e disposizioni di massima, pubblicate o diramate nelle provincie venete, vol. 29, Venezia 1838

Corbelli, A., 'I partiti politici in Lombardia nel '48', *Rassegna Storica del Risorgimento*, 12 (1935)

Correnti, C., *L'Austria e la Lombardia*, Italia 1847

Cornoldi, A., 'Canti politici e patriottici del Polesine (1848–1866)', *Lares*, 13 (1965)

Correr, G. (ed.), *Venezia e le sue lagune*, 2 vols., Venezia 1847
'Correspondence respecting the affairs of Italy, 1846–9', *Accounts and Papers*, 28 (1849)
Cossar, R. M., 'Riflessi goriziani della rivoluzione del 1848', in *La Venezia Giulia e la Dalmazia nella rivoluzione nazionale* (q.v.)
Costi, M., *Della illegalità della Assemblea convocata in Venezia pel giorno 11 ottobre 1848*, Venezia 1848
Curato, F., 'L'insurrezione e la guerra del 1848', in *Storia di Milano*, vol. 14, Milano 1960

D'Agostini, E., *Ricordi militari del Friuli*, 2 vols., Udine 1881
Dalla Pozza, A. M., *Nostro Risorgimento. Lettere dal carteggio dei marchesi Gonzati su Vicenza nel '48*, Firenze 1941
Dall'Ongaro, F., *Venezia l'undici agosto 1848*, Capolago 1850
Epistolario (ed. A. De Gubernatis), Firenze n.d.
D'Azeglio, M., *Dell'emancipazione civile degl'Israeliti*, Firenze 1848
Debrunner, J., *Aventures de la compagnie suisse pendant la siège*, Lugano 1849
De Castro, G., *Giuseppe Sirtori*, Milano 1892
De Franceschi, C., 'G. Revere e il Circolo italiano di Venezia', in *La Venezia Giulia e la Dalmazia nella rivoluzione nazionale* (q.v.)
De Giorgi, A., 'Venezia nel 1848 e 1849', *Archivio Veneto*, 11 (1876)
Della Marmora, A., *Alcuni episodi della guerra nel Veneto* (ed. M. Degli Alberti), Milano, Roma, Napoli 1915
Della Peruta, F., 'Le condizioni dei contadini lombardi nel Risorgimento', *Società*, 8 (1951)
I democratici e la rivoluzione italiana, Milano 1958
'Il pensiero sociale di Mazzini', *Nuova Rivista Storica*, 48 (1964)
'I contadini nella rivoluzione lombarda del 1848', in his *Democrazia e socialismo nel Risorgimento*, Roma 1965
Mazzini e i rivoluzionari italiani: Il 'partito d'azione', 1830–1845, Milano 1974
De Luna, F., *The French Republic under Cavaignac, 1848*, Princeton 1969
Depoli, A., *I rapporti tra il regno di Sardegna e Venezia negli anni 1848–9*, 2 vols., Modena 1959
De Rosas, R., 'Strutture di classe e lotte sociali nel Polesine preunitario', *Studi Storici*, 18 (1977)
De Stefani, L., *La campagna dei Sette Comuni nel 1848*, Pisa 1898
Diario del nono congresso degli scienziati italiani convocato in Venezia nel settembre 1847, Venezia 1847
Dizionario biografico degli italiani, 16 vols., Roma 1960–73
Dizionario del Risorgimento nazionale, 4 vols., Milano 1931–7

Ellesmere, Earl of (trans.), *Military Events in Italy, 1848–9*, London 1851; English translation of *Die Ereignisse in Italien im Jahre 1848* (anon.), Zürich 1848

Ember, G., 'Louis Kossuth à la tête du comité de la défense nationale', *Studia Historica Academiae Scientarium Hungaricae*, 6 (1953)

Emerson, D. E., *Metternich and the Political Police: Security and Subversion in the Hapsburg Monarchy, 1815–30*, The Hague 1968

Errera, A., *Storia e statistica delle industrie venete e accenni al loro avvenire*, Venezia 1870

Errera, A. and Finzi, C., *La vita e i tempi di Daniele Manin, 1804–1848*, Venezia 1872

Fabris, C., *Gli avvenimenti militari del 1848 e 1849*, 3 vols., Torino 1898–1904

Faleschini, A., 'Corrispondenze di Licurgo Zannini e Leonardo Andervolti dopo l'assedio di Osoppo del 1848', *Atti dell'Accademia di Scienze, Lettere e Arti di Udine*, 10 (1945–8)

'L'Assedio di Osoppo nelle memorie di Leonardo Andervolti', *Atti dell'Accademia di Scienze, Lettere e Arti di Udine*, 10 (1945–8)

Fasanari, R., *Il Risorgimento a Verona, 1797–1866*, Verona 1958

Federigo, F., *Del periodo politico e della vita intima di D. Manin*, Venezia 1868

Fedrigoni, A., *L'industria e il commercio della carta nel Veneto durante la seconda dominazione austriaca*, Torino 1970

Fejtö, F., 'Hungary, the war of independence', in F. Fejtö (ed.), *The Opening of an Era, 1848*, London 1948

Ferrari, G. E., 'Spunti di riforma economico-sociale negli scritti d'un funzionario veneto ai margini della rivoluzione', *Rassegna Storica del Risorgimento*, 44 (1957)

Ferrari, G. E., 'L'attitudine di Padova verso Venezia nella crisi veneta del quarantotto', *Miscellanea in onore di Roberto Cessi*, vol. 3, Roma 1958

Ferrari, V. (ed.), *Carteggio Casati–Castagnetto*, Milona, 1909

Filipuzzi, A., 'Luoghi comuni nella storia del Risorgimento italiano', *Memorie Storiche Forogiviliesi*, 56 (1971)

Freschi, G., 'Intorno i mezzi di cui abbisogna l'agricoltura per conseguire da vero i progressi che lo stato attuale della scienza le ha preparato', *Atti dell'I.-R. Istituto Veneto di Scienze, Lettere ed Arti*, 7 (1847–8)

Fulin, R., 'Venezia e Daniele Manin', *Archivio Veneto*, 9 (1875)

Gambarin, G., 'Il Mazzini, il Tommaseo, il Manin e la difesa di Venezia', *Archivio Veneto*, 5 (1929)

'Il giornale *San Marco*', *Archivio Veneto*, 75 (1964)

Garnier Pagès, L. A., *Histoire de la révolution de 1848*, vols. 9 and 10, Paris 1869 and 1872.

Georgelin, J., 'Une grande propriété en Vénétie au xviiie siècle: Anguillara', *Annales, Economies, Sociétés, Civilisations*, 23 (1968)

Gianelli, G. L., 'Dei miglioramenti sociali efficaci e possibili a vantaggio degli agricoltori e degli operai', *Giornale dell'I.-R. Istituto Lombardo di Scienze, Lettere ed Arti e Biblioteca Italiana*, 1 (1847)

Giusti, R., 'L'agricoltura e i contadini nel Mantovano (1848–66)', *Movimento Operaio*, 7 (1955)

'Le vicende della Repubblica romana del 1849 nel carteggio di Benedetto Musolino, G. Battista Castellani, Filippo de Boni ed altri democratici', *Archivio Veneto*, 66 (1960)

Glazier, I. A., 'Il commercio estero del Regno lombardo-veneto dal 1815 al 1865', *Archivio Economico dell'Unificazione Italiana*, 15 (1966)

Gloria, A., *Il comitato provvisorio dipartimentale di Padova dal 25 marzo al 13 giugno 1848*, Padova 1927

Gooch, G. P. (ed.), *Later Correspondence of Lord John Russell*, vol. 1, London 1925

Gramsci, A., *Selections from the Prison Notebooks*: see Q. Hoare and G. Nowell Smith

Grandi, T., *Gustavo Modena, attore patriota, 1803–61*, Pisa 1968.

Grandi, T. (ed.), *Epistolario di Gustavo Modena, 1827–61*, Roma 1955

Greenfield, K. R., 'Commerce and new enterprise at Venice, 1830–48', *Journal of Modern History*, 11 (1939)

Economics and Liberalism in the Risorgimento. A Study of Nationalism in Lombardy, 1815–1848, Baltimore 1965 (first edition 1934)

Guiccioli, A., 'Diario inedito', *Nuova Antologia*, 163 (1932)

Guida commerciale di Venezia, Venezia 1848

Hearder, H., 'La rivoluzione veneziana del 1848 vista dal console generale inglese', *Rassegna Storica del Risorgimento*, 46 (1957)

Helfert, J. A., *Zur Geschichte des Lombardo-Venezianischen Königsreich*, Wien 1908

Hillard, G. S., *Six Months in Italy*, Boston 1853

Hoare, Q. and Nowell Smith, G. (eds.), *Selections from the Prison Notebooks of Antonio Gramsci*, London 1971

Hobsbawm, E. J., *The Age of Revolution, 1789–1848*, London, New York, 1962

Howells, W. D., *Venetian Life*, 2 vols., London 1891

Hübner, J. A. von, *Une année de ma vie, 1848–9*, Paris 1891

Il 22 marzo. Cenni biografici e sul massacro di Giovanni Marinovich, Venezia 1850

Imbriani, V., *Alessandro Poerio a Venezia*, Napoli 1884

Jäger, E., *Storia documentata dei corpi militari veneti ed i loro alleati, 1848–9*, Venezia 1880

Jászay, M., *L'Italia e la rivoluzione ungherese del 1848–9*, Budapest 1948

Jennings, L. C., *France and Europe in 1848*, Oxford 1974

La Forge, A. de, *Histoire de la République de Vénise sous Manin*, 2 vols., Paris 1852–3

Laing, S., *Notes of a Traveller on the Social and Political State of France, Prussia, Switzerland, Italy, etc.*, London 1842

Laing, S., *Observations on the Social and Political State of the European People in 1848 and 1849*, London 1850

La Marmora, A., *Alcuni episodi della guerra nel Veneto* (ed. M. Degli Alberti), Milano 1915

La Masa, G., *Documenti della rivoluzione siciliana del 1847-9*, 3 vols., Torino 1850-1

Lamartine, A. de, *Histoire de la révolution de 1848*, 2 vols., Bruxelles 1849

Lamennais, M. F. de, *Affaires de Rome*, Paris 1836-7

   Des maux de l'Eglise et de la société, et des moyens d'y remédier, Paris 1836-7

La Repubblica veneta nel' 1848-9 (ed. Il comitato regionale veneto per la celebrazione centenaria del 1848-1849), vol. 1, *Documenti diplomatici*, Padova 1949; vol. 2, *Documenti diplomatici, carteggio di G. B. Castellani*, Padova 1954

La Venezia Giulia e la Dalmazia nella rivoluzione nazionale del 1848-9 (ed. Il comitato triestino per le celebrazioni del centenario), 3 vols., Trieste 1949

Lazzarini, C., *N. Bixio*, Forlì 1910

Le assemblee del Risorgimento (ed. La camera dei deputati), vol. 2, *Venezia*, Roma 1911

Leoni, C., 'Cronaca, 1848', in his *Epigrafi e prose edite e inedite* (ed. G. Guerzoni), Firenze 1879.

Levi, A., *La politica di Daniele Manin*, Milano 1933

Levi Minzi, G., 'I giornali veneziani nel 1848-9', *Rassegna Nazionale*, 43 (1921)

Lizier, A., 'Prodromi e primi momenti del '48 a Treviso', *Archivio Veneto*, 42-3 (1948)

Lucas, F. L., *The Decline and Fall of the Romantic Ideal*, 2nd edn, Cambridge 1948

Lucchetta, M., *Arte tipografica e movimento politico-letterari a San Vito di Tagliamento*, Udine 1973

Lucchini, A., 'Memoriale del maresciallo Radetzky sulle condizioni d'Italia al principio del 1848', *Nuova Rivista Storica*, 14 (1930)

Lutyens, M. (ed.), *Effie in Venice*, London 1965

Luzzatto, G., 'Le vicende del porto di Venezia dal primo medioevo allo scoppio della guerra 1914-18', in his *Studi di storia economica veneziana*, Padova 1954

Macartney, C. A., *The Habsburg Empire, 1790-1918*, London 1968

Mack Smith, D., *Modern Sicily after 1715*, London 1968

Mack Smith, D. (ed.), *Garibaldi*, New Jersey 1969

Malamani, V., 'La censura austriaca delle stampe nelle provincie venete', *Rivista Storica del Risorgimento Italiano*, 1 (1896) and 2 (1897), and *Il Risorgimento Italiano*, 2 (1909)

Mangini, N., 'La politica scolastica dell'Austria nel Veneto dal 1814 al 1848', *Rassegna Storica del Risorgimento*, 46 (1957)

Manni, M., *La commissione militare dittatoriale dal giugno all'agosto del 1849*, Lodi 1883

Marchesi, V., *Settant'anni della storia di Venezia, 1798–1866*, Torino 1892
  Storia documentata della rivoluzione e della difesa di Venezia negli anni 1848–9, Venezia 1916

Marchesi, V. (ed.), 'Diario di un anonimo (Venezia dal maggio al 16 agosto 1849), *Miscellanea veneziana (1848–9)*, Roma 1936

Mariutti, A., *Organismo ed azione delle società segrete del Veneto durante la seconda dominazione austriaca, 1814–47* (Miscellanea di storia veneta, vol. 3), Venezia 1930

Martin, H., *Daniele Manin and Venice in 1848–9*, 2 vols., London 1862

Marx, K., 'The class struggles in France, 1848–1850' (first published 1850), in his *Surveys from Exile* (ed. D. Fernbach), London 1973

Massarani, T., *Cesare Correnti nella vita e nelle opere*, Milano 1890

Massimo d'Azeglio alla guerra d'indipendenza nel '48. Documenti inediti, Modena 1911

Mazzini, G., 'Royalty and republicanism in Italy', in *Life and Writings of Joseph Mazzini*, vol. 5, London 1869
  Scritti editi ed inediti, 100 vols., Imola 1906–43

Medin, D., *Schiarimento relativo ad una storia vecchia*, Padova 1885

Memorie istoriche dell'artiglieria Bandiera–Moro, assedio di Marbhera e fatti del ponte a Venezia, 1848–9 (Documenti della Guerra Santa d'Italia, vol. 10), Capolago 1849

Meneghello, V., *Il quarantotto a Vicenza*, Vicenza 1898

Meneghetti, N. (ed.), *Il Cavaignac di Venezia. Diario inedito del generale Mengaldo, 1848–49*, Venezia 1910

Meneghini, P., *Bozzetti di un crociato*, Vicenza 1879

Menghini, M., *Lodovico Frapolli e le sue missioni diplomatiche a Parigi 1848–9*, Firenze 1930

Metternich, K. von, *Mémoires, documents et écrits divers laissés par le prince de Metternich*, 8 vols., Paris 1880–4

Modena, G., *Epistolario, see* T. Grandi

Molon, F., *Un ricordo del 1848*, Lonigo 1883

Montanelli, G., *Memorie sull'Italia*, Firenze 1963 (first edn, Torino 1853)

Monteleone, G., 'La carestia del 1816–17 nelle provincie venete', *Archivio Veneto*, 86–7 (1969)

Monterossi, P. A., *Memorie storico-biografiche di Daniele Manin*, Venezia 1848

Monti, A., *Un dramma fra gli esuli*, Milano 1921
  Un italiano: Francesco Restelli, 1814–90, Milano 1933

Morandi, A., *Il mio giornale*, Modena 1867

Moreno, G., *Calvi e la difesa del Cadore*, Roma 1892

Morley, J., Viscount, *The Life of Richard Cobden*, 2 vols., London 1881

Mosca, R., *Le relazioni del governo provvisorio di Lombardia con i governi d'Italia e di Europa*, Milano 1950

Moscati, R., *La diplomazia europea e il problema italiano nel 1848*, Firenze 1947

388   *Bibliography*

Murray, R. G., 'Carlo Cattaneo and His Interpretation of the Milanese Revolution of 1848', Ph.D. dissertation, Cambridge 1963
Mutinelli, F., *Annali delle provincie venete dal 1801 al 1840*, Venezia 1843

Natali, G., 'Corpi franchi del quarantotto', *Rassegna Storica del Risorgimento*, 13 (1935)
Noaro, A., *Dei volontari in Lombardia e nel Tirolo e della difesa di Venezia nel 1848-49*, Torino 1850
Nobili, M., 'Corrispondenza tra Emanuele e Carlo Fenzi nel 1849', *Rassegna Storica del Risorgimento*, 26 (1939)
Normanby, Marquis of, *A Year of Revolution from a Journal Kept in Paris in 1848*, 2 vols., London 1857

Ottolenghi, A., 'Abraham Lattes nei suoi rapporti colla repubblica di Daniele Manin', *Rassegna Mensile di Israel*, 5 (1930); off-print version, Città di Castello 1930
L'azione di Tommaseo a Venezia per la emancipazione degli Israeliti, Venezia 1933
Ottolini, V., *La rivoluzione lombarda del 1848 e 1849*, Milano 1887

Palumbo-Fossati, C., 'Un amore giovanile di Daniele Manin per una Fossati di Morcote', *Bollettino Storico della Svizzera Italiana*, 28 (1953)
Passerin D'Entrèves, E., 'Qualche ulteriore riflessione sull'amicizia tra Mazzini e George Sand', in *Mazzini e i repubblicani italiani. Studi in onore di Terenzio Grandi*, Torino 1976
Pecchiai P., 'Caduti e feriti nelle cinque giornate di Milano: ceti e professioni cui appartennero', *Atti e memorie del XXVII congresso dell'Istituto per la storia del Risorgimento italiano*, Milano 1948
Pecorari, P., 'Motivi d'intransigimentismo nel pensiero del patriarca di Venezia Jacopo Monico durante il biennio 1848-9, *Archivio Veneto*, 93 (1971)
Pepe, G., *L'Italia militare e la guerra di sollevazione*, Paris 1836
Histoire des révolutions et des guerres d'Italie, 1847-9, Paris 1850
Pierantoni, A., *Il colonnello Alessandro Monti e la legione italiana in Ungheria*, Roma 1903
Pieri, P., 'La guerra regia nella pianura padana', in *Il 1848 nella storia italiana ed europea* (ed. E. Rota), Milano 1948
'Carlo Cattaneo storico militare della prima guerra d'indipendenza', *Studi sul Risorgimento in Lombardia*, vol. 1, Modena 1949
Storia militare del Risorgimento, Torino 1962
Pilosio, L., *Il Friuli durante la Restaurazione, 1813-47*, Udine 1943
Pilot, A., 'Venezia nel blocco del 1813-14. Da noterelle inedite del Cicogna', *Archivio Veneto*, 27 (1914)
'Il patriarca cardinale G. Monico contro *Sior Antonio Rioba*', *Rassegna Nazionale*, 43 (1923)
'L'assalto al palazzo del patriarca cardinale Monico a Venezia nel agosto 1849', *Rassegna Storica del Risorgimento*, 11 (1924)

'Il *Per tutti* di G. Vollo', *Rassegna Storica del Risorgimento*, 14 (1927)

Pino-Branca, A., 'La finanza di guerra del governo provvisorio veneto (1848–9)', in *Studi in onore di Gino Luzzatto*, vol. 3, Milano 1950

Pirri, P., 'La missione di mons. Corboli-Bussi in Lombardia nel 1848', *Rivista di Storia della Chiesa in Italia*, 1 (1947)

Pisacane, C., *Guerra combattuta in Italia negli anni 1848 e 1849*, Genova 1851

Pitocco, F., *Utopia e riforma religiosa nel Risorgimento. Il sansimonismo nella cultura toscana*, Bari 1972

Piva, E., 'La cacciata degli austriaci da Rovigo nel marzo del 1848 e la costituzione del comitato dipartimentale del Polesine', *Archivio Veneto*, 32 (1916)

'Prime armi 1848 (dalle memorie del generale Domenico Piva)', in *1848–1948, Celebrazioni polesane del centenario*, Rovigo 1948

Planat de la Faye, F. (ed.), *Documenti e scritti autentici lasciati da Daniele Manin*, 2 vols., Venezia 1877; first edition, in French, *Documents et pièces authentiques laissés par Daniel Manin*, 2 vols., Paris 1860

Polver, G., *Radetzky a Verona nel 1848*, Verona 1913

Priuli, N., *Venezia all'Italia. Discorso pronunziato nell'adunanza del consiglio comunale di Venezia il giorno 6 nov. 1848*, Venezia 1848

Quadri, A., *Prospetto statistico delle provincie venete*, Venezia 1826

Quazza, G., 'La missione Martini a Venezia e il problema della fusione', *Il Risorgimento*, 3 (1951)

Radaelli, C., *Storia dell'assedio di Venezia*, Napoli 1865

Radvany, E., *Metternich's Projects for Reform in Austria*, The Hague 1971

Rath, R. J., 'The Habsburgs and the great depression in Lombardy-Venetia, 1814–18', *Journal of Modern History*, 13 (1941)

'L'amministrazione austriaca nel Lombardo-Veneto, 1814–21', *Archivio Economico dell'Unificazione Italiana*, 9 (1959)

The Provisional Austrian Regime in Lombardy-Venetia, 1814–15, Austin and London 1969

Renier, G., *La cronaca di Mestre degli anni 1848 e 1849*, Treviso 1896

Revolutions of 1848. Document Collection, The Open University Press, Milton Keynes 1976

Rigobon, P., *Gli eletti alle assemblee veneziane del 1848–9*, Venezia 1950

Rizzi, D., *Adria e lo stabilimento agrario dei fratelli Scarpa*, Rovigo 1838

Lettera a co. Gherardo Freschi sui lavori di agricoltura e le industrie campestri, Venezia 1848

Sui miglioramenti agrari delle due tenute di Sabbion e Desmonta nel distretto di Cologna del nob. co. Giovanni Papadopoli, Verona 1861

Roberts, J. M., 'Lombardy', in A. Goodwin (ed.), *The European Nobility in the Eighteenth Century*, London 1953

Romani, M., 'L'economia milanese nell'età del Risorgimento', *Storia di Milano*, vol. 14, Milano 1960

Romeo, R., *Cavour e il suo tempo*, vol. 1, Bari 1969

Ronchi, C., *I democratici fiorentini nella rivoluzione del 1848-9*, Firenze 1963

Rosaroll, C., *Assedio di Malghera 1849. Lettere di colonnello barone Cesare Rosaroll-Scorza, comandante la lunetta n. 13*, Padova 1894

Rossi, G., *Lettere del sacerdote Giovanni Rossi, profugo in Firenze, a Valentino Pasini a Parigi, ottobre-novembre 1848*, n.p. 1915

Rota, E., 'Del contributo dei lombardi alla guerra del 1848; il problema del volontarismo', *Nuova Rivista Storica*, 12 (1928)

Rothenberg, G. E., 'The Austrian army in the age of Metternich', *Journal of Modern History*, 40 (1968)

Rovani, V., *Daniele Manin*, Capolago 1850

Rutto, G., 'Tommaseo e la "Fratellanza de' popoli"', *Rassegna Storica del Risorgimento*, 62 (1975)

Sabbatini, M., *Profilo politico dei clericali veneti, 1866-1913*, Padova 1962

Salvatorelli, L., *La rivoluzione europea, 1848-1849*, Milano, Roma 1949

Salvemini, G., 'Giuseppe Mazzini dall'aprile 1846 all'aprile 1848', in his *Scritti sul Risorgimento*, Milano 1961

'I partiti politici milanesi nel secolo XIX', in his *Scritti sul Risorgimento*, Milano 1961

Sandonà, A., *Il regno Lombardo-Venet, 1814-59. La costituzione e l'amministrazione*, Milano 1912

Sanseverino, F., 'Delle fabbriche di pannilana in Follina nella provincia di Treviso, 1840', *Annali Universali di Statistica, Economia Pubblica ecc.*, 67 (1841)

Santalena, A., *Treviso nel 1848*, Treviso 1888

Treviso nella seconda dominazione austriaca, Treviso 1890

Memorie del quarantotto. Il fatto d'armi di Cornuda, Treviso 1898

Sanzin, L. G., 'F. e L. Seismit-Doda nelle vicende del 1848-9', in *La Venezia Giulia e la Dalmazia nella rivoluzione nazionale* (q.v.)

Sardagna, S., 'I primi errori militari dei Veneti nel 1848, 22 marzo – 8 aprile 1848', *Rivista di Fanteria*, 1904; off-print version, Torino 1904

Sarti, T., *Il parlamento subalpino e nazionale. Profile e cenni biografici di tutti i deputati e senatori creati dal 1840 al 1890*, Roma 1896

Scarpa, G., *L'agricoltura del Veneto nella prima metà del XIX secolo. L'utilizzazione del suolo* (Archivio economico dell'unificazione italiana, vol. 8), Torino 1963

Senior, N., *Conversations with M. Thiers, M. Guizot and Other Distinguished Persons during the Second Empire*, 2 vols., London 1878

Serena, A., *Una cronaca inedita del '48*, Treviso 1910

Shelley, P. B., 'Lines written amongst the Euganean hills', in Shelley, *Poetical Works* (ed. T. Hutchinson), Oxford 1970

Simpson, F. A., *Louis Napoleon and the Recovery of France*, 3rd edn, London 1951 (1st edn, 1923)

Sinclair, J. D., *An Autumn in Italy*, Edinburgh 1829

Smyth, H. M., 'Austria at the crossroads; the Italian crisis of June, 1848', in

Essays in the History of Modern Europe (ed. D. C. McKay), New York 1936

Soboul, A., 'Les troubles agraires de 1848', in his *Paysans, sans-culottes et jacobins*, Paris n.d.

Soldani, S., 'Contadini, operai e "popolo" nella rivoluzione del 1848-9 in Italia', *Studi Storici*, 14 (1973)

Spellanzon, C., *Storia del Risorgimento e dell'unità d'Italia*, 5 vols., Milano 1933-50

Il vero segreto di re Carlo Alberto, Firenze 1953

Stefani, G., 'Leone Pincherle', in *1831-1931. Il centenario delle Assicurazioni Generali*, Trieste 1931

Leone Pincherle e Daniele Manin, Trieste 1933

'Documenti ed appunti sul quarantotto triestino', in *La Venezia Giulia e la Dalmazia nella rivoluzione nazionale* (q.v.)

'Giuliani e Dalmati nella guerra d'indipendenza', in *La Venezia Giulia e la Dalmazia nella rivoluzione nazionale* (q.v.)

'La flotta sardo-veneta nell'Adriatico e il blocco di Trieste', in *La Venezia Giulia e la Dalmazia nella rivoluzione nazionale* (q.v.)

Stern, D., *Histoire de la révolution de 1848*, 2 vols., Paris 1862

Taylor, A. J. P., *The Italian Problem in European Diplomacy*, Manchester 1934

Tegoborski, M. L. de, *Des Finances et du crédit public de l'Autriche*, 2 vols., Paris 1843

Tessitori, T., 'Zaccario Bricito (celebrazione del centenario del 1848)', in *Atti e Memorie dell'Accademia di Udine*, 10 (1945-8)

Thompson, E. P., 'The peculiarities of the English', *Socialist Register*, 2 (1965); full version in his *The Poverty of Theory & other essays*, London 1978

Tivaroni, C., *L'Italia durante il dominio austriaco*, 3 vols., Torino, Roma 1892

Tommaseo, N., *Appel à la France*, Paris, Aug. 1848

Venezia negli anni 1848 e 1849, vol. 1 (ed. P. Prunas), Firenze 1931, vol. 2 (ed. G. Gambarin), Firenze 1950

Tommaseo, N. and Capponi, G., *Carteggio inedito dal 1833 a 1874*, vols. 1 and 2, Bologna 1911, Firenze 1914

Trevelyan, G. M., *Garibaldi's Defence of the Roman Republic*, London 1907

Manin and the Venetian Revolution of 1848, London 1923

Trotsky, L., *Results and Prospects*, London 1971

Tucci, U., 'Le emissioni monetarie del governo provvisorio di Venezia (1848-9)', *Archivio Economico dell'Unificazione Italiana*, 1 (1956)

'Le monete del regno lombardo-veneto dal 1815 al 1866', *Archivio Economico dell'Unificazione Italiana*, 2 (1956)

Uggè, A., 'Le entrate del regno lombardo-veneto dal 1840 al 1864', *Archivio Economico dell'Unificazione Italiana*, 1 (1956)

Ulloa, G., *Guerre de l'indépendence italienne, 1848–9*, 2 vols., Paris 1859

Valussi, P., *Rapporto della camera di commercio e d'industria della provincia del Friuli, all'ecc. I.-R. ministero del commercio, ecc . . . 1851–2*, Udine 1853
Dalla memoria d'un vecchio giornalista dall'epoca del Risorgimento italiano, Udine 1967
Van Nuffel, R. O. J., 'Intorno alla perdita della flotta a Venezia', *Rassegna Storica del Risorgimento*, 44 (1957)
Vanzetti, C., *Due secoli di storia dell'agricoltura veronese*, Verona 1965
Venezia, A., 'Il '48 nel Friuli orientale', in *La Venezia Giulia e la Dalmazia nella rivoluzione nazionale* (q.v.)
Venezia e le sue lagune, see G. Correr
Ventura, A., *Lineamenti costituzionali del governo provvisorio di Venezia nel 1848–9*, Padova 1955
'L'Avesani, il Castellani e il problema della fusione', *Archivio Veneto*, 45 (1955)
'Daniele Manin e la Municipalità nel marzo '48', *Rassegna Storica del Risorgimento*, 44 (1957)
'La formazione intellettuale di Daniele Manin', *Il Risorgimento*, 9 (1957)
Ventura, A. (ed.), *Verbali del consiglio dei ministri della Repubblica veneta, 27 marzo – 30 giugno 1848*, Venezia 1957
Visconti Venosta, G., *Memoirs of Youth, 1847–60*, London 1914

Whyte, A. J., *The Evolution of Modern Italy*, Oxford 1950
Wingate, A., *Railway Building in Italy before Unification* (Centre for the Advanced Study of Italian Society, University of Reading, Occasional Papers no. 3), Reading 1970

Zago, F., *L'archivio storico della camera di commercio di Venezia. Inventario (1806–70)*, Venezia 1964
Zalin, G., *Aspetti e problemi della economia veneta dalla caduta della Repubblica all'annessione*, Vicenza 1969
L'economia veronese in età napoleonica, Milano 1973

Note on documents and newspapers

DOCUMENTS

The archives are dealt with in alphabetical order, as listed in the table of abbreviations at the beginning of the book. What follows is not a list of every primary source that I have consulted, but a commentary on the archives where I have worked and the documents they contain.

Archivio comunale, Pordenone

When I visited this archive in September 1974 it was in the most complete disorder. All the *buste* containing the documents of the archive, dating back to the Middle Ages, were lying on the floor of one room, waiting to be shelved. Amidst clouds of dust and with the help of Rag. Gasparini I managed to find the papers of the Guardia Nazionale for March and April of 1848. There were doubtless other documents referring to 1848 which I did not find. In general, the communal archives of the Veneto must contain an enormous wealth of material which has never been tapped, at least for the nineteenth century. One can only hope that natural disasters (the recent earthquakes in Friuli), man-made disasters (the fighting in this area in the first World War), and sheer neglect have not taken too heavy a toll of this historical patrimony.

Archivio comunale, Venezia

This archive is housed in a large semi-derelict building in Castello. I worked there in the summer of 1974 and conditions were insalubrious, to put it mildly. The building was rat-infested and I was shown some very large specimens of the species. The staff was as friendly as possible in a situation where the heat and the smell drove us all out into the *campo* at regular intervals. There is a good index to the bulk of the archive, the Atti di Ufficio, but no guide to the papers of the Casa di Industria or the Atti del Consiglio Comunale.

Archivio storico del Risorgimento, Firenze

This houses the Archivio Fenzi which is of interest because of Carlo Fenzi's presence in Venice in 1849. His correspondence with his father has been published by M. Nobili ('Corrispondenza tra Emanuele e Carlo Fenzi nel 1849', *Rassegna Storica del Risorgimento*, 26 (1939)).

Archivio di stato, Torino

Contains an enormous amount of material dealing with Piedmont in 1848–9. For the historian of Venice, see in particular: *Carte Bianchi* (inventory 174), serie II, mazzo 10, no. 15: Relazioni con Venezia 1848; serie II, mazzo 13, no. 6: Documenti sulle due missioni sostenute nel Veneto nel 1848 da Carlo Gonzales a nome del Gov. Provv. della Lombardia; *Carte politiche diverse* (inventory 165), cart. 24, no. 132: Lettere politiche del Sig. Ponzio Vaglia, 1848; cart. 25, no. 150: Lettere del Gov. Provv. di Venezia e di alcuni citta-dini veneziani 1848–9. There is also a separate section of the archive called the *Sezioni riunite*, housed in Via Santa Chiara 40 and containing the letters of the Piedmontese consul at Venice for the period 1848–9.

Archivio di stato, Udine

This important and efficient archive contains all the *buste* from the communal archive of Udine, as well as those of a number of other communes of Friuli: Forni di Sopra, S. Giorgio della Richinvelda, Forame and Venzone. *Buste* 578–83 of the communal archive of Udine contain the material dealing with 1848. There are also a number of collections of family papers, with inventories. In the Archivio Florio, b. 55 contains the journal of Count Francesco di Toppo; volume 22 of this journal deals with the period 1 Jan. 1846 – 31 Dec. 1849. The Archivio Caimo contains letters to and from Count Giacomo Caimo Dragoni for the period 1802–66.

Archivio di stato, Venezia

Before dealing with the separate *fondi* in this, the Mecca for all historians of Venice, I would like to explain the remarks made on p. 32 of this book. Until very recently it was impossible to consult a number of nineteenth-century *fondi* which are of great importance for reconstructing the social history of Venice and the Veneto. This was true of the papers of the Magistrato Camerale, the Monte di Pietà, the Arsenale, the Tribunale Criminale and Tribunale d'Appello, the Commissione d'Este, etc. These papers were housed on the Giudecca in a warehouse which gradually fell into disrepair. The roof did not keep out all the rain, nor did it protect the dampened *buste* from the heat of the sun. As a result numbers of documents were stuck together and irremediably destroyed. Also in various parts of the old deposit rats set up home amongst the documents. In this way significant and irreparable damage was done, in particular to the papers of the Monte di Pietà and the Magistrato Camerale.

The present staff of the archive have now done everything in their power to remedy this situation. The papers have been moved to a new deposit on the Giudecca and some have been transferred to the main archive at the Frari. On my last visit to Venice, in December 1977, I was informed that a small reading room has been set up in the new Giudecca deposit, and that it is now possible to obtain permission from the director of the archive to go and work there. In this way the mass of the Giudecca *fondi* has been saved from further decay and has at last been made available to students of nineteenth-century Venice.

Camera di commercio. It has become relatively easy to find one's way around this collection, thanks to the work of F. Zago, *L'Archivo storico della camera di commercio di Venezia. Inventario (1806–70)*, Venezia 1964.

Imperiale-Regia commissione governativa di commercio, agricoltura e industria, 9 Dec. 1832 – 25 Jan. 1848. This collection contains eleven *buste* without an index, but it is a mine of information on economic conditions in the pre-revolutionary period.

Governo 1814–48. A huge collection. For the period 1845–9 alone there are 835 *buste*.

Presidio di governo, 1814–48. Another large and very important collection. I have used it only for the period 1845–8 and found that the easiest way to tackle it was to work through the alphabetical subject index (*rubrica*).

Governo provvisorio, 1848–9. There are 856 *buste* and 554 *registri.* I have certainly not read them all. There is a good index, no. 177.

Prefettura centrale ordine pubblico – sorvegliati e sospetti. These extensive papers have only recently been discovered by Adolfo Bernardello. They are not listed in any index. Although there are more than 30 *buste* and many thousands of documents, the contents are less interesting than might have been hoped.

Presidenza della Luogotenenza veneta, 1849–66. A descriptive index to this collection has only recently been compiled. *Buste* 586–8 are the papers of the Austrian military government in the Veneto, 1848–9.

Carte Avesani. Two *buste*, containing the papers of G. F. Avesani from 1830–52.

Fondo Mocenigo. The papers of Alvise Mocenigo, more than 150 *buste* in all. When I looked at the *fondo* (July 1973) there was as yet no index, but Professor L. Lanfranchi had compiled a rough guide for his own use, which he was willing to make available. The collection is an immensely rich one, from which it would be possible to reconstruct the social, economic and cultural activity of one of the most interesting of Venetian noble landowners.

Archivio di stato, Verona

Contains the papers of the Austrian Delegazione Provinciale and those of the city's Congregazione Municipale. While in Verona it is also worth working in the Biblioteca Comunale, which has a number of diaries relevant to 1848 and a collection of contemporary letters for which there is an alphabetical card index.

Biblioteca Ambrosiana, Milano

Houses the papers of Giuseppe Sirtori, deposited in 1910 by the parish priest of Arosio, who burned many of the more controversial letters, etc., before handing over the collection. The first three *buste* (1815–48, 1848 – June 1849, July–Aug. 1849) contain material relevant to the Venetian revolution.

Biblioteca civica Bertoliana, Vicenza

Does not have a modern catalogue with a complete list of manuscripts. The student of 1848 has to consult three inventories – those entitled Mazzatinti and Capparezzo, and that of the MSS Gonzati. When I worked there it was only possible to request one item at a time – a crippling restriction for anyone who does not have unlimited time. This rule did not apply in any of the other libraries and archives in which I worked. I found three chronicles of particular interest: that of A. Magrini for Vicenza (Gonz. 25.9.44); that of G. Soster for Valdagno (Gonz. 24.7.19); and the anonymous 'Cronaca riguardante Bassano nel 1848' (Gonz. 22.10.27). There are probably many other manuscripts of interest.

Biblioteca comunale, Udine

There is a recent catalogue: G. M. Del Basso, *Manoscritti Risorgimentali della Biblioteca comunale di Udine*, Udine 1966. Unfortunately the library is nowhere near as rich as that of Vicenza with regard to 1848. Only Conti's diary (Fondo corrente no. 3851) is of real interest.

British Library

No manuscript sources, but broadsheets and handbills, now moved to Woolwich. A fine collection of secondary sources, built up by Antonio Panizzi, one-time *carbonaro*, later Sir Anthony Panizzi, librarian of the British Museum, friend of Gladstone and special constable against the Chartists in 1848.

Biblioteca nazionale, Firenze

Houses the papers of Nicolò Tommaseo. The main catalogue of letters, manuscripts, etc. contains a good index to Tommaseo's correspondence.

Fondazione Querini-Stampalia, Venezia

Housed in the palace which was sacked in the famous riot against the patriarch on 3 Aug. 1849. A painting of this event is to be found in the office of the vice-librarian. In the manuscript collection there are only a few items that are relevant, but the library is the only one in Venice to remain open in the evenings.

Haus-, Hof- und Staatsarchiv, Wien

I have only scratched the surface here, and much work remains to be done on Austrian administration and policy before and during the revolution. However, it must be remembered that the bulk of material on Austrian government in the period 1815–48 (Governo, Presidio di Governo, etc.) was moved to Venice after the first world war. In Vienna I consulted the following collections: *Staatskanzlei Provinzen Lombardo-Venezien*, box files nos. 15, 31, 35, 37 and 40; *Informations-Büro, Kart. Korrespond. mit Polizei-Hofstelle*, nos. 23–5: mostly reports on individuals, but one wodge of copies of intercepted letters of Feb. 1849, including letters of Mazzini and Gustavo Modena; *Staatskanzlei Interiora Intercepte*, 1847–8, box file no. 38: in this, alt Fasz. 64 contains copies of intercepted Italian letters from 13 Dec. 1847 to 19 March 1848, including good descriptions by Contessa Verri and P. Mantegazza of the tense atmosphere in Milan at the beginning of 1848 and the fighting of 3 Jan.; *Kabinettsarchiv, Separat Protokoll*, 1848: Band I, Anspruchsliste, summaries of all the reports that arrived in the period Jan.–April 1848; Band II, the same continued until Dec. 1848.

For those who wish to pursue Austrian military policy in much more depth than I have done, a period of study in the Kriegsarchiv would be essential. This forbidding building houses an enormous collection of documents, including the unpublished diary of General Nugent, written during the campaign in the Veneto in the spring of 1848.

Museo Correr, Venezia

Carte della polizia austriaca, 1799–1848. These are the original documents from which a selection was made for the published work, *Carte segrete e atti ufficiali della polizia austriaca in Italia dal 4 giugno 1814 al 22 marzo 1848*, 3 vols., Capolago 1851–2.

Documenti Manin. Manin's papers. 4,246 documents, bound in fourteen volumes. The numbering is consecutive, except at the beginning of vol. 9.

Aggiunte Manin. Forty-nine *buste*, of less importance than the above, but containing some vital material.

Documenti Pellegrini. Forty-eight *buste*, many of them containing the personal letters of Manin written before the revolution.

Documenti Pellegrini, miscellanea. Ten *buste*, for the most part typed transcripts of the documents in the larger Pellegrini collection.

These last four *fondi* constitute the Manin papers. There is a card index for the first three of them, called the *schedario Manin*. This is certainly a useful alphabetical guide, but is by no means complete.

Archivio Bernardi. The papers of Monsignor Jacopo Bernardi. This is an archive of recent acquisition and has no index. There are 112 *buste*, of which I have only managed to look at 54 (1–43, 60–64, 75, 81, 109–112). The majority of this vast collection, as far as I am able to judge, deals with the period after 1860.

Cicogna diary. The diary of a Venetian gentleman, Emanuele Cicogna, for the whole period. Cicogna was secretary to the Venetian court of appeal.

Provenienze diverse, 716/c/11. A selection of papers from the Austrian chiefs of police, 1814–48.

Museo del Risorgimento, Milano

Contains the archive of the Lombard provisional government of 1848, with a complete index. The Cattaneo, Correnti and Bertani private archives are also of great interest for 1848, and it is worth going through the three volumes of the general catalogue (entries in alphabetical order). Of the *fondi piccoli organici* those of Martini and Restelli are of obvious importance, even if they have already been used extensively by historians.

Museo del Risorgimento, Roma

Housed at the top of the Victor Emanuel II monument. There is a large and comprehensive card index to the many thousands of letters which the museum contains. Not much of the correspondence of the principal figures of the Venetian revolution seems to have found its way to Rome, but there are some letters of Manin and the Fabrizi archive contains interesting letters from Ulloa.

Private archives and manuscripts

MS Olivi. An account of Giuseppe Olivi's economic and political activity, written by him some years after the revolution. I am grateful to avv. Olivi of Padua and Professor Lanfranchi, former director of the Archivio di Stato, Venezia, for allowing me to consult this document.

Archivio Dubois de Dunilach. This archive, which contains the papers of the two French brothers who settled in Venice to build up their banking house, is the private property of Professor Lanfranchi. Again, I am very grateful to him for letting me have a look at it.

NEWSPAPERS

There is a good list in G. M. Trevelyan, *Manin and the Venetian Revolution of 1848*, pp. 272–3, giving the political complexion of many of the most important newspapers of the revolution. I have read large sections of *Il Libero Italiano*, *L'Indipendente*, *Fatti e parole*, *Sior Antonio Rioba*, *San Marco*, *Per tutti* and *L'Operaio*. For further information, see G. Levi Minzi, 'I giornali veneziani nel 1848–9', *Rassegna Nazionale*, 43 (1921); G. Baccini, 'La stampa periodica in Venezia nel 1848–9', *Rivista delle Biblioteche e degli Archivi*, 27 (1916); and D. Bertoni Jovine (ed.), *I periodici popolari del Risorgimento*, vol. 1, Milano 1959, who reprints a number of articles from Venetian newspapers of the period.

Index

Abercromby, Ralph, 148n
action party, 259, 376
Adige, river, 11, 78
Adria, 16, 42, 155, 164n, 170n, 207
Aglebert, Augusto, 217, 248n
Agordo, 26, 163, 165, 212
Albert (member of the French provisional government), 112
Albini, G. B., 222, 263, 337
Albrizzi, Carlo, 71n
Albrizzi (delegate from the meeting at the Casino dei Cento), 261
Aleardi, Aleardo, 88n, 189n, 267n, 284
Alessandri (deputy from the Veneto to the Italian Club at Venice), 274
Alexandria, 237
Alfieri, Vittorio, 317
Alvisi, Luigi, 315
Ambrogio, Friar, 316n
Amigo, Colonel, 172n, 248n
Ancona, 330n
Andervolti, Leonardo, 243, 244n
Andreola (printer to the Venetian government), 229
Andreotta, Bernardo, 230n
Andretta (textiles firm), 17
Anelli, Luigi, 141
Anglo-French mediation in Italy, 282–4, 286, 291, 296, 316, 374
Anguillara, 14n
Antonini, Giacomo, 219, 220, 248, 257
Antonini, Prospero, 92n, 103n, 123, 173n
Apponyi, Antal Rudolf, 6
Aragon, d' (French deputy), 150
Armandi, Pietro, 195n, 216, 217, 241n, 248n, 341
army of the Alps, *see* French republic

Arnstein (Austrian banker), 53, 57
Asiago, 110, 162, 207
Asolo, 11, 78n, 191n
Aubin, Karl, 35n
Auronzo di Cadore, 174, 211
Austrian army, 9, 27
  Nugent's (then Thurn's), 178–9, 182–4, 187–8, 191, 199–202, 209, 214, 218–20, 239, 245, 251, 370
  Radetzky's, 10, 80, 153, 171, 191, 239–41, 345, 364
  and the siege of Venice (1849), 337–8, 353
  Welden's, 199, 212, 218, 255, 296, 332, 344
Austrian navy, 222, 300, 359–60, 362
Austrian taxation, 45, 63
  direct, 47–8
  indirect, 42
  on land, 19–20
  personal tax, 28, 63, 74n, 78, 243, 369
  on salt, 28, 42, 369
  on stamped paper (*carta bollata*), 27–8, 36, 42
Austro-Hungarian empire, 27, 56, 125, 142, 178, 205, 210, 295–6, 374
  bureaucracy of, 10, 19, 36, 45, 64
  centralisation in, 4, 45, 47
  decay in the administration of, 47
  economy of, 3, 15, 20–1, 47–8, 63, 74n, 246
  and French intervention in Italy (1848), 286–7, 290–1
  and the kingdom of Lombardy-Venetia (1815–48), 2–11, 18–21, 27–9, 36, 45–6, 62–4, 67, 70, 79–80, 95, 183, 210, 242–3, 245–6, 365, 397

Austro-Hungarian empire, *cont.*
  and the Milan–Venice railway, 52–3, 57–8
  and negotiations with the Venetian government (1849), 346–7
  peasant revolts in (1847), 61
Avesani, Gian Francesco, 71, 96n, 97, 100–3, 112, 124, 169, 175, 237–8, 250, 316, 318n, 329, 351, 356, 366, 395

Badini, Captain, 181n
Bagnoli, 168n
Balbo, Cesare, 70
Baldisserotto, Francesco, 298n, 340, 342, 350n, 351, 357, 359–60
Bandiera, Attilio and Emilio, 50, 96, 141, 219, 236, 269
Barnaba, Domenico, 111
Bartelloni (Livornese popular leader), 334
Baruffaldi, L., 358, 361
Bassano, 105, 123, 169, 174, 191, 196n, 200, 242, 396
  civic guard of, 163, 169n, 181
  population of, 42
  provincial committee of, 191
Bassi, Ugo, 214, 229, 298n, 310
Basso, G. M. del, 396
Bastide, Jules, 245, 246n, 278–84, 286–93, 373
Bava, Eusebio, 253
Beauharnais, Eugène de, 1, 269
Bedolo, Sebastiano, 100n
Belgioioso, Cristina di, 285
Bellati (bishop of Ceneda), 165
Bellegarde, Heinrich Joseph, 47
Bellinato, Antonio, 103, 236
Bellotto, 171n
Belluno, city of, 44, 108, 200, 204, 211
  adheres to the Venetian republic, 123
  population of, 42
Belluno, province of, 63–4, 181, 194, 233
  departmental committee of, 152, 174, 181n, 200, 211
  grain prices in, 59–60
  seasonal emigration from, 26
Belluzzi, Domenico, 218, 241n, 357, 370
Beltrame, 111n, 154

Bem, Jozef, 345
Bentivoglio family, 76n
Benvenuti brothers, 78n, 90n, 236
Benvenuti, Bartolomeo, 82, 93, 100, 166, 187, 236n, 274, 357
Benvenuti, G. B., 16n
Beretta, Antonio, 247n
Beretta, Luciano, 248n
Bergamo, 53, 55–7, 58n, 206
Berici hills, 220, 240
Berlinghieri, R., 145, 146
Bernardello, Adolfo, 395
Bernardi, Jacopo, 27n, 96n, 165n, 353, 359, 397
Bernardini, Antonio, 227n
Berti, G., 237n
Berti (president of the committee for provisioning the Giudecca), 362n
Bertoncelli (Venetian lawyer), 57
Bertone, S., 285n
Bertuch, Friedrich, 35, 233n, 237n, 350–1, 352n
Bertuzzi, Angelo, 122n
Bevilacqua, Guglielmo and Girolamo, 232
Bianchetti, Giuseppe, 189
Bigaglia, Pietro, 31n, 34n, 52, 310, 352n, 373
Biscaro (lawyer), 57
Bixio, Alessandro, 149, 260
Bixio, Nino, 260
Blanc, Louis, 112, 149n
Bohemia, 2n, 59, 367
Bologna, 198, 218n, 221, 287, 297, 332, 367
Bolognini, Eugenia, 77n
Bonaparte, Napoleon, 1, 30, 31n, 57n, 69, 87, 124n, 219n, 221, 243
Bonelli, Antonio, 198n, 199n, 216n
Boniotti, Lodovico, 168n
Bonlini, Pietro, 310n
Borgo, 200
Borromeo, Maria, 130
Borromeo, Vitaliano, 56, 129, 130
Bortoloni, Eugenio, 176
Bottrighe, 164n
Bovolenta, 207
Bowring, Sir John, 15n
Bragadin, Colonel, 272
Braida, Francesco, 230n

Brambilla (Venetian banker), 57
Brasil, Luigi, 113
Bratich, General, 345
Brenier, Anatole, 141n
Brenta canal, 163
Brenta, river, 11, 174, 242
Brescia, 206, 207n, 337
Bricito, Zaccaria, 183
Brignole Sale, Antonio, 281–2, 285
Brocchi, Virginio, 9n
Brofferio, Carlo, 317
Brondolo, fort, 352
Brunetti, Luigi, 322
Brusoni, Giacomo, 189n
Brussels, 292, 325
Bua, Giorgio, 168n, 188n, 270, 340–1
Bucchia, Admiral, 342, 359–61
Budapest, 30, 344
Buia, 111
Buja, Baldassare, 27n
Buol, C. F., 79n
Burani, Giovanni, 92n, 103n
Burano, 44, 117, 170n, 239, 314
Burri, Maria, 77n
Byron, George Gordon, Lord, 57n

Cadore, the, 123, 174, 207, 302
    defence of, 199, 210–13, 217, 369
Cadorin, G. B., 302
Caffi, Ippolito, 179n, 183n, 354
Caffi, Michele, 340
Caffo, Luigi, 174n, 189n
Caimo Dragoni, Giacomo, 394
Calabria, 50, 222
Caldiero, 110n
Call (Austrian police chief at Venice),
    60n, 61, 63, 65, 68, 76n, 77, 243n
Calucci, Giuseppe, 88, 156, 204, 224n,
    225n, 226n, 235, 236n, 245n, 314n,
    329, 346–7
Calvi, Pier Fortunato, 211–13, 217, 257,
    332, 369–70
Camerata, Francesco, 112–14, 188, 204,
    226, 254
Campbell, Robert, 186n
Campoformio, treaty of, 224, 247
Campone, 111
Canal, Bernardo, 312–13, 363
Canal, Pietro, 347
Canini, Marc'Antonio, 311–13, 315

Canino, prince of, 68
Canizzano, 196
Cantù, Cesare, 69, 141n, 147
Caorle, 14n
capitalism
    agrarian, 13, 129
    English, 48
    in north-east Italy, 45
    and the railway question, 52
Capponi, Gino, 68n, 188n, 303n, 319
carbonari, 9, 50, 221
Carinthia, 26, 40, 345
Carnevali, Antonio, 139
Carnia, 11, 180
Carrano (deputy from Naples to the
    Italian Club in Venice), 274
Carrer, Giovanni, 145n
carta bollata, see Austrian taxation
Cartura, 175
Casale, 106
Casanova, Colonel, 201
Casarini, Giorgio, 97n, 266, 268n, 359
Casati, Agostino, 180n
Casati, Gabrio, 56, 128, 130, 133, 135–
    41, 144, 160, 184n, 205, 206, 245n,
    246, 281, 284, 297, 367–8
Cassola (Brescian republican), 337
Castagnetto, Cesare, 135n, 136, 140,
    152, 186n, 188
Castelfranco, 163, 170n, 218n
Castellani clan, *see* Venice
Castellani, G. B., 202, 203n, 224n,
    233n, 248n, 270n, 275, 317n,
    324–5, 330–1, 335–6, 377
Castell'Arzignano, 196
Castelli, Jacopo, 56, 96n, 112–14, 146–7,
    156, 158, 188, 190, 195, 204, 249–
    50, 254–7, 261–6, 269n, 270n,
    273n, 276–7, 278, 317
Castelnuovo, 190–1
Cattabeni, Vincenzo, 265, 298
Cattaneo, Carlo, 48, 205–6, 376, 398
    and the *cinque giornate* of Milan, 128,
        134, 137–41, 366–8, 373
    and the *lotta legale*, 69, 86
    and Mazzini, 258
    in Paris, 285, 291n
    political beliefs of, 89, 129–30, 140,
        377
    and the railway question, 56–8

Cavaignac, Louis Eugène, 245n, 247, 268, 279–86, 288–91, 293–4, 373–4
Cavalletto, 356
Cavarzere, 78, 175
Cava Zuccherina, 195
Cavedalis, Giovanni Battista, x, 180n, 195n, 269, 270, 297–9, 311, 316, 327, 329–30, 332, 339–41, 343, 362, 374
Cavour, Camillo Benso di, 127, 376–7
Cazzano, 60
Cempini, Leopoldo, 319
Cencenighe, 163
Ceneda, 25n, 177, 359
Cenedese (member of the Italian Club in Venice), 271
Cernuschi, Enrico, 130, 132–4, 137, 138n, 139, 140, 158n, 206, 322
Ceroni, Ricardo, 139
Cerrini, C., 123n
Cerutti (Venetian glass manufacturer), 34n
Cervignano, 63n
Cesenatico, 358
Charles II, duke of Parma, 144n
Charles Albert, king of Piedmont, 126–9, 141, 145, 157–9, 153, 155–6, 187, 189, 190n, 216, 220, 222, 256–7, 268, 294, 326
  abdicates, 332
  character of, 135
  and the *cinque giornate* of Milan, 135–7, 139
  and the first war of independence, 186–8, 221, 239–41, 246–7, 252–4, 261, 284, 331–2, 364, 368, 373, 375
  and French intervention in Italy, 245, 278–82
  and Lombardy, 204–6, 247n
  political programme of, 135, 142–3, 184, 185, 186, 193
  proclaims the *statuto*, 81, 132
  sends papal army into the Veneto, 198, 209
  and the Venetian provinces, 207–8, 244–5
  and the Venetian republic, 223–6, 237, 252, 255, 264, 369, 373
Chieregin, Nicola, 189n

Chioggia, 38, 44, 62, 95n, 123, 237, 239, 314, 331, 358, 361n
  military commission of (1849), 342
  population of, 42
cholera
  epidemic of 1835–6, 22, 31
  epidemic of 1849 in Venice, 333, 355–6, 361–2; *see also* Venice
Chrzanowski, Wojciech, 331
Cialdini, Enrico, 240
Cibrario, Luigi, 263–8
Cicconi, Antonio, 118
Ciceruacchio (Roman popular leader), 322
Cicogna, Emanuele, 8n, 41n, 85n, 213n, 267, 301, 302n, 350, 353n, 354, 398
Ciconi, G. D., 18, 26n, 44n, 189n
Cilento, the, 222
Cittadella, Giovanni, 69, 187
Cividale del Friuli, 18n
Clam (Austrian statesman), 10
Clerici, Carlo, 131, 132
Clerici, Giorgio, 134, 138n, 139
Cobden, Richard, 67–9
Coccaglio, 58n
Codroipo, 111, 181
Coen di Benedetto brothers, 34n, 302
Coen, M. P., 48n, 249, 315
Coletti, Giovanni, 207, 212n
Colledani, Doctor, 163
Colles (textiles firm), 17
Colli, Vittorio, 263–6, 268
Cologna Veneta, 107n, 196
Coluzzi (commander of the S. Antonio battery), 339
Comacchio, 358
Comello, Angelo, 34, 120, 234, 236
Comello, Giuseppe, 12n
Comello, Valentino, 16n, 34, 234
Comin, Francesco, 191
communism, 149n, 229, 237, 299n, 312
Como, 133, 258
Concordia, 175
Conegliano, 11, 57, 122, 170n, 243n
Confalonieri, Federico, 128
Conselve, 168n
consulta, see Venetian republic (1848)
Conti, A., 180n, 182, 396
Contratti (Brescian republican), 337
Corfu, 20n, 50

Cornuda, 78, 105, 200–2, 204, 210, 218, 221, 370
corpi franchi, see Venetian republic (1848)
Corrao, Domenico, 85, 235, 236n
Correnti, Cesare, 48, 129n, 130n, 131, 138–9, 160, 224, 247n, 257n, 260, 261n, 324, 398
Correr, Giovanni, 5n, 16n, 67n, 68, 75, 76, 90, 95, 97, 100, 102n, 130n, 145n, 234
Correr, Pietro, 76n, 94, 248n
Corsini, Luigi, 199n
Corsini, Neri, 245
Cosa, Admiral, 222
Cosenz, Enrico, 338–9, 342
Costabili (Roman patriot), 68
Costantini (president of provisional government of Vicenza), 123n
Cracow, republic of, 79
Crema, 141
Cremona, 133, 206
crociati, see Venetian republic (1848)
Csányi (Hungarian nobleman), 344
Culoz, Karl, 101, 201, 211, 240, 241
Curtatone, 172, 239, 319
Cusani, Marquis, 137
Custozza, 252, 258, 263, 268, 282, 284, 290, 317, 319, 331, 364

Da Camin, Giuseppe, 316, 329
Da Camino, Bianca, 336n
D'Adda, Carlo, 132, 136
Dahleroup, Admiral, 359, 362
Dall'Ongaro, Francesco, 180n, 206, 207, 214, 256, 272, 273n, 274, 276, 374
Dalmistro (Venetian glass manufacturer), 34n
Dalvecchio, Benedetto, 189n
Da Mosto, A., 378
Dandolo, Enrico, 336n
Dandolo, Enrico (Doge of Venice), 255
Dandolo, Girolamo, 353
D'Aspre, Lieutenant-Marshal, 109, 110, 334
Dawkins, Clinton, 76, 132, 352
D'Azeglio, Massimo, 35n, 50n, 198, 200, 203, 209, 240
De Bruck (Austrian minister), 346–7, 362

De Castro, Vincenzo, 77n
Decupil, Vincenzo, 92
De Domini, Gianpiero, 181n
Degli Antoni, Francesco, 96n, 100n, 103
Delacour (French ambassador to Vienna), 245, 286, 290
Del Basso, G. M., 396
Della Vida, Cesare, 73, 306
De Madice, Captain, 197
De Marchi, Alessandro, 121n
Denois, F., 132n, 245n
De' Simoni, Bianca, 136, 186n
Desperati (ex-chief of police at Modena), 213
Dobbiaco, 199, 211
Dolfin, Leonardo, 71n
Dolfin Boldù, Girolamo, 275
Dolo, 57, 60n, 176n, 239
Dolomites, the, 11, 162
Donà, Luigi, 102n, 234
D'Onigo, Guglielmo, 78n, 181, 190, 193, 202n, 318
Drouyn de Lhuys, 325, 336, 337n
Dubois de Dunilach, Henri and Pierre (Pietro Dubois), 31n, 350n, 398
Duodo, Giacomo, 355
Duodo, L., 180n
Durando, Giovanni, 198, 199n, 200–3, 209, 215, 218–20, 240–1, 251
Durini, Giuseppe, 56, 144, 145n, 147, 190n, 195n

Edeles, Emmanuel, 176
Emilii, Pietro, 77, 109
Énego, 242
England, 48, 142, 281
    and French intervention in Italy, 281–3, 284n, 287–90, 374
    and Venice, 246, 282, 292, 320, 336–7, 376
English Channel, the, 283
Errera (Venetian glass manufacturer), 34n
Erskeles (Austrian banker), 53, 57, 58n
'Esperia' (secret society), 50, 96, 100
Este, 192, 213
Eugène, prince of Savoy, 136

Fabris, Gaetano, 112
Fabris, Pietro, 93

Fabrizi, Luigi, 214
Fabrizi, Nicola, 261n, 274, 339, 374
Faccanoni, Antonio, 92, 97n
Faccioli, Girolamo, 198n
Falghera (landowner), 196n
Falmouth, 63
Fanti (member of Milanese committee of defence), 252
Farini (bishop of Padua), 165
Fauché, G. B., 99n
Federigo, Ermolao, 168n, 195n
Feltre, 27, 123, 200–1, 204
Fenzi, Carlo, 274n, 307n, 326, 329n, 339n, 343, 355, 393
Fenzi, Emanuele, 326n, 393
Ferdinand I, emperor of Austria, 34, 47, 66n, 71, 245
Ferdinand II, king of the Two Sicilies, 80, 81, 221, 222–3, 261n, 322, 364
Ferrara, 64n, 70
Ferrari, Andrea, 172n, 198, 200–2, 213–14, 218, 248, 251, 257, 370
Ferrari, Giuseppe, 158n, 205–6
Ferrari-Bravo, Giovanni, 264, 277n, 316, 328–9, 350
Ferro, Francesco, 122
Ficquelmont, Karl Ludwig, 4n, 80
Fiesso, 60, 175
Fincati, Luigi, 300
Fiume, 345
Florence, 232, 244–5, 299n, 319, 323–5, 344–5
Fogazzaro, Giuseppe, 108
Follina, 17, 25n
Fontana, Galeazzo, 168n, 195n
Foramiti, Francesco, 54
Forbes, Hugh, 214, 216n
Foretti, Jacopo, 165n
Formani (member of the Italian Club at Venice), 276
Foscolo, Giorgio, 346
Fossati family, 54–5
Fossati, Carolina, 54, 55n
France, 48, 80, 171, 377
Francesconi, 356
Francis I, emperor of Austria, 4–5, 7, 9, 10, 19, 30, 32, 34, 47, 69
Francis V, duke of Modena, 144n
Franz Joseph, emperor of Austria, 241n
Franzini, Antonio, 187, 198n, 246

Frapolli, Lodovico, 149n, 151, 272, 280, 285
French republic, first, 113, 127, 156–7, 161
French republic, second, 298
    army of the Alps, 150, 278, 279n, 365, 367
    intervention in northern Italy, 87, 134, 135n, 143, 148–51, 160, 210, 244–6, 254, 278–93, 295, 336–7, 364, 367–8, 373–4
    journée of 15 May 1848, 150
    nature of, 88
    proclamation of, 81, 87, 127, 132
    and the Roman republic, 334, 337
Freschi, Gherardo, 13, 14, 21, 28, 72, 169, 177, 189n, 194, 244, 302, 317, 326n
Friuli, 11, 18, 22, 26n, 29n, 40, 72, 154, 170, 173n, 194, 199–200
    agrarian society of, 13n
    defence of, 177–84
    departmental committee of, 179–80
    events of March 1848, 111, 163
    manufacturing industry in, 18n
    nobility of, 14n
    seasonal emigration from, 26
    silk production in, 15n, 16n
Fusinato, Arnaldo, 196–7

Gabussi, Giuseppe, 336n, 377n
Gaeta, 291, 312, 322, 324
Galicia, 2n, 79, 130, 242
Galletti, Giuseppe, 322, 334
Galli, Girolamo, 315
Gambarare, 175–6
Gar, Tommaso, 88n, 267n, 324, 345n
Garašanin, Ilija, 346
Garibaldi, Giuseppe, 215, 243, 253, 259–60, 263, 267–8, 287n, 294, 320–2, 333–5, 358, 375–6
Gaspare Gaspari, Luigi, 189n
Gatte, Albano, 114
Gattersburg Morosini, Loredana, 39n, 234, 303, 304
Gavazzi, Alessandro, 216, 229, 311, 319
Gemona, 26, 174n
Genoa, 17, 34, 53, 71, 136, 145, 197n, 224n, 230, 236, 237n, 271, 367
    insurrection in (1849), 333, 376

Germany, 20, 215
Gerschenkron, A., x
Ghilardi (Livornese popular leader), 334
Giacomuzzi, Antonio, 303
Giannini (delegate from the meeting at the Casino dei Cento), 261
Gioberti, Vincenzo, 49, 206, 224n, 273, 316–18, 323–6
Giovanelli family, 232, 234n, 373
Giovanelli, Andrea, 121n, 230, 234, 303, 304n
Giovanelli, Pietro, 234, 303, 304n
Giuriati, Giuseppe, 82, 90n, 93, 100, 176, 192, 196, 236, 261, 316, 354, 363n
Giustinian, Elisabetta, 76
Giustinian, Giambattista, 102n, 350n
Giustiniani, Luigi, 57
glassware, from Murano, 33, 230
Gobbetti, Lorenzo, 189n
Godego, 163
Goito, 239
Gonars, 180
Gonzales, Carlo, 197, 198n, 202
Görgey, Arthur, 343, 346
Gorizia, 169, 183n
Gorzowsky, General, 363
Gradenigo, Girolamo, 94, 116, 117n, 119
Gramsci, Antonio, ix–x, 126, 214, 369–70, 371n
Graziani, Leone, 269, 270n, 300, 327, 329, 339, 342, 359
Gregoretti (delegate from the meeting at the Casino dei Cento), 261
Gregori, Gabriele, 212n
Grimani, Marco, 232
Gritti, Giovanni, 234
Grondoni, Ernesto, 179n, 182n
Groppler, Count, 174n
Grossmajer (factory owner), 43
Guerrazzi, Francesco Domenico, 224, 319, 334
Guerrieri Gonzaga, Anselmo, 69, 89, 139, 280–1, 285
Guiccioli, Alessandro, 96n, 330
Guidotti, Alessandro, 214
Guizot, Francois Pierre, 364
Gyulai, Ferencz, 104n, 362n

Hablitschek, Major, 211–12

Hanau, M. B., 186n
Hartig, Franz von, 183, 242, 243n
Haynau, Julius Jakob von, 298, 337, 345
Hess, Heinrich Hermann, 239, 362
Holm, Thomas, 35, 62n
Hugo, Victor, 82n, 86
Hummelauer, Karl, 246, 282, 367
Hungary, 22, 26, 153, 295, 331, 343–6, 365, 367, 369, 373
   Diet of, 5, 37, 45
   and Venice, 345–6, 351, 362
   (*see also* Austro-Hungarian empire)

Innsbruck, 67, 71, 129, 245–6
Italian Club at Venice, 261–2, 264, 266–7, 270–7, 298n, 300, 310, 315–16, 323n, 327–8, 335, 340–1, 374
Italian constituent assembly, 319–27
Ivancich, Antonio Luigi, 35, 230, 234

Jelačic (Croatian leader), 295, 344, 346
Jesuits, 7, 118
Jews, 12; *see also* Venice
Joseph II, emperor of Austria, 10, 128

kingdom of upper Italy, 126, 128, 149, 210, 226, 235–7, 246, 250, 252, 258, 260, 281, 321, 323, 364
Kolb (Württemburg consul at Rome), 335
Kolowrat, Franz Anton, 3, 42, 47
Kossuth, Lajos, 84, 295, 343–5, 367, 369
Kubeck, Karl Friedrich, 4, 8, 47

La Forge, Anatole de, 55
La Marmora, Alberto, 197n, 198n, 199–200, 244, 333
Lamartine, Alphonse de, 87, 88, 112, 127, 148–51, 245, 260, 279, 367–8, 373
La Masa, Giuseppe, 214, 215, 217, 242
Lamon, 27
Lamoricière (French minister of war), 279, 289
Landriani, Lieutenant, 217n
Lanza (political prisoner), 90n
Lanzetti (former actor), 196
Latisana, 25n, 181n

Lattes, Abramo, 120
Lattis, Girolamo, 14n, 175n
Lazansky, Count, 6, 7n
Lazzaneo, Abbot, 340
Lazzaris, Bortolo, 303n
Lecco, 133
Ledru Rollin, Alexandre Auguste, 312
Leghorn (Livorno), 1, 34, 71, 230, 271, 319, 334, 367
Legnago, 43, 110
Legnaro, 176
Leoni, Carlo, 59, 255-6, 306-7
Leopold II, grand duke of Tuscany, 319, 324, 326, 334
Levi, Abramo, 61
Levi, Angelo Adolfo, 237
Levi, Cesare, 14n, 238
Levi, Jacopo, 35, 234, 302
Lido, Venetian, 116, 227, 228n, 248, 257
Lissoni, Antonio, 139
Litta, Pompeo, 137, 139
Liverpool, 63
Lloyd's company, of Trieste, 38n, 68, 237, 359
Locatelli, Tommaso, 8
Lodi, 141
Lombard provisional government (1848), 141, 143-6, 160, 190, 280, 398
foundation of, 139, 152
and France, 148, 151, 245
and fusion with Piedmont, 143, 184-5, 194, 204-7
offered independence by Austria, 245-7, 370
and the peasantry, 205
and the policy of *a guerra finita si deciderà*, 139-40, 142, 204, 368
and the Venetian republic, 187, 195
Lombardo (Venetian emissary to France), 300
Lombardy, 10, 45, 56-7, 73, 121, 126, 128, 140, 146, 147n, 154, 178, 205-6, 252, 262, 281-2, 366, 373
Casse di Risparmio of, 130
child employment in, 25
clergy of, 131
economic development of, 129
manufacturing industry in, 17
under Napoleonic rule, 1

nobility of, 18, 57
peasantry of, 61, 79, 130, 133, 205-6, 253, 258-9
schools in, 8n
silk production in, 15, 20
union with Venetia, 123
(*see also* Austro-Hungarian empire)
Lombardy-Venetia, kingdom of, *see* Austro-Hungarian empire
London, 15, 17, 20, 63, 115, 246, 304
Longo, G. B., 92, 93n
Lonigo, 106, 164
lotta legale, 69-74; *see also* Cattaneo, Milan, Tommaseo
Louis Napoleon (Napoleon III), 291, 334, 364, 378
Louis Philippe, king of France, 81
Lubati, Giambattista, 189n
Lugano, 258, 269, 272
Luino, 259
Luzzatto, Leone, 53n
Lyons, 15, 279, 287

Maestri, Pietro, 130, 132, 252, 272, 274, 322, 374
Maffei, Massimiliano, 103, 104n
Magrini, A., 396
Mainardi (member of the committee of defence), 270
Maiset, Francesco, 187n
Malamocco, port of, 32n, 36, 71
Malcolm, Alexander, 35, 237n
Malenza, G. B., 189n
Malfatti, Bartolomeo, 329, 330n
Malutta, Luigi, 193, 207
Mamiani, Terenzio, 305n, 321-2
Manara, Luciano, 133, 336n
Manetti, Antonio, 71n
Manetti, G. D., 236
Manin, Daniele, 37, 65, 75, 79-80, 108, 110, 115, 121, 126-7, 130n, 150n, 168n, 182, 221, 257, 264, 291, 297n, 301-2, 304, 319, 333, 339, 349-51, 378, 397-8
arrested by the Austrians, 74, 131
assumes supreme power in Venice (August 1849), 356-7
and the Cadore, 174, 211, 213, 217
character of, 54
childhood and youth of, 54

Manin, Daniele, *cont.*
  chooses first government (March 1848), 112–14
  death of, 377
  and elections in Venice, 249, 314–16
  in exile, 377
  and French intervention in Italy, 86, 148, 244, 247, 268, 289, 300, 368, 373
  and Hungary, 345–6
  his ignorance of the countryside, 158, 369, 371
  imprisonment of, 74–5, 79–80, 82–3
  and internal order in Venice, 306–8, 321, 372–6
  and the Italian Club, 271, 275–7, 340
  and the Italian constituent assembly, 320–1, 323–4, 326
  and Italian nationalism, 55, 89, 144, 147, 161, 377
  leads the revolution in Venice (March 1848), 89–91, 93–7, 99–104, 124, 138, 365–6
  and Mazzini, 225, 266–7, 293
  and the military commission, 340–1
  and military strategy, 152–3, 155, 157–9, 208–9, 215–18, 298, 369–70, 372
  organises opposition in Venice (March 1847 to January 1848), 67–74
  and the peasantry, 176–7
  and the 'permanent' assembly in Venice, 327–32
  personal life of, 54, 377
  and Piedmont, 184–5, 188, 222, 224–6, 244, 248, 250, 317–18, 326, 327, 371
  and the policy of *a guerra finita si deciderà*, 143–8, 155, 159, 188, 204, 250, 368–9
  political attributes of, 84–5, 238, 251, 365, 372
  and the railway question, 56–8, 129
  returns to power in Venice (11 August 1848), 266–7, 372–3
  and the Roman republic, 322, 325, 334–7
  social conservatism of, 267–8, 309–13
  and the surrender of Venice, 362–3
  treats with the Austrians, 346–7
  and the Venetian army, 119, 125, 195, 197, 251, 311n
  and the Venetian clergy, 118
  and the Venetian lower classes, 227–30, 235–6, 251, 255–6, 267, 308, 329, 354, 372, 375
  and the Venetian navy, 300, 359–60
  and the Venetian provinces, 122, 151–2, 189–90, 192–3
  and Vicenza, 219–20
Manin, Emilia, 55, 90, 377
Manin, Giorgio, 55, 99
Manin, Lodovico (Doge of Venice), 83
Manin, Pietro, 54
Manin, Teresa, 54, 55, 87, 96n, 99n, 186n, 377
Mantua, 43, 110, 133, 213n, 239
Manzini (engineer), 340
Manzoni, Alessandro, 129
Marchesi, Vincenzo, x
Marchetti, Giovanni, 245
Marghera, fort, 107, 248, 298, 337–8, 346
Maria del Pedro, Giovanni, 223
Maria Teresa, empress of Austria, 10, 32
Marinovich, Giovanni, 98–100
Marseilles, 81, 151, 287, 289
Marsich, General, 272, 342
Marson, Cesare, 78n
Martelli (member of Venetian electoral commission), 314n
Martinengo, Leopardo, 189n, 219, 226n, 234, 236n, 237n, 238n, 254, 301, 310
Martini, Enrico, 132, 135, 136–8, 184, 248, 255, 256, 257n, 398
Martini, Vice-admiral, 99–100
Marzani, Count, 6, 63n, 95n
Marzotto, Gaetano, 17, 106
Maser, 78, 163
Masi, Luigi, 68, 193, 274, 334
Massa, 106, 207
Matarazzo, F., 223n
Mathieu, Major, 363n
Mattei, Giacomo, 237n
Mauria Pass, 212
Mazzini, Giuseppe, 127, 147, 149, 206, 219n, 266, 269, 274, 298, 324, 397
  arrives in Milan (April 1848), 141

Mazzini, Giuseppe, *cont.*
  and French intervention in Italy, 285, 293
  influence amongst Milanese poor, 130n
  and Manin, 225
  political beliefs of, 49–50, 89, 141–2, 254, 257–9, 293
  and the Roman republic, 330–1, 333–7, 376
  and Venice, 272–3, 276, 330–1, 335–7, 374
  and the 'war of the people', 258–60
Mazzinianism, 49–50, 130, 135, 259, 277, 364
  in Venice, 260–4, 267, 270–7, 294, 327, 374
Mazzucchelli, Captain, 274
Medin, Dataico, 67n, 102n, 362
Meneghini, Andrea, 90n, 121, 241n
Mengaldo, Angelo, 16n, 57, 84, 93–5, 102n, 103, 119–20, 154n, 228n, 232n, 243n, 249, 265n, 272n, 278–9, 284, 288–9, 341, 345n
Messina, 376
Messola, 358
Mestre, 3n, 55, 58, 95n, 107, 168n, 175, 244n, 338, 346, 362
  coachmen of, 191–2
  sortie to, 297–8, 316, 329n
Metternich, Clemence de, 1, 2, 4, 6, 7, 9–10, 13, 32n, 34, 47, 66n, 79n, 80, 82, 104, 364
Metternich, Melanie, 32n, 34
Mezzacapo, Carlo, 270, 356n
Miara, Alessandro, 189n
Michiel, Luigi, 40, 62n, 67n, 102n, 234, 236n
Milan, 3n, 16, 30, 32, 145, 187, 206, 236, 244
  Austrian garrison in, 128
  bourgeoisie of, 58, 129, 132
  the *cinque giornate* of (March 1848), 96, 126–41, 149, 151, 155, 160–1, 254, 260, 336n, 366–8
  clergy of, 129
  democrats and republicans in, 127, 130–4, 138, 139–42
  economic crisis in (1846–7), 62n

  learned journals of, 48
  lotta legale in, 69–70
  municipality of, 33, 58, 79, 128–35, 137–8, 367
  non-smoking campaign in, 72, 75–8, 131, 397
  and the railway question, 52–3, 55–7
  reoccupied by Radetzky, 252–4, 259, 265, 280, 284, 290, 331
  silk market at, 15, 17, 34
  university of, 130
  working classes of, 128n, 130–1, 133, 138
Milani (member of the committee of defence), 195n, 270
Milanopolo, 350n
Milesi (patriarch of Venice), 39
military council for all volunteer corps, 214–18, 251, 260, 342
Minotto, Giovanni, 110n, 300n, 315, 316, 357
Minto, Gilbert Elliott, Lord, 246
Mira, 163
Mirano, 60, 118n
Mocenigo, Alvise, 32, 71n, 175, 232, 234n, 235, 299n, 395
Modena, 44, 56n, 70, 126, 144, 213–14, 269
Modena, Gustavo, 97n, 115, 123, 179n, 199n, 214, 215, 315n, 335, 396
Moga, General, 295
Molin (Venetian painter), 92
Mondolfo, Giuseppe, 62n
Monico, Jacopo, 8, 31n, 66, 91, 94, 103, 179, 232, 302n, 310, 353, 377
Montanara, 172, 239, 319
Montanars, 26
Montanelli, Giuseppe, 265, 303n, 305n, 318–23, 327
Montebello, 170–2, 187, 190, 209, 370
Montebelluna, 195, 201
Montello, 173
Montereale, 122
Monti, Alessandro, 345
Monza, 28, 53, 133
Morandi, Antonio, 214–16, 217n, 218, 342, 357, 370
Morazzone, 260
Mordini, Antonio, 214, 216n, 260–1, 265–7, 272, 274, 275–7, 326n, 374

Moro, Domenico, 50, 120
Morosini, Giovan Battista, 71n
Morosini, Nicolo, 93–4
Mortegliano, 181
Motta, 180
Murano, 33, 38, 239, 307–8, 314, 363; *see also* glassware
Murat, Joachim, 69, 124n, 221
Muti (patriarch of Venice), 66n
Muzzarelli, 325

Nani (Venetian envoy to Paris), 148, 149n, 300
Naples, 34, 81, 145, 159, 198, 224
 counter-revolution in, 22–3, 364
 lazzaroni of, 39, 222
 (*see also* Two Sicilies, kingdom of)
Napoleon, *see* Bonaparte, Napoleon
Nazari, Giovan Battista, 70, 131
Negri, Professor, 318
neo-Guelph movement, 49, 65, 129, 378
Nice, 149, 282n
Nicholas I, Czar of Russia, 346
Nicolini, G. B., 193, 194, 216
Nicolotti clan, *see* Venice
Noaro, Agostino, 241n, 260
Normanby, Lord, 280, 282–4, 287–90, 325
Novara, 331–3, 375
Noventa, 78
Noventa Vicentina, 164n
Nugent, Laval, 169, 177–9, 182–3, 186–8, 191, 198–202, 209, 212, 214, 218, 220, 245, 251, 369–70, 397

Occhiobello, 207
Oexle, Federico, 35, 61, 62n, 349
Oliverò, General, 299, 326
Olivi, Giuseppe, xiv, 6n, 16, 61, 69n, 77n, 108, 112, 180n, 190, 216n, 398
Olivieri, General, 253
Olmo, 219
Olper, Samuele, 239n, 262, 264, 266, 309n, 329, 335, 336n
Oriani, G. B., 155
Orlandini (Triestine patriot), 104n, 194
Orsini, Felice, 199n
Ortis, Domenico, 183n
Osoppo, 107, 183–4, 199, 243

Oudinot, Nicolas Charles Victor, 187n, 334, 336
Padua, city of, 9n, 43, 57, 60n, 192–3, 198n, 372
 adheres to the Venetian republic, 123
 bakers' trade union in (1846), 43
 capitulation of, 241, 244
 defence of, 170n
 events in (February–March 1848), 77, 109, 112
 hostility to Venice, 121, 223
 population of, 42
 university of, 8, 43, 53, 55, 72, 77, 92, 115n, 311, 312n
Padua, province of, 19, 23n, 163, 194, 196, 233
 departmental committee of, 152, 155, 168n, 175, 235, 372
 votes for fusion with Piedmont, 207–8
Paita, Lieutenant, 360
Palatini, Captain, 181n
Palatini, Giuseppe, 189n, 212n
Paleocapa, Pietro, 55, 64, 112–14, 146, 156, 188, 204, 249n, 250, 254, 257, 263, 269n, 273n, 297n, 317
Palermo, 80–1, 214, 215n, 244, 364
Palffy, Aloys, 6, 63n, 64n, 73, 77n, 79n, 82, 90, 92n, 93–5, 100–3, 104n, 107, 124, 366
Palladio, Andrea, 43, 123
Palmanova, 107, 179, 182–4, 199, 243–4, 253
Palmerston, Henry, Viscount, 76n, 246, 282–3, 284n, 287–8, 290–2, 336–7, 367, 374, 376
Panizzi, Antonio (later Sir Anthony), 396
Paolucci, Antonio, 96, 98–9, 100, 112, 114, 167, 168n, 188n, 216, 249, 254
Papa, Captain, 197
Papadopoli family, 34, 55, 303, 373
Papadopoli, Angelo, 234, 302
Papadopoli, Giovanni, 34n, 120
Papadopoli, Spiridione, 20, 21, 35n, 52, 62n, 119–20, 157, 230, 234, 301, 310, 352, 365
Papal States, 11, 15n, 59, 68, 198, 230, 305, 333–7, 358
 army of, 198–202, 208–9, 213–14, 217, 220, 240–1, 250, 299, 369–70

Paravia, P. A., 77n, 224n
Pareto, G., 184n
Pareto, Lorenzo, 136, 142, 143, 184n, 185, 186n, 238n, 247n, 250, 257n, 279n
Paris, 61n, 148–51, 156, 217n, 219n, 223, 279, 283–4, 290, 325
  June days in (1848), 210, 247, 249, 267, 311n, 364
  revolution in (February 1848), 81–2, 86, 364
Parma, 44, 65, 70, 126, 144n, 317
Parolari (archpriest of Godego), 163
Pascotini, 77n
Pasini, Eleonoro, 17
Pasini, Lodovico, 314n, 347
Pasini, Valentino, 55–6, 57, 68, 69n, 74n, 108–9, 123, 189n, 190, 194, 195n, 237n, 238n, 284n, 291, 299n, 300, 305n, 325, 365
Passo della Morte, the, 212
Pasta, Giuditta, 258n
Pavan, Francesco, 316n
Pavia, 132n, 144, 145n
Pázmándy (Hungarian nobleman), 344
peasantry, *see* Austro-Hungarian empire, Lombardy, Venetia
Pelizzo, G., 14, 18n, 26n, 29n, 44n
pellagra, 22
Pellestrina, 117n, 314
Pellico, Silvio, 11n, 54
pensionatico, the, 21n, 73
Penso, Domenico, 239
People's Club, 311, 312n, 313, 327–8
Pepe, Guglielmo, 221, 223, 241n, 248, 255, 257, 263, 270, 276, 296–8, 299n, 331–2, 339, 341n, 342n, 357–8, 363, 374
Perissinotti, Teresa, *see* Manin, Teresa
Perrone di San Martino, Ettore, 321, 323
Pesaro Maurogonato, Isacco, 73, 169, 239n, 303, 306, 314n, 329, 349n, 351, 356
Peschiera, 43, 110, 239
Petitti di Roreto, Carlo, 52, 53, 205
Petrillo, Alessandro, 163
Petronio, Matteo, 191n
Pettorazza Grimani, 208
Pezzato, Jacopo, 145, 231n
Piacenza, 184

Pian delle Fugazze, pass of, 196
Piansi, Antonio Milani detto, 354
Piave, river, 11, 181, 197, 200, 211
Piazzola, 202, 218
Piedmont, kingdom of, 21, 53, 65, 70, 126, 151–2, 160, 230, 281, 284–5, 298, 335, 367, 376, 394
  army of, 132, 141, 147, 178–9, 181, 184n, 186, 187, 191, 208, 219, 239, 252–3, 258, 265n, 278, 317–18, 331–2
  and the *cinque giornate* of Milan, 136–7, 139–40, 159
  constitution proclaimed in, 81, 132
  fleet of, 222, 263, 278, 300, 337, 375
  and the Italian constituent assembly, 321, 323, 325
  and Lombardy, 184, 187, 225, 320
  and Venice, 155, 184–5, 187–9, 305, 326–7
Piermartini, Giovanni, 312–13
Pieve, 60
Pieve di Cadore, 211
Pigazzi brothers, 34, 234, 303, 304n
Pigozzi, Francesco, 274n
Pillersdorff, Franz von, 24, 178, 246
Pincherle, Leone, 90, 97, 100, 103, 112, 114, 158, 187–8, 204, 273n, 318
Pinelli, Pierdionigi, 317, 323
Pinzani (parish priest), 7
Pisacane, Carlo, 158n, 368, 377
Pisani, Vettore, 234, 303, 304n, 373
Pittoni, Marco Natale, 124n
Pius IX (Pio Nono), 59, 65–7, 69, 70, 75, 76, 81, 89, 106, 128, 131, 165, 185, 198, 202–4, 261n, 291, 302n, 310, 321–4, 334–5, 364, 366, 379
Planat de la Faye, F., 375
Pletti, Domenico, 112
Po, river, 11, 14n, 59–60, 68, 106, 168n, 221, 223
Poerio, Alessandro, 222n, 224, 298n
Poerio, Carlo, 224
Pojana, 103–4, 222
Poland, 150, 223, 364, 367
Polesella, 60
Polesine, *see* Rovigo, province of
Ponsonby, Lord, 80, 246, 286
Pontebba, 184
Ponti, Giuseppe, 96

Ponzio Vaglia, Marquis, 140, 185, 186n, 198n
Ponzoni (secretary of the Italian Club at Venice), 271
Porcia, Alfonso, 77n
Porcia de Brugnera, Lugrezia, 77n
Pordenone, 18, 124n, 163, 243n, 299, 393
Porro, Alessandro, 205n
Porro, Luigi, 148
Porte Grandi, 216
Portogruaro, 175, 177
Portosecco, 117n
Prague, 30n, 62n, 245
Prata, 124n
Primolano, 200–1
Priuli, Nicolò, 305n, 347, 352n, 362
Prussia, 3n, 20
Puato (merchant from Este), 213

Quadrilateral (of fortresses), 43, 146n
Querini Stampalia, Alvise, 30n
Querini Stampalia, Giovanni, 232n, 354
Quero, 200

Radaelli, Carlo, 100, 236
Radetzky, Josef, 10, 80, 155, 169, 171, 179, 186, 188, 200, 205, 218, 245, 286, 319, 331, 338, 346, 366, 370, 373
  and the *cinque giornate* of Milan, 96n, 109, 128, 133–4
  intransigence of, 178, 247
  military strategy of, 182n, 190, 239–41, 252–4, 332
  plans a peasant militia, 79
  and Vicenza, 220
railway bridge, across the Venetian lagoon, 31, 38, 42, 58, 338–9
railway company, Milan–Venice, 14n, 52, 57–8, 230, 233
railway question, the, 51–8, 113
Ranier, Josef, 4, 20n, 28, 63n, 64n, 80, 92n, 94, 105, 109, 110n
Raspail, François Vincent, 312
Ravenna, 330
Reali, Giuseppe, 14, 18, 20–1, 33, 34, 50, 52, 62n, 69n, 157, 189n, 230, 234, 254, 276–7, 302, 304n, 310, 350, 352, 365

Rebizzo, Lazzaro, 110n, 185, 186n, 198n, 326n
Recoaro, 171, 196
Rederer (factory owner), 43
Reggio, 184, 213
Reiset, Gustave, 280
Renier, G., 168n
Rensovich, Nicolò, 315, 336n, 341n
Restelli, Francesco, 170n, 172n, 184, 188n, 204n, 221, 245n, 247, 252, 258, 398
Revere, Giuseppe, 274, 275n, 276
revolution, 140, 237
  bourgeois, ix, 14, 45, 126, 160, 367–8, 370–1, 377
  in Italy (1831–2), 9, 55, 108, 158, 214
  passive, ix, 366, 368
  proletarian, 371n
  (*see also* Paris, Milan, Venice, Vienna)
Ricci, Alberto de', 178, 279n, 281–2, 285
Ridolfi, Cosimo, 319
Rifembergo, 173n
Rizzardi, General, 316, 338
Romagnosi, G. D., 48
Rome, 49, 65, 67, 159, 198, 244–5, 248n, 291, 319, 321
  republic of (1849), 312, 322–5, 327, 330, 334–7, 345, 358, 365, 375–6
Romeo, Rosario, x, 127n
Rosada, Angelo Maria, 234
Rosada, Giovanni d'Angelo, 62n
Rosaroll, Cesare, 298, 338n, 339
Rosmini, Antonio, 129
Rosmini (commander of volunteer battalion), 181n
Rossetti (delegate from the meeting at the Casino dei Cento), 261
Rossi family, 25n
Rossi, Alessandro, 299n
Rossi, Francesco, 17
Rossi, Pellegrino, 321–3, 334
Rossini, Gioachino, 8, 352
Rothschild, James, 61, 62n
Rothschild, Salomon, 33
Rovigo, city of, 44, 68n, 168, 192
  adheres to the Venetian republic, 123
  events in (March 1848), 108
  grain prices in, 60n

Rovigo, city of, *cont.*
  population of, 42
Rovigo, province of (Polesine), 9, 13, 19,
    23n, 44, 64n, 155, 169, 175, 194,
    199n, 233, 332
  carbonari lodges in, 50
  civic guards in, 164–5
  grain prices in, 59, 60n
  provincial committee of, 164, 223–4,
    235
  votes for fusion with Piedmont, 208
Ruffoni (Venetian emissary to Paris),
    272n, 285
Ruskin, Effie, 31, 58n
Ruskin, John, 31
Russell, John, Lord, 246, 288n, 289n
Russia, 346

Sacile, 243n
Sagredo, Agostino, 31n, 75n
Saint-Simon, Claude-Henri de, 66
Salasco, Carlo Caneva di, 253
Salasco armistice, 253, 264, 288, 300,
    305, 317
Salm (civil governor of Trieste), 104n
Salvi, G. B., 118n
San Daniele del Carso, 173n
San Daniele del Friuli, 7, 11
San Donà di Piave, 14n, 24, 62n, 163,
    176
Sanfermo, Marcantonio, 170–2, 209,
    370
San Michele (di Portogruaro), 175
San Pietro in Viminario, 175
San Pietro in Volta, 117, 314, 361
Santi, Bonifacio, 230n
San Vito di Tagliamento, 13
Sardinia, 197n
Sasso, Andrea, 92
Savoy, 115n, 149, 245, 282n
Sbardelà, Gaetano, 189n
Scapinelli (ex-governor of Reggio), 213
Scarpa brothers, 16
Sceriman, Fortunato, 177
Sceriman, G. B., 234
Schiavo, Alessandro, 194n, 212n
Schio, 17, 25n, 55, 171–2, 196,
    299n
Schwarzenberg, Felix, 247n, 291–3,
    295–6, 346

scientific congress, ninth Italian, 68–9,
    79
Scotti, G. B., 164n
Seismit-Doda, Federico, 220n, 268, 336n
Serbo-Croatia, 344–6
Serena, A., 69n, 105n, 291n, 300
Sernagiotto (member of the Venetian
    civic guard), 113n
Serravalle, 27n
Serravalle, Jacopo, 343n
Sette Comuni, the, 162, 171, 242
Settimo, Ruggero, 245
Sicily, 81, 105n, 145, 215, 217, 221–2,
    243, 245
Siena, 271
Silesia, 59
silk, 15–17, 19–20, 24–5, 33, 34, 35n,
    45, 62, 64, 230–1; *see also* Friuli,
    Milan, Lombardy, Venetia, Venice,
    Vienna
Sirtori, Giuseppe, 167–8, 198, 316,
    338–9, 363, 377, 396
  character of, 260
  early years of, 260
  and Garibaldi, 358
  and 11 August 1848, 165–6
  and the Italian Club, 262n, 272, 376
  and the military commission, 340–2,
    376
  and the 'permanent' assembly in
    Venice, 327–30, 356–7, 375
  political ideas of, 261, 327
  and the sortie from Brondolo, 352–3
socialism, 66, 311–13, 315
Solagna, 298–9
Soler (Albertist), 269n
Soler, Giuseppe, 113n
Solera, Francesco, 112, 114, 119
Solerni (Sicilian delegate from the
    meeting at the Casino dei Cento),
    261
Sondrio, 133
Sophie, archduchess of Austria, 7, 82
Sorio, 170, 172, 175, 370
Soster, G., 171n., 194n, 396
Spilimbergo, 111, 165, 180, 269
Stadion, Franz, 104n
Stecchini, Pietro, 168n
Stefani, Guglielmo, 343n
Stefani (political prisoner), 90n

Strassoldo, Giulio, 6
Strigelli, Gaetano, 144–5
Styria, 26, 345
Suardi, Francesco, 230n
Sugana, Count, 152
Susegana, 157
Switzerland, 20–1, 134, 136, 171, 186n, 285
Szarvady, Frederic, 345n

Tagliamento, river, 11, 183–4, 197, 199, 200
Taglio Mira, 176
Talamini (delegate from the meeting at the Casino dei Cento), 261
Tecchio, Sebastiano, 108, 305n, 326
Tedeschi, Vincenzo, 189n
Teleki, Count, 344
Terzaghi, Giulio, 134, 137, 138n, 139
Tezze, 110n
Thom (Austrian chargé d'affaires in Paris), 288, 290, 296
Thurn, Count (Austrian official in Venice), 5, 6, 11, 24
Thurn, General, 108, 218–20, 239
Ticino, river, 136, 253, 318
tithe, the, 21, 28, 73
Tocqueville, Alexis de, 286n, 363n
Toffoli, Angelo, 90n, 112–13, 118n, 119
Toggenburg, de (lieutenant of the Venetian provinces), 66n, 307n
Tolmezzo, 212
Tommaseo, Nicolò, 59, 87, 89, 95, 104, 151, 153, 190, 215, 239, 264, 273n, 275, 297n, 301, 304, 316, 338, 344, 348, 351, 365
   alienation from Manin, 268, 340, 396
   arrested by the Austrians, 74, 131
   character of, 66
   distrusts Charles Albert, 147–8
   and the *Fratellanza dei Popoli*, 344n
   and freedom of the press, 256
   and French aid, 244n, 268–9, 278–9, 284–6, 288, 291, 303n, 373
   his ignorance of rural conditions, 158
   imprisonment of, 74–5, 79–80, 82
   and the *lotta legale*, 71, 73n, 74
   and Mazzini, 226, 262
   as minister of culture and education, 112–14, 232n, 309n

and the 'permanent' assembly in Venice, 327, 329, 356–8
   and Pius IX, 66–7, 323
   political opinions of, 66, 85–6, 90, 114–15, 116, 188, 190n, 204, 226, 250, 372, 377
   proposes a rationing system for Venice, 349
   and the riot at the Palazzo Querini Stampalia, 353–4
   and the Venetian clergy, 118
   and the Venetian lower classes, 255
   and the Venetian navy, 360
   and Vicenza, 219–20
Toppo, Francesco di, 394
Torcello, 314, 316n
Torelli, Luigi, 130, 139
Tornielli, G. B., 229, 236, 249, 309n, 349, 357
Torre, 18, 164
Torre, Ridolfo, 92
Toulon, 148, 287, 289
Trecenta, 199n
Trent, 200
Treporti, 116, 227, 353
Trevelyan, G. M., x
Treves, Isacco, 120, 234, 303, 304n
Treves, Jacopo, 34, 52, 55, 57, 69n, 120, 157, 230, 234, 301–3, 304n, 352, 365
Treves de Bonfili brothers, 16n, 373; *see also* Treves, Isacco and Jacopo
Treviglio, 57, 58n
Trevignano, 180
Trevisan, Major, 164
Treviso, city of, 16, 44, 57, 62, 108, 122, 158, 171, 180–1, 197, 201, 213, 218
   adheres to the Venetian republic, 123
   under Austrian rule, 6n
   capitulation of, 241–2, 244
   civic guard of, 106, 190
   defence of, 170n, 200, 202
   and the military council for all volunteer corps, 213–17
   nationalist demonstrations in (1847–8), 76–7
   political battles in, 193, 207, 208n, 216
   population of, 42

Treviso, province of, 17, 23n, 60, 194, 196, 233
  departmental committee of, 152, 155, 189
Tribano, 168n
Tricesimo, 26
Trieste, 26, 29–30, 34, 36, 45, 52–3, 67, 71, 95, 111, 345–6, 370
  blockade of, 222–3
  events in (March 1848), 104n
  organisation of Nugent's army in, 177–8
Trivignano, 107
Trolli, Carlo, 112, 113, 269
Tron, Andrea, 14
Turin, 81, 132, 135, 148n, 149, 186, 206, 263, 273, 317–18, 323
Tuscany, 15n, 65, 68, 70, 305, 311, 318–20, 323–5, 327, 330–1, 333–4, 336, 375
Two Sicilies, kingdom of the, 80–1, 221–3
Tyrol, the, 2n, 10n, 30, 64n

Uccelli, Fabio, 307n, 339
Udine, city of, 26n, 44, 62, 72, 77, 107, 112, 155, 177, 180, 209, 269, 369, 394, 396
  adheres to the Venetian republic, 123
  capitulation of, 183, 188, 193, 211, 218
  civic guard of, 105n
  population of, 42
Ulloa, Girolamo, 154n, 261, 270, 332n, 338–40, 351, 356–8, 363, 398
Urbino, Fortunato, 206

Valdagno, 17, 106, 171, 194n, 396
Val d'Intelvi, 277, 298, 374
Valdobbiadene, 27n
Valle, 181
Valstagna, 110
Valussi, Pacifico, 18n, 73, 256, 313, 363
Valvason, Nicolò di, 14
Vanni, Sante, 189n
Vanzo, 175
Varè, Giambattista, 82, 238, 264, 266, 267n, 271, 275n, 315, 316, 328, 347
Vasseur (French consul at Venice), 278n, 307n, 330n, 341n, 352n, 363n

Venas, 212
Vendramini (Austrian police chief at Rovigo), 68n
Venerio, Girolamo, 14
Venetia (the Veneto), 51, 56–7, 282
  agriculture of, 12–29
  artisans of, 191–2
  bourgeoisie of, 14, 19, 59, 107, 113, 124, 157, 378
  chambers of commerce in, 13–14, 21n, 46, 120
  child employment in, 25
  clergy in, 7–8, 66, 69, 77–8, 105–6, 118, 165, 199, 369
  economic crisis in (1846–7), 59–64
  geography of, 11
  Jews of, 12
  landowners in, 12–21, 24, 45–6, 59, 157, 177, 191
  manufacturing industry in, 17–18
  under Napoleonic rule, 1
  nobility of, 24, 57, 107, 124, 191
  peasantry of, 2, 21–9, 60–1, 64, 67, 78–9, 99, 106–7, 110–11, 121–2, 124–5, 154, 157–60, 162–70, 173–7, 180–2, 184, 195–7, 199n, 200, 214, 217, 242–3, 298–9, 369–71, 378
  and Pius IX, 65
  population of, 21, 22, 45
  prices of grain and maize in, 29
  revolution in (March 1848), 104–12
  schools in, 8n
  silk production in, 15–17, 19–20, 24–5, 230
  sugar refineries in, 230n
  union with Lombardy, 123
  (*see also* Austro-Hungarian empire)
Venetian navy, (1848–9), 96, 103–4, 125, 249n, 267, 270, 299–300, 340, 342, 351, 358–61, 375
Venetian provisional government (August 1848 to August 1849), 275, 278
  army of, 255, 257, 296–7, 299, 341–3, 374
  central provisioning committee of, 308, 349, 350n, 361
  civic guard of, 271, 306, 310, 339–40, 342

Venetian provisional government, *cont.*
committee of public vigilance of, 307, 310, 313, 328, 341, 349, 354
creation of, 269–70
and elections, 313–16
finances of, 301–6, 345, 351, 362
and freedom of the press, 310–13
and French aid, 284, 287, 288–9, 292–3
and Hungary, 345–6
and the Italian constituent assembly, 323–4
the military commission of, 339–43, 352, 356, 374
the 'permanent' assembly, 316, 327–31, 332, 335, 340–1, 346–7, 349, 351, 356–7
and the Roman republic, 334–7
surrender of, 362–3
triumvirate of, 269–70, 278, 314, 317, 328
and the Venetian working classes, 310
Venetian republic (1848), 208–9
absence of an army, 119, 125, 153–60, 166–7, 172, 181n, 191, 194–9, 202, 236, 250–1
anti-clericalism in, 118
civic guards in (mobile), 167, 181n, 209; (rural), 162–70, 173, 209, 369, 393; (of Venice), 179, 192, 195, 232, 249
committee of defence of, 159, 168, 169–72, 194–5, 197, 211, 270
committee of public vigilance of, 229, 249, 372
and conscription, 154–5, 157, 194–5, 209
consultative council (*consulta*) of, 147, 151–2, 169n, 189–90, 194–5, 244, 264, 317
corpi franchi of, 168, 171–2, 176
crociati of, 168, 170, 179, 197, 229n
elections in, 235–9
finances of, 232–5, 247
freedom of the press in, 162, 231, 249n
French intervention in, 151
and Friuli, 179
government of, 151–2, 156–7, 162
internal order of, 120

July assembly of, 226, 238, 247–50
and Lombardy, 204, 226
ministers of, 112–14
nature of, 114–16, 122–5, 368
and Piedmont, 184–5, 187–8, 204, 226, 247–50
and the policy of *a guerra finita si deciderà*, 143–8, 226
proclamation of, 101–4, 134, 145, 162, 366
and the provinces, 169, 189–94, 223–4, 241
social tensions in, 116–17, 173–7, 191–2
unpopularity of in Italy, 224
Venice, city of, 9, 26, 29–42, 50–1, 58, 66, 85, 112, 131, 158, 187, 210, 214–15, 223, 226–32, 294, 368
arsenal, 29–30, 38, 96–100, 124, 138, 154, 171, 237, 308, 352, 370, 394
arsenal workers of, 38, 96, 98–100, 110, 117, 124–5, 228, 338n, 366
Ateneo Veneto, 37, 67, 71
Austrian garrison in, 91–2, 95–6, 99, 101–2
bank of, 230, 303
bourgeoisie of, 12, 33–7, 39, 45–6, 50–1, 58–9, 61, 64, 67, 76, 91, 103, 119–20, 125, 162, 229–31, 236–7, 239, 262, 306, 350, 365, 373
bombardment of (1849), 351–3, 359, 361
Cassa di Risparmio, 31, 117n
central congregation of, 20n, 45, 70–3, 93
chamber of commerce of, 14n, 31n, 34–8, 45–6, 50, 52, 61, 64, 71, 74, 119, 157, 230–1, 234, 237, 302, 350, 365, 395
cholera in (1849), 333, 355–6, 361–2
civic guard of, 93–4, 98–100, 102, 104, 119–20, 232, 249; *see also* Venetian republic
clergy in, 7n, 74, 118, 232, 238–9, 313–14
commercial company of, 35, 55, 61
commission of public charity of, 30, 39, 40, 349
Doges' palace, 69, 249, 328, 332

Venice, city of, *cont.*
  economic crisis in (1846–7), 61–2
  Fenice opera house, 8, 32, 36n, 72,
    76, 81, 352
  Florian, café, 76, 92, 95, 103, 354
  free port of, 30–1
  gondoliers of, 38–9, 82, 228, 235,
    315–16, 338n
  grain and bread prices in, 59, 74, 228,
    307–8, 347–8
  Jews of, 34–5, 73–4, 120, 154, 239
  manufacturing industry in, 33, 71, 120
  Monte di Pietà, 117, 229, 394
  municipality of, 34, 38–40, 45, 68,
    90–1, 94–5, 96n, 97, 101, 102, 113,
    117n, 119, 126, 229n, 236n, 304–5,
    307–8, 310, 314n, 339, 356
  nationalist agitation in, 69–76, 81–3
  Nicolotti and Castellani clans, 41, 75,
    85, 92, 235
  nobility of, 12, 14, 18–19, 32–3, 45,
    58, 76, 91, 113, 121, 125, 162, 232,
    234, 237, 350, 353, 357–8
  petty bourgeoisie of, 37–8
  Piazza San Marco, 10–11, 29, 31, 82,
    85, 88–9, 91–3, 95, 100–3, 118,
    229, 231n, 235, 250, 265–6, 302,
    307, 310, 327, 331–2, 347, 351,
    354, 357–8, 361, 363
  political traditions of, 84–5, 88–9,
    126, 130
  population of, 30–1, 41n
  and the railway question, 53, 56–8
  revolution in (March 1848), 84–104,
    124–5, 135, 141, 160
  Riva degli Schiavoni, 54, 75, 101,
    352–3
  siege of (1813–14), 1, 29
  siege of (1849), 306, 333, 337–9,
    347–53, 358–9, 361–3, 375
  silk production in, 3, 41, 61, 230
  tobacco factory in, 38, 116, 227
  trade and commerce of, 33–4, 36, 45,
    50, 61, 67, 120
  workhouse in, 40, 309, 393
  working classes of, 38–42, 61, 64, 67,
    74, 82, 84, 88, 91–3, 94n, 104,
    116–17, 125, 226–31, 235–6, 249–
    51, 255, 262, 267, 306–11, 313,
    337, 348, 350, 354–5, 366, 375
Venice, July government of (1848), 254–
  66
Venice, province of, 19
Venturi, Francesco, 323–6
Verdi, Giuseppe, 32, 72, 76
Verona, city of, 9n, 11, 42–3, 45, 57,
    64n, 67, 77, 94, 123, 155, 169–72,
    178–9, 196, 200, 202, 218–20,
    239–41, 245, 251, 347, 364, 395
  economic crisis in (1846–7), 62
  events in (March 1848), 109–10, 124,
    366
  manufacturing industry in, 43
  population of, 42
Verona, province of, 15–16
  landholding in, 23n, 24
  rural thefts in, 29n
Vianello, Ferdinando, 92
Vicenza, city of, 9n, 43–4, 55, 57–8, 94,
    171–2, 193–4, 197, 200, 202,
    396
  adheres to the Venetian republic, 123
  civic guard of, 105
  defence of, 170n, 196, 218–20, 240–1,
    369
  events in (March 1848), 108–9, 366
  population of, 42
Vicenza, province of, 17, 194, 233
  departmental committee of, 152, 190n
  votes for fusion with Piedmont, 207–
    8
Victor Emmanuel II, king of Piedmont,
    332, 333, 377
Victoria, queen of England, 282
Vienna, 3, 5, 15, 28, 31, 34, 53, 57,
    67, 124, 178, 211
  chestnut sellers in, 26, 52
  events in (May 1848), 240, 245
  population of, 30
  revolution in (March 1848), 82, 91,
    94, 364; (October 1848), 291, 295,
    320, 365
  silk production in, 20
Vieusseux, Giovan Pietro, 54, 325
Villafora, 164n
Virgili (Neapolitan delegate from the
    meeting at the Casino dei Cento),
    261
Visco, 182
Vittorelli, Giuseppe, 230n

Vollo, Giuseppe, 256, 309n, 312, 329, 363n
Volpe, G., 243n

Watt, James, 17
Welden, Franz Ludwig von, 199, 212, 218, 242–3, 255, 264, 296, 344
Wessenberg, Johann von, 2, 245–6, 247n, 286, 288, 290–1, 370
Windischgrätz, Alfred, 295
Winkler, Lajos, 345
Wolowski, Ludwik, 150

Young Italy, 9n, 49

Zambaldi, Carlo, 341
Zambeccari, Livio, 199n, 219, 242
Zanardini (Venetian envoy to Paris), 148–9, 150n, 300
Zanchi, Luigi, 110n

Zanellato (chief of volunteers at Vicenza), 257
Zanetti, Alessandro, 93n, 96n, 231n, 301n, 363n
Zanetti, Francesco, 230n
Zannini, Dionisio, 255, 262, 269n
Zannini, Licurgo, 243, 244n
Zannona, Marc'Antonio, 34n
Zen, Pietro, 71n, 234
Zennari (secretary of the Venetian provisional government), 235, 236n, 238, 358n
Zerman, Francesco, 99n
Zichy, Lieutenant-Marshal, 6, 91, 95, 98, 100–2, 104n, 107–8, 124
Zoia, Giovanni, 192, 372
Zoldo, 212
Zucchelli, Francesco, 52
Zucchi, Carlo, 107, 108n, 182, 183n, 197, 243, 253